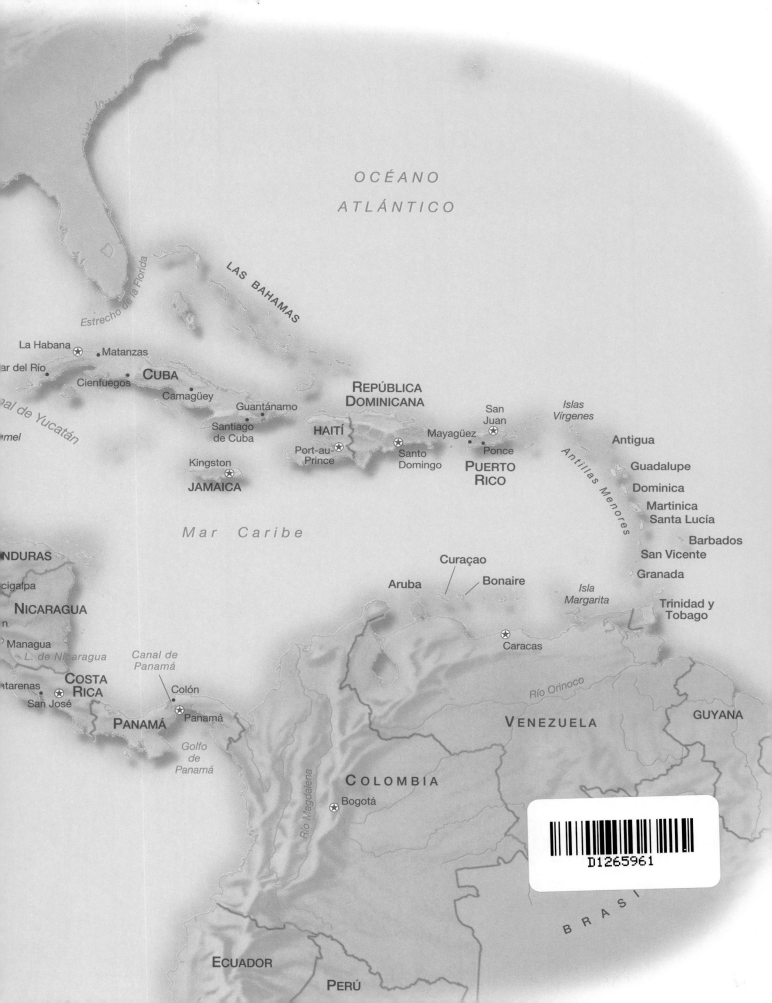

MOSAICOS

FOURTH EDITION

MOSAICOS

Spanish as a World Language

Matilde Olivella de Castells
Emerita, California State University, Los Angeles

Elizabeth Guzmán
College of Saint Benedict, St. John's University

Paloma Lapuerta
Central Connecticut State University

Carmen García
Arizona State University

ANNOTATED INSTRUCTOR'S EDITION

PEARSON
Prentice
Hall

Upper Saddle River, NJ 07458

Executive Editor: *Bob Hemmer*
Sr. Director of Market Development: *Kristine Suárez*
Director of Editorial Development: *Julia Caballero*
Production Supervision: *Amy Rose of Interactive Composition Corporation*
Project Manager: *Claudia Dukeshire*
Asst. Director of Production: *Mary Rottino*
Supplements Editor: *Meriel Martínez Moctezuma*
Media Editor: *Samantha Alducin*
Media Production Manager: *Roberto Fernández*
Prepress and Manufacturing Buyer: *Brian Mackey*
Prepress and Manufacturing Assistant Manager: *Mary Ann Gloriande*
Interior Design: *Andrew Ogus*
Cover Design: *Ximena Tamvakopoulos*
Line Art Coordinator: *Maria Piper*

Illustrator: *Mari Isabel Rodriguez Martin*
Director, Image Resource Center: *Melinda Reo*
Manager, Rights and Permissions IRC: *Zina Arabia*
Manager, Visual Research: *Beth Boyd Brenzel*
Manager, Cover Visual Research & Permissions: *Karen Sanatar*
Image Permissions Coordinator: *Debbie Hewitson*
Photo Researcher: *Elaine Soares*
Cover image: Antonio Gaudi y Cornet. Mosaics in Park Guell, Barcelona, Spain. Date created: 1900-1914. Photographer: *Charles Lenars*
Sr. Marketing Manager: Jacquelyn Zautner
Marketing Assistant: *William J. Bliss*
Publisher: *Phil Miller*

This book was set in Sabon by *Interactive Composition Corporation* and was printed and bound by *Courier Kendallville*. The cover was printed by *Coral Graphics*.

Student Text, Regular Edition: ISBN 0-13-192324-2
Student Text, Brief Edition: ISBN 0-13-154420-9
Annotated Instructor's Edition: ISBN 0-13-192325-0

Pearson Education LTD., *London*
Pearson Education Australia PTY, Limited, *Sydney*
Pearson Education Singapore, Pte. Ltd.
Pearson Education North Asia Ltd., *Hong Kong*
Pearson Education Canada, Ltd., *Toronto*
Pearson Educación de México, S.A. de C.V.
Pearson Education–Japan, *Tokyo*
Pearson Education Malaysia, Pte. Ltd.
Pearson Education, Upper Saddle River, *New Jersey*

BRIEF CONTENTS

SCOPE AND SEQUENCE

LECCIÓN	OBJETIVOS COMUNICATIVOS	A PRIMERA VISTA
P **Bienvenidos 2** 	Introducing oneself and others Greetings and good-byes Expressions of courtesy Spelling in Spanish Identifying people and classroom objects Locating people and objects Using numbers from 0–99 Expressing dates Telling time Using classroom expressions	
1 **Los estudiantes y la universidad 22** 	Asking for and providing information Expressing needs Asking for prices Talking about daily activities Asking about and expressing location	Los estudiantes y los cursos 24 La vida estudiantil 26 En la universidad 29
2 **Los hispanos en los Estados Unidos 58** 	Asking about and describing persons, animals, places, and things Expressing nationality and place of origin Expressing where and when events take place Expressing possession Expressing likes and dislikes	Mis amigos y yo 60 ¿Cómo son...? 62 ¿De qué color son...? 64 ¿De dónde son...? 65

LECCIÓN	OBJETIVOS COMUNICATIVOS	A PRIMERA VISTA
3 **Las actividades y los planes 92** 	Asking about and discussing leisure activities Communicating by phone Ordering food in a restaurant Making suggestions and future plans Accepting and rejecting invitations Using numbers 100 and above	Diversiones populares 94 La comida 97
4 **La familia 128** 	Identifying and describing family members Describing routine activities Expressing preferences, desires, and feelings Asking and giving permission Expressing when, where, or how an action is done Expressing how long events and states have been going on	Las familias 130 ¿Qué hacen los parientes? 133
5 **La casa y los muebles 164** 	Asking about and describing housing and household items Discussing daily activities in the home Asking about and discussing daily schedules Expressing ongoing actions Describing physical and emotional states Expressing obligation	En casa 166 Las tareas domésticas 169

LECCIÓN	OBJETIVOS COMUNICATIVOS	A PRIMERA VISTA
9 **El trabajo** 318 	Talking about the workplace and professions Discussing job skills and abilities Giving formal orders and instructions Expressing intention Avoiding repetition	Las profesiones 320 La entrevista 325
10 **La comida y la nutrición** 356 	Discussing food, shopping, and planning menus Expressing wishes and hope Making requests and expressing opinions Expressing doubt Giving advice	En el supermercado 358 La mesa 361 ¿Dónde se compra? 362 Antes de seguir... 364
11 **La salud y los médicos** 392 	Talking about the body Describing health conditions and medical treatments Expressing emotions, opinions, and attitudes Expressing expectations and wishes Giving informal orders and instructions Expressing goals and purposes	Las partes del cuerpo 394 La salud 395

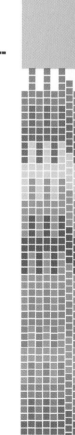

LECCIÓN	OBJETIVOS COMUNICATIVOS	A PRIMERA VISTA
15 **La ciencia y la** **tecnología 532** 	Talking about advances in science and technology Giving opinions and making suggestions Hypothesizing about the present and the future Softening requests and statements Expressing unexpected occurrences Expressing contrary-to-fact conditions in the present	La conservación del medio ambiente 534 La ciudad del futuro 536 Nuevas fronteras 538

	OBJETIVOS COMUNICATIVOS	CONTENIDO LINGÜÍSTICO
Expansión gramatical A1	Telling informally two or more people to do something (in Spain) Expressing an indirect wish so that a third party do something Suggesting that someone do something with two or more people, including the speaker Reacting to a past occurrence or event Hypothesizing about an occurrence or event in the past Expressing contrary-to-fact conditions in the past Emphasizing a fact resulting from the action of someone or something	*Vosotros* commands A1 Indirect commands A2 The Spanish equivalents of English *let's* A4 The present perfect subjunctive A6 The conditional perfect and the pluperfect subjunctive A8 *If*-clauses (using the perfect tenses) A10 The passive voice A11

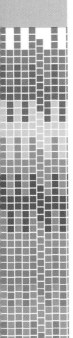

EXPLICACIÓN Y EXPANSIÓN

MOSAICOS

ENFOQUE CULTURAL

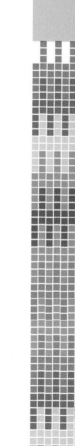

PREFACE

About the Mosaicos Program

With each new edition, more and more instructors across North American are discovering that *Mosaicos* offers a distinct and better alternative for their elementary Spanish classes. Why? **Because Mosaicos enables instructors to emphasize communication while taking into account the realities of the classroom!** In most classrooms, the goal is communication, but the realities are . . . that students are taking the course because of a language requirement . . . . that students come to class with questions about grammar . . . . that students feel anxious about communicating in a second language . . . and that students need help developing their reading, writing, and listening skills. With Mosaicos' commonsense communicative approach, the beginning classroom becomes a setting for true communication and cultural exchange. *Mosaicos* combines the best elements of language instruction in a highly interactive approach. An emphasis on frequently used vocabulary, practical applications of grammar, illustrated language contexts, and engaging activities to help successfully develop good communication skills.

Mosaicos is built on a foundation of interaction, communication, and culture. Its functional grammatical syllabus provides an understanding of the language in a clear, concise format. Structures are presented as a means to effective communication and valuable class time can be spent interacting as well as developing and improving language skills in Spanish.

Highlights of the Program

The fourth edition of Mosaicos continues the successful tradition of the first three editions, retaining and enhancing the core features, and integrating many new and exciting features.

Contextualized Vocabulary

The *Mosaicos* program features a lively and visual communicative format for presenting and practicing new language. Abundant activities in the *A primera vista* section of each chapter foster use of newly-acquired and previously-learned words and expressions in a variety of contexts. These contexts provide a natural environment for learning and practicing new vocabulary, as well as for recycling previously-taught language and previewing new structures.

- **WHAT'S NEW!** Active vocabulary words are now highlighted in boldface type to help students quickly identify active vocabulary within each thematic unit and negotiate the meaning of the word as it is presented in the context of words they already know.

- **WHAT'S NEW!** Recordings of the dialogues and language samples in *A primera vista* are now included in the *Mosaicos* audio program. The recordings give students opportunity to hear vocabulary pronounced in context, as well as giving them exposure to a variety of native speakers.

- **WHAT'S NEW!** *En directo* boxes throughout the chapter introduce colloquial expressions and ideas and encourage students to use them in communicative activities such as Situaciones, A conversar, and others.

Integrated Grammar

Mosaicos presents grammar as a means to communicate effectively. The clear and concise bulleted explanations are easy to understand and are designed to be studied at home, yet their integration into the text enables students to use them for quick reference as they practice communication in class.

The carefully sequenced, communicative activities that practice the grammar in the *Explicación y expansión* section of each chapter have been a hallmark feature of *Mosaicos* since the first edition. They develop the ability to use linguistic structures for direct communicative purposes.

WHAT'S NEW! The first activity in each activity sequence in *A primera vista* and *Explicación y expansión* is now consistently an input-oriented comprehension check requiring minimal output from the student. This helps students recognize new forms and meanings based on language input before progressing to activities requiring guided output, then open-ended communication.

WHAT'S NEW! The open-ended *Situaciones* activities that culminate the activity sequence for each grammar point have been thoroughly revised to focus more on real-life situations. Direction lines for these activities are now consistently in English.

The grammatical scope and sequence in *Mosaicos* has always been dictated by the perceived communicative needs of beginning students. Based on reviewer suggestions we have retained the third edition scope and sequence of grammatical topics in *Mosaicos, Fourth Edition*, with one exception.

WHAT'S NEW! The indirect commands and the equivalents of English *let's* have been moved from chapters 10 and 11, respectively, to the *Expansión gramatical* section at the back of the text. Many instructors no longer consider these structures necessary to the elementary year language acquisition process, and we have responded accordingly. However, these structures, as well as others in the *Expansión gramatical* section, use the same format as the grammatical material throughout *Mosaicos* and may easily be incorporated, if desired.

Integrated Culture

The fourth edition of *Mosaicos* continues with the successful integration of culture and language of the third edition. Each chapter focuses on a country or region and numerous examples from that country or region are used consistently throughout the chapter in language samples, photos, maps, and realia. Related cultural content is interwoven throughout the text in activities and readings.

Mosaicos also includes a section called *Enfoque cultural* in each chapter that provides practical knowledge of specific cultural topics of the Spanish-speaking world as well as an orientation to the countries that make up that world.

WHAT'S NEW! **Enfoque cultural** sections of each chapter are now less textual and more visual; they feature several large, colorful photographs and an attractive topographical map highlighting the country or countries that forms the focus of the chapter. This section whets students' appetites and creates interest in cultural features without turning itself into a serious reading activity.

WHAT'S NEW! **Notas**, a new section within the *Enfoque cultural*, features a song corresponding to the Hispanic country or region of the chapter, along with pre-, during-, and post-listening activities. *Notas* uses music to motivate student interest in Hispanic culture.

A four-skills synthesis

Following the *A primera vista* and *Expansión gramatical* sections is the 4-skills section called *Mosaicos*. This section provides the student with a unique opportunity to bring all the pieces of the chapter together: vocabulary, grammar, and culture. The fourth edition of *Mosaicos* retains the core elements of skill-building, skill-using and skill chaining for listening, speaking, reading, and writing and adds new features to enhance and extend the effectiveness of this section.

WHAT'S NEW! The *process approach* is applied to the acquisition of all four skills. Pre-, during, and post-activities for listening, speaking, reading, and writing are included in each chapter.

WHAT'S NEW! In the *Mosaicos* section of each chapter, explicit strategies are provided for listening, reading and writing. In addition to skill-building activities, "strategies" for speaking are addressed in new *En directo* boxes.

Listening. In *Escuchar* in the *Mosaicos* skills section, students listen for different purposes, for example: to make inferences, to distinguish between facts and opinion, identify the speaker, listen for specific details, etc. In many cases, students are asked to fill in charts, comment on, or otherwise process the information they hear after completing the specific listening task, integrating listening with productive skills.

WHAT'S NEW! New scripts, audio recordings, and accompanying activities have been created for practically all listening sections. Scripts now simulate authentic discourse. Their short conversations, announcements, etc. all relate to the topics and content of each chapter.

Speaking. Open-ended activities in every chapter provide opportunities for individuals, pairs and groups of students to gather, process and share information in Spanish, stimulating real communication in the classroom. Conversation activities in the *Conversar* section of each chapter encourage interaction on a personal level combining newly acquired structures and vocabulary in discussions of chapter topics.

Reading. Pre- and post-reading activities provide opportunities and strategies for developing reading skills. Reading selections include a greater number of authentic texts and reflect a variety of discourse types and styles ranging from journalistic to literary.

WHAT'S NEW! **Visual Advance organizers** have been added to the pre-reading activities in every chapter to help students activate their background knowledge and prepare them to comprehend the reading passage that follows.

WHAT'S NEW! The last three chapters of the full version *Mosaicos* now have **literary readings.** (Chapters 1-12 offer cultural readings.) Chapters 13-15 expose students to Hispanic literature and serve as a transition to Intermediate Spanish while continuing to develop their abilities to read literature in Spanish.

WHAT'S NEW! Many **new readings** have been selected to reflect greater diversity of topics and appeal to a broader range of students.

WHAT'S NEW! Readings in early chapters are now shorter and simpler, with length and difficulty of readings increasing consistently from chapter to chapter. This allows students to develop confidence gradually in their ability to read materials in the target language.

Writing. Carefully-crafted process writing activities conclude each *Mosaicos* section. Pre- and post-writing activities are a guide through critical steps in the writing process. Throughout, extensive annotations guide instructors to teach writing as a recursive—rather than linear—process.

WHAT'S NEW! Writing tasks have been simplified and revised to relate more directly to chapter theme. The writing task is now more realistic—assignments are realistic in both scope and content, ensuring that students can complete the task with confidence.

WHAT'S NEW! Sample texts have been included in the pre-writing activity of each chapter and function as input for the writing process. The sample texts also give students a model so that they have clear guidelines to successfully complete the task.

Other features of the fourth edition are:

WHAT'S NEW! New *En directo* boxes highlight formulaic expressions that will help students sound more "adult-like," and more spontaneous in their speech. The *En directo* boxes are found throughout the text and are placed alongside the activity in which students can put them to immediate use. Learning these expressions will help students carry out their interpersonal or presentational exchanges more effectively.

The range of the *Cultura* boxes has been expanded in the third edition and they now appear in each chapter to ensure students gain an understanding and appreciation of people and cultures while building linguistic skills.

Acentos boxes are placed strategically throughout *Mosaicos*. The stress and accent rules in Spanish are presented on an as-needed basis. A complete presentation of accents is located in Appendix 1.

Lengua boxes, which inform learners of socio-linguistic distinctions in the Spanish language, appear at strategic intervals throughout the fourth edition, just as they did in the third edition.

Extensive, practical teachers' annotations provide instructors with lively ideas and pertinent information to facilitate their task in getting the most out of the *Mosaicos* Program.

 Vínculos are a new type of annotation. Located in the Annotated Instructor's Edition, the *Vínculos* correlate appropriate sections of supplementary materials with the activities in the Student Text.

Organization of the Text

The full version of *Mosaicos* consists of a preliminary chapter (*Bienvenidos*) and fifteen regular chapters.

 A brief version of *Mosaicos* is now available for those instructors who wish to cover less material during the first year of instruction. The brief edition contains the preliminary chapter and chapters 1-12 of the full edition.

Through a variety of visual stimuli, the *Bienvenidos* chapter allows instructors to conduct classes in Spanish from the very first day. Each regular chapter maintains the following consistent structure:

A primera vista.   This opening section of each chapter provides a richly contextualized, cultural framework for learning and practicing new language. New material is presented within two or three thematic groupings, which make use of photos, illustrations, and authentic documents. Comprehensible input is provided through a wide variety of language samples (dialogs, brief narratives, brochures, comic strips, captions, etc.). Within each thematic grouping, activities provide opportunities to practice the new vocabulary and in some cases preview grammar points which are formally presented later in the chapter. The last activity in this section is a listening activity that recycles vocabulary in an authentic conversational framework while providing practice of global listening skills. Previously-taught material is consistently recycled and reinforced.

Explicación y expansión.   The *Explicación y expansión* sections consist of concise grammar explanations focused on usage and followed by immediate practice of each new structural item within a contextualized framework. The exercises and activities in this section develop students' abilities to use linguistic structures for direct communicative purposes. Contextualized and personalized, the exercises focus student attention on a variety of useful tasks and provide practice for communicating effectively in pairs or small groups in a variety of real-life situations. These activities reinforce both vocabulary introduced in the *A primera vista* section of the chapter and vocabulary presented in previous chapters.

Mosaicos.   Students get an opportunity to "bring all the pieces together" in this process-oriented, strategy-focused section. Skills and topics are interwoven at the end of each chapter into a series of skill-building and skill-chaining activities that bring together the chapter vocabulary, structures, and cultural content:

Escuchar develops students' ability to listen to and understand spoken Spanish in a variety of authentic contexts: brief exchanges and longer conversations between two or more speakers, telephone messages, radio broadcasts, literary texts, etc.

Conversar includes open-ended speaking activities based on naturally-occurring discourse situations and authentic written texts. Students learn to express and discuss their own needs and interests. This section provides many opportunities for personalized expression.

Leer teaches students how to become independent readers by introducing basic strategies for understanding the general meaning of a text as well as for extracting specific information from it. The activities guide students to develop their ability to read a variety of high-interest, authentic Spanish texts, from simple documents such as advertisements to the extended discourse of brochures, newspaper and magazine articles, letters, literary texts, etc.

Escribir provides step-by-step activities in which students learn to compose messages and memos, postcards and letters, journals, simple expository paragraphs and brief essays. Activities guide students through critical steps in the writing process, including: brainstorming (to develop ideas for topics); defining one's purpose, means of communication, tone, and reader; making an outline; revising; and conferencing and peer editing. Additionally, useful tips in **Leer** provide students with specific lexicon, structures, and points of syntax relevant to the writing task at hand.

Enfoque cultural. This lively and informative section focuses on contemporary cultural issues related to the chapter theme. Each section of the *Enfoque cultural* includes activities that encourage students to explore the cultural topics and compare and contrast them with their own.

Temas introduces students to a broad variety of topics ranging from distinctive and changing aspects of daily life, such as family, housing, shopping, and travel, to broader social, political, and economic issues in Hispanic countries. Pre- and post-activities accompany the short illustrated reading.

Vistas employs a graphic layout, combining photos, maps, and captions to capture students' interest and expose them to key cultural information.

 Fortunas, a storyline video, is now integrated into the student texts with pre-, during–, and post-activities included in the text.

 Notas exposes beginning students to the various rhythms and topics of Hispanic music.

The Complete Program

Mosaicos is a complete learning and teaching program that includes the following components.

For the student
Mosaicos: Spanish as a World language (0-13-192324-2)
The full Student edition consists of a preliminary chapter followed by Chapters 1-15.

Mosaicos: Spanish as a World Language (0-13-154420-9)
The brief Student text consists of a preliminary chapter followed by Chapters 1-12 (the same content as the full edition).

Student Activities Manual (0-13-192326-9)
The new Student Activities Manual includes both workbook and lab manual materials in a single convenient volume, with all materials for a given chapter grouped together, saving students money and simplifying navigation. The *Mosaicos* Workbook parallels the organization of the text and provides more reading comprehension activities, sentence building and completion exercises, fill-ins, realia and art-based activities as well as composition exercises. Each chapter of the *Mosaicos* Lab Manual contains activities based on recordings of native speakers in situations thematically related to the corresponding chapters in the text. The listening material for the Lab Manual, the student audio for the in-text listening activities, and recordings of all the text's active vocabulary is provided for free on the *Mosaicos* Companion Website™.

Answer Key to Accompany Student Activities Manual (0-13-196985-4)
A separate Answer Key to the *Mosaicos* SAM is available, giving instructors the option of providing their students with answers to check their homework. The Answer Key now includes answers to both Workbook and Lab Manual activities.

Supplementary Activities Book (0-13-193045-1)
The Supplementary Activities Book consists of a range of fun, engaging activities that complement the vocabulary and grammar themes of each chapter and offers instructors additional in-class activities that serve to energize and enrich students' classroom experience.

Audio CDs to Accompany Text (0-13-196984-6)
These CDs correspond to the in-text listening activities and include recordings of the end-of-chapter vocabulary.

Audio CDs to Accompany Student Activities Manual (0-13-154642-2)
These CDs correspond to the Lab Manual portion of the Student Activities Manual.

Student Video CD-ROM (0-13-196979-X)
The Student Video CD-ROM contains the entire *Fortunas* video as well as the *Entrevistas* interview segments together with interactive comprehension activities. The *Fortunas* video will be accompanied by new comprehension activities and increased pedagogical support. The video is displayed using the Divace® media player developed by Sanako—the only media player on the market that was designed specifically for the language learner.

For the instructor
Annotated Instructor's Edition (0-13-192325-0)
The Annotated Instructor's Edition now includes *Vínculos* boxes with cross-references to related material in other components of the *Mosaicos* program. This enables instructors to see at a glance what material is available for homework assignments or additional practice, as well which specific materials are available for instructor use. Marginal annotations in the Annotated Instructor's Edition include warm-up and expansion exercises and activities, teaching tips and additional cultural information. The annotations are specifically designed for novice teaching assistants and adjunct faculty teaching from *Mosaicos* for the first time or who may have limited course preparation time. Answers to discrete point activities and the tapescript for the in-text listening activities are also provided for the instructor's convenience.

Instructor's Resource Manual (0-13-196982-X)
The Instructor's Resource Manual now contains complete lesson plans for all chapters as well as helpful suggestions for foreign and new instructors. Additionally, there are new video activities for the *Fortunas* video, and video activities will also be provided for the new *Entrevistas* and cultural videos. The Instructor's Resource Manual is a comprehensive source that contains everything from information on the philosophy behind the textbook to a complete Testing Program, Video Manual, and full, integrated syllabi and lesson plans.

Testing Audio CD (0-13-154643-0)
These CDs correspond to the listening comprehension portions of the Testing Program.

Image Resource CD (0-13-196983-8)
All illustrations from the textbook are provided on the CD. Instructors can use the images to create their own activities, implement in testing, create unique transparencies, etc.

Spanish Picture File (0-13-931313-3)
A beautifully crafted photo file of 50 full-color photographs mounted on cardboard and indexed by theme also accompanies *Mosaicos*. These can be used in the classroom in order to provide practice using the target vocabulary while discussing lesson themes and culture.

Instructor's Music CD (0-13-193419-8)
The Instructor's Music CD contains recorded versions of the songs found in the *Notas* section of each chapter, giving instructors convenient access to music for classroom use. The songs on this CD represent a variety of musical styles from a range of Spanish-speaking countries.

***Fortunas* VHS Video Cassette** (0-13-196980-3)
Written and filmed specifically for *Mosaicos*, the *Fortunas* video is an ongoing drama that features four contestants competing to locate three fortunes within Mexico. The three fortunes correspond with the three cultural periods of Mexican history (Pre-colonial, Colonial and Contemporary). Clues highlight and teach students about these cultural periods while the contest atmosphere provides students with a dynamic, interesting environment in which to learn the target grammar and vocabulary. New video activities are included in the IRM that include pre-, during–, and post-viewing exercises designed for in-class or lab use.

Online resources
Mosaicos OneKey is available in CourseCompass, WebCT, and Blackboard.

Companion Website™ *www.prenhall.com/mosaicos*

The *Mosaicos* Web site contains a wealth of practice and expansion exercises for students. Each chapter of the web site complements a chapter in the text and contains automatically graded exercises that practice and reinforce the vocabulary and grammar in each chapter. The section *Para investigar* includes link-based activities that take the student to a wealth of Spanish-language websites for linguistic and cultural discovery. In addition, the complete audio program to accompany the text and the Student Activities Manual is available for free, as well as an interactive soccer game and flashcard module.

National Standards

The National Standards in Foreign Language Education Project published *Standards for Foreign Language Learning: Preparing for the 21st Century* which identified five goal areas for programs of foreign language instruction: Communication, Cultures, Connections, Comparisons, and Communities. These goal areas inform the pedagogy of the fourth edition of *Mosaicos*.

Communication. Throughout the text, students engage in meaningful conversations, providing and obtaining information, expressing their opinions and feelings, and sharing their experiences. Students also listen to, read, and interpret language on a variety of topics. Through *informes* as part of many activities and in compositions in **Escribir,** students present information and ideas in both written and oral communication.

Cultures. *Cultura* boxes and the *Enfoque cultural* sections of each chapter give students an understanding of the relationship between culture and language throughout the Spanish-speaking world.

Connections. Realia, readings, and conversation activities throughout the text provide opportunities for making connections with other discipline areas. Students gain information and insight into the distinctive viewpoints of Spanish speakers and their cultures.

Comparisons. *Lengua* boxes often provide students with points of comparison between English and Spanish. *Para pensar* activities in the *Enfoque cultural* sections encourage students to reflect on aspects of daily life in their own culture before reading about and investigating similar aspects of daily life in Spanish-speaking countries.

Communities. The text encourages students to go beyond the classroom through Internet activities, and the *Mosaicos* Website provides abundant opportunities for exploration, personal enjoyment, and enrichment. Instructors are reminded to encourage students to explore and become a part of Spanish-speaking communities in their areas.

Acknowledgments

The fourth edition of *Mosaicos* is the result of a collaborative effort between ourselves, our publisher, and you, our colleagues. We are sincerely appreciative of all the comments and suggestions from first, second, and third edition users, and we look forward to continuing the dialog and having your input on this edition. We are especially indebted to the many members of the Spanish teaching community whose reviews and comments at various stages throughout the preparation of the first, second, third, and fourth editions have made *Mosaicos* the solid program that it is. We especially acknowledge and thank:

Shannon Álvarez, Monmouth College

Jorge Arbujas, Louisiana State University

Antonio Baena, Louisiana State University

Cora Bauza, Louisiana State University

Heather Beal, Louisiana State University

Betty Becker-Theye, University of Maine Hutchinson Center

Dr. Joan Cammarata, Manhattan College

Olga Casanova-Burgess, Baruch College City University of New York

José J. Colín, University of Oklahoma

Michelle Connolly, Community College of Rhode Island

David Cruz de Jesús, Baruch College/CUNY

Mark Del Mastro, The Citadel

Claudia Díaz, Texas Tech University

Carmen Eblen, Oxnard College

José Antonio Fábres, College of Saint Benedict/St. John's University

Sara Fernández-Medina, Texas Tech University

Wayne Finke, Baruch College (CUNY)

Jill Gauthier, Miami University—Hamilton

Jim Gregory, Texas Tech University

Janis Hanson, University of WI—La Crosse

María Hernández, Louisiana State University

Kelly Holmquist, Idaho State University

Hildegart Hoquee, San Jacinto College Central

Casilde Isabelli, University of Nevada, Reno

Kyra Kietrys, Davidson College

Nancy Laguna-Luque, Louisiana State University

Miguel Lechuga, Germanna Community College

Armanda Lewis, Columbia University

Nuria López Ortega, Miami University

Magdalena Maíz-Pena, Davidson College

Paola Marin, Gustavus Adolphus College

Rosa-María Moreno, Cincinnati State Technical & Comm. College

Jeanne Mullaney, Community College of Rhode Island

William O'Donnell, Canisius College

Carimer Ortiz Cuevas, Columbia University

María Pérez, Iowa Western Community College

Silvia Peart, Texas Tech University

Michelle Petersen, Arizona State University

Silvia T. Pulido, Brevard Community College

M. Mercedes Rahilly, Lansing Community College

Marilyn Reit, Shasta Tehama Junior College

Maria Rippon, The Citadel

Patricia Romero, Columbia University

Raúl Rosales, Columbia University

Linda Stewart, Idaho State University

Julie Sykes, Arizona State University

Andrew Tabor, Louisiana State University

Helen Tarp, Idaho State University

Glenn Thompson, Texas Tech University

Janos Welsch, Louisiana State University

Angela Willis, Davidson College

Hilma-Nelly Zamora, Valparaiso University

Sally Zengaro, University of Alabama

We would like to thank Blanca and César Gómez Villegas, Ana María and Juan Jorge Sanz, Gloria Toriello de Herrera, Johanna Herrera, Miguel Ordóñez, Benjamín Guzmán, and Raúl E. Salas for their help in obtaining authentic materials, and their advice regarding elements of current Spanish usage in their respective countries; Ninon Larché for her English language advising and technical support.

We would also like to thank all the editorial, production, and marketing staff at Prentice Hall who have contributed to the *Mosaicos* program. The authors of *Mosaicos, Fourth Edition* are deeply grateful to Bob Hemmer, Executive Editor, for his insightful guidance, invaluable support, and tireless work, particularly considering the special circumstances under which the fourth edition of *Mosaicos* was written. Many thanks to Julia Caballero, Director of Editorial Development, for her organization and continued encouragement.

We are also grateful to Mercedes Roffe, Development Editor, and Sarah Ramsey, for their dedication and meticulous work on the manuscript; Mary Rottino, Assistant Director of Production, who supervised all phases of the book's production; Claudia Dukeshire, Production Editor, for her careful and resourceful attention to every detail; Ximena de la Piedra Tamvakopoulos for the beautiful cover design; Meriel Martínez Moctezuma, Supplements Editor, for her calm efficiency and good humor in managing the print and audio supplements; Samantha Alducin, Media Editor, for her creativity, dedication, and many hours of hard work on the exciting online materials and videos; Roberto Fernández, Media Production Manager, for his commitment to the success of the Web site and CD-ROM projects; Kristine Suárez, Senior Director of Market Development, for her keen observations and market knowledge; and Jacquelyn Zautner, Senior Marketing Manager, for her many excellent ideas for the marketing campaign.

We are also grateful for the work of our talented colleagues at other institutions who have contributed to the supplementary materials for *Mosaicos, Fourth Edition.* Thanks to Mónica Prieto (Florida International University), Silvia Sobral (Brown University), JoAnne Flanders, Rebecca Williams and María Luisa Torres (all of Coastal Carolina University), Michelle Petersen (Arizona State University), Lina Lee (University of New Hampshire), James Crapotta (Barnard College), and Nurial López-Ortega (Miami University).

The coauthors of *Mosaicos* would like to express their thanks and admiration to Matilde Castells for her strength, love of life, and disposition to bringing *Mosaicos, Fourth Edition,* to a successful completion.

P

LECCIÓN PRELIMINAR
BIENVENIDOS

Objetivos comunicativos

- Introducing oneself and others
- Greetings and good-byes
- Expressions of courtesy
- Spelling in Spanish
- Identifying people and classroom objects

- Locating people and objects
- Using numbers from 0–99
- Expressing dates
- Telling time
- Using classroom expressions

Contenido

VÍNCULOS

To practice las presentaciones
- SAM-OneKey: WB: P-1, P-2 / LM: P-29, P-30
- Companion Website: AP P-1
- IRCD: Preliminary chapter; pg. 4

Goals. *Bienvenidos* is designed to make students' first exposure to the Spanish classroom a successful, enjoyable experience. Establish a comfortable atmosphere by using a variety of supportive techniques to lower students' anxiety level. Never underestimate the importance of praise and encouragement. Help students access meaning to unknown words by making frequent use of gestures or visuals—particularly in the beginning stages of learning.

Suggestions. Model *me llamo* by pointing to yourself and saying your name. Then write *me llamo* on the board and repeat the sentence. Now ask individual students for their names. Accept their answers if they say only their name, but encourage them to use *me llamo*, pointing to the board to guide them. Introduce yourself to a student, asking his or her name; answer with *mucho gusto*. Write *mucho gusto* on the board, and encourage the same response from the student. You may shake the student's hand to make the introduction more realistic. Repeat with another student, but this time encourage the student to say *mucho gusto* after his or her name; you respond with *igualmente*. Repeat it again before asking students to introduce themselves to a classmate. They may refer to the dialog if needed.

Suggestion. Quickly compare the uses of *tú* and *usted* by using pictures of people of various ages. Tell students to use *tú* when addressing each other. Then model the second dialog. Perform the dialog with a female and a male to show the change in *encantado/a*. Write both forms on the board.

Alternate. Model the third dialog. Write *amigo/a* on the board. Do the dialog again with one female student, using *amiga*. Then, in groups of three, one student introduces the other two, using their real names.

Expansion. You may introduce the phrase, *Su (Tu) nombre, por favor.* For further practice, you may have a student ask you your name or ask the names of two classmates.

Suggestion. When the need arises, use the *Expresiones útiles en la clase*, pages 19–20. Try to speak Spanish as much as possible from the first day of class.

Las presentaciones

AUDIO ANTONIO: **Me llamo** Antonio Mendoza.
Y tú, ¿cómo te llamas?
BENITO: Benito Sánchez.
ANTONIO: **Mucho gusto.**
BENITO: **Igualmente.**

PROFESOR: **¿Cómo se llama usted?**
ISABEL: Me llamo Isabel Mendoza.
PROFESOR: Mucho gusto.
ISABEL: **Encantada.**

LAURA: María, **mi amigo** José.
MARÍA: Mucho gusto.
JOSÉ: **Encantado.**

- Spanish has more than one word meaning *you*. Use **tú** when talking to someone on a first-name basis (close friend, relative, child). Use **usted** when talking to someone you address in a respectful or formal manner; for example, **doctor, doctora, profesor, profesora, señor, señora,** and so on. Finally, use it to address individuals you do not know well.

- Young people normally use **tú** when speaking to each other.

- **Mucho gusto** is used by both men and women when they are meeting someone for the first time. A man may also say **encantado,** and a woman, **encantada.**

- When responding to **mucho gusto,** you may use either **encantado/a** or **igualmente.**

¿Qué dice usted?

② P-1 Presentaciones. Complete the following conversation with the appropriate expressions from the box on the right. Then move around the classroom, introducing yourself to several classmates and introducing classmates to each other.

ALICIA: Me llamo Alicia. Y tú, ¿cómo te llamas?
ISABEL: Isabel Pérez. _Mucho gusto_.
ALICIA: _Igualmente_.

| Igualmente |
| Mucho gusto |

ALICIA: Isabel, _mi amigo Pedro_.
ISABEL: Mucho gusto.
PEDRO: _Encantado_.

| Encantado |
| mi amigo Pedro |

Los saludos

SEÑOR: **Buenos días, señorita** Mena.
SEÑORITA: Buenos días. **¿Cómo está usted, señor** Gómez?
SEÑOR: **Bien, gracias. ¿Y usted?**
SEÑORITA: **Muy** bien, gracias.

MARTA: **¡Hola,** Inés! **¿Qué tal? ¿Cómo estás?**
INÉS: **Regular,** ¿y tú?
MARTA: **Bastante** bien, gracias.

SEÑORA: **Buenas tardes,** Felipe. **¿Cómo estás?**
FELIPE: Bien, gracias. Y usted, ¿cómo está, **señora?**
SEÑORA: **Mal,** Felipe, mal.
FELIPE: **Lo siento.**

- Use **buenos días** until lunch time.

- Use **buenas tardes** from noon until nightfall. After nightfall, use **buenas noches** (*good evening, good night*).

- **¿Qué tal?** is a more informal greeting. It is normally used with **tú**, but it may also be used with **usted.**

- Use **está** with **usted** and **estás** with **tú.**

AUDIO

¿Qué dice usted?

P-2 Saludos. You work as a receptionist in a hotel. Which greeting (**buenos días, buenas tardes, buenas noches**) is appropriate at the following times?

a. 9:00 a.m   c. 4:00 p.m.   e. 1:00 p.m.
b. 11:00 p.m.   d. 8:00 a.m   f. 10:00 p.m.

Las despedidas

adiós	*good-bye*
hasta luego	*see you later*
hasta mañana	*see you tomorrow*
hasta pronto	*see you soon*

- **Adiós** is generally used when you do not expect to see the other person for a while. It is also used as a greeting when people pass each other but have no time to stop and talk.

- **Chao** (also spelled **chau**) is an informal way of saying good-bye. It is very popular in South America.

Expresiones de cortesía

con permiso	*pardon me, excuse me*
de nada	*you're welcome*
gracias	*thanks, thank you*
lo siento	*I'm sorry*
perdón	*pardon me, excuse me*
por favor	*please*

Con permiso and **perdón** may be used "before the fact," as when asking a person to allow you to go by or when trying to get someone's attention. Only **perdón** is used "after the fact," as when you have stepped on someone's foot or have interrupted a conversation.

¿Qué dice usted?

P-3 ¿Perdón o con permiso? Would you use **perdón** or **con permiso** in these situations?

Warm-up for P-3. As you pass through the classroom, bump into chairs and so forth. Model uses of *con permiso* or *perdón*.

Note. Whenever possible, students should work in pairs, taking turns to provide the appropriate answer. This will give them additional opportunities to communicate in Spanish. Then the whole class reviews the activity.

a. perdón **b.** perdón, con permiso **c.** perdón

d. perdón, con permiso **e.** perdón, con permiso

P-4 Expresiones de cortesía, y despedidas. Which expression(s) would you use in the following situations?

gracias	de nada	por favor
adiós	hasta luego	lo siento

1. Someone thanks you. de nada
2. You say good-bye to a friend you will see later this evening. hasta luego
3. You are asking a classmate for his/her notes. por favor
4. You hear that your friend is sick. lo siento
5. You receive a present from a friend. gracias
6. Your friend is leaving for a vacation in Spain. adiós, hasta pronto

② P-5 Encuentros. You meet the following people on the street. Greet them, ask them how they are, and then say good-bye. Switch roles.

1. su (*your*) amigo Miguel 3. su amiga Isabel
2. su profesor/a 4. su doctor/a

Warm-up for P-5. Model activity with a student before beginning the activity.

Note. Point out the importance of developing listening comprehension through regular use of the student audio CDs that accompany the text.

A escuchar.
The audioscript for each *A escuchar* is printed in the margin so the instructor may read the activity aloud instead of playing the audio CD.

Conversación 1
—*Buenos días, señora Gómez.* —*Buenos días. ¿Cómo está usted, señor Jiménez?* —*Bastante bien, gracias. ¿Y usted?* —*Bien, gracias.*

Conversación 2
—*¡Hola, Felipe! ¿Qué tal? ¿Cómo estás?* —*Regular, ¿y tú?* —*Bien, gracias.*

Conversación 3
—*Buenas tardes, señora Mena. ¿Cómo está usted?* —*Bastante bien, gracias. Y usted, ¿cómo está, señora?* —*Regular, regular.* —*Lo siento.*

Conversación 4
—*Me llamo Carlos Martínez. Y tú, ¿cómo te llamas?* —*Me llamo Cristina Camacho.* —*Mucho gusto.* —*Igualmente.*

Distinguishing Registers

AUDIO When you talk to different people, you use different registers. For example, when you talk to a professor, you most likely use more formal language than when you talk to your classmates or friends. In Spanish, one way of marking this difference is by using **tú** (informal) and **usted** (formal).

Now you will hear four brief conversations in which people greet each other. But before you listen, complete the following chart with the pronoun you think you would use.

WHEN TALKING TO YOUR . . .	TÚ	USTED
1. brother or sister		
2. doctor		
3. coach		

Saludos. As you listen to the four brief conversations, mark the appropriate column to indicate whether the greetings are formal (with **usted**) or informal (with **tú**). Do not worry if you do not understand every word.

FORMAL   INFORMAL
1. _X_   ____
2. ____   _X_
3. _X_   ____
4. ____   _X_

VÍNCULOS

To practice el alfabeto
• SAM-OneKey: WB: P-7 / LM: P-36, P-37
• Companion Website: AP P-5

Suggestion. The Image Resource CD contains the images on this page. Contrast *ñ* with *n*, giving examples of words students know (e.g., *señor, mañana*).

Note. The Spanish alphabet included *ch* and *ll* as letters until 1994, when the *Real Academia Española* deleted them. Dictionaries published after that date alphabetize *ch* and *ll* as in English. Point out the pronunciation of *ch* and *ll*, giving examples of words students know (e.g., *mucho, llamo, llamas*). Point out that since *b* and *v* are pronounced alike *(be)*, many Spanish speakers say *be larga* for *b* and *ve corta* for *v* when spelling.

Note. Point out the importance of good pronunciation, and remind students of the pronunciation section in the Student Activities Manual. Explanation and practice of the Spanish vowels is in the Student Activities Manual.

AUDIO *El alfabeto*

a	a	**o**	o
b	be	**p**	pe
c	ce	**q**	cu
d	de	**r**	ere, erre
e	e	**s**	ese
f	efe	**t**	te
g	ge	**u**	u
h	hache	**v**	ve, uve
i	i	**w**	doble ve,
j	jota		doble uve
k	ka		uve doble
l	ele	**x**	equis
m	eme	**y**	i griega, ye
n	ene	**z**	zeta
ñ	eñe		

■ The Spanish alphabet includes **ñ,** a letter that does not exist in English. Its sound is similar to the pronunciation of *ni* and *ny* in the English words *onion* and *canyon.*

■ The letters **k** and **w** appear mainly in words of foreign origin.

¿Qué dice usted?

P-6 ¿Cómo se escribe? Ask your classmate how to spell these Spanish last names.

MODELO: Zamora
               E1: ¿Cómo se escribe Zamora?
               E2: Con z.

1. Celaya
2. Montalvo
3. Salas
4. Bolaños
5. Henares
6. Velázquez

Note for P-6. Point out that Spanish speakers often do not spell out the whole word, but give only the letter(s) that may cause confusion. Model the activity by using some Spanish last names.

P-7 Los nombres. Ask three of your classmates their names. Write down their names as they spell them.

MODELO: E1: ¿Cómo te llamas?
               E2: Me llamo David Robinson.
               E1: ¿Cómo se escribe Robinson?
               E2: R-o-b-i-n-s-o-n

Suggestion for P-7. Have students move around the classroom for this activity.

Identificación y descripción de personas

AUDIO

CARLOS: **¿Quién es ese chico?**
SANDRA: Es Julio.
CARLOS: ¿Cómo es Julio?
SANDRA: Es romántico y sentimental.

LUIS: ¿Quién es **esa chica?**
QUIQUE: Es Carmen.
LUIS: ¿Cómo es Carmen?
QUIQUE: Es activa y muy seria.

VÍNCULOS

To practice identificación y descripción de personas
- SAM-OneKey: WB: P-8, P-9, P-10 / LM: P-38, P-39
- Companion Website: AP P-6
- IRCD: Preliminary chapter; pp. 9, 10

Note. The goal of this section is to introduce students to the verb *ser* and to preview the notion of gender and its relationship to adjective endings.

Suggestions. Use pictures of well-known people, as well as your own students, to practice *¿Quién es?* Use the pictures again to ask the following questions: *¿Cómo es X, serio/a o cómico/a? ¿X es activo/a o inactivo/a? ¿Es sentimental? ¿Es optimista o pesimista?* When presenting cognates with -o and -a endings, write words on the board, point to a male student using the appropriate adjective, and then point to a female student. Contrast with *¿Cómo está?* (e.g. *¿Cómo es Carmen? Es inteligente y seria. ¿Cómo está Carmen? Está muy bien.*) Model and personalize the short dialogs by pointing to individual students and having classmates respond (use only positive traits).

Note. Here only the *yo, tú, usted, él,* and *ella* forms of the verb *ser* are presented since these are the forms students will need for communication at this stage. You may present the other verb forms if you believe your students can profit from them. The formal presentation of the verb *ser* and its uses is found in *Lección 2, p. 69.*

Suggestion. Introduce and model *soy* by pointing to yourself as you describe yourself, sometimes using *yo* and sometimes omitting it: *Yo soy activo/a y serio/a. No soy impulsivo/a. Soy optimista. No soy pesimista.*

Introduce *eres* and *es* by varying model exchanges above and substituting names of different students.

SER *(to be)*			
yo	**soy**	*I*	*am*
tú	**eres**	*you*	*are*
usted	**es**	*you*	*are*
él, ella	**es**	*he, she*	*is*

■ Use **ser** to describe what someone is like.

Es Carmen. Ella **es** activa y muy seria.

■ To make a sentence negative, place the word **no** before the appropriate form of **ser.** When answering a question with a negative statement, say *no* twice.

Ella es inteligente. → Ella **no** es inteligente.
¿Es rebelde? → **No, no** es rebelde.

VÍNCULOS

To practice cognados
● SAM-OneKey: WB: P-11, P-12 / LM: P-40, P-41
● Companion Website: AP P-7

Suggestion. Explain how students can make good use of Spanish cognates. Ask them to come up with words they already know in Spanish. Focus their attention on adjectives by introducing *elegante, importante,* and *inteligente.* Use well-known people to introduce new cognates. You may also use visuals to present some of the cognates (e.g., a secretary *es responsable, es muy eficiente;* a poet or a writer *es idealista y sentimental, es creativo;* a musician or singer *es rebelde y romántico;* a priest *es religioso y tranquilo).* Well-known fictional characters may also be used (e.g., Sherlock Holmes *es inteligente y paciente, es muy valiente).* Ask yes/no questions to check understanding.

When presenting *extrovertido* you may mention that the form *extravertido* is also used.

Note. You may wish to add that the equivalent in Spanish for "lecture" is *conferencia,* and for "exit" is *salida.*

Cognados

Cognates are words from two languages that have the same origin and are similar in form and meaning. Since English shares many words with Spanish, you will discover that you already recognize many Spanish words. Here are some cognates that are used to describe people.

The following cognates use the same form to describe a man or a woman.

arrogante	**importante**	**optimista**	**popular**
eficiente	**independiente**	**paciente**	**responsable**
elegante	**inteligente**	**perfeccionista**	**tradicional**
idealista	**interesante**	**pesimista**	**valiente**

The following cognates have two forms. The **-o** form is used to describe a man, and the **-a** form to describe a woman.

ambicioso/a	**creativo/a**	**impulsivo/a**	**religioso/a**
atlético/a	**dinámico/a**	**introvertido/a**	**sincero/a**
atractivo/a	**extrovertido/a**	**moderno/a**	**tímido/a**
cómico/a	**generoso/a**	**pasivo/a**	**tranquilo/a**

There are also some words that appear to be cognates but do not have the same meaning in both languages. These are called false cognates. **Lectura** *(reading)* and **éxito** *(success)* are examples of this kind. You will find some examples in future lessons.

¿Qué dice usted?

Warm-up for P-8. Give a visual of a person to each pair of students, and have them describe the person.

② **P-8 Conversación.** Ask each other about your classmates. Describe them by using cognates from the lists above.

MODELO: E1: ¿Cómo es... ?
E2: Es...

❷ **P-9 ¿Cómo es mi compañero/a?** Choose from the cognates list on page 10 to ask the person next to you about his/her personality traits.

MODELO: E1: ¿Eres pesimista?
            E2: No, no soy pesimista. *o* Sí, soy (muy) pesimista.

Then find out what he/she is really like.

MODELO: E1: ¿Cómo eres (tú)?
            E2: Soy activo, optimista y creativo.

SITUACIÓN

You are walking through campus, and you run into a friend from your hometown. Your friend is walking with a person you do not know. As your friend is doing the introductions, your Spanish professor walks by. Your friend asks you who she/he is. Describe your professor to your friend and his/her companion, using at least three cognates.

¿Qué hay en el salón de clase?

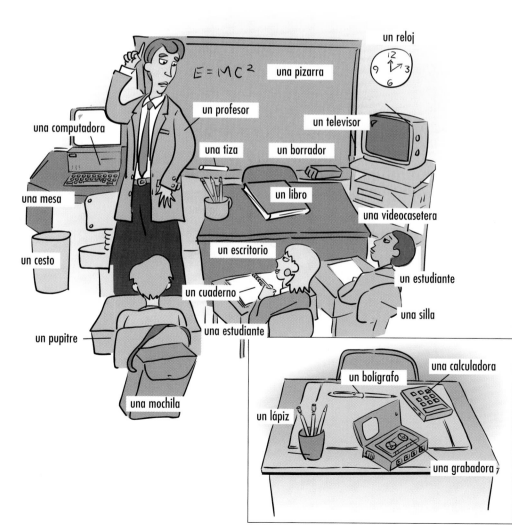

un reloj
una pizarra
un profesor
un televisor
una computadora
una tiza
un borrador
un libro
una mesa
una videocasetera
un cesto
un escritorio
un estudiante
un cuaderno
una silla
un pupitre
una estudiante
una mochila
un bolígrafo
una calculadora
un lápiz
una grabadora

Follow-up for P-9. After doing this activity, students get together in groups of four to exchange information.

Note. In the *Situaciones,* students are presented with a communicative task in which they must interact with each other. The *Situaciones* are presented in English to ensure that the students know what is requested of them and also so as not to give away vocabulary and linguistic constructions. The pedagogic purpose of the *Situaciones* is to provide students with ample opportunities to practice the vocabulary and language structures learned in the chapter, within a realistic context.

VÍNCULOS

To practice ¿Qué hay en el salón de clase?
• SAM-OneKey: WB: P-13, P-14 / LM: P-42, P-43
• Companion Website: AP P-8
• IRCD: Preliminary chapter; pp. 11, 12

Suggestion. Always strive to present new vocabulary in context. Experience has shown that students can become overwhelmed if too many new vocabulary items are presented at once. We suggest introducing three to four items at a time, checking for understanding before continuing.

The Image Resource CD contains the images on this page that can serve as a springboard for presentation of people and items typically found in the classroom. To check for recognition, mention different objects in the classroom and have students identify them.

Note. You may wish to point out that *computador* and *computadora* are used (also *ordenador* in Spain). Gender of nouns is presented in *Lección 1*; for now, use *un* and *una* without detailed explanation.

¿Qué dice usted?

Follow-up. Have students identify classroom objects or furniture that is found in their rooms.

Answers for P-10. a. *un reloj* b. *una calculadora* c. *un cuaderno* d. *un lápiz* e. *un bolígrafo* f. *un libro*

2 P-10 Identificación. With a partner, identify the items on this table.

Suggestion for P-11. Provide additional vocabulary if needed (e.g., *el casete, un diccionario, un CD*).

2 P-11 Para la clase de español. Write down a list of the things you need for this class. Compare your list with that of your partner.

VÍNCULOS

To practice ¿Dónde está?
• SAM-OneKey: WB: P-15, P-16 /
  LM: P-44, P-45, P-46
• IRCD: Preliminary chapter; pg. 12

Suggestions. Present the contrasting pair *enfrente de/detrás de* by standing in front of a student. Say *¿Dónde está el/la profesor/a? Está enfrente de...* Then move behind a student and ask the same question. *Está detrás de...* Reinforce understanding by asking three students to form a line in front of the class. The remaining students in the class respond with *sí* or *no*, according to whether your statements about the position of students are correct.

Ask either/or questions about students and objects: *¿Está Manuel enfrente de Carolina o detrás de ella?*

Ask questions using *¿Dónde está... ?* You may want to do some of the following: review *quién;* introduce other expressions such as *encima de, dentro de, a la derecha (de), a la izquierda (de);* or preview *están* by asking questions regarding the location of students: *¿Dónde están David y Elena?*

¿Dónde está?

To ask about the location of a person or an object, use **dónde + está.**

¿Dónde está la profesora?	Está en la clase.
¿Dónde está el libro?	Está sobre el escritorio.

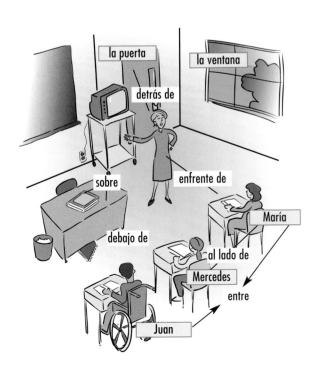

¿Qué dice usted?

P-12 ¿Sí o no? Primera fase. Indicate whether each of the following statements is true or false, based on the relative position of people or objects in the drawing.

	Sí	No
1. El televisor está detrás de la profesora.	X	
2. Juan está al lado de la profesora.		X
3. El libro está sobre el escritorio.	X	
4. María está entre Mercedes y Juan.		X
5. Mercedes está enfrente de la ventana.		X
6. El cesto está debajo de un pupitre.		X

Segunda fase. Now complete the following sentences, based on the relative position of people or objects in the drawing.

1. La pizarra está __detrás de__ la profesora.
2. María está __enfrente de__ la profesora.
3. Mercedes está __entre__ Juan y María.
4. Juan está __al lado de__ Mercedes
5. El cesto está __enfrente de__ Juan.
6. El televisor está __entre__ la pizarra y la puerta.

② P-13 La clase de español. Look at the seating chart below, and then follow the instructions.

María	Juan	Ester		Susana	Pedro
Carlos	Cristina	Ángeles		Alberto	Anita
Mercedes	Victoria	Roberto		Rocío	Pablo
		Profesor Gallegos			

1. Tell where Juan, Ángeles, Rocío, and Pedro are seated.
2. Ask questions about the location of other students.

② P-14 ¿Dónde está? Take turns asking where several items in your classroom are. Answer by giving their position in relation to a person or another object.

MODELO: E1: ¿Dónde está el libro?
                    E2: Está sobre el escritorio.

② P-15 ¿Quién es? Based on what your partner says regarding the location of another student, guess who he/she is.

MODELO: E1: Está al lado de Juan. ¿Quién es?
                    E2: Es María.

Suggestion for P-13. Prepare students by telling where some of the students on the chart are seated. They should answer *sí* or *no*. You may clarify that there are several possible statements for each name (e.g., *Alberto está entre Anita y Ángeles; Alberto está al lado de Anita/Ángeles; Alberto está detrás de Rocío*). Then they should do the first part of the activity (#1). Finally, students can ask either one or several classmates for the location of other students on the chart.

Suggestion for P-14. Students can also perform this activity in groups of four. The first student asks the person to the right, who answers and then asks the student to his/her right, and so forth. Students who are not asking can check that responses are correct.

Warm-up for P-15. Model the activity with students before they pair up. You may wish to introduce the expressions *cerca (de)* and *lejos (de)* and use them in this guessing game: *Está lejos de Susana. Está lejos de Arturo. Está muy cerca de Amelia. ¿Quién es?* Students take turns providing information and guessing.

A Escuchar

AUDIO Listening with Visuals

When you are talking with someone, you can understand what is being said by paying attention to the pictures or objects that the people point or refer to. Sometimes these objects are around you, but other times they are not. You have only a mental representation of them. For example, when a friend describes his/her Spanish classroom, an image of a classroom comes to your mind from your experience of being a student.

In Spanish, make a list of the people and objects you expect to see in a regular classroom.

_____

_____

_____

Now look at the drawing of the classroom on page 12. As you hear the different statements about the location of several people and objects, mark the appropriate column to indicate whether each of the statements is true (**cierto**) or false (**falso**).

	CIERTO	FALSO			CIERTO	FALSO
1.	X	___		4.	X	___
2.	X	___		5.	___	X
3.	___	X		6.	___	X

VÍNCULOS

To practice los números 0–99
- SAM-OneKey: WB: P-17, P-18, P-19 / LM: P-47, P-48, P-49
- Companion Website: AP P-9
- *Gramática viva*: Grammar Points 25 and 26: Numbers 1–20; Numbers 20–100
- IRCD: Preliminary chapter; pp. 14, 16

AUDIO

Los números 0–99

0 cero	11 once	21 veintiuno
1 uno	12 doce	22 veintidós
2 dos	13 trece	30 treinta
3 tres	14 catorce	31 treinta y uno
4 cuatro	15 quince	40 cuarenta
5 cinco	16 dieciséis	50 cincuenta
6 seis	17 diecisiete	60 sesenta
7 siete	18 dieciocho	70 setenta
8 ocho	19 diecinueve	80 ochenta
9 nueve	20 veinte	90 noventa
10 diez		

- Numbers from sixteen through twenty-nine are usually written as one word. Note the spelling changes and the written accent on some forms.

    18: **dieciocho** 22: **veintidós**

- Beginning with thirty-one, numbers are written as three words.

    31: **treinta y uno** 45: **cuarenta y cinco**

- The number *one* has three forms in Spanish: **uno, un,** and **una.** Use **uno** when counting: **uno, dos, tres...** Use **un** or **una** before nouns: **un borrador, una mochila, veintiún libros, veintiuna mochilas.**

- Use **hay** for both *there is* and *there are.*

    Hay un libro sobre la mesa. *There is a book on the table.*
    Hay dos libros sobre la mesa. *There are two books on the table.*

¿Qué dice usted?

P-16 ¿Qué número es? Your instructor will read a number from each group. Circle the number.

a.	8	4	3	5
b.	12	9	16	6
c.	37	59	41	26
d.	54	38	76	95
e.	83	62	72	49
f.	47	14	91	56

P-17 Una lista. This is a list of items you might need for your new office. Choose five items and tell your partner (the acquisitions manager) how many of each you want. Exchange roles.

MODELO: 4–7 mesas: Necesito cuatro mesas.

a. 6–10 teléfonos
b. 8–12 escritorios
c. 14–18 sillas
d. 6–12 calculadoras
e. 10–20 cestos

f. 24–48 bolígrafos
g. 9–15 computadoras
h. 1–2 computadora(s) portátiles
i. 1–3 reloj(es)
j. ...

P-18 Problemas. Take turns in solving the following problems. Use **y** (+), **menos** (–), and **son** (=).

MODELO: 2 + 4 = 12 − 5 =
    dos y cuatro son seis doce menos cinco son siete

a. 11 + 4 = 15
b. 8 + 2 = 10
c. 13 + 3 = 16
d. 20 − 6 = 14
e. 39 + 50 = 89
f. 80 − 1 = 79
g. 50 − 25 = 25
h. 26 + 40 = 66
i. 90 − 12 = 78

Suggestion for P-16. Have students hold up one, two, three, or four fingers to show each number's position.

Suggestions for P-17. Point out that *una* is used before feminine nouns by modeling appropriate examples. Write numbers on the board, making sure to include *uno* (*un bolígrafo, una silla, veintiún relojes*).

Note. An ellipsis (...) next to an item number in activities signals an opportunity for students to provide their own cue or response.

Suggestion for P-19. You may want to point out and discuss the use of both paternal and maternal surnames in most Spanish-speaking countries.

CULTURA

In Spanish-speaking countries, the name of the street precedes the house or building number. At times, a comma is placed before the number.

Calle Bolívar 132
132 Bolívar Street
Paseo de Gracia, 18
18 Paseo de Gracia

Telephone numbers are generally not stated as individual numbers, but in groups of two whenever possible. This also depends on how the numbers are written or on the number of digits, which varies from country to country.

12-24-67:
doce, veinticuatro, sesenta y siete

243-89-07:
dos, cuarenta y tres, ochenta y nueve, cero siete

VÍNCULOS

To practice los días de la semana y los meses del año
- SAM-OneKey: WB: P-20, P-21, P-22, P-23 / LM: P-50, P-51, P-52
- Companion Website: AP P-10
- IRCD: Preliminary chapter; pg. 16

Suggestion. Using a Spanish calendar or the Image Resource CD, model days of the week, pointing out that Monday is normally the first day of the week. You may preview ordinal numbers (presented in *Lección 5*) by saying *El lunes es el primer* (hold up index finger) *día de la semana. El martes es el segundo día,* etc. Introduce *último: el último día es el domingo.*

Follow-up. Point out that some Spanish calendars show the name of a saint for each day.

Suggestion. Introduce *Hoy es...* and *Mañana es...* by modeling appropriate days. You may also wish to introduce *Ayer fue...*

Note. Point out that the spelling *setiembre* is also correct.

❷ **P-19 Los números de teléfono y las direcciones.** Ask each other the addresses and phone numbers of some of these people. Use the chart below.

MODELO: Castellanos Rey, Carlos   Colón 62   654-6416
E1: ¿Cuál es la dirección de Carlos Castellanos Rey?
E2: Calle Colón, número 62.
E1: ¿Cuál es su teléfono?
E2: (El) 6-54-64-16

●	Cárdenas Alfaro, Joaquín	General Páez 40	423-4837
●	Cárdenas Villanueva, Sara	Avenida Bolívar 7	956-1709
●	Castelar Torres, Adelaida	Paseo del Prado 85	218-3642
●	Castellanos Rey, Carlos	Colón 62	654-6416
●	Castelli Rivero, Victoria	Chamberí 3	615-7359
●	Castillo Montoya, Rafael	Santa Cruz 73	956-3382

Los meses del año y los días de la semana

enero	*January*	mayo	*May*	septiembre	*September*
febrero	*February*	junio	*June*	octubre	*October*
marzo	*March*	julio	*July*	noviembre	*November*
abril	*April*	agosto	*August*	diciembre	*December*

ENERO CALENDARIO

lunes	martes	miércoles	jueves	viernes	sábado	domingo
		1 AÑO NUEVO	2	3	4	5
6 LOS SANTOS REYES	7	8	9	10	11	12
13	14	15	16	17	18	19
20	21	22	23	24	25	26
27	28	29	30	31		

Days of the week and months of the year are not generally capitalized in Spanish, but sometimes they are capitalized in advertisements and invitations.

- Monday (**lunes**) is normally presented as the first day of the week.

- To ask what day it is, use **¿Qué día es hoy?** Answer with **Hoy es...**

- To ask about the date, use **¿Qué fecha es?** or **¿Cuál es la fecha?** Respond with **Es el (14) de (octubre).**

- Express *on + a day of the week* as follows:

el lunes	*on Monday*
los lunes	*on Mondays*
el domingo	*on Sunday*
los domingos	*on Sundays*

- Cardinal numbers are used with dates (e.g., **el dos, el tres**) except for the first day of the month, which is **el primero**. In Spain the first day is also referred to as **el uno**.

LENGUA

When dates are given in numbers, the day normally precedes the month: *11/8* = **el 11 de agosto.**

¿Qué dice usted?

P-20 ¿Qué día de la semana es? Take turns asking and answering the following questions. Use the calendar on page 16.

1. ¿Qué día de la semana es el 2?
2. ¿Qué día de la semana es el 5?
3. ¿Qué día de la semana es el 22?
4. ¿Qué día de la semana es el 18?
5. ¿Qué día de la semana es el 10?
6. ¿Qué día de la semana es el 13?
7. ¿Qué día de la semana es el 28?
8. ¿Qué día de la semana es el... ?

P-21 Preguntas. Take turns asking and answering these questions.

1. ¿Qué día es hoy?
2. Hoy es... ¿Qué día es mañana?
3. Hoy es el... de... ¿Qué fecha es mañana?
4. ¿Hay clase de español los domingos? ¿Y los sábados?
5. ¿Qué días hay clase de español?

P-22 Fechas importantes. Tell each other the dates on which these events take place.

MODELO: la reunión de estudiantes (10/9)
   E1: ¿Cuándo es la reunión de estudiantes?
   E2: (Es) el 10 de septiembre.

1. el concierto de Cristina Aguilera (12/11) (Es) el 12 de noviembre.
2. el aniversario de Carlos y María (14/4) (Es) el 14 de abril.
3. el banquete (18/3) (Es) el 18 de marzo.
4. la graduación (22/5) (Es) el 22 de mayo.
5. la fiesta de bienvenida (24/8) (Es) el 24 de agosto.

P-23 El cumpleaños. Find out when your classmates' birthdays are. Write your classmates' names and birthdays in the appropriate space in the chart.

MODELO: E1: ¿Cuándo es tu cumpleaños?
   E2: (Es) el 3 de mayo.

CUMPLEAÑOS			
enero	febrero	marzo	abril
mayo	junio	julio	agosto
septiembre	octubre	noviembre	diciembre

Suggestion for P-20. Use the Image Resource CD that contains the image of the calendar; students may also work in pairs, taking turns.

Follow-up. Use a hypothetical class schedule and ask questions: *¿Qué día es la clase de español? ¿Cuándo es la clase de economía? ¿Y la de filosofía?* This will help students practice more cognates and serve as a preview for the vocabulary presented in *Lección 1.* You may also use cognates that could appeal more to your older students: *¿Qué día es el ballet? ¿Cuándo es el concierto?*

Note. You may wish to point out that Roman numerals can also be used to represent the month; for example, 11/X/05.

Warm-up for P-21. Ask *¿Hoy es...?* using the wrong day; students will answer *no.* Then say *¡Ah! Hoy es...* using another wrong day. Students answer *no.* Then ask *¿Qué día es hoy?* After a volunteer answers, students work in pairs, changing roles.

Follow-up for P-23. Each student should find out his/her partner's birthday. Then in groups of four, they should exchange the information.

VÍNCULOS

To practice la hora
- SAM-OneKey: WB: P-24, P-25, P-26 / LM: P-53, P-54, P-55
- Companion Website: AP P-11
- *Gramática viva*: Grammar Point 11: Expressions of time and location
- IRCD: Preliminary chapter; pp. 18, 19

Suggestions. Model *¿Qué hora es?* by using a clock with movable hands, using the Image Resource CD, or pointing to a clock or watch. Answer *Es la una, Son las...* Then give true or erroneous times using a clock with movable hands; students respond *sí* or *no*. Follow with either/or questions (e.g., *¿Son las tres o las cuatro?*) while indicating times. Finally, introduce and practice *y cuarto/y quince, y media/y treinta.*

Suggestions. Point out that there are alternate expressions for the time after the half hour: *son las tres menos diez, son las dos y cincuenta.* You may also introduce *faltan diez minutos para las tres.*

You may present *en punto* and *más o menos* using gestures. Follow with an introduction of *de la mañana/tarde/noche* and indicate *a.m.* or *p.m.* on the board.

You may point out that it is also common to say *siete de la tarde* if there is still daylight.

You may introduce the expressions *mediodía* for noon and *medianoche* for midnight.

CULTURA

In Spanish-speaking countries, events such as concerts, shows, classes, and professional meetings begin on time. Normally, medical appointments are also kept at the scheduled hour. However, informal social functions such as parties and private gatherings do not usually begin on time. In fact, guests are expected to arrive at least one half hour after the appointed time. When in doubt, you may ask either **¿Hora latina? ¿Hora americana?** or **¿En punto?** to find out whether you should be punctual.

La hora

- Use **¿Qué hora es?** to inquire about the hour. To tell time, use **es la...** from one o'clock to one thirty and **son las...** with the other hours.

Es la una.	*It is one o'clock.*
Son las tres.	*It is three o'clock.*

- To express the quarter hour, use **y cuarto** or **y quince**. To express the half hour, use **y media** or **y treinta**.

Son las dos **y cuarto.**	*It is two fifteen.*
Son las dos **y quince.**	
Es la una **y media.**	*It is one thirty.*
Es la una **y treinta.**	

- To express time after the half hour, subtract minutes from the next hour, using **menos**.

Son las cuatro **menos** diez.	*It is ten to four.*

- Add **en punto** for the exact time and **más o menos** for approximate time.

Es la una **en punto.**	*It is one o'clock sharp.*
Son las cinco menos cuarto, **más o menos.**	*It is about quarter to five.*

- For *a.m.* and *p.m.*, use the following:

de la mañana	(from midnight to noon)
de la tarde	(from noon to nightfall)
de la noche	(from nightfall to midnight)

¿Qué dice usted?

P-24 ¿Qué hora es en...? What time is it in the following cities?

Los Ángeles, A.M.

México, P.M.

San Juan, P.M.

Buenos Aires, P.M.

Madrid, P.M.

② **P-25 El horario de María.** Take turns to ask and answer questions about María's schedule.

MODELO: E1: ¿A qué hora es la clase de español?
E2: Es a las nueve.

	LUNES
9:00	clase de español
10:15	receso
10:30	clase de matemáticas
11:45	laboratorio
1:00	almuerzo
2:00	clase de física
5:00	partido de tenis

② **P-26 Mi horario.** Write down your Monday schedule, omitting the time each class meets. Exchange schedules with your partner, and find out what time each of his/her classes starts.

Expresiones útiles en la clase

Siéntese.

Levántese.

Abra el libro en la página 10.

Cierre el libro.

Escuche.

Pregúntele a su compañero.

Warm-up. Introduce *¿A qué hora es...?* and *(Es) a la(s)...* by writing on the board (in appropriate order):

clase de español   (time)
almuerzo   1:00 p.m.
clase de física   2:00 p.m.

Clarify *almuerzo* by using appropriate gesture for eating and by writing *cafetería* on the board. Then model questions and answers for the schedule.

Students will have additional opportunities to practice time in *Lección 1*.

LENGUA

To ask the hour at which an event takes place or something happens, use **¿A qué hora es...?** To answer, use **A la(s)...**
¿A qué hora es la clase?
At what time is (the) class?
(Es) **a las** nueve y media.
It is at 9:30.

VÍNCULOS

To practice expresiones útiles en la clase
• SAM-OneKey: WB: P-27, P-28 / LM: P-56, P-57
• Companion Website: AP P-12
• IRCD: Preliminary chapter; pg. 19

Suggestions. Use Total Physical Response (TPR) procedures to model the expressions in this section: *escuchen* (cup hand behind ear), *contesten* (make motion of calling students to yourself with both hands), *abran el libro* (open a book), *vayan a la pizarra* (go to the board).

Point to several students, give a command, and have students follow it. Write the word (e.g., *escuchen*). Then point to one student, give the command (without the final -*n*) and cross out or erase the -*n* on the board so students can hear and understand the difference between plural and singular commands.

Instructors who feel more comfortable using *tú* when addressing students may use informal commands to present these classroom expressions.

Vaya a la pizarra.

La tarea, por favor.

Conteste.

Repita.

Levante la mano.

Lea.

Escriba.

Note. Vocabulary lists at the end of *Bienvenidos* and *Lecciones 1* to *15* contain the active words and expressions used throughout the lesson, with the exception of obvious cognates.

■ When asking two or more people to do something, the verb form ends in **-n: vaya → vayan, conteste → contesten, repita → repitan.**

■ Although you may not have to use all these expressions, you should be able to recognize them and respond accordingly. Other expressions that you may hear or say in the classroom include the following:

Más alto, por favor.	*Louder, please.*
Otra vez.	*Again.*
¿Comprende(n)?	*Do you understand?*
¿Tiene(n) alguna pregunta?	*Do you have any questions?*
No comprendo.	*I do not understand.*
No sé.	*I do not know.*
Tengo una pregunta.	*I have a question.*
Más despacio, por favor.	*More slowly, please.*
¿En qué página?	*On what page?*
¿Cómo se dice... en español?	*How do you say . . . in Spanish?*
¿Cómo se escribe...?	*How do you spell . . . ?*
Presente.	*Here (present).*

VOCABULARIO*

Presentaciones

¿Cómo se llama usted?	*What's your name?* (formal)
¿Cómo te llamas?	*What's your name?* (familiar)
encantado/a	*delighted*
igualmente	*likewise*
me llamo...	*my name is . . .*
mucho gusto	*pleased/nice to meet you*

En el salón de clase

el bolígrafo	*ballpoint pen*
el borrador	*eraser*
la calculadora	*calculator*
el cesto	*wastepaper basket*
la computadora	*computer*
el cuaderno	*notebook*
el escritorio	*desk*
la grabadora	*tape recorder, cassette player*
el lápiz	*pencil*
el libro	*book*
la mesa	*table*
la mochila	*backpack*
la pizarra	*chalkboard*
la puerta	*door*
el pupitre	*student's desk*
el reloj	*clock*
la silla	*chair*
el televisor	*television set*
la tiza	*chalk*
la ventana	*window*
la videocasetera	*VCR*

La dirección

la calle	*street*
el número	*number*

Personas*

el/la amigo/a	*friend*
la chica	*girl*
el chico	*boy*
él	*he*
ella	*she*
el/la estudiante	*student*
el/la profesor/a	*professor*
señor (Sr.)	*Mr.*
señora (Sra.)	*Mrs.*
señorita (Srta.)	*Miss*
tú	*you* (familiar)
usted	*you* (formal)
yo	*I*

Posición

al lado (de)	*next to*
debajo (de)	*under*
detrás (de)	*behind*
enfrente (de)	*in front of*
entre	*between, among*
sobre	*on, above*

Tiempo, hora y fecha**

el año	*year*
cuarto	*quarter*
el día	*day*
en punto	*sharp*
la fecha	*date*
la hora	*hour, time*
hoy	*today*
mañana	*tomorrow*
la mañana	*morning*
media	*half*
menos	*minus, to* (for telling time)
el mes	*month*
la semana	*week*

Verbos

eres	*you are* (familiar)
es	*you are* (formal), *he/she is*
está	*he/she is, you are* (formal)
estás	*you are* (familiar)
hay	*there is, there are*
son	*they, you* (plural) *are*
soy	*I am*

Palabras útiles

a	*at, to*
en	*in*
ese/a	*that* (adjective)
mi	*my*
sí	*yes*
tu	*your* (familiar)
un/una	*a, an*
y	*and*

Expresiones útiles

¿Cómo es?	*What is he/she/it like?*
¿Dónde está...?	*Where is . . . ?*
más o menos	*more or less*
¿Quién es...?	*Who is . . . ?*

*See page 10 for cognates.
**See pages 14 and 16 for numbers, days of the week, and months of the year.

1

LOS ESTUDIANTES Y LA UNIVERSIDAD

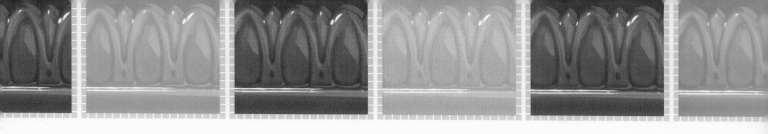

Objetivos comunicativos

- Asking for and providing information
- Expressing needs
- Asking for prices

- Talking about daily activities
- Asking about and expressing location

Contenido

A primera vista

- Los estudiantes y los cursos
- La vida estudiantil

- En la universidad

Explicación y expansión

- Subject pronouns
- Present tense of regular -*ar* verbs
- Articles and nouns: Gender and number

- Present tense of the verb *estar*
- Question words
- Algo Más: Some regular -*er* and -*ir* verbs

Mosaicos

- Escuchar: Listening for the gist
- Conversar: Summarizing the results of a poll

- Leer: Identifying the format and content of a text to guess meaning; identifying cognates to improve reading comprehension
- Escribir: Identifying basic aspects of writing; writing an email to a friend to talk about classes

Enfoque cultural

- Temas: Las universidades en España y en Hispanoamérica
- Vistas: España

    Para investigar en Internet

- Fortunas: Episodio 1
- Notas: Cuéntame alegrías, *Tachú*

Vocabulario

A PRIMERA VISTA

Los estudiantes y los cursos

Me llamo Carmen Granados. **Estudio sociología** en la **Facultad** de **Humanidades** de la **Universidad** de Salamanca. **Llego** a la universidad a las ocho y media. Mis cursos este semestre son **economía, ciencias políticas, psicología, antropología** y **estadística.** La clase de **economía** es mi **favorita.** La clase de antropología es **difícil,** pero el profesor es muy bueno. La clase de psicología es **fácil** y muy interesante. Por las tardes **trabajo** en una **oficina.**

Este chico es mi amigo. Se llama David Thomas. Es **norteamericano** y estudia español en mi universidad. **También** estudia **literatura, historia** y **geografía.** David es un chico muy responsable y **estudioso.** Generalmente llega a la universidad a las diez. Habla español y **practica todos los días** con sus **compañeros** de clase, sus profesores y sus amigos de la universidad. Por la tarde, estudia con uno de sus compañeros y **escucha** música o programas en español.

¿Qué dice usted?

1-1 ¿Qué sabe usted de Carmen? First circle all of the classes above that Carmen is taking. Then match the courses in the right column with the information on the left.

1. _____ nombre completo
2. _____ universidad
3. _____ clase favorita
4. _____ clase difícil
5. _____ clase fácil

a. antropología
b. psicología
c. Salamanca
d. economía
e. Carmen Granados

1-2 ¿Y David? Indicate whether each statement is true (**Cierto**) or false (**Falso**).

1. David es norteamericano. (C)
2. David habla español. (C)
3. David estudia literatura, historia y geografía. (C)
4. David llega a la universidad a las nueve. (F)
5. David practica español con sus amigos. (C)
6. David escucha música por la mañana. (F)

AUDIO David y Carmen hablan de sus clases

DAVID: Hola, Carmen. ¿Cómo estás?

CARMEN: Hola, David. **¿Cómo te va?**

DAVID: Bueno... bastante bien, **pero** mi clase de historia es muy difícil.

CARMEN: ¿Quién es tu profesor?

DAVID: Se llama Pedro Hernández. Es inteligente, pero la clase es **aburrida**.

CARMEN: ¡Vaya! Lo siento. ¿Estudias bastante?

DAVID: Estudio mucho, pero **saco malas notas**.

CARMEN: **¡Qué lástima!** Mis cinco clases son excelentes. Y tú, **¿cuántas clases tienes?**

DAVID: **Tengo sólo** cuatro.

CARMEN: ¡Uy! Son las once. Tengo un **examen** de economía **ahora**. Hasta luego.

DAVID: Hasta pronto. **¡Buena suerte!**

¿Qué dice usted?

1-3 ¿En qué clase... ? Match the words on the left with the appropriate class on the right.

1. __c__ casete y CD
2. __e__ números
3. __a__ mapa digital
4. __b__ animales
5. __f__ Freud
6. __d__ Napoleón

a. geografía
b. biología
c. español
d. historia
e. matemáticas
f. psicología

Ⓖ 1-4 Mis clases. Make a list of your classes. Next to each one, indicate the days and time it meets. Also say whether the class is easy, difficult, interesting or boring. You will find some subjects in the box below. Compare your list with those of your classmates.

ciencias
bioquímica
física
artes plásticas
contabilidad

comunicaciones
geografía
cálculo
estadística
astronomía

historia contemporánea
historia del arte
genética
seminario
filosofía

CLASE	DÍAS	HORA	¿CÓMO ES?

A INVESTIGAR

Look up **Universidad de Salamanca** on the Internet (**www.usal.es**).

1. Go to **Centros y Departamentos** and write down six of the departments listed.
2. Find the name of one professor in each department. Share your findings with those of other classmates.
3. Did you notice any differences between the last names used in the United States and those from Spain?

Warm up for 1-5. Before doing this activity you may want to have students practice the first person singular of *-ar* verbs and the forms *tengo* and *tienes,* which appear in the photo captions and the dialog at the beginning of this lesson. You can make comparisons with Carmen and David: *Carmen tiene cuatro clases, ¿cuántas clases tiene usted? David saca malas notas, ¿y usted?*

Suggestion. Remind students that the word *ordenador* is used in Spain. Have students share the information they got with other classmates. You may wish to preview third person plural forms. *Los estudiantes de esta clase estudian mucho. Trabajan con computadoras y escuchan casetes en el laboratorio. Uds. estudian español.*

2 **1-5 Las clases de mis compañeros/as. Primera fase.** Use the following questions to interview one of your classmates. Take notes. Then switch roles.

1. ¿Qué estudias este semestre?
2. ¿Cuántas clases tienes?
3. ¿Cuál es tu clase favorita?
4. Tu clase de español, ¿es fácil, difícil, interesante o aburrida?
5. ¿Trabajas con computadoras/ordenadores?
6. ¿Escuchas casetes en el laboratorio?
7. ¿Sacas buenas notas?
8. ¿Tienes muchos exámenes?

G **Segunda fase.** First, introduce your new friend to another classmate and give him/her one piece of information about your new friend that you find interesting. Your classmate will ask your friend questions about his/her classes.

MODELO: Él es Pedro, estudia ciencias políticas y tiene cuatro clases este semestre.

La vida estudiantil

Suggestion. Use the Image Resource CD to provide comprehensible input.

Note. Point out that some Spanish speakers say *tomar notas* in place of *tomar apuntes.*

AUDIO **En la biblioteca**

Unos **alumnos** estudian en la **biblioteca.** No **conversan porque** está prohibido. Estudian, **toman apuntes** y trabajan en sus **tareas. A veces buscan** palabras en el **diccionario.**

¿Y qué hacen los fines de semana?

Los estudiantes **toman algo** en un **café**.

Miran televisión en **casa**.

Bailan en una **discoteca** con amigos.

Caminan en la **playa**.

Montan en bicicleta.

¿Qué dice usted?

1-6 Para escoger. Look at the illustrations above and on the previous page. Then choose the word or phrase that makes sense.

1. Los estudiantes ___b___ en la biblioteca.
   a. toman café
   b. estudian
   c. hablan

2. Buscan palabras en ___b___.
   a. el reloj
   b. el diccionario
   c. el laboratorio

3. Miran televisión en ___c___.
   a. la biblioteca
   b. la playa
   c. casa

4. Montan en bicicleta ___a___.
   a. los fines de semana
   b. en el café
   c. los jueves

AUDIO En la librería

ESTUDIANTE: **Necesito comprar** un diccionario **para** mi clase de español.

DEPENDIENTE: **¿Grande** o **pequeño?**

ESTUDIANTE: Grande y todo en español.

DEPENDIENTE: **Este** diccionario es muy bueno.

ESTUDIANTE: **¿Cuánto cuesta?**

DEPENDIENTE: Cuarenta y ocho euros.

¿Qué dice usted?

1-7 Para completar. Complete the following statements, based on the previous conversation.

1. El estudiante necesita _____ un diccionario _____.
2. Es un diccionario _____ grande *or* para la clase de español *or* muy bueno _____.
3. Es para su clase de _____ español _____.
4. El diccionario cuesta _____ 48 euros _____.

1-8 ¿Cuánto cuesta? You are at the university bookstore. Ask the salesclerk how much each of the following items costs.

MODELO:

ESTUDIANTE:
¿Cuánto cuesta la grabadora?

DEPENDIENTE/A:
Cuesta cincuenta euros.

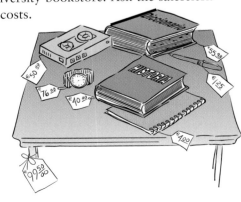

En la universidad

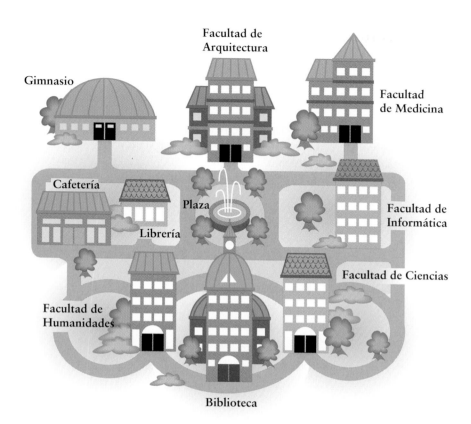

Gimnasio

Facultad de Arquitectura

Facultad de Medicina

Cafetería

Plaza

Librería

Facultad de Informática

Facultad de Ciencias

Facultad de Humanidades

Biblioteca

Suggestion for En la universidad. Using the Image Resource CD, point to various buildings, and recycle expressions from *Bienvenidos: La Facultad de Humanidades está al lado de la biblioteca. La plaza está detrás de la biblioteca.* Remind students that *la librería es donde compramos los libros* while *la biblioteca es donde estudiamos y consultamos libros.*

Bring copies of your school's campus map, and have students label various buildings in Spanish.

Note. You may point out that in some countries the word *computación* is used more often than *informática.*

¿Qué dice usted?

1-9 Entrevista (*Interview*). Ask a classmate where and when he/she does each of the following activities.

MODELO: practicar frisbi
E1: ¿Dónde practicas frisbi?
E2: Practico frisbi en la plaza.
E1: ¿Cuándo practicas?
E2: Practico por las tardes.

Note for 1-9. In the few cases where a new word appears in an activity, its English equivalent will appear in parenthesis next to the word, except for cognates (e.g., *frisbi*).

Follow-up. Additional items: 7. *montar en bicicleta* 8. *caminar con tus amigos* 9. *practicar español* 10. *tomar apuntes*

ACTIVIDAD	DÓNDE	CUÁNDO
1. estudiar para un examen difícil		
2. mirar televisión		
3. tomar café/chocolate		
4. bailar salsa		
5. escuchar música		
6. comprar un diccionario		

Follow-up for 1-10. Divide students into groups of three or four. Ask them to listen to each other's answers, comparing information. Students may share their stories in class.

1-10 En la universidad. Tell your partner about your classes. Take turns completing the following sentences.

1. Llego a la universidad a la(s)...
2. Mi clase favorita es...
3. El/La profesor/a se llama...
4. La clase es muy...
5. Practico español en...
6. Para mi clase de composición en español, necesito...

Follow-up for 1-11. Ask additional questions to recycle vocabulary and introduce new words: ¿Qué métodos usan en el centro? ¿Cuál es la clase más difícil en su opinión? ¿Cuál es la más fácil?

1-11 Busco una escuela. With a classmate, read the following brochure and look for the following specific information: name of the school, classes offered, school's address, and school's telephone number.

Suggestion for 1-12. As a pre-listening activity, divide the class in pairs or small groups and have them draw three columns: work, studies, and free time. Ask them to write—in 3 minutes—as many words as possible that they associate with each column. You may want students to compare their lists. Or, you may provide words and have students place them in the appropriate column (e.g., *oficina, clase, discoteca, televisión*).

Audioscript for *A escuchar*

1. Por las mañanas camino a la oficina. Trabajo en el departamento de informática de una compañía muy importante. Llego a la oficina a las nueve menos diez, y a las nueve ya estoy frente a la computadora. Mi trabajo es muy interesante.

2. Estudio biología y alemán. Mis clases son por la mañana y por la tarde. La clase de biología es difícil, pero no es aburrida. Hay muchos alumnos en mis clases de biología y de química, pero hay menos alumnos en las prácticas de laboratorio.

3. Los sábados por la mañana, practico fútbol con mis amigos. Por la tarde, miro televisión y hablo con mi amiga Alicia. Por la noche, Alicia y unos amigos toman algo en un café y yo bailo en una discoteca.

AUDIO **1-12 ¿Qué hacen estas personas?** You will hear three people talking about their activities during the week and on weekends, but before you listen, complete the following chart with your own activities.

MIS ACTIVIDADES DE TODOS LOS DÍAS	MIS ACTIVIDADES DEL FIN DE SEMANA
1.	
2.	
3.	

Now pay attention to the general idea of what is said. As you hear the three people talking about their activities, determine what they are talking about. Then write the number of the description next to the appropriate heading.

_____2_____ los estudios

_____3_____ el tiempo libre

_____1_____ el trabajo

EXPLICACIÓN Y EXPANSIÓN

1. Subject pronouns

SINGULAR		PLURAL	
yo	*I*	nosotros, nosotras	*we*
tú	*you*	vosotros, vosotras	*you* (familiar)
usted	*you* (formal)	ustedes	*you* (formal/familiar)
él	*he*	ellos	*they* (masculine)
ella	*she*	ellas	*they* (feminine)

- In Spain, the plural of **tú** is **vosotros** or **vosotras**. In other Spanish-speaking countries, the plural of both **tú** and **usted** is **ustedes**.

- Except for **ustedes**, the plural pronouns have masculine and feminine endings. Use **-as** for a group composed only of females; use **-os** for a mixed group or one composed only of males.

- Because the endings of Spanish verbs indicate the subject (the doer of the action), subject pronouns are generally used only for emphasis, clarification, or contrast.

¿Qué dice usted?

1-13 ¿Qué pronombre usa usted? Primera fase. You are talking *about* the people in the left column. Match the pronouns on the right with the people on the left.

1. __d__ Alfredo y Juana   a. él
2. __b__ la Sra. Gómez   b. ella
3. __e__ usted (*yourself*)   c. ellas
4. __a__ el Sr. Martínez   d. ellos
5. __f__ Ana y usted   e. yo
6. __c__ Alicia y Susana   f. nosotros/as

Segunda fase. Now you are talking *with* the following people. Match the pronouns on the right with the people mentioned on the left.

1. __b__ su profesor de historia   a. tú
2. __a__ su amigo íntimo   b. usted
3. __c__ dos doctores   c. ustedes
4. __b__ una senadora
5. __c__ dos compañeros
6. __a__ un niño (*a child*)

Note. Grammar explanations are brief and are followed by practice within a carefully focused, contextualized framework. Additional practice is given in the Activities Manual. Class time should be reserved for communicative/task-oriented activities. If a grammar point is to be presented in class, it should take a minimal amount of time. Ask students to read grammar explanations outside of class, preferably before the class meets.

Note. You may wish to mention that the pronoun *vos* is used in several Central and South American countries.

Suggestion. Review singular and plural pronouns by pointing to students in the class and having classmates provide the appropriate pronouns.

VÍNCULOS

To practice subject pronouns
- SAM-OneKey: WB: 1-6, 1-7/LM: 1-36, 1-37
- Companion Website: AP 1-2
- *Gramática viva*: Grammar Point 50: Subject Pronouns
- IRCD: Chapter 1; pg. 31

Note for 1-14. In this activity, students are only required to produce the subject pronouns in the answer. Students have practiced the singular forms of the verb *ser* in the *Lección preliminar* and some of them may answer with complete sentences using the singular forms of *ser*. The complete conjugation of the verb *ser* is presented in *Lección 2*. The formal presentation of the plural of nouns is in the next section of this lesson, but students have used *estudiantes* and *alumnos* in the previous section of *A primera vista*. You may preview these linguistic forms now, depending on your students and your program.

Note. *Vosotros/as* forms are presented in charts throughout *Mosaicos*; however, activities do not require that students produce *vosotros/as* forms since the majority of Spanish speakers do not use them. Instructors who wish to use *vosotros/as* in class can easily incorporate them into the activities.

Suggestion. To familiarize students with the verb forms, say: *Yo hablo español.* Point to a student or to a picture of a well-known Hispanic person and say: *Él/Ella habla español.* Point to the student or picture and to yourself and say: *Nosotros hablamos español. También hablamos inglés. No hablamos italiano.* Write *hablamos* on the board, circling the *-amos* ending. Point to another student and to yourself, and give another example: *Nosotros miramos la televisión.* Write *miramos* on the board, circling *-amos*. Point to one student and say: *Él/Ella habla inglés.* Point to another student and repeat the same sentence. Then point to both students and say: *Ellos/Ellas hablan inglés, pero no hablan portugués.* Write *hablan* on the board, circling the *-an*.

Note. The use of the present tense to express future actions is presented in *Lección 3*.

Suggestion. Model the use of *nunca* before the verb (*Juan nunca llega a las ocho de la mañana. Llega a las nueve.*).

Suggestion. You may wish to do a brainstorming activity to remember and reactivate all the *—ar* verbs students have seen so far. Write them down on the board as students say them. You may ask them to choose three of them and write sentences that they can share with the class.

VÍNCULOS

To practice present tense of regular *-ar* verbs
- SAM-OneKey: WB: 1-8, 1-9, 1-10 / LM: 1-38, 1-39
- Companion Website: AP 1-3
- *Gramática viva*: Grammar Point 34: Present tense of regular verbs in *-ar*
- IRCD: Chapter 1; pg. 32

Ⓖ 1-14 Mis compañeros. Ask questions to find out what your classmates are like. Every student will take notes to share answers with the class.

MODELO: E1: ¿Quién es optimista?
                   E2: Yo (*o* él, ella, nosotros, etc.).
COMENTARIO: Hay tres estudiantes optimistas. *o*
                   No hay estudiantes optimistas en el grupo.

	TOTAL	COMENTARIO
responsable	3	Hay 3 estudiantes responsables.
pesimista		
estudioso/a		
hiperactivo/a		
perfeccionista		
tolerante		
creativo/a		

2. Present tense of regular *-ar* verbs

HABLAR			
yo	hablo	nosotros/as	hablamos
tú	hablas	vosotros/as	habláis
él, ella, Ud.	habla	ellos, ellas, Uds.	hablan

■ Use the present tense to express what you and others generally or habitually do or do not do. You may also use the present tense to express an ongoing action. Context will tell you which meaning is intended.

Ana trabaja en la oficina.   *Ana works in the office.*
                   Ana is working in the office.

■ Here are some expressions you may find useful when talking about what you and others habitually do or do not do.

siempre	*always*	muchas veces	*often*
todos los días/meses	*every day/month*	a veces	*sometimes*
todas las semanas	*every week*	nunca	*never*

■ Other common -ar verbs are **bailar, buscar, caminar, comprar, conversar, escuchar, estudiar, llegar, montar, practicar, tomar, trabajar.**

¿Qué dice usted?

1-15 Preferencias. Primera fase. Rank the following activities from 1 to 8, according to your preferences (1 = most interesting, 8 = least interesting).

_____ bailar en una discoteca
_____ mirar televisión en casa
_____ conversar con amigos en los cafés
_____ caminar en la playa
_____ montar en bicicleta los fines de semana
_____ escuchar música rock
_____ comprar casetes y videos
_____ hablar por teléfono con amigos

❷ Segunda fase. Now compare your answers with those of a classmate according to the model.

MODELO: E1: Para mí, caminar en la playa es número 1. ¿Y para ti?
                   E2: Para mí, conversar con amigos en los cafés es número 1.

1-16 Mis actividades. Primera fase. Indicate with a check mark the activities that are part of your routine at the university.

1. _____ Llego a la universidad a las nueve de la mañana.
2. _____ Tomo notas en todas las clases.
3. _____ Converso con mis amigos en la plaza.
4. _____ Hablo con mis compañeros en la cafetería.
5. _____ Estudio en la biblioteca por las mañanas.
6. _____ Practico español con el CD-ROM en el laboratorio de computadoras.
7. _____ Miro programas cómicos en la televisión.
8. _____ A veces camino en el parque con un amigo.

② Segunda fase. Now compare your answers with those of a classmate. The expressions in the box will help you react to the information you hear as your classmate tells you about himself/herself. Report your findings to the class.

MODELO: Daniel y yo somos (muy) similares. Él y yo miramos programas cómicos en la televisión. o Daniel y yo somos (muy) diferentes. Yo estudio por las mañanas; él estudia por las tardes.

1-17 A preguntar. Find one classmate who does each of the following activities. Write his/her name in the corresponding column. The expressions in the box will help carry out a more spontaneous conversation.

MODELO: mirar televisión por la noche
      E1: ¿Miras televisión por la noche?
      E2: Sí, miro televisión por la noche.
          No, miro televisión por la tarde.

PERSONA	ACTIVIDAD
_____	estudiar español los fines de semana
_____	llegar a la universidad a las 9:30 a.m.
_____	escuchar música clásica en casa por la noche
_____	trabajar en una oficina por la tarde

② 1-18 Unos estudiantes excelentes. Make a list of things that the excellent students in your class do. Then, compare your lists.

MODELO: Siempre toman apuntes.

1-19 Mis actividades. Primera fase. Place a check mark in the space that indicates the frequency with which you do the following activities.

ACTIVIDADES	A VECES	MUCHAS VECES	SIEMPRE	NUNCA
estudiar con amigos				
sacar buenas notas				
llegar a la facultad a las ocho				
mirar televisión por la noche				
bailar los sábados				
montar en bicicleta los fines de semana				

Suggestions for 1-15. Additional items: *estudiar por la noche, tomar notas en mis clases, hablar con mis amigos en el café, llegar en taxi/caminar a la universidad, escuchar la radio.*

The inclusion of *para mí* and *para ti* in the model gives students the opportunity of using more authentic language as they exchange their opinions. Students only follow the model, and *para mí* and *para ti* are not considered active vocabulary at this stage.

Note. Both *vídeo* and *video* are used in Spanish; *Mosaicos* uses *video*.

You may wish to have students work in small groups to find out which is the most and the least interesting activity for the group. Afterward, you may have the whole class tally their responses.

EN DIRECTO

To express disbelief:
¡Qué increíble!
To show surprise at a coincidence:
¡Qué coincidencia!
To express interest at a finding:
¡Qué interesante!

Warm-up for 1-17. Model the activity by asking one student *¿Practicas español con tus amigos?* If he/she responds *sí*, say: *Yo escribo el nombre de... en el libro.* If he/she says *no*, ask another student. Then say: *Ahora ustedes les preguntan a sus compañeros. Levántense, por favor.* Signal for them to get up and move around to ask their classmates.

EN DIRECTO

To call the attention of someone or to interrupt to ask questions:
¡Oye! (*to someone around your age or younger*)
Oiga, por favor. (*to someone unknown to you*)
Perdón, tengo unas preguntas.
To agree to answer:
Con mucho gusto.

Follow-up for 1-17. After students complete the activity, have them report their results to the class. To practice plural verb forms, students can work in groups and pull together their findings: *Marta y Lucía llegan a la universidad a las 9:30.* Students can also find out if they are excellent students or not by checking with their classmates' lists.

Follow-up for 1-19. For additional practice, divide the class into groups of four. After each pair has asked and answered the questions, they change partners. Each new partner should tell the other the information he/she gathered.

Suggestion for 1-21. Have students observe the whole series of pictures to infer the context of the scene. Encourage students to give descriptions of the setting and the action(s) in each picture. Emphasize the importance of guessing when short of vocabulary (e.g., the words in illustrations 1 and 3). You may point out that part of the routine of many Spaniards is meeting with friends at a *bar de tapas* after work or school, before going home for dinner (*cena*). You may also mention that a) offices normally close from 1:30 to 4:30 p.m., b) employees usually stay until 8:00 p.m., and c) dinner is normally at around 9:30 P.M.

Segunda fase. Now, take turns telling the frequency with which you do the previous activities. Then, find out where he/she does them.

MODELO: E1: Yo estudio con amigos a veces, ¿Y tú?
          E2: Yo siempre estudio con amigos.
          E1: ¿Dónde estudias/estudian?
          E2: Estudio/Estudiamos en la biblioteca.

1-20 Tengo mucha curiosidad. You are really curious about how busy or quiet Friday evenings/nights are for one of your classmates. Write down four questions and ask him/her. Be prepared to answer his/her questions as well.

MODELO: ¿Estudias los viernes por la noche?

Segunda fase. Determine what activities are common to both of you. Then share them with another couple.

1-21 Un día típico en la vida de Luisa. Primera fase. Describe what Luisa does on a typical day.

MODELO: Luisa llega a la oficina a las nueve menos diez.

Note. This provides the students with a good opportunity to practice telling time as presented in *Bienvenidos*.

1.   2.   3.

Note for 1-21, Segunda fase. This is a good opportunity to recycle some of the cognates presented in *Bienvenidos* (*eficiente, independiente, inteligente, activa, moderna*), as well as others presented in this lesson (*estudiosa, responsable*).

4.   5.   6.

Segunda fase. Now, based on a typical day in her life, say what Luisa is like. Then explain what you normally do on a regular workday.

SITUACIONES

Use the expressions you have learned to sound more natural and spontaneous.

1. Your friend tells you that he/she works in the afternoons and you would like to know more about his/her job. Ask him/her a) where he/she works, b) the days of the week and the hours that he/she works, and c) how interesting/boring/difficult/easy the job is.

2. Greet your partner and ask a) how he/she is, b) what subjects he/she is studying this semester, c) the time of his/her first class **(primera clase)**, and d) what the professor is like.

3. Greet a new friend on campus and ask what he/she and his/her friends normally do on weekends (**¿Qué hacen...?**). Explain to him/her what you and your friends normally do on weekends.

4. You need to buy some school supplies at the university bookstore. Ask the salesperson for at least three items. Be specific and ask for prices. He/She will give you some choices and inform you of the prices.

Suggestion for Situaciones. Students should read the information for each situation and role-play with a partner. Make sure that students play at least two different roles.

3. Articles and nouns: Gender and number

Nouns are words that name a person, place, or thing. In English all nouns use the same definite article, *the,* and the indefinite articles *a* and *an.* In Spanish, masculine nouns use **el** or **un** and feminine nouns use **la** or **una.** The terms masculine and feminine are used in a grammatical sense and have nothing to do with biological gender.

Gender

Suggestions. Write *el/un* on the board or on a transparency next to the word *libro,* circling or underlining the *o.* Write *la/una* and the word *tarea,* circling the *a.* Give other examples of vocabulary presented in the chapter. Write *el mapa* and say *excepción;* do the same thing with *el día.* Continue with *la actividad, la lección,* and *la televisión,* underlining the endings **-dad, -ción,** and **-sión,** pointing out that words with these endings use the articles *la/una.*

As a mnemonic device, write the following words in a vertical column on the board, *el cereal, el libro, el salón, el pupitre, el borrador, el tenis.* Circle the final letters of each word to spell "loners"; point out that words ending in these letters are usually masculine.

	MASCULINE	FEMININE	
SINGULAR DEFINITE ARTICLES	el	la	*the*
SINGULAR INDEFINITE ARTICLES	un	una	*a/an*

- Generally, nouns that end in **-o** are masculine and require **el** or **un,** and those that end in **-a** are feminine and require **la** or **una.**

| el/un libro | el/un cuaderno | el/un diccionario |
| la/una mesa | la/una silla | la/una ventana |

- Nouns that end in **-dad, -ción, -sión** are feminine and require **la** or **una.**

| la/una universidad | la/una lección | la/una televisión |

- Some nouns that end in **-a** and **-ma** are masculine.

| el/un día | el/un mapa |
| el/un programa | el/un problema |

- In general, nouns that refer to males are masculine and require **el/un,** whereas nouns that refer to females are feminine and require **la/una.** Masculine nouns ending in **-o** change the **-o** to **-a** for the feminine; those ending in a consonant add **-a** for the feminine.

| el/un amigo | la/una amiga |
| el/un profesor | la/una profesora |

- Nouns ending in **-ante** and **-ente** normally share the same form (**el/la estudiante**), but sometimes they have a feminine form ending in **-a** (**el dependiente, la dependienta**).

- Use definite articles with titles (except **don** and **doña**) when you are talking about someone. Do not use definite articles when addressing someone directly.

<table>
<tr><td>

La señorita Andrade trabaja en
el Departamento de Lenguas.
Cuando **el** profesor Jones llega
por la mañana, ella dice:
"Buenos días, profesor Jones",
y él contesta: "Buenos días,
señorita Andrade".

</td><td>

*Miss Andrade works in the
Department of Languages.
When Professor Jones arrives in
the morning, she says, "Good
morning, Professor Jones," and
he answers, "Good morning,
Miss Andrade."*

</td></tr>
</table>

Number

	MASCULINE	FEMININE	
PLURAL DEFINITE ARTICLES	los	las	*the*
PLURAL INDEFINITE ARTICLES	unos	unas	*some*

- Add **-s** to form the plural of nouns that end in a vowel. Add **-es** to nouns ending in a consonant.

la silla	→ las sillas	el cuaderno	→ los cuadernos
la actividad	→ las actividades	el señor	→ los señores

- Nouns that end in **-z** change the **z** to **c** before **-es**.

  el lápiz → los lápi**c**es

- To refer to a mixed group, use masculine plural forms.

  los chi**c**os   *the boys and girls*

¿Qué dice usted?

② **1-22 Conversaciones incompletas.** Complete the following dialogs with the appropriate articles.

A. Supply the appropriate definite articles (**el, la, los, las**).

E1: ¿Dónde está María?
E2: Está en ___la___ clase de ___la___ profesora Sánchez.
E1: ¡Qué lástima! Necesito hablar con ella. Es urgente.
E2: Bueno, ella está en ___el___ salón de clase hasta ___la___ una, y por ___la___ tarde trabaja en ___el___ laboratorio.
E1: ¿Y a qué hora llega?
E2: Llega a ___las___ dos, más o menos.

B. Supply the appropriate indefinite articles (**un, una, unos, unas**).

E1: Necesito comprar ___una___ grabadora y ___unos___ lápices.
E2: Y yo necesito ___un___ bolígrafo y ___un___ diccionario, pero no sé qué diccionario comprar.
E1: Para el primer curso, ___unos___ profesores usan ___un___ diccionario pequeño y otros usan ___un___ diccionario grande. Habla con tu profesor.

C. Supply the appropriate definite or indefinite articles.

E1: Tengo ___un___ examen de matemáticas mañana y necesito sacar ___una___ buena nota en esa clase.

E2: ¿Quién es ___el___ profesor?

E1: Es ___la___ doctora Solís.

E2: ¡Ah! Es ___una___ profesora excelente.

E1: Sí, pero ___la___ clase es muy difícil. Estudio y reviso ___las___ tareas todos ___los___ días, pero no saco buenas notas.

E2: ¡Vaya! Lo siento mucho.

2 **1-23 ¿Qué necesitan?** Take turns saying what these classmates need.

MODELO: Alicia tiene que escuchar unos casetes.
            Necesita una grabadora.

1. Mónica tiene que tomar apuntes en la clase de historia.
2. Carlos y Ana tienen que hacer (*to do*) la tarea de matemáticas.
3. Alfredo tiene que estudiar para el examen de geografía.
4. Isabel tiene que escribir una composición para su clase de inglés.
5. Blanca y Lucía tienen que encontrar (*find*) dónde está Salamanca.
6. David tiene que copiar un programa de su computadora para un compañero.

SITUACIONES

To sound more natural and spontaneous in your conversation use the expressions you have learned.

1. **Role A.** You have missed the first day of class. Ask one of your classmates a) at what time the class is, b) who the professor is, and c) what you need for the class.

   Role B. Tell your classmate a) the time of the class, and if the class is in the morning, afternoon, or evening; b) the name of the professor and what he/she is like; and c) at least three items that your classmate will need for the class.

2. **Role A.** You work for the student newspaper at your college and you have been asked to interview students to find out what they typically do on weekends. After introducing yourself, find out from your interviewee a) if he/she works, and where; b) what he/she studies; and c) what he/she does on Saturdays and Sundays.

   Role B. Tell the interviewer a) if you work, and where you work; b) the classes you take; and c) the things you do on weekends, where you do them, and with whom you do them.

Note for 1-23. The expression *tener que + infinitive* is presented here for recognition purposes only and to provide each situation with a context. Students are not expected to use it. A thorough presentation of the verb *tener* and *tener que + infinitive* is found in *Lecciones 4* and *5*. Students have seen and used *tiene(s)* in *A primera vista*; therefore they should have no difficulty in recognizing *tienen* since they are familiar with the conjugation of verbs.

Answers for 1-23. Responses may vary. Possible answers: 1. *un lápiz, un bolígrafo, un cuaderno* 2. *una calculadora, un cuaderno* 3. *un libro, un mapa* 4. *un cuaderno, un bolígrafo, una computadora* 5. *un mapa* 6. *un disquete, una computadora*

Follow-up for *Situaciones*. Beginning with this *Situaciones* section, you will find a blend of open-ended, semiguided and guided role-plays. The purpose of the former is to allow for personalization of information and/or the completion of a communication gap; the latter aim at obtaining specific output from the student, that is, they are thought to assess the use of particular vocabulary and structures. However, care should be taken that students follow appropriate patterns of oral exchanges in Spanish in both kinds of situations.

For the second *Situación*, students should interview at least two classmates. Afterwards, students may form groups, gather their findings, and share information with the class.

Note. Remind students that they have been using two verbs, both translated as "to be" in English. Write *ser* and *estar* on the board. Ask basic questions that students practiced in the previous lesson (*¿Cómo está usted? ¿Dónde está...? ¿Cómo es...?*) while pointing to the appropriate verb. Have students answer.

Suggestion. Use photos, illustrations, or the Image Resource CD of people in various places to introduce *estar*. Also practice plural forms: *Ellos están en un café, y estas chicas están en una oficina* (write *están* on the board). *Pero ustedes están en la clase de español. Nosotros* (use gesture) *estamos en la clase de español.*

Cross-reference. The use of *ser* and *estar* are contrasted in *Lección 2*, page 69.

4. Present tense of the verb *estar*

ESTAR			
yo	**estoy**	*I*	*am*
tú	**estás**	*you*	*are*
Ud., él, ella	**está**	*you are, he/she*	*is*
nosotros/as	**estamos**	*we*	*are*
vosotros/as	**estáis**	*you*	*are*
Uds., ellos, ellas	**están**	*you, they*	*are*

■ Use **estar** to express the location of persons or objects.

¿Dónde **está** el gimnasio?   *Where is the gym?*
Está al lado de la cafetería.   *It is next to the cafeteria.*

■ Use **estar** to talk about states of health.

¿Cómo **está** el señor Mora?   *How is Mr. Mora?*
Está muy bien.   *He is very well.*

¿Qué dice usted?

VÍNCULOS

To practice present tense of the verb *estar*
- SAM-OneKey: WB: 1-15, 1-16, 1-17 / LM: 1-42, 1-43
- Companion Website: AP 1-5
- *Gramática viva*: Grammar Point 15: *Hay/está*
- IRCD: Chapter 1; pg. 38

2 **1-24 En la cafetería.** In the cafeteria, you run across a former classmate whom you have not seen for some time. Complete the following conversation, using the correct forms of **estar**.

estoy	estás	está	estamos	están

ROBERTO: Hola, Carlos. ¿Qué tal? ¿Cómo __estás__?
  CARLOS: __Estoy__ muy bien. ¿Y tú?
ROBERTO: Muy bien, muy bien. ¿Y cómo __está__ tu hermana *(sister)* Ana?
  CARLOS: Ella y mamá __están__ en España ahora.
ROBERTO: ¡Qué suerte! Y nosotros __estamos__ en la universidad, ¡y en la semana de exámenes!

Note for 1-25. This activity gives students an opportunity to recycle vocabulary and expressions, such as *al lado de, detrás de,* and *entre,* which were presented in *Bienvenidos.*

2 **1-25 Lugares en el campus. Primera fase.** Determine four places on campus that in your view are frequently visited by students in your university.

Segunda fase. You run across a classmate in the hallway. Tell him/her what you need from two of the buildings mentioned in **Primera fase,** and then ask where these buildings are located. He/She will answer as specifically as possible. Do not forget to address him/her appropriately as you approach him/her and ask for help. Also, thank him/her for the information.

MODELO: E1: Necesito un mapa. ¿Dónde está la biblioteca?
         E2: Está _____.

2 **1-26 Horas y lugares. Primera fase.** Ask where your classmate usually is at the following times and days.

MODELO: 8:00 a.m. / los lunes
         E1: ¿Dónde estás a las ocho de la mañana los lunes?
         E2: Estoy en la clase de física. ¿Y tú?
         E1: Estoy en casa.

a. 9:00 a.m. / los martes
b. 11:00 a.m. / los miércoles.
c. 1:00 p.m. / los viernes

d. 3:00 p.m. / los domingos
e. 9:00 p.m. / los lunes
f. ...

G **Segunda fase.** Ask two classmates where they usually are a) in the morning, b) in the afternoon, and c) in the evening on weekends. Then share this information with the class.

❷ 1-27 Conversación. Look at the following drawings. Ask a classmate where these people are, how they feel, and what they are doing.

MODELO:　　E1: ¿Dónde está María Luisa?
　　　　　　　E2: Está en la biblioteca.
　　　　　　　E1: ¿Cómo está?
　　　　　　　E2: Está regular.
　　　　　　　E1: ¿Qué hace?
　　　　　　　E2: Estudia.

Suggestion for 1-27. Encourage students to guess how to say the location in drawing 2 (*el hospital, la clínica*), telling them only that it is a cognate. Once a student guesses either word, model pronunciation and spelling of both. Do the same thing for *basquetbol* in drawing 3. You may also give the word *baloncesto*.

María Luisa

1. 　Berta　　Lorena

2. 　Carlos　　el Dr. Núñez

3.　Marcelo　　Eduardo

SITUACIONES

1. **Role A.** You are the university representative who has to give directions to a graphic designer for the new student handbook. Explain to him/her the location of the various buildings below.

la cafetería	la biblioteca	la Facultad de Humanidades
la Facultad de Ciencias	la librería	el gimnasio

   Role B. You are the graphic designer for the campus map. Ask questions about the location of these buildings as you draw the new map. When you have finished, show the map to the university representative to check if you have understood his/her explanations.

2. **Role A.** You are a new student at the university and you do not know where the bookstore is. Introduce yourself to one of your classmates. Then, a) tell him/her that you need to buy some books and b) ask where the bookstore is. Thank him/her for the help **(Gracias por la ayuda).**

   Role B. A new student will greet you and ask questions. Make your answers as complete and specific as possible.

Suggestion. Students should switch roles, so the university representative can play the role of the designer, and vice versa.

Suggestions. Ask students questions such as the following: *¿Dónde está la pizarra? ¿Y quién(es) está(n) al lado de la pizarra? ¿Cuántos alumnos hay en esta fila? ¿Quiénes son? ¿Cómo es...?* Point out the difference in stress and meaning between *¿por qué?* and *porque.*

To practice asking for definitions, provide students with words such as *lugar* and *objeto: ¿Qué es una librería? Es un lugar donde compramos libros. ¿Qué es un lápiz? Es un objeto que usamos para escribir.* In small groups, have students practice giving very simple definitions (e.g., *oficina, tiza*).

Ask questions using *cuál(es): ¿Cuál es la mochila de Alberto? ¿Y cuáles son los libros de Ana y Pedro?*

Point out that intonation rises at the end of yes/no questions. Indicate this by lifting your hand as you raise intonation asking sample yes/no questions with subjects following and preceding the verb.

To practice interrogative tags you may wish to ask several questions of the same student: *Usted es David, ¿verdad? Y usted es norteamericano, ¿no?*

Practice the use of *¿cómo?* to request repetition or clarification.

Follow-up for 1-28. Have students create questions using the question words in the directions.

Suggestion for 1-29. Students interview each other in pairs, then report to other students in groups of four. Encourage students to be creative and ask additional questions.

5. Question words

cómo	how/what	cuál(es)	which
dónde	where	quién(es)	who
qué	what	cuánto/a	how much
cuándo	when	cuántos/as	how many

■ If a subject is used in a question, it normally follows the verb.

> ¿Dónde **trabaja Elsa?** *Where does Elsa work?*

■ Use **por qué** to ask *why* and **porque** to answer *because.*

> ¿**Por qué** está Pepe en la biblioteca? *Why is Pepe at the library?*
> **Porque** necesita estudiar. *Because he needs to study.*

■ Use **qué + ser** when you want to ask for a definition or an explanation.

> ¿**Qué es** la sardana? *What is the sardana?*
> Es un baile típico de Cataluña. *It is a typical dance of Catalonia.*

■ Use **cuál (es) + ser** when you want to ask which one(s).

> ¿**Cuál es** tu mochila? *Which (one) is your backpack?*
> ¿**Cuáles son** tus papeles? *Which (ones) are your papers?*

■ Questions that may be answered with **sí** or **no** do not use a question word.

> ¿Trabajan ustedes los sábados? *Do you work on Saturdays?*
> No, no trabajamos. *No, we do not.*

■ Another way to ask a question is to place an interrogative tag after a declarative statement.

> Tú hablas inglés, ¿**verdad?** *You speak English, don't you?*
> David es norteamericano, ¿**no?** *David is an American, isn't he?*

¿Qué dice usted?

2 1-28 Entrevista. Look at the cues in the right column before completing the questions using **quién, cuándo, cuántos/as, cuál, por qué,** as needed. Then walk around the room to interview two classmates.

1. ¿ _Cuántas/Qué_ clases tomas? Tomo...
2. ¿ _Cuándo_ son tus clases? Por la...
3. ¿ _Cuál_ es tu clase favorita? La clase de...
4. ¿ _Quién_ es tu profesor favorito? El/La profesor/a...
5. ¿ _Por qué_ estudias español? Porque...
6. ¿ _Cuántos_ estudiantes hay en tu clase de español? Hay...

2 1-29 Entrevista. Ask appropriate questions to find out the following information. Use the appropriate expressions to show: disbelief, coincidence, how interesting the answers you hear are, etc.

1. número de clases que toma este semestre
2. su clase favorita y por qué
3. número de alumnos en la clase favorita
4. nombre del/de la profesor/a favorito/a
5. lugar donde estudia y cuántas horas
6. lugar donde trabaja

1-30 Entrevista. You are conducting a survey for a Spanish television station. Ask appropriate questions to find out the information requested below.

1. Dirección _____
2. Teléfono _____
3. Número de personas en la casa/el apartamento _____
4. Número de televisores en la casa/el apartamento _____
5. Programas favoritos _____
6. Número de horas que miran televisión durante la semana _____
7. Número de horas que miran televisión los fines de semana _____

  **SITUACIONES**

1. You have just run across a Spanish-speaking friend that you have not seen for a long time. Tell him/her about a) your university (location and size), b) your courses, and c) your activities. Ask him/her questions to get the same information.

2. **Role A:** It is the beginning of the term, and you missed yesterday's class. As usual, you expect some minor changes in the course schedule and syllabus. Ask your partner a) if there is homework, b) if there is an exam soon **(pronto)**, and c) when the exam is.

   Role B: Answer your classmate's questions being as specific as possible. You may add that the exam will take place in a different classroom and give him/her the classroom location.

 **ALGO MÁS**

Some regular -er and -ir verbs

The verb form found in dictionaries and in most vocabulary lists is the infinitive: **hablar, estudiar,** etc. Its equivalent in English is the verb preceded by *to: to speak, to study.* In Spanish, most infinitives end in **-ar;** other infinitives end in **-er** and **-ir.**

So far you have practiced the present tense of regular **-ar** verbs. Now you will practice the **yo, tú,** and **usted/él/ella** forms of some **-er** and **-ir** verbs: **leer,** *to read;* **comer,** *to eat;* **aprender,** *to learn;* **escribir,** *to write;* **vivir,** *to live;* **asistir,** *to attend.*

■ As you did with **-ar** verbs, use the ending **-o** when talking about your daily activities.

   Leo y **escribo** en la clase todos los días.   *I read and I write in class every day.*

■ For the **tú** form, use the ending **-es.**

   ¿**Comes** en la cafetería o en tu casa?   *Do you eat in the cafeteria or at home?*

   Vives en una casa, ¿verdad?   *You live in a house, right?*

■ For the **usted/él/ella** form, delete the final **-s** of the **tú** form.

   Ella **vive** en la calle Salud.   *She lives on Salud Street.*

Suggestion for 1-30. After exchanging the information in pairs, students may get together with another pair and compile the information of the group. As a last step, they may compare their findings with those of other groups and find out a) the average number of hours that each individual watches TV, b) the number of hours they watch TV in weekdays vs. weekends, and c) which is their favorite program.

VÍNCULOS

To practice question words
● SAM-OneKey: WB: 1-18, 1-19, 1-20, 1-21 / LM: 1-44, 1-45
● Companion Website: AP 1-6
● *Gramática viva:* Grammar Point 22: Interrogatives

Remind Students to use those expressions that will help you sound more natural and spontaneous.

Note for Algo más. In the *Algo más* section, some key structures needed for communication are previewed and introduced in increments. For example, in the *Algo más* section for this lesson, students practice some high-frequency regular *-er* and *-ir* verbs, which will enable them to improve their ability to talk about their studies and daily life. A formal presentation of regular *-er* and *-ir* verbs is found in *Lección 3.*

VÍNCULOS

To practice some regular *-er* and *-ir* verbs
● SAM-OneKey: WB: 1-22, 1-23 / LM: 1-46, 1-47
● Companion Website: AP 1-7
● *Gramática viva:* Grammar Point 37: Present tense of regular *-er, -ir* verbs

A conversar

G **1-43 Entrevista.** Ask all members of your group what courses they are taking and what their classes are like. Complete the chart with the results of your poll.

MODELO: E1: ¿Estudias estadística?
E2: Sí, estudio estadística./No, no estudio estadística. Estudio...
E1: ¿Es una clase difícil?
E2: No, es (una clase) fácil.
E1: ¿Es una clase obligatoria?
E2: Sí, (es obligatoria). / No, (es optativa).

MATERIAS	ESTUDIANTE	DIFÍCIL	FÁCIL	OBLIGATORIA	OPTATIVA
ciencias políticas					
economía					
español					
literatura inglesa					
matemáticas					

Después de conversar

G **1-44 Resultados de la entrevista.** Now summarize the results of your poll and share them with the class.

1. ¿Cuántos/as compañeros/as estudian economía, física, etc.?
2. Según la opinión del grupo, ¿qué clases son fáciles? ¿Qué clases son difíciles?
3. ¿Qué clases son obligatorias? ¿Y qué clases son optativas?

 Leer ▪▪

Introduction to reading

Reading is an important skill that you will develop as you study Spanish. You should not expect to be able to read proficiently at first; however, it is important to begin developing this ability early in the language learning process.

In each chapter of *Mosaicos,* you will be focusing on one or two reading strategies to improve your reading skills in Spanish. As the term unfolds, you will also review previously learned strategies that are necessary to face more complex texts.

In *Lección 1,* you will do the following:

- Draw on your experience and knowledge of the world to comprehend an unfamiliar text. Use what you know about the topic as you read; this will help you predict and/or discover new meanings.

- Pay attention to cognates; that is, words that are spelled similarly in Spanish and English and that bear the same meaning. Such words will help tremendously with comprehension of the text. Beware that there are also false cognates (words with the same or almost the same spelling), which may hinder your interpretation of meaning.

- Pay close attention to visual cues like photographs, illustrations, and charts that may accompany the reading, or to the size of type used for headings, and so on. These visual cues will help you make educated guesses about the content and meaning of the text.

- Get used to reading every text at least twice. First read the text to get the general sense and main ideas. When you read the second time, underline or jot down unfamiliar expressions that block your comprehension of the text. Make hypotheses about possible meanings and read the text a third time. This last reading should serve as a confirmation of your guesses.

Guía de prelectura

1. As you take a quick look at the text in 1-46, rely on your previous knowledge to answer these questions:

   A. Does the following text appear in a newspaper? Yes No

   B. What information led you to answer the way you did?
   1. the format of the text   Yes   No
   2. some cognates in the text   Yes   No
   3. the illustrations   Yes   No

2. Use your knowledge of the English language for comprehension.
   If cognates helped you figure out the kind of text this is, can you write at least three of the cognates that facilitated your work?

   a. _____   b. _____   c. _____

Suggestion for Guía de prelectura. Since this may be the first time your students read a whole text in Spanish, we suggest you discuss reading strategies in English. Doing so will allow your students to understand information that will help them improve their reading proficiency.

Antes de leer

1-45 Preparación. Which of the classes below should be mandatory for students majoring in the following careers? Write the classes under the corresponding career.

fisiología
diseño gráfico
drogas tóxicas
conflictos sociales contemporáneos
la estructura del español

muralistas mexicanos
anatomía
medicinas alternativas
historia de las lenguas modernas
la depresión

Answers for 1-45. *Medicina: fisiología, anatomía; Bellas Artes: diseño gráfico, muralistas mexicanos; Farmacia: drogas tóxicas, medicinas alternativas; Psicología: conflictos sociales contemporáneos, la depresión; Filologios: la estructura del español, historia de las lenguas modernas*

MEDICINA	BELLAS ARTES	FARMACIA	PSICOLOGÍA	FILOLOGÍA

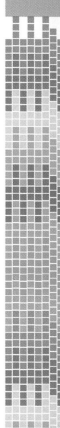

A leer

1-46 Primera mirada. Underline the correct response in each statement taken from the Web page of a Spanish educational institution.

1. Esta página web es de una escuela secundaria/de una universidad/del gobierno español.
2. El logo indica que esta institución es muy nueva/muy antigua.
3. Esta página web presenta una lista de clases/una lista de carreras.
4. La información de esta página web es muy específica/muy general.
5. Esta institución tiene un campus/más de un campus.
6. Es posible/No es posible escribir un correo electrónico (*e-mail*) para obtener información sobre las carreras.

1-47 Segunda mirada. According to the information on the Web page, answer the following questions.

1. ¿Qué palabras de esta página Web son probablemente nombres de ciudades?
2. Al final (*the bottom*) de esta página Web hay varias teclas (*keys*). ¿Qué tecla usan los estudiantes para conversar con personas que trabajan en la Universidad de Salamanca?
3. Imagínese que usted necesita información sobre su especialidad en la Universidad de Salamanca. ¿Qué facultad tiene la información que usted necesita?

Después de leer

1-48 Ampliación. In general, most of the words ending in **-ía, -cia, -ción** are feminine in Spanish. Find the names of some careers that have a feminine ending. Write them below.

-ÍA	-CIA	-CIÓN

 *Escribir*

Identifying basic aspects of writing

Writing is an act of communication in every language. In order for your writing to be effective, you need to consider the following questions before you begin:

1. **Purpose:** Why are you writing? To communicate with a friend? To request something in a business situation? To complain? To inform?
2. **Medium of communication:** What medium of communication are you using? Is it a letter, a postcard, an essay? Are you filling out a form, writing a report?
3. **Reader:** Are you writing to a friend, a business person, a young or an old person?
4. **Topic:** What is the content of your writing? Are you writing about your personal experience or about a broader, more general topic?
5. **Language:** What vocabulary and structures will you potentially need to develop your topic? When writing in a language other than your own, you will find it helpful to list these before you begin. For example, if you are interviewing a classmate about his or her background, you will find it useful to make a list of the questions for requesting personal information: *¿Dónde vives? ¿Qué estudias?*, and so on.

In this chapter, you have talked about your life at school, outside school, and your daily routine. Now, you will have the opportunity to do it in writing.

Antes de escribir

1-49 Preparación. Primera fase. Imagine that this is your first year in college and you would like to write your Spanish-speaking pen pal an e-mail about your new life as a university student. To show your pen pal that your Spanish skills have improved greatly, think about the following information and complete what's missing.

1. Specify the purpose of your message/writing.
2. Determine your reader.
3. Determine the topic of your message.

Segunda fase. Now plan the language you will probably use.

1. Think of two ways to tell your friend how things are going for you. Write them down.
2. Make a list in Spanish of the classes you are taking this term.
3. Write some expressions that you would use to describe what your professors and your classes are like.
4. Make a list of the activities that you routinely do . . .
    a. during the week: When and where do you do them? Do you do them in the morning, in the afternoon, or at night? Do you do them with a friend or with a classmate?
    b. on weekends: How different is your weekend from the rest of the week? Do you break up your routine? How?

Suggestion for 1-49. Primera fase. Primera fase intends to help students concentrate on the rhetorical aspects of their text, that is, the organization of content and ideas.

Suggestions for 1-49, Segunda fase and 1-50. You may wish to have students do this writing task in pairs or small groups (three at the most). You may also want to model the process. If so, explain how you would go through the various steps during the actual writing process. Keep input (teacher-talk) as natural and spontaneous as possible so students become comfortable with discussing the writing process. Accept any complete or partial response. Keep in mind that this is probably the students' first formal experience writing in Spanish. Elicit information from students rather than giving it yourself. If you decide to do the task in small groups, have students approach it as if they were one writer, in the first person singular.

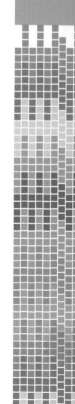

A escribir

Note for 1-50. Let students know that they will be writing more than one draft for each task and will need a reader/peer editor to comment on their work. Either appoint an editor or have students choose their own. Once students have received input from their peer editor, have them edit their text. To facilitate the work of peer editors and writers, you may wish to design an error correction code or use the one provided in the Appendix.

1-50 Manos a la obra. Now write your Spanish-speaking pen pal an e-mail telling him/her about your new life at the university. You may use the information you gathered in Activity 1-49. Do not forget to tell him/her . . .

■ how things are going for you.

■ about your university or college, the number and names of your classes, when you are taking them, how interesting (or not) your classes and professors are.

■ what your daily routine at school is like, what you do after (*después de*) class and on weekends, where and with whom you do these activities, and so on.

Para:

Asunto:

Querido/a....,

Hasta pronto.....

Después de escribir

Suggestion for 1-51. You may wish to guide peer editors as to what to pay attention to while reading a classmate's text. They should read the text holistically first, concentrating on how successfully (or not) the writer met his/her communicative purpose: Did peer editors (or did they not) comprehend the text as a whole? Is there any information that peer editors, as readers, would like to have that they were not provided with? What is it that they would like to know? Have them write the questions. It is not advisable that students, at this stage, edit their classmates' language forms. Language forms are, for the most part, simple at this level; therefore, the student writer should revisit his/her text to check for grammatical inaccuracies.

2 **1-51 Revisión.** After writing your e-mail, discuss it with a classmate. Then make any necessary changes.

■ Make sure you have provided all the information requested in 1-50 or any other you may deem necessary.

■ Revise any possible inaccuracies you may find regarding language use, spelling, punctuation, accentuation, and so on.

■ Finally, make any necessary changes that will make your text clear and comprehensible to your e-mail pen pal.

ENFOQUE CULTURAL

Para pensar

¿Cómo se llama su universidad? ¿Es grande o pequeña? ¿Nueva o antigua? ¿Privada o pública? ¿Es difícil ingresar (*be admitted*) a la universidad en los Estados Unidos? ¿Qué examen toman los estudiantes de secundaria para entrar a la universidad?

Algunas universidades españolas son modernas, pero también hay otras que son muy antiguas. Entre las universidades más antiguas está la Universidad de Salamanca, fundada en el siglo XIII.

En Hispanoamérica, las primeras universidades se fundan en el siglo XVI: la Universidad de Santo Tomás de Aquinas (en la foto), en Santo Domingo, República Dominicana; la Universidad de San Marcos, en Lima, Perú; y la Universidad de México.

Algunas universidades son muy grandes, como, por ejemplo, la Universidad Complutense de Madrid, donde estudian más de 120.000 estudiantes. Otras son mucho más pequeñas y tienen menos estudiantes.

Para contestar

A. Las universidades. Responda a las siguientes preguntas:

1. ¿Cómo son las universidades en el mundo hispano? Explique.
2. ¿Hay muchas universidades antiguas en los países hispanos? Dé un ejemplo.

(G) **B. Riqueza cultural.** Mencionen dos cosas similares y alguna diferencia entre las universidades de los Estados Unidos y las de España o Hispanoamérica.

Para pensar

¿Sabe usted dónde está España? ¿Qué ciudades importantes hay? ¿Qué museos y parques importantes hay? ¿Conoce usted (*do you know*) alguna actividad típica española? ¿Cuál es?

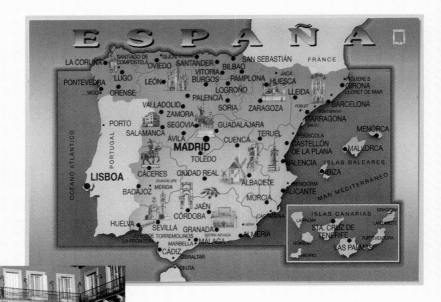

Café al aire libre en la Plaza Mayor de Madrid.

El Museo del Prado en Madrid.

Madrid, la capital de España, es una ciudad de gran vitalidad y energía. Durante el día los madrileños se reúnen en los cafés y terrazas y en la noche, hasta la madrugada, en los bares y discotecas.

Expresiones españolas:

ir de tapas	¡Vamos de tapas!	*Let's go have some tapas!*
catear	¡Me han **cateado**!	*They've flunked me!*
majo/a	Ella es muy **maja**.	*She's a very nice person.*
vale	Te llamo luego, ¿**vale**?	*I'll call you later, OK?*
chaval	¿Dónde está ese **chaval**?	*Where's that kid?*

Para contestar

En el mapa

1. Busque tres ciudades importantes de España. Indique dónde están.
2. Diga qué ciudad está más cerca de (*near*) Portugal. ¿Y de Francia?

Ahora diga...

1. ¿Por qué es famosa Sevilla?
2. ¿Qué lugar de Madrid le gustaría (*would you like*) visitar?

Los madrileños también disfrutan de los muchos museos, palacios, iglesias, y de las impresionantes plazas, fuentes y parques de su ciudad.

En el sur de España está Sevilla, ciudad de un encanto sin par. Sevilla es famosa por sus históricos edificios y también por sus celebraciones de Semana Santa con sus procesiones religiosas. En la Feria de abril, las sevillanas, que son los bailes típicos, y las corridas de toros llenan de alegría la ciudad. Visitar España es una experiencia cultural muy importante.

¿Qué dice Ud...

1. para describir a una persona agradable?
2. si quiere comer algo con sus amigos?
3. si saca una nota muy mala en un examen?

Para investigar en Internet

Busque información en *www.prenhall.com/mosaicos* sobre elementos importantes en la vida universitaria en España y en Hispanoamérica (eventos deportivos, bibliotecas, cafés, exposiciones de arte, conferencias, etc.). Informe a sus compañeros de alguna actividad interesante.

¡Prepárese!

1-52 Cognados. Before watching the first episode of *Fortunas*, look at the following list of cognates. Can you guess the meaning of these words?

a. la fortuna   fortune

b. el misterio   mystery

c. la competencia   competition

d. el/la participante   participant

e. el público   audience

1-53 Diccionario. Now use a bilingual dictionary or the glossary at the back of the book to learn the meanings of the following words, which will also be helpful as you participate in *Fortunas*.

a. la pista   clue

b. el premio   prize

c. el concurso   contest

d. la regla   rule

e. la encuesta   poll

Ángela y Manolo trabajan en la producción del video.

Tito anuncia que el concurso es en México.

Sabrina es de España.

Carlos es de Colombia.

Efraín es de Argentina.

Katie es de los Estados Unidos.

¡Responda!

1-54 Participantes. After watching the first episode of *Fortunas,* answer the following questions in Spanish, based on what you saw.

1. ¿Cómo es Manolo?
2. ¿Cómo es Ángela?
3. ¿De qué habla Tito?
4. ¿Cuántos participantes hay?
5. ¿Cuál es su participante favorito y por qué?

The rhythms and singing style of this song (*canción*) reflect the influence of Spanish flamenco music, which originated in southern Spain.

¡Prepárese!

(G) **1-55 Estilos musicales.** What other styles of music besides flamenco do you know that are popular in Spain and other countries of the Spanish-speaking world? Work in groups to generate a list and then compare your list to those of other groups. Which group has the longest list?

Suggestion. Have students compete against each other to see who can come up with the most answers in a specific time period.

¡Escuche!

1-56 Parejas. Primera fase. Look at each of the following words you will hear in *Cuéntame alegrías*. Then, match them to the English equivalents.

1. corazón ___b___   a. *flower*
2. flor ___a___   b. *heart*
3. amor ___d___   c. *happiness*
4. luz ___e___   d. *love*
5. alegría ___c___   e. *light*

Segunda fase. Thinking of the words in the **Primera fase**, what will the song that you will hear probably refer to? Mark your answer.

a. love ___X___   b. nature _____   c. sorrow _____

Cuéntame alegrías, mi "vía",
y dame tu amor.
Hazme una caricia, sonrisa,
dame el corazón.
Tienes mi alma, caramba,
hay para ti un rincón
y siempre presente en mi mente
Ahí te mantengo yo.

No quiero que llegue el día
¡Ay! que me digas que en la vida
todo tiene que acabar.
Que me digas que el cariño
igual que viene se va,

que ese amor que compartimos
lo arrastra una tempestad,
que ese amor tú lo compartas
con una persona más.

Eres luz del día, mi "vía",
flor de mi jardín
donde guardo flores y olores
sólo para ti.
Entre tierra y cielo, te quiero.
¡Ay! Nunca podrá haber
amor más sincero, espero
que nuestro querer

Note: The purpose of introducing songs in each lesson of the text is to familiarize students with the music and rhythms of the Spanish-speaking world. Since the songs are meant for a Hispanic population, their linguistic context is above the level of students at this stage. The students are simply asked, especially in the beginning lessons, to get the gist of the song and enjoy it.

You may point out that "*mi vía*" is a colloquial form of "*mi vida*." Terms of endearment such as this are common when addressing the person you love (e.g., *mi cielo, mi corazón*). In *Lección 3*, more terms of endearment are presented.

¡Responda!

1-57 Cantar, escuchar... After listening to the song, write sentences in Spanish, using the words of the two columns provided and adding some further information.

MODELO: Los chicos escuchan *Cuéntame alegrías* en la radio.

SUBJECTS	VERBS
yo	escuchar
la cantante (*singer*)	bailar
la canción (*song*)	cantar (*to sing*)
la música española	hablar
el flamenco	ser
mis compañeros y yo	estar

Suggestion. Ask students to read their sentences aloud to the class and then ask questions that will allow them to expand their answers, like *¿Dónde?, ¿Cuándo?, ¿Por qué?*, etc.

VOCABULARIO

AUDIO **En la clase**

el diccionario	*dictionary*
el examen	*test, examination*
el mapa	*map*
la nota	*note, grade*
la tarea	*homework*

Materias o asignaturas

la antropología	*anthropology*
las ciencias políticas	*political science*
la economía	*economics*
el español	*Spanish*
la geografía	*geography*
la historia	*history*
la literatura	*literature*
la (p)sicología	*psychology*
la sociología	*sociology*

Lugares

la biblioteca	*library*
el café	*coffee house*
la cafetería	*cafeteria*
la casa	*house, home*
la discoteca	*dance club*
el gimnasio	*gymnasium*
el laboratorio	*laboratory*
el laboratorio de lenguas	*language lab*
la librería	*bookstore*
la oficina	*office*
la playa	*beach*
la universidad	*university*

Facultades

arquitectura	*architecture*
ciencias	*sciences*
humanidades	*humanities*
informática	*computer science*
medicina	*medicine*

Personas

el/la alumno/a	*student*
el/la compañero/a	*partner, classmate*
el/la dependiente/a	*salesperson*
ellos/ellas	*they*
nosotros/nosotras	*we*
ustedes	*you* (plural)

Descripciones

aburrido/a	*boring*
difícil	*difficult*
estudioso/a	*studious*
excelente	*excellent*
fácil	*easy*
grande	*big*
malo/a	*bad*
norteamericano/a	*American*
pequeño/a	*small*

Verbos*

bailar	*to dance*
buscar	*to look for*
caminar	*to walk*
comprar	*to buy*
conversar	*to talk, to converse*
escuchar	*to listen (to)*
estar	*to be*
estudiar	*to study*
hablar	*to speak*
llegar	*to arrive*
mirar	*to look (at)*
montar	*to ride*
montar en bicicleta	*to ride a bicycle*
necesitar	*to need*
practicar	*to practice*
sacar	*to get, to take (out)*
tomar	*to take, to drink*
tomar apuntes	*to take notes*
trabajar	*to work*

Palabras y expresiones útiles**

algo	*something*
buena suerte	*good luck*
¿Cómo te va?	*How is it going?*
con	*with*
¿Cuánto cuesta?	*How much is it?*
este/a	*this*
el fin de semana	*weekend*
para	*for, to*
pero	*but*
¡Qué lástima!	*What a pity!*
su	*his, her, their, your* (formal)
también	*also*
tengo/tienes	*I/you have*
¿Verdad?	*Right?*

Suggestion. You may wish to encourage students to use empty space on the vocabulary pages to write down any words and expressions they've acquired through classroom work beyond those activated in each *Lección*. Students can use the heading *Vocabulario personal*.

*See page 32 for expressions of frequency.
**See page 41 for some *-er* and *-ir* verb forms.
***See page 40 for question words.

2

LOS HISPANOS EN LOS ESTADOS UNIDOS

Objetivos comunicativos

- Asking about and describing persons, animals, places, and things
- Expressing nationality and place of origin
- Expressing where and when events take place
- Expressing possession
- Expressing likes and dislikes

Contenido

A primera vista

- Mis amigos y yo
- ¿Cómo son...?
- ¿De qué color son...?
- ¿De dónde son...?

Explicación y expansión

- Adjectives
- Present tense and some uses of the verb *ser*
- *Ser* and *estar* with adjectives
- Possessive adjectives
- Algo Más: Expressions with *gustar*

Mosaicos

- Escuchar: Listening for specific information
- Conversar: Describing appearance and personality
- Leer: Scanning a text; inferring meaning
- Escribir: Responding to an ad; addressing an unknown reader

Enfoque cultural

- Temas: Los hispanos en los Estados Unidos
- Vistas: La influencia hispana en los Estados Unidos
  Para investigar en Internet
- Fortunas: Episodio 2
- Notas: Oh Naná, *Millo Torres y el Tercer Planeta*

Vocabulario

AUDIO *Mis amigos y yo*

Me llamo Mario Quintana. Soy de Puerto Rico, y tengo veintidós años. **Me gusta** escuchar música y mirar televisión. Estudio en una universidad americana y **deseo ser** profesor de historia. Los **chicos** en estas fotografías son **mis amigos. Ellos también** son **hispanos y** estudian en la universidad. **Todos** somos **bilingües.**

Esta chica es Amanda Martone. Es **alta, delgada,** tiene los **ojos de color café** y el **pelo castaño** y muy **largo.** Amanda es una chica muy **agradable.** Estudia mucho y desea ser economista. Su familia es argentina, pero vive en los Estados Unidos.

Este chico se llama Ernesto Fernández. Ernesto es **moreno, bajo, fuerte,** muy **conversador y simpático.** Le gusta **usar** la computadora para conversar con sus amigos de aquí y de México.

Esta amiga se llama Ana Villegas. No es alta ni baja, es **mediana** y usa **lentes de contacto.** Es **pelirroja,** tiene pelo **corto** y ojos **negros.** Ana es **callada, trabajadora** y muy inteligente. Sus padres son cubanos.

Esta chica es Marta Chávez Conde. Es española y tiene veintiún años. Es **rubia,** tiene los ojos **azules,** y es muy **divertida.** Este año está en los Estados Unidos con su familia.

Note. In some countries, *moreno/a* refers to African ancestry and skin color. In others, it refers to a person's hair color, meaning brunet / brunette. *Corto/a* generally refers to length (*pelo corto*), while *bajo/a* refers to height (*Ella es baja*).

Marta Chavez's ID card provides the opportunity of reentering the use of two last names in Spanish.

ESPAÑA

NOMBRE MARTA
PRIMER APELLIDO CHÁVEZ
SEGUNDO APELLIDO CONDE
16533103-J
EXPED. 03-06-1997 VAL 02-06-2002
16533103-J **II** MINISTERIO DEL INTERIOR

NACIÓ EN SANTA CRUZ DE TENERIFE
PROVINCIA STA C TENERIFE 24-07-1983
HIJA DE INOCENCIO Y ROSARIO SEXO F
DIRECCIÓN C CÓRCEGA 397 11
LOCALIDAD BARCELONA
PROVINCIA BARCELONA EQUIPO 08055A606
ID<ESP<<<<<<<<<<<<<<<<<<<<<<<<<<<
16533103-J<<<<<<<<<<<<<<<<<<<<<<<

¿Qué dice usted?

2-1 Asociaciones. To whom do the descriptions on the left refer?

1. __b__ Tiene el pelo largo.
2. __a__ Tiene veintidós años.
3. __e__ Es de España.
4. __c__ Es bajo y fuerte.
5. __d__ Es callada y muy inteligente.
6. __c__ Habla mucho.
7. __b__ Tiene los ojos de color café.
8. __e__ Es rubia.
9. __e__ Tiene los ojos azules y es muy divertida.
10. __a__ Desea ser profesor de historia.

a. Mario Quintana
b. Amanda Martone
c. Ernesto Fernández
d. Ana Villegas
e. Marta Chávez

Follow-up for 2-1. Name the person described by the following questions: *¿Quién tiene veintiún años?* (Marta), *¿... es alta?* (Amanda), *¿... es muy conversador?* (Ernesto), *¿... es callada?* (Ana), *¿... tiene ojos azules?* (Marta), *¿... tiene ojos negros?* (Ana).

VÍNCULOS

To practice vocabulario—Mis amigos y yo
• SAM-OneKey: WB: 2-1, 2-2, 2-3, 2-4 / LM: 2-29, 2-30, 2-31, 2-32
• Companion Website: AP 2-1
• IRCD: Chapter 2; pp. 62, 63, 64, 66

Note for 2-2. Depending on the size of your class, do this activity in small groups (4 students) or with the whole class. This is an exercise that students particularly enjoy doing, and, at times, some of them get carried away and talk in English. Guide them back to Spanish and provide them with vocabulary as needed.

Note for 2-3. The *gustar* construction is presented in *Lección 6*. Here students should use phrases with *gustar* as set expressions. Refer to *Algo más*, page 76, for a brief introduction.

Warm-up. Say what you like and do not like to do: *Me gusta caminar. También me gusta escuchar música popular. Por las noches me gusta mirar televisión. No me gusta trabajar por las noches.* Ask students what they like to do: *¿Le gusta estudiar español? ¿Le gusta estudiar en la biblioteca/ caminar/ mirar televisión por las noches/ bailar en las discotecas?* Point out that since they address their classmates as *tú*, they will use *¿te gusta?* Practice with one or two students prior to doing the activity. Students take turns asking and answering.

Warm-up. Describe yourself and/or students using adjectives and expressions introduced in this section. To present words such as *alto/bajo, rubio/moreno,* and *tengo* or *tiene pelo negro/castaño/corto/largo* you may point to students who fit those descriptions. To check comprehension of new vocabulary, select students by name, describe them correctly or incorrectly, and ask the class to evaluate your description with *sí* or *no.* To recycle the question word *¿quién?,* ask questions using adjectives: *¿Quién es alto y moreno? ¿Quién tiene pelo castaño?* Students can answer using names of their classmates. Recycle numbers by asking *¿Cuántos son altos? ¿morenos?,* etc.

Suggestion. Name several famous people and describe them using the adjectives in this lesson. Ask students to name and describe other people.

Alternate. Ask students to describe themselves using the adjectives in this section.

Expansion. Tape the name of a famous person to the back of each student. Students move around the room asking "yes/no" questions that will help them discover their "identity." You may want to first demonstrate by having them choose a name for you and answering your questions first.

2-2 ¿Quién es? Primera fase. Read again the texts on pages 60–61 and write a list of at least eight expressions that you may use to describe people in regards to: a) their physical appearance and b) their personality traits.

Ⓖ Segunda fase. Now, without mentioning his/her name, describe a classmate in at least three sentences, using the vocabulary from **Primera fase,** or any other that you may need. The rest of the group will guess who this person is. If they cannot guess his/her identity, they should ask Yes/No questions to the student who made the description. He/She will answer using **Sí** or **No.**

MODELO: E1: Es alto y delgado. Tiene pelo negro. Es fuerte y callado.
                 E2: Es...

❷ 2-3 ¿Qué (no) me gusta? Indicate whether you like or dislike each of the following activities. Then ask a classmate, and compare your answers.

MODELO: estar en casa por las noches
                 E1: ¿Te gusta estar en casa por las noches?
                 E2: Sí, me gusta. /No, no me gusta.

ACTIVIDADES	USTED		COMPAÑERO/A	
	Sí	No	Sí	No
1. mirar televisión por la tarde				
2. estudiar español				
3. practicar tenis/fútbol/béisbol				
4. escribir en la computadora				
5. trabajar los fines de semana				
6. tomar café por la noche				
7. bailar los sábados por la noche				
8. hablar con los amigos en los cafés				

¿Cómo son...

estas personas?

fuerte   débil

joven   vieja/mayor

lista

tonto

trabajador

perezoso

Alternate. Have students complete the following sentences with an adjective: *Juana no tiene dinero* (show money). *Es...; Me gusta mucho trabajar. Soy...; Rigoberta tiene quince años. Es muy...; Manuela y Marcos siempre están en el laboratorio. Son muy...*

Note. Some Spanish speakers consider *viejo/a* offensive when describing people, and prefer to use *mayor*.

antipático

simpático

alegre

triste

rica

pobre

casado

soltero

LENGUA

Spanish uses the words **bonita** and **guapa** when referring to a female. When referring to a male, the expressions **buen mozo** and **guapo** are used.

estos animales?

el hipopótamo

Es feo.

la gata

Es muy bonita.

la serpiente

Es delgada.

el oso

Es gordo.

Suggestion. Bring photos of different people and animals into the class or ask students to bring them. Distribute them and have the students work in groups of three to describe each item. They should describe people by giving both physical characteristics and personality traits; for fun, you may wish to have students assign animals some human personality traits, for example: *el gato es callado y perezoso, el perro es romántico,* etc.

¿De qué color son...

Suggestion. Bring brochures and ads for various cars. Ask students about their preferences. Encourage them to describe the cars giving colors and features. You may also introduce words such as *suéter, blusa, camisa,* and ask questions *¿De qué color es el suéter de...? ¿Y la blusa de...?*

estos autos?

Es rojo.

Es amarillo.

LENGUA

There are several Spanish words, depending on the country, to express the color brown: **café, marrón, carmelita, castaño,** and **pardo/a.** The words **naranja** and **rosa** are also used instead of **anaranjado** and **rosado.**

Otros colores

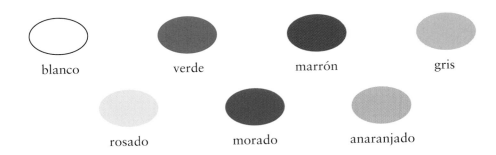

blanco   verde   marrón   gris

rosado   morado   anaranjado

2-4 Opuestos. Complete the following statements.

MODELO: Shakira no es vieja, es joven.

1. __c__ Penélope Cruz no es gorda, es...
2. __a__ El presidente no es perezoso, es...
3. __f__ Jennifer López no es antipática, es...
4. __b__ Madonna no es tonta, es...
5. __d__ Bill Gates no es pobre, es...
6. __e__ Enrique Iglesias no es feo, es...

a. trabajador
b. lista
c. delgada
d. rico
e. guapo
f. simpática

② **2-5 Autodescripción. Primera fase.** You are appearing on the TV program **Cita a ciegas** (*Blind Date*). Describe yourself to make a good first impression. Your partner should take notes.

1. Me llamo...
2. Soy... No soy...
3. Tengo...
4. Estudio...
5. Trabajo...
6. Me gusta...

Segunda fase. Use your notes to describe your partner to the rest of the class.

1. Se llama...
2. Es... No es...
3. Tiene...
4. Estudia...
5. Trabaja...
6. Le gusta...

2-6 Vamos a describir. Look at the following photos and describe the people in them.

Alberto

Nicolás

Marisol

Mirta

2-7 ¿Quién soy? Write down a brief description of yourself (physical and personality wise). **Do not** include your name. Give the piece of paper to your instructor. He/She will ask each of you to pick a description, read it, and match the description with the name of your classmate who wrote it.

MODELO: Soy alta y morena; llevo lentes, tengo el pelo corto; soy muy trabajadora.

¿De dónde son...?

¿Qué dice usted?

2-8 ¿Quiénes son? Primera fase. Identify the following people (map pg. 65).

1. jugador (*player*) de béisbol dominicano f
2. diseñadora (*designer*) famosa de Venezuela g
3. escritor de Perú; autor de *La ciudad y los perros* b
4. actriz mexicana, protagonista de *Frida* i
5. activista guatemalteca, Premio Nobel de la Paz, 1992 d
6. bailarín argentino h
7. cofundador de Microsoft a
8. ex-presidenta de Nicaragua j
9. escritor colombiano, autor de *Cien años de soledad*, Premio Nobel, 1982 e
10. novelista chilena, autora de *La casa de los espíritus* c

a. Bill Gates
b. Mario Vargas Llosa
c. Isabel Allende
d. Rigoberta Menchú
e. Gabriel García Márquez
f. Sammy Sosa
g. Carolina Herrera
h. Julio Bocca
i. Salma Hayek
j. Violeta Chamorro

Segunda fase. Which of the public personalities in **Primera fase** is interesting to you? Why?

MODELO: Para mí, ... es interesante. Es un/a actor/actriz famoso/a.

2-9 Adivinanzas. Think of a well-known person. A classmate will try to guess his or her identity by asking you questions.

MODELO: E1: ¿De dónde es?
E2: Es española.
E1: ¿Cómo es?
E2: Es bonita, morena y muy inteligente.
E1: ¿En qué trabaja?
E2: Es actriz.
E1: ¿Es Penélope Cruz?
E2: ¡Sí!

Warm-up for 2-10 As a pre-listening activity, divide the class in pairs or small groups and have them draw three columns: Hispanic names, physical descriptions, different areas of study. Ask them to write—in 3 minutes—as many words they associate with each column as possible. You may have students compare their lists. Or, you may provide words and have students place them in the appropriate column (e.g., names, physical descriptions, areas of study).

Audioscript for 2-10. ¡Hola! Me llamo Miguel Jiménez. Soy de Buenos Aires, Argentina, y tengo 26 años. Estudio medicina en la Universidad de Virginia. Estoy en el tercer año de la carrera. Soy alto, delgado y muy trabajador.

Answers may vary in *Antes de escuchar* column.

AUDIO **2-10 ¿Quiénes son?** Before you listen to a student describing himself, mark in the appropriate **Antes de Escuchar** column the information you think he will provide.

	ANTES DE ESCUCHAR		DESPUÉS DE ESCUCHAR	
	Sí	No	Sí	No
1. name			X	
2. age			X	
3. his parents' names				X
4. physical description			X	
5. country where he was born			X	
6. place where he will work in the future				X

Now, pay attention to the general idea of what is said. Then, in the **Después de escuchar** column in the chart, indicate if the information was or was not provided.

EXPLICACIÓN Y EXPANSIÓN

1. Adjectives

Adjectives are words that describe people, places, and things. Like articles (**el, la, un, una**) and nouns (**chico, chica**), they generally have more than one form. In Spanish an adjective must agree in gender (masculine or feminine) and number (singular or plural) with the noun or pronoun it describes. Adjectives that describe characteristics usually follow the noun.

■ Most masculine adjectives end in **-o**, and most feminine adjectives end in **-a** when used with feminine words. To form the plural, these adjectives add **-s**.

	MASCULINE	FEMININE
SINGULAR	el chico alto	la chica alta
PLURAL	los chicos altos	las chicas altas

■ Adjectives that end in **-e** and some adjectives that end in a consonant are both masculine and feminine. To form the plural, adjectives that end in **-e** add **-s**; adjectives that end in a consonant add **-es**.

	MASCULINE	FEMININE
SINGULAR	un amigo interesante	una amiga interesante
	un chico popular	una chica popular
PLURAL	unos amigos interesantes	unas amigas interesantes
	unos chicos populares	unas chicas populares

■ Other adjectives that end in a consonant add **-a** to form the feminine and **-es** and **-as** to form the plurals.

	MASCULINE	FEMININE
SINGULAR	el alumno español	la alumna española
	el alumno trabajador	la alumna trabajadora
PLURAL	los alumnos españoles	los alumnas españolas
	los alumnos trabajadores	las alumnas trabajadoras

■ Adjectives that end in **-ista** are both masculine and feminine. To form the plurals, add **-s**.

Pedro es muy optim**ista**,   *Pedro is very optimistic,*
    pero Alicia es pesim**ista**.   *but Alicia is pessimistic.*
Ellos no son material**istas**.   *They are not materialistic.*

Note. Adjectives and adjective agreement have been previewed in the *A primera vista* section of this lesson.

Suggestions. Use visuals to practice noun-adjective agreement or personalize by describing some students in the class: *José es un chico alto y simpático.* Write the words *chico alto* on the board underlining or circling the *o.* Do the same with a feminine noun and adjective. Write the plural. Ask yes/no and either/or questions regarding students in the classroom. Do the same with adjectives ending in *-e* such as *interesante.* Ask questions regarding subject matters: *¿Es interesante la historia? Y el español, ¿es interesante? Y las ciencias, ¿son interesantes?* Working in pairs, have students find out subjects that their partners think are *interesante*(s) or *aburrido/a*(s) and share their opinions with the class. Practice adjectives that end in a consonant and adjectives of nationality. Give examples: *Antonio Banderas es español. Penélope Cruz es española. Ella es una actriz excelente. Antonio Banderas y Penélope Cruz son muy famosos.* Students working in groups find out what programs, sports figures, actors, or singers are popular within each group and compare their findings.

VÍNCULOS

To practice adjectives
● SAM-OneKey: WB: 2-5, 2-6, 2-7, 2-8 / LM: 2-33, 2-34
● Companion Website: AP 2-2
● *Gramática viva*: Grammar Points 2 and 3: Adjectives (gender and number); Adjectives of nationality
● IRCD: Chapter 2; pg. 67

Note. Adjectives of nationality are presented on page 69.

¿Qué dice usted?

2-11 ¿Cómo son estas personas? Choose the correct completion to describe the following people. In some cases, there is more than one possible answer.

1. Muchos de los alumnos de mi universidad son...
   a. alto   (b.) hispanos   c. norteamericanas   (d.) mexicanos

2. Mi profesora favorita es muy...
   (a.) joven   b. perezosas   (c.) atractiva   d. delgado

3. En mi clase de español, los estudiantes son...
   a. trabajadora   b. calladas   (c.) agradables   (d.) simpáticos

4. Mi amigo Nicolás es muy...
   a. tonta   (b.) fuerte   (c.) callado   d. antipática

5. Mi amiga Isabel es...
   a. rubio y guapo   (b.) simpática y divertida
   c. joven y soltero   (d.) baja y pelirroja

6. Las dos chicas más populares de la clase son...
   a. activos y trabajadores   (b.) inteligentes y estudiosas
   c. altos y morenos   d. anaranjadas y verdes

Expansion for 2-12. You may tell students that before beginning their descriptions, they should think of the people they are describing: Are the people male or female? Is it one person or more?

Encourage students to provide additional adjectives. They may also use the negative with the opposite quality: *La directora de relaciones públicas no es antipática. Es muy simpática.*

Also encourage students to ask questions, such as: *¿Es joven/Son jóvenes? ¿Habla(n) español bien? ¿Cómo se llama(n)?*

2 2-12 Descripciones. You are the personnel manager of a Hispanic company in California and you have just hired some staff. Mark the qualities that you think these people have and then describe them to a partner, making all the necessary changes. Answer the questions he/she may have.

1. La directora de relaciones públicas
   _____ activo   _____ competente   _____ pasivo   _____ agradable
   _____ bilingüe   _____ callado   _____ antipático _____ trabajador
   _____ extrovertido _____ atractivo   _____ casado   ...

2. Dos empleados para la oficina de ventas (*sales*)
   _____ perezoso   _____ inteligente   _____ débil   _____ hablador
   _____ tímido   _____ perfeccionista _____ tonto   _____ simpático
   _____ imparcial   _____ eficiente   _____ joven   ...

Note for 2-13. Some well-known Americans have been included for those students that may not be familiar with the Hispanic personalities presented in the activity. You may explain that Shakira is a very popular Colombian singer that has made the crossover and has recorded CD's in English and Spanish. Students can find additional information about her in the Internet.

Expansion for 2-13. Choose other well-known people or characters such as Julia Roberts, Brad Pitt, Denzel Washington, and Bruce Willis, and ask students to describe them. You may ask other students if they agree or not with the description given introducing the question *¿Está de acuerdo?*

Have students use one adjective to describe two people in order to practice plural forms: *Salma Hayak y Julia Roberts son bonitas y simpáticas.*

Suggestion for 2-13, Segunda fase. Since asking questions is a difficult skill for beginners, you may wish to have students write down some questions before the **Segunda fase** to make the most of this activity. Point out to students that they should listen attentively to what their classmates say in order to ask appropriate follow-up questions. Be prepared to give students additional vocabulary they may need.

2 2-13 Personas importantes. Primera fase. Take turns describing the people below, using at least three of the following adjectives or expressions for each one. Compare your description with those of other classmates.

serio	trabajador	cómico
inteligente	simpático	atlético
guapo	extrovertido	liberal
tiene ojos...	tiene pelo...	...

1. Christina Aguilera
2. Toni Morrison
3. Alex Rodríguez

4. Shakira
5. Antonio Banderas
6. Tiger Woods

Segunda fase. Now, take turns describing someone important in your life. Your partner will ask questions to get more information about the person you describe and to find out why he/she is important to you.

SITUACIONES

1. **Role A.** You have just rented a two bedroom apartment near campus and are looking for a roommate (**compañero de cuarto**). You receive a call from a student who is interested. Verify his name and ask him a) where he is from, b) what his personality traits are, c) if he currently works; if so, where, and d) what he likes to do in his free time (**tiempo libre**).

   Role B. Through an ad (**anuncio**) on a campus bulletin board, you found out that someone is looking for a roommate (**compañero de cuarto**) to share an apartment. You call the person in the ad. Answer your potential roommate's questions in detail and ask any questions you may have.

2. **Role A.** Your best friend has called to tell you that she has a new boyfriend (**novio**). Ask a) where your best friend's boyfriend is from, b) what he is like, c) what he studies, d) if he has a car, and e) what car he has.

   Role B. You call your best friend to tell him about your new boyfriend. Your friend wants to know more about him. Answer all of your friend's questions in as much detail as possible.

2. Present tense and some uses of the verb *ser*

SER (*to be*)			
yo	soy	nosotros/as	somos
tú	eres	vosotros/as	sois
Ud., él, ella	es	Uds., ellos/as	son

You have practiced some forms of the verb **ser** and have used them for identification (**Ese señor es el dependiente**) and to tell time (**Son las cuatro**). Below you will learn other uses of the verb **ser.**

■ **Ser** is used with adjectives to describe what a person, a place, or a thing is like.

¿Cómo **es** ella?	*What is she like?*
Es inteligente y simpática.	*She is intelligent and nice.*
¿Cómo **es** la casa?	*What is the house like?*
La casa **es** grande y muy bonita.	*The house is big and very beautiful.*

■ **Ser** is used to express the nationality of a person; **ser + de** is used to express the origin of a person.

NATIONALITY

Luis **es** chileno.	*Luis is Chilean.*
Ana **es** mexicana.	*Ana is Mexican.*

ORIGIN

Luis **es** de Chile.	*Luis is from Chile.*
Ana **es** de México.	*Ana is from Mexico.*

Suggestion. Ask questions to practice the use of *ser* to express possession: *¿De quién es esa mochila? ¿Y de quién es ese bolígrafo?*

Suggestion. Make sure students understand the difference between location of an event and location of a person or object: *¿Dónde es la clase de español? ¿Dónde está el profesor de español? ¿Dónde es la clase de inglés? ¿Dónde están los estudiantes?*

■ **Ser + de** is also used to express possession. The equivalent of the English word *whose* is **¿de quién?**

¿De quién es la casa?	*Whose house is it?*
La casa es de Marta.	*The house is Marta's.*

■ **Ser** is also used to express the location or time of an event.

El baile es en la universidad.	*The dance is (takes place) at the university.*
El examen es a las tres.	*The test is (takes place) at three.*

3. *Ser* and *estar* with adjectives

■ **Ser** and **estar** are often used with the same adjectives. However, the choice of verb determines the meaning of the sentence.

■ **Ser** + *adjective* states the norm—what someone or something is like.

Manolo es delgado.	*Manolo is thin.* (He is a thin boy.)
Sara es muy nerviosa.	*Sara is very nervous.* (She is a nervous person.)
El libro es nuevo.	*The book is new.* (It is a new book.)

■ **Estar** + *adjective* expresses a change from the norm, a condition, or how one feels about the person or object being discussed.

Manolo está delgado.	*Manolo is thin.* (He lost weight recently.)
Sara está muy nerviosa.	*Sara is very nervous.* (She has been nervous lately.)
El libro está nuevo.	*The book is/looks new.* (It seems like a brand new book.)

■ The adjectives **contento/a, cansado/a, enojado/a** are always used with **estar**.

Ella está contenta ahora.	*She is happy now.*
El niño está cansado.	*The boy is tired.*
Carlos está enojado.	*Carlos is angry.*

■ Some adjectives have one meaning with **ser** and another with **estar**.

Ese señor es malo.	*That man is bad/evil.*
Ese señor está malo.	*That man is ill.*
El chico es listo.	*The boy is clever.*
El chico está listo.	*The boy is ready.*
La manzana es verde.	*The apple is green.*
La manzana está verde.	*The apple is not ripe.*
Ella es aburrida.	*She is boring.*
Ella está aburrida.	*She is bored.*

¿Qué dice usted?

2-14 ¿Cómo somos? Primera fase. Look at the following descriptions and write an X under the appropriate heading.

	Sí	No
1. Soy muy estudioso/a y trabajador/a.	___	___
2. A veces soy callado/a.	___	___
3. Mi familia es muy religiosa y tradicional.	___	___
4. Mi mejor amigo es muy simpático y conversador.	___	___
5. Él y yo somos agradables.	___	___
6. Mis clases de este semestre son interesantes.	___	___

Segunda fase. Now compare your answers with those of a classmate. Ask questions to get additional information about your classmate.

2-15 Descripciones. Ask what the following people and places are like.

MODELO: tu profesor/a de inglés
E1: ¿Cómo es tu profesor de inglés?
E2: Es alto, moreno y muy simpático.

1. la oficina del Departamento de Lenguas
2. tu cuarto (*bedroom*)
3. tu compañero/a de cuarto
4. tu auto/bicicleta
5. los chicos/las chicas de la clase
6. el laboratorio de lenguas

2-16 ¿De quién es/son...? You walk into your room and find several objects that do not belong to you. Ask your classmate (roommate) whose they are. He/She will ask you at least two questions to help you identify the owner.

MODELO: computadora portátil (*laptop*)
E1: ¿De quién es la computadora?
E2: No sé. ¿De qué color es?
E1: Es negra.
E2: ¿Es grande o pequeña?
E1: Es pequeña.
E2: Entonces es la computadora portátil de Luis.

1.

2.

3.

4.

5.

6.

VÍNCULOS

To practice *ser* and *estar* with adjectives
- SAM-OneKey: WB: 2-12, 2-13, 2-14, 2-15 / LM: 2-37, 2-38
- Companion Website: AP 2-4

Follow-up for 2-15. Students change partners. Each new partner should tell the other the information he/she gathered.

Suggestion for follow up for 2-15. To make the report of information more natural, you may wish to teach and model the following: *X dice que el laboratorio está al lado de la cafetería.*

Warm-up for 2-16. Ask students ¿*De quién es/son...?* questions using classroom objects. Use *ese/a* since students practiced it in *Bienvenidos.* You may want to use *esos/as* as well.

Suggestion. Encourage students to use *entonces* as it is used in the model to make their speech more authentic.

4. Possessive adjectives

POSSESSIVE ADJECTIVES	
mi(s)	*my*
tu(s)	*your* (familiar)
su(s)	*your, his, her, its, their*
nuestro(s), nuestra(s)	*our*
vuestro(s), vuestra(s)	*your* (familiar plural)

■ These possessive adjectives always precede the noun they modify.

   mi casa   **tu** bicicleta

■ Possessive adjectives change number to agree with the thing possessed, not with the possessor.

   mi casa, **mis** casas

■ The **nosotros** and **vosotros** forms must agree also in gender.

   nuestro profesor, **nuestros** amigos; **nuestra** profesora, **nuestras** amigas

■ **Su** and **sus** have multiple meanings. To ensure clarity, you may use **de** + the name of the possessor or the appropriate pronoun.

   su compañera = la compañera +
   { **de ella** (la compañera de Elena)
   de él (la compañera de Jorge)
   de usted
   de ustedes
   de ellos (la compañera de Elena y Jorge)
   de ellas (la compañera de Elena y Olga)

¿Qué dice usted?

2-21 Mi mundo. Primera fase. Write down two things that you own and two different people that you value very much.

POSESIONES	PERSONAS
1. _____	1. _____
2. _____	2. _____

❷ Segunda fase. Take turns describing the two objects and the people you value.

Posesiones

   E1: Mi bicicleta es nueva y muy bonita. ¿Y cómo es tu bicicleta?
   E2: Mi bicicleta es azul y bastante vieja.

Personas

   E1: Mi madre es muy alegre y activa. ¿Y tu mamá, cómo es?
   E2: Es tranquila y muy inteligente.

2-22 Mi familia. First, mark your answers in the appropriate column. Then interview each other and compare your answers.

	YO		MI COMPAÑERO/A	
	Sí	No	Sí	No
1. Mi familia es grande.	_____	_____	_____	_____
2. Otros miembros de la familia viven en nuestro barrio (*neighborhood*).	_____	_____	_____	_____
3. A veces pasamos las vacaciones con mis abuelos (*grandparents*).	_____	_____	_____	_____
4. Siempre conversamos sobre temas políticos.	_____	_____	_____	_____
5. A veces no estamos de acuerdo y discutimos.	_____	_____	_____	_____
6. Nuestros amigos visitan la casa frecuentemente.	_____	_____	_____	_____

Suggestion for 2-22. There are some new words in the activity that students should recognize because they are cognates or near cognates. Point out to students the importance of guessing the meaning of words through context. When a new word —whose meaning will be difficult for students to guess— is presented, its meaning is glossed, as in the case of *barrio*.

Ask questions about students' vacations: *¿Dónde pasa Ud. las vacaciones? ¿Por qué? ¿Le gusta el lugar? ¿Qué hace Ud. allí?*

2-23 Nuestra universidad. Primera fase. In preparation for **Segunda fase**, write down some words that describe in general the following at your university.

1. profesores: _____
2. clases: _____
3. estudiantes: _____
4. equipo (*team*) de béisbol/basquetbol/fútbol: _____

Segunda fase. Now, prepare a short oral presentation—to a group of students from another college/university—about your university, using the correct form of **nuestro**.

SITUACIONES

1. **Role A.** You are looking for a new apartment. One of your classmates is trying to talk you into moving in with him/her into his/her apartment. Before making a decision, ask questions regarding a) size, b) location c) cost, and d) color.

    Role B. You would like your classmate to move in with you. Answer his/her questions regarding your apartment trying to make it look as spacious and desirable as possible.

2. **Role A.** You are planning to give your best friend a surprise birthday party at your house and would like to invite one of your classmates. Tell your classmate a) that your friend's birthday is on Sunday, and b) where the party will take place.

    Role B. You've been invited to a party. Find out a) the exact address, b) the time of the party, c) who the other guests (**otros invitados**) are, and d) thank your classmate for the invitation (**por la invitación**).

EN DIRECTO

To emphasize a characteristic, use the adverb **muy**.
El apartamento es **muy** grande.
Está **muy** cerca (*near*) de la Universidad, etc. . .

To initiate the conversation:
Mira, el domingo es el cumpleaños de...
¿Sabes? (*You know?*) El domingo es el cumpleaños de, ...
To acknowledge information by showing surprise:
Ah, ¿sí?
¡No me digas! (*Oh, really?*)

Note. In *A primera vista*, students used *me gusta* and *te gusta* as lexical items. Here they will find an introduction of the forms that they will need for communication at this stage. It is not advisable to go into a detailed grammar explanation.

A INVESTIGAR

The number of Hispanics has increased tremendously in the last few years. Find out the percentage of Hispanics in the population of your state according to the last census and the one before. Has it increased? Can you give some examples of the Hispanic presence in this country?

Suggestion for 2-24. Tell students about the kind of music you like. Ask them about their preferences. Play some typical music from the Spanish-speaking world (*pasodoble* from Spain, *ranchera* from Mexico, *tango* from Argentina, *son* and *chachachá* from *Cuba*, etc.). Local radio stations in areas where there is a large Hispanic population play popular music from many of the Spanish-speaking countries.

VÍNCULOS

To practice expressions with *gustar*
- SAM-OneKey: WB: 2-20, 2-21 / LM: 2-41, 2-42
- Companion Website: AP 2-6
- *Gramática viva*: Grammar Point 1: *(A mí) me interesa, gusta*

EN DIRECTO

To compare:
M y N son semejantes.
Los/Las dos hablan mucho por teléfono.
M y N son diferentes.
M estudia mucho toda la semana. N estudia de lunes a viernes.

 **ALGO MÁS**

Expressions with gustar

- To express what you like to do, use **me gusta** + *infinitive*. To express what you don't like to do, say **no me gusta** + *infinitive*.

Me gusta bailar.	*I like to dance.*
No me gusta mirar la televisión.	*I don't like to watch television.*

- To express that you like something, use **me gusta** + *singular noun* or **me gustan** + *plural noun*.

Me gusta la música clásica.	*I like classical music.*
Me gustan las fiestas.	*I like parties.*

- To ask a classmate what he/she likes, use **¿Te gusta/n...?** To ask your instructor, use **¿Le gusta/n...?**

¿Te gusta/Le gusta tomar café?	*Do you like to drink coffee?*
¿Te gustan/Le gustan los chocolates?	*Do you like chocolates?*

¿Qué dice usted?

2-24 Mis preferencias. Fill in the following chart, based on your preferences. Compare your answers with those of a classmate.

ACTIVIDAD	ME GUSTA MUCHO	ME GUSTA	NO ME GUSTA
escribir correos electrónicos			
hablar por teléfono			
bailar salsa			
leer libros sobre Hispanoamérica			

2-25 ¿Te gusta...? Ask a classmate if he/she likes the following things. Do not forget to ask follow-up questions as appropriate.

1. el gimnasio de la universidad
2. las discotecas
3. la informática
4. los autos de este año
5. los animales
6. los conciertos de música pop

2-26 ¿Qué te gusta hacer? Primera fase. Write down some questions that you would ask a classmate to find out the following:

1. What he/she likes to do during the week: in the morning, afternoon, night.
2. What he/she likes to do over the weekend: Saturdays and Sundays.

Segunda fase. Interview two classmates and ask each of them the questions you prepared in **Primera fase.** Compare their responses and be prepared to share your conclusions regarding how your classmates spend their time with the rest of the class or with another group. The expressions in the box may help you express your conclusions.

MOSAICOS

 *Escuchar*

Listening for specific information

When you are asking specific questions, you need to understand only the answer to the question you have asked; that is, you need to understand the specific information you have requested. For example, if you want to know the name or place of origin of a new friend, you might want to focus only on his/her name or the place he/she is from. Although you might understand everything else, you just need to understand what you are interested in.

Antes de escuchar

2-27 ¿Quiénes son? You will listen to a conversation between two Hispanic students, Rafael and Laura. First write down the names of four Spanish-speaking countries and the nationality of the people born in each of them.

Countries: _____

Nationalities: _____

VÍNCULOS

For materials related to the Mosaicos section, see

- SAM-OneKey: WB: 2-22, 2-23, 2-24, 2-25, 2-26, 2-27 / LM: 2-43

A escuchar

AUDIO 2-28. Now, listen to the conversation and complete the following chart.

NOMBRE	NACIONALIDAD	FACULTAD	UNIVERSIDAD
Rafael	boliviano	arquitectura	de la Florida
Laura	española	informática	de Maryland

Audioscript for A escuchar 2-28. RAFAEL: ¡Hola! Me llamo Rafael. ¿Cómo te llamas? LAURA: Me llamo Laura. ¿De dónde eres, Rafael? RAFAEL: Soy de Bolivia. ¿Y tú? LAURA: De España, de Madrid. ¿Dónde estudias? RAFAEL: En la facultad de Arquitectura, en la Universidad de la Florida. LAURA: ¡Qué interesante! Yo estudio informática en la Universidad de Maryland.

Después de escuchar

2-29 ¿Y usted? Answer the following questions.

1. ¿Cómo se llama usted? _____
2. ¿De dónde es? _____
3. ¿Dónde estudia? _____

Antes de escuchar

2-30 ¿Cómo son? In **2-31,** you will listen to a conversation between a student and her mother. The student is talking about how different her roommates are. Before listening to their conversation, write your roommate(s)' name(s) and a sentence that describes her/him/them.

_____

_____

A escuchar

Audioscript for A escuchar 2-31. AUDIO
ESTUDIANTE: ¡Hola, mamá! ¿Cómo estás? MAMÁ: Bien, muy bien. Y tú, ¿cómo estás, hija? ESTUDIANTE: Aquí muy contenta con mis nuevas compañeras de la universidad. Son muy agradables, pero muy diferentes. MAMÁ: ¿Sí? ¿Por qué? ESTUDIANTE: Bueno, Rita es mexicana y estudia economía. Es muy seria y trabajadora. Ella es alta, delgada y tiene el pelo rubio. Es callada y muy tranquila. No le gusta salir mucho. Marcela es de Honduras. Es baja, morena, tiene el pelo largo y ojos negros. Ella es muy activa y le gusta la música moderna, el rock y la salsa. Le gusta bailar y salir con sus amigos todos los fines de semana. Mamá: ¿Y qué estudia Marcela? Estudiante: Estudia arte moderno MAMÁ: Bueno, veo que son diferentes, pero las dos son agradables, ¿no? ESTUDIANTE: Sí, y yo las quiero mucho a las dos. MAMÁ: Bueno, me alegro, hija.

2-31 Dos personas diferentes. Now, listen to the conversation between a student and her mother. Mark the appropriate column(s) to indicate whether the following statements describe Rita, Marcela, or both.

	RITA	MARCELA
1. Estudia economía.	X	
2. Le gusta bailar.		X
3. Es baja, morena y tiene los ojos negros.		X
4. Es alta, delgada y es muy seria.	X	
5. Estudia arte moderno.		X

Después de escuchar

2-32 ¿Semejantes o diferentes? Complete the following ideas, according to your experience.

1. (No) Me gusta(n) mi(s) compañero/a(s) de cuarto porque _____

_____

2. Es/Son semejantes/diferentes porque _____

_____

Conversar

Antes de conversar

🄖 **2-33 ¿Descripción física o de personalidad?** Classify the following expressions under the appropriate column in the chart below.

Es inteligente.   Es guapa.
Tiene buen humor.   Es listo.
Tiene los ojos marrones. Es pelirroja.
Es simpático.   Es muy delgada.
Le gusta bailar.   Tiene el pelo largo.

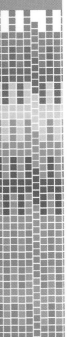

CARACTERÍSTICAS FÍSICAS	CARACTERÍSTICAS DE PERSONALIDAD
Tiene los ojos marrones; Es guapa;	Es inteligente; Tiene buen humor;
Es pelirroja; Es muy delgada; Tiene el pelo largo	Es listo; Es simpático; Le gusta bailar

A conversar

2-34 Adivinen quién es. Describe a student in the class or a public figure that everyone knows. The class will guess who this person is.

Después de conversar

2-35 Descripción. Choose one of the persons described and write a complete paragraph about him/her. Describe the person physically as well as his/her personality. Also indicate whether or not you like the person and why.

Note for 2-34. This activity does not require that students use words associated with family kinship in Spanish. Family relationships are presented in *Lección 4*. However, some students may want to use them. As the need arises, you may wish to provide students with words such as *padre, madre, hermano/a, primo/a, abuelo/a*, etc.

Antes de conversar

2-36 Condorito y sus amigos. *Condorito* is a comic strip magazine named after its central character. *Condorito* is very popular among children and adults in many Spanish-speaking countries. Go to www.prenhall.com/mosaicos, choose one of the characters shown in the picture below, and read the description about him/her.

Suggestion for 2-36. Assign this as homework ahead of time. Students should read the brief description of the character they chose. To avoid repetition, you may wish to show a picture of the cartoon characters in class and have students choose one in pairs/small groups. The characters are the following: *Pepe Cortizona, Garganta de lata, Don Cuasimodo, Che copete, Washington, Yayita, Huevoduro, Doña Tremebunda, Comegatos, El loro Matías, Coné, Don Chuma, Yuyito, Ungenio.*

World Editors®

A conversar

2-37 Mi personaje (*character*) favorito. Describe physically and in personality terms the *Condorito* character you read about in **2-36**. Your classmate will ask questions or make comments when appropriate.

Después de conversar

2-38 Mi visión de un personaje cómico. Find out about another popular comic character, like those mentioned in the *Cultura* box, page 80, and make a small information poster that includes a description of the character.

Leer

Accurate, fluent reading is an important skill that must be developed to become proficient in another language. It is important to develop this skill from the earliest stages of learning a new language.

Reading proficiently means more than just knowing words. It represents an active process in which linguistic and non-linguistic variables intervene while you are trying to make sense of a written text.

Before proceeding with the following activities, review some of the reading tips you practiced on pp. 46–47 of *Lección 1*. Then, in *Lección 2*, you will skim a text and infer meaning from context clues.

Guía de prelectura

Skim the texts in activity 2-40 and answer the questions, based on what you know from your own experience.

1. What type of texts are the following?
   a. e-mail messages
   b. for sale ads
   c. personal ads

2. What helped you identify the type of text?
   a. the format
   b. some expressions used
   c. the length

3. What do the people in the texts probably need?
   a. to find a lost relative
   b. to find someone to marry
   c. to make friends

4. Now, use your knowledge of the English language to comprehend what you read.

What cognates helped you figure out the answer to question 3 in the previous section?

   a. _____　　b. _____　　c. _____

Possible answers for 4. *sin compromiso, explorar, mantener correspondencia, etc.*

Antes de leer

2-39 Preparación. Primera fase. Read the following list and mark with an X those aspects that you find desirable in a friend.

1. _____ las características físicas
2. _____ el dinero (*money*)
3. _____ la ideas políticas
4. _____ el lugar de origen
5. _____ la educación
6. _____ la raza (*race*)
7. _____ la personalidad
8. _____ la fidelidad

2 Segunda fase. Now interview each other to find out the qualities that your best friends have. Mark your choices with an X. Then, determine which aspects in **Primera fase** are important for both of you. Do both of you value the same characteristics in a friend?

MODELO: E1: Tu mejor amigo/a, ¿es generoso/a?
E2: Sí, es generoso/a. *o* No, no es generoso/a. Es tacaño (*stingy*).

1. _____ moreno/a
2. _____ rubio/a
3. _____ simpático/a
4. _____ conservador/a
5. _____ liberal
6. _____ rico/a
7. _____ alegre
8. _____ extranjero/a
9. _____ trabajador/a
10. _____ ...

A leer

2-40 Primera mirada. Read the ads below and find one person you would like as your friend or as a friend of someone you know. Fill in the form below. In some cases, it may not be possible to provide all the information requested.

	SU CANDIDATO/A	CANDIDATO/A PARA OTRA PERSONA
Nombre		
Edad		
Forma de comunicación		
Estado civil		
¿Por qué?		

Suggestion for 2-40. Before the activity, tell students that the purpose of the activity is to scan the personal ads for specific information. Encourage them to guess the meaning of unfamiliar words from context and not to concern themselves with those words not needed to complete the task. To check comprehension, you may have students read aloud or write their responses directly from the ads. Do not force them to paraphrase the information as they give it to you, since this is not a speaking activity, and they may not be ready to do it. In case some students would like to respond in their own words, you may wish to teach them *El anuncio dice...* Make the activity as communicative as possible by having students answer *No sé* or *No sabemos* when the information is not provided.

LENGUA

Y changes to **e** when it precedes a word beginning with **i** or **h**.

inglés y español, but **español e inglés**

inteligente y agradable, but **agradable e inteligente**

hipócrita y ambicioso, but **ambicioso e hipócrita**

Amigos sin fronteras

Soltera, sin hijos y sin compromiso. Me llamo Susana y tengo 24 años. Busco amigos extranjeros, solteros, separados o divorciados, jóvenes o mayores. Soy amable, cariñosa y muy trabajadora. Por mi trabajo, viajo mucho, pero me gusta la compañía de otras personas. Soy bilingüe. Hablo español e inglés. Escriban a sincompromiso@comcast.net.

Soy Ricardo Brown. 21 años, sincero, dedicado. Me gustan las fiestas. Deseo conocer a una chica de unos 23 años. Prefiero una mujer activa e independiente. Me gusta practicar deportes y explorar lugares nuevos. Escríbanme a amigosincero@msn.com.

Me llamo Pablo Sosa, tengo 31 años, y soy chileno. Soy agradable y muy trabajador. Me gusta hacer mi trabajo a la perfección, pero soy tolerante. Mi pasión son los autos convertibles. Deseo mantener correspondencia por correo electrónico con jóvenes del extranjero para intercambiar información sobre los convertibles europeos o americanos. Mi dirección electrónica es locoporlosautos@yahoo.com.

Soy Xiomara Stravinsky, decoradora y fotógrafa. Soy joven, dinámica, agradable y generosa, pero tengo pocos amigos porque tengo dos trabajos y paso muchas horas con mis clientes. Necesito un cambio en mi vida. ¿Deseas ser mi amigo/a? Por favor, escríbeme a xiomarastravinsky@hotmail.com.

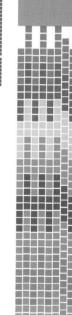

Después de leer

❷ **2-41 Ampliación.** What qualities do you associate with Susana (**S**), Ricardo (**R**), Pablo (**P**), and Xiomara (**X**)? Why? With a classmate, write the initial(s) next to each quality, and support your opinions.

1. __S, R__ sociable
2. __S, X__ simpático/a
3. __R__ divertido/a
4. __P__ perfeccionista
5. __P__ mayor
6. __S, R__ flexible
7. __S, P, X__ trabajador/a
8. __S, X__ ocupado/a

 *Escribir*

Writing a Description

Writing a description is similar to painting a picture, except we use words instead of paint. There are many ways to write a description, but in general a good written description . . .

■ presents enough information about the object so the reader may visualize the characteristics of what is described: colors, physical characteristics, personality traits, etc.

■ places the object described in a particular space and time: an empty classroom after classes are over looks and feels different from a crowded one during class time. The physical or psychological description of an individual helps the reader visualize what is described. Through the use of adjectives, the writer may cause the reader to like, dislike, enjoy, remember, etc.

■ requires organization of information, and a good selection of vocabulary and structures (nouns, adjectives, verbs, adverbs, etc.).

■ is always made with the reader in mind: What does the reader need to know? How much information should be provided? Why will he/she read our description?

As you gain more experience with the language, you will start focusing on ways to approach the writing task more effectively with your peers and your instructor. The following will be very useful in discussing your writing:

■ to state the purpose (**propósito**) of your writing: **describir, narrar, explicar,** etc.

■ to describe the means of communication (**medio de comunicación**): **carta** (*letter*), **anuncio** (*ad*), **correo electrónico**, etc.

■ to determine the reader (*lector/a*): **amigo/a, conocido/a** (*acquaintance*), **familiar,** etc.

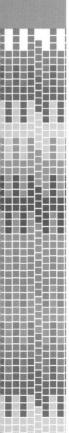

Antes de escribir

2-42 Enfoque (*Focus*). Primera fase. A male movie fan writes the following ad in the local newspaper to meet other people with whom he can share his passion and with whom he can have fun outdoors. First, read the ad and the response he got from a female reader of the ad. Then, follow the instructions.

Fanático del cine necesita amigos para discutir películas los fines de semana. Tengo 24 años y estudio cinematografía. Me fascinan las películas de acción y también las románticas. Soy fuerte, activo, atlético y aventurero. Me gusta practicar deportes, especialmente el tenis y el esquí. Siempre estoy muy ocupado, pero tengo unas horas todas las semanas para conversar sobre películas y hacer deportes. Interesados, favor de enviar correo electrónico a fanaticodelcine@yahoo.com.

```
Para: fanaticodelcine@yahoo.com
De: Marta20@chat.com
Asunto: anuncio

Estimado fanaticodelcine,

Me llamo Marta y me gustan mucho las películas y los deportes. Tengo
20 años y estudio en la universidad. Tú y yo somos similares. Yo soy
atlética, aventurera, pero muy responsable. Me gusta tener muchos
amigos y explorar lugares con ellos.

Este semestre tomo seis clases y tengo mucho trabajo, pero siempre
miro películas o practico deportes. Los fines de semana tengo un poco
de tiempo para hacer actividades interesantes. Vivo cerca de la
universidad y me gusta mucho mi apartamento. No necesito tomar el
bus para asistir a clase. También me gusta mucho caminar. Por favor,
responde a mi dirección de correo electrónico: marta20@chat.com

Hasta pronto.
```

Segunda fase. Answer the following questions based on Marta's response.

1. Does Marta describe herself appropriately in her response to *fanaticodelcine*?
        Yes   No
2. Mark with an X the reason for your response or write your own response:
   _____ Marta describes herself as a physically attractive young woman.
   _____ Marta provides *fanaticodelcine* with a description of the potential friend he is looking for.
   _____ Marta addresses the needs of *fanaticodelcine* by telling him how compatible their free time activities are.
   _____ Marta plans her ideas carefully. She specifies her free time activities and hobbies, talks about her personality features, etc. to match the person *fanaticodelcine* is looking for.
   _____ . . .

Possible answers for 2-42. Segunda fase 1. Yes; 2. Marta provides *fanaticodelcine* with a description of the potential friend he is looking for. Marta addresses the needs of *fanaticodelcine* by telling him how compatible their free time activities are. Marta plans her ideas carefully: She specifies her free time activities and hobbies, talks about her personality features, etc. to match the person *fanaticodelcine* is looking for.

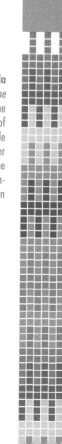

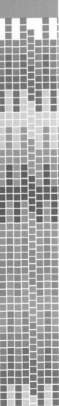

Suggestion for 2-43. To lower the affective filter, you may wish to ask that students adopt a new identity, that is, that they think of a physical or psychological description of someone imaginary/ideal.

2-43 Preparación. Reread the ads in **Amigos sin fronteras**, page 81, and choose one ad you would like to respond to. Then, make a list of words that will help you describe yourself (or someone you'd like to be) to become friends with the person who wrote the ad.

1. one way to tell your age
2. indicate your place of origin
3. some words (adjectives) that describe you physically
4. some expressions (adjectives) that describe your personality
5. some activities (verbs) that you like to do that match the needs of the person in the ad

A escribir

2-44 Manos a la obra. Now answer the ad using the information you prepared in the previous activity.

```
Para: _____

De: _____

Asunto: Anuncio

Hola _____,

Respondo a tu anuncio del periódico. Me llamo _____.

Primero, aquí tienes alguna información personal: _____
_____
_____

En segundo lugar, éstas son algunas de las actividades similares a
tus actividades que me gustan en mi tiempo libre: _____
_____

En tercer lugar, por las tardes/noches, o los fines de semana, me gusta
_____
_____

Finalmente, deseo ser tu amigo/a. Por favor, escríbeme un correo
electrónico a mi dirección: _____

Hasta pronto.
```

Después de escribir

2-45 Revisión. After completing your letter or e-mail, read it at least twice. Check the following:

■ The content of the letter or e-mail: Did you include all the information your reader needs?

■ The form of the text: Did you use punctuation correctly? Did you verify that there are no spelling or grammatical mistakes?

Finally, discuss your letter or e-mail with a classmate.

ENFOQUE CULTURAL

TEMAS: LOS HISPANOS EN LOS ESTADOS UNIDOS

Para pensar

¿Tiene usted amigos hispanos? ¿De qué países son? ¿Hay estudiantes hispanos en su universidad? ¿Sabe usted el nombre de una comida hispana?

Las personas de origen hispano viven en muchos estados de los Estados Unidos: Arizona, California, Colorado, Illinois, Nueva York, Nueva Jersey, Nuevo México, Texas, etcétera.

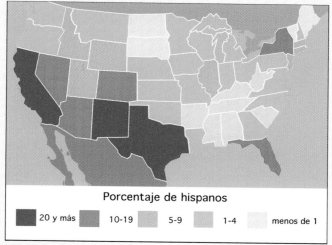

Porcentaje de hispanos

| 20 y más | 10-19 | 5-9 | 1-4 | menos de 1 |

Los hispanos en los Estados Unidos vienen de todos los países de Hispanoamérica, pero no todos son inmigrantes; los chicanos (personas de ascendencia mexicana) son ciudadanos desde que la región del suroeste pasó a ser territorio norteamericano en 1848. Los puertorriqueños son ciudadanos norteamericanos desde 1917.

Algunos hispanos abandonan sus países por razones políticas o económicas. Otros buscan mejores oportunidades de trabajo o una educación especializada.

Los hispanos traen su rica y valiosa cultura, su voluntad de trabajo y deseo de superación, y contribuyen a la vida cultural, política, artística y deportiva de los Estados Unidos.

Para contestar

2 **Los amigos hispanos.** Respondan a las siguientes preguntas:

1. ¿De qué países vienen los hispanos que viven en los Estados Unidos?
2. ¿Cómo contribuyen los hispanos a la vida de los Estados Unidos?

G **Riqueza cultural.** Mencionen las ventajas y desventajas (*advantages and disadvantages*) que tiene un país con muchos inmigrantes.

VÍNCULOS

For materials related to the Enfoque cultural, see

- SAM-OneKey: WB: 2-28
- IRCD: Chapter 2; pg. 85

Para pensar

¿Conoce usted alguna ciudad en los Estados Unidos con una gran influencia hispana? ¿Cómo se refleja esa influencia?

Al lado del Viejo San Juan está el San Juan moderno, una ciudad con una intensa vida nocturna y hermosas playas.

El Viejo San Juan es una parte muy hermosa de la capital de Puerto Rico. En esta zona hay muchas tiendas, cafés al aire libre y museos.

La influencia de la población cubana en Miami es inmensa. Hay muchos festivales donde la gente baila, come y disfruta de muchas tradiciones de su país de origen.

Expresiones puertorriqueñas:

cabuya	No le des **cabuya**.	*Don't give him/her ammunition to bother you.*
macacoa	Yo no compro la lotería porque tengo una **macacoa** terrible.	*I don't buy the lottery because I have horrible bad luck.*
majarete	Dejó su cuarto hecho un **majarete**.	*He/she left his/her room a complete mess.*
babada	No hagas caso. Es una **babada**.	*Don't pay attention. It is something foolish.*

Expresiones chicanas:

Ando brujo.	*I have no money.*
¡Ándale, güero!	*Let's go, blondey (male).*

En San Diego, California, y San Antonio, Texas, la población y la arquitectura de origen mexicano son partes integrales de estas ciudades.

Para contestar

En el mapa

1. Busque una ciudad en los Estados Unidos con una alta población hispana. Indique dónde está.
2. Diga qué ciudad con una alta población hispana está más cerca de su ciudad.

Ahora diga...

1. qué ciudad de los Estados Unidos con una alta población hispana quiere visitar y por qué.
2. una actividad de los cubanos en Miami.

¿Qué dice usted si...

1. no tiene dinero?
2. su compañero/a de cuarto no limpia (*clean*) su cuarto?

Para investigar en Internet

Busque el nombre de diez personas importantes de origen hispano en el gobierno, en la empresa privada, en los deportes, en el arte o en el mundo de la moda de los Estados Unidos. Seleccione una persona y después informe a la clase sobre esta persona.

¡Prepárese!

3 **2-46 Misterios y pistas.** Before watching the second episode of *Fortunas*, read the first mystery (*misterio*) and the four clues (*pistas*). In groups of three, discuss the meanings of the *misterio* and the *pistas* and possible relationships between them. Use the following questions as a guide for your discussion. Remember that the first mystery is related to the history of the Aztecs.

Misterio No. 1: Cinco es suficiente.

Pistas:
a. Destrucción de los gigantes por el viento (monos)
b. Destrucción por la lluvia (pájaros)
c. Destrucción por el diluvio (peces)
d. Destrucción por el jaguar

1. ¿El número cinco tiene un significado especial en la cultura o en la sociedad?
2. ¿Qué importancia tiene el número cinco, u otros números, para usted personalmente?
3. ¿Qué tienen en común el viento, la lluvia y el diluvio?
4. ¿Es importante la idea de la destrucción en la historia de los aztecas?
5. ¿Qué tipo de animal es el jaguar?

Manolo y Ángela hablan del comienzo del concurso.

Tito habla con Sabrina y Efraín sobre el concurso.

Sabrina y Efraín están en Xochimilco.

A Sabrina le gustan mucho los misterios pero a Efraín no.

Efraín no es mucha competencia para Sabrina.

Sabrina desea ganar el concurso, pero su plan es un secreto.

¡Responda!

2-47 Ser o estar. Primera fase. After watching the second episode of *Fortunas*, complete the following sentences with the correct form of **ser** or **estar**.

1. Manolo y Ángela __están__ contentos con el concurso.
2. Tito __está__ en Xochimilco para hablar con los participantes.
3. Efraín __es__ de Argentina, y Sabrina __es__ española.
4. Efraín __es__ músico.
5. Sabrina __es__ una persona inteligente y agresiva.

Segunda fase. Now, write complete sentences in Spanish to describe the following people and things related to the *Fortunas* contest. Use adjectives from the list or any others that you can think of.

MODELO: E1: concurso
          E2: El concurso es muy interesante.

alegre	listo/a	joven
simpático/a	divertido/a	tonto/a
interesante	nervioso/a	misterioso/a
contento/a	hablador/a	ridículo/a

1. Ángela y Manolo
2. Xochimilco
3. Tito
4. misterio número 1
5. Efraín y Sabrina
6. la entrevista de Sabrina

The music of this Puerto Rican group combines several musical styles like rock, reggae, ska, and Afro-Caribbean rhythms. Their songs frequently comment on social problems.

2-48 ¡Prepárese! Try to match the following themes from *Oh Naná* with their Spanish equivalents. Use a bilingual dictionary if necessary.

1. sadness
2. the enjoyment of life
3. happiness

a. __3__ respira alegría
b. __2__ ríe también, vive, goza
c. __1__ la pena

What things do you associate with these themes? Do you know any songs in your own language with the same themes?

> Hoy desperté con la pena
> de mi corazón, que entre latidos me
> decía no pierdas la razón.
> Me dijo, mira el cielo brillando está
> y si llueve no temas, ya el sol vendrá,
> que yo te digo, canta conmigo
> Oh Naná, Oh Nanananá.
> Y luego en la noche un viejo amigo que
> me visitó. Y aunque vestía su sonrisa,
> su rostro demostró, entró y lloró.
> Yo le dije, oye, mira, escucha bien
> respira alegría y luego ven
> que yo te digo, canta conmigo
> Oh Naná, Oh Nanananá.
> No sé por qué desperté con tanta
> tristeza, me lastimé el corazón,
> perdí la cabeza, pero alguien dijo así.
> Si sufres llora, ríe también, vive, goza,
> tiene que ser, y yo te digo,
> canta conmigo...
> Oh Naná, Oh Nanananá.

2-49 ¡Escuche! As you listen to *Oh Naná,* indicate with an X which adjectives from the list below you would use to describe the song.

_____ agradable	_____ bonita	_____ aburrida
_____ interesante	_____ corta	_____ divertida
_____ feliz	_____ fuerte	_____ enojada
_____ tranquila	_____ triste	_____ seria
_____ alegre	_____ simpática	_____ lenta

2-50 ¡Responda! Now, using the adjectives you have chosen and the verb **ser,** write five questions to ask your partner to find out how he/she would characterize the song (*la canción*), the lyrics (*la letra*), and/or the rhythm (*el ritmo*). Then answer the questions your partner has written.

MODELO: E1: ¿Es bonita la canción?
E2: Sí, es bonita./No, no es bonita.

VOCABULARIO

AUDIO Descripciones

agradable	*nice*
alegre	*happy, glad*
alto/a	*tall*
antipático/a	*unpleasant*
bajo/a	*short* (in stature)
bilingüe	*bilingual*
bonito/a	*pretty*
callado/a	*quiet*
cansado/a	*tired*
casado/a	*married*
contento/a	*happy, glad*
conversador/a	*talkative*
corto/a	*short* (in length)
débil	*weak*
delgado/a	*thin*
divertido/a	*funny, amusing*
enojado/a	*angry*
feliz	*happy*
feo/a	*ugly*
fuerte	*strong*
gordo/a	*fat*
guapo/a	*good-looking, handsome*
joven	*young*
largo/a	*long*
listo/a	*smart, ready*
mayor	*old*
mediano/a	*average, medium* (height)
moreno/a	*brunet, brunette*
nervioso/a	*nervous*
nuevo/a	*new*
pelirrojo/a	*redhead*
perezoso/a	*lazy*
pobre	*poor*
rico/a	*rich, wealthy*
rubio/a	*blond*
simpático/a	*nice, charming*
soltero/a	*single*
tonto/a	*silly, foolish*
trabajador/a	*hardworking*
tranquilo/a	*calm, tranquil*
triste	*sad*
viejo/a	*old*

Verbos

desear	*to wish, to want*
ser	*to be*
usar	*to use*

El cuerpo

los ojos	*eyes*
ojos azules	*blue eyes*
ojos verdes	*green eyes*
ojos (de color)	
café	*brown eyes*
el pelo	*hair*
pelo castaño	*brown hair*
pelo negro	*black hair*

Nacionalidades*

argentino/a	*Argentinean*
chileno/a	*Chilean*
colombiano/a	*Colombian*
cubano/a	*Cuban*
dominicano/a	*Dominican*
español/a	*Spanish*
guatemalteco/a	*Guatemalan*
mexicano/a	*Mexican*
nicaragüense	*Nicaraguan*
peruano/a	*Peruvian*
puertorriqueño/a	*Puerto Rican*
venezolano/a	*Venezuelan*

Palabras y expresiones útiles

ahora	*now*
de	*of, from*
¿de quién?	*whose?*
del	*of the* (contraction of *de* + *el*)
le gusta(n)	*you* (formal) *like*
los lentes de contacto	*contact lenses*
me gusta(n)	*I like*
mucho/a	*much, a lot*
no (ni)... ni	*neither . . . nor*
pero	*but*
que	*that*
te gusta(n)	*you* (familiar) *like*
Tengo... años.	*I am . . . years old*
tiene	*he/she has, you* (formal) *have*

*Other adjectives of nationality can be found in the English-Spanish and Spanish-English glossaries at the end of the book.
See pages 63–64 for animals and additional colors.
See pages 74 for possessive adjectives.

3

LAS ACTIVIDADES Y LOS PLANES

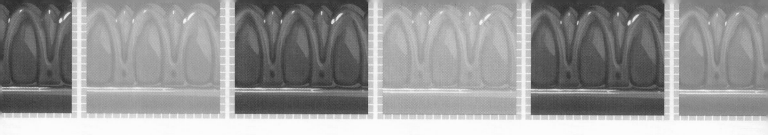

Objetivos comunicativos

Contenido

A PRIMERA VISTA

AUDIO *Diversiones populares*

VÍNCULOS

*En las **fiestas** y **reuniones,** los jóvenes bailan, escuchan **música** o conversan. A veces **tocan** la **guitarra** y **cantan canciones** populares.*

*Estas chicas **van** a la playa en su **tiempo libre** y también **durante** las **vacaciones.** Allí, caminan y conversan mientras otras personas **toman el sol, nadan en el mar, corren** o **descansan.***

*Este señor **lee** el **periódico al aire libre.** Y usted, ¿lee el periódico? ¿Qué periódicos o **revistas** lee?*

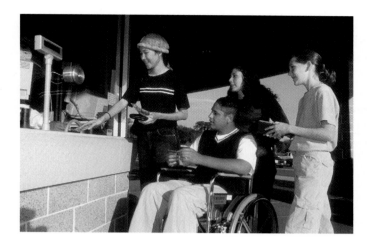

*Muchos jóvenes van al **cine**, especialmente los fines de semana. También es común **alquilar películas** para **ver** en casa.*

Follow-up. The following are some questions you may ask after presenting this photo: *¿Va usted al cine los fines de semana? ¿Va usted por la tarde o por la noche? A mí me gusta ver películas románticas. También me gustan las películas de misterio, pero no me gusta ver películas de ciencia-ficción. Y a usted, ¿le gusta ver películas de acción? ¿Cuáles son sus películas favoritas?*

Suggestion. Point out that telephone greetings vary from country to country. *¡Diga!, ¡Dígame!* (Spain); *¡Bueno!* (Mexico); *¡Aló!* (Argentina, Peru, Chile); *¡Oigo!, ¿Qué hay?* (Cuba). You may also want to point out the use of terms of endearment such as *mi amor* (in this dialog), *corazón, mi vida, querido/a,* and *mi cielo.*

AUDIO **Una conversación por teléfono**

TERESA: ¿**Aló**?

JAVIER: Hola, Teresa, ¿qué te parece si **vamos** al cine esta tarde y **después** vamos a **cenar** a un restaurante de **comida** peruana para **celebrar** tu **cumpleaños**?

TERESA: ¡Ay, Javier, qué bien! ¿Y qué vamos a ver?

JAVIER: Tú decides, mi amor; es tu **cumpleaños.**

TERESA: Pues, la película nueva de Alfonso Cuarón.

JAVIER: **Fabuloso.** Voy para la casa ahora. Hasta pronto.

TERESA: Chao.

¿Qué dice usted?

3-1 Asociaciones. What activities do you associate with the following places?

1. __c__ la playa
2. __e__ la fiesta
3. __a__ el cine
4. __b__ la biblioteca
5. __b, d__ la casa

a. ver una película
b. leer el periódico
c. tomar el sol
d. mirar televisión
e. bailar y conversar

❷ 3-2 Mis actividades. What do you do in the following places? Take turns asking each other questions.

MODELO: las fiestas
          E1: ¿Qué haces en las fiestas?
          E2: En las fiestas bailo mucho. ¿Y tú?
          E1: Bailo y hablo con mis amigos.
          E2: Y tú, ¿qué haces en… ?

1. la universidad por las mañanas
2. la biblioteca pública de tu ciudad
3. casa el fin de semana
4. un parque de tu ciudad
5. la playa durante las vacaciones
6. la discoteca con tus amigos

CULTURA

There are many outstanding Spanish-language films. Traditionally, Mexico, Spain, and Argentina have had an important industry, but there are films from other Spanish-speaking countries too. Directors like Pedro Almodóvar or Icíar Bollaín in Spain; Alfonso Cuarón or Alejandro González in Mexico; Sergio Cabrera in Colombia; and Juan Carlos Tabío in Cuba, are internationally known.

Expansión for 3-2. 7. una reunión, 8. el cine, 9. un restaurante elegante, 10. el auto, 11. el centro de la ciudad, 12. el laboratorio de lenguas

Note for 3-3. Film titles are not literally translated from other languages into Spanish. An example is *The recruit*, which has been translated as *La prueba* (test, proof, evidence).

Suggestion for 3-3. You may wish to review some ways to accept or reject an invitation. Write two columns: *Aceptar, No aceptar* on the board. Give a few examples of each. *Aceptar: Sí, gracias; ¡Qué bueno! ¡Fabuloso! No aceptar: No, gracias; Lo siento.* You may also wish to introduce, *No puedo; Debo estudiar/trabajar…*

3-3 ¿Adónde vamos? Primera fase. Look at the cultural section of a Peruvian newspaper below. Underline three activities that you would like to do on the weekend. Then fill in the information in the following chart, including the day and the time that you are planning to do them.

EL Diario de Trujillo

Muestras y Exposiciones

Exposición del séptimo concurso de artes visuales. *Pasaporte para un artista,* que este jueves, a las 7:30 p.m., se inaugura en la Casona Orbegoso.

Los monstruos de Salid. Muestra del pintor Sadid Luján. Lugar: Casa de la Emancipación. Horario al público: De 9 a.m. a 1 p.m. y de 4 a 7 p.m.

Presencia colombiana en nuestro país. Cuadros de los pintores colombianos Félix Ángel y Jenaro Mejía. Lugar: Sexto piso de El cultural.

Sarita & Co. Muestra colectiva con motivo del Día Internacional de la Mujer. Lugar: Casa de la Emancipación.

Música y Teatro

Orquesta Sinfónica de Trujillo. (OST), Dirigida por el maestro Teófilo Álvarez: Suite No. 1 de la ópera Carmen de Bizet y Obertura de Rossini. Teatro Municipal de Trujillo a las 10:30 de la mañana.

Compañía Regional del Ballet. Escenas de la ópera rock, *Jesucristo Superstar.* La coreografía pertenece a Stella Puga, la música a Andrew Lloyd Webber y la letra a Timothy Rice.

Cine

La prueba (*The Recruit*). Un thriller que nos muestra los secretos de la CIA: cómo se recluta a los agentes, cómo se entregan para el espionaje y cómo aprenden las reglas de la supervivencia. Con Colin Farrell y Al Pacino. V.O.S. A las 5 p.m., 8 p.m. y 10 p.m. En los Minicines Trujillo.

Las horas (*The Hours*). Tres mujeres que viven en épocas y lugares diferentes, pero están vinculadas entre sí porque las tres buscan el sentido de sus vidas. Con Nicole Kidman, Julianne Moore y Meryl Streep. V.O.S. A las 12 p.m, 4 p.m. y 7 p.m. En los Minicines Trujillo.

Mi vida sin mí de la directora catalana Isabel Coixet. Sobre una mujer que decide vivir a fondo los pocos meses que le quedan de vida. Con Sarah Polley y Mark Ruffalo. A las 2 p.m. 8 p.m. y 10 p.m. En los Minicines Trujillo.

¿ADÓNDE VAMOS?	¿QUÉ VAMOS A VER/ HACER/ ESCUCHAR?	¿CUÁNDO?

EN DIRECTO

To invite a friend over the phone:

Te llamo para ver si quieres (*if you would like*) + *infinitive.*

Tengo una idea. ¿Por qué no… (nosotros *form, present tense*)?

② Segunda fase. Phone a classmate and invite him/her to one of the events you chose in *Primera fase.* He or she will give you an excuse as in the model.

MODELO: E1: ¿Aló?

E2: Hola, Pedro. Soy María. ¿Vamos el viernes por la tarde a la exposición "Los monstruos de Salid"?

E1: Lo siento, María, el viernes Carlos y yo vamos al cine a las cuatro. Vamos a ver *Las horas.*

La comida

ESPECIALIDADES DE LA CASA

ENTRADAS

Ceviche de pescado S/.15
Papa a la huancaína S/.10
Causa a la limeña S/.12

PLATO PRINCIPAL

Chupe de camarones S/.25
Ají de gallina S/.18
Lomo saltado S/.17

POSTRES

Suspiro de limeña S/.8
Alfajor S/.8
Mazamorra morada S/.6

BEBIDAS

Chicha morada S/.4
Jugo de maracuyá S/.4
Inca Kola S/.3

En el restaurante. Ahora Javier y Teresa están en el restaurante *El jardín limeño* para **celebrar** el **cumpleaños** de Teresa.

CAMARERO: Buenas noches. ¿Qué desean los señores?

JAVIER: Teresa, ¿qué vas a comer?

TERESA: Para mí, una **ensalada** primero y después **pollo** con **verduras.**

JAVIER: Yo, para empezar, **ceviche** de camarones. Y luego un **bistec** con **papas.**

CAMARERO: ¿Y para **beber**?

JAVIER: Vamos a beber **vino.** Y también **agua** con gas, por favor.

A INVESTIGAR

"S/." is the abbreviation for the monetary unit in Peru. What is the name of the monetary unit? What is the current rate of exchange?

CULTURA

Peruvian cooking uses mainly regional ingredients and follows the traditional ways of preparing them inherited from various indigenous cultures. A very typical dish of Peru and other countries in Latin America is *ceviche*. It is generally made with seafood that is not cooked, but cured in lime and spices. For more information about this dish and its variations, see www.prenhall.com/mosaicos

Tap water is generally not brought to the table in restaurants in the Spanish-speaking world as it is in the United States. Most restaurant-goers order bottled mineral water (*agua mineral*) to drink with their meal, in either its carbonated (*con gas*) or noncarbonated (*sin gas*) form.

Suggestion. Introduce new vocabulary: *El camarero les pregunta a Javier y a Teresa qué desean comer y qué van a beber* (make gestures). *Ellos van a beber vino para celebrar el cumpleaños de Teresa.* Point out that *beber* and *tomar* may be used interchangeably for "to drink." Have students act out the dialog in groups of three. They can imagine they are in a restaurant and order from the Peruvian menu. The explanation of the various Peruvian dishes is in the IRM. In some countries, the word *bife* is used to refer to steak; in others, *bistec* and *bisté* are used. Inform students that eating hours vary in the Hispanic countries.

La comida rápida

La comida rápida es muy popular entre la gente joven. Las "hamburgueserías" de tipo norteamericano existen en muchas **ciudades** del mundo hispano. Los restaurantes de comida rápida en los **países** hispanos frecuentemente combinan comida de los Estados Unidos con comidas **típicas** de cada país. Por ejemplo, usted puede comer una **hamburguesa** con **papas fritas** o con **arroz** y frijoles negros. En muchos países, usted puede tomar vino o **cerveza** en estos restaurantes.

Ají de gallina

Papas a la huancaína

Suggestion. You may wish to talk about *tapas*, the Spanish version of fast food (the word *tapas* was introduced in activity 1-21 in *Lección 1*). Ask questions that compare American fast food with variations in other countries: *¿Le gusta comer arroz con frijoles negros? ¿Es posible comer eso en un restaurante de comida rápida aquí en los Estados Unidos? ¿Es una buena idea tomar cerveza o vino en McDonald's?* Ask who eats fast food and how often.

Suggestions. On page 97 and on this page, some Peruvian dishes were introduced as part of the cultural content of the chapter (Peru is the country presented in the *Enfoque cultural*). In this section, the different foods that are normally part of the students' experience are presented so they can talk about what they normally eat or drink. In *Lección 10*, the food theme will be revisited. Use the Image Resource CD to introduce food vocabulary, providing comprehensible input; you may wish to have students repeat the names of each item. Ask questions such as, *¿Toma Ud. café en el desayuno? ¿Come Ud. cereal? ¿Qué come Ud. a la hora del almuerzo? ¿Qué comida no le gusta? ¿Cuál es su bebida/comida favorita? ¿Qué comida es rica en vitaminas?* Introduce *caliente* and *frío/a: La sopa está caliente. La cerveza está fría. Y el café, ¿está frío o caliente?*

Ceviche de pescado

Suggestion. You may wish to have students bring pictures of food items to class. Divide the class into (small) groups and have them put together breakfast, lunch and dinner menus with their corresponding food labels in Spanish. Finally, have the groups compare their menus with those of other groups and decide which one(s) they like best.

Más comidas y bebidas

el desayuno

el cereal

la leche

el jugo de naranja

el café caliente

el pan tostado/las tostadas

los huevos fritos

el almuerzo

la ensalada de lechuga y tomate

el sándwich de jamón y queso

una cerveza fría

las papas fritas

el refresco

la hamburguesa

la fruta

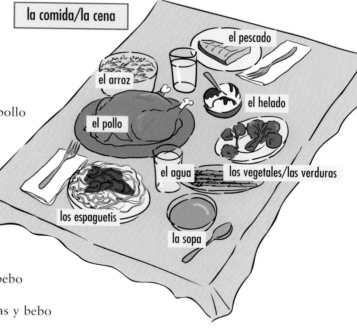

la comida/la cena

el pescado

el arroz

el helado

el pollo

el agua

los vegetales/las verduras

los espaguetis

la sopa

¿Qué dice usted?

3-4 La dieta. Primera fase. Which of the
following contains more calories? Underline
your response.

1. la sopa de tomate, <u>las hamburguesas</u>, la sopa de pollo
2. <u>el pollo frito</u>, el pescado, la ensalada
3. los vegetales, la fruta, <u>las papas fritas</u>
4. <u>la cerveza</u>, la leche, el café
5. <u>el helado de chocolate</u>, el cereal, el arroz

❷ Segunda fase. Mention one food item or drink
in *Primera fase* that you eat or drink frequently.
Do you and your classmate like to eat and drink
the same foods?

❷

MODELO: E1: Frecuentemente como ensaladas y bebo
                      cerveza. ¿Y tú?
              E2: Yo frecuentemente como papas fritas y bebo
                      refrescos.

3-5 Las comidas. Tell a classmate what you have for breakfast, lunch, and
dinner. Then find out what he/she has.

MODELO: En el desayuno, como tostadas y bebo café. ¿Y tú?

Warm-up for 3-4. Provide a calorie chart and
have students look up the number of calories for
each item, working in pairs. Numbers from 100
to 2 million are presented in *Explicación y
expansión;* you may wish to preview some of
them here.

Suggestion for 3-4. You may wish to ask
students to talk about meals that have fewer
calories as well.

Alternate for 3-6. Have students enact the following situations in pairs (results to be reported to the class later): 1. *Su amigo/a está a dieta porque está un poco gordo/a. ¿Qué debe comer en el desayuno, en el almuerzo y en la cena?* 2. *Su madre tiene un nivel de colesterol muy alto. ¿Qué comidas no debe comer? (Huevos, leche, bistec, queso.)*

Suggestion for 3-6. Ask who in the class is a vegetarian. Discuss what he/she eats.

2 **3-6 Dietas especiales.** Look at the menu below and decide which would be the best option for the following people.

SOPAS	
Sopa de pollo	S/. 12
Sopa de tomate	S/. 10
Sopa de vegetales	S/. 10
Sopa de pescado	S/. 14

ENSALADAS	
Ensalada de lechuga y tomate	S/. 8
Ensalada de pollo	S/. 14
Ensalada de atún	S/. 12

PLATOS PRINCIPALES	
Bistec con papas y vegetales	S/. 20
Hamburguesa con papas fritas	S/. 16
Pescado con papas fritas	S/. 18
Arroz con vegetales	S/. 15

1. Su padre y usted son un poco delgados y desean subir de peso (*gain weight*) ¿Qué van a comer de este menú?
2. Su mamá es alérgica a los productos del mar. ¿Cuál de las ensaladas va a comer?
3. Su mejor amigo/a está un poco gordo/a y quiere bajar de peso (*lose weight*). ¿Cuál de los platos principales no debe comer?
4. El/La profesor/a de español está enfermo/a (*sick*) hoy. ¿Qué debe comer?

2 **3-7 ¿Qué te gusta más?** Using the words below, ask a classmate what he/she prefers to drink **por las mañanas, a la hora del almuerzo, por las noches.** Alternate asking questions and taking notes. Then in small groups decide which are the most popular drinks.

MODELO: E1: ¿Qué te gusta más por las mañanas, el té o el café?
          E2: Me gusta más el café.

el té	un vaso (*a glass*) de leche	una cerveza	un chocolate caliente
el café	el agua mineral con gas	un refresco	un batido (*shake*) de fruta
el jugo de naranja	el agua mineral sin gas	una copa de vino	un té de hierbas

Alternate for 3-8. Have students work in pairs to decide what they will order at a restaurant, using the *ir a* + infinitive construction.

Follow-up for 3-8. Ask additional questions such as *La hora de comer: ¿A qué hora es el desayuno? ¿el almuerzo? ¿la cena? Las bebidas: ¿Cuándo tomamos vino? ¿leche? ¿jugo de naranja? ¿cerveza? ¿agua? La sopa: ¿Cuántas variedades de sopa hay? (de tomate, vegetales, pollo, pescado). El postre: ¿Cuál es su postre favorito?*

Suggestions for 3-8. Bring menus to class or have students prepare them in groups of three, using poster board and markers. Have half the students play the role of customers in a restaurant. They should sit and order from the menus as other students (waiters/waitresses) take orders. Have students switch roles.

2 **3-8 En el café.** It is 8:00 Saturday morning, and a friend and you are in your favorite café. Ask your friend what he or she would like to order. Then say what you would like to order.

MODELO: E1: El desayuno es muy bueno aquí. ¿Qué deseas comer?
          E2: _____ ¿Y tú?
          E1: _____ ¿Y qué vas a tomar?
          E2: _____

café	S/.4
té	S/.4
café con leche	S/.6
jugo de naranja	S/.5
chocolate	S/.7
tostadas	S/.5
pan con mantequilla	S/.5
pan dulce	S/.6
cereal	S/.8
huevos fritos	S/.10

G **3-9 Una excursión.** You are spending a few days in Peru, and you are planning a day trip to Machu Picchu. Make arrangements to take some food and beverages for a picnic.

a. Make a list of the food and beverages that you need to take.
b. Talk about the things that you are going to see.

La ciudad de Machu Picchu en los Andes

2 **3-10 Nuestro menú.** Your roommate and you want to have guests for dinner tonight. First decide whom each of you is going to invite; then ask each other the guests' phone numbers so one of you can make the calls later. Decide what you are going to serve. Finally, compare your menu with that of another pair of classmates.

UDIO **3-11 ¿Qué hacen estos estudiantes?** You will listen to two students, Rafael and Miguel, talking about their daily and leisure activities. Before you listen, write down three activities you do in your leisure time, and three activities other students you know do.

Mis actividades: _____
_____

Las actividades de otros estudiantes: _____
_____

Now, listen to the audio and pay attention to the general idea of what is said. Then, in the chart below, mark **Sí** next to the activities they mention they will do during the weekend and **No** next to those ones they will not do.

	Sí	No
1. leer el periódico al aire libre		X
2. estudiar para los exámenes		X
3. ir a la playa y nadar	X	
4. descansar y conversar	X	
5. trabajar en la librería		X

RAFAEL: ¡Ah! ¡Qué bien! Entonces voy con ustedes. El fin de semana va a ser de descanso para todos. Vamos a tomar el sol, nadar y conversar mucho. No vamos a hablar de estudios ni de exámenes. Después de tanto trabajo, todos necesitamos un buen descanso.
MIGUEL: ¡Así se habla! Nos vemos el viernes, entonces.
RAFAEL: Sí, y gracias, ¿eh?

Suggestion for 3-9. Prepare students for this activity by showing photos of Machu Picchu in Peru or by reading the *Enfoque cultural* section. You may also wish to have students do some research on the Incas and the famous ruins.

LENGUA

Both *Perú* and *el Perú* are used when referring to the country. Also, both *Cuzco* and *Cusco* are accepted spellings for the Peruvian city that was the capital of the Inca empire.

Alternate for 3-10. Encourage students to be outrageous and extravagant in what they'll serve, whom they'll invite, etc. Make sure that they come up with complete menus, and not just with one-course meals.

Warm-up for 3-11. Before listening to the conversation, have students provide information about themselves: weekend plans, favorite restaurants, and favorite food.

After students write down what is asked from them in the prelistening activity, ask students to read the statements in the chart before they listen to the conversation.

Audioscript for 3-11.

RAFAEL: ¡Hola! Miguel, ¿cómo estás?
MIGUEL: Muy bien, Rafael. ¿Y tú?
RAFAEL: Bien, pero cansado. Tú sabes que mis clases de economía son muy difíciles, y además trabajo en una librería los martes y jueves por la tarde. Esta semana es terrible porque tengo mucho trabajo. Tengo exámenes y voy a estudiar con un amigo todas las noches.
MIGUEL: ¿Y qué vas a hacer este fin de semana?
RAFAEL: No sé. Pienso que voy a descansar.
MIGUEL: Perfecto. Mira, Rafael, mi familia tiene una casa en la playa de San Bartolo. Voy a ir con un grupo de amigos el viernes, después del último examen. El viernes por la noche vamos a cenar en un restaurante que está en la playa, al lado del mar. Es mi restaurante favorito porque la comida es excelente, especialmente el pescado, y los camareros son muy amables. Siempre que vamos a ese restaurante, comemos pescado y bebemos cerveza. ¿Por qué no vienes con nosotros?

EXPLICACIÓN Y EXPANSIÓN

Suggestions. Review **-ar** verbs and person markers (**-s, -mos, -n**). Point out the similarities and differences between **-er** and **-ir** verbs. Contextualize your speech as you present the conjugation. *¿Lee Ud. mucho? ¿Qué libros lee? Y sus amigos, ¿leen mucho también? ¿Lee usted el periódico por la mañana? ¿Qué periódico lee? ¿Dónde vive usted? ¿Vive en una casa o en un apartamento?*

You may remind students that the singular forms of these verbs were presented in the *Algo más* section of *Lección 1* and revisited in *Lección 2*. This gave students opportunities to familiarize themselves with these forms and to use them when communicating with their instructor and classmates before being formally presented in this lesson.

VÍNCULOS

To practice present tense of regular *-er* and *-ir* verbs
- SAM-OneKey: WB: 3-6, 3-7, 3-8, 3-9 / LM: 3-31, 3-32, 3-33
- Companion Website: AP 3-3
- *Gramática viva*: Grammar Point 37: Present tense of regular **-er, -ir** verbs
- IRCD: Chapter 3; pg. 102

Follow-up for 3-12. Students may form groups and prepare a list on what they consider an ideal student's routine, and then compare their list with those of other groups.

1. Present tense of regular *-er* and *-ir* verbs

COMER (*to eat*)			
yo	como	nosotros/as	comemos
tú	comes	vosotros/as	coméis
Ud., él, ella	come	Uds., ellos/as	comen

VIVIR (*to live*)			
yo	vivo	nosotros/as	vivimos
tú	vives	vosotros/as	vivís
Ud., él, ella	vive	Uds., ellos/as	viven

■ The endings for **-er** and **-ir** verbs are the same, except for the **nosotros** and **vosotros** forms.

■ The verb **ver** has an irregular **yo** form.

ver: **veo**, ves, ve, vemos, veis, ven

■ Use **deber** + *infinitive* to express what you *should* or *ought to* do.

Debes beber mucha agua.   *You should (must) drink lots of water.*

■ Other common **-er** and **-ir** verbs are **aprender, correr, leer, asistir,** and **escribir.**

¿Qué dice usted?

3-12 Mi profesor/a modelo. Primera fase. Indicate which of the following activities are or are not part of an ideal instructor's routine.

	Sí	No
1. Lee el periódico en la clase.		X
2. Nunca está en su oficina.		X
3. Siempre prepara sus clases.	X	
4. Saca libros de la biblioteca y lee mucho.	X	
5. Comprende los problemas de los estudiantes.	X	
6. Bebe café en la clase todo el tiempo.		X
7. Escribe ejemplos muy buenos en la pizarra.	X	
8. Come papas fritas en la clase.		X

2 **Segunda fase.** Compare your answers with those of a classmate. Do both of you agree? Finally, write down two more features of an ideal instructor's academic life and ask your instructor if they are part of his/her real routine.

3-13 Para pasarlo bien ***(To have a good time).*** **Primera fase.** Indicate which of the following activities your classmates do to have a good time.

1. ______ Estudian español hasta las dos de la mañana.
2. ______ Escriben y leen correos electrónicos.
3. ______ Van de vacaciones con sus amigos.
4. ______ Asisten a conferencias y exposiciones de arte.
5. ______ Corren en el gimnasio o en el parque.
6. ______ Leen el periódico y revistas para jóvenes.
7. ______ Alquilan películas para ver en casa.
8. ______ Comen en restaurantes donde la comida es buena.
9. . . .
10. . . .

Suggestion for 3-13. Note that *pasarlo bien* is introduced as a lexical item. Before the activity, explain the meaning of the expression and exemplify its use: *Hay muchas maneras de pasarlo bien. Yo, por ejemplo, para pasarlo bien, escucho música, voy al cine con amigos, tengo fiestas en mi casa, etc. ¿Y usted, lee o baila para pasarlo bien? ¿Qué hace usted para pasarlo bien los fines de semana/durante las vacaciones?*

Alternate for 3-13. Students may ask partners if and when they do some of the activities listed. Then they switch partners and tell each other about the information they gathered.

Segunda fase. Compare your answers with those of a classmate. Then get together with another pair and exchange information about the activities that all of you do to have a good time. Use the expressions in *En directo* to help you react more naturally to your classmates' responses.

MODELO: PAREJA 1: Nosotros bailamos en discotecas los sábados por la noche. ¿Y ustedes?
PAREJA 2: Bebemos cerveza y conversamos con amigos en un café.

EN DIRECTO

To react to what someone said:

¡Qué interesante!
¡Qué divertido! (*How funny!*)
¡Qué aburrido!

3-14 Lugares y actividades. Ask a classmate what he/she does in the following places. He/She will respond with one of the activities listed. Then ask your classmate what he/she does not do in each place.

MODELO: en la clase/ver videos
E1: ¿Qué haces en la clase?
E2: Veo videos en español.
E1: ¿Y qué no haces en la clase?
E2: No hablo inglés (ni leo el periódico).

LUGARES	ACTIVIDADES
en la playa	beber cerveza
en un café	tomar el sol y descansar
en una discoteca	bailar salsa
en una fiesta	mirar televisión
en el cine	leer el periódico
en la casa	comer un sándwich y tomar algo
en un restaurante	ver películas españolas y argentinas
en la biblioteca	escuchar música clásica

Note for 3-14. Students have used *¿Qué hace(s)?* and *¿Qué hacen?* in controlled situations beginning with *Lección 1.* This gives them more opportunities for communication since they respond without using the verb *hacer.* You may wish to incorporate these expressions as part of their active vocabulary.

Suggestion for 3-14. Encourage students to expand their answers (e.g., *En la playa, descanso y también tomo el sol.*)

Expansion for 3-14. Additional places: *la librería, el laboratorio de lenguas, el trabajo, el gimnasio.* You can also ask questions using *dónde;* students answer by giving the appropriate place: *¿Dónde come(s) los sábados? ¿Dónde escribe(s)?*

Follow-up for 3-14. Students ask each other when they do some of these activities. Then they switch partners and tell new partners which activities are part of their routine and which are not: *Felipe y yo leemos el periódico por la mañana. Yo tomo el sol los sábados por la mañana, pero Felipe no toma el sol. Él nada.*

3-15 Las diversiones estudiantiles. Primera fase. Working in a small group, appoint a secretary to tally responses. Then find out which of you do the following things in your free time. Next get together with another group, compare your findings, and tally responses once again.

MODELO: nadar en la playa
E1: ¿Nadas en la playa los fines de semana?
E2: Sí, nado (en la playa) los fines de semana.

	Sí	No
1. beber café y conversar con amigos	_____	_____
2. tocar la guitarra	_____	_____
3. comer en restaurantes peruanos	_____	_____
4. ver programas cómicos en la televisión	_____	_____
5. tomar cerveza con amigos	_____	_____
6. leer libros de misterio	_____	_____

Segunda fase. Finally, as a class, discuss the following:

1. ¿Cuál es la actividad favorita de la clase?
2. ¿Cuál es la actividad que le gusta menos a la clase?

3-16 ¿Qué deben hacer? Read the situations in the column on the left and select the appropriate advice for each person(s) from the column on the right.

1. ___e___ Mariela desea estar delgada.
2. ___d___ Los turistas están en Lima y desean visitar Machu Picchu.
3. ___f___ Mónica estudia música y canta muy bien.
4. ___b___ Mis amigos están aburridos.
5. ___c___ Emilia y yo siempre estamos cansados.
6. ___a___ Yo tengo problemas de estómago porque bebo mucho café.

a. Debes beber té o café sin cafeína.
b. Deben ir al cine o alquilar una película cómica.
c. Deben tomar vitaminas y descansar más.
d. Deben ir a Cuzco primero.
e. Debe caminar todos los días y beber mucha agua.
f. Debe aprender canciones en español.

3-17 Sugerencias. What should or should not the following people do?

MODELO: Luis está muy cansado.
E1: ¿Qué debe hacer Luis?
E2: Debe descansar o No debe trabajar hoy.

1. Juan tiene un examen el lunes.
2. Francisco está débil y muy delgado.
3. Manuel y Victoria no tienen trabajo.
4. Marta ve televisión todos los días y saca malas notas.
5. Luis y Emilia desean aprender español.
6. Isabel y Lucía desean visitar Perú.

❷ **3-18 Un/a compañero/a nuevo/a.** Get together with a classmate you do not know very well and ask him/her questions to find out more about him/her.

1. lugar donde vive
2. si ese lugar le gusta o no le gusta
3. lugar donde come fuera de casa
4. si le gusta o no le gusta la comida de ese lugar
5. comida favorita
6. bebida favorita
7. …
8. …

ACENTOS

You have probably noticed that the words **examen, casas, fruta** do not have a written accent, whereas **débil, sándwich, López** do. In Spanish, words stressed on the next-to-last syllable do not have a written accent if they end in **n, s,** or a vowel (**examen, casas, fruta**). If they end in any other letter, they carry an accent mark (**débil, sándwich, López**).

Expansión for 3-17. *7. Susana está a dieta, 8. Rolando es perezoso.* Encourage students to provide different answers to the various situations.

Alternate for 3-18. Students may do this activity with a Hispanic person outside the class (a neighbor; another teacher; someone who works at a store, restaurant, or office; etc.). Advise students to prepare their questions in advance. Afterward, they should present a short oral report to the class.

SITUACIONES

1. You meet one of your classmates at the library. After greeting him/her, find out (a) if your partner likes to read, (b) when he/she reads, (c) what newspapers and magazines he/she reads, and (d) if he/she reads newspapers or magazines in Spanish. If the answer is yes, find out the names of the newspapers or magazines.

2. You are a waiter/waitress at a café. Two of your classmates will play the part of the customers. Greet your customers and ask them what they would like to eat and drink. Be prepared to answer any questions they may have.

2. Present tense of the verb *ir*

IR (*to go*)			
yo	**voy**	nosotros/as	**vamos**
tú	**vas**	vosotros/as	**vais**
Ud., él, ella	**va**	Uds., ellos/as	**van**

- Use **a** to introduce a noun after the verb **ir.** When **a** is followed by the article **el,** the two words contract to form **al.**

  Voy **a la** fiesta de María. *I am going to María's party.*
  Vamos **al** gimnasio. *We are going to the gymnasium.*

- Use **adónde** when asking *where to* with the verb **ir.**

  ¿**Adónde** vas ahora? *Where are you going now?*

3. *Ir* + *a* + infinitive to express future action

- To express future action, use the present tense of **ir** + **a** + the infinitive form of the verb.

  Ellos **van a nadar** después. *They are going to swim later.*
  ¿**Vas a ir** a la fiesta? *Are you going to go to the party?*

4. The present tense to express future action

- You may also express future action with the present tense of the verb. The context shows whether you are referring to the present or the future.

  Mañana **tengo** un examen. *I have a test tomorrow.*
  ¿**Vas** al cine esta noche? *Are you going to the party tonight?*

- The following expressions denote future time:

después	*afterwards, later*
más tarde	*later*
esta noche	*tonight*
mañana	*tomorrow*
pasado mañana	*the day after tomorrow*
la próxima semana	*next week*
el próximo mes/año	*next month/year*

EN DIRECTO

Expressions to take an order:
¿Qué desean los señores?
¿Qué van a tomar/beber?

Expressions to order food:
Para mí, una ensalada, arroz con…
Me gustaría comer/tomar…
(*I would like to eat/drink . . .*)
Yo quiero…

VÍNCULOS

To practice present tense of *ir*
- SAM-OneKey: WB: 3-10, 3-11 / LM: 3-34, 3-35
- Companion Website: AP 3-4
- IRCD: Chapter 3; pg. 105

VÍNCULOS

To practice *ir* + *a* + infinitive to express future action
- SAM-OneKey: WB: 3-12, 3-13 / LM: 3-36, 3-37
- Companion Website: AP 3-5
- *Gramática viva*: Grammar Point 23: *ir a* + infinitive

Suggestions. You may use a calendar to practice the use of *ir a* + *infinitive* or the present tense to refer to future events. Say what you or another person will do tomorrow, on Saturday, and so on. Personalize by asking students about themselves.

When asking questions, point out how, in normal speech, *va a hacer (vaacer)* runs together. Make students aware that it is similar to English "Whaddayagonnado?"

VÍNCULOS

To practice the present tense to express future action
- SAM-OneKey: WB: 3-14, 3-15 / LM: 3-38, 3-39
- Companion Website: AP 3-6
- IRCD: Chapter 3; pg. 107

¿Qué dice usted?

3-19 Lugares y actividades. Match where the following people are going with the activities that they are probably going to do there.

1. ___d___ Victoria va a su casa.
2. ___f___ Elena y Alberto van a la biblioteca.
3. ___b___ Rodrigo y Berta van a la playa.
4. ___a___ Alina va a una librería hispana.
5. ___c___ Nosotros vamos al cine.
6. ___e___ Estela va a un café.

a. Va a comprar un libro sobre Perú.
b. Van a tomar el sol y a nadar.
c. Vamos a ver una película española.
d. Va a descansar y a mirar televisión.
e. Va a tomar un refresco.
f. Van a estudiar para un examen.

Suggestion for 3-20. Practice asking and accepting or rejecting invitations with your better students before doing the activity.

Follow-up for 3-20. Have students prepare their own agenda for the upcoming week. Then have them work in pairs to find out about each other's plans.

Ⓖ 3-20 Mi agenda para la semana. Primera fase. Invite six classmates individually to do the following activities with you. Each will accept or reject your invitation according to his/her agenda for the week. Write down your plans in the chart, indicating the activity and the name of the classmate who accepted your invitation.

MODELO:　estudiar en la biblioteca el lunes
　　　　　E1: ¿Vamos a estudiar en la biblioteca el lunes?
　　　　　E2: Lo siento, Miguel, el lunes voy a ir al cine con David. Pero, ¿por qué no comemos en un restaurante peruano el martes?
　　　　　E3: Buena idea. Hablamos después.

1. ir al cine
2. mirar televisión en casa
3. tomar algo en un café
4. estudiar para la clase de español
5. bailar en la discoteca
6. correr una milla

EN DIRECTO

To accept an invitation:
¡Estupendo! ¿Dónde quedamos? (*Where do we meet?*)
Sí, gracias, ¡qué bien!

To turn down an invitation politely:
Lo siento, pero no tengo tiempo/tengo mucho trabajo, etcétera.
Ese día no puedo (*I can't*); debo estudiar para un examen.

DÍA	¿QUÉ VA A HACER?	¿CON QUIÉN?
martes	comer en un restaurante peruano	Miguel

❷ Segunda fase. Prepare your own agenda for the upcoming week. Take turns asking questions to find out what your partner is going to do.

Follow-up for 3-21. Students work in groups of four to exchange information. They could also indicate a restaurant they all like and why they like it.

❷ 3-21 Vamos a comer fuera. A friend and you are planning to eat out tonight. Each one should suggest a restaurant and mention the dishes they prepare, the prices (*precios*), and so on. Decide on the time and where you will go. Finally, tell other classmates about your plans.

3-22 Los planes de Maribel. Primera fase. Take turns to tell what Maribel is going to do. Ask questions to get additional information from your partner regarding Maribel.

Warm-up for 3-22. Use the Image Resource CD or posters of people engaged in a variety of activities to solicit spontaneous descriptions of what each person is going to do. Then ask students to compare their activities with those shown in the visuals.

Segunda fase. Tell your classmate what you are going to do on Friday. Are your plans similar or different from Maribel's?

3-23 Este fin de semana. With a classmate, discuss what each of you is going to do this weekend. Expand the conversation by asking questions of each other to get more details, if necessary. Take notes about each other's plans. Then share your findings about your partner with another classmate.

Expansion for 3-24. Ask students to get information on the Internet about the places they are planning to visit on their next vacation, and have them exchange the information with their classmates. They may also go to www.prenhall.com/mosaicos to get information about interesting places in Peru and plan a visit to that country.

3-24 ¡Vivan los feriados! Choose a new classmate with whom you would like to share information about your plans for the next holiday; for example **Navidad (Christmas), Januká, Ramadán, el Año Nuevo, el Día de la Independencia.** Get as much information as possible about each other's plans. Make sure to address the following points.

1. lugar adonde va a ir
2. con quién(es) va a ir
3. cuánto tiempo va a estar allí
4. qué va a hacer

SITUACIONES

1. Your friend is planning to go to a concert **(un concierto).** Call him/her to find out a) where and when the concert is going to be, b) who is going to sing, c) who is going to play an instrument, and d) how much the ticket **(el boleto/billete, la entrada)** costs.

2. A friend calls you on the phone. Tell him/her about your plans for tonight. Tell him/her a) what you are planning to do, b) with whom, and c) how much money **(dinero)** you are going to need. Inquire about his/her plans too.

VÍNCULOS

To practice numbers 100 to 2,000,000
- SAM-OneKey: WB: 3-16, 3-17 / LM: 3-40, 3-41
- Companion Website: AP 3-7
- IRCD: Chapter 3; pg. 110

Note. Point out the exceptions: *quinientos, setecientos, novecientos.* Also point out that *y* is not used after *cien* or *ciento,* only between tens and units (*ciento cuarenta y cinco*).

LENGUA

In Spanish, numbers higher than one thousand are not stated in pairs as they often are in English. For example, 1942 must be expressed as **mil novecientos cuarenta y dos,** whereas in English it is often given as "nineteen forty-two."

5. Numbers 100 to 2.000.000

100	cien/ciento	1.000	mil
200	doscientos/as	1.100	mil cien
300	trescientos/as	2.000	dos mil
400	cuatrocientos/as	10.000	diez mil
500	quinientos/as	100.000	cien mil
600	seiscientos/as	150.000	ciento cincuenta mil
700	setecientos/as	500.000	quinientos mil
800	ochocientos/as	1.000.000	un millón (de)
900	novecientos/as	2.000.000	dos millones (de)

■ Use **cien** to say 100 used alone or followed by a noun, and use **ciento** for numbers from 101 to 199.

100	cien
100 chicos	cien chicos
120 profesoras	ciento veinte profesoras

■ Multiples of 100 agree in gender with the noun they modify.

200 periódicos	doscientos periódicos
1.400 revistas	mil cuatrocientas revistas

■ Use **mil** for *one thousand.*

1.000	mil alumnos, mil alumnas

■ Use **un millón** to say *one million*. Use **un millón de** when a noun follows.

    1.000.000   **un millón**
    1.000.000 (personas)   **un millón de personas**

■ In many Spanish-speaking countries, a period is used to separate thousands, and a comma to separate decimals.

    $1.000 $19,50

¿Qué dice usted?

3-25 Para identificar. Your instructor will say a number from each of the following series. Identify each one.

a. 114	360	850	524
b. 213	330	490	919
c. 818	625	723	513
d. 667	777	984	534
e. 1.310	1.420	3.640	6.860
f. 10.467	50.312	100.000	2.000.000

Suggestion for 3-25. Students hold up one, two, three, or four fingers to show if the number is the first, second, third, or fourth in the group, or they write down each number said by the instructor, who then writes the number on the board to confirm. Then students work in pairs, taking turns to identify the number said by the partner.

3-26 ¿Cuándo va a ocurrir? Exchange opinions with a classmate about when each of the following events will occur.

MODELO: Todos los libros van a ser electrónicos.
               E1: En el año 2010.
               E2: Estoy de acuerdo. *o* No estoy de acuerdo. Va a ser en el 2020.

Note for 3-26. Some Spanish speakers use *el* with the year 2000 and subsequent years: *Voy a visitar Machu Picchu en el 2009.* Before students do the activity, introduce and practice the use of *(no) estar de acuerdo.*

1. Las personas van a trabajar sólo 20 horas a la semana.
2. Los estudiantes no van a ir a clases. Van a estudiar en universidades virtuales.
3. Todos los autos van a ser eléctricos y muy rápidos.
4. Los turistas van a ir de un país a otro sin pasaporte.
5. La contaminación va a ser muy grande, y las personas van a usar máscaras (*masks*) en los parques y en las calles.
6. Los robots, y no los camareros, van a servir la comida en los restaurantes.
7. Las personas van a comunicarse por telepatía.

3-27 Unas vacaciones. Primera fase. Your classmate has chosen one of the destinations in the ad on page 111 for his/her next vacation. To find out where he/she is going, ask him/her the following questions. Switch roles.

1. ¿Adónde vas?
2. ¿Con quién vas?
3. ¿Qué lugares vas a ver?
4. ¿Cuándo vas?
5. ¿Cuántos días vas a estar allí?
6. ¿Por qué vas a ir a ese lugar?
7. ¿Cuánto cuesta la excursión?
8. …

Suggestion for 3-27. Students can get information on Peru in the *Enfoque cultural*, pages 121–126 and also at www.prenhall.com/mosaicos.

Segunda fase. Based on your classmate's answers, fill in the information requested and share it with the rest of the class.

1. Su compañero/a necesita…
    a. _____ sacar un pasaporte.
    b. _____ obtener una visa.
    c. _____ hacer reservaciones.

2. Lugar(es) que va a visitar: _____
3. Tiempo que va a estar allí: _____
4. Costo de la excursión: _____
5. Dinero extra que usted cree que su compañero va a necesitar: _____

AGENCIA MUNDIAL

A SU SERVICIO SIEMPRE
20 años de experiencia, responsabilidad y profesionalismo

TODOS LOS PRECIOS INCLUYEN PASAJES AÉREOS Y SERVICIOS TERRESTRES POR PERSONA

PERÚ Y BOLIVIA

LIMA, AREQUIPA, CUZCO, MACHU PICCHU, PUNO, LA PAZ, 15 días. La Ruta del Inca. Hoteles de 3 y 4 estrellas. Desayuno incluido.
$1.960

PERÚ

LIMA, CUZCO, MACHU PICCHU, NAZCA, 12 días. Visite fortalezas incas. Vea las misteriosas líneas de Nazca desde el aire. Hoteles de primera. Desayuno y cena incluidos.
$2.250

LIMA, NAZCA, AREQUIPA, LAGO TITICACA, 10 días. Admire la arquitectura colonial de Lima y Arequipa. Vea las líneas de Nazca desde el aire. Navegue en el lago más alto del mundo. Hoteles de primera.
$1.650

ARGENTINA

BUENOS AIRES, BARILOCHE, MENDOZA, 12 días. Disfrute de una gran metrópoli. Esquíe en uno de los lugares más bellos del mundo. Hoteles de 4 y 5 estrellas. Desayuno y cena.
$2.990

CHILE Y ARGENTINA

SANTIAGO, PUERTO MONTT, BARILOCHE, BUENOS AIRES, 12 días. Excursión a Viña del Mar y Valparaíso. Cruce de los Andes en minibús y barco. Hoteles de 3 y 4 estrellas.
$3.190

CARIBE

JAMAICA, 7 días. Happy Inn, todo incluido. Exclusivo para parejas.
$1.750

PUERTO RICO

SAN JUAN, 5 días. Hotel de 5 estrellas. Excursión a Ponce. Visita con guía al Viejo San Juan. Desayuno incluido.
$1.250

MÉXICO

MÉXICO, TAXCO, ACAPULCO, 7 días. Hoteles de 3 y 4 estrellas. Excursión a Teotihuacán. Desayuno bufet incluido.
$1.450

CANCÚN, 5 días. Hotel de 4 estrellas. Excursión a Cozumel. Visita a ruinas mayas. Las mejores playas.
$1.150

Solicite los programas detallados con variantes de hoteles e itinerarios a su agente de viajes.

Tel. 312-785-4455 Fax: 312-785-4456

Note for Situaciones. Since this is an information-gap type of activity, assign students roles and have each read instructions for his/her role. To make the task more meaningful, have each student cover his/her partner's role. Give them reasonable time to prepare for the task (2 to 3 minutes). Do not interrupt students during the exchange. You may wish to record the students' role-playing, or you may jot down their errors for further discussion with individual students or with the whole class. Pay close attention to the use of register (*usted* or *tú*), vocabulary, and appropriate use of negotiation strategies (to clarify meaning, to agree, disagree, refuse politely, etc.) between students.

EN DIRECTO

To call the attention to an unusual fact:
¡Fíjate qué noticia! (*Imagine the news!*)
¡Imagínate!

To express happiness upon hearing good news:
¡Qué suerte!
¡Qué maravilla!
¡Qué bien!

To convince someone:
¡Ven/Anda, anímate! (*Come on!/Come along, cheer up!*)
Lo vamos a pasar muy bien. (*We are going to have a good time.*)

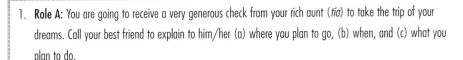

SITUACIONES

1. **Role A:** You are going to receive a very generous check from your rich aunt (*tía*) to take the trip of your dreams. Call your best friend to explain to him/her (a) where you plan to go, (b) when, and (c) what you plan to do.

   Role B: Your classmate is going to receive a large sum of money from his/her wealthy aunt (*tía*) to take a trip. Ask him/her (a) with whom he/she is planning to go, (b) what places he/she is going to visit, and (c) what he/she is planning to buy.

2. **Role A:** A friend and you are making plans for Saturday. Your friend is going to tell you what he/she plans to do. Tell your friend that you need to rest and want to spend (*pasar*) the day at the beach. He/She will try to convince you to change your mind. Inquire about specifics of his/her plan, such as: where he/she is going, with whom, and so on. Politely, be firm about your original plans.

   Role B: Your friend and you are making plans for Saturday. Tell him/her that you want to go to a fancy restaurant and to a discotheque afterward. Try to convince your friend to change plans. Answer his/her questions. Finally, tell him/her that you are going to go along with his/her plans.

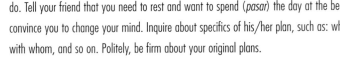

ALGO MÁS

Some uses of por and para

In previous activities, you used **para** as an equivalent of *for*, with the meaning *intended* or *to be used for*:

Necesito un diccionario **para** la clase. *I need a dictionary for the class.*

You used **por** in expressions such as **por favor, por teléfono,** and **por la mañana/tarde/noche.** Other fixed expressions with **por** that you will find useful when communicating in Spanish are:

por ejemplo	*for example*	por lo menos	*at least*
por eso	*that is why*	por supuesto	*of course*
por fin	*finally, at last*	por ciento	*percent*

Por and **para** can also be used to express movement in space and time.

- Use **para** to indicate movement toward a destination.

  Caminan **para** la playa. *They walk toward the beach.*
  Vamos **para** el túnel. *We are going toward the tunnel.*

- Use **por** to indicate movement through or by a place.

  Caminan **por** la playa. *They walk along the beach.*
  Vamos **por** el túnel. *We are going through the tunnel.*

- You may also use **por** to indicate length of time or duration of an action. Many Spanish speakers omit **por** in this case, or they use **durante.**

  Necesito el auto (**por**) tres días. *I need the car for three days.*

¿Qué dice usted?

3-28 ¿Para dónde van? Read the following, guess where these people are going, and compare your guess with that of your classmate. Are the guesses similar? Then find out where a classmate is going after class, and why.

MODELO: *Jorge busca su uniforme de fútbol.*
 Va para el estadio.

1. Es la una de la tarde, y Pedro desea comer.
2. Sebastián lleva una mochila con sus libros de química y una calculadora.
3. Magdalena y Roberto van a consultar unos libros porque tienen un examen.
4. Gregorio va a comprar un libro para su clase de español.
5. Ana María va a ver una película de su actor favorito.
6. Amanda y Clara están muy elegantes y contentas. En este momento llegan Arturo y Felipe en su auto.

3-29 Caminante. Your classmate likes to walk. Ask him/her the following questions. Then, switch roles.

1. ¿Por dónde caminas?
2. ¿Te gusta caminar por la playa o por un parque?
3. ¿Caminas por la mañana?
4. ¿Caminas con amigos o solo/a (*by yourself*)?
5. ¿Caminas durante media hora o más?

Note. Since the correct use of *por* and *para* is not easy for students to master, these prepositions are presented throughout several lessons. In this first presentation, only those uses necessary for communication about the theme of the chapter are explained. In *Lección 6,* more uses are presented and subsequent lessons. In *Lección 11,* there is a complete presentation of *por* and *para,* including the uses that students are familiar with.

Suggestion. Use visuals to contrast the use of *por* and *para* to express movement (e.g., *Josefina está en su casa ahora. Ella va para la playa* (show visual of a beach) *después. Ella camina con su amiga por la playa* (show photo on p. 94 or visual of young women walking on the beach).

VÍNCULOS

To practice some uses of *por* and *para*
- SAM-OneKey: WB: 3-18, 3-19 / LM: 3-42, 3-43
- Companion Website: AP 3-8

Escuchar

Using background information

When you are listening to a conversation, you use your background knowledge of the situation to understand what is happening or what is being said. For example, it is probably much easier for you to understand what your roommate tells you about his/her daily activities than to understand a neurosurgeon talking about his/her day in the operating room. This is because you have much more experience with the activities of a college student than with the activities of a neurosurgeon.

Antes de escuchar

3-30 Las grabaciones telefónicas. In 3-31, you will be calling several museums in Lima to find out their days and hours of operation, addresses, and phone numbers. Use your knowledge of museum hours to write down what days and hours you think the museums you are calling will be open.

Horario: _____

A escuchar

3-31 Exhibiciones y horarios. Now listen to the automated recorded messages and fill in the following chart with the missing information.

	DÍAS	HORAS	DIRECCIÓN	TELÉFONO
Museo de Arte	martes a domingo	10:00 A.M.–6:00 P.M.	Avenida Ponce de León 1782	423-4586
Museo de Historia	todos los días	9:00– 4:00 P.M.	San Martín 600	
Museo de Antropología	los lunes, martes y viernes	desde las 12:00 hasta las 8:00 P.M.	Mercaderes 102	
Museo de Ciencias Naturales	lunes a viernes y sábado	9:30 A.M.–5:00 P.M. 12:00–6:00 P.M.	Avenida Bolívar 840	

VÍNCULOS

For materials related to the Mosaicos section, see
- SAM-OneKey: WB: 3-20, 3-21, 3-22, 3-23, 3-24, 3-25 / LM: 3-44
- IRCD: Chapter 3; pg. 117

Audioscript for 3-31. 1. Buenos días. El Museo de Arte abre de martes a domingo, desde las 10:00 de la mañana hasta las 6:00 de la tarde. Los invitamos a ver nuestra exhibición de oro del Perú. Se encuentra en el salón centenario. El museo está situado en la Avenida Ponce de León 1782. Para más información, llame al 423-45-86. 2. Usted se ha comunicado con el Museo de Historia. El museo está abierto todos los días de las 9:00 de la mañana a las 4:00 de la tarde. La entrada principal está en la calle San Martín 600. 3. Museo de Antropología: Buenos días. El Museo de Antropología está abierto los lunes, martes y viernes desde las 12:00 hasta las 8:00 de la noche. Nuestra dirección es Mercaderes 102. 4. Muy buenos días. El Museo de Ciencias Naturales está abierto al público de lunes a viernes, desde las 9:30 de la mañana a las 5:00 de la tarde, y los sábados desde las del día a las de la tarde. Nuestra dirección es Avenida Bolívar 840.

Después de escuchar

3-32 ¿Y usted? Answer the following questions.

1. ¿Qué museo desea visitar? _____

2. ¿Qué museo tiene un horario conveniente para usted? _____

Antes de escuchar

3-33 Diferentes precios. In **3-34**, you will listen to a recorded announcement of ViajaMás, a travel agency. The recording will provide the name of the destination cities in Latin America, the flight numbers, the days of the flights, and the price of the ticket from Miami. Before you listen, using your knowledge of Latin American countries and your knowledge of traveling costs, write down the names of three large cities you think the recording may mention and the probable cost of the ticket.

Ciudad: _____ Precio del pasaje: _____

Ciudad: _____ Precio del pasaje: _____

Ciudad: _____ Precio del pasaje: _____

A escuchar

3-34 Días y vuelos. Now listen to the recording and complete the following chart with the information provided.

CIUDAD	VUELO #	DÍAS	PRECIO DEL PASAJE
Lima	881	**sábados y domingos**	$730
Buenos Aires	**479**	todos los días	$980
Caracas	963	todos los días	**$250**
Bogotá	1247	lunes, martes y sábados	$455

Audioscript for 3-34. Agencia ViajaMás anuncia sus precios especiales para las siguientes ciudades: Lima, vuelo número 881, sólo sábados y domingos, precio especial: $730. Buenos Aires, vuelo número 479, todos los días, precio: $980. Caracas, vuelo número 963, todos los días, precio especial: $250. Bogotá, vuelo 1247, lunes, martes y sábados, precio: $455. ¡Gracias por llamar a la Agencia ViajaMás!

Después de escuchar

3-35 ¡Ahora usted! Your best friend, who is studying Spanish, would like to visit a large capital city in Latin America, but he/she is unsure where to go. After listening to the ad in **3-34**, you would like to suggest a city to him/her. Complete the following e-mail for your best friend.

```
De: ........................
A:.........................
Asunto: Una ciudad interesante en América Latina
Hola......,
¡Tengo una información excelente para ti! Hay tarifas fantásticas para
visitar ................. Los vuelos salen ............. y los
boletos cuestan ............. Hablamos por teléfono este fin de semana,
¿OK?

............................
```

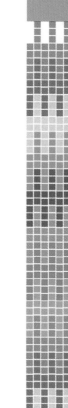

Conversar

Antes de conversar

3-36 ¿Qué comen sus compañeros? A new cafeteria is going to open on campus. You have been hired to do a random survey on the most popular foods so the cafeteria may include them on the menu. First find out what your classmates like to eat and drink at different meals on campus. Write down the names of students who answer **Sí** or **No** in the appropriate column.

MODELO: E1: Susana, ¿comes cereal en el desayuno?
           E2: Sí, como cereal en el desayuno./No, no como cereal.

	DESAYUNO		ALMUERZO		CENA	
	SÍ	NO	SÍ	NO	SÍ	NO
cereal con leche						
café/chocolate caliente						
jugo de naranja/tomate/manzana						
hamburguesas						
ensalada de frutas						
vino						
pan						
...						

A conversar

2 **A la cafetería.** Analyze the information you collected in *Primera fase* and go to see the new cafeteria supervisor (your classmate). Explain what most students eat and drink. Discuss with him/her a possible menu for breakfast, lunch, and dinner. Write down your menu.

Después de conversar

G **3-37 ¿Cuál es el menú más saludable (*the healthiest*)?** Compare your menu with those of other classmates. Then vote on which menu is the healthiest and the most complete. Explain why.

CULTURA

Despite the differences from country to country, mealtimes in Hispanic countries differ from those in the United States. People typically eat breakfast at around 7:00 or 8:00 a.m. Breakfast normally consists of *café con leche* (hot milk with strong coffee), *té*, or *chocolate caliente* with bread, a sweet roll, and sometimes juice or fruit. This is a light breakfast, so people sometimes have a snack in the late morning. Cereals are becoming more popular, especially among the younger generation.

In some countries, the main meal of the day is lunch (*el almuerzo* or *la comida*), eaten between 12:30 and 3:00 p.m. Supper (*la cena* or *la comida*) is served after 7:00 or 8:00 p.m., and sometimes as late as 10:00 or 11:00 p.m.

Antes de conversar

❷ 3-38 ¿Cómo pasarlo bien? Go to www.prenhall.com/mosaicos and find out how to have fun in any of the countries whose websites have been provided, or in another of your choice. Take notes on at least the following information.

1. Nombre del lugar o evento: _____
2. Dirección: _____
3. Teléfono: _____
4. Actividad(es) que las personas hacen allí: ¿Son actividades culturales, deportivas (*sports*), etcétera? _____

Note for 3-38 Some Web sites do not provide students with all the information requested in the activity. However, some do not.

A conversar

3-39 ¡Vamos a pasarlo bien! Invite a classmate to the event or place you researched in activity **3-38**. Explain to him/her (a) what type of event or place it is, (b) where it is, (c) how you are planning to get there. He/She may accept or reject the invitation. Make sure to review expressions on pages 106 and 110.

Después de conversar

3-40 Planes excepcionales. Write a postcard to a friend, explaining what you are planning to do, with whom, where, how you are going to get there, and so on. Include as much information as possible.

 # Leer

In *Lección 1* and *Lección 2* you used some basic reading strategies to help you comprehend a text better: a) drawing on your knowledge of the world to anticipate the content of a text; b) identifying cognates; and c) determining the kind of text and the text format. It is important to remember that successful second-language readers systematically use these strategies as they face the reading of a variety of texts. Therefore, as you gain insights and experience with other reading strategies, keep in mind the ones you have practiced before and utilize them.

In this chapter, you will practice identifying key words to comprehend the message of the text. Do not worry if you do not answer correctly the first time. Over time, practice will help you improve this crucial reading skill in Spanish.

Guía de pre-lectura. Skim the texts in activity **3-42** and answer the questions, based on your knowledge of the world.

1. What type of texts are included in **3-42**?
   a. brochures
   b. ads advertising services
   ⓒ entertainment ads

2. In what section of the newspaper would you find these texts?
   a. in the sports section
   b. in the business section
   ⓒ in the recreations section

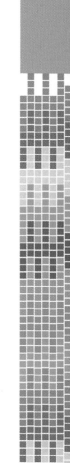

3. What is the purpose of the ads? Use an X to mark all that apply.
a. __X__ to get the attention of adults with children
b. __X__ to catch the attention of ethnic food restaurant goers
c. _____ to entice potential actors
d. __X__ to advertise a play in Spanish

4. Now, use your knowledge of the English language for comprehension. What words *in each text* helped you figure out the answer to question 3 above?
Text 1. _____   Text 3. _____
Text 2. _____   Text 4. _____

Antes de leer

Note for 3-41, *Primera fase.* Students may not be able to answer without some hints. Help students find the answer by giving more input such as the following: *Es una de las capitales más antiguas de la América hispana; está en la costa del Pacífico. Es una ciudad muy grande con personas de diversos orígenes étnicos: hay indígenas, negros, mulatos, mestizos, europeos, asiáticos, etc. En esta ciudad está la universidad más antigua de la América del Sur (la Universidad de San Marcos). En las casas y lugares públicos las personas hablan español y quechua.*

3-41 Preparación. Primera fase. Look at the picture and follow the instructions.

1. La fotografía muestra (*shows*) una ciudad importante de Perú. ¿Qué ciudad peruana es probablemente? Lima
2. Marque con una X los lugares de diversión (*entertainment*) que probablemente hay en esta ciudad.
a. __X__ museos para los aficionados (*fans*) al arte
b. __X__ discotecas para bailar y pasar el tiempo libre
c. _____ hospitales modernos
d. __X__ teatros que presentan dramas y comedias nacionales e internacionales
e. __X__ cines que pasan películas nacionales y extranjeras
f. __X__ parques de diversión para los niños
g. __X__ restaurantes de comida étnica
h. _____ universidades excelentes

② Segunda fase. Take turns answering the following questions.

1. En la opinión de usted, ¿cuál es la mejor hora para divertirse (*to have fun*)?
2. ¿Qué hace usted para divertirse?

A leer

3-42 Primera mirada. Read these ads from a Peruvian newspaper, and offer a solution for each of the problems.

NIÑOS

CORPORACIÓN CULTURAL DE LIMA. Santa María y Gálvez. 2209451. A las 12 y 16 horas. Bagdhadas. S/. 12.

TEATRO INFANTIL A DOMICILIO. 2390176. El patito feo. Adaptación del cuento de Andersen. Compañía Arcoiris.

CENTRO LIMA. Av. Grau y Velásquez. A las 12, show especial de Navidad.

FANTASÍA DISNEY. Desde las 15. Niños, S/. 8; adultos, S/. 14. Parque de entretenimientos.

EL MUNDO FANTÁSTICO DE MAFALDA. Desde las 10. Entrada general a todos los juegos. Niños, S/. 12. Calle Domingo Sarmiento 358.

PLANETARIO DEL MORRO SOLAR. A las 12, 17 y 19. Gratis para niños; adultos, S/. 15. Circunvalación, Nuevo Perú. Tel. 5620841.

PARQUE DE LAS LEYENDAS (ZOO). De 9 a 19 hrs. Niños y 3ra edad, S/. 5; S/. 10, otro público. Cerro Tongoy, 3701725.

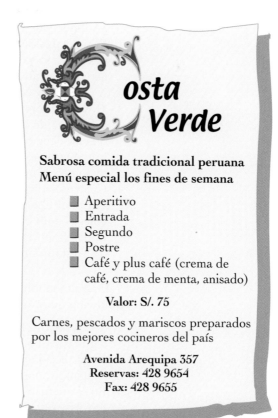

Costa Verde

Sabrosa comida tradicional peruana
Menú especial los fines de semana

- Aperitivo
- Entrada
- Segundo
- Postre
- Café y plus café (crema de café, crema de menta, anisado)

Valor: S/. 75

Carnes, pescados y mariscos preparados por los mejores cocineros del país

Avenida Arequipa 357
Reservas: 428 9654
Fax: 428 9655

TEATRO MUNICIPAL
CORPORACIÓN CULTURAL DE LA
ILUSTRE MUNICIPALIDAD DE LIMA

Directores: ALBERTO ISOLA, OSWALDO CATTON

Presenta
EL HOMBRE DE LA MANCHA
Con **DAVID Y ETTY ELKIN**

| Lunes 20 Dic., 7:00 p.m. | Martes 21 Dic., 6:00 p.m. |
| Miércoles 22 Dic., 8:00 p.m. | Jueves 23 Dic., 7:00 p.m. |

ENTRADAS EN VENTA DESDE S/.20–40

Boleterías en Teatro Municipal
Fonoventas: 7624901 (con tarjetas de crédito)

El Chifa Lungfung

La más exquisita, variada y exótica carta de comida cantonesa-peruana: finas carnes, pescados y todo tipo de mariscos.

SÁBADOS Y DOMINGOS:

Almuerzos y cenas familiares

...los esperamos

AIRE ACONDICIONADO
MÚSICA AMBIENTAL
CAMAREROS PROFESIONALES
AV. REPÚBLICA DE PANAMÁ 8720
RESERVAS 3817543, 3816532, 3814241

PROBLEMAS

1. El señor y la señora Molina tienen cuatro hijos entre tres y ocho años. A los niños les fascinan los animales, en particular las especies que no existen en Perú. Toda la familia desea salir este fin de semana, pero tiene poco dinero. ¿Adónde van a ir ellos probablemente? ¿Por qué?

2. El señor Liskin, un turista norteamericano, visita Lima por primera vez. Él desea ver todo lo típico de Perú. Este fin de semana va a poder hacer sus actividades favoritas. Al señor Liskin le gusta mucho escuchar música clásica, ir al teatro y comer bien. ¿Qué debe hacer durante el fin de semana?

3. Hoy es el cumpleaños de Carlitos, el hijo de Paloma. ¡Ya tiene ocho años! A diferencia de otros años en esta fecha, hoy el niño está en casa. El doctor dice que no debe caminar porque se fracturó una pierna. Carlitos está muy triste porque no va a celebrar su fiesta de cumpleaños con sus amigos, pero su mamá tiene una sorpresa para él. ¿Qué va a hacer Paloma?

4. Cuatro médicos alemanes visitan el Centro de Investigaciones del Cáncer del Hospital Central. El Dr. Moreira, director del Centro, desea invitar a sus colegas a un buen lugar esta noche para comer productos del mar peruanos. Él desea un restaurante cómodo, con buena comida y excelente atención. ¿A qué restaurante va a invitarlos? ¿Por qué?

3-43 Segunda mirada. Go back and read the ads (3-42) again to answer the following questions.

1. ¿Cuál de los anuncios es básicamente para menores (*minors*)? Indique algunas palabras que indican esta idea. The first ad.

2. En la sección de niños, Parque de las Leyendas, ¿qué significa 3ra edad? ¿Cuántos años tiene como mínimo una persona de la 3ra edad? Senior citizens.

3. En el anuncio del restaurante Costa Verde, identifique la expresión que indica que este restaurante prepara comida nacional. Tradicional peruana.

4. Chifa Lungfung es probablemente un restaurante de excelente calidad (*quality*). ¿Qué expresiones en el anuncio se refieren a la buena calidad del restaurante? Exquisita, exótica carta, todo tipo de mariscos, camareros profesionales, etc.

5. En el anuncio de Chifa Lungfung, ¿qué palabra significa *reservation*? Reservas.

Después de leer

2 **3-44 Expansión.** With a classmate, answer the following questions on the ads in activity **3-42.**

1. ¿Cuál de las siguientes actividades desean hacer ustedes en Lima: ir a un parque de entretenimiento (*entertainment park*), comer comida tradicional peruana, ver teatro o comer comida china? ¿Por qué?

2. ¿Cuál de los dos restaurantes sirve comida que a ustedes les gusta, Costa Verde o Chifa Lungfung?

 *Escribir*

The writing process

The series of steps you follow to produce a clear and effective piece of writing is the same in any language. First you organize your thoughts, perhaps by writing an outline. Then you write a first draft. As you write, or once you finish, you may revise to find better ways of expressing your ideas. For example, you may change the organization, rewrite sentences, or choose better words. Finally, you correct any content inaccuracies or errors in spelling, punctuation, accent marks, and so on.

In *Lección 3* you will have the opportunity to write a letter to a friend. Although correspondence to friends tends to be less formal, well-written messages always follow writing conventions such as including the date, a salutation, an introduction, a body, a closing line, and so on. What follows is an example of a letter to a friend.

Antes de escribir

3-45 Enfoque. Primera fase. Juanita recently took a trip to Peru with her family. She wrote the following letter to a friend about her trip. Read Juanita's letter and do as indicated.

Cuzco, 8 de enero de 2005

Querida María Fernanda,

¿Cómo están tú y tu familia? ¿Cómo van tus clases? Espero que fantástico.

¡Sorpresa! En estos momentos, mi familia y yo estamos en Perú, un país increíble. Esta semana visitamos Cuzco y Machu Picchu, lugares con una historia muy interesante.

Muchos turistas visitan Cuzco y Machu Picchu para aprender sobre la cultura de los incas. En Cuzco, algunos visitan los mercados artesanales, compran productos indígenas y caminan por las antiguas calles de la ciudad. Otros montan en bicicleta y hacen excursiones por las montañas. Por las noches, muchos comen en restaurantes de comida típica de Perú. Los cuzqueños son muy amables y simpáticos. Muchos hablan español y quechua, su lengua nativa. En Machu Picchu, algunos escalan los Andes y escuchan a los expertos que hablan sobre la historia del lugar.

Tengo muchas fotografías de los Andes, de los mercados artesanales, de algunos restaurantes peruanos, etcétera. María Fernanda, debes visitar Perú. Te va a gustar. Es un lugar ideal para vacaciones, con mucha historia y tradiciones antiguas.

Bueno, ahora vamos a una excursión a Tambopata, una reserva natural con muchos animales autóctonos. Te llamo pronto. Chao.

Tu amiga,
Juanita

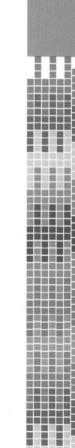

Segunda fase. Answer the following questions about Juanita's letter.

1. Mark with an X the purposes of Juanita's letter to María Fernanda.
   ___X___ To describe her vacation activities.
   ___X___ To describe a vacation spot that she likes.
   ___X___ To inform her friend of fun leisure activities people can do in Cuzco and Machu Picchu.
   ___X___ To suggest that her friend visit Peru.
   ___X___ To provide a profile of Peruvian people.

2. Based on its purpose, is Juanita's letter effective? _____ Yes _____ No
   Mark some possible reasons for your response.
   ___X___ Juanita organizes the information clearly.
   _____ The letter is poorly organized.
   ___X___ Juanita describes Cuzco and Machu Picchu very well.
   ___X___ The tone of the letter is friendly.
   _____ Juanita informs María Fernanda of the way her days are spent in Peru.
   ___X___ Juanita presents a positive portrait of Cuzco and Machu Picchu so María Fernanda may visit them in the future.

3. What salutation did María Fernanda use with her friend? How would you write the salutation to a male friend? Do you know any other way to say hello to a friend in Spanish? What is it?

4. How does María Fernanda say good-bye to her friend in the letter? Do you know any other way to say good-bye to a friend in Spanish? What is it?

Suggestion for 3-46. Depending on your approach or your students' proficiency, you may wish to give this activity a more cultural orientation. To that end, you may ask that students do some research on the Internet.

3-46 Preparación. Choose a vacation spot or any other fun place you know well. Pretend that you are visiting the place. To prepare to write a letter to a friend informing him/her of your vacation, do the following:

1. Identify the place: Is it a beach, a park, a city, a historical landmark?
2. Make a list of words (adjectives) that describe the place: Is it small, big, beautiful, comfortable?
3. Write down some fun activities (verbs) that people do there: Are they outdoor activities, sports, culturally oriented (museums, explorations, fairs)?
4. Indicate some of the activities in #3 that you personally like.
5. Write down possible salutations and closings you may use.

A escribir

3-47 Manos a la obra. Now write a brief letter to your best friend, informing him/her of your vacation. Use the information you prepared in **activity 3-46.** Do not forget to date your letter and write the salutation and closing.

Después de escribir

Suggestions for 3-48. If you would rather have students revise their text in class, have them exchange letters with a peer editor that you may appoint or one that they choose. Give students enough time to read their classmate's letter so they can discuss it later. If time poses a constraint, you may assign the reading of the text as homework, followed by a class discussion. Remind peer editors to concentrate on content first and form second.

3-48 Revisión. After completing your letter, read it at least twice with your reader in mind. Check the following:

■ The content of the letter: Did you include information your friend would like to read about? Is there any new information for your friend?

■ The form of the text: Did you use punctuation correctly? Did you verify that there are no spelling or grammatical mistakes?

Finally, discuss your letter with one of your peers.

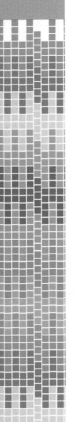

ENFOQUE CULTURAL

TEMAS: EL CINE, EL TEATRO, LAS PEÑAS

Para pensar

¿Qué hace usted cuando quiere pasar un rato agradable? ¿Adónde va—A la playa, al cine, al teatro, a la discoteca, al parque? ¿Con quién va a estos lugares?

Muchas familias peruanas pasan los meses de verano en las playas cerca de sus ciudades.

En los países hispanos, una costumbre muy popular entre los jóvenes y los adultos es ir al cine con amigos. Generalmente después del cine las personas van a un café a conversar y disfrutar del ambiente.

En Perú, unos lugares muy atractivos para jóvenes y adultos son las peñas, donde se presentan cantantes de música criolla y conjuntos de bailes folclóricos (marinera, huayno, tondero, por ejemplo), y donde las personas escuchan música, cantan, bailan y comen comida criolla. Si prefieren conversar con sus amigos y disfrutar al mismo tiempo de una obra de teatro, van a los café-teatros donde se presentan comedias cortas y se puede comer y tomar un café o una copa.

Para contestar

2 Los amigos hispanos. Responda a las siguientes preguntas:

1. Si uds. son personas muy activas y visitan Perú, ¿a qué lugares les gustaría ir?
2. Si prefieren actividades más tranquilas, ¿qué pueden hacer en un país hispano?

G Riqueza cultural. Hablen sobre las actividades que pueden hacer en los países hispanos y que no pueden hacer en los Estados Unidos.

Para pensar

¿Conoce usted a alguna persona del Perú? ¿Sabe dónde está el Perú? ¿Qué lugares le gustaría visitar en el Perú?

El Perú es un país de geografía muy variada. Tiene una larga costa, una zona andina y una selva amazónica.

Lima, la capital del Perú, tiene zonas antiguas de gran belleza y valor histórico, y también tiene zonas modernas. Hay muchos museos importantes. El Museo de Oro tiene una excelente colección de joyería (jewelry) y objetos precolombinos; el Museo de la Nación exhibe joyería, artesanía y gran variedad de objetos de las civilizaciones que se desarrollaron en el Perú.

Otro lugar de gran interés en la costa del Perú es Nazca, al sur de Lima, muy conocida por sus famosas líneas de origen desconocido en el desierto.

Una de las ciudades más importantes del Perú es Cuzco, la antigua capital del imperio de los incas. Cerca de Cuzco se encuentran las ruinas de la ciudad inca de Machu Picchu y la fortaleza de Sacsayhuamán.

Expresiones peruanas

chamba	Me conseguí una chamba.	*I got myself a job.*
maldita	¡La película estuvo maldita!	*The movie was great!*
bacán	¡Ella es bacán!	*She is great / a lot of fun!*
chancón	¡Él es un chancón!	*He studies all the time.*

VÍNCULOS

For materials related to the Enfoque cultural, see
- SAM-OneKey: WB: 3-26
- IRCD: Chapter 3; pg. 122

Para contestar

En el mapa

1. Busque tres ciudades del Perú: una en la costa, otra en la zona andina y otra en la selva amazónica.
2. Diga qué países están al norte, al sur y al este del Perú.

Ahora diga...

1. si le gustaría visitar las líneas de Nazca o las ruinas de Machu Picchu, y por qué.
2. qué ciudad del Perú le gustaría visitar, y por qué.

¿Qué dice usted si...?

1. le gusta mucho su nuevo auto
2. su compañero/a de cuarto es muy estudioso

Para investigar en Internet

Busque información *www.prenhall.com/mosaicos* sobre los espectáculos que hay en una peña en Lima esta semana. Averigüe el nombre de la peña, dónde está, a qué hora abre, qué artistas se presentan, cuánto cuesta el espectáculo, etcétera. Traiga a clase la información e informe a la clase.

¡Prepárese!

3-49 Los personajes. Before watching the *Fortunas* video segment for *Lección 3*, conjugate the verbs in parenthesis for the following sentences that go with the video images below.

1. A Ángela no le _____gusta_____ (gustar) la reacción del público.
2. Carlos y Katie _____caminan_____ (caminar) por Coyoacán.
3. Katie _____debe_____ (deber) decidir colaborar o no colaborar con Carlos.
4. Ellos _____van_____ (ir) a investigar la mitología para solucionar el misterio.
5. Carlos _____lee_____ (leer) un libro sobre la mitología de los aztecas.
6. Los padres de Efraín _____viven_____ (vivir) en diferentes países.

Ángela está preocupada sobre la reacción del público.

Carlos y Katie están en Coyoacán.

Hay una posible colaboración entre Carlos y Katie.

Las pistas tienen una posible relación con la mitología.

Carlos sabe bastante sobre la mitología azteca.

Efraín habla sobre sus padres y sus problemas familiares.

¡Responda!

3-50 Katie y Carlos. Keeping in mind the concept of collaboration discussed by Katie and Carlos, after watching the *Fortunas* video segment for *Lección 3*, work together in groups of three on the following word association activity.

Asociación de palabras:
Take turns saying the following words. After each word the members of your group should say aloud any words or phrases that come to mind. Record your answers.

destrucción / gigantes / viento / monos / global / jaguar

Look at your lists. Discuss possible connections and relations to see if you can form an idea of what the first *misterio* means. Share your ideas with the class.

In your opinion, what are the advantages and disadvantages of collaborating with your classmates?

The title of *Camino de la montaña,* which means "mountain journey," is a metaphor for the journey we take in life. The country and people of Peru are closely associated with the Andes mountains; thus, the symbolic mountain of the song is related to Peruvian culture and tradition.

¡Prepárese!

3-51 Metáforas. Before listening to *Camino de la montaña* think about the idea of metaphor and what it means to you. The mountain journey is a metaphor for life's journey. Based on your personal experience, what are some possible metaphors for the following concepts from the song? Refer to the lyrics if necessary.

1. *la libertad* / freedom
2. *la verdad* / truth
3. *el peregrino* / pilgrim
4. *el destino* / destiny

> Camino de la montaña, camino de libertad
> Yo quiero subir por ella en busca de mi verdad
> Ser el santo y peregrino en busca de mi destino
> Y unos ojos soñadores que mi vida me alumbran
> Camino de la montaña, camino de libertad
> Yo quiero subir por ella en busca de mi verdad
> Ser el santo y peregrino en busca de mi destino
> Y unos ojos soñadores que mi vida me alumbran
> Hay amores en la vida que se buscan locamente
> Que andan perdidos sin rumbo por los caminos del mundo
> Más buscarán sus destinos, quizás por otros caminos
> Porque la vida misma es un camino por andar
> Más buscarán sus destinos, quizás por otros caminos
> Porque la vida misma es un camino por andar

¡Escuche!

3-52 Los instrumentos. Indicate with an X the instruments you hear as you listen to the song.

__X__ el piano	__X__ la quena*	__X__ la guitarra
_____ el clarinete	_____ la trompeta	_____ las maracas
__X__ el tambor		

Which instrument do you like most, and why? Describe it in your own words in Spanish, using adjectives you have learned.

¡Responda!

3-53 La entrevista. Imagine that you are a journalist who has been assigned to interview the artists of Los Kjarkas. Use the **ir + a** + *infinitive* construction with the verbs from the list to find out what their plans are. Present your questions and answers to the class.

MODELO: ¿Van Uds. a cantar en un concierto en EE.UU.?

cantar / escribir / ir / tocar / vivir / celebrar

*an Andean flute prominent in Peruvian music

VOCABULARIO*

Comunicación

el periódico	newspaper
la revista	magazine
el teléfono	telephone

Diversiones

la canción	song
el cumpleaños	birthday
la fiesta	party
la guitarra	guitar
la música	music
la película	film
la reunión	meeting, gathering
las vacaciones	vacation

Personas

e/la camarero/a	waiter/waitress
el/la joven	young man/woman

En un café o restaurante

el agua	water
el almuerzo	lunch
el arroz	rice
la bebida	drink
el bistec	steak
el café	coffee
la cena	dinner, supper
la cerveza	beer
el ceviche	raw fish dish
la comida	dinner, supper
el desayuno	breakfast
la ensalada	salad
la fruta	fruit
la hamburguesa	hamburger
el helado	ice cream
el huevo	egg
el jugo	juice
la leche	milk
la lechuga	lettuce
la naranja	orange
el pan	bread
la papa	potato
las papas fritas	French fries
el pescado	fish
el pollo	chicken
el refresco	soda
la sopa	soup
el tomate	tomato
la tostada	toast

el vegetal/la verdura	vegetable
el vino	wine

Lugares

el cine	movies
la ciudad	city
el mar	sea
el país	country, nation

Descripciones

caliente	hot
fabuloso/a	fabulous, great
frío/a	cold
frito/a	fried
rápido/a	fast
típico/a	typical

Verbos

alquilar	to rent
beber	to drink
cantar	to sing
celebrar	to celebrate
cenar	to have dinner
comer	to eat
correr	to run
deber	ought to, should
descansar	to rest
escribir	to write
ir	to go
leer	to read
nadar	to swim
tocar	to touch
tocar (un instrumento)	to play (an instrument)
tomar el sol	to sunbathe
ver	to see
vivir	to live

Palabras y expresiones útiles

¿Aló?	Hello
¿Adónde?	Where (to)?
al	to the (contraction of a + el)
al aire libre	outdoors
otro/a	other, another
si	if
tiempo libre	free time

*See page 105 for expressions that denote future time.
**See page 111 for expressions with por.

4

LA FAMILIA

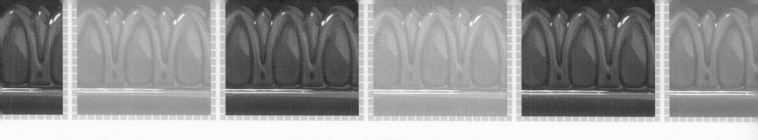

Objetivos comunicativos

- Identifying and describing family members
- Describing routine activities
- Expressing preferences, desires, and feelings
- Asking and giving permission

- Expressing when, where, or how an action is done
- Expressing how long events and states have been going on

Contenido

AUDIO *Las familias*

Una foto familiar de tres generaciones: **abuelos, hijos** y **nietos.** ¿Cuántos **niños** hay? ¿Hay muchos niños en la familia de usted? ¿Es el **perro** parte de la familia?

Una familia colombiana celebra el **bautizo** de su hija. En estas ceremonias participan los **padres,** los **padrinos** y los **ahijados.** Para muchas familias hispanas, el bautizo es un día muy especial.

La familia de Pablo

UDIO Pablo habla de su familia

Me llamo Pablo Méndez Sánchez y vivo con mis padres, mi **hermana** y mis **abuelos** en un apartamento en Bogotá, la capital de Colombia.

Mi **madre** tiene un hermano, mi **tío** Jorge. Su **esposa** es mi tía María. Tienen tres hijos y viven también en Bogotá. Mi **primo** Jorgito es el **menor.** Mis primas Elenita y Ana son **gemelas.** Mis primos son muy simpáticos y **pasamos** mucho tiempo **juntos.**

Mis tíos tienen sólo dos **sobrinos** en Bogotá, mi hermana Inés y yo. Su otra **sobrina,** la hija de mi tía Lola, vive en Cartagena, al norte del país.

La **nieta** favorita de mis abuelos es mi hermanita Inés. Tiene sólo tres años y es la **menor** de todos sus nietos.

¿Qué dice usted?

4-1 Asociación. Asocie la descripción a la izquierda con la expresión correcta.

1. __c__ la esposa de mi papá
2. __a__ el hermano de mi prima
3. __d__ los padres de mi papá
4. __b__ el hijo de mi hijo
5. __e__ el hermano de mi mamá

a. mi primo
b. mi nieto
c. mi madre
d. mis abuelos
e. mi tío

4-2 La familia de Pablo. Complete las siguientes oraciones de acuerdo con el árbol genealógico (*family tree*) de Pablo.

1. La hermana de Pablo se llama __Inés__.
2. Don José y doña Olga son los __abuelos__ de Pablo. Ellos tienen __dos__ hijas y __un__ hijo.
3. Pablo es el __hijo__ de Jaime.
4. Jaime es el __padre__ de Pablo, y Elena es su __madre__.
5. Inés y Ana son __primas__. Elenita y Ana son __hermanas gemelas__.
6. Don José y doña Olga tienen __dos__ nietos y __tres__ nietas en Bogotá.
7. Elena es la __tía__ de Jorgito, Elenita y Ana.
8. Lola es la __hermana__ de Jorge y Elena.

❷ **4-3 ¿Quién es y cómo es?** Escoja (*Choose*) a un miembro de la familia de Pablo. Su compañero/a debe decir cuál es su relación familiar con Pablo y usar su imaginación para dar información adicional.

MODELO: E1: ¿Quién es Elenita?
E2: Es la prima de Pablo. Tiene dieciocho años y estudia psicología. Es muy simpática y tiene muchos amigos.

Warm-up for 4-3. You may want to begin this exercise by choosing a family member yourself and asking for descriptions from the class at large. Then, have students work in small groups to describe Pablo's family. Have each group report back to the class on one member of his family.

Follow-up for 4-3. Have students describe members of their own families.

Otros miembros de la familia de Pablo

Suggestion. Use the Image Resource CD to present Pablo's aunt and her family.

Note. You may point out that *hermanastro/a* is used in some countries in place of *medio/a hermano/a*, despite the differences involved in both terms: *medios/as hermano/as* have a common parent, *hermanastros/as*, do not.

Paula   Sergio   Lola   Osvaldo

Roberto   Sofía

AUDIO La única hermana de mi mamá es mi tía Lola. Lola y Sergio están **divorciados** pero tienen una hija, mi prima Sofía. Ahora tía Lola está casada con Osvaldo, el **padrastro** de Sofía. Sergio está **casado** con Paula y tienen un hijo, Roberto. Paula es la **madrastra** de Sofía, y Roberto es su **medio hermano**.

¿Qué dice usted?

4-4 ¿Cierto o falso? Marque la columna adecuada de acuerdo con la información sobre la familia de Lola.

	CIERTO	FALSO
1. La tía Lola está casada con Sergio.	____	X
2. Osvaldo es el papá de Roberto.	____	X
3. Paula es la madrastra de Roberto.	____	X
4. Lola es la madre de Sofía.	X	____
5. Sofía tiene un medio hermano.	X	____

4-5 El arte de preguntar. Primera fase. Preparen las preguntas necesarias para obtener la siguiente información.

1. Tengo cuatro abuelos vivos (*alive*).
2. No, no soy hija única.
3. Tengo dos hermanos.
4. Vivo con mi madre y mi padrastro.
5. Mis abuelos no viven con nosotros.
6. Tengo muchos primos.
7. Tengo una media hermana, pero no vive con nosotros.
8. Mi media hermana vive con su madre.

Note for 4-5. *Primera fase* will give students the opportunity to practice individual questions and to prepare for more personal questions in *Segunda fase.*

❷ **Segunda fase** Ahora intercambien preguntas para obtener información sobre sus propias familias. Después, compartan (*share*) esta información con la clase.

A INVESTIGAR

■ ¿Sabe Ud. que el apellido Fernández viene del nombre Fernando?

■ Asocie cada apellido con el nombre correspondiente.

_3_ Hernández   1. Ramiro
_4_ Álvarez   2. Martín
_2_ Martínez   3. Hernán
_5_ González   4. Álvaro
_1_ Ramírez   5. Gonzalo

■ ¿Hay apellidos en inglés que tienen origen en un nombre? ¿Cuáles?

■ ¿Dónde va el apellido de la madre en español?

■ ¿Hay personas en su cultura que usan el apellido materno y paterno? ¿Tiene usted ejemplos? ¿Hay mujeres casadas que mantienen el apellido paterno?

2 **4-6 Mi familia.** Preparen un árbol genealógico individualmente. Luego, deben intercambiar su árbol. Finalmente, cada uno/a debe hacerle preguntas a su compañero/a sobre su familia para obtener la siguiente información.

1. nombre de los abuelos vivos
2. nombre de los padres (padrastro/madrastra)
3. número y nombre de los hermanos o medios hermanos
4. número y nombre de los primos
5. descripción de dos familiares

¿Qué hacen los parientes?

Mis abuelos viven en una casa al lado del parque. Normalmente, ellos **pasean** por las mañanas y **almuerzan** muy temprano. Después, **duermen** una siesta, y por la tarde **visitan** a sus **parientes.**

Jorgito es mi primo favorito. Es **un poco** menor que yo, pero corremos y **jugamos** mucho **juntos.** También nos gusta ver el fútbol en la televisión y montar en bicicleta los domingos.

Hace dos años que mi prima Ana tiene **novio, y** **frecuentemente** dice que **quiere casarse** muy pronto. Elena, su hermana gemela, **piensa** que Ana no debe casarse porque es muy joven.

Mi tío Jorge es un hombre muy **ocupado. Sale** de casa muy **temprano** y **vuelve** **tarde** todos los días. Mi tía María, su esposa, dice que él **prefiere** el trabajo a su familia. Pienso que en todas las familias hay problemas. En la mía también, pero me gusta mi familia.

Follow-up for 4-12. Each pair of students chooses the better of the two answers for each item and compares them with those of another pair. Then they choose the best answers and share them with the class.

¿Qué dice usted?

4-11 Preferencias de la familia. Primera fase. En la casilla (*box*) adecuada, escriba una **Y** para indicar lo que usted prefiere beber y comer, y una **F** para lo que prefiere otro miembro de su familia.

¿QUÉ PREFIERO BEBER YO Y QUÉ PREFIERE...?			
EN EL ALMUERZO	leche	chocolate caliente	café
DESPUÉS DE CORRER	jugo	refresco	agua
PARA CELEBRAR UN CUMPLEAÑOS	vino	cerveza	champaña

¿QUÉ PREFIERO COMER YO Y QUÉ PREFIERE...?			
EN EL DESAYUNO	cereal	tostadas	huevos
LOS DOMINGOS	comida mexicana	comida italiana	comida española
EN UN RESTAURANTE	pollo	pescado	espaguetis

Segunda fase. Túrnense para decirle a su compañero/a qué prefieren beber y comer usted y otro miembro de su familia en cada situación. Después pregúntele a su compañero/a cuáles son sus preferencias.

MODELO: Por la mañana: jugo, café, té
E1: Por la mañana, yo prefiero tomar té, pero mi hermano prefiere tomar café. ¿Y tú?
E2: Pues yo prefiero té.

4-12 ¿Qué piensan hacer estas personas? Túrnense para decir qué piensa hacer cada persona en las situaciones siguientes. Cada uno debe dar una respuesta diferente.

MODELO: Mi hermano desea estar delgado.
E1: Piensa correr mucho.
E2: Piensa empezar una dieta.

1. Mi hermana tiene un examen de matemáticas mañana.
2. Mi hermana estudia bastante, pero no entiende muchos de los problemas.
3. Mi tía está muy débil y cansada.
4. Mis abuelos están de vacaciones en Colombia.
5. Mis primos quieren ir a Cartagena para visitar a los abuelos.

2 **4-13 Comidas y bebidas.** Túrnense para preguntarle a su compañero/a qué pide para comer y beber en estos lugares. Él/Ella debe contestarle y además decir lo que pide algún miembro de la familia que tiene gustos diferentes.

MODELO: en un partido de béisbol
E1: ¿Qué pides en un partido de béisbol?
E2: Pido un perro caliente y un refresco, pero mi hermano pide una hamburguesa.

1. en un restaurante español muy elegante
2. en un McDonald's si quieres estar delgado/a
3. en un bar con tus amigos
4. en un restaurante en una playa
5. en una pizzería

Suggestion for 4-13. Provide comprehensible input to clarify *partido de béisbol.* Students should be able to guess the meaning of *perro caliente.*

Follow-up for 4-13. In small groups decide which are the most popular dishes and drinks for each place.

2 **4-14 Entrevista.** Túrnense para entrevistarse entre ustedes (*each other*). Deben cubrir los siguientes puntos en su entrevista y después compartir la información con otro/a compañero/a.

1. hora del desayuno y qué prefiere beber y dónde
2. lugar donde almuerza y qué prefiere comer
3. bebida que prefiere a la hora del almuerzo
4. sus actividades después del almuerzo
5. hora de la cena, dónde y con quién
6. número de horas que duerme por la noche

Suggestion for 4-14. Provide time for students to prepare the questions they are going to ask.

2 **4-15 ¿Cuándo y con quién? Primera fase.** Háganse preguntas entre ustedes para obtener la siguiente información sobre lo que cada uno hace con sus amigos.

1. lo que hacen juntos durante el año académico durante la semana y los fines de semana
2. si practican algún deporte (*sport*), qué días y dónde
3. actividades preferidas del fin de semana

Follow-up for 4-15. Primera fase. Encourage students to try to get as much information as possible from their partners.

Segunda fase. Comparen sus actividades. ¿Cuáles son semejantes o diferentes? Compártanlas con otra pareja.

MODELO: Durante la semana, nosotros almorzamos en la cafetería de la universidad.

G **4-16 Una reunión.** Imagínense que todos son miembros de una misma familia y determinen cuál es la relación entre ustedes (hermanos, primos, tíos, etc.). Ahora, organicen una reunión familiar para celebrar el aniversario de los abuelos y decidan lo siguiente:

1. lugar y hora de la reunión
2. número de niños y adultos que participan (especifiquen la relación familiar)
3. obligaciones de los adultos antes de la reunión
4. comida y bebida que van a servir
5. actividades y diversiones para los niños y para los adultos

1. You and a/some member(s) of your family are planning to take a trip abroad. Your partner should find out a) when you are planning to go, b) with whom you are going, c) what country and cities you prefer to visit, d) why, and e) if the other family member(s) prefer(s) to go to other places.

2. **Role A:** Your grandparents are celebrating their 50th wedding anniversary and the entire family has gathered for a party. You encounter an old aunt who is very curious about your life in college. After commenting on the party and several family members, answer her questions politely.

   Role B: You are very happy to see your young nephew/niece who is studying in college. After commenting on the party and several family members, ask him/her the following questions about college life: a) the classes he/she is taking; b) which one(s) he/she prefers; c) the type of job he/she wants to do in the future; d) where he/she normally eats; e) when vacations start; f) what he/she is planing to do; and g) when he/she is coming back.

EN DIRECTO

These expressions may help you maintain the flow of your conversation:

¡Cuánto me alegro! (*I am so happy for you!*)

Claro, claro. . . (*But of course . . .*)

¡Qué bien/bueno!

VÍNCULOS

To practice adverbs
- SAM-OneKey: WB: 4-9, 4-10, 4-11 / LM: 4-34, 4-35
- Companion Website: AP 4-3

Suggestions. Point out secondary stress on *-mente.*

You may also provide some practice by giving students an adjective and asking them to give the corresponding adverb form. Ask questions to elicit adverbs: *¿Cómo camina usted a clase? ¿Cómo juega al tenis? ¿Cómo habla español?*

You may present the expressions *con frecuencia* and *por lo general* as equivalents of *frecuentemente* and *generalmente,* respectively.

ACENTOS

Adjectives with a written accent retain it when forming adverbs ending in **-mente:**

difícil → difícilmente

2. Adverbs

- Adverbs are used to describe when, where, and, how an action/event takes place. You have used Spanish adverbs when expressing time (**mañana, siempre, después**) and place (**detrás, debajo**). You have also used adverbs when expressing how you feel (**bien, muy mal, regular**). These same adverbs can be used when expressing how things are done.

  Rafael nada **bien.**   *Rafael swims well.*

- Spanish also uses adverbs ending in **-mente**, which corresponds to the English *-ly*, to qualify how things are done. To form these adverbs, add **-mente** to the feminine form of the adjective. With adjectives that do not have a special feminine form, simply add **-mente**.

  María lee **lentamente.**   *María reads slowly.*
  Cantan **alegremente.**   *They sing happily.*

- Some commonly used adverbs ending in **-mente** are:

básicamente	normalmente	relativamente
frecuentemente	perfectamente	simplemente
generalmente	realmente	tradicionalmente
lógicamente	regularmente	tranquilamente

¿Qué dice usted?

4-17 ¿Está de acuerdo o no? Primera fase. Indique si está de acuerdo (**Sí**) o no (**No**) con las siguientes afirmaciones.

1. _____ Los padres deben hablar frecuentemente con sus hijos adolescentes.
2. _____ Los nietos deben visitar regularmente a sus abuelos.
3. _____ Normalmente los hijos solteros viven con sus padres.
4. _____ Los padres siempre hablan lentamente cuando están enojados con sus hijos.
5. _____ Generalmente las familias grandes son más felices que las familias pequeñas.
6. _____ Los padres deben tener reuniones con los profesores de sus hijos regularmente.

❷ Segunda fase. Compare sus respuestas con las de su compañero/a y diga por qué están o no están de acuerdo.

4-18 ¿Lenta o rápidamente? Primera fase. Escriba tres actividades que usted hace rápidamente y tres que hace lentamente.

RÁPIDAMENTE	LENTAMENTE
1. _____	1. _____
2. _____	2. _____
3. _____	3. _____

❷ Segunda fase. Compare sus actividades con las de su compañero/a. Puede usar las actividades de la **Primera fase** o usar los verbos que aparecen más abajo.

MODELO: Nado lentamente.
E1: Yo nado lentamente cuando estoy cansado/a.
E2: Pues, yo siempre nado rápidamente.
E1: ¡Qué impresionante!

almorzar	beber	estudiar
bailar	caminar	nadar
hablar español	tomar apuntes	leer el periódico
escribir composiciones	pasear	...

❷ 4-19 Entrevista. Primera fase. Hágale estas preguntas a su compañero/a. Después él/ella le debe hacer las mismas preguntas a usted.

1. ¿Qué haces normalmente por la tarde?
2. ¿A qué lugares vas regularmente y con quién?
3. Generalmente, ¿adónde vas por la noche?
4. ¿Adónde vas para conversar tranquilamente con tus amigos?
5. ¿A quiénes llamas por teléfono más frecuentemente, a tus amigos o a tu familia?

Segunda fase. Ahora escriba una breve comparación entre usted y su compañero/a con respecto a cada pregunta en la **Primera fase.** ¿Hacen ustedes actividades semejantes (*similar*) o diferentes? ¿Van ustedes a los mismos (*same*) lugares? ¿Quién de ustedes es más sociable: usted o su compañero/a? ¿Por qué?

Note for 4-18. You may want to point out the activity title and tell students that when two or more adverbs are used in a series, only the last shows the *-mente* ending.

Alternate for 4-18. You may wish to have students work in pairs and then share with the rest of the class what they do *lenta o rápidamente* in the following places: 1. *la casa,* 2. *la biblioteca,* 3. *el gimnasio,* 4. *un restaurante.*

EN DIRECTO

To express surprise at what you hear:
¡Qué increíble! *Incredible!*
¡Qué impresionante! *How impressive!*

Note for 4-19. Although comparatives are presented in *Lección 8,* students can use them in this activity since the structures are similar in both languages. To compare and contrast, you may wish to model the use of *y* and *pero* talking about yourself and your significant other: *Mi esposo/a y yo hacemos actividades semejantes por la tarde. Él y yo trabajamos. Pero hacemos algunas actividades diferentes. Regularmente él va a los partidos de fútbol con sus amigos, pero yo voy a los centros comerciales con mis amigas. Mi esposo/a es más sociable y le gusta salir con amigos y hablar por teléfono. Yo prefiero estar en casa y escuchar música.*

SITUACIONES

1. Your class is conducting a survey regarding students' movie habits. Ask a classmate a) when he/she goes to the movies, b) with whom he/she generally goes, c) the type of movies he/she normally prefers (romantic, dramas, science fiction, etc.), d) what he/she eats or drinks at the movies, and e) the name of his/her favorite movie theater.

2. You are conducting a survey regarding family customs and activities for your Sociology class. Ask a classmate a) if the members of his/her immediate family generally eat together, b) if they visit other family members frequently (grandparents, aunts, uncles, cousins), c) who is the family member that normally organizes family reunions, and d) if there are traditions in his/her family and what they are.

VÍNCULOS

To practice present tense of *hacer, poner, salir, traer,* and *oír*
- SAM-OneKey: WB: 4-12, 4-13, 4-14 / LM: 4-36, 4-37
- Companion Website: AP 4-4
- IRCD: Chapter 4; pp. 140–141.

3. Present tense of *hacer, poner, salir, traer,* and *oír*

El padre pone la mesa.

La madre oye música y también las noticias.

La hija trae las tostadas a la mesa.

El hijo hace la cama.

El abuelo pone la televisión.

La familia desayuna y sale.

Note. Some of the house chores shown in the illustration serve as a preview for those that will be presented in the next lesson, where students will be talking about their home/apartment and the house chores they do.

You may wish to present the expression *tender la cama*. Point out that *tender* is a stem-changing verb.

HACER (*to make, to do*)			
yo	**hago**	nosotros/as	**hacemos**
tú	**haces**	vosotros/as	**hacéis**
Ud., él, ella	**hace**	Uds., ellos/as	**hacen**

Suggestion. Present these verbs using the Image Resource CD. Talk about the various activities of the people in the illustrations as well as your own activities. For example: *El padre pone la mesa. Yo no pongo* (write *pongo* on the board) *la mesa. Mi hijo pone la mesa. Yo preparo la comida. Y en su casa, ¿quién pone la mesa?*

PONER (*to put*)			
yo	**pongo**	nosotros/as	**ponemos**
tú	**pones**	vosotros/as	**ponéis**
Ud., él, ella	**pone**	Uds., ellos/as	**ponen**

- **Poner** normally means *to put.* However, with some electrical appliances, **poner** means *to turn on.*

Note. You may want to present *encender,* another stem-changing verb and a synonym of *poner* for "to turn on."

Yo **pongo** los platos en la mesa a la hora de la cena. — *I put the plates on the table at dinner time.*

Mi abuelo siempre **pone** la televisión después de la cena. — *My grandfather always turns on the T.V. after dinner.*

SALIR (*to leave*)			
yo	**salgo**	nosotros/as	**salimos**
tú	**sales**	vosotros/as	**salís**
Ud., él, ella	**sale**	Uds., ellos/as	**salen**

- **Salir** can be used with several different prepositions: to express that you are leaving a place, use **salir de;** to express the place of your destination, use **salir para;** to express with whom you go out or the person you date, use **salir con;** to express what you are going to do, use **salir a.**

Yo **salgo de** mi cuarto ahora. — *I am leaving my room now.*
Salgo para la librería. — *I am leaving for the bookstore.*
Mi hermana **sale con** Mauricio. — *My sister goes out with Mauricio.*
Ellos **salen** a bailar los sábados. — *They go out dancing on Saturdays.*

TRAER (*to bring*)			
yo	**traigo**	nosotros/as	**traemos**
tú	**traes**	vosotros/as	**traéis**
Ud., él, ella	**trae**	Uds., ellos/as	**traen**

Suggestion. You may want to point out the spelling of *traigo,* as well as the accent mark and the use of *y* in some forms of the verb *oír.*

OÍR (*to hear*)			
yo	**oigo**	nosotros/as	**oímos**
tú	**oyes**	vosotros/as	**oís**
Ud., él, ella	**oye**	Uds., ellos/as	**oyen**

¿Qué dice usted?

4-20 El rey (*king*) de la organización. Primera fase. Alberto es una persona muy organizada, considerada, estudiosa y puntual. Marque con una X las afirmaciones que Alberto probablemente hace sobre sí mismo (*about himself*).

1. _____ Yo no **hago** mi cama.
2. _____ Yo **hago** mi cama temprano por la mañana.
3. _____ Para concentrarme en mis estudios, yo no **pongo** música.
4. _____ Siempre **pongo** música rock cuando estudio.
5. _____ Para ayudar (*help*) a mi madre, **pongo** la mesa para el desayuno.
6. _____ No **pongo** la mesa porque no me gusta trabajar en casa.
7. _____ Generalmente, **traigo** el periódico a la mesa porque me gusta leer las noticias mientras desayuno.
8. _____ En general, no **traigo** el periódico a la mesa mientras desayuno porque prefiero conversar con mi familia.
9. _____ Después de desayunar **salgo** rápidamente para la universidad porque no me gusta llegar tarde.
10. _____ Desayuno lentamente y luego **salgo** para la universidad porque tengo suficiente tiempo para llegar a la hora que la clase empieza.

❷ **Segunda fase.** Túrnense para comparar las actividades de Alberto con las actividades de ustedes. ¿Son ustedes organizados/as, considerados/as, estudiosos/as y puntuales como Alberto?

MODELO: E1: Yo también... ¿Y tú?
E2: Pues yo también... o No, yo no...

4-21 ¿Familias tradicionales o modernas? Primera fase. Indique quiénes hacen estas actividades en su familia: los hombres (H), las mujeres (M) o ambos (*both*) (A).

1. _____ comprar la comida
2. _____ poner la mesa
3. _____ hacer el desayuno
4. _____ salir solo/a porque no le gusta la compañía de otras personas
5. _____ hacer las camas
6. _____ oír los chismes (*gossip*) más recientes sobre los famosos en la radio
7. _____ traer el periódico a la casa
8. _____ poner la televisión para ver las noticias

❷ **Segunda fase.** Comparen sus respuestas. Determinen cuál de las familias es más tradicional y cuál es más moderna. ¿Por qué?

❷ **4-22 Intercambio. Primera fase.** Hoy la familia de su compañero/a está muy ocupada. Hágale preguntas a su compañero/a para saber a qué hora salen y para dónde van las personas que aparecen en la tabla.

MODELO: E1: ¿A qué hora sale Juan?
E2: (Sale) a las 8 de la mañana.
E1: ¿Para dónde va Juan?
E2: Va para el gimnasio.

NOMBRE	HORA	LUGAR
Juan	8:00 a.m.	gimnasio
Alicia	9:30 a.m.	laboratorio de computadoras
tu sobrino	2:00 p.m.	café
Cristina	8:30 p.m.	oficina
tú	...	...

Segunda fase. Respondan a las siguientes preguntas sobre las personas de la **Primera fase.**

1. ¿Quién hace ejercicio (*exercise*)? ¿Por qué?
2. ¿A quién le gusta socializar?
3. ¿Quién es fanático/a del trabajo? ¿Por qué?
4. ¿A quién le gusta usar las computadoras?

2 **4-23 Las clases de español de mi hermano.** Hable sobre las actividades escolares de su hermano, y después pregúntele a su compañero/a sobre sus actividades.

MODELO: tener la clase de español por la mañana
E1: Mi hermano tiene la clase de español por la mañana. ¿Y tú?
E2: Yo tengo la clase (de español) por la tarde. *o* Yo también tengo la clase (de español) por la mañana.

1. hacer la tarea por la noche
2. salir para la universidad a las nueve frecuentemente
3. poner la tarea sobre el escritorio del profesor generalmente
4. traer los libros a la casa
5. salir de la clase a las diez normalmente

2 **4-24 Entrevista.** Usted quiere saber qué hace su compañero/a en su tiempo libre y él/ella quiere saber qué hace usted. Háganse preguntas para averiguar (*to find out*) lo siguiente:

1. hora de salida de la universidad
2. lugares para donde va
3. actividades en esos lugares
4. actividades en su casa por las noches
5. programas de televisión favoritos
6. ...

4-25 ¿De dónde salen, con quién y para dónde? Mire el dibujo y complete el siguiente párrafo (*paragraph*) con la forma correcta de **salir + de, salir + para** o **salir + con.**

1. Javier y Marcelo son amigos. Ellos <u>salen de</u> la casa de Javier. <u>Salen para</u> el cine. Javier siempre <u>sale con</u> Marcelo los domingos por la tarde.

Ahora complete el siguiente párrafo de acuerdo con sus propias actividades y su propio horario. Compare sus respuestas con las de su compañero/a.

2. Yo _____ casa a las _____ de la mañana. _____ la universidad. Llego a la universidad a las _____. Las clases terminan a las _____. A esa hora _____ casa. Por las noches _____ mi novio/a.

SITUACIONES

1. Find out the following information about your partner's family: a) who sets the table, b) who prepares breakfast, c) who makes the beds, and d) what time each family member leaves the house in the morning.

2. **Role A.** You are participating in a school play in which you act out the part of a character who has many family problems. In this scene, you are telling your counselor: a) that you have a stepsister/brother that is very lazy and unpleasant, b) that you work a lot in the house, c) that your stepmother is not nice to you and explain why, and d) that you talk with your father about these problems, but he thinks you exaggerate (**exagerar**). Then ask your counselor what you should do in this situation.

   Role B. You play the part of the family counselor. After listening to your client, you ask for the following information: a) the number of family members, b) what they are like, and c) the things he/she does at home. Then, tell your client to be nice to his/her step sister/brother for two weeks, to write down the work her sister/brother should do in the house and to note whether he/she does it or not.

4. *Hace* with expressions of time

■ To say that an action/state began in the past and continues into the present, use **hace** + *length of time* + **que** + present tense.

    Hace dos horas que juegan.　　*They've been playing for two hours.*

■ If you begin the sentence with the present tense of the verb, do not use **que.**

    Juegan hace dos horas.　　*They've been playing for two hours.*

■ To find out how long an action/state has been taking place, use **cuánto tiempo** + **hace que** + *present tense.*

    ¿Cuánto tiempo hace que juegan?　　*How long have they been playing?*

¿Qué dice usted?

4-26 Éste soy yo. Primera fase. Lea la siguiente descripción y contesta las preguntas.

Me llamo Jaime Caicedo. Soy de Cali, Colombia, pero mis padres viven ahora en Bogotá. Hablo español, pero deseo aprender inglés para poder hablar con personas de los Estados Unidos. Estudio inglés **hace** dos años, pero debo estudiar más para hablar, leer y escribir inglés correctamente. Para aprender más, siempre miro programas de televisión en inglés en los canales del cable. Mi programa favorito es *Friends*. **Hace** dos años **que** miro el programa y me gusta mucho. En mi tiempo libre, voy al cine y a fiestas. Tengo un auto un poco viejo **hace** un año, pero salgo en él con mis amigos y también con mi novia. **Hace** cuatro meses **que** somos novios. Somos muy felices.

1. Jaime Caicedo es de...
   a. los Estados Unidos   (b.) Bogotá   c. *Friends*

2. Hace dos años que Jaime...
   a. tiene novia   b. va al cine   (c.) mira *Friends*

3. En su tiempo libre, jaime...
   (a.) va a fiestas   b. estudia inglés   c. estudia español

❷ Segunda fase. Ahora escriba su propia descripción, siguiendo el modelo. Luego, comparta su descripción con un/a compañero/a.

Me llamo _____. Soy de _____, _____ (ciudad y país). Hablo _____ (su lengua materna), pero deseo aprender _____ (lengua extranjera) para _____ (razón). Estudio _____ **hace** _____ (lengua extranjera y período de tiempo), pero debo estudiar más para hablar, leer y escribir en la lengua correctamente. Para aprender más, siempre miro _____ (programa que usted escucha o mira para aprender más). Mi programa favorito es _____. **Hace dos años que** _____ el programa y me gusta mucho. En mi tiempo libre, _____ Tengo _____ (vehículo/objeto o animal) **hace** _____. También **hace** _____ (período de tiempo) **que** tengo _____ (novio/a o nuevo amigo/a). _____ (Describa sus sentimientos sobre esta relación).

❷ 4-27 Entrevista. Túrnense para hacerse las siguientes preguntas. Después compartan la información con otra pareja.

1. ¿Dónde vives? ¿Cuánto tiempo hace que vives allí?
2. ¿Dónde trabaja tu padre/madre? ¿Cuánto tiempo hace que trabaja allí?
3. ¿Cuánto tiempo hace que estudias en esta universidad?
   ¿Y por qué estudias español?
4. ¿Practicas algún deporte? ¿Cuánto tiempo hace que juegas al...?
   ¿Juegas bien?

Suggestion for Situaciones. Before students do this situation, you may explain that *ajiaco de pollo* is a chicken soup made with two kinds of potatoes, corn, cream and capers; *papas chorreadas* are boiled potatoes covered with a sauce made with butter, chopped onions, tomatoes and milk; for *arroz con coco*, the rice is cooked in coconut milk. Students may also go to www.prenhall.com/mosaicos or the Web to get additional information about these typical Colombian dishes or others.

  **SITUACIONES**

1. You are a new student at the university, and a cousin from Colombia is coming to visit you. Since you are not familiar with the area, ask your friend about the good Colombian restaurant where he/she usually goes. Ask a) how long he/she has been going to this restaurant, b) what Colombian dishes they serve (e.g., **ajiaco de pollo, papas chorreadas, arroz con coco**) and how much they cost, and c) thank him/her for the information. Your friend will answer giving as much information as possible.

 **ALGO MÁS**

Some reflexive verbs and pronouns

Note. This is an introduction to reflexive verbs and pronouns so students can start using them when talking about daily activities. There is a complete presentation of true reflexive verbs and other verbs that use reflexive pronouns in *Lección 7*. At this stage, practice them as lexical items. You may wish to introduce other reflexive verbs as the need arises.

LAVARSE		
yo	**me lavo**	*I wash myself*
tú	**te lavas**	*you wash yourself*
Ud.	**se lava**	*you wash yourself*
él/ella	**se lava**	*he/she washes himself/herself*

■ Reflexive verbs are those that express what people do to or for themselves.

Suggestions. Remind students that they have been using the reflexive forms: *¿Cómo te llamas? Me llamo. . . ¿Cómo se llama usted?*

REFLEXIVE
Mi hermana **se lava.**   *My sister washes herself.*
                                       (She is the doer and the receiver.)

Write different times on the board and say what you do on a typical morning: *Por la mañana, a las siete y cuarto más o menos, yo busco el periódico y preparo el café. A las siete y media me baño y me visto. A las ocho como cereal y bebo otra taza de café. A las nueve salgo para la universidad.* Ask questions to check comprehension. Then ask students to recall at what time they do each activity: *¿Qué hace Ud. a las ocho? ¿A qué hora desayuna? ¿Se baña por la mañana o por la tarde? ¿A qué hora?*

NONREFLEXIVE
Mi hermana **lava** el auto.   *My sister washes the car.*
                                       (She is the doer and the car is the receiver.)

■ A reflexive pronoun refers back to the subject of the sentence. In English this may be expressed by pronouns ending in *-self* or *-selves*; in many cases, Spanish uses reflexives where English does not.

Yo **me levanto, me baño, me seco** y **me visto** rápidamente.   *I get up, take a shower, dry myself, and get dressed quickly.*

VÍNCULOS

To practice some reflexive verbs and pronouns
• SAM-OneKey: WB: 4-16, 4-17 / LM: 4-39
• Companion Website: AP 4-6
• *Gramática viva*: Grammar Point 45: Reflexive verbs
• IRCD: Chapter 4; pg. 146

■ Place reflexive pronouns after the word **no** in negative constructions.

Tú **no te peinas** por la mañana.   *You don't comb your hair in the morning.*

■ The pronoun **se** attached to the end of an infinitive shows that the verb is reflexive.

lavar   *to wash*
lavarse   *to wash oneself*

¿Qué dice usted?

4-28 La rutina diaria de mi compañero/a. Primera fase. Indique con un número (1, 2, 3, . . .) el orden en que, según usted, su compañero/a hace lo siguiente.

_____ desayuna   _____ sale

_____ se peina   _____ se baña

_____ se seca   _____ se viste

_____ se levanta

Segunda fase. Ahora hágale preguntas a su compañero/a para verificar el orden.

4-29 ¿Qué hace? Escoja a un miembro de su familia de quién va a hablar en esta actividad. Intercambie preguntas con su compañero/a sobre las actividades de este pariente y llene la tabla.

Miembro de la familia _____

	7:00 A.M.	8:00 A.M.	?
Se levanta			
Desayuna	hora	comida	bebida
Se baña	mañana	tarde	noche
Actividades	lavar el auto	hacer la cama	poner la mesa
Sale para	trabajo	universidad	?

MOSAICOS

Escuchar

Filling in charts or forms

Listening for specific information is a much-needed skill in many settings and contexts such as special events (sports, academic, religious), traveling, shopping, and so on. Once you have determined what information you are interested in, you listen to it, screen it, and select only those bits and pieces that you need. You let go what is irrelevant or unnecessary.

In an academic setting (your chemistry class, for example), you may listen to your professor's lecture and fill in a chart or a form in order to solve a problem later.

Antes de escuchar

4-30 Un bautizo. In **4-31,** you will listen to a conversation between two friends talking about the christening of one of their relatives. Before you listen, and using your knowledge of this or a similar type of ceremony, state who participates and where the event takes place.

Participantes: _____

Lugar: _____

A escuchar

AUDIO 4-31 Now, listen to the recording and circle the correct information in the following chart.

Nombre del niño	a. Rafael José	b. Álvaro Mejía
Fecha de nacimiento	a. 12 de agosto	b. 11 de octubre
Lugar de nacimiento	a. Bogotá	b. Santa Clara
Nombre de la madre	a. Mónica	b. Ana María
Nombre del padre	a. Miguel	b. Rafael
Nombre de la madrina	a. María Elena	b. Rosa
Nombre del padrino	a. Álvaro	b. José

Después de escuchar

4-32 ¿Y usted? With a classmate, share your answers to the following questions.

1. ¿Tiene usted sobrinos? ¿Cuántos?
2. ¿Tiene usted una madrina o un padrino? ¿Cómo se llama(n)?
3. ¿Qué ocasión es más importante para usted: un bautizo o un cumpleaños? ¿Por qué?

VÍNCULOS

For materials related to the Mosaicos section, see
• SAM-OneKey: WB: 4-18, 4-19, 4-20, 4-21, 4-22, 4-23 / LM: 4-40

Audioscript for 4-31.

ANA MARÍA: ¿Cómo estás, María Elena? ¿De dónde vienes? ¡Estás muy elegante!

MARÍA ELENA: Muy bien, gracias. Vengo del bautizo de mi sobrino Rafael José, que nació el 11 de octubre en Bogotá.

ANA MARÍA: ¡Qué bien! ¿Quiénes son los padres de Rafael José?

MARÍA ELENA: Mi prima Mónica Caicedo y su esposo, Rafael Mejía.

ANA MARÍA: ¡Uhm! ¿Y tú eres la madrina?

MARÍA ELENA: No, no, no. La madrina es Rosa Puertas, una amiga de mi prima. El padrino es Álvaro Guzmán, un amigo de la familia.

ANA MARÍA: ¿Y quién bautizó a tu sobrino?

MARÍA ELENA: El padre Miguel García, un amigo de la familia. La ceremonia fue muy bonita.

ANA MARÍA: ¡Cuánto me alegro! ¡Felicitaciones!

MARÍA ELENA: Gracias.

Antes de escuchar

4-33 El mensaje telefónico. In **4-34,** you will listen to a message Pedro left on Julio's answering about a surprise party he is organizing. Before you listen, write down the arrangements that would generally be made for such a party.

_____

_____

_____

A escuchar

JDIO **4-34** Now, complete the chart below with the correct information as you listen to the message. Do not worry if you do not understand every word.

La fiesta va a ser en la casa de:	Pedro
La dirección es:	calle 12, número 127
El día de la fiesta es:	domingo
José debe llegar a la casa a las:	ocho y media
Julio debe llevar (*take*):	CDs de música típica de Colombia

Audioscript for 4-34.

¡Hola, José! Habla Pedro. Te llamo porque mi prima Josefina llega hoy de Colombia y mi hermano y yo queremos darle una fiesta sorpresa. Mi hermana y mi madre van a preparar la comida, así que te va a gustar. Yo sólo me ocupo de los refrescos.

La fiesta va a ser el domingo, en mi casa. Debes llegar temprano, a las ocho y media, más o menos porque Josefina va a venir a las nueve y como es una sorpresa todos debemos estar aquí antes que ella. Dice mi hermano que tienes unos CDs de música típica de Colombia. ¿Puedes traer algunos? Bueno, recuerda, la hora: ocho y media, en mi casa: calle 12, número 127. Te esperamos el domingo. Chao.

Después de escuchar

4-35 ¿Y usted? You are going to give a surprise party for one of your friends in your Spanish class, and you would like to invite your Spanish professor. Complete the following note you will leave in your professor's campus mailbox.

Estimado/a profesor/a ..._____:

Este fin de semana, pienso dar una fiesta sorpresa para _____.

¿Le gustaría venir? Vamos a comer _____ y _____. Vamos a tener

refrescos para todos.

La fiesta va a ser el _____ en mi casa/apartamento a la(s) _____ de la

mañana/ tarde/ noche. Mi dirección es _____.

Lo/La espero el _____.

Hasta pronto.

_____

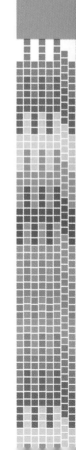

Conversar

Antes de conversar

4-36 ¿Quién de mi familia? En cada espacio en blanco, escriba el nombre de un familiar, incluyendo el parentesco (*family relationship*) y la actividad que hace.

MODELO: _____ en restaurantes los fines de semana.
Mi primo David come *en restaurantes los fines de semana.*

1. _____ cerveza frecuentemente cuando mira(n) fútbol en la televisión.
2. _____ mucho y con frecuencia está(n) cansado/a(s).
3. _____ a conciertos de música popular.
4. _____ en casa los fines de semana. Descansan, leen, escuchan música, etc.
5. _____ ejercicio físico tres o cuatro veces por semana.
6. _____ con amigos o con la familia en casa el día de su cumpleaños.
7. _____ música romántica a todas horas.
8. _____ por el teléfono celular.

A conversar

Warm-up for 4-37. Ask questions about students' families: *¿Cuántos hermanos tiene usted? ¿Dónde viven?* Ask other students to recall information given by their classmates.

4-37 ¿Cómo es familia? Respondan a las siguientes preguntas.

1. ¿Quiénes son más activos en su familia: las mujeres o los hombres?
2. ¿Qué miembros de la familia pasan más tiempo en casa: los jóvenes o los mayores?
3. ¿Quiénes son más sociables: las mujeres o los hombres, los jóvenes o los mayores? ¿Por qué?

Después de conversar

Suggestion for 4-38. You may wish to have students discuss their responses and draw conclusions with the class as a whole.

4-38 Nuestras familias. Completen un pequeño informe con la información que obtuvieron (*got*) en la actividad **4-37** y compártanlo con el resto de la clase.

- En nuestras familias (los hombres/las mujeres) _____ son más activos/as porque _____.

- (Los jóvenes/los mayores) _____ pasan más tiempo en casa porque _____.

- Las mujeres/los hombres/los jóvenes/los mayores) _____ son más sociables porque _____.

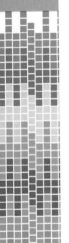

Antes de conversar

2 **4-39 Generalizaciones.** A continuación hay algunas generalizaciones sobre la familia hispana. Léanlas y luego escriban algunas generalizaciones sobre las familias de su comunidad.

LA FAMILIA HISPANA	LAS FAMILIAS DE MI COMUNIDAD
1. La religión es una parte importante de la vida.	1. _____
2. Para los padres, la educación de sus hijos es vital.	2. _____
3. Los jóvenes respetan mucho a los mayores. Cuando los padres hablan, los hijos escuchan.	3. _____ _____
4. Los hijos viven en casa con los padres mientras estudian.	4. _____
5. Muchas madres trabajan doble, en casa y fuera de ella.	5. _____
6. Los miembros de las familias celebran ocasiones especiales juntos como cumpleaños, bautizos, etc.	6. _____
7. Las hijas colaboran con la madre en el trabajo de la casa. Los hijos reparan cosas (*things*) con el padre.	7. _____ _____
8. Los padres que son mayores viven frecuentemente con sus hijos.	8. _____

A conversar

G **4-40 ¿De acuerdo o no?** Ahora compartan con otro grupo sus ideas sobre la familia de su comunidad (actividad **4-39**). ¿Están de acuerdo en sus generalizaciones? ¿En qué están de acuerdo? ¿En qué no están de acuerdo?

Después de conversar

4-41 ¿Son las familias semejantes o diferentes? Escriba un breve informe sobre las diferencias y semejanzas de las familias hispanas y las familias de su comunidad.

EN DIRECTO

To agree or disagree with someone:

(No) Estoy de acuerdo.
Tiene(s) razón. (*You are right*)
Está(s) equivocado/a. (*You are wrong.*)

Suggestion for 4-41. This is a culture-oriented activity. Give students the tools to compare by providing them with the vocabulary and idiomatic expressions they may need as they write their report. Research shows that the culture of the target language is what really motivates students taking foreign languages. You may be pleasantly surprised to see how engaged they get in the conversation.

📖 Leer

In *Lecciones 1* through *3* you used a variety of basic reading strategies to become a more proficient reader in Spanish such as 1) relying on your knowledge of the world to anticipate the content of a text, 2) identifying cognates, 3) determining the kind of text and the text format, 4) using visuals to comprehend better, and 5) skimming and scanning. Remember to use these strategies as the need arises.

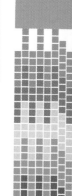

Guía de prelectura

Read the title of the article in activities **4-45** and **4-46** and answer the following questions, based on your previous knowledge.

1. Thinking of the theme of *Lección 4* and after reading the title of the article, can you guess what the theme of the article will be?
   a. communication between friends
   (b.) communication among family members
   c. communication with peers at work

2. Can you anticipate some ideas that the article probably contains? Circle all that may apply. Do not worry if you miss some answers. You may come back and verify your responses after reading the article.
   a. Today, adults and children communicate better than in the past.
   (b.) Children do not talk about their problems with their parents because the latter are busy all the time.
   (c.) Modern life has affected communication between parents and children.
   (d.) There is lack of communication between family members today, although communication is very important.

3. Now, use your knowledge of the English language to comprehend the text. What words in the title helped you figure out the answers to question 2? Write them down.

   <u>importancia, comunicación, familiar</u>

   Are they cognates?   Yes   No

4. Judging from the title, in what kind of printed media can an article on this topic be found?
   a. ___X___ in a family magazine
   b. _____ in a journal of medicine
   c. _____ in a sports magazine

Antes de leer

❷ **4-42 Preparación.** Mire esta fotografía con su compañero/a. Luego respondan a las preguntas.

1. Este niño y su padre, ¿tienen una buena o mala relación? ¿Por qué?
2. ¿Cuántos años tienen los padres del niño probablemente? En su opinión, ¿es más fácil para los padres jóvenes comprender a sus hijos?
3. Generalmente, ¿cuándo conversan los hijos con sus padres?
4. Probablemente, ¿de qué temas conversan? ¿De problemas familiares o de problemas escolares? ¿De otros temas?
5. ¿A qué edad es más difícil la comunicación entre padres e hijos? ¿Por qué?

② 4-43 Asociación. Marque con una X las actividades que usted asocia con una buena relación entre padres e hijos. Luego, compare sus respuestas con las de un/a compañero/a.

1. __X__ conversar
2. __X__ pasar tiempo juntos
3. __X__ hablar por teléfono
4. _____ pelear (*argue*)
5. __X__ escribir correos electrónicos a un miembro de la familia que vive lejos (*far*)
6. _____ comprar regalos (*presents*)
7. __X__ expresar amor
8. _____ estar conectados a Internet por muchas horas

Suggestion for 4-43. To help students compare responses, you may wish to write the following on the board: *Es necesario...; No es necesario...* You may wish to provide an example: *Es necesario estar en contacto con la familia. No es necesario hablar por teléfono todos los días.*

Possible answers for 4-43. Answers may vary. Accept any logically supported answers.

A leer

4-44 Primera etapa. El siguiente artículo es de una revista que se dedica a los temas de familia. Lea los dos primeros párrafos y siga las instrucciones.

Subraye (*Underline*) ...

1. las palabras en el título que probablemente indican el tema del artículo
2. una palabra que describe la condición de la familia de hoy
3. una palabra que indica la importancia de la comunicación dentro de la familia

Escriba...

4. una causa de los problemas de comunicación en la familia
5. tres necesidades de los hijos que tienen padres que trabajan fuera
6. dos efectos de la ausencia de los padres de la casa

Suggestion for 4-44. Remember that students may comprehend much more than they can verbalize or write. Therefore, it is advisable not to force them to respond to questions in their own words or paraphrase at this stage. They will do so when they are ready. Instead they may quote their answers directly from the text.

Answers for 4-44. 1. *importancia, comunicación, familiar;* 2. *crisis;* 3. *vital;* 4. *la madre y el padre trabajan largas horas fuera de casa y los hijos están solos mucho tiempo;* 5. *la compañía, la orientación y la supervisión;* 6. *cierta independencia en los hijos y una distancia emocional*

La importancia de la comunicación familiar

(1) Los expertos afirman que la familia de nuestros días está en crisis por la falta[1] de comunicación entre sus miembros o por la mala comunicación que existe entre ellos. También coinciden en que la comunicación es vital en todas las relaciones, especialmente en la familiar.

(2) Pero, ¿por qué existen problemas de comunicación en las familias? Las razones son varias. Una es que la madre y el padre trabajan largas horas fuera de casa y los hijos están solos mucho tiempo, sin la compañía, la orientación y la supervisión de sus mayores. La ausencia casi diaria de los padres puede crear cierta independencia en los hijos y una distancia emocional que dificulta la comunicación entre padres e hijos.

[1]lack

Note. This text has been divided into two parts to facilitate the students' focused reading task and for pedagogical reasons. In *Primera etapa*, students will practice anticipating and inferring about a topic through key terms. In *Segunda etapa*, they will guess the meaning of new words through context clues and the identification of suffixes.

4-45 Segunda etapa. Ahora lea el resto del artículo y siga las indicaciones. En el párrafo número tres, el artículo presenta otra razón de la mala comunicación entre padres e hijos.

Indique...

1　una palabra asociada con los problemas de comunicación familiares.
2　por qué la tecnología probablemente afecta las relaciones de la familia.
3　dos ejemplos de cómo la tecnología causa problemas cuando no se usa bien.
4　dos palabras que indican la calidad (*quality*) de la comunicación cuando usamos el correo electrónico.

En el párrafo número cuatro, el artículo indica algunas formas de usar la tecnología en beneficio de la relación familiar.

5　¿Cómo es posible usar la tecnología positivamente en la comunicación con la familia?

---

(3) Un segundo factor es la tecnología. Nuestro mundo está controlado por la tecnología, en casa, en el trabajo, etc. Evidentemente la tecnología facilita mucho la vida, pero su uso excesivo puede complicar nuestra existencia. En las sociedades donde el uso de la tecnología tiene un costo bajo, un gran número de hogares[2] están conectado a Internet. Así, muchos jóvenes tienen acceso ilimitado a la Red y al correo electrónico. Idealmente, el bajo costo de conexión debería afectar positivamente la comunicación en la familia, pero la realidad indica que, en general, la comunicación por correo electrónico, por ejemplo, tiende a ser más breve y más superficial. Los hijos prefieren no discutir por correo electrónico su depresión o sus malas notas en la universidad. Prefieren hablar directamente con sus padres, si es que estos tienen el tiempo. Lo mismo ocurre con el teléfono celular. La comunicación es casi instantánea. Es cierto que muchos jóvenes usan celulares para llamar a sus padres, pero, ¿cuántos de ellos hablan 15 minutos sobre temas importantes como sus problemas, alegrías, éxitos, etc.? ¡Muy pocos!

(4) En conclusión, el tiempo limitado que los padres pueden dar a sus hijos y la naturaleza impersonal de la comunicación electrónica pueden afectar negativamente las relaciones familiares. Por eso es importante crear oportunidades para una comunicación real y profunda dentro de la familia. Use la tecnología de manera positiva para expresar el amor y el cariño que siente por sus padres, hijos, abuelos, tíos. Su familia va a ser más fuerte y unida.

[2]*homes*

4-46 Identificación. Primera fase. La terminación (*ending*) de las palabras revela información importante sobre ellas: si la palabra es un nombre, un adjetivo, un verbo o un adverbio, por ejemplo. Observe las siguientes palabras del artículo y, luego, clasifíquelas en la columna correspondiente.

facilita　　　　orienta**ción**　　impersonal　　electrónico
supervi**sión**　　ausen**cia**　　　afectar　　　ilimit**ado**
dificult**a**　　　negativa**mente**　socie**dades**　positiva**mente**

NOMBRES	ADJETIVOS	FORMAS VERBALES	ADVERBIOS
orientación	impersonal	facilita	negativamente
supervisión	electrónico	dificulta	positivamente
ausencia	ilimitado	afectar	
sociedades			

Segunda fase. Las siguientes terminaciones indican que las palabras son nombres femeninos en español: **-sión, -ción, -cia, -ía, -dad.** Escriba abajo otros nombres con estas terminaciones que aparecen en el artículo.

_____

_____

_____

Después de leer

4-47 Expansión. Lea el siguiente texto incompleto sobre las relaciones familiares y, luego, seleccione la palabra que corresponde lógicamente en cada espacio en blanco.

supervisión	ausencia	electrónico	trabajo
trabajan	facilita	compañía	positivamente

Mi familia es como una pequeña sociedad. Todos los miembros colaboran a la felicidad del grupo. Mis padres (1) ___trabajan___ mucho fuera de casa cada día, y nosotros necesitamos su (2) ___compañía___. Pero su (3) ___ausencia___ es solamente de lunes a viernes. Cuando ellos están en su (4) ___trabajo___, ellos realizan la (5) ___supervisión___ de sus hijos por teléfono. Siempre llaman por teléfono para verificar nuestro trabajo en casa y nuestras tareas. El teléfono celular (6) ___facilita___ mucho nuestra comunicación. Mi padre, en particular, se comunica con nosotros por correo (7) ___electrónico___. Cuando hay pequeños problemas entre nosotros, nuestros padres siempre reaccionan (8) ___positivamente___. Hablan pacientemente con nosotros para resolver nuestros conflictos.

Escribir

In _Lección 3_, you practiced writing a letter to a friend. Any correspondence with friends usually lacks formality. However, writing to elders in your family, such as your parents, older aunts and uncles, may be more formal. To show love and respect, you choose your language more carefully, you may talk about different issues more seriously, and you address your elders differently from the way you address your friends.

Although there is no standard manner of addressing your elders in Spanish, since family relationships are unique to each home, the expressions in _En directo_ constitute some common address forms to elders with whom you maintain a close relationship.

In letter writing, closings are also important. Again, as is the case with salutations, closings also reflect a certain degree of formality and closeness to the person to whom you are writing. _En directo_ has some common closing lines you may wish to use when writing to elders in your family or close older friends.

EN DIRECTO

Querido abuelo/ tío: _Dear . . ._
Querida abuela/ mamá:

EN DIRECTO

Con cariño,
Affectionately;
Con mucho cariño,
With much love,
Abrazos y besos,
Hugs and kisses,
Te recuerdo con cariño,
I remember you (familiar),
with affection.

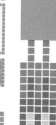

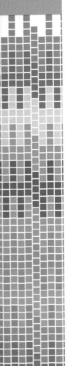

Antes de escribir

4-48 Preparación. Primera fase. La madre de Julián, un alumno universitario colombiano, escribe la siguiente carta a su hijo. La madre está triste y preocupada porque su hijo estudia en la Universidad de Los Andes y vive lejos de casa. Lea la carta y siga las instrucciones.

> *Querido Julián:*
>
> *¿Qué tal estás? ¿Cómo van tus clases? Hace un mes que no tenemos información sobre ti. ¡No escribes correos electrónicos, no llamas por teléfono! ¿Qué ocurre?*
>
> *Bueno, es el fin del semestre y debes tener mucho trabajo. ¿Estás muy estresado? ¿Duermes suficiente? ¿Comes bien en la universidad? Un estudiante necesita una buena dieta. En tu próxima visita, voy a preparar tus platos favoritos. Tu hermana Mariela, tus abuelos y tíos van a estar con nosotros y vamos a conversar largas horas.*
>
> *Tengo una sorpresa para ti. Tu hermano Marcos tiene novia; se llama Alicia. Es una chica fascinante. Pasan mucho tiempo juntos; van al cine, pasean por el parque de la universidad, salen a comer por las noches, etc. A Marcos le gusta mucho Alicia. La semana próxima Marcos y Alicia tienen vacaciones y, para conocerla un poco más, Marcos piensa ir a Cartagena con ella por unos días. Las temperaturas allí están perfectas para nadar y descansar un poco.*
>
> *Debo confesarte que tu padre y yo pensamos mucho en ti. ¿Por qué no escribes? ¿Tienes problemas en tus clases? ¿Sacas buenas notas en tus exámenes? ¿Trabajas mucho y no tienes tiempo para estudiar? ¿Estás desconectado de Internet? Por favor, escribe o llama pronto.*
>
> *Un beso de papá, Mariela y toda la familia.*
>
> *Abrazos,*
>
> *Tu madre*

Segunda fase. Imagínese que usted es Julián. Después de leer la carta de su madre, usted está muy triste. Prepárese para responder a la carta. Haga lo siguiente:

1. Identifique las preguntas de su madre a las que usted va a responder y escriba algunas ideas o información para la respuesta.
2. Escriba algunas preguntas que usted quiere hacerle a su madre: sobre su padre, sus hermanos, sus abuelos, su perro o gato, etc.

A escribir

4-49 Manos a la obra. Ahora en una hoja de papel responda a la carta de su madre. Use la información de la **Segunda fase** de la **Actividad 4-48**. Incluya la fecha, un saludo y una despedida (*closing*) apropiados.

Después de escribir

Note for 4-50. Some Spanish speakers use a comma after the salutation instead of a colon for less formal letters.

4-50 Revisión. Antes de darle su carta a su compañero/a editor/a, revise:

- primero, la coherencia de sus ideas y la cantidad de información que su madre necesita.
- luego, la precisión gramatical (el vocabulario apropiado al contexto, la estructura de las oraciones, la concordancia, etc.).
- finalmente, la ortografía y la acentuación.

ENFOQUE CULTURAL

TEMAS: LA FAMILIA HISPANA

Para pensar

¿Tiene usted una familia grande o pequeña? ¿Quiénes forman parte de su familia? ¿Dónde viven? ¿Con qué frecuencia ve usted a los miembros de su familia? ¿Quiénes trabajan fuera de la casa? ¿Quiénes se ocupan de las tareas domésticas?

La familia es una de las instituciones sociales más importantes del mundo hispano. En general, las familias pasan bastante tiempo juntas y es común verlas en almuerzos, paseos, fiestas y otras actividades.

La familia hispana incluye a los padres e hijos, pero también a abuelos, primos, tíos y padrinos. La familia hispana tiene una larga tradición de ser numerosa y unida.

En la familia tradicional los hombres trabajan fuera de la casa, y las mujeres hacen las tareas domésticas y crían (raise) a los niños.

Para contestar

2 **4-51 La familia hispana.** Responda a las siguientes preguntas:

1. Compare la familia hispana tradicional y la moderna con respecto al tamaño, la persona que hace las tareas domésticas, etc.
2. Compare la familia hispana moderna y la familia americana con respecto al tamaño, la persona que hace las tareas domésticas, etc.
3. Además de los padres y los hijos, ¿qué otras personas forman parte de la familia hispana?

G **Riqueza cultural.** Hablen de las ventajas y desventajas para los padres y para los hijos de vivir con los abuelos, tíos y primos en una misma casa.

En la actualidad muchas mujeres tienen menos hijos y trabajan fuera de la casa, pero también se ocupan de las tareas domésticas.

5

LA CASA Y LOS MUEBLES

Objetivos comunicativos

- Asking about and describing housing and household items
- Discussing daily activities in the home
- Asking about and discussing daily schedules

- Expressing ongoing actions
- Describing physical and emotional states
- Expressing obligation

Contenido

A primera vista
- En casa

- Las tareas domésticas

Explicación y expansión
- Present progressive
- Expressions with *tener*
- Direct object nouns and pronouns

- Demonstrative adjectives and pronouns
- *Saber* and *conocer*
- Algo Más: More on adjectives

Mosaicos
- Escuchar: Matching descriptions with pictures
- Conversar: Looking for housing

- Leer: Looking at visuals; getting informed about a topic
- Escribir: Describing an imaginary house to an expert audience

Enfoque cultural
- Temas: Las casas y la arquitectura
- Vistas: Nicaragua, El Salvador y Honduras
  Para investigar en Internet

- Fortunas: Episodio 5
- Notas: Marimba con Punta, *Los Profesionales*

Vocabulario

A PRIMERA VISTA

AUDIO *En casa*

Una casa de estilo colonial en Granada, Nicaragua. Algunas personas prefieren vivir **cerca** del **centro**, generalmente en **edificios** de apartamentos. Creen que los **barrios** de las **afueras** están muy **lejos** del **trabajo** y de los centros de **diversión**.

Bienes Raíces Su Casa

En Altos de Castaños,
moderna residencia
con piscina, vista, jardín y terraza con bar,
sala, comedor, estudio, baño visitas,
3 habitaciones, 3 baños,
cocina completa,
garaje para 2 autos,
400 mts. de construcción,
$300.000.00 o su equivalente
en lempiras.

☎ TEL. 232-3277, 232-5551 • FAX 232-5154

CULTURA

Notice that the first floor is normally called **la planta baja** in most Hispanic countries. The second floor is called **el primer piso**.

décimo: Rodríguez
noveno: Peralta
octavo: Elizondo
séptimo: Díaz
sexto: Gómez
quinto: Lizaur
cuarto: Sánchez
tercero: Carreras
segundo: Iglesias
primero: Olmos
planta Baja

Alquilo

Apartamento Edificio Venecia, Lomas de Miraflores Sur, sala-comedor, cocina con muebles, dos **dormitorios**, dos baños, dormitorio y baño para empleada, portón eléctrico, **estacionamiento**, TV cable, L. 6.500.00. Tel. 239-3367

Ordenando la casa

RICARDO: ¿Aló?

CATALINA: Hola, Ricardo, ¿qué estás haciendo?

RICARDO: ¡Ay, Catalina! Estoy trabajando en la casa, **limpiando** todo, el baño, la cocina, un clóset y mi **cuarto.**

CATALINA: Pero, ¿no tienes que estudiar para el examen de matemáticas?

RICARDO: ¡**Claro** que tengo que estudiar! Pero mañana mis padres **regresan** de sus vacaciones, y tengo que tener la casa **limpia** y **ordenada** porque todo está **sucio.** Tú **sabes** que mi madre es muy maniática con la limpieza.

CATALINA: Sí, ya lo sé, pero es muy tarde. ¿No tienes **sueño?**

RICARDO: Sí, pero **todavía** tengo que **ordenar** la cocina, pasear al perro, y **regar** las plantas... ¡Uf, para qué hablar!

CULTURA

In general, Hispanic homes tend to be smaller and built more closely together than homes in the United States, but spacious homes can be found in affluent neighborhoods. Living quarters for domestic help are especially characteristic of upper middle class homes, although this is less common in new constructions.

VÍNCULOS

To practice vocabulario—En casa
- SAM-OneKey: WB: 5-1, 5-2, 5-3, 5-4, 5-5, 5-6 / LM: 5-32, 5-33, 5-34, 5-35, 5-36
- Companion Website: AP 5-1
- IRCD: Chapter 5; pp. 166, 167, 169, 171

Suggestion. After presenting the names of rooms, tell students to imagine that the classroom is a house. Walk around and "identify" the different "rooms." First, whisper to individual students what activities they will charade in each part of the house. Later, you may ask the rest of the class questions as follows: *Mark y Susan están en la cocina. ¿Qué están haciendo? Están preparando la comida. Ésta es la sala y aquí están María y Carlota. ¿Qué están haciendo en la sala? Están mirando la televisión.*

Suggestion. You may introduce some additional vocabulary, such as *pared, congelador, ventilador.* You may also review colors using the illustration or the Image Resource CD, and/or having students give the color of rooms and furniture in their house or apartment.

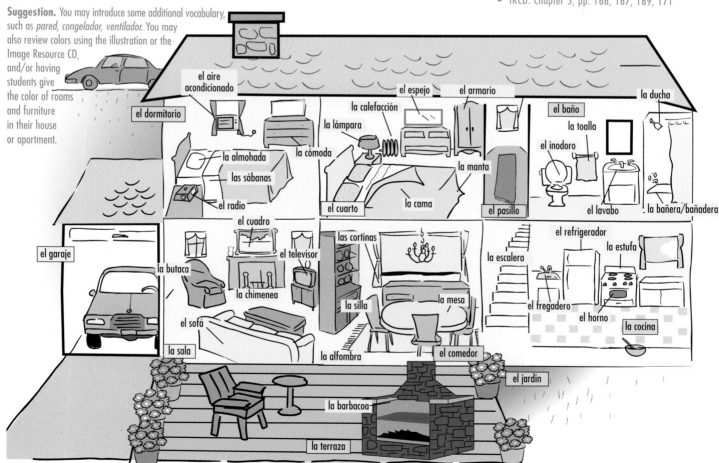

¿Qué dice usted?

Warm-up for 5-1. Have students name rooms or parts of a house associated with the following activities: *preparar la comida, escuchar música, almorzar, dormir, cultivar vegetales, conversar,*

5-1 ¿En qué parte de la casa están? Primera fase. Marque con una X el lugar donde generalmente están los siguientes objetos.

	TERRAZA	COCINA	BAÑO	SALA	DORMITORIO	COMEDOR	JARDÍN
la estufa y el lavaplatos		X					
la barbacoa	X						X
el sofá y las butacas				X			
la mesa de comer		X				X	
las toallas y el jabón (*soap*)			X				
la cama y la cómoda					X		
el televisor		X		X	X		
las almohadas y las sábanas					X		

leer el periódico, ver televisión, correr y jugar. Expand with other activities: *estacionar el auto (el garaje).* Mention other vocabulary items (*refrigerador, lavabo, alfombra, cortinas*) and ask where they are located.

Note for 5-2. Point out that vocabulary items often have more than one acceptable form. *Dormitorio* may be referred to as *cuarto, alcoba, recámara,* or *habitación. Piscina* is also called *alberca* and *pileta.*

Segunda fase. Ahora describan qué actividades ocurren normalmente en cada cuarto de la casa. ¿Qué parte de la casa prefieren ustedes? ¿Por qué?

5-2 ¿Aparatos eléctricos, muebles o accesorios? Primera fase. Escriba cada una de las siguientes palabras en la columna apropiada.

el cuadro	el armario	las cortinas
la cómoda	la silla	la alfombra
el refrigerador	el radio	el horno

APARATOS ELÉCTRICOS	MUEBLES	ACCESORIOS
el refrigerador	el armario	el cuadro
el radio	la cómoda	las cortinas
el horno	la silla	la alfombra

Segunda fase. Con su compañero/a responda a las siguientes preguntas relacionadas con la **Primera fase.**

1. ¿Qué aparato eléctrico cuesta más dinero?
2. ¿Qué muebles necesita un estudiante que estudia cada día?
3. ¿Qué accesorios tienen ustedes en su cuarto?

5-3 El curioso. Intercambien preguntas para describir los cuartos de la casa/apartamento de cada uno/a. Traten de obtener la mayor información posible.

MODELO: E1: ¿Cómo es la sala de tu casa?
E2: Es pequeña. La alfombra es verde, y hay un sofá grande, dos sillas modernas y una mesa con una lámpara. ¿Y tu dormitorio?

2 **5-4 La casa ideal. Primera fase.** Dibujen un plano de su casa/apartamento ideal. Hablen para ponerse de acuerdo sobre los siguientes puntos:

1. número de habitaciones
2. número de baños
3. distribución de los cuartos
4. localización de los muebles
5. color de las paredes

6. otras características (garaje, jardín, sótano (*basement*), ático, etc.)
7. localización de la casa en relación a la universidad

Segunda fase. El alquiler de la casa cuesta mucho dinero y ustedes deben compartir los gastos con otro/a compañero/a. Escriban un anuncio—similar a los de la página 166—para encontrar (*find*) a una persona. Expliquen las condiciones del alquiler.

G **5-5 Ventajas y desventajas (*Advantages/disadvantages*).** Discutan los aspectos positivos y negativos de las siguientes opciones. Escriban una o dos frases en la tabla. Después compartan sus opiniones con el resto de la clase.

	VENTAJAS	DESVENTAJAS
1. vivir en un apartamento		
2. vivir en una casa		
3. tener una piscina		
4. vivir con un/a compañero/a de cuarto/casa		

Las tareas domésticas

Gustavo **lava** los platos.

Beatriz **seca** los platos.

el (horno) microoondas
el lavaplatos

Beatriz **cocina**. Ella usa mucho los **electrodomésticos**.

Gustavo **limpia** el baño y **pasa** la **aspiradora.**

Gustavo **saca** la **basura.**

Gustavo **barre** la terraza.

Beatriz **tiende** la **ropa.**

la lavadora   la secadora

Después la **dobla** cuando está seca.

Beatriz **plancha** la ropa.

Suggestion. Use the Image Resource CD or posters to illustrate vocabulary. Personalize questions: *¿Quién limpia su casa? ¿Qué días limpia la casa? ¿Barre usted la terraza? ¿Y pasa la aspiradora también? ¿Quién cocina en su familia? ¿Lava usted los platos? ¿Quién lava la ropa? ¿... plancha la ropa? ¿... saca la basura?*

Point out *colgar/tender la ropa.* Mention that in Hispanic countries, domestic help may do some of these chores.

Suggestion for 5-6. Ask the students to use the following expressions to organize their answers and to recycle vocabulary (*primero, luego, más tarde, después, finalmente*) when communicating with their classmates.

Follow-up for 5-7. What does everyone do in the various rooms? Come to a consensus and report, using *nosotros.* You may also introduce some expressions with *tener: ¿Qué haces cuando tienes sueño? ¿Dónde?*

¿Qué dice usted?

2 5-6 Por la mañana. ¿En qué orden hace usted estas cosas según los debujos en la página 169? Compare sus respuestas con las de su compañero/a.

_____ lavar los platos	_____ desayunar
_____ preparar el café	_____ secar los platos
_____ salir para la universidad	_____ hacer la cama

2 5-7 Actividades en la casa. Pregúntele a su compañero/a dónde hace estas cosas normalmente.

MODELO:　E1: ¿Dónde ves televisión?
　　　　　　E2: Veo televisión en mi cuarto. ¿Y tú? *o* No veo televisión. ¿Y tú?

1. dormir la siesta
2. escuchar música
3. planchar
4. estudiar para un examen
5. almorzar durante la semana
6. desayunar el fin de semana
7. vestirse
8. hablar por teléfono con amigos/as

5-8 Preparativos. Primera fase. Usted va a casarse pronto y tiene que comprar muchos muebles, accesorios y electrodomésticos para su nueva casa. Póngalos en los lugares adecuados de la tabla.

	MUEBLES	ACCESORIOS	ELECTRODOMÉSTICOS
para el dormitorio			
para la sala			
para el comedor			
para la cocina			

2 Segunda fase. Comparta la lista con su compañero/a. Él/Ella le va recordar otras cosas que probablemente va a necesitar.

MODELO:　E1: Tengo que comprar una cama nueva para el dormitorio.
　　　　　　E2: ¿Y no tienes que comprar sábanas y mantas?

5-9 De compras (*Shopping*). Ahora usted va a una mueblería para comprar algunas cosas de su lista. Pregúntele al/a la dependiente/a dónde están los muebles, los accesorios y los electrodomésticos que necesita comprar. Él/Ella le va a contestar de acuerdo con el directorio de la tienda a continuación.

MODELO: E1: Perdón, ¿en qué piso están las lámparas?
               E2: Están en el primer piso.

Note for 5-9. Ordinal numbers were introduced as lexical items in the first part of *A primera vista* p. 166. A formal presentation of ordinal numbers is found in the *Algo más* section, p. 187. Remind students that the *planta baja* is the equivalent of the first floor in the United States and the *primer piso* or *primera planta* is the equivalent of the second floor. The expression *tener que* + infinitive is presented in the dialog on p. 167. Have students look at the ad and guess the meaning of *sótano*.

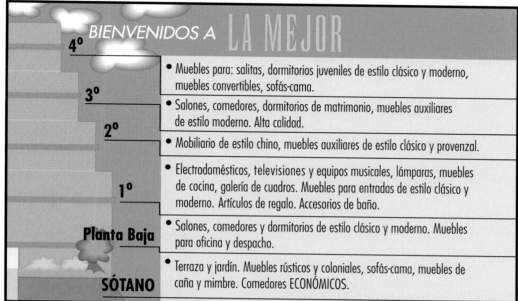

BIENVENIDOS A **LA MEJOR**

4º • Muebles para: salitas, dormitorios juveniles de estilo clásico y moderno, muebles convertibles, sofás-cama.

3º • Salones, comedores, dormitorios de matrimonio, muebles auxiliares de estilo moderno. Alta calidad.

2º • Mobiliario de estilo chino, muebles auxiliares de estilo clásico y provenzal.

1º • Electrodomésticos, televisiones y equipos musicales, lámparas, muebles de cocina, galería de cuadros. Muebles para entradas de estilo clásico y moderno. Artículos de regalo. Accesorios de baño.

Planta Baja • Salones, comedores y dormitorios de estilo clásico y moderno. Muebles para oficina y despacho.

SÓTANO • Terraza y jardín. Muebles rústicos y coloniales, sofás-cama, muebles de caña y mimbre. Comedores ECONÓMICOS.

5-10 El agente de bienes raíces. You will listen to a conversation between a couple and a real estate agent in El Salvador. Before you listen, write down some of the questions the couple might be interested in asking.

_____

_____

_____

Now, as you listen to the conversation, circle the letter next to the correct information.

1. Los señores Mena quieren comprar…
    (a.) una casa.
    b. un apartamento.

2. El señor y la señora Mena prefieren vivir…
    (a.) en una buena zona.
    b. lejos de un parque.

3. El agente de bienes raíces…
    a. no sabe cómo ayudarlos.
    (b.) tiene una casa buena para ellos.

4. El agente dice que la casa del barrio La Mascota…
    a. cuesta mucho.
    (b.) tiene un buen precio.

Warm-up for 5-10. As a pre-listening activity, students get into groups of four and describe the places where they live. Then, they may write a description of their own house/ apartment/room.

Audioscript for 5-10. El agente de bienes raíces.

AGENTE: Sr. Mena, creo que esta casa es una buena compra. Además está cerca de su trabajo.

SRA. MENA: Sí, pero no me gusta la zona donde está. Nosotros preferimos comprar algo más pequeño, pero en una buena zona, especialmente por los niños.

AGENTE: Es que una casa con tres habitaciones, dos baños, sala, comedor y garaje para dos autos en un barrio bueno cuesta bastante... ¿Y un apartamento? Hay unos apartamentos nuevos, muy buenos, en la calle Sol.

SR. MENA: Mire, preferimos una casa. Los niños necesitan estar al aire libre para jugar; por eso queremos una casa con un jardín pequeño, o por lo menos una que esté cerca de un parque.

AGENTE: Pues hay una casa en la Colonia La Mascota que no es muy grande, 200 metros cuadrados, pero que tiene dos habitaciones grandes, una tercera habitación más pequeña y dos baños.

SR. MENA: La Mascota es un barrio muy bueno, a diez o quince minutos de mi oficina. ¿La casa tiene jardín?

AGENTE: Sí, un jardín pequeño.

SRA. MENA: ¿Y cuánto piden?

AGENTE: Déjeme ver... 1.200.000 colones, un buen precio para esa zona.

SR. MENA: Pues, creo que debemos verla.

EXPLICACIÓN Y EXPANSIÓN

1. Present progressive

Suggestions. Use visuals or the chalkboard to show the present participle endings. Give additional examples in context referring to your class or to people in illustrations or photos. For example: *Ahora yo estoy hablando y ustedes están escuchando. En esta foto el chico está cocinando y la chica está lavando los platos. Este chico está corriendo y ese chico está bebiendo agua.* Point out that the present participle is invariable, always ending in *-o.* Ask yes/no and either/or questions based on the visuals using the present progressive.

You may personalize presentation of the present progressive as follows: *Yo estoy hablando español y ustedes están escuchando. Pedro está mirando la pizarra. María está escribiendo en su cuaderno.* Then ask questions: *¿Estoy hablando español? Y ustedes, ¿están escuchando? ¿Están contestando preguntas?*

VÍNCULOS

To practice present progressive
- SAM-OneKey: WB: 5-7, 5-8, 5-9 / LM: 5-37, 5-38
- Companion Website: AP 5-2
- *Gramática viva*: Grammar Point 42: Progressive forms (*estar* + gerund)
- IRCD: Chapter 5; pg. 172

ESTAR (*to be*)		PRESENT PARTICIPLE (*-ando/-iendo*)
yo	estoy	
tú	estás	hablando
Ud., él, ella	está	comiendo
nosotros/as	estamos	escribiendo
vosotros/as	estáis	
Uds., ellos/as	están	

- Use the present progressive to emphasize an action in progress at the moment of speaking, as opposed to a habitual action.

Marcela **está limpiando** la casa.	*Marcela is cleaning the house.* (at this moment)
Marcela **limpia** la casa.	*Marcela cleans the house.* (normally)

- Spanish does not use the present progressive to express future time, as English does; Spanish uses the present tense instead.

Salgo mañana.	*I am leaving tomorrow.*

- Form the present progressive with the present of **estar** + *the present participle.* To form the present participle, add **-ando** to the stem of **-ar** verbs and **-iendo** to the stem of **-er** and **-ir** verbs.

hablar	→	**hablando**
comer	→	**comiendo**
escribir	→	**escribiendo**

- When the verb stem of an **-er** or an **-ir** verb ends in a vowel, add **-yendo**.

leer	→	**leyendo**
oír	→	**oyendo**

- Stem-changing **-ir** verbs (o → ue, e → ie, e → i) change o → u and e → i in the present participle.

dormir (duermo)	→	**durmiendo**
sentir (siento)	→	**sintiendo**
pedir (pido)	→	**pidiendo**

¿Qué dice usted?

5-11 ¿Qué están haciendo y por qué? Primera fase. Asocie las acciones de la columna de la izquierda con las explicaciones de la columna de la derecha.

1. __d__ La Sra. Villa está preparando una cena deliciosa.
2. __e__ Su hijo Marcelo está barriendo la terraza.
3. __b__ Su hija Ana está lavando los platos en el fregadero.
4. __c__ Alicia está regando las plantas.
5. __a__ Pedro está estudiando en su cuarto.

a. Tiene un examen mañana.
b. El lavaplatos no está funcionando.
c. Están muy secas.
d. Es el cumpleaños de su esposo.
e. Está muy sucia y vienen unos amigos esta tarde.

Segunda fase. Piense en dos actividades que uno o dos miembros de su familia está(n) probablemente haciendo en este momento. Comparta estas ideas con su compañero/a. ¿Están las personas en las que ustedes piensan haciendo actividades semejantes?

MODELO: Probablemente mi padre está lavando el auto en este momento y mi madre está mirando televisión.

5-12 La vida activa. Túrnense para decir qué están haciendo las personas en los dibujos y lo que ustedes piensan que van a hacer después.

MODELO: E1: Ellos están cantando en una fiesta.
E2: Después van a bailar y a conversar con sus amigos.

Suggestion for 5-12. You may use the Image Resource CD when doing this activity. The English present participle is called *gerundio* in Spanish.

Efraín   Madela   Memo

Oscar   Felipe

Suggestion for 5-13. It will be easier for students to describe a place they are familiar with; however, depending on your class, you may encourage students to describe a place presented in this lesson. They could bring pictures of the place to class, find information in the *Enfoque cultural* or visit www.prenhall.com/mosaicos. Students may do their research outside of class and come prepared to the next class meeting.

5-13 Lugares y actividades. Primera fase. Piense en un lugar de su país, de España o de Hispanoamérica, y haga lo siguiente:

■ Escriba dos o tres palabras que describen el lugar.

■ Escriba dos o tres actividades que típicamente se asocian con este lugar.

❷ Segunda fase. Descríbale el lugar a su compañero/a y diga dos o tres actividades que las personas probablemente **están haciendo** en este lugar en este momento. Su compañero/a debe adivinar el nombre del lugar.

MODELO:　E1: Ésta es una ciudad muy antigua que está en América del Sur. Es muy popular entre los turistas. Está en los Andes, y en este momento muchos turistas están visitando la ciudad.
　　　　　　E2: ¡Ah! Es Machu Picchu./ Es Cuzco.

SITUACIONES

1. **Role A.** Your best friend calls you to find out what you are doing. Respond that you are doing a major cleaning of the apartment that you share with other friends. Explain to her/him the chores that each one of you is doing.

   Role B. Call your best friend to find out what she/he is doing. Inquire about who is doing what and tell your friend to remind the others what they should do in case they are not doing it.

2. You cannot attend a big reunion that your family is having and you feel homesick. You call home; your partner is the family member who answers the phone. a) Greet him/her, b) excuse yourself for not being there, c) find out who is at the reunion and how everyone is, and d) ask what each family member is doing right now.

VÍNCULOS

To practice expressions with *tener*
● SAM-OneKey: WB: 5-10, 5-11, 5-12 / LM: 5-39, 5-40, 5-41
● Companion Website: AP 5-3
● *Gramática viva*: Grammar Point 56: *Tener, tener que*
● IRCD: Chapter 5; pg. 174

Suggestion. Use visuals to present the expressions with *tener*. Personalize these expressions as follows: *¿Tiene usted calor? ¿Tiene sed? ¿Qué toma usted cuando tiene sed?* Ask other students about their classmates' answers.

Suggestion. You may wish to explain that *mucha prisa* is the Spanish equivalent of being in a rush/great hurry. Provide an example: *Son las ocho menos cinco y Emilio está corriendo por el pasillo para llegar a su clase de español. Hay un examen a las ocho y él no quiere llegar tarde. Emilio tiene mucha prisa.*

Review *ser* and *estar* with *frío* and *caliente*. Visuals can be very helpful.

Suggestion. Ask a few questions using *tener que*, *querer*, and *pensar* with infinitive. Begin by telling what you have to, want to, and intend to do.

2. Expressions with *tener*

■ You have already seen the expression **tener... años:** *Eduardo tiene veinte años.* Spanish uses **tener** + *noun* in many cases where English uses *to be* + *adjective*.

TENER + NOUN			
tener	hambre	to be	*hungry*
	sed		*thirsty*
	sueño		*sleepy*
	miedo		*afraid*
	calor		*hot*
	frío		*cold*
	suerte		*lucky*
	cuidado		*careful*
	prisa		*in a hurry/rush*
	razón		*right, correct*

- With these expressions use **mucho(a)** to indicate *very*.

| Tengo **mucho** calor (frío, miedo, sueño, cuidado). | *I am very hot (cold, afraid, sleepy, careful).* |
| Tienen **mucha** hambre (sed, suerte). | *They are very hungry (thirsty, lucky).* |

- Use **tener + que +** *infinitive* to express obligation.

Tengo que regresar hoy.   *I have to return today.*

¿Qué dice usted?

5-14 Asociaciones. Asocie las oraciones de la izquierda con las expresiones de la derecha.

1. __f__ Mi hermano va a comer mucho.
2. __d__ Mi hermana siempre duerme diez horas.
3. __e__ Mis primos están en el Polo Norte.
4. __a__ Mis abuelos toman mucha agua cada día.
5. __c__ Mi mamá siempre gana (*wins*) cuando juega a la lotería.
6. __b__ Son las 8:00 y tengo que estar en casa a las 8:10.

    a. Tienen sed.
    b. Tengo prisa.
    c. Tiene mucha suerte.
    d. Tiene sueño.
    e. Tienen mucho frío.
    f. Tiene hambre.

5-15 ¿Cómo están estas personas? Primera fase. Use una expresión con el verbo **tener** para decir cómo están estas personas.

MODELO: Pablo tiene frío.

Suggestion for 5-15. Encourage students to talk about the various illustrations before using the *tener* expressions. You may wish to give them additional vocabulary, as needed. For the last illustration, students may say that the baby is sleepy, hungry, or thirsty. You may try to elicit such responses.

Pablo

Lázaro

Sixto y Daniel

Josefina

Julio

Aida

Suggestion. Have students identify the direct object nouns in the drawings asking questions using *¿Qué?*, e.g., *Juan lava el auto. ¿Qué lava Juan? (Lava) el auto. Alicia saca la basura. ¿Qué saca Alicia? (Saca) la basura. ¿A quién ayuda la niña? (Ayuda) a su padre.* For additional practice with *¿a quién?*, have one student look at another and ask questions, e.g., *Juan, mire a María. ¿A quién mira Juan? (Mira) a María.*

EN DIRECTO

To express discontent or to complain:

Tengo que decirte que...
Debemos hablar sobre algunos problemas/asuntos (*issues*).
Mira, tengo un problema.

To give excuses:

Lo siento, pero...
Perdona/Disculpa, pero...

You may use the Image Resource CD to talk about the drawings and ask questions to check comprehension.

Suggestion. To practice direct object pronouns, a) distribute some of your classroom items among the students and then ask questions: *¿Tiene usted mi lápiz? Sí, lo tengo./No, no lo tengo. Y usted, ¿tiene mi libro?* b) ask students if they use certain

② **Segunda fase.** Dígale a su compañero/a cómo se siente (*feel*) usted en este momento y qué va a hacer para sentirse mejor (*better*).

MODELO: Tengo sueño. Voy a caminar un poco.

② **5-16 Agenda.** Haga una lista de todas las cosas que tiene que hacer cada día de la semana próxima. Después intercambie información con un/a compañero/a.

MODELO: E1: ¿Qué tienes que hacer el lunes?
E2: Tengo que estudiar para el examen de matemáticas. ¿Y tú?

SITUACIONES

Role A: You share an apartment with a messy friend. Complain to him/her about the fact that a) his/her books, backpack, etc. are always all over the living room, b) that he/she uses dishes, but does not wash them, c) that his/her dirty clothes are always in the washer, etc., and c) that you have to do that extra work.

Role B: The friend with whom you share an apartment has some complaints about you. a) Apologize to him/her by saying that you will be more careful in the future and explain how, b) suggest to your friend making a list of house chores, and c) say for which chores you will be responsible.

3. Direct object nouns and pronouns

¿Qué hacen estas personas?

¿Quién saca **la basura**?
Alicia **la** saca.

¿Quién lava **el auto**?
Juan **lo** lava.

household items, e.g., *¿Usa usted la aspiradora en su casa? Sí, la uso./No, no la uso. ¿Y el horno microondas?* Help them if necessary. You may also ask if they eat certain items, e.g., *¿Come usted cereal en el desayuno...? Sí, lo como. ¿Y, frutas?* Introduce *me* afterwards by asking *¿Me ve usted? ¿Me escucha?*, and then guide students to ask each other the same questions to practice both *me* and *te*.

During the rest of the course be sure to integrate direct object pronouns into regular speech.

Miguel corta **el césped** y su hija recoge las hojas.
¿Quien ayuda **a Miguel**?
Su hija **lo** ayuda.

■ Direct object nouns and pronouns answer the question **what?** or **whom?** in relation to the verb.

¿Qué lava Pedro?	*What does Pedro wash?*
(Pedro lava) **los platos**.	*(Pedro washes) the dishes.*

■ When direct object nouns refer to a specific person, a group of persons, or to a pet, the word **a** precedes the direct object. This **a** is called the personal **a** and has no equivalent in English. The personal **a** followed by **el** contracts to **al**.

Amanda seca **los platos**.	*Amanda dries the dishes.*
Amanda seca **a la niña**.	*Amanda dries off the girl.*
¿Ves la piscina?	*Do you see the swimming pool?*
¿Ves **al** niño en la piscina?	*Do you see the child in the swimming pool?*

■ Direct object pronouns replace direct object nouns. These pronouns refer to people, animals, or things already mentioned, and they are used to avoid repeating the noun.

DIRECT OBJECT PRONOUNS			
me	*me*	nos	*us*
te	*you* (familiar, singular)	os	*you* (familiar plural, Spain)
lo	*you* (formal, singular), *him, it* (masculine)	los	*you* (formal and familiar, plural), *them* (masculine)
la	*you* (formal, singular), *her, it* (feminine)	las	*you* (formal and familiar, plural), *them* (feminine)

■ Place the direct object pronoun before the conjugated verb form.

¿Limpia Mirta **el baño**?	*Does Mirta clean the bathroom?*
No, no **lo** limpia.	*No, she does not clean it.*
¿Quieres mucho **a tu perro**?	*Do you love your dog a lot?*
Sí, **lo** quiero mucho.	*Yes, I love him a lot.*

■ With compound verb forms (a conjugated verb and an infinitive or present participle), a direct object pronoun may be placed before the conjugated verb, or be attached to the accompanying infinitive or present participle.

¿Vas a ver **a Rafael**?	*Are you going to see Rafael?*
Sí, **lo** voy a ver./Sí, voy a ver**lo**.	*Yes, I am going to see him.*
¿Están limpiando **la casa**?	*Are they cleaning the house?*
Sí, **la** están limpiando.⎱	
Sí, están limpiándo**la**.⎰	*Yes, they are cleaning it.*

■ Since the question word **quién(es)** refers to people, use the personal **a** when **quién(es)** is used as a direct object.

¿**A** quién(es) vas a ver?	*Whom are you going to see?*
Voy a ver a Pedro.	*I am going to see Pedro.*

VÍNCULOS

To practice direct object nouns and pronouns
- SAM-OneKey: WB: 5-13, 5-14, 5-15, 5-16 / LM: 5-42, 5-43, 5-44, 5-45
- Companion Website: AP 5-4
- *Gramática viva*: Grammar Points 9 and 28: Direct object pronouns; Personal *a*
- IRCD: Chapter 5; pg. 177

ACENTOS

You have learned that words that stress the next-to-the-last syllable do not have a written accent if they end in a vowel: lav**a**ndo. If we attach a direct object pronoun, the stress falls on the third syllable from the end and a written accent is needed: lav**á**ndolo.

Suggestions for 5-17. You may point out to students that although all alternatives are grammatically correct, only one of them contains the correct direct object pronoun appropriate to the context.

¿Qué dice usted?

5-17 La división del trabajo. Tres de sus compañeros comparten un apartamento y usted les hace las siguientes preguntas para saber cómo dividen las tareas domésticas entre ellos. Escriba la letra de la respuesta correcta.

1. ¿Quién lava los platos?
   a. Yo lo lavo.   (b.) Pedro los lava.   c. Julio y yo las lavamos.

2. ¿Quién prepara las comidas?
   a. Pedro la prepara.   b. Yo los preparo.   (c.) Martín las prepara.

3. ¿Quién limpia el baño?
   (a.) Los tres lo limpiamos.   b. Pedro los limpia.   c. Martín la limpia.

4. ¿Quién saca la basura?
   a. Martín lo saca.   b. Pedro las saca.   (c.) Julio la saca.

5. ¿Quién pasa la aspiradora?
   a. Martín y yo las pasamos.   (b.) Julio la pasa.   c. Yo lo paso.

5-18 ¿Qué es lógico hacer? Primera fase. Las afirmaciones de la columna de la izquierda describen algunas situaciones domésticas. Léalas y, luego, asocie cada una de ellas con una acción lógica para resolverlas.

1. ___b___ Las camas están sin hacer.
2. ___d___ La ropa está seca.
3. ___a___ Los dormitorios están desordenados.
4. ___f___ El aire acondicionado no funciona.
5. ___d___ Las ventanas están sucias.
6. ___f___ No pueden poner el auto en el garaje porque hay muchos muebles viejos y cajas (boxes) con libros.

a. Los hijos los van a ordenar.
b. La madre las hace después de leer el periódico.
c. El padre las va a limpiar.
d. Hay que plancharla.
e. Los hijos lo van a limpiar.
f. El hijo mayor lo va a reparar.

Segunda fase. Dígale a su compañero/a cuál(es) de las afirmaciones de la **Primera fase** describe(n) mejor su apartamento o casa en este momento. Luego, explíquele qué va a hacer usted y cuándo.

Suggestion for 5-19. Encourage student 1 to use *también* when answering a question affirmatively if his/her partner has given the same answer previously (e.g., E1: *¿Sacas la basura?* E2: *Sí, la saco. ¿Y tú?* E1: *Sí, yo la saco también.*). You may wish to preview *tampoco* for negative answers (e.g., E2: *No, no la saco. ¿Y tú?* E1: *No, yo no la saco tampoco.*).

5-19 Mis responsabilidades en casa. Primera fase. Averigüe si su compañero/a es responsable de las siguientes tareas domésticas en su casa.

MODELO: sacar la basura
   E1: ¿Sacas la basura?
   E2: Sí, la saco./No, no la saco. ¿Y tú?

1. limpiar la cocina
2. lavar los platos
3. secar los platos

4. tender las camas
5. lavar la ropa
6. cortar el césped

Follow-up for 5-19, Segunda fase. Have students compare their answers and then tell another pair what both of them do or do not do in their homes.

Segunda fase. Ahora, comparen sus respuestas. Después díganle a otra pareja cuáles son las tareas domésticas que ustedes dos hacen y averigüen si ellos las hacen también.

MODELO: E1: Nosotros no lavamos los platos en casa porque tenemos lavaplatos. ¿Y ustedes los lavan?
   E2: Sí, nosotros los lavamos y hacemos las camas también.

2 **5-20 El apartamento de mi compañero/a.** Usted va a cuidar el apartamento de su compañero/a por una semana, y quiere saber cuáles son sus responsabilidades y lo que puede o no puede hacer allí.

MODELO: E1: ¿Debo sacar la basura?
　　　　　 E2: Sí, la debes sacar/debes sacarla todos los días.
　　　　　 E1: ¿Puedo usar tu estéreo?
　　　　　 E2: Claro que lo puedes usar.

Note for 5-20. Many Spanish speakers use *sacar al perro* instead of *pasear al perro*.

Follow-up for 5-20. In groups of four, students compare the answers they got. If they feel that some answer is not fair, they should ask their classmate to explain the reason for his/her answer.

¿DEBO O NO DEBO?	SÍ	NO	¿PUEDO O NO PUEDO?	SÍ	NO
regar las plantas	___	___	leer los libros	___	___
pasear al perro	___	___	usar los electrodomésticos	___	___
limpiar el apartamento	___	___	invitar a un/a amigo/a	___	___
poner la alarma	___	___	hacer la tarea en la computadora	___	___
...	___	___	...	___	___

5-21 Los preparativos para la visita. La familia Granados está muy ocupada porque espera la visita de unos parientes. Conteste las preguntas de su compañero/a sobre lo que está haciendo cada miembro de la familia.

MODELO: E1: ¿Quién está preparando la comida?
　　　　　 E2: La abuela la está preparando/está preparándola.

Suggestion for 5-21. You may use the Image Resource CD to do this activity.

Suggestion for 5-22, Primera fase. Have students share their answers in small groups.

2 5-22 Una mano amiga. Primera fase. Conteste las preguntas de su compañero/a sobre sus relaciones con otras personas y lo que ellas hacen por usted.

MODELO: ayudar económicamente   mis padres
E1: ¿Quién te ayuda económicamente?
E2: Mis padres me ayudan económicamente.

1. querer mucho
2. escuchar en todo momento
3. llamar por teléfono con frecuencia
4. ayudar con los problemas
5. aconsejar (*advise*) cuando estás indeciso/a
6. entender siempre

a. mi padre
b. mi madre
c. mi mejor amigo/a
d. mi novio/a
e. ...

Segunda fase. Dígale a su compañero/a lo que usted hace por las siguientes personas. Indique en qué circunstancias lo hace.

MODELO: su esposo/a
E1: Lo/La ayudo cuando está cansado/a.
E2: Y yo lo/la escucho cuando tiene problemas en el trabajo.

1. su papá
2. su mamá
3. su mejor amigo/a
4. su novio/a
5. sus vecinos (*neighbors*)

EN DIRECTO

To assist a customer in a shop:
¿Qué desea?
¿En qué puedo ayudarlo/a?

To request a product:
Quisiera...
¿Podría ver/mostrarme (*show me*) . . . ?

SITUACIONES

Role A. You are at a furniture store buying a sofa. Tell the salesperson which sofa you want and ask him/her when they can deliver (**entregar**) it. Tell the salesperson you are not going to be home at that time, but that you can be home in the afternoon. Agree to the time and thank the salesperson.

Role B. You are a salesperson at a furniture store. Tell the customer that the sofa he/she wants is a very good one and that you can deliver it next Monday morning. Since the convenient time for the customer is the afternoon, tell him/her that you can deliver it between three and five o'clock.

4. Demonstrative adjectives and pronouns

Demonstrative adjectives

Esta silla tiene que estar
aquí y esa mesa allí.

Los otros muebles están allá,
en aquel edificio.

- Demonstrative adjectives agree in gender and number with the noun they modify. English has two sets of demonstratives (*this, these* and *that, those*), but Spanish has three sets.

this	{**este** cuadro **esta** butaca	*these*	{**estos** cuadros **estas** butacas
that	{**ese** horno **esa** casa	*those*	{**esos** hornos **esas** casas
that (over there)	{**aquel** edificio **aquella** casa	*those* (over there)	{**aquellos** edificios **aquellas** casas

- Use **este, esta, estos,** and **estas** when referring to people or things that are close to you in space or time.

Este escritorio es nuevo.	*This desk is new.*
Traen el sofá **esta** semana.	*They will bring the sofa this week.*

VÍNCULOS

To practice demonstrative adjectives and pronouns

- SAM-OneKey: WB: 5-17, 5-18, 5-19 / LM: 5-46, 5-47, 5-48, 5-49
- Companion Website: AP 5-5
- *Gramática viva*: Grammar Points 7 and 8: Demonstrative Adjectives; Demonstrative Pronouns
- IRCD: Chapter 5; pp. 181, 182

Suggestion. Point to objects in class, relating demonstrative adjectives to their location: *Este libro es mi libro de español. Ese cuaderno es su cuaderno de ejercicios, ¿no? Aquellas mochilas son de los estudiantes.* Walk around the room to show how demonstratives change in relation to the speaker and the person spoken to.

Suggestion. As you walk around the classroom pointing to different objects, you may introduce the words *aquí, acá, allí,* and *allá* along with the corresponding demonstrative adjective.

LENGUA

Some Spanish speakers also use the word **este** or **pues** as pause fillers when trying to remember a word while speaking.

Voy a ver la película en el cine... este... Riviera.

What do English speakers do in this situation?

- Use **ese, esa, esos,** and **esas** when referring to people or things that are not relatively close to you. Sometimes they are close to the person you are addressing.

> **Esa** lámpara es muy bonita. *That lamp is very pretty.*

- Use **aquel, aquella, aquellos,** and **aquellas** when referring to people or things that are more distant.

> **Aquel** edificio es muy alto. *That building (over there) is very tall.*

Demonstrative pronouns

Note. Remind students that the pronoun refers to an already mentioned noun and, therefore replaces it: *Necesito este cuaderno y ése (cuaderno).*

Note. The written accent on demonstrative pronouns is falling into disuse in Spanish. The *Real Academia Española* in conjunction with the academies of this hemisphere stated in 1999 that the written accent mark is not required on demonstrative pronouns any longer. Since it is optional, many Spanish speakers still use it. Students may see demonstrative pronouns without accents in recent publications.

- Demonstratives can be used as pronouns. A written accent mark may be placed on the stressed vowel to distinguish demonstrative pronouns from demonstrative adjectives.

> Compran este espejo y **ése.** *They are buying this mirror and that one.*

- To refer to a general idea or concept, or to ask for the identification of an object, use *esto, eso,* or *aquello.* These pronouns do not take an accent.

> Trabajan mucho y **eso** es muy bueno. *They work a lot and that is very good.*
> ¿Qué es **esto?** *What is this?*
> Es un espejo. *It is a mirror.*

¿Qué dice usted?

5-23 Cerca, relativamente cerca o lejos. Decida qué adjetivo demostrativo debe usar de acuerdo con el lugar donde se encuentran los siguientes objetos.

Cerca de usted

1. ___a___ mesa es de Honduras.   a. Esta   b. Esa   c. Aquella
2. ___a___ cuadros también son de Honduras.   a. Estos   b. Esos   c. Aquellos

Relativamente cerca de usted

3. ___b___ sofá es muy cómodo (*comfortable*).   a. Este   b. Ese   c. Aquel
4. ___b___ alfombra tiene unos colores muy alegres.   a. Esta   b. Esa   c. Aquella

Lejos de usted

5. ___c___ espejo es nuevo.   a. Este   b. Ese   c. Aquel
6. ___c___ lámparas son antiguas.   a. Estas   b. Esas   c. Aquellas

2 **5-24 En una mueblería en Managua.** Usted y su compañero/a van a hacer los papeles de cliente/a y dependiente/a. El/La cliente/a pregunta los precios de algunos muebles y accesorios (usando los demostrativos correctos). El/La dependiente/a le hace preguntas para saber específicamente a qué se refiere.

MODELO: CLIENTE/A: ¿Cuánto cuesta esa mesa?
DEPENDIENTE/A: ¿Cuál? ¿La mesa que está al lado de la silla?
CLIENTE/A: No, la mesa que está entre la butaca y la silla pequeña. *o* Sí, ésa.
DEPENDIENTE/A: Cuesta 750 córdobas. *o* Cuesta 2.150 córdobas.

A INVESTIGAR

¿Managua es la capital de qué país? ¿Cuál es la unidad monetaria de ese país? ¿A cuánto está el cambio (*rate of exchange*) en estos momentos?

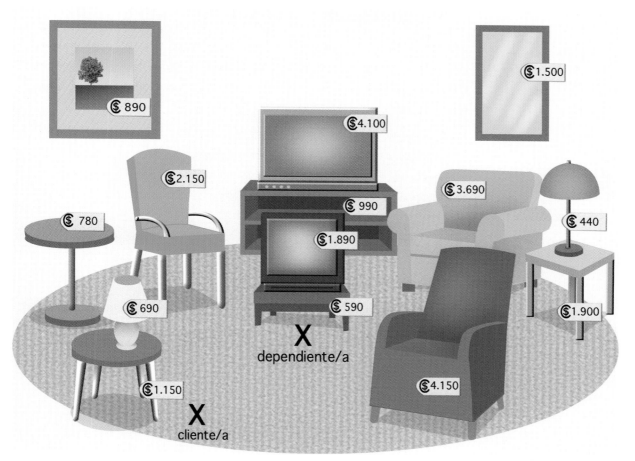

2 **5-25 ¿De quién es?** En su tiempo libre, usted y un/a compañero/a están trabajando de asistentes en una escuela primaria. Al final del día ustedes revisan el salón de clase y notan que los niños dejaron (*left*) varios objetos en diferentes lugares. Pregúntense (*ask each other*) de quién es cada objeto.

MODELO: E1: ¿De quién es este/ese/aquel bolígrafo?
E2: Éste/ése/aquél es de David. *o* Es de Miguel.

un cuaderno	unos lentes	una mochila azul	una grabadora
un libro	unos apuntes	una calculadora	unos lápices

Note for 5-24. You may explain that the name *córdoba* is in memory of the Spanish conquistador Francisco Hernández de Córdoba. The symbol for the *córdoba* is a dollar with a C on the left side, as shown in the illustration.

Suggestion for 5-24. You may introduce the words *rectangular, redondo/a,* and *cuadrado/a* to help students describe the tables. Students may use demonstrative adjectives or pronouns as shown in the model.

⚫ 5-26 Descripciones. Piense en un objeto o mueble y diga en qué parte de la casa está. Su compañero/a va a hacerle preguntas para adivinar qué es. Cada uno/a debe pensar en tres objetos.

MODELO: E1: Este mueble está generalmente en el comedor.
               E2: ¿Es grande?
               E1: Puede ser grande o pequeño.
               E2: ¿Lo usamos para comer?
               E1: Sí.
               E2: Es la mesa.

SITUACIONES

Role A. You are planning to buy a larger home. A real estate agent has already shown you pictures of one house and is now showing you pictures of a second one. Discuss with him/her a) the price, b) the number of rooms, and c) facilities such as laundry room (**lavandería**), garage, and pool, of both houses. Tell him/her which of the two houses you want to see and say why.

Role B. You are a real estate agent. You already showed your client pictures of one house and now are showing him/her pictures of a second house. Answer his/her questions by saying a) that the first house is $145,000 dollars and the second one is $150,000, b) that both houses have three bedrooms, and c) that the first house has a one-car garage while this one has a two-car garage. Also tell him/her the advantages of each of the two houses.

5. *Saber* and *conocer*

Both **saber** and **conocer** mean *to know*, but they are not used interchangeably.

	SABER	CONOCER
yo	sé	conozco
tú	sabes	conoces
Ud., él, ella	sabe	conoce
nosotros/as	sabemos	conocemos
vosotros/as	sabéis	conocéis
Uds., ellos/as	saben	conocen

■ Use **saber** to express knowledge of facts or pieces of information.

    Él **sabe** dónde está el edificio.   *He knows where the building is.*

■ Use **saber** + *infinitive* to express that you know how to do something.

    Yo **sé** reparar electrodomésticos.   *I know how to repair appliances.*

■ Use **conocer** to express acquaintance with someone or something. **Conocer** also means *to meet*. Remember to use the personal **a** when referring to people.

    Conozco a mis vecinos.   *I know my neighbors.*
    Conozco bien ese libro.   *I am very familiar with that book.*
    Ella quiere **conocer a** Luis.   *She wants to meet Luis.*

Suggestion. Students should use *esa casa* to refer to the first house (the one they saw before) and *esta casa* or *ésta* to refer to the pictures of the house that they are looking at now.

VÍNCULOS

To practice *saber* and *conocer* (to know)
- SAM-OneKey: WB: 5-20, 5-21, 5-22 / LM: 5-50, 5-51
- Companion Website: AP 5-6
- *Gramática viva*: Grammar Point 47: Saber vs. conocer
- IRCD: Chapter 5; pg. 184

Suggestion. Use visuals of well-known people to practice *saber* and *conocer*, for example, a picture of Bill Gates: *Yo sé quién es esta persona. Es Bill Gates. Sé que es muy rico y que su compañía se llama Microsoft. También sé que vive en una casa muy grande en el estado de Washington. Yo sé quién es, pero no lo conozco.*

Point out the irregular first person of both verbs. Remind students that a *c* has the sound of *k* when used with *o*. Point out the *z* (not *s*) in *conozco*.

ACENTOS

Sé, the **yo** form of the verb **saber,** has a written accent to distinguish it from the pronoun **se.**
Yo **sé** que su hermano **se** llama José.

¿Qué dice usted?

5-27 Un encuentro en un pasillo. Raúl, un estudiante nuevo en la universidad, necesita información, y le hace preguntas a Sergio, otro estudiante. Escoja la respuesta correcta para completar la conversación.

RAÚL: Soy un estudiante nuevo y no _____ donde está la librería.	(a.) sé	b. conozco
SERGIO: Es muy fácil. Tú _____ dónde está la cafetería, ¿no? Pues está al lado.	(a.) sabes	b. conoces
RAÚL: Gracias. ¿Y _____ si hay un club de español?	(a.) sabes	b. conoces
SERGIO: Sí, claro, y _____ que esta noche tiene una reunión.	(a.) sé	b. conozco
RAÚL: Magnífico. Sólo _____ a dos o tres compañeros de clase.	a. sé	(b.) conozco
SERGIO: Pues allí vas a _____ a muchos estudiantes.	a. saber	(b.) conocer

② **5-28 ¿Sabes quién es...?** Túrnense para preguntarle a su compañero/a si sabe quién es la persona mencionada y si la conoce.

MODELO: el actor principal de *Troya*
E1: ¿Sabes quién es el actor principal de *Troya?*
E2: Sí, sé quién es. Es Brad Pitt.
E1: ¿Lo conoces?
E2: No, no lo conozco. *o* Sí, lo conozco.

1. tu representante en el congreso
2. el/la decano/a de la facultad
3. el/la jefe/a (*boss*) de tu papá o de tu mamá
4. el rey de España
5. el/la presidente/a de Nicaragua
6. ...

Ⓖ **5-29 Adivina, adivinador.** En grupos pequeños, túrnense para leer las siguientes descripciones y adivinar de quién se habla.

MODELO: E1: Es una chica muy pobre que va a un baile. Allí conoce a un
príncipe, pero a las 12:00 de la noche ella debe volver a su casa.
E2: Sí, sé quién es. Es Cenicienta (*Cinderella*).

1. Es un gorila gigante con sentimientos (*feelings*) humanos. En una película aparece en el edificio Empire State de Nueva York. King Kong
2. Es una actriz y cantante puertorriqueña. Es joven, bonita y canta en inglés y español. En 2003, actuó con el actor Ben Affleck en la película *Una relación peligrosa.* Jennifer López
3. Es una diseñadora de ropa y joyas, hija de un famoso pintor español. Su perfume más famoso lleva su nombre. Paloma Picasso
4. Es un hombre de otro planeta con doble personalidad. Trabaja en un periódico, pero cuando se pone una ropa azul especial, puede volar (*fly*). Superman
5. Es un hombre joven y fuerte, educado por los gorilas en la jungla. Nada muy bien y su compañera se llama Jane. Tarzán
6. Fue (*She was*) una mujer muy importante en Argentina. Su esposo gobernó ese país por varios años. Hay un musical con su nombre y también una película donde Madonna la representa. Eva Perón/ *Evita*

Note for 5-28. Students should have no difficulty in understanding the cognates (e.g., *representante, congreso*). Other words may need some explanation, for example, *rey. En España hay un rey, Juan Carlos I. Su esposa es la reina Sofía* (bring pictures if possible). *Su hijo es el príncipe Felipe.*

Note for 5-29. There are three three preterit verb forms (*actuó, fue, gobernó*) in this activity. In the section on pronunciation in *Lección 2* of the Lab Manual, students were introduced to the effect of stress and the written accent in changing the tense of a verb. They should have no difficulty in understanding the sentences. There is a complete presentation of the preterit of regular verbs and the verbs *ir* and *ser* in *Lección 6.*

Note for 5-29. The new words *gigante, pintor, jungla* were not glossed since they can be considered cognates or near cognates. The context will help students guess their meaning.

Expansion for 5-29. Use gestures to clarify. *7. Es un animal de los dibujos animados. Es gris, corre muy rápido y tiene orejas muy largas (Bugs Bunny). 8. Es una chica muy bonita y buena que vive en el bosque con siete enanitos. Tiene una madrastra muy mala (Blancanieves).*

Follow up for 5-29. In pairs or groups of four, students prepare a description of a character or person. Then they read it aloud without saying who it is and the other students try to guess.

Suggestion for 5-30. Use visuals and personalized questions to elicit the use of *saber* + infinitive: *¿Sabe nadar esta persona? Y usted, ¿sabe nadar? ¿Sabe nadar muy bien?* Ask some students to name one thing they can do.

❷ 5-30 ¿Qué sabes hacer? Pregúntele a su compañero/a si sabe hacer las siguientes cosas. Si responde que sí, hágale más preguntas para obtener (*get*) más información.

MODELO: bailar música rock
E1: ¿Sabes bailar música rock?
E2: Sí, sé bailar música rock. *o* No, no sé bailar música rock. ¿Y tú?

1. tocar la guitarra
2. jugar al tenis
3. nadar
4. preparar tacos
5. cocinar platos muy elaborados
6. trabajar con computadoras
7. usar el microondas
8. ...

Suggestion for 5-31. You may ask students to consult the *Enfoque cultural* (pp. 197–198) or the WWW prior to doing this activity so they will be able to answer the questions on Central America.

5-31 Bingo. Para ganar el Bingo, usted debe llenar vertical, horizontal o diagonalmente tres casilleros (*boxes*) con los nombres de los/las compañeros/as que contestan afirmativamente las preguntas y dan la respuesta correcta.

¿Sabes dónde está la ciudad de Tegucigalpa? Honduras.	¿Sabes cuál es la capital de El Salvador? San Salvador.	¿Sabes dónde está la ciudad de Managua? Nicaragua.
¿Conoces a los padres de tu mejor amigo/a? Answers may vary.	¿Sabes cuál es la unidad monetaria de Nicaragua? El córdoba.	¿Sabes el nombre de un lago importante que está en Nicaragua? EL lago Nicaragua.
¿Sabes preparar platos centroamericanos? Answers may vary.	¿Conoces algún país hispanoamericano? Answers may vary.	¿Sabes dónde están las ruinas mayas de Copán? Honduras.

Suggestion for 5-32. You may wish to give examples of the use of the new words *entonces* and *tampoco*.

❷ 5-32 Saber y conocer. Complete con su compañero/a el siguiente diálogo con las formas correctas de **saber** y **conocer**.

E1: ¿_____Conoces_____ a esa chica?
E2: Sí, yo _____conozco_____ a todas las chicas aquí.
E1: Entonces, ¿_____sabes_____ dónde vive?
E2: No, no lo _____sé_____.
E1: Pero _____sabes_____ su número de teléfono, ¿verdad?
E2: No, tampoco lo _____sé_____.
E1: Y... ¿_____sabes_____ cómo se llama?
E2: Pues, la verdad es que no lo _____sé_____.
E1: ¿Cómo dices que la _____conoces_____? Tú no _____sabes_____ dónde vive, tú no _____sabes_____ su nombre.
E2: Es que tengo muy mala memoria.

 **SITUACIONES**

Your partner wants to set a blind date for you with his/her friend from Honduras but you want to have some information about the person before agreeing to a date. Using **saber** or **conocer**, ask your partner if he/she knows: a) the person's family, b) how old the person is, and c) how long he/she has known this person, d) from what part of Honduras he/she comes, and e) if he/she speaks English. Also, find out if the person knows how to play tennis, and if he/she likes to dance.

ALGO MÁS

VÍNCULOS

To practice more on adjectives
- SAM-OneKey: WB: 5-23, 5-24 / LM: 5-52
- Companion Website: AP 5-7
- IRCD: Chapter 5; pg. 187

More on adjectives

- Ordinal numbers are adjectives and agree in gender and number with the noun they modify (e.g., **la segunda casa, el cuarto edificio**). **Primero** and **tercero** drop the final **o** when used before a masculine singular noun.

  el **primer** cuarto   el **tercer** piso

- When **bueno** and **malo** precede masculine singular nouns, they are shortened to **buen** and **mal**.

  Es un **buen** edificio.   *It is a good building.*
  Es un **mal** momento para comprar. *It is a bad time to buy.*

- **Grande** shortens to **gran** when it precedes any singular noun. Note the meaning associated with each position.

  Es una casa **grande**.   *It is a big house.*
  Es una **gran** casa.   *It is a great house.*

¿Qué dice usted?

5-33 ¿En qué piso viven? Pregúntele a su compañero/a dónde viven las diferentes personas. Su compañero/a debe contestarle de acuerdo con el dibujo.

MODELO: E1: ¿Dónde viven los Girondo?
          E2: Viven en el cuarto piso, en el apartamento 4-A.

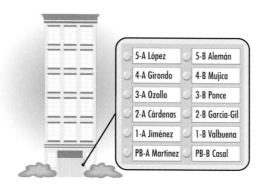

5-A López	5-B Alemán
4-A Girondo	4-B Mujica
3-A Ozollo	3-B Ponce
2-A Cárdenas	2-B García-Gil
1-A Jiménez	1-B Valbuena
PB-A Martínez	PB-B Casal

Suggestion for 5-33. Review the ordinal numbers by drawing a building on the chalkboard or using visuals to present the various floors. Ask questions to personalize: *¿Vive usted en un edificio de apartamentos? ¿En qué piso vive usted?*

5-34 Opiniones. Túrnense para explicar qué o quiénes son las siguientes personas y lugares. Después, den su opinión sobre cada uno. Usen algunas de las siguientes palabras.

buen	bueno/a	gran	grande	mal	malo/a	primer	primero/a

MODELO: el Parque El Imposible
          Es una gran reserva natural donde hay muchos animales en peligro de extinción. El Parque El Imposible está en El Salvador. Es muy grande y es una reserva natural muy importante de América Central.

1. el Parque Central
2. Antonio Banderas
3. la Casa Blanca
4. Daniel Ortega
5. el lago Nicaragua
6. ...

MOSAICOS

 Escuchar

Matching descriptions with pictures

You have already learned that you can understand what is being said by paying attention to the pictures or objects that people point or refer to. Sometimes these objects are around you, but sometimes they are not. For example, when you hear a description of somebody's house, an image of a house comes to your mind from your experience.

Antes de escuchar

5-35 La casa de los Esquivel. In **5-36,** you will listen to a description of a house. Before you listen, and using your knowledge of what houses look like, make a list of **four** rooms and **three objects** (furniture, appliances, accessories) you expect to hear about **in each** room.

PARTE DE LA CASA	OBJETOS
_____	_____
_____	_____
_____	_____
_____	_____

A escuchar

AUDIO **5-36** Now, look at the following drawing, and as you hear the different statements about the location of several pieces of furniture and objects, mark the appropriate column to indicate whether each of the statements is true (**Sí**) or false (**No**).

VÍNCULOS

For materials related to the Mosaicos section, see
• SAM-OneKey: WB: 5-25, 5-26, 5-27, 5-28, 5-29, 5-30 / LM: 5-53
• IRCD: Chapter 5; pp. 188, 189, 193

Audioscript for 5-36.

1. La casa de los Pérez Esquivel tiene dos dormitorios y un baño.
2. En la sala hay un televisor y un sofá grande.
3. En el comedor hay una alfombra.
4. Un dormitorio tiene una cama grande y dos mesas de noche.
5. En los baños de esta casa hay bañadera.
6. Hay cuadros en la sala y en el comedor.
7. La ventana del comedor no tiene cortinas.
8. La cocina está entre un dormitorio y el comedor.

	Sí	No
1.	____	X
2.	X	____
3.	____	X
4.	____	X
5.	X	____
6.	X	____
7.	____	X
8.	X	____

Después de escuchar

5-37 ¿Y tu casa? Ask each other these questions and compare your answers.

1. ¿Cómo es tu casa/apartamento? ¿Cuántos dormitorios tiene?
2. ¿Qué muebles hay en tu dormitorio?
3. ¿Qué electrodomésticos hay en tu casa/apartamento?

Antes de escuchar

5-38 Un apartamento cómodo. In **5-39**, you will listen to some descriptions of an apartment. Before you listen, look at the picture and in the lines below write down the number of bedrooms, bathrooms and closets this apartment has.

dormitorios __3__   baños __2__   armarios __3__

A escuchar

5-39 El apartamento. Now, you will listen to four different descriptions of this apartment. As you listen, mark the appropriate column to indicate whether the description is true (**Sí**) or false (**No**).

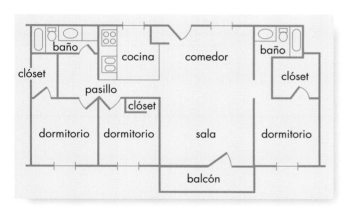

	Sí	No
1.		X
2.		X
3.	X	
4.		X

Audioscript for 5-39.

1. Este apartamento tiene un dormitorio, un baño y un balcón.
2. Este apartamento es muy cómodo porque tiene cinco dormitorios.
3. Este apartamento tiene tres dormitorios, tres armarios, dos baños, una cocina, una sala y un comedor.
4. No me gusta este apartamento porque no tiene balcón.

Después de escuchar

5-40 ¿Y usted? Imagine you buy the apartment of your dreams. Discuss where this apartment is located, how many bedrooms it has, and what furniture, appliances and conveniences the apartment has.

Conversar

Antes de conversar

5-41 Busco apartamento. Usted necesita alquilar un apartamento. En cada columna, escriba algunas características esenciales y algunas secundarias del apartamento que usted necesita.

CARACTERÍSTICAS ESENCIALES	CARACTERÍSTICAS SECUNDARIAS
_____	_____
_____	_____
_____	_____
_____	_____

Suggestion for 5-41. Ask students to review in advance the vocabulary related to the house on p. 167. You may wish to ask that students be as specific as possible as they write their lists. On a transparency, provide them with an example. As you explain, write under the corresponding column: *Para mí, el alquiler es esencial.* (Write down *alquiler*) *Busco un apartamento que no cueste mucho. También el color es muy importante. Deseo un apartamento de color...* (Write down *color*) *Los muebles y los electrodomésticos son esenciales también.* (Write down the names of some pieces of furniture). *Un garaje es esencial porque tengo un auto. Un balcón, un ascensor, aire acondicionado y dos baños son secundarios.*

As a follow-up you may wish to ask students to compare their lists in pairs. This will help them review vocabulary more thoroughly.

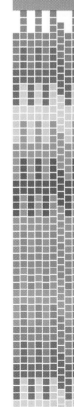

A conversar

5-42 Buscando vivienda (*housing*). Su mejor amigo/a (su compañero/a) siempre lee los anuncios de los periódicos. Llámelo/la por teléfono y hágale preguntas para obtener información sobre las características esenciales y secundarias del apartamento que usted busca. Puede usar las siguientes ideas. Su mejor amigo/a va a responder con información sobre **dos** apartamentos de los siguientes anuncios. Luego, cambien de papel.

- alquiler
- localización del apartamento
- piso en el edificio
- número de habitaciones y baños
- con muebles o sin muebles
- aire acondicionado/calefacción
- otras características esenciales para usted
- número de teléfono o dirección de contacto
- ¿?

ALQUILERES

Se alquila apartamento en zona céntrica, cuarto piso: amueblado, 2 habitaciones, 2 baños, 5.000 colones mensuales. Tfno. 2 33 14 78

Se arrienda apartamento espacioso para familia: quinto piso, ascensor, excelente ubicación, cerca de centros comerciales, sin muebles, 3 dormitorios, dos baños, aire acondicionado, jardín, garaje para dos autos. 6.500 colones. Tfno. 2 54 22 83

Alquilo apartamento cerca de centro comercial. Transporte público a la puerta. Ideal para profesionales. 1 dormitorio, 1 baño con jacuzzi, con muebles y electrodomésticos, terraza, sistema de seguridad, garaje doble. 7.500 colones. Tfno. 2 65 16 92

Se alquila habitación en casa particular. Amplia, cómoda, iluminada, enorme clóset, cable gratis. Se comparten cocina, baño y garaje. Muebles finos. Preferible mujer soltera. Tfno. 2 38 84 29

Suggestion for 5-42. Have students read the ads and exchange roles asking for information over the phone to a friend. You may wish to review the formulaic expressions used in phone conversations.

You may wish to review ways to describe different options, for example: *Hay un apartamento que cuesta... Tiene dos habitaciones, un baño. También hay otro apartamento que tiene una terraza y muebles finos.*

Suggestion for 5-43. You may wish to do **5-43** in class or outside of class. Again, you may provide students with a model.

Después de conversar

5-43 ¡Éste me gusta! Escríbale una breve nota a su mejor amigo/a para informarle sobre el apartamento que usted piensa alquilar. Explíquele por qué. Déle las gracias (*Thank him/her*) por su ayuda.

Fecha: _____, 200_____

De: _____

A: _____

Asunto: Mi nuevo apartamento

_____

_____

_____

_____

Adiós,

_____

Antes de conversar

5-44 La casa o apartamento ideal. Ustedes son un grupo de buenos amigos que piensan vivir juntos durante sus estudios universitarios. Piensen en su casa ideal y descríbanla. Incluyan la siguiente información en su descripción:

- la ciudad o pueblo (*town*) donde va a estar la casa
- los cuartos y comodidades (*comforts*) que la casa va a tener
- los muebles, los electrodomésticos, etc.
- la(s) persona(s) que va(n) a vivir en ella

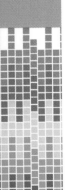

A conversar

5-45 Mi casa ideal en imágenes. Ahora hagan un dibujo (o un collage) de su casa ideal para compartirlo con la clase. Indiquen el número de cuartos, garajes, y para quién es cada cuarto. Especifiquen cómo va a ser la sala, el comedor, la cocina, etc.

Suggestion for 5-45. Take advantage of students with artistic skills. With the help of computer software, they may design very fancy homes for their group.

Después de conversar

5-46 Ésta es mi casa ideal. Preséntenle su casa ideal a la clase y respondan a sus preguntas.

 ## Leer

In this chapter, you will practice the following strategies to aid your reading comprehension in Spanish: 1. looking at visuals, and 2. informing yourself about a topic.

Looking at visuals in a written text enables foreign language readers to anticipate and comprehend the text message. Pictures, signs, schedules, charts, arrows, and color may provide you with essential information at a department store where you are doing shopping, a train station or an airport when traveling, etc.

Besides visuals, getting acquainted with a topic may greatly facilitate your comprehension. Imagine that you are planning to study in a Spanish-speaking country. Since, as you may know, most students usually do not live on campus, you are faced with the task of finding housing for yourself. Where do you start? How do you go about renting an apartment or a room? Should you seek help from a housing office on campus? What if there isn't one? Also, what commodities or basic needs should you expect when you rent an apartment or a room, for example: a private bathroom, a phone in your room, or one to share with someone else? The most efficient manner to accomplish this task is by informing yourself, by asking people, by reading about the topic in your own language, etc. Keep in mind the importance of visuals and of informing yourself as you read or before you read a text.

Guía de prelectura

Read the title of the article in activity **5-49** and answer the questions, using your knowledge of the topic.

1. Thinking of the theme of *Lección 5* and looking at the picture that accompanies the article, can you anticipate its content?
   a. The wide use of computers by women at home
   b. Technology at the service of humans at home
   c. Houses that communicate with human beings

2. The article contains some of the following ideas. Circle all that may apply, in your opinion. In case you miss some answers, you will be able to verify your responses later.
   a. Today's homes have nothing in common with those of the future.
   b. Future homes will be much more automated than those of today.
   c. Human beings will have much more free time due to the abundance of technology at home.
   d. Electrical appliances and electronic devices will duplicate their functions in the house of the future.

3. Now, use your background knowledge to comprehend the text. On what did you base your answers to question 2?
   a. The cognates in the title
   b. The photo that accompanies the article
   c. Your knowledge of technology

Answers for Guía de prelectura:
3. Answers may vary. However, you may expect students to answer a, b, c.

Antes de leer

Answers for 5-47.

1. Aparatos eléctricos: *lámpara*; Aparatos electrónicos: *computadora, fotocopiadora*
2. Aparatos eléctricos: *cafetera, aspiradora*; Aparatos electrónicos: *microondas*
3. Aparatos eléctricos: *ventilador*; Aparatos electrónicos: *aire acondicionado, sensor de temperatura*
4. Aparatos electrónicos: *teléfono inalámbrico*,
5. Aparatos electrónicos: *televisor, aparato de DVD*

5-47 Preparación. Muchas casas modernas tienen aparatos eléctricos y electrónicos. Clasifiquen los siguientes aparatos en la columna correspondiente.

sensor de temperatura	microondas	teléfono inalámbrico	ventilador (*fan*)
aire acondicionado	computadora	televisor	fotocopiadora
lámpara	aparato de DVD	aspiradora	cafetera

FUNCIÓN	APARATOS ELÉCTRICOS	APARATOS ELECTRÓNICOS
1. para trabajar desde (*from*) casa	_____	_____
2. para hacer trabajos domésticos	_____	_____
3. para controlar la temperatura de la casa	_____	_____
4. para comunicarse con otras personas	_____	_____
5. para entretenerse (*have fun*) en casa	_____	_____

Answers for 5-48. Answers may vary. Accept any responses that are logically supported.

5-48 Anticipación. Primera fase. Indique con una X las características que, según usted, va a tener la casa del futuro.

1. _____ múltiples dispositivos (mecanismos) para controlar la energía
2. _____ puertas automáticas
3. _____ sensores de temperatura y humedad
4. _____ sensores de voz (*voice*)
5. _____ sistema de seguridad activado por la voz
6. _____ música ambiental en todos los cuartos

Segunda fase. Ahora, comparen sus respuestas. ¿Están de acuerdo o no?

A leer

Answers for 5-49. 1. Answers may vary. Students may highlight the following words: *inteligentes, electrónicos, eléctricos, computadora, avances, dispositivos, sensores, funcionar, electrodomésticos, cafeteras, microondas, ventiladores, aire acondicionado, calefacción, aparatos, refrigeradores, Internet, red, mensajes electrónicos, servidores, banda ancha, almacenamiento;* 2. **AC**: *cafeteras, ventiladores, frigoríficos;* **EL**: *computadora, dispositivos, sensores, microondas, servidores*

5-49 Primera fase. El siguiente artículo describe la casa del futuro. Léalo y siga las instrucciones.

1. Pase un marcador (*highlighter*) por las palabras que se asocian con tecnología en cada párrafo.
2. Escriba **AC** si una palabra se refiere a un aparato eléctrico y **EL** si indica un aparato electrónico.

La casa inteligente del futuro

Las casas inteligentes o automatizadas ya existen en el presente. Los expertos las describen con un gran número de aparatos eléctricos y electrónicos —controlados por una computadora— que se comunican entre ellos. Pero, muchos se preguntan, ¿cuáles son las diferencias entre una casa tradicional y una inteligente?

Básicamente, la casa inteligente incorpora los últimos avances tecnológicos en beneficio de las personas que viven en ella. A través de complejos dispositivos y sensores, estas casas facilitan el trabajo doméstico de sus dueños: abren y cierran cortinas y puertas, hacen funcionar electrodomésticos (cafeteras, microondas, ventiladores, etc.), el aire acondicionado y la calefacción, por ejemplo.

Además, la casa inteligente ofrece un uso más eficiente y múltiple de los aparatos eléctricos y electrónicos en su interior. Un microondas se puede usar para calentar comida y también para ver televisión. De la misma manera, un refrigerador puede conectarse a Internet y permitir a una persona navegar por la red o enviar mensajes electrónicos.

Si a la familia le gusta escuchar música mientras descansa o mirar películas en su tiempo libre, basta conectar dispositivos de red a servidores con suficiente ancho de banda y capacidad de almacenamiento[1] como para distribuir música y películas a cada habitación de la casa.

En resumen, la casa del futuro es una versión técnicamente más sofisticada de la casa del presente. Es difícil predecir con exactitud cómo vamos a vivir en 50 años más. Sin embargo, muchos se preguntan si esta abundancia de tecnología va a afectar nuestra vida positiva o negativamente.

[1]*storage space*

Answers for 5-49, Segunda fase. 1. *Casas con un gran número de aparatos eléctricos y electrónicos —controlados por una computadora— que se comunican entre ellos. 2. La casa inteligente incorpora los últimos avances tecnológicos en beneficio de las personas que viven en ella. 3. Abren y cierran cortinas y puertas, hacen funcionar electrodomésticos (cafeteras, microondas, ventiladores, etc.), el aire acondicionado y la calefacción. 4. Answers will vary. 5. El ser humano debe conectar dispositivos de red a servidores con suficiente ancho de banda y capacidad de almacenamiento como para distribuir música y películas a cada habitación de la casa.*

Segunda fase. Lea el artículo otra vez y haga lo siguiente.

1. En el primer párrafo, el autor del artículo da una definición de una casa inteligente. Escriba la definición.
2. El segundo párrafo contrasta la casa inteligente con la casa tradicional. ¿Cuál es la diferencia? Escríbala.
3. El párrafo dos también indica algunas formas en que la casa inteligente ayuda a las personas que viven en ella. Indique una función útil para una persona de su familia. ¿Por qué es útil?
4. En el tercer párrafo, se mencionan algunas de las funciones múltiples de los aparatos eléctricos y electrónicos. ¿Cuál de estas funciones múltiples es más beneficiosa para un estudiante? ¿Por qué?
5. En el cuarto párrafo, el autor presenta un ejemplo que indica la superioridad del ser humano sobre la tecnología. Subraye el ejemplo.

2 5-50 Búsqueda (*Search*). Busquen en el artículo algunas palabras con las siguientes terminaciones y, luego, clasifíquenlas en la tabla: **-ado/a, -cia, -ción/-sión, -ar, -al, -ico, -dad, -mente.**

SUSTANTIVOS	ADJETIVOS	FORMAS VERBALES RELACIONADAS CON LA TECNOLOGÍA	ADVERBIOS
diferen**cias**, calefac**ción**,	automatiz**adas**, contro**ladas**,	funcion**ar**, us**ar**, calent**ar**,	técnica**mente**,
televi**sión**, capaci**dad**,	eléct**ricos**, electrón**icos**,	conect**ar(se)**, naveg**ar**, envi**ar**, etc.	negativa**mente**
habita**ción**, ver**sión**,	tradicion**al**, domést**ico**,		
abundan**cia**	acondicion**ado**		

Después de leer

5-51 Expansión. Lea la siguiente nota que el arquitecto de una casa inteligente le escribe a uno de sus colegas. Complete los espacios en blanco con la palabra adecuada.

urgentemente	funcionar	inteligente	ventanas	tecnológicos
ideal	construir	sensores	funciones	

Manolo,

¡Te tengo una gran sorpresa! Oscar de la Renta necesita (1) __urgentemente__ una casa (2) __inteligente__ en Managua. Como sabes, de la Renta es muy rico y quiere los últimos avances (3) __tecnológicos__ en ella. Desea una casa con dispositivos para abrir y cerrar puertas y (4) __ventanas__. También quiere incorporar electrodomésticos con (5) __funciones__ múltiples. Quiere calefacción controlada por (6) __sensores__. Tú sabes mucho de sistemas automatizados y yo de construcción, y pienso que eres la persona (7) __ideal__ para ayudarme en este proyecto. Vamos a (8) __construir__ una casa espectacular. Todo va a (9) __funcionar__ perfectamente.

Debemos responder pronto. Llámame.

Ricardo

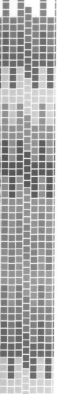

Escribir

In *Lección 4*, you practiced writing a letter to a family member older than you. You also paid attention to ways of addressing a family member and appropriate closings. Writing to the public at large is somewhat similar to writing to elders in your family. When you do not know your audience personally, you can do the following:

- Anticipate what your audience knows or may not know about the topic you are writing. Provide as much detail as necessary.

- Accommodate the language of your text to your audience. Use less technical language with an audience who is not an expert on the topic; be more technical with an expert audience.

- Use a more formal tone. In Spanish, a formal tone may be signaled, among others, by the use of the pronoun **Ud.**

In this chapter, you will write a descriptive pamphlet for a general, unknown audience. As you plan and write your pamphlet, keep in mind the amount of information and degree of formality of your text.

Antes de escribir

5-52 Preparación. Primera fase. En el siguiente panfleto, la Facultad de Arquitectura de la Universidad Católica de Honduras, en Tegucigalpa, invita a los alumnos a participar en el concurso (*contest*) ***La casa automatizada del futuro***. Lea los requisitos del concurso.

Departamento de Arquitectura
Universidad Católica de Honduras
Campus Tegucigalpa

Concurso: **La casa automatizada del futuro**

Bases del concurso:

Los participantes deben enviar la siguiente información por fax (233-2210) a la Facultad de Arquitectura, Campus Tegucigalpa:

1. una ficha con información personal: nombre completo, dirección, teléfono, facultad donde estudia y dirección de correo electrónico
2. una descripción de la casa automatizada con la siguiente información:
   a. tamaño de la casa (pies [feet] o metros cuadrados [square meters])
   b. número y nombre de las habitaciones
   c. aparatos eléctricos y electrónicos de la casa y sus funciones
   d. dispositivos y sensores y su(s) función(es)
3. si es posible, un dibujo o foto digital de la casa automatizada

Fecha límite: el 30 de marzo
Premio: Un semestre de estudios gratis en la Facultad de Arquitectura de la Universidad de Milán, Italia

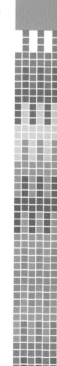

Segunda fase. Usted decide participar en el concurso con un proyecto excepcional. Para preparar su proyecto, haga lo siguiente:

1. Imagine la casa automatizada que usted desea construir.
   a. ¿Qué tamaño (*size*) tiene? Indíquelo en pies (*feet*) o metros cuadrados (*square meters*) ¿Qué cuartos va a tener esta casa? ¿Cuántas habitaciones, salas, terrazas, etc.? ¿Cuántos garajes, áticos, etc.?
   b. ¿Qué aparatos eléctricos y electrónicos va a tener? ¿Dónde va a estar cada uno de ellos?
   c. ¿Qué función(es) va a tener cada aparato eléctrico y electrónico? (Por ejemplo: Una aspiradora que limpia las alfombras y seca platos también.)
   d. Esta casa automatizada, ¿va a tener dispositivos y sensores? ¿Qué función(es) va a tener cada dispositivo y sensor? (Por ejemplo: ¿Un dispositivo para encender y apagar el televisor? ¿Un sensor que determina la calidad del aire dentro de la casa?)

2. ¿Sabe usted dibujar? Dibuje con lápiz o digitalmente su casa automatizada.

A escribir

5-53 Manos a la obra. Ahora prepare su descripción de *La casa automatizada del futuro* para el comité que selecciona a los ganadores (*winners*). Use sus ideas de la **Segunda fase** de la actividad **5-48**. Recuerde incluir toda la información que pide el concurso.

Después de escribir

Suggestion for 5-54. If Activity **5-53** has been done in pairs, then you may ask that students exchange the first draft of the description with another pair. If the activity has been done individually, then have each student submit his/her project to a peer editor.

5-54 Revisión. Antes de presentar su proyecto, revise:

- primero, la claridad de sus ideas y la cantidad de información dada
- luego, la precisión gramatical (el vocabulario común y corriente y el vocabulario más técnico, la estructuras que utiliza para describir, la concordancia, etc.)
- finalmente, la ortografía y la acentuación

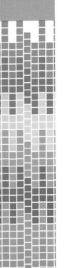

ENFOQUE CULTURAL

TEMAS: LAS CASAS Y LA ARQUITECTURA

Para pensar

¿Vive Ud. en un apartamento o en una casa? ¿Cómo es, grande
o pequeño/a? ¿Moderno/a o antiguo/a? ¿Hay apartamentos/casas
semejantes al/a la suyo/a en su vecindario? ¿Dónde está su casa
o apartamento, cerca del centro de la ciudad o en las afueras?

*Hay mucha variedad de viviendas
en los países hispanoamericanos.
En esta foto se ve la influencia de la
época colonial. Se puede admirar
una casa con hermosos balcones de
madera, grandes patios interiores,
azulejos* (tiles) *en los pisos y paredes
y bellas rejas* (iron work) *exteriores.*

*En algunos lugares se puede ver la influencia de la
cultura española y las culturas precolombinas en
la arquitectura.*

Para contestar

2 **Las casas.** Con su
compañero/a responda a
las siguientes preguntas:

*Generalmente no hay gran variedad de
electrodomésticos en las casas, debido
principalmente a su alto costo pero también a la
posibilidad de tener empleados que ayudan con las
tareas domésticas.*

1. ¿Cómo son las casas
   coloniales? ¿Hay casas de estilo colonial en su vecindario?
2. ¿Qué electrodomésticos hay en su casa? ¿Cuáles probablemente se pueden
   encontrar en la mayoría de las casas hispanoamericanas, según ustedes?
   ¿Por qué?
3. En España e Hispanoamérica, ¿en qué lugares de la casa pasa más tiempo
   conversando o tomando algo la familia?

G **Riqueza cultural.** En grupos de tres, describan cómo es su casa ideal, usando la
información de **Las casas y la arquitectura**.

*En España e Hispanoamérica,
la familia pasa mucho tiempo
conversando, tomando un refresco
en el patio o jardín o viendo
televisión en la sala de su casa.*

Esta canción es un ejemplo de "punta rock", una música regional bailable de Centroamérica en la cual se toca la marimba, un instrumento típico del oeste de África.

¡Prepárese!

5-57 Música regional. ¿Qué ejemplos de música "regional" de su país o de otros conoce? ¿Por qué se considera regional?

¡Escuche!

5-58 La canción. Mientras escucha *Marimba con punta* complete las siguientes estrofas de la canción con las palabras de la lista.

chicas	discotecas	ritmo	gorditos	rico	verano
ricos	sabroso	cocineros	casa	muchachos	

Este es un _____ _____
que el mundo lo baila ya.
[...]
Que el mundo entero lo baila ya.
Lo bailan los _____
_____ y pobres, ¡Qué _____ está!
Bailamos flacos, _____
altos, bajitos, ¡Oye mamá!

Todos en este _____
Se apresuran a bailar.
Todos en este verano
se apresuran a bailar.

Las _____ que hay en la playa
con los _____ la gozarán
otros lo bailan en _____,
en _____ en cualquier lugar.

5-59 La letra. Ahora conteste en español las siguientes preguntas, según la letra de la canción.

1. ¿Cómo es el ritmo de esta canción?
2. ¿Quién baila "punta rock"?

3. ¿Cuándo lo baila(n)?
4. ¿Dónde lo baila(n)?

¡Responda!

5-60 Expresiones con tener. Imagínese que usted y sus amigos están en una fiesta donde están tocando y bailando "punta rock" hasta muy tarde en la noche. Indique con una cruz (X) qué expresiones con **tener** pueden usar Uds. para describir cómo se sienten al final de la fiesta.

_____ tener hambre   _____ tener prisa
_____ tener sed   _____ tener cuidado
_____ tener frío   _____ tener sueño
_____ tener calor   _____ tener suerte
_____ tener miedo   _____ tener razón

5-61 Nosotros tenemos... Ahora escriba cinco oraciones completas y lógicas en español usando algunas de las expresiones de arriba y los sujetos siguientes.

1. mis amigos
2. yo
3. mis amigos y yo

4. los músicos
5. todo el mundo (*Everybody*)

Suggestion. You may wish to clarify some of the vocabulary prior to students listening to the song. You may also clarify that *flaco* is another word for expressing *delgado*.

VOCABULARIO*

En una casa

el aire acondicionado	air conditioning
el armario	closet, armoire
el baño	bathroom
la barbacoa	barbecue
la basura	garbage, trash
la calefacción	heating
el césped	lawn
la chimenea	fireplace
la cocina	kitchen
el comedor	dining room
el cuarto/dormitorio	bedroom
el garaje	garage
el jardín	backyard, garden
la piscina	swimming pool
el piso	floor
la planta baja	first floor
la sala	living room
la terraza	terrace

Muebles y accesorios

la alfombra	carpet, rug
la butaca	armchair
la cama	bed
la cómoda	dresser
la cortina	curtain
el cuadro	picture
el espejo	mirror
la lámpara	lamp
la mesa de noche	night stand
el sofá	sofa

Electrodomésticos

la aspiradora	vacuum cleaner
la lavadora	washer
el lavaplatos	dishwasher
el (horno) microondas	microwave oven
el/la radio	radio
el refrigerador	refrigerator
la secadora	dryer

Para la cama

la almohada	pillow
la manta	blanket
la sábana	sheet

En el baño

la bañadera	tub
la ducha	shower
el inodoro	toilet
el lavabo	washbowl, bathroom sink
la toalla	towel

En la cocina

la estufa	stove
el fregadero	kitchen sink
el plato	dish, plate

Lugares

las afueras	outskirts
allá	over there
allí	there
el apartamento	apartment
aquí	here
el barrio	neighborhood
el centro	downtown, center
cerca (de)	near (close to)
el edificio	building
lejos (de)	far (from)

Descripciones

limpio/a	clean
ordenado/a	tidy
seco/a	dry
sucio/a	dirty

Verbos

ayudar	to help
barrer	to sweep
cocinar	to cook
conocer (zc)	to know, to meet
cortar	to cut
creer	to believe
doblar	to fold
limpiar	to clean
ordenar	to tidy up
pasar la aspiradora	to vacuum
planchar	to iron
preparar	to prepare
recoger (j)	to pick up
regar (ie)	to water
regresar	to come back
saber	to know
secar	to dry
sentir (ie, i)	to feel
tender (ie)	to hang (clothes); to make (a bed)

Palabras útiles

¡Claro!	of course
el perro	dog

*For expressions with **tener**, see page 174
**For direct object pronouns, see page 176
***For demonstrative adjectives and pronouns, see pages 181–2
****For ordinal numbers, see page 187

6

LA ROPA Y LAS TIENDAS

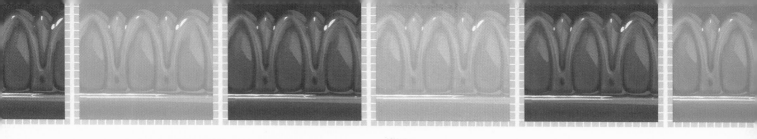

Objetivos comunicativos

- Talking about clothing and shopping
- Asking for and telling prices
- Expressing measurements
- Expressing likes and dislikes
- Expressing satisfaction and dissatisfaction
- Expressing opinions

Contenido

A primera vista

- La ropa
- De compras

Explicación y expansión

- Preterit tense of regular verbs
- Preterit of *ir* and *ser*
- Indirect object nouns and pronouns
- The verb *dar*
- *Gustar* and similar verbs
- Algo Más: More uses of *por* and *para*

Mosaicos

- Escuchar: Taking notes to recall important information
- Conversar: Haggling; determining what clothing is appropriate in a particular context
- Leer: Finding specific information to accomplish a task; identifying word endings that indicate places where certain products are sold or services rendered
- Escribir: Writing a letter of complaint to a store; narrating chronologically

Enfoque cultural

- Temas: De compras en el mundo hispano
- Vistas: Venezuela
  Para investigar en Internet
- Fortunas: Episodio 6
- Notas: Caminito de Guarenas, *Orquesta Billo's Caracas Boys*

Vocabulario

La ropa

... de mujer

Suggestions. You may use the Image Resource CD when doing this activity to talk about articles of clothing. Identify and describe each piece. Ask questions to check comprehension. Describe the clothes you're wearing and then personalize by commenting on similar items worn by students: *¿De qué color es el vestido de...? Es bonita la blusa de..., ¿no?* Use some expressions such as *de lunares* and *de color entero/un solo color* to make your description of clothing more interesting.

Pretend you are going on a trip; bring a packed backpack or suitcase to class and identify each item of clothing as you remove it. Follow up by having students identify items.

Describe a student's clothing without mentioning his or her name. Other students guess who the person is.

As necessary, you may introduce additional vocabulary such as: *ropa interior, de manga corta (larga), bolsillo, de tacón alto.*

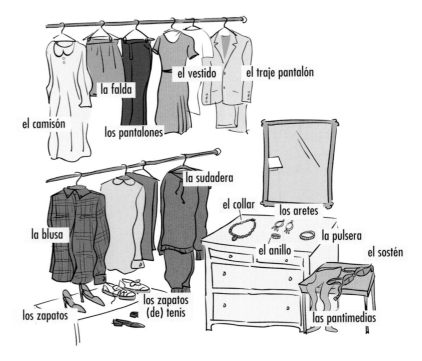

... de hombre

Las estaciones y la ropa

En el **invierno hace frío**. ¿Qué ropa **llevamos**?

el suéter · los guantes · la chaqueta · las botas · el abrigo · la bufanda

Y cuando **hace calor** en el **verano**, ¿qué **nos ponemos** para ir a la playa?

las gafas de sol · la gorra · el sombrero · el traje de baño · los pantalones cortos · las sandalias

En la **primavera** y el **otoño llueve mucho**.

el impermeable · el paraguas

¿Qué dice usted?

6-1 ¿Cuándo se usa? Asocie cada prenda de vestir de la columna de la izquierda con una situación o un lugar de la columna de la derecha.

1. __e__ los guantes
2. __c__ las gafas de sol
3. __b__ el piyama
4. __a__ la bata
5. __f__ el impermeable
6. __d__ el traje de baño

a. después de bañarse y antes de vestirse
b. para ir a dormir
c. para ver cuando hace mucho sol
d. en la piscina o en la playa
e. en los lugares fríos durante el invierno
f. cuando llueve

Note. Weather related terms are formally introduced in *Lección 7*.

Suggestions. Use visuals and/or the Image Resource CD to illustrate weather expressions and the clothes people wear. You may tell students what you wear in the wintertime: *En el invierno, yo llevo un suéter y una falda. Cuando hace mucho frío me pongo un abrigo y unos guantes. A veces llevo una bufanda.* Ask yes/no and either/or questions to check understanding. Personalize by asking students what they wear and do in winter. Contrast by asking what they do and wear in summer.

You may wish to point out the following regional variations:
medias (both stockings and socks)
aretes = pendientes, pantallas
cartera = billetera
playeras = zapatos de tenis
piyama/pijama/payama
bolso = bolsa, cartera
jersey (Spain) = *suéter*
cachucha (Mexico) = *gorra*
chamarra (Mexico) = *chaqueta*
traje = flux (Venezuela).

VÍNCULOS

To practice vocabulario—la ropa & de compras
• SAM-OneKey: WB: 6-1, 6-2, 6-3, 6-4 / LM: 6-26, 6-27, 6-28, 6-29
• Companion Website: AP 6-1, AP 6-2
• IRCD: Chapter 6; pp. 207, 209, 210, 211, 212

2 **6-2 ¿Qué deben llevar estas personas? Primera fase.** Escriban el nombre de dos prendas de vestir y un accesorio que se asocian con las siguientes ocasiones.

1. una graduación: ———————————————————————
2. un partido de tenis: ———————————————————————
3. un día de reparaciones en casa: ———————————————————————
4. una reunión con el decano de la facultad: ———————————————————————

Expansion for 6-2, Segunda fase. 7. Unos estudiantes van a ir a Alaska en diciembre. 8. Alicia va a cenar por primera vez en casa de los padres de su novio. 9. Unos jóvenes piensan jugar voleibol por la tarde. 10. Dos muchachas van a pasar el fin de semana en la playa.

2 **Segunda fase.** Ahora, digan (*say*) qué deben llevar estas personas, de acuerdo con las situaciones.

MODELO: Raúl y Rosa van a ir a una fiesta en casa del rector de la universidad.
E1: Raúl debe llevar pantalones, una camisa y una corbata.
E2: Rosa debe llevar un vestido o un traje pantalón y una blusa.

1. Dos estudiantes van a ir a un picnic.
2. Una chica y un chico tienen una entrevista para un trabajo en una oficina.
3. Dos mujeres van a un desfile de modas de la diseñadora Carolina Herrera.
4. Pedro va a jugar tenis con unos amigos, y Carmen va a visitar a sus parientes.
5. Los Sres. Montes van a ir a un té muy elegante en la Embajada de Venezuela.
6. El Sr. Jiménez y su esposa van a trabajar en el jardín de su casa.

2 **6-3 Vacaciones en Venezuela. Primera fase.** Usted y su amigo/a van a pasar sus vacaciones en Venezuela. Primero escojan el plan que más les interesa de las siguientes opciones.

1. Quince días en la isla Margarita. Por el día: ir a la playa; por la noche: ir a las discotecas.
2. Tomar un curso de verano en la Universidad de Caracas. Por la mañana: clases de español; por las tardes: lugares de interés turístico.
3. Explorar la fauna y flora de la región de Canaima. Por el día: caminar mucho; por las noches: estar en un campamento.

EN DIRECTO

To suggest something different:
¿Y qué te parece(n) un suéter/ zapatos de tenis? (*And how about . . .*)

To praise someone for a good suggestion:
¡Buena/Excelente/Fabulosa idea!

Suggestions for 6-3. You may show *Isla Margarita* on a map and explain to the students that it is an island in the Caribbean, north of Venezuela, and that Canaima is in the western part of Venezuela. You may also mention that the highest waterfall in the world, *El salto del Ángel*, is there.

Students could expand their lists by describing the items. Have students plan a trip in another season, focusing on the different articles of clothing they will need.

Segunda fase. Ahora, preparen una lista de la ropa y/o accesorios que van a necesitar de acuerdo con el plan que seleccionaron en la **Primera fase.**

PLAN # ____	YO	MI COMPAÑERO/A
por la mañana		
por la tarde		
por la noche		

Tercera fase. Informen al resto de la clase sobre sus **planes** y la ropa y accesorios que van a necesitar.

MODELO: Mi compañero/a y yo vamos a ir a la ciudad venezolana de Mérida. Yo necesito unos zapatos de tenis para caminar por la ciudad. Mi compañero/a necesita unos pantalones cortos. También necesitamos un traje para salir por las noches.

De compras

AUDIO ... a lo moderno

Un **centro comercial** moderno donde
venden de todo. Hay ropa para la familia,
muebles, accesorios y **electrodomésticos**
para la casa, **juguetes** para los niños y, en
algunos **almacenes**, a veces también hay
hasta un **supermercado.**

DEPENDIENTA: **¿En qué puedo servirle?**

CLIENTE: Quisiera comprar un
regalo para una muchacha
joven. Un **bolso** o una
billetera, por ejemplo.

DEPENDIENTA: Hay unos bolsos **de cuero**
preciosos y no son muy
caros. Enseguida le
muestro los que tenemos.

(La dependienta trae unos bolsos.)

CLIENTE: Me gustaría comprar éste,
pero no puedo **gastar**
mucho. ¿Cuánto cuesta?

DEPENDIENTA: Sólo vale 45.000 bolívares.
El precio es muy bueno.

CLIENTE: Sí, no es mucho dinero.

DEPENDIENTA: Y están muy **de moda.**
Las chicas jóvenes los
llevan mucho.

CLIENTE: Bueno, lo voy a
comprar.

DEPENDIENTA: Muy bien, señor.
¿Va a pagar con
tarjeta de crédito
o en **efectivo**?

CLIENTE: En efectivo.

A INVESTIGAR

¿Sabe usted en qué país el
bolívar es la moneda oficial?
Averigüe cuál es el equivalente
de 90.000 bolívares en
dólares.

LENGUA

To soften requests, Spanish
uses the forms **me gustaría**
(instead of **me gusta**) and
quisiera (instead of **quiero**).
English does this by adding
would.

Me gustaría/Quisiera ir a esa
tienda. *I would like to go to
that store.*

Suggestions. Use visuals and comprehensible input to introduce *escaparate* and some of the vocabulary in the dialog (*talla, probarse, quedar bien/mal, cambiar*). Have students enact the dialog in pairs, then have them exchange roles and create a similar dialog, substituting some elements in it. Also personalize: *¿Se prueba Ud. la ropa en las tiendas? ¿Va a las tiendas cuando hay rebajas? ¿Cuál es su tienda favorita? ¿Qué talla usa?*

You may explain that the approximate equivalent of size 38 is an 8. Sizes 40, 42, and 44 are similar to sizes 10, 12, and 14 respectively.

Suggestion. Discuss shopping at markets. **AUDIO** Introduce the word *regatear* (*haggling*) and give examples. Then have students work in pairs, pretending they want to buy something and bargaining to reduce the price. Students will get more practice haggling in activities 6-32 and 6-33.

Note. Argentina, Paraguay, and Uruguay are known for their leather goods. In Bolivia, Peru, Ecuador, and Guatemala, one can find beautiful Indian weavings. There are excellent wines in Chile and Argentina. Some countries are known for their quality stones and silver work: Colombia for its emeralds and Peru and Mexico for silver. Isla Margarita in Venezuela is known for its miniature handicrafts.

AUDIO **... a lo tradicional**

Muchas personas prefieren ir de compras a los **mercados** al aire libre. En estos mercados venden productos como comida, ropa, aparatos electrónicos, etc. Otras personas prefieren ir a los **centros comerciales** o a las **megatiendas**.

Telas y diseño

MARTA: Las **rebajas** son magníficas. Mira esa chaqueta. Está **rebajada** de 120.000 bolívares a 90.000. ¿Por qué no vemos si tienen tu **talla**?

ANA: Sí, y **me pruebo** la chaqueta para ver si **me queda** bien. Uso la talla 38 y a veces es difícil encontrarla. Esta chaqueta está **muy barata** y es **preciosa**.

MARTA: O te pruebas la chaqueta en casa y si te queda mal, la **cambias**. (Entran en la tienda.)

ANA: Buenos días; señorita, **quisiera** probarme esa chaqueta en la talla 38.

DEPENDIENTA: Lo siento, pero las únicas tallas que **nos quedan** son más grandes, la 42 y la 44.

ANA: ¡Qué lástima! Gracias.

Le queda estrecha.

Le queda ancha.

Suggestion. Present vocabulary by commenting on articles of clothing students are wearing: *Pedro lleva una camisa de cuadros. Es muy bonita. Y Juan, ¿lleva una camisa de cuadros? No, es de rayas. Le queda muy bien. No le queda ancha. Y a Pedro, ¿le queda ancha? ¿Le queda estrecha?*

Note: *apretado/a* is also used for "tight."

¿Qué dice usted?

6-4 ¡Lo mejor (*The best*)! Asocie las afirmaciones de la columna de la izquierda con una terminación lógica de la columna de la derecha.

1. __c__ Elisa necesita una falda en la talla 12. La tienda tiene la talla 10.
2. __a__ Raúl quiere regalarle un suéter de buena calidad a su mejor amigo.
3. __e__ Mamá prefiere las telas naturales. No va a comprar esa blusa.
4. __f__ Nos gustaría ver zapatos finos.
5. __b__ Quisiera una camisa elegante para mi graduación.
6. __d__ Necesito unos vaqueros a la moda.

a. Quisiera uno de lana fina.
b. Una de un solo color, por favor.
c. No la va a comprar porque le queda estrecha.
d. Los prefiero azules y anchos.
e. Es de nilón.
f. Solamente de cuero.

❷ 6-5 El cumpleaños de Nuria. Ustedes van a una tienda para comprarle un regalo a una buena amiga, pero cada artículo que ven presenta un problema. Analicen cada problema y piensen en la solución.

ARTÍCULO	PROBLEMA	SOLUCIÓN
collar	es muy caro	Debemos buscar uno rebajado/más barato.
impermeable	le queda ancho	
vaqueros	son de poliéster	
sudadera	es pequeña	
blusa	las rayas son muy anchas	
bolso	no es de cuero	
falda	le queda estrecha	

Suggestions for 6-5. To help students' speech sound more natural, you may wish to review with them ways to express agreement/disagreement as they work together to find solutions to the problems presented in the chart.

Start by brainstorming and writing on the board students' suggestions for gifts, especially clothes and accessories. Then, brainstorm kinds of problems shoppers face.

While doing the activity, encourage students to be creative and expand on their answers: *En el almacén El Encanto hay unos collares muy bonitos. ¿Por qué no miramos los collares allá?* Have them think of other gifts and come to a conclusion: *¿Le vamos a regalar un suéter? ¿Le interesan las sandalias? ¿Qué le vamos a dar?* You may wish to have students do this exercise in groups of three or four.

Follow-up for 6-6. Ask students to estimate the price of various other items of clothing, selecting some of the less-frequently used words. Follow up by asking if they have such an item and, if so, when and where they wear it. Ask them to name a store where it can be purchased: *¿Cuánto cuestan las gafas de sol? ¿Usted las usa? ¿Dónde y cuándo las usa? ¿Dónde las compró?*

Variation for 6-6. If time allows, recycle vocabulary for school supplies and household items. Follow the questioning pattern as shown in the model, asking how much an item costs, if the student has one, where/when he/she uses it, and where he/she purchased it.

Note. You may want to practice some preterit *yo* forms before this activity if students have not read the *Explicación y expansión* section on the preterit: *Yo compré este cinturón en septiembre. Pagué sólo $10.* Contrast *compro* and *compré.*

2 6-6 **¿Cuánto cuesta/n... ?** Su compañero/a le va a preguntar el precio de algunos de los artículos que aparecen en el siguiente dibujo. Contéstele que usted tiene el mismo artículo y dígale cuánto pagó. Dé una breve descripción y diga cuándo lo usa. Después cambien de papel.

MODELO:　　E1: ¿Cuánto cuesta/vale la bufanda?
　　　　　　　E2: Cuesta/Vale 6.000 bolívares.
　　　　　　　E1: ¡Qué cara!
　　　　　　　E2: Sí, está cara. Yo tengo una igual y pagué 5.000. Es de seda y la uso mucho en el invierno.
　　　　　　　E1: ¿Dónde la compraste?
　　　　　　　E2: En... ¿Por qué no vamos allí?

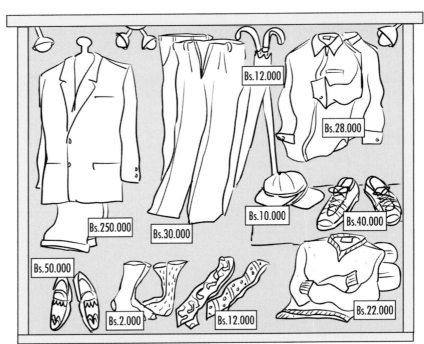

2 **6-7 Unos regalos.** Cada uno de ustedes debe hacer unos regalos. Primero, escojan A o B. Lean los anuncios de abajo. Luego explíquele a su compañero/a para quiénes son los regalos. Su compañero/a le va a dar algunas ideas de qué comprar y el lugar donde puede comprar, según la información de los anuncios.

A. REGALOS PARA	B. REGALOS PARA
1. un sobrino que tiene cinco años	1. un hermano que va a pasar unos días en el Caribe
2. su mamá para el Día de la Madre	2. su padre para su cumpleaños
3. un/a amigo/a que necesita ropa informal	3. su novio/a para el Día de los enamorados

Note for 6-7. A *guayabera* is a short or long-sleeved man's shirt often worn in place of a shirt or a coat and tie in areas where the weather is very hot.

6-8 Vestuario apropiado. Primera fase. Imagínese que usted es un/a experto/a en moda. Usted les da recomendaciones a sus clientes sobre la ropa apropiada para las diferentes ocasiones. Escriba algunas preguntas que usted les hace normalmente a sus clientes para ayudarlos.

MODELO: ¿Dónde va a ser la recepción? *o* ¿La recepción va a ser en un club elegante o en una casa de familia?

Para saber...

1. la hora del evento/ de la actividad
2. el tipo de personas que van a asistir al evento/ a la actividad
3. la ropa que la persona piensa/va a llevar
4. los accesorios que la persona tiene
5. cómo va a llegar la persona al lugar del evento/ de la actividad
6. ¿...?

Suggestion for 6-8. Segunda fase. Each student should play the role of the designer and the client.

Have students bring in magazine photos of the outfits they, as designers, would like to sell to their customers. In small groups, instruct them to present their item by describing it completely: size, color, fabric, sizes available, price. One member of the group could be the customer and pretend to try the outfit on, commenting on whether he/she likes it, how it fits, etc. Guide the conversation by suggesting that the customer ask questions such as *¿Me queda bien? ¿Me queda bien este color? ¿Lo/La debo comprar?* If time allows, test your students' ability to sell something that they do not want anymore: an old car, their Spanish book, a pair of worn jeans, etc.

Follow-up for 6-8. Segunda fase. Tell students that the designer has a newspaper column in which he/she answers e-mails. Have the clients send e-mails to the designers explaining the event they have to attend and asking for advice. The designer should reply via e-mail.

Warm-up for 6-9. As a pre-listening activity, have students get in groups of four and describe the clothes they wear for these events: parties, classes, family reunions, weddings, graduations.

Audioscript for 6-9. Conversación 1 BERTA: Alfredo, dime una cosa ¿vas a la fiesta en la embajada esta noche? ALFREDO: Sí. Tú también vas, ¿verdad? BERTA: Sí, y no sé qué me voy a poner. Supongo que es formal. ALFREDO: Sí, es formal. Yo voy a ir con un traje azul y mi hermana va a llevar un traje de la diseñadora Carolina Herrera, sencillo pero elegante. BERTA: ¡Qué bien! Yo no sé todavía qué me voy a poner. ¿Y a qué hora van a ir? ALFREDO: A las nueve más o menos. BERTA: Bueno, nos vemos entonces.

② Segunda fase. Uno/a de ustedes va a hacer el papel de cliente/a, y va a describir la ropa que piensa llevar para una ocasión especial. El/la experto/a le hace preguntas y recomendaciones sobre qué ropa es más apropiada para el evento/ la ocasión.

MODELO: Una recepción a las 8:00 en un hotel
E1: El sábado próximo tengo que ir con mi esposo a una recepción en un hotel. Tengo un vestido negro corto muy bonito. ¿Es apropiado para la ocasión?
E2: Un vestido negro siempre es apropiado para una recepción, especialmente en el invierno. ¿Tiene un collar y unos aretes bonitos?
E1: Sí, tengo un collar y una pulsera muy bonitos.
E2: Va a necesitar un bolso pequeño y zapatos del mismo color del bolso.
E1: ¡Excelente idea! Mil gracias.

1. una invitación a un picnic con varias celebridades del mundo de la política
2. una cena de gala con el cónsul/embajador de Venezuela
3. la graduación de su mejor amigo/a
4. un crucero por el Mediterráneo
5. la primera cita (*date*) con un/a chico/a que a usted le gusta

6-9 Ropa para cada ocasión. You will listen to a brief conversation regarding the clothes people will wear for an event. Before you listen, list what you would wear on the following occasions.

Fiesta elegante _____
Fiesta informal _____

Now as you listen to the conversation, write a check mark next to the appropriate clothes and to the event mentioned.

ROPA	EVENTO
__X__ ropa elegante	_____ entrevista de trabajo
_____ falda y chaqueta	_____ reunión de jóvenes
_____ traje pantalón y blusa	_____ excursión de fin de semana
_____ pantalones cortos y camiseta	__X__ fiesta formal

1. Preterit tense of regular verbs

Spanish has two simple tenses to express the past: the preterit and the imperfect (**el pretérito y el imperfecto**). Use the preterit to talk about past events, actions, and conditions that are viewed as completed or ended.

	HABLAR	COMER	VIVIR
yo	hablé	comí	viví
tú	hablaste	comiste	viviste
Ud., él, ella	habló	comió	vivió
nosotros/as	hablamos	comimos	vivimos
vosotros/as	hablasteis	comisteis	vivisteis
Uds., ellos/as	hablaron	comieron	vivieron

- Note that the **nosotros** form of the preterit of -ar and -ir verbs is the same as the present **nosotros** form. Context will help you determine if it is present or past.

  Llegamos a la tienda a las tres.   *We arrive at the store at three.*
      We arrived at the store at three.

- Stem-changing -ar and -er verbs in the present do not change in the preterit.

  pensar: pensé, pensaste, pensó, pensamos, pensasteis, pensaron
  volver: volví, volviste, volvió, volvimos, volvisteis, volvieron

- Verbs ending in -car and -gar have a spelling change in the **yo** form to show how the word is pronounced. The spelling change of verbs ending in -zar (**empecé**) shows that Spanish rarely uses a z before e or i.

  sacar: saqué, sacaste, sacó...
  llegar: llegué, llegaste, llegó...
  empezar: empecé, empezaste, empezó...

- Some expressions that you can use with the preterit to denote past time are:

anoche	*last night*
anteayer	*day before yesterday*
ante(a)noche	*night before last*
ayer	*yesterday*
el año/mes pasado	*last year/month*
la semana pasada	*last week*

Suggestion. Begin by describing what you generally do each morning. Then, to contrast, mention how today differed from the routine: *Normalmente desayuno en casa, pero hoy desayuné en la cafetería. Generalmente tomo té, pero hoy tomé un café y conversé con unos estudiantes* (write preterit forms on the board or a transparency). *Después caminé a mi oficina y hablé por teléfono.* Ask questions to check understanding and then ask personal questions using the verb forms on the board: *¿Tomó usted café en el desayuno? Y usted, ¿tomó café o té? ¿Desayunó en casa o en un café?* If necessary, point to the verb forms on the board. Afterwards, repeat information provided by students using the *él/ella* verb form: *Pedro tomó té, pero Arturo tomó café.*

VÍNCULOS

To practice preterit tense of regular verbs
- SAM-OneKey: WB: 6-5, 6-6, 6-7 / LM: 6-30, 6-31, 6-32
- Companion Website: AP 6-3
- *Gramática viva:* Grammar Point 39: Preterit tense of regular verbs + regular verbs with spelling changes
- IRCD: Chapter 6; pg. 215

ACENTOS

The **yo** and the **Ud., él/ella** preterit verb forms are stressed on the last syllable and end in a vowel. Therefore, they carry a written accent: **hablé, comí, viví, habló, comió, vivió.**

2. Preterit of *ir* and *ser*

IR AND SER			
yo	**fui**	nosotros/as	**fuimos**
tú	**fuiste**	vosotros/as	**fuisteis**
Ud., él, ella	**fue**	Uds., ellos/as	**fueron**

Suggestion. Mention places that you went to last weekend, writing *fui* on the board. Ask students if they went to the same places: ¿*Fue usted a...?* (write *fue* on the board). Point out that the lack of accent marks is due to the fact that monosyllabic words normally do not have an accent mark unless they are written exactly alike, but have a different meaning and grammatical function: *dé* (of the verb *dar*) vs. *de* (preposition). You may use visuals showing various places to elicit answers and practice other verb forms.

VÍNCULOS

To practice preterit of *ir* and *ser*
- SAM-OneKey: WB: 6-8, 6-9 / LM: 6-33, 6-34
- Companion Website: AP 6-4
- *Gramática viva:* Grammar Point 38: Preterit tense of irregular verbs *ser, ir, tener, estar*
- IRCD: Chapter 6; pg. 216

Ir and **ser** have identical forms in the preterit. Context will help determine the meaning.

Ernesto **fue** a la tienda.   *Ernesto went to the store.*
Fue vendedor en esa tienda.   *He was a salesman at that store* (for some time).

¿Qué dice usted?

6-10 Ayer yo... Primera fase. Marque cuáles fueron sus actividades ayer y añada una actividad en cada grupo.

1. POR LA MAÑANA	2. POR LA TARDE	3. POR LA NOCHE
_____ Desayuné.	_____ Almorcé en la cafetería.	_____ Preparé la cena.
_____ Escribí una composición.	_____ Saqué libros de la biblioteca.	_____ Miré televisión.
_____ Tomé el sol en la playa.	_____ Lavé unas camisas.	_____ Planché unos pantalones.
_____ Estudié español.	_____ Fui al cine.	_____ Salí con mis amigos.

Follow-up for 6-10. After students compare their answers, they get together with another pair and exchange information regarding what both of them did yesterday.

Answers for 6-11. Primera fase. Answers may vary. Accept any logical responses.

❷ **Segunda fase.** Comparen sus respuestas. ¿Fueron sus actividades semejantes o diferentes? Expliquen.

❷ **6-11 ¡Visita inesperada (*unexpected*)! Primera fase.** El gerente (*manager*) general de la cadena *La última moda* visitó una de sus tiendas y encontró muchas irregularidades. En la columna A están los problemas que encontró. Expliquen qué hicieron, probablemente, los empleados para tratar de resolver cada problema.

MODELO: uno de los dependientes ausente
E1: Probablemente los otros dependientes lo llamaron por teléfono a su casa.
E2: Sí, pero el dependiente probablemente no contestó el teléfono. *o* El dependiente contestó el teléfono y explicó todo.

indicar	limpiar	lavar	marcar
depositar	ordenar	sacar	llamar

A   PROBLEMAS

1. la ropa rebajada sin los nuevos precios
2. la ropa de niños muy desordenada
3. el baño público sucio
4. unos cheques en el mostrador (*counter*)
5. uno de los dependientes en el teléfono con un amigo
6. los probadores (*fitting rooms*) con ropa

B   ¿QUÉ HICIERON?

1. _____
2. _____
3. _____
4. _____
5. _____
6. _____

② **Segunda fase.** Ahora digan qué hizo el gerente general con las siguientes personas. Pueden usar los siguientes verbos u otros.

conversar	hablar	explicar
ayudar	decidir	cambiar

1. la persona que limpia los baños
2. el empleado en el teléfono
3. la persona responsable de la ropa de niños

② **6-12 El sábado pasado. Primera fase.** Yolanda y Pedro son una pareja moderna y muy activa. Mire los dibujos con su compañero/a y describan cómo pasaron Yolanda y Pedro el fin de semana.

Suggestion for 6-12. Encourage students to ask follow-up questions and expand on their answers.

Answers for 6-12. (Answers may vary slightly).

1. *Pedro pasó la aspiradora.*   2. *Barrió la terraza.*   3. *Se bañó/duchó.*   4. *Yolanda miró televisión.*

5. *Escuchó la radio y estudió.*   6. *Fue a la playa.*   7. *Comieron en un restaurante elegante.*

② **Segunda fase.** Ahora hablen sobre el fin de semana de ustedes. ¿Fue un fin de semana igual o diferente al de Yolanda y Pedro?

1. ¿Qué actividades hizo cada uno de ustedes el fin de semana pasado?
2. ¿Quién pasó un mejor fin de semana, ustedes o Yolanda y Pedro? ¿Por qué?

② **6-13 Un día de compras. Primera fase.** Usted y su compañero/a fueron de compras el sábado. Para recordar sus actividades ese día, deben hacer lo siguiente:

- Escribir una lista de todas las cosas que hicieron durante su día de compras

- Anotar qué compraron, dónde, cuánto gastaron, etc.

G **Segunda fase.** En grupos de cuatro estudiantes intercambien información.

■ Comparen sus actividades y contesten las preguntas de sus compañeros sobre sus compras y actividades.

■ Explíquenle a la clase si hicieron cosas similares o diferentes y qué grupo gastó más.

SITUACIONES

1. You went to a party last Saturday. Your friend would like to know a) where the party was, b) what time the party started, c) with whom you went, d) what clothes you wore, d) what time the party ended, and f) where you went after the party. Answer his/her questions in as much detail as possible.

2. **Role A.** You are at the store trying to get your best friend the same kind of sweat suit you wear for your exercise class, but you don't see it among the sports clothes. Explain to the salesperson a) when you bought your sweat suit, b) what it looks like, and c) give him/her the brand name **(marca)** and size of the product.

   Role B. After listening to the customer, explain that a) you don't have that brand name any more, b) that you received a similar one that costs less, c) that you have all sizes and colors, and d) ask if he/she would like to try it on.

EN DIRECTO

To persuade a customer/client:
Es de excelente calidad.
Tiene muy buen precio.
¡Pruébeselo/la!
¡Lléveselo/la !

VÍNCULOS

To practice indirect object nouns and pronouns
- SAM-OneKey: WB: 6-10, 6-11 / LM: 6-35, 6-36, 6-37
- Companion Website: AP 6-5
- *Gramática viva:* Grammar Point 19: Indirect object pronouns
- IRCD: Chapter 6; pg. 218

Suggestions. Act out this situation in class: *Yo le doy el bolígrafo a Mercedes. Mercedes le da el bolígrafo a Juan. ¿Qué le da Mercedes a Juan? ¿A quién le da el bolígrafo Mercedes?* (if necessary, point to Juan) *Mercedes le da un lápiz a Luisa. ¿Qué le da Mercedes a Luisa? ¿A quién le da un lápiz Mercedes?* Write on the board one or two sentences you have used, or have them on a transparency. Circle *le* and the indirect object noun. Draw an arrow connecting *le* and the indirect object noun.

Talk about the illustration: *Hoy es el cumpleaños del amigo de Ana María. Ella le da un regalo a su amigo.* Have students answer the two questions.

Start yourself a chain drill by saying: *Le doy mi lápiz a X. ¿Qué le da usted a Y?* Next student continues the chain: *Yo le doy... a Y. ¿Qué le das (tú) a Z?,* etc.

3. Indirect object nouns and pronouns

Ana María le da un regalo a su amigo.
¿Qué le dice su amigo?
¿Qué le contesta Ana María?

INDIRECT OBJECT PRONOUNS	
me *to/for me*	**nos** *to/for us*
te *to/for you* (familiar)	**os** *to/for you* (familiar)
le *to/for you* (formal), *him, her, it*	**les** *to/for you* (formal), *them*

■ Indirect object nouns and pronouns tell *to whom* or *for whom* an action is done.

Mi madre **me** compró ropa la semana pasada.
My mother bought me clothes last week.

Yo **te** presto mis zapatos para la fiesta.
I will lend you my shoes for the party.

■ Indirect object pronouns have the same form as direct object pronouns except in the third person: **le** and **les**.

¿El dependiente? Ella **lo** ve por la mañana. (direct object)

She sees him in the morning.

¿El dependiente? Ella **le** da los recibos por la mañana. (indirect object)

She gives him the receipts in the morning.

■ Place the indirect object pronoun before the conjugated verb form. It may be attached to an infinitive or to a present participle.

Te voy a comprar un regalo.
Voy a comprar**te** un regalo.

I am going to buy you a present.

Juan **nos** está preparando la cena.
Juan está preparándo**nos** la cena.

Juan is preparing dinner for us.

Note. Point out the accent mark over the vowel directly preceding -*ndo* when an indirect object pronoun is attached and remind students about the rule of accentuation for *llanas* and *esdrújulas*, which were presented and practiced in *Lección 2* and *Lección 3* of the Student Activities Manual.

■ Use indirect object pronouns even when the indirect object noun is stated explicitly.

Yo **le** compré un regalo a **Victoria**.

I bought Victoria a present.

■ To eliminate ambiguity, **le** and **les** are often used with the preposition **a** + *pronoun*.

Le hablo **a usted**.
Siempre **les** compro algo **a ellos**.

I am talking to you. (not to him)
I always buy them something. (not you)

■ For emphasis, use **a mí**, **a ti**, **a nosotros/as**, and **a vosotros/as** with indirect object pronouns.

Pedro **te** habla **a ti**.

Pedro is talking to you (not to someone else).

Note. Double object pronouns are introduced in *Lección 9*.

4. The verb *dar*

DAR (*to give*)		
	PRESENT	PRETERIT
yo	doy	di
tú	das	diste
Ud., él, ella	da	dio
nosotros/as	damos	dimos
vosotros/as	dais	disteis
Uds., ellos, ellas	dan	dieron

VÍNCULOS

To practice the verb *dar*
- SAM-OneKey: WB: 6-12, 6-13 / LM: 6-38
- Companion Website: AP 6-6
- *Gramática viva*: Grammar Point 33: Present irregular: hacer, saber, dormir, volver, dar, ir
- IRCD: Chapter 6; pg. 219

■ **Dar** is almost always used with indirect object pronouns. Notice the difference in meaning between **dar** (*to give*) and **regalar** (*to give as a gift*).

Ella **le da** la camisa a Pedro.
Ella **le regala** la camisa a Pedro.

She gives (hands) Pedro the shirt.
She gives Pedro the shirt (as a gift).

■ In the preterit, **dar** uses the endings of **-er** and **-ir** verbs.

Suggestion. Obtain three items and select a student to give them to. Narrate as you give him or her each item: *Le doy el papel a él/ella. Le/Te doy la mochila a usted/ti.* The student then reports your actions: *Me da el papel a mí. Me da los lápices a mí.* Have the whole class work on giving things back and forth, using *me/te, a mí/a ti.*

¿Qué dice usted?

6-14 Una clase optativa (*elective*). Imagínense que están tomando la clase optativa *Elegancia con poco dinero.* Marquen las sugerencias que les da su instructor a usted y a sus compañeros/as.

1. _____ Nos da nombres de tiendas de ropa buena y barata.
2. _____ A mí me recomienda artículos sobre la moda actual.
3. _____ Nos dice los secretos para ser elegantes y gastar poco.
4. _____ Nos muestra telas que son elegantes y baratas.
5. _____ A mí me da ejemplos de cómo combinar ropa y accesorios.
6. _____ A mí me explica cómo comprar ropa por Internet.

6-15 Expertos en moda. Primera fase. Imagínense que ustedes tienen un/a experto/a que siempre les da recomendaciones para estar a la moda. En la siguiente lista, marquen las cosas que esta persona hace por ustedes. Después deben añadir una actividad más y compartir sus ideas con otros/as compañeros/as.

MODELO: hacer preguntas sobre la ropa que necesitamos
           Nos hace preguntas sobre la ropa que necesitamos.

1. _____ dar nombres de tiendas famosas en los países hispanos
2. _____ hablar sobre las cosas que venden en los mercados al aire libre
3. _____ comprar ropa
4. _____ dar ideas sobre accesorios
5. _____ decir las telas que debemos comprar
6. _____ mostrar fotos de almacenes y tiendas en varios países hispanos
7. _____ regalar libros sobre la moda
8. ...

Segunda fase. Ahora, ustedes desean recompensar (*compensate*) a este/a experto/a. Indiquen qué es lo que van a hacer por él/ella.

1. ordenar su oficina
2. preguntar cómo está
3. lavar su auto
4. hacer pequeños favores
5. comprar regalos por su cumpleaños
6. contestar el teléfono de su oficina
7. comprar revistas de moda en español
8. mandar correos electrónicos

6-16 Para estar a la última moda. Primera fase. Imagínense que cada uno de ustedes tiene los deseos o necesidades de la lista de abajo. Explíquense entre ustedes la situación. Después pidan y den una recomendación.

MODELO: E1: Quiero llevar ropa a la última moda. ¿Qué me recomiendas?
           E2: Te recomiendo comprar ropa de colores claros.
           E1: ¿Me recomiendas alguna marca en especial?
           E2: Te recomiendo comprar ropa de diseñadores venezolanos.

1. Quiero llevar pantalones a la moda.
2. Necesito zapatos cómodos y modernos.
3. Deseo protegerme del sol.
4. Quiero ropa buena y barata
5. Quiero estar más delgado/a.
6. Me gustaría llevar ropa elegante y fina a la entrevista de trabajo.

Segunda fase. Comparta con otro/a compañero/a tres buenas recomendaciones que recibió en la **Primera fase.**

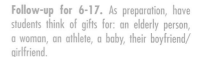

6-17 Afortunados. Primera fase. Ustedes acaban de (*have just*) ganar la lotería y quieren compartir su fortuna con su familia y sus compañeros de clase.

- Hagan una lista de los miembros de su familia a quienes desean regalarles algo.

- Indiquen el regalo que piensan hacerle a cada uno.

MODELO: E1: A nuestros padres les vamos a regalar/vamos a regalarles un crucero por el Caribe.

E2: A Sara le vamos a comprar/vamos a comprarle una mochila.

Segunda fase. Ahora, hagan una lista de cuatro compañeros/as a quienes ustedes les quieren dar algo. Indiquen en la siguiente lista el regalo que piensan hacerle a cada uno. Compartan la información con otra pareja.

1. una invitación para un desfile de moda (*fashion show*)
2. la revista de moda *En voga*
3. una entrada para ver el concurso Señorita Venezuela
4. 150.000 bolívares para gastar en el Centro Sambil en Caracas
5. un perfume de Óscar de la Renta o Carolina Herrera

6-18 Entrevista. Basándose en la siguiente lista, háganse preguntas sobre sus hábitos de compras y los regalos que hacen y reciben de otras personas. Después comparen sus respuestas.

1. Ir de compras: ¿adónde? ¿cuándo?
2. Tienda(s) favorita(s): ¿cuál(es)?
3. Comprar regalos caros: ¿a quién(es)?
4. Le compran regalos a usted: ¿quién(es)?

SITUACIONES

1. **Role A.** You are a customer at a department store. Tell the salesperson that a) you are looking for a present for a young man/lady, b) you are not sure what you should buy, and c) the amount that you can spend.

   Role B. You are a salesperson. A customer comes into the store to ask for your advice: a) inquire about the young man's/lady's age, taste, size, favorite color, or any other pertinent information; b) make reasonable suggestions to your customer; and c) give him/her information about the quality of the products, prices, sales, etc.

2. **Role A.** You are starting a new job and you go to the store to get some new clothes. Tell the salesperson a) that you saw a suit/dress at the shop window (**escaparate**) and b) inquire if he/she has your size. Answer all the salesperson's questions and decide which suits/dresses you would like to try on.

   Role B. You are a salesperson. First, a) ask the client for more details to identify the suit/dress the customer is referring to, b) tell him/her that you have it in brown, blue, gray, and black, c) that you also have some new suits/dresses that you can show him/her (describe the styles), and d) ask him/her if she would like to see them.

Follow-up for 6-17. As preparation, have students think of gifts for: an elderly person, a woman, an athlete, a baby, their boyfriend/ girlfriend.

5. *Gustar* and similar verbs

Suggestions. Using visuals, identify a few of your favorite foods. Poll students, eliciting responses as to what they like and dislike (and why).

Point out that in *gustar* constructions the definite article is used, and that the subject usually follows the verb: *Me gustan los niños. Nos gusta la música.*

To reinforce the *gustar* construction, practice *interesar, encantar,* and *parecer;* they offer a better parallel to English: Your story interests me. *Me interesa tu cuento.*

VÍNCULOS

To practice *gustar* and similar verbs
- SAM-OneKey: WB: 6-14, 6-15, 6-16 / LM: 6-39, 6-40, 6-41
- Companion Website: AP 6-7
- *Gramática viva*: Grammar Point 1: *(A mí) me interesa, gusta*
- IRCD: Chapter 6; pg. 222

¿Le gusta esta camisa?
No, no me gusta.

Me gustan éstas. ¿Y a usted?
Me gustan mucho.

- In previous lessons you have used the verb **gustar** to express likes and dislikes. As you have noticed, **gustar** is not used the same way as the English verb *to like.* **Gustar** is similar to the expression *to be pleasing (to someone).*

  Me gusta ese vestido.   *I like that dress.*
  (That dress is pleasing to me.)

- In this construction, the subject is the person or thing that is liked. The indirect object pronoun shows to whom something is pleasing.

me		*I*
te		*you* (familiar)
le	gusta el traje.	*you* (formal), *he/she*
nos		*we*
os		*you* (familiar)
les		*they, you*
		(formal and familiar)

like/s the suit.

- The most frequently used forms of **gustar** in the present are **gusta** and **gustan** and for the preterit **gustó** and **gustaron.** If one person or thing is liked, use **gusta/gustó.** If two or more persons or things are liked, use **gustan/gustaron.** To express what people like or do not like to do, use **gusta** followed by infinitives.

Me **gusta** ese **collar.**	*I like that necklace.*
No me **gustaron** los anillos.	*I did not like the rings.*
Nos **gusta caminar** por la mañana.	*We like to walk in the morning.*
¿No te **gusta correr** y **nadar?**	*Do not you like to run and swim?*

- Some other Spanish verbs that follow the pattern of **gustar** are **encantar** (*to delight, to love*), **interesar** (*to interest, to matter*), **parecer** (*to seem*), and **quedar** (*to fit, to have something left*).

- To express that you like or dislike a person, you may also use **caer bien** or **caer mal,** which follow the pattern of **gustar.**

Les cae bien Miriam.	*They like Miriam.*
La dependienta **me cae mal.**	*I do not like the salesclerk.*

Note. Many Spanish speakers use *caer bien/mal* exclusively to talk about liking/disliking people in a general sense, reserving the use of *gustar* for talking about physical attraction.

■ To emphasize or clarify to whom something is pleasing, use **a + mí, a + ti, a + él/ella,** etc. or **a +** *noun*.

> **A mí** me gustaron mucho los zapatos, pero **a Pedro** no le gustaron.

> *I liked the shoes a lot, but Pedro did not like them.*

¿Qué dice usted?

6-19 Mis preferencias en la ropa. Primera fase. Complete la siguiente tabla según sus preferencias.

ROPA	ME ENCANTA/N	ME GUSTA/N	NO ME GUSTA/N
la ropa deportiva			
los aretes			
las chaquetas de cuero			
los suéteres de lana			
las blusas/camisas de seda			
los vaqueros			
los pantalones cortos			

(G) Segunda fase. Comparen sus preferencias, y luego, explíquenle al resto de la clase si ustedes coinciden en sus gustos.

MODELO: E1: A dos de nosotros nos gustan los colores fuertes.
E2: Y también nos encanta la ropa deportiva. *o* A todos nos encantan los vaqueros.

(2) 6-20 Problemas. Lean estos problemas y busquen la solución.

MODELO: Pilar tiene 50.000 bolívares. Paga 25.000 bolívares por una blusa y 10.000 por unos aretes. ¿Cuánto dinero le queda? 15.000 bolívares.

1. Ernesto tiene 75.000 bolívares. Le da 15.000 a su hermano. ¿Cuánto dinero le queda? 60.000
2. Érica tiene 25.000 bolívares. Va al cine y a cenar con una amiga. El cine cuesta 5.000 bolívares y la cena 12.000. ¿Cuántos bolívares le quedan? 8.000 bolívares
3. Gilberto tiene 40.000 bolívares. Compra un suéter por 39.000 bolívares. ¿Cuánto dinero le queda? 1.000 bolívares
4. Mis amigos tienen 30.000 bolívares. Van a la playa y almuerzan en un restaurante por 25.000 bolívares. ¿Cuántos bolívares les quedan? 5.000 bolívares

Follow-up for 6-20. Play a game to see who can follow money transactions and answer quickly. 1. *Ud. Tiene $26. Compra un video por $21. ¿Cuánto dinero le queda?* 2. *Ud. Sale de casa con $75. Gasta $10 en el almuerzo, compra un suéter que cuesta $35 y paga $20 por unas gafas de sol. ¿Cuánto dinero le queda?* 3. *Tengo $200 y quiero salir esta noche. Gasto $40 en el restaurante, las entradas al teatro cuestan $60 y le pago $15 al taxista. ¿Cuánto dinero me queda?* 4. *Ud. Tiene $150 en total, $50 en la cartera y $100 en la chaqueta. Alguien le roba la chaqueta. ¿Cuánto dinero le queda?*

G **6-21 ¿Qué opinan ustedes?** Primero, pregúntense y den su opinión sobre los siguientes temas. Luego, intercambien sus opiniones en grupos pequeños.

MODELO: el uso de uniformes en las escuelas
E1: ¿Qué piensas del uso de uniformes en las escuelas?
E2: Me parece que es una idea excelente. Y tú, ¿qué opinas?
E1: Pues yo creo que cada estudiante debe llevar la ropa que le gusta.

1. los almacenes de descuento
2. la ropa que llevan los artistas a la ceremonia de los Óscares
3. los precios de la ropa de los diseñadores famosos
4. los desfiles de moda en la televisión
5. los chicos que llevan aretes
6. las personas que se pintan el pelo de colores fuertes

2 **6-22 ¿Qué planes tienes?** Ustedes van a ir a una recepción muy elegante el sábado próximo. Averigüe qué ropa piensa llevar o comprar su compañero/a y qué le gustaría hacer después de la recepción. Después él/ella debe hacerle a usted las mismas preguntas.

SITUACIONES

1. One of you is shopping at a clothing store, the other is the clerk. Tell the clerk a) what you need (e.g., pants, shoes, and so on), b) ask the price of each item, c) say whether or not you like each item, and d) decide if you will buy it/them. He/She will ask you pertinent questions.

2. **Role A:** You are at the store where you bought a pair of jeans last week. Tell the clerk that a) you tried them on at home and they didn't fit, and b) that you would like to exchange them. Listen to the clerk and respond accordingly.

   Role B: You are the clerk at a store. A customer comes to you to exchange a piece of clothing. Listen to his/her case and tell the customer that you don't have any other sizes in that style. Try to interest the customer in another style.

ALGO MÁS

VÍNCULOS

To practice some more uses of *por* and *para*
- SAM-OneKey: WB: 6-17, 6-18 / LM: 6-42
- Companion Website: AP 6-8

More uses of por *and* para

- Use **por** to indicate the reason or motivation for an action.

  No le compra el collar **por** el precio.

  He is not buying her the necklace because it is too expensive (because of the price).

- If you use a verb to express the reason or motivation, you must use **porque.**

  No le compra el collar **porque** es muy caro.

  He is not buying her the necklace because it is very expensive.

- Use **para** to indicate for whom something is intended or done.

  Compró otro collar **para** su novia.

  He bought another necklace for his girlfriend.

¿Qué dice usted?

6-23 ¿Cuál es el motivo? Usen **por** o **porque** para terminar las oraciones de la columna de la izquierda con un motivo lógico de la columna de la derecha.

MODELO: Pedro compró un traje   lo invitaron a una fiesta
          Pasamos el fin de semana preocupados   el examen del lunes

          Pedro compró un traje porque lo invitaron a una fiesta.
          Pasamos el fin de semana preocupados por el examen del lunes.

1. Pepito quiere una bicicleta b   a. le queda grande
2. No va a comprar los pantalones e   b. sus buenas notas
3. Rebeca va a cambiar el vestido a   c. el tráfico
4. Ellos llegaron tarde c   d. la ropa es más barata
5. Voy a ir de compras hoy f   e. son muy cortos
6. Isabel prefiere comprar en un mercado d f. las rebajas

6-24 Unos regalos. Usted fue a Caracas la semana pasada y su compañero/a quiere saber para quién son los regalos que usted compró.

MODELO: una pulsera
          E1: ¿Para quién es la pulsera?
          E2: Es para mi hermana.

1. los libros de español
2. la billetera
3. las camisetas
4. el collar
5. los discos compactos del Puma
6. ...

Follow-up for 6-24. Ask students why they bought each present: *¿Por qué le compró una pulsera?* If they have difficulty answering, ask additional questions: *¿Le gustan las pulseras a su hermana? ¿Son baratas las pulseras en Venezuela?*

 ## *Escuchar*

Taking notes to recall important information

Sometimes when you want to remember something that somebody tells you, you benefit from taking notes. For example, when you ask for directions to go somewhere, you might remember better what you hear if you take notes.

VÍNCULOS

For materials related to the Mosaicos section, see
- SAM-OneKey: WB: 6-19, 6-20, 6-21, 6-22, 6-23, 6-24 / LM: 6-43
- IRCD: Chapter 6; pg. 230

Antes de escuchar

6-25 En el Centro Comercial Sambil. In 6-26, Irma—a working mother who takes good care of her clothes and accessories—is at a big department store in Caracas. She is asking one the employees where to find different items. Before you listen, make a list of the different items of clothing and accessories that she might be interested in buying.

accesorios _____

ropa _____

A escuchar

Audioscript for 6-26. IRMA: Señor, por favor, ¿me puede decir dónde están los artículos de cuero? EMPLEADO: En el tercer piso están nuestro artículos de cuero. Allí puede encontrar bolsas, zapatos, botas, guantes y chaquetas. En el tercer piso también puede encontrar abrigos de lana, paraguas y sombreros. IRMA: ¡Ah, qué bien! Y, ¿dónde está la ropa deportiva? EMPLEADO: En el primer piso puede encontrar pantalones, pantalones cortos, sudaderas, camisas, blusas. IRMA: ¿Y la ropa interior? EMPLEADO: La ropa interior está en el segundo piso. Allí esta la ropa interior para hombres y para mujeres. En el segundo piso también están los accesorios; aretes, anillos, collares y pulseras. IRMA: Muy bien, muchas gracias. EMPLEADO: A sus órdenes.

AUDIO **6-26** Now, listen to Irma asking an employee at Centro Comercial Sambil where she can find different items she needs. As you listen to the conversation, look at her incomplete notes and complete them stating what items are on each floor. You do not have to remember all the items mentioned!

Primer piso _ropa deportiva, pantalones, pantalones cortos, sudaderas, camisas, blusas_
Segundo piso _ropa interior para hombres y para mujeres, aretes, anillos, collares, pulseras_
Tercer piso _artículos de cuero, bolsas, zapatos, botas, guantes, chaquetas, abrigos de lana, paraguas y sombreros_

Después de escuchar

2 **6-27 ¿Y usted?** Conversen sobre la última vez que cada uno de ustedes fue a un centro comercial.

1. ¿Cuándo fue la última vez que usted fue a un centro comercial?
2. ¿Qué compró? ¿Compró regalos? ¿Para quién?
3. ¿Qué le gustó pero no pudo comprar?

Antes de escuchar

6-28 De compras. In **6-29** you will listen to a conversation between Andrea and her parents in which Andrea talks about her needs for school. Before you listen, make a list of things you had to buy before you came to school this semester.

_____
_____
_____

A escuchar

6-29 Now, you will listen to the conversation between Andrea and her parents. As you listen, complete the notes her parents are taking. You don't have to remember all the items Andrea mentions!

Para ir a clases Andrea necesita <u>guantes, una chaqueta, una bufanda y un abrigo</u>
Para practicar deportes Andrea tiene que comprar <u>pantalones cortos, camisetas, una sudadera, medias</u>
Para salir con sus amigos Andrea quiere <u>pantalones vaqueros, blusas, zapatos y muchas cosas más</u>

Después de escuchar

6-30 ¿Y usted? Converse con su compañero/a sobre sus compras antes de venir a la universidad.

1. ¿Qué compró usted antes de venir a la universidad este semestre: ropa, muebles para su cuarto, aparatos electrónicos?
2. ¿Compró accesorios? ¿Qué accesorios compró usted? ¿Dónde los compró?
3. ¿Fue usted a unas rebajas? ¿Gastó mucho dinero? ¿Cuánto gastó?

Conversar

Antes de conversar

6-31 En un mercado. Usted tiene que comprar un regalo, algo para su apartamento/casa, etc. en un mercado al aire libre. Complete la tabla con la información de los productos que desea comprar.

¿QUÉ DEBE COMPRAR?	¿PARA QUIÉN(ES)?	DESCRIPCIÓN DEL PRODUCTO

Audioscript for 6-29. ANDREA: Mamá, ustedes saben que necesito muchas cosas. Por ejemplo, para ir a mis clases ahora en invierno, necesito unas botas, guantes y una chaqueta. También necesito una bufanda y un abrigo. MAMÁ: Pero Andrea, si el año pasado te compramos ropa de invierno. Todavía la puedes usar. ANDREA: No, mamá. Quiero estar a la última moda, y mi ropa ya está vieja. Quiero ir a una boutique elegante y comprarme toda mi ropa allí. PAPÁ: Me parece muy bien, Andrea. Puedes comprar todo lo que quieras, pero dime, ¿de dónde vas a sacar dinero para pagar por esa ropa? Tú no trabajas. ANDREA: ¡Papá, por favor ! Tú me puedes prestar dinero o me puedes dar tu tarjeta de crédito. Además necesito ropa para practicar deportes. Quiero comprar pantalones cortos, camisetas, una sudadera, medias y... MAMÁ: Andrea, ¿estás loca? Nosotros no tenemos tanto dinero. No podemos pagar todo eso ni prestarte dinero y mucho menos darte la tarjeta de crédito. ANDREA: Mamá, escucha, para salir con mis amigos necesito pantalones vaqueros, blusas, zapatos y muchas cosas más. PAPÁ: Todo me parece muy bien, Andrea. Trabaja, ahorra y gasta tu dinero, pero yo no te voy a dar ni un solo bolívar. ANDREA: Pero, papá, comprende, por favor. PAPÁ: Ni una palabra más.

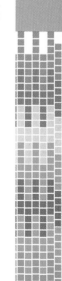

A conversar

6-32 ¡A ahorrar! (*Let's save*). Usted ya está en un mercado al aire libre. Pregúntele al/ a la vendedor/a (su compañero/a) el precio de los productos que usted desea comprar. Regatee (*Haggle*) para obtener el mejor precio posible. Use las expresiones más apropiadas. Luego, cambien del papel.

Después de conversar

6-33 ¡Qué experiencia! Conversen sobre su experiencia de regateo en el mercado al aire libre de la actividad **6-32.** Cuéntense lo siguiente:

1. qué productos pudo comprar y para quién los compró.
2. cuánto le pidió el/la vendedor/a por cada producto.
3. cuánto dinero le ofreció usted.
4. cuánto pagó finalmente.

Antes de conversar

6-34 ¿Apropiado o inapropiado? Elimine la ropa y los accesorios que, según usted, son inapropiados en las siguientes ocasiones. Luego, compare sus respuestas con las de su compañero/a.

1. Un chico fue a escalar montañas en sus vacaciones de verano con botas, pantalones cortos, un sombrero, un cinturón, una chaqueta de lana.
2. Unas chicas fueron de picnic al lago Sinamaica en Venezuela. Todas se pusieron minifalda de color entero, zapatos de tenis, un collar de perlas, una blusa de algodón a rayas.
3. La semana pasada, el presidente de una corporación tuvo una reunión importante con los ejecutivos de la filial (*branch office*) en Caracas. Se puso un impermeable verde, zapatos negros, vaqueros azules, una guayabera, un sombrero mexicano.

A conversar

6-35 Inspector/a de la moda. Lean las siguientes descripciones y comenten si las personas llevan la ropa y los accesorios apropiados (A) o inapropiados (I) para la ocasión. Indiquen cuál(es) es/son inapropiado(s) para cada situación y digan por qué.

1. _____ Una actriz famosa fue a la ceremonia de los premios Óscar en traje de baño, gafas de sol y sandalias.
2. _____ El presidente de los Estados Unidos invitó a unos estudiantes a visitar la Casa Blanca. Los estudiantes se pusieron traje, corbata y zapatos de tenis.
3. _____ Usted y sus hermanos/as prepararon una gran fiesta para celebrar las bodas de plata (25 aniversario) de sus padres. Su padre llevó vaqueros, una camiseta blanca y botas tejanas; su madre se puso un vestido negro largo, un collar de perlas y unos aretes finos.
4. _____ A su primera entrevista de trabajo, su mejor amiga llevó una falda y una chaqueta azul, unos aretes pequeños, unas pantimedias oscuras, zapatos negros y una bolsa pequeña del color de los zapatos.

Después de conversar

6-36 ¿Elegante o de mal gusto? Usted trabaja en la revista *A la moda* y debe escribir un artículo para la sección **Inspector de la moda** de este mes. Seleccione una de las situaciones de la actividad **6-35** y escriba un breve informe sobre la situación para los lectores de su revista. Incluya como mínimo la siguiente información.

1. ¿Sobre qué persona(s) es la noticia?
2. ¿Cuál fue el evento/la situación y dónde fue?
3. ¿Qué ropa y accesorios usó/usaron la(s) persona(s)?
4. Según usted, ¿fueron apropiados los accesorios y la ropa? ¿Por qué?

 Leer

In this chapter, you will practice finding specific information to accomplish a task, and identifying word endings that indicate places where certain products are sold or services rendered.

As the need arises, remember to apply all the strategies you have learned so far.

Guía de prelectura

Skim the text in activity **6-38** and answer the questions, using your previous knowledge and experiences.

1. Thinking of the theme of *Lección 6* and looking at the text format and illustrations, can you anticipate the type of text it is?
   a. Guidelines to buy on online
   b. Online advertising for one store
   c. A listing of stores that sell online

2. Now, use your background knowledge to comprehend the text. On what did you base your answers to question 1?
   a. The cognates in the title
   b. Visuals in the text
   c. The use of key words for online shopping

3. The text probably contains the following information for shoppers. Circle all that may apply. You will be able to verify your responses later.
   a. Products and prices
   b. Method of payment for online purchases
   c. Bargains
   d. Alphabetically arranged list of online stores

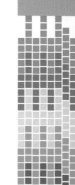

EN DIRECTO

To state that something is appropriate or inappropriate:
(No) Es apropiado + *infinitivo*
Es inapropiado + *infinitivo*...

To explain why some clothes or accessories are inappropriate:
... no es/son apropiado/a(s) porque la ocasión es formal/informal.
En un/a... (evento/ocasión) no es elegante/apropiado llevar/usar...
(Clothing/accesory)... no va(n) bien con... (*Clothing/accesory*)

Antes de leer

6-37 Megatiendas. Primera fase. ¿Qué productos o servicios se pueden obtener en una megatienda de su ciudad? Escriba **Sí** o **No** al lado del producto o servicio.

1. _____ ropa de mujer/hombre
2. _____ electrodomésticos
3. _____ camisetas para niños
4. _____ máquinas fotográficas
5. _____ seguros (*insurance*) de auto
6. _____ frutas y verduras
7. _____ ropa de fiesta
8. _____ muebles
9. _____ juguetes para niños
10. _____ acceso a Internet

2 Segunda fase. Converse con su compañero/a sobre lo siguiente:

1. ¿Les gusta comprar en las megatiendas o prefieren las tiendas más pequeñas? ¿Por qué?
2. En su ciudad o país, ¿hay megatiendas en internet? ¿Cuál(es) es/son?
3. ¿Cuáles son algunas ventajas de comprar en las megatiendas?

A leer

6-38 Primera mirada. Lea la siguiente página de Internet y, luego, siga las instrucciones.

Bienvenido a CompreenInternet.net

Menú	Nuestro Proceso	Beneficios
• Nuestra compañía	1. Hágase miembro	• Excelentes precios
• Nuestros Servicios	2. Busque su producto	• Pagos en bolívares
• Cómo puede comprar	3. Calcule los gastos de su envío	• Entrega en todo el país
• Recomendaciones prácticas	4. Pague con tarjeta de crédito	• Nuestras filiales de Nueva York o Miami hacen los envíos
• Preguntas frecuentes	5. Espere su envío y disfrútelo	
• Regulaciones de compras		
• Nuestras filiales		

3. Calcule los gastos de su envío

2. Busque su producto

4. Pague con tarjeta de crédito

1. Hágase miembro

5. Espere su envío y disfrútelo

Servicios

Compra de una gran variedad de productos en Internet:

• Aparatos eléctricos/electrónicos
• Muebles accesorios, ropa, juguetes, software, etc.
• Asistencia de expertos mientras y después de su compra
• Envío gratis en Venezuela
• Descuentos por recomendarnos a otras personas
• Lista de las mejores tiendas en Internet
• Ofertas y gangas de la semana

• Póngase en contacto con nosotros
• Recomiéndenos y gane puntos
• Búsqueda

Dirección en EE.UU.
1438 Flagger St.
Miami, Florida (Fl)
Código Zip: 33166
Tel : 305-328-6289
Utilice esta dirección para su envío (shipping)

• Asistencia para afiliados
• Actualizar datos personales
• Modificación de clave
• Salida

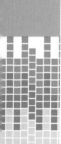

Indique si las siguientes afirmaciones son correctas (C) o incorrectas (I), según el contenido de la página Web. Si son incorrectas (I), corrija la información.

1. _____ Los productos y servicios que **CompreenInternet.com** ofrece son básicamente para personas que viven fuera de Venezuela.
2. _____ La sección **Nuestro proceso** de la página de Web les indica a los clientes las diversas fases de una compra en Internet.
3. _____ Las tiendas que promociona (*advertises*) **CompreenInternet.com** sólo incluyen tiendas que están en Venezuela.
4. _____ **CompreenInternet.com** tiene su oficina central en Venezuela.
5. _____ Los clientes de **CompreenInternet.com** solamente pueden comprar ropa.
6. _____ Los clientes ahorran dinero si compran en internet.

Answers for 6-38. 1. I: *clientes en Venezuela*; 2. C.; 3. I: *están en los EE.UU.*; 4. C.; 5. I: *una variedad de productos y servicios*; 6. C.

6-39 Segunda mirada. Lea otra vez la página de **CompreenInternet.com** y seleccione la alternativa correcta.

1. Los clientes que compran en **CompreenInternet.com** pagan solamente en...
   a. dólares   b. bolívares   c. dólares y bolívares

2. En el **Menú** de **CompreenInternet.com,** la palabra **búsqueda** probablemente es un nombre derivado del verbo...
   a. bañar   b. buscar   c. barrer

3. La expresión **envío gratis** significa que los clientes...
   a. pagan por recibir los productos en su casa.
   b. no pagan por recibir los productos en su casa.
   c. pagan sólo un 10% del costo por recibir sus productos en casa.

4. La expresión **Hágase miembro** en la sección **Nuestro proceso** probablemente significa que para comprar, las personas deben...
   a. subscribirse a una lista de clientes de la tienda en Internet.
   b. tener a un miembro de la familia en la tienda.
   c. comprar un mínimo al año.

❷ 6-40 Tercera mirada. Lean una vez más el menú de la página de **CompreenInternet.com** y completen la tabla con las categorías de tiendas que, según ustedes, las chicas, los chicos o ambos visitan con más frecuencia. Compartan sus respuestas con las de otra pareja.

Answers for 6-40. Answers may vary. Accept any response that is supported.

Suggestions for 6-40. After students have compared responses with another couple, you may wish to discuss responses with the whole class. Encourage students to support their answers.

LAS CHICAS	LOS CHICOS	AMBOS

Después de leer

6-41 Ampliación. Adivinen a qué tipo de tienda van a ir estas personas. Completen la tabla.

PERSONA QUE BUSCA UN PRODUCTO O SERVICIO	TIPO DE TIENDA
Modelo: El constructor civil necesita una herramienta (*tool*).	ferrete**ría**
1. El señor Fonseca desea comprar un **mueble** nuevo para su casa.	mueblería
2. La señora Méndez debe comprarle un **juguete** a su nuevo sobrino.	juguetería
3. Mauricio necesita comprar una **joya** (*jewel*) para su novia.	joyería
4. Ustedes desean comprar **pescado** para la cena.	pescadería
5. Doña Sara quiere comprarle a su esposo unos **zapatos** elegantes.	zapatería
6. Ustedes quieren comprar **fruta** para su madre.	frutería

 Escribir

In *Lección 5*, you practiced writing for a general, unknown audience. However, writing for a specific reader, particularly one with whom you have done business, to fulfill a specific need requires attention to the following, among others:

- The use of a formal, business tone. In Spanish, a business tone is signaled by the use of **Señores**, and the pronoun **usted/ustedes**, for example.

- The length of the message to be communicated. Most business correspondence tends to be brief and straight to the point.

- Clear descriptions and/or explanations. To meet their needs, customers must describe accurately and clearly the product/service they need or explain precisely what is wrong with a product they bought that did not meet their expectations.

In this chapter, you will write a letter of complaint to a store, agency, etc. As you plan and write your letter of complaint, keep in mind the degree of formality of business correspondence, and the accuracy and amount of information you will provide.

Antes de escribir

6-42 Enfoque. Primera fase. Hace dos semanas el señor Contreras compró un traje en Internet. Cuando lo recibió, él se dio cuenta de (*realized*) algunos problemas. Él le escribió una carta al Departamento de Ventas de la tienda en línea. Lea la carta y siga las instrucciones.

Avenida Simón Bolívar 1439, Apt. B
Maracaibo VENEZUELA
28 de enero de 2005

Alamoda.com
Departamento de ventas
Bulevar Las Américas # 392, Oficina 801
Caracas VENEZUELA

Estimados señores:

Les escribo para informarles sobre un problema con el traje que compré en la página Web de su tienda el 13 de enero de este año. Después de mirar la gran variedad de trajes que ustedes tienen, escogí uno con esta descripción:

> Estilo: 7635; talla: 48, color: azul marino, material: lana inglesa, detalles del saco: doble abotonadura[1], bolsillos[2] pequeños, detalles del pantalón: pliegues[3], bolsillos sin botón.

Desafortunadamente, el 27 de enero recibí un traje que no corresponde a la descripción que ustedes me dieron en Internet. El traje que me mandaron tiene los siguientes problemas: Primero, es de poliéster, no de lana como yo lo pedí. Segundo, los pantalones no tienen bolsillos. Tercero, yo pedí un traje azul marino, pero recibí uno gris de rayas.

Yo necesito con urgencia el traje que les pedí. Les envío una copia del recibo por la cantidad de 190.000 bolívares que pagué con mi tarjeta VISA.

Por favor, mándenmelo a la dirección que incluí arriba.

Espero una solución rápida a este problema.

Muy agradecido por su pronta respuesta, los saluda muy atentamente,

Alberto Contreras

P.S.: Por favor, confirmen el envío a mi dirección electrónica: ras81@ter.com

[1]*double-breasted* [2]*pockets* [3]*pleats*

Segunda fase. Answer the following questions based on Mr. Contreras' letter.

1. Mark with an X the intended purpose of Mr. Contreras' letter to the Sales Department of **Alamoda.com**:

   _____ to describe the clothes he would like to order

   ___X___ to complain about a discrepancy between the description of the product online and the actual product they shipped to him

   ___X___ to request that **Alamoda.com** ship the right product to him

   _____ to inform **Alamoda.com** of a forthcoming lawsuit

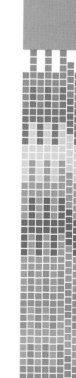

2. Based on its purpose, is Mr. Contreras' letter effective?

(Yes)　　No

Mark some possible reasons for your response.

___X___ He narrates his shopping experience chronologically, starting with the present and moving toward the past.

___X___ He provides the sales department with the exact online description of the product.

___X___ He pinpoints the differences between the online description of the product and the actual product he received.

___X___ The tone of his letter is businesslike.

_____ He writes to **Alamoda.com** as a friend.

___X___ His letter of complaint is brief and straight to the point.

3. What salutation did Mr. Contreras use in his letter? _____Estimados señores_____

4. How does he close the letter? What does this sentence probably mean in English? _Muy agradecido por su pronta respuesta; I'm looking forward to your prompt reply_

5. How does he say good-bye in the letter? Do you know any other way to say good-bye in a business letter in Spanish? What is it? _Atentamente. Cordialmente, Sinceramente_

Suggestion for 6-43. As customary, we advise that the preparation phase be done either outside of class or in class in a workshop format. For this particular writing task, you may ask that students prepare to write about an imaginary purchase gone wrong or a real experience they had. In either case, help students with the vocabulary they may need.

6-43 Preparación. Como Alberto Contreras, usted compró un producto en Internet (ropa, un mueble, un accesorio, etc.), pero el producto resultó ser diferente de sus expectativas. Usted decide escribir una carta de queja al Departamento de Ventas de la tienda en línea. Haga lo siguiente:

1. Escriba el nombre de la tienda donde usted compró los producto(s).

2. Indique el producto que compró en línea: ¿Qué compró? ¿Cuánto(s)/(as) compró?

3. Prepare una lista de expresiones (nombres y adjetivos) para describir cada producto que usted compró: ¿Un vestido negro largo? ¿Una camisa blanca ancha? ¿Un plato decorativo de cerámica?

4. Narre los hechos (*facts*) en orden cronológico: ¿Cuándo hizo la compra en internet? ¿Cómo describe los productos la tienda en internet? ¿Cuánto costó/costaron el/los producto(s)? ¿Cómo pagó usted? ¿Usó una tarjeta de crédito o llamó a un número gratis para pagar?

5. Escriba la(s) razón(es) de su insatisfacción con el/los producto(s).

A escribir

6-44 Manos a la obra. Ahora escríbale una carta de queja a la persona encargada del Departamento de Ventas de la tienda en línea. Use la información que preparó en la actividad **6-43**. Incluya la fecha, el saludo, el cierre de la carta y la despedida.

Después de escribir

6-45 Revisión. Ahora lea su carta por lo menos dos veces. Piense en la persona que la va a leer. Verifique lo siguiente:

■ El contenido: ¿Incluyó usted toda la información necesaria?

■ El tono de la carta: ¿Escribió su carta formalmente?

■ La forma de la carta de queja:
  a. ¿Revisó la gramática de su texto: el vocabulario correcto, algunas expresiones que indican cronología en la narración, la concordancia (*agreement*), el tiempo (presente, pasado, futuro), etc.?
  b. ¿Usó la puntuación y ortografía correctas?

Finalmente, comente su carta con un/a compañero/a.

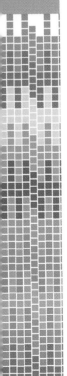

ENFOQUE CULTURAL

TEMAS: DE COMPRAS EN EL MUNDO HISPANO

Para pensar

¿Cuáles son los lugares más populares para ir de compras en los Estados Unidos? ¿Qué puede usted comprar allí? ¿Cómo paga usted sus compras? ¿Pide rebajas?

En las metrópolis de los países hispanos hay grandes y lujosos centros comerciales donde se pueden comprar muchos productos nacionales o importados. Frecuentemente venden artículos de muy buena calidad y a precios muy altos. Se puede pagar en efectivo o con tarjeta de crédito.

En todas las ciudades hispanas, a lo largo de las avenidas del centro, hay innumerables tiendas pequeñas que se especializan en determinados productos. En las tiendas del Bulevar de Sabana Grande en Caracas, uno puede comprar muchas cosas.

Para contestar

2 **Las tiendas.** Hagan lo siguiente.

1. Comparen los centros comerciales, las tiendas pequeñas y los mercados al aire libre de los países hispanos con respecto a productos que se pueden comprar, localización de las tiendas, costo de los productos, forma de pago. Mencionen cuáles son las ventajas y las desventajas de cada lugar.
2. ¿En qué lugares se puede pedir rebaja en los países hispanos? Y en los Estados Unidos, ¿se puede pedir rebaja? ¿Dónde?

G **Riqueza cultural.** Comparen los lugares donde uno puede ir de compras en los Estados Unidos y en los países hispanos. Hablen de lo que se puede comprar en esos lugares y la forma de pago.

En estos mercados al aire libre se ofrece una gran variedad de productos: ropa, juguetes, perfumes, artículos de ferretería (hardware), artesanías, comida, etc. Los precios son más bajos y es posible regatear, pero por lo general sólo aceptan el pago en efectivo.

VÍNCULOS

For materials related to the Enfoque cultural, see
- SAM-OneKey: WB: 6-25
- IRCD: Chapter 6; pg. 236

Para pensar

¿Qué sabe usted acerca de Venezuela? ¿Sabe usted dónde está? ¿Sabe usted cuál es su principal producto de exportación?

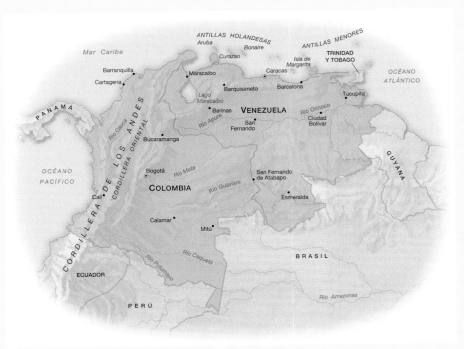

Venezuela está en la parte norte de América del Sur. Es un país que tiene hermosas playas caribeñas, tranquilos pueblos andinos, selvas amazónicas y grandes ciudades cosmopolitas.

En la parte oriental del país se encuentra el Parque Nacional Canaima, donde están las cataratas del Salto del Ángel, las más altas del mundo, con una caída de 807 metros (16 veces más altas que las cataratas del Niágara).

En la zona de los Andes está Mérida, llamada "la Ciudad de los Caballeros", una ciudad colonial, tranquila y muy agradable.

Maracaibo es el centro de la industria petrolera. Venezuela es un país de enormes recursos económicos; además del petróleo, hay oro, piedras preciosas, minerales, etc.

Expresiones venezolanas:

cónchale	¡Cónchale!	*Darn!*
la cara amarrada	Amaneció con la cara amarrada.	*He woke up in a bad mood.*
corotos	¿Dónde están mis **corotos**?	*Where are my things?*

Para contestar

En el mapa

1. Busque una isla de Venezuela que está en el Mar Caribe.
2. Diga qué países están al sur, al este y al oeste de Venezuela.

Ahora diga...

1. por qué se dice que Venezuela es un país privilegiado.
2. qué lugar de interés le gustaría visitar en Venezuela y por qué.

¿Qué dice usted si...

1. no encuentra sus cosas.
2. su amigo/a está de mal humor.

Para investigar en Internet

Busque ofertas de ropa o productos para el hogar en los periódicos de Caracas. Haga una copia de los anuncios para presentarlos en clase y comentar los precios. Describa el anuncio y diga en qué se parece o se diferencia de los anuncios que se publican en los periódicos de los Estados Unidos.

¡Prepárese!

6-46 Impresiones. En este episodio va a ver que los jefes de Ángela quieren cambios en el concurso porque desean algo impresionante, con más impacto. ¡Son muy exigentes (*demanding*)! Imagínese que es uno/a de los jefes de Ángela y exprese sus impresiones sobre el programa hasta este momento. Use los verbos **gustar, interesar, parecer, caer bien/mal** y el complemento indirecto.

MODELO: **Me parece** difícil el Misterio 3.

1. _____
2. _____
3. _____
4. _____
5. _____

Manolo y Ángela tienen que hacer cambios en el programa.

¿Es Katie simpática o agresiva?

En el Parque Chapultepec...

Sabrina y Efraín no están de acuerdo.

Efraín piensa que la solución no puede ser muy obvia.

Si no van a las pirámides de Teotihuacán, ¿adónde van?

¡Responda!

6-47 ¿Qué pasó? En las oraciones siguientes sobre el Episodio 6, use la forma correcta del pretérito del verbo apropriado.

hablar	ir	entrevistar
salir	mencionar	enseñar

1. Los jefes de Ángela le _hablaron_ de cambios en el concurso.
2. Manolo le _enseñó_ a Angela el video del Episodio 6.
3. En el video, Tito _entrevistó_ a Katie.
4. Sabrina y Efraín _fueron_ al Parque Chapultepec.
5. Sabrina _mencionó_ las tres pistas y la Pirámide del Sol en Teotihuacán.
6. Los dos _salieron_ del Parque Chapultepec.

Esta canción de los años 50 en la cual el cantautor lamenta la ausencia de su novia, María Luisa, se refiere a un amor perdido.

¡Prepárese!

6-48 Los diminutivos. En el capítulo 4 vimos como la terminación "-ito/-ita" (el diminutivo) puede usarse para indicar afecto o tamaño o edad. En el título de esta canción hay un diminutivo. ¿Cuál es? Escriba los diminutivos de los siguientes nombres y palabras de la letra de *Caminito de Guarenas*.

PALABRA:	DIMINUTIVO:
María Luisa	María Luisita
la morena	la morenita
una rosa	una rosita
solo (*alone*)	solito/a

¡Escuche!

6-49 ¿Qué pasó? Escuche la canción y después complete los espacios en blanco con la forma correcta del pretérito de los verbos que faltan.

jurar   perder   abandonar   olvidar   encontrar

Caminito de Guarenas
donde (1) _encontré_ la novia mía,
María Luisa la morena,
la que (2) _juró_ que me quería,
y yo recuerdo aquella tarde
cuando una rosa deshojaba
pregúntandole al camino
si era verdad que yo la amaba.
Caminito de Guarenas
que yo encontré,
Caminito de Guarenas
que se me fue.

Caminito de Guarenas,
ya no te acuerdas de nosotros.
María Luisa la morena
me (3) _abandonó_ y se fue con otro.
Ha pasado mucho tiempo
de aquella flor no queda nada,
y en el alma sólo siento,
que tú solito te quedabas.

Ay! caminito que se (4) _perdió_,
Caminito que me (5) _olvidó_.

¡Responda!

6-50 Un club. Imagínese que usted fue a un club a escuchar la música de la orquesta Billo's Caracas Boys. Complete los espacios en blanco con la forma correcta del pretérito de los verbos entre paréntesis.

El sábado pasado mis amigos y yo (ir) _fuimos_ a un club para escuchar la música de la Billo. (Bailar) _Bailamos_ mucho y también (tomar) _tomamos_ algo. Allí yo (bailar) _bailé_ con Julia, una muchacha bonita y simpática. Julia me (dar) _dio_ su número de teléfono. Yo la (llamar) _llamé_. Nosotros (conversar) _conversamos_ mucho y (decidir) _decidimos_ volver al club el sábado siguiente.

VOCABULARIO*

Los accesorios

el anillo	ring
el arete	earring
la billetera	wallet
la bolsa	purse
la bufanda	scarf
el cinturón	belt
el collar	necklace
las gafas de sol	sunglasses
la gorra	cap
el guante	glove
el pañuelo	handkerchief
el paraguas	umbrella
la pulsera	bracelet
el sombrero	hat

Las compras

el almacén	department store
el centro comercial	shopping center
el mercado al aire libre	open-air market
el precio	price
la rebaja	sale
el regalo	present
la talla	size
la tarjeta de crédito	credit card
la tienda	store

Telas y diseño

el algodón	cotton
de color entero	solid color
de cuadros	plaid
de cuero	leather
la lana	wool
de lunares	polka-dotted
el poliéster	polyester
de rayas	striped
la seda	silk

La ropa

el abrigo	coat
la bata	robe
la blusa	blouse
la bota	boot
el calcetín	sock
el calzoncillo	boxer shorts
la camisa	shirt
la camiseta	T-shirt
el camisón	nightgown
la chaqueta	jacket
la corbata	tie
la falda	skirt
el impermeable	raincoat
las medias	stockings, socks
los pantalones	pants
los pantalones cortos	shorts

las pantimedias	pantyhose
el saco	blazer
la sandalia	sandal
el sostén	bra
la sudadera	jogging suit, sweatshirt
el suéter	sweater
el traje	suit
el traje de baño	bathing suit
el traje pantalón	pantsuit
los vaqueros/jeans	jeans
el vestido	dress
la zapatilla	slipper
el zapato	shoe

Verbos

cambiar	to change, to exchange
contestar	to answer
dar	to give, to hand
encantar	to delight, to love
encontrar (ue)	to find
entrar	to go in, to enter
gastar	to spend
gustar	to be pleasing to, to like
interesar	to interest
llevar	to wear, to take
mostrar (ue)	to show
pagar	to pay
parecer (zc)	to seem
ponerse	to put on
probarse (ue)	to try on
quedar	to fit, to be left over
regalar	to give (a present)
valer	to be worth
vender	to sell

Descripciones

ancho/a	wide
barato/a	inexpensive, cheap
caro/a	expensive
estrecho/a	narrow, tight
magnífico/a	great
precioso/a	beautiful
rebajado/a	marked down

Palabras y expresiones útiles

así	this way
el dinero	money
en efectivo	cash
¿En qué puedo servirle(s)?	How may I help you?
enseguida	immediately
estar de moda	to be fashionable
ir de compras	to go shopping
Me gustaría...	I would like . . .
Quisiera...	I would like . . .

*A list of expressions denoting past time can be found on page 215.

EL TIEMPO Y LOS DEPORTES

Objetivos comunicativos

- Expressing and describing physical activities
- Asking and answering questions about weather conditions
- Expressing more measurements
- Talking about past events
- Expressing how long ago events and states occurred

Contenido

A PRIMERA VISTA

AUDIO Los deportes

El **fútbol** es el **deporte** número uno en los países hispanos.

Hay excelentes equipos de fútbol en España, Argentina, Uruguay, Colombia, México y otros países latinoamericanos. Los mejores **jugadores** de los equipos locales forman un **equipo** nacional. Esta selección representa al país en **campeonatos** internacionales y participa, cada cuatro años, en la Copa Mundial.

En la zona del Caribe, el béisbol es el deporte más popular, y muchos de sus jugadores, como Sammy Sosa y Pedro Martínez, forman parte de los mejores equipos de los Estados Unidos.

El **esquí** es un deporte que practican muchas personas en Argentina, Chile y España. Aquí vemos a unos jóvenes que van a **esquiar** en las **pistas** de Bariloche, Argentina, uno de los centros de esquí más importantes de la América del Sur.

El **ciclismo,** el tenis y el golf son otros deportes que cuentan con figuras renombradas en Hispanoamérica y España. Los españoles Aitor González y Roberto Heras son algunos de los líderes del Tour de France. En esta **carrera,** que dura más de 20 días, los ciclistas recorren a veces unos 200 kilómetros, el equivalente de 120 millas, en un solo día.

En cuanto al tenis, Juan Ignacio Chela, argentino, y Fernando González, chileno, son dos de los tenistas más conocidos del Cono Sur.

Sergio García, conocido como "El niño", es la promesa más joven del golf español.

Deportes y equipos necesarios

el béisbol — el bate

los jugadores

el guante

el golf — los palos de golf

la raqueta

la cancha

el tenis

el cesto/
la cesta

el basquetbol / el baloncesto

la pelota

la red

el vóleibol

You may use the Image Resource CD to provide input about baseball and other sports: *El béisbol es el deporte más importante en el área del Caribe* (show on map). *Los jóvenes practican este deporte todo el año. En los Estados Unidos hay muchos jugadores profesionales del Caribe, especialmente de la República Dominicana, como los hermanos Pedro y Ramón Martínez, Sammy Sosa y Vladimir Guerrero. De Puerto Rico, Bernie Williams, Javy López y Jorge Posada; y de Cuba, Rey Ordóñez y los hermanos Liván y Orlando Hernández, este último más conocido como El Duque. ¿Va Ud. a los partidos de béisbol o prefiere verlos en la televisión? ¿Conoce a algún jugador famoso? ¿Juega Ud. al béisbol? ¿Quiénes más juegan al béisbol? ¿Y al baloncesto?* You may ask about other sports, such as *boxeo, tenis, golf, natación,* and *campo y pista.*

VÍNCULOS

To practice vocabulario—Los deportes, Deportes y equipos necesarios, El tiempo y las estaciones & Un partido importante

- SAM-OneKey: WB: 7-1, 7-2, 7-3, 7-4 / LM: 7-24, 7-25, 7-26, 7-27
- Companion Website: AP 7-1, AP 7-2, AP 7-3, AP 7-4
- IRCD: Chapter 7; pp. 245, 247, 248, 249, 250, 251

Note. While the majority of people use *jugar + al + deporte*, some Spanish speakers omit *al*, saying *jugar tenis, golf,* etc. In Spain, *jugar a tenis, golf,* etc.

Note. Some Spanish speakers say *básquetbol*, with the stress on the antepenultimate syllable.

Note. Some Spanish speakers say *volibol*.

¿Qué dice usted?

7-1 Deportes: ¿Quién es? Primera fase. Asocie los deportes de la columna de la izquierda con los jugadores hispanos de la columna de la derecha.

1. __d__ ciclismo
2. __c, e__ tenis
3. __b__ béisbol
4. __a__ golf

a. Sergio García
b. Pedro Martínez
c. Fernando González
d. Aitor González
e. Juan Ignacio Chela

Segunda fase. Ahora elijan dos deportes e intercambien datos sobre sus jugadores favoritos del deporte. Luego descríbale a la clase los jugadores favoritos de su compañero/a.

7-2 ¿Qué necesitamos para jugar? Primera fase. Además de una pelota, necesitamos ciertas cosas para practicar estos deportes. Indíquelo al lado de cada deporte en la siguiente tabla.

DEPORTE	EQUIPO
béisbol	
golf	
vóleibol	
baloncesto	
tenis	

Segunda fase. Entreviste a su compañero/a sobre los deportes que él/ella practica.

1. ¿Qué deporte(s) practicas?
2. ¿Dónde compras el equipo y la ropa que necesitas para practicarlo(s)?
3. ¿Por qué compras tu equipo allí?

7-3 ¿Qué deporte es? Túrnense para identificar los siguientes deportes.

1. Hay nueve jugadores en cada equipo y usan un bate y una pelota. béisbol
2. Es un juego para dos o cuatro personas; necesitamos raquetas y una pelota. tenis
3. En este deporte los jugadores no pueden usar las manos. fútbol
4. Para practicar este deporte necesitamos tener una bicicleta. ciclismo
5. En cada equipo hay cinco jugadores que pueden lanzar (*throw*) la pelota a un cesto. baloncesto
6. Para este deporte necesitamos una red y una pelota; mucha gente lo juega en la playa. vóleibol

7-4 Su deporte favorito. Háganse las preguntas necesarias para averiguar lo siguiente.

1. deporte favorito
2. lugar donde lo practica, con quién y cuándo
3. otros deportes que practica
4. nombres de sus jugadores/as favoritos/as

Ⓖ 7-5 Encuesta. En grupos de tres o cuatro, intercambien preguntas para completar la siguiente encuesta. Después, comparen los resultados de su grupo con los de otros.

1. deporte favorito
2. jugador/a favorito/a
3. equipo favorito
4. asistencia a los partidos
   a. todos b. pocos c. ninguno (*none*)
5. ver los partidos por televisión
   a. todos b. pocos c. ninguno
6. saber jugarlo bien
   a. Sí b. No

Suggestion for 7-5. You may introduce the new words *asistencia* and *ninguno* to facilitate the students' work.

El tiempo y las estaciones

ⒹⒾⓄ Verano

¿Qué tiempo hace? Hace buen tiempo y hace calor. Es un día perfecto para jugar al vóleibol en la playa. El cielo está despejado y hace mucho sol.

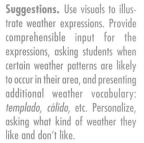

Suggestions. Use visuals to illustrate weather expressions. Provide comprehensible input for the expressions, asking students when certain weather patterns are likely to occur in their area, and presenting additional weather vocabulary: *templado, cálido,* etc. Personalize, asking what kind of weather they like and don't like.

Suggestions. Recycle months by asking students when the following occur; for each, you may also want to ask what the weather is like both in your area and in the Southern Hemisphere: 1. *Termina el año escolar.* 2. *Empieza la temporada de béisbol.* 3. *Ud. celebra su cumpleaños.* 4. *Sale de vacaciones.* 5. *Se juega el campeonato de fútbol americano "Super Bowl".* 6. *Se celebra el día de San Patricio.* 7. *Se celebra el día de Martin Luther King.* 8. *Es el cumpleaños de su mejor amigo/a.* 9. *Este mes tiene el día más corto del año.*

You may point out that the Celsius system is used in Hispanic countries, while pointing to the illustrations.

Note. Some Spanish speakers use *hay* instead of *hace: Hay mucho sol.*

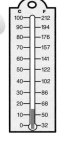

Otoño

Hace fresco y mucho viento. No es fácil jugar al golf cuando hace viento. Pero el otoño es muy bonito porque muchos árboles cambian de color antes de perder las hojas.

Invierno

Hace mal tiempo. Anoche nevó y hoy hace frío. Hay mucha nieve y hielo en las calles. Los lagos también se congelaron y algunas personas aprovechan para patinar en el hielo.

Note. In some Spanish speaking countries the expressions *jugar (al) boliche* or *ir de bowling* are preferred to *jugar a los bolos.*

A INVESTIGAR

¿En qué estación son los campeonatos de béisbol en el Caribe? ¿Por qué cree usted que se realizan en esa estación?

Suggestions for 7-7. You may wish to review phone-calling expressions in Spanish. To make the conversation as realistic as possible, you may have pairs sit back to back. Videotape a TV weather report in Spanish and have students watch it before this activity.

You may wish to present additional weather-related vocabulary such as *tornado, ciclón, humedad, huracán, granizo, nevada, llovizna, sequía, neblina, escampar, llovizar, truenos, relámpagos.*

EN DIRECTO

To express happiness and gratitude for someone's call:
Mil gracias por llamar. ¡Fue un gusto escucharte!
Gracias por llamar. ¡Qué placer escucharte!

Follow-up for 7-8. You may wish to ask students to choose a country or city in the Spanish-speaking world and do this exercise using weather conditions in that part of the world.

Variation for 7-8. Have students complete the following open-ended statements with ideas not related to sports, such as *Cuando llueve..., Cuando nieva..., Cuando hace mal tiempo..., Cuando hace mucho calor...;* they may also match activities and appropriate weather conditions: *¿Qué tiempo hace en el verano cuando juega vóleibol en la playa?*

Primavera

Hoy **está nublado** y **está lloviendo;** por eso estos chicos no pueden jugar al fútbol y están jugando a los **bolos.** Pero **la lluvia** es muy buena para las plantas y las **flores,** y además limpia la atmósfera contaminada.

¿Qué dice usted?

7-6 Asociación. Asocie la situación de la columna de la izquierda con el estado del tiempo de la columna de la derecha.

1. __e__ Todo el césped está blanco.
2. __c__ Las personas llevan impermeable y paraguas.
3. __d__ La casa es un horno y vamos a ir a la playa.
4. __b__ Está lloviendo, pero es imposible abrir el paraguas.
5. __a__ Vamos a celebrar mi cumpleaños en el parque porque el clima está perfecto.
6. __f__ El cielo está muy oscuro. No vamos a jugar al golf hoy.

a. Hace muy buen tiempo.
b. Hace mucho viento.
c. Está lloviendo.
d. Hace mucho calor.
e. Está nevando.
f. Está nublado.

7-7 ¿Qué tiempo hace? Uno/a de sus amigo/as lo/la llama por teléfono desde otra ciudad o país. Pregúntele qué tiempo hace donde él/ella está y averigüe cuáles son sus planes. Su amigo/a debe hacerle preguntas a usted.

MODELO: E1: ¡Qué sorpresa! ¿Dónde estás?
E2: _____
E1: ¿Qué tiempo hace allí?
E2: _____
E1: ¿Y qué piensas hacer esta tarde/noche/este fin de semana?
E2: _____
E1: Mil gracias por llamar.

7-8 Las estaciones y los deportes en mi ciudad. Primera fase. Háganse preguntas sobre las estaciones del año en su ciudad de origen y los deportes que practican en cada estación. Después, cambien de papel.

MODELO: E1: ¿De dónde eres?
E2: _____.
E1: ¿Y qué tiempo hace allí en _____?
E2: _____.
E1: ¿Qué deportes practicas?
E2: _____.

G **Segunda fase.** Sin mencionar el nombre de su compañero/a, escriba un resumen de la información que obtuvo en la **Primera fase.** El resto de la clase va a adivinar sobre quién escribió. Siga el modelo.

MODELO: Es una persona de... En su ciudad/país, ... en invierno. En primavera, ... y... En otoño, ... y... En el invierno, el clima es... ¿Con quién conversé?

2 7-9 Las temperaturas. Escojan una ciudad del mapa y completen la siguiente conversación.

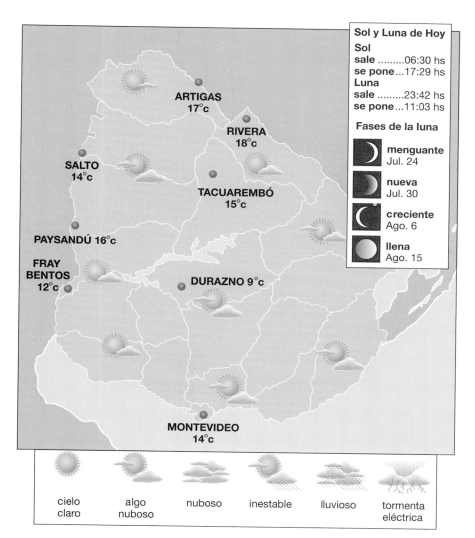

E1: ¿Qué temperatura hace en _____?
E2: _____ grados, más o menos.
E1: ¿Por el día o por la noche?
E2: Por _____.
E1: ¿Cuál es el equivalente en Fahrenheit?
E2: _____.
E1: ¿Y qué tiempo hace allí?
E2: _____.

Las actividades diarias

AUDIO Un partido importante

Hoy es el juego decisivo del campeonato de fútbol.

Rigoberto **se despierta** temprano.

Se levanta.

Se lava los dientes.

Se **afeita.**

Se viste.

Se sienta a desayunar. Después se va para el campo de fútbol.

El partido está terminando y el equipo de Rigoberto gana. Los aficionados aplauden porque están muy emocionados. Un jugador del equipo contrario está discutiendo con el **árbitro** porque no **está de acuerdo** con su decisión.

Rigoberto **se quita** el uniforme.

Se baña.

Se seca.

Se peina.

Note. You may wish to point out that some Spanish speakers would make a distinction between *se baña* and *se ducha.*

Se pone la ropa.

Va a una fiesta para celebrar el triunfo.

Vuelve a casa muy tarde.
Está muy cansado y **se acuesta.**

¿Qué dice usted?

7-10 ¿Qué significa? Lean estas palabras relacionadas con los deportes con su compañero/a. Asocien cada palabra con su significado.

1. __c__ ganar
2. __f__ equipo
3. __e__ decisión
4. __d__ partido
5. __b__ árbitro
6. __a__ campeón/campeona

a. jugador/a número 1 en un deporte
b. persona que mantiene el orden en un partido
c. tener más puntos al terminar un juego
d. juego entre dos equipos o individuos
e. la palabra final del árbitro
f. un grupo de jugadores

7-11 Las actividades de Rigoberto. Primera fase. Contesten las preguntas sobre las actividades de Rigoberto el día del partido.

1. ¿Qué es lo primero que hace Rigoberto? Se despierta.
2. Después de levantarse, ¿se lava los dientes o se viste? Se lava los dientes.
3. ¿Se afeita por la mañana o por la noche? por la mañana
4. ¿Qué usa para secarse? una toalla
5. ¿Adónde va después de bañarse y vestirse? a una fiesta
6. ¿Cuándo se acuesta? a medianoche

G **Segunda fase.** Indiquen qué actividad(es) de Rigoberto muestra(n) que es una persona...

1. limpia
2. puntual
3. responsable
4. que cuida su salud (*health*)

¿Hacen ustedes lo mismo?

Suggestions for 7-12. As you go around the class monitoring pair work encourage conversation by asking: *¿A qué hora se levanta Ud.? ¿Quién se baña por la mañana, usted o él/ella? ¿Usted se sienta a desayunar o no se sienta? ¿Y su compañero/a?*

Talk about yourself to encourage students to talk about themselves: *Yo me despierto a las seis.* Write *yo me despierto* on the board, underlining *yo, me, -o.* *¿A qué hora se despierta Ud.?* Write *Ud. se despierta* also, underlining *Ud., se, -a.* Continue this pattern for other questions without writing *yo/usted.*

2 7-12 Mi rutina diaria. Primera fase. Intercambien información sobre lo que hace cada uno/a de ustedes todos los días desde que se levanta hasta que se acuesta. Háganse preguntas sobre lo siguiente:

1. hora de despertarse y de levantarse
2. actividades que hace por la mañana y por la tarde
3. número de horas de estudio
4. deporte(s) que practica y frecuencia con que lo(s) practica
5. actividades que hace con otras personas y frecuencia con que las hace

2 Segunda fase. Después, comparen su rutina diaria, contestando las siguientes preguntas:

1. ¿Quién de ustedes está más ocupado/a durante el día? ¿Por qué?
2. Normalmente, ¿quién se levanta más temprano? ¿Quién se acuesta más tarde?
3. ¿Quién estudia más? ¿Quién practica más deportes?
4. ¿Quién es más sociable? ¿Por qué?

Warm-up for 7-13. As a prelistening activity, have students get together in groups of four and describe the weather in their cities during spring, summer, fall, and winter and the clothes they wear.

Audioscript for 7-13: ANUNCIADOR: Y ahora el pronóstico del tiempo para las capitales hispanas. Lima: El día está muy nublado. No llueve, pero hace mucho frío. La temperatura es de 14 grados centígrados con 95% de humedad. Es un buen día para ponerse un suéter de lana y una chaqueta. Buenos Aires: Está lloviendo. La temperatura es de 10 grados centígrados. Esta noche va a hacer mucho frío. La temperatura bajará a 5 grados centígrados. Póngase un impermeable y no olvide su paraguas. ¡Lo va a necesitar! Caracas: Hace mucho sol y no hace ni frío ni calor. La temperatura es de 20 grados centígrados y esta tarde va a ser de unos 22 grados. Un día ideal para pasear por la ciudad. Madrid: El sol está muy fuerte y hace mucho calor. La temperatura es de 42 grados centígrados. Un día perfecto para quedarse en casa.

AUDIO **7-13 El clima en América Latina.** You will listen to the weather forecast for four Latin American cities. Before you listen, write down the phrases that you might hear in a weather forecast in the following seasons:

primavera _____
verano _____
otoño _____
invierno _____

Now, pay attention to the general idea of what is said. Then, as you listen to the weather forecast, use a check mark to indicate whether each forecast predicts good or bad weather.

	BUEN TIEMPO	MAL TIEMPO
Lima		X
Buenos Aires		X
Caracas		X
Madrid	X	

1. Preterit of *-er* and *-ir* verbs whose stem ends in a vowel

LEER			
yo	leí	nosotros/as	leímos
tú	leíste	vosotros/as	leísteis
Ud., él, ella	leyó	Uds., ellos/as	leyeron

OÍR			
yo	oí	nosotros/as	oímos
tú	oíste	vosotros/as	oísteis
Ud., él, ella	oyó	Uds., ellos/as	oyeron

The preterit endings of verbs whose stem ends in a vowel are the same as those of regular -er and -ir verbs, except for the **usted, él, ella** form and the **ustedes, ellos, ellas** form, which end in **-yó** and **-yeron**.

2. Preterit of stem-changing *-ir* verbs (e → i) (o → u)

PREFERIR			
yo	preferí	nosotros/as	preferimos
tú	preferiste	vosotros/as	preferisteis
Ud., él, ella	prefirió	Uds., ellos/as	prefirieron

DORMIR			
yo	dormí	nosotros/as	dormimos
tú	dormiste	vosotros/as	dormisteis
Ud., él, ella	durmió	Uds., ellos/as	durmieron

- The preterit endings of stem-changing **-ir** verbs are the same as those for regular **-ir** verbs.

- Stem-changing **-ir** verbs (e → ie, e → i, o → ue) change e → i and o → u in the **usted, él, ella** and **ustedes, ellos, ellas** preterit forms.

Marta prefirió salir temprano.	*Marta preferred to leave early.*
José durmió tranquilamente.	*José slept calmly.*

Suggestions. You may wish to review the discussion of diphthongs and written accents in *Student Activities Manual Lección 6* by pointing out the two distinct vowel sounds and written accent on first- and second-person forms (lei, leíste) and on the infinitive *oír*.

VÍNCULOS

To practice preterit tense of -er and -ir verbs whose stem ends in a vowel
- SAM-OneKey: WB: 7-5 / LM: 7-28
- Companion Website: AP 7-5
- *Gramática viva:* Grammar Point 39: Preterit tense of regular verbs + regular verbs with spelling changes
- IRCD: Chapter 7; pg. 253

Suggestions. Use visuals or colored chalk to highlight preterit stem changes. Compare with the present tense. Additional verbs: *morir, pedir, repetir, sentir, servir, vestir.* Remind students that there is no stem change for -ar and -er verbs in the preterit. Present progressive: *Está pidiendo, sirviendo, repitiendo.*

VÍNCULOS

To practice preterit tense of stem-changing -ir verbs (e → i) (o → u)
- SAM-OneKey: WB: 7-6, 7-7 / LM: 7-29
- Companion Website: AP 7-6
- IRCD: Chapter 7; pg. 253

¿Qué dice usted?

Follow-up for 7-14. Ask additional questions based on students' answers: *¿Qué periódico leyó? ¿Leyó todas las secciones? Y usted, ¿leyó el mismo periódico? ¿Leyó usted las mismas secciones que su compañero/a?*

Expansion for 7-14. 7. *¿Quiénes oyeron música clásica anoche? 8. ¿Quiénes durmieron bien/mal? 9. ¿Quiénes pidieron cerveza en un bar? 10. ¿Quiénes leyeron algo en español?*

G 7-14 Encuesta. Primera fase. En grupos pequeños, hagan la siguiente encuesta. Anoten los datos.

¿QUIÉNES EN EL GRUPO...?	TOTAL DEL GRUPO
1. ... leyeron el periódico ayer	_____
2. ... oyeron las noticias esta mañana	_____
3. ... fueron a un partido de tenis o béisbol recientemente	_____
4. ... practicaron un deporte esta semana	_____
5. ... durmieron siete horas o más anoche	_____
6. ... durmieron menos de seis horas anoche	_____

G Segunda fase. Ahora, calculen y comenten lo siguiente. Luego, compartan sus datos con el resto de la clase.

1. ¿Qué porcentaje de ustedes practicó un deporte esta semana o fue a un partido recientemente?
2. ¿Qué porcentaje oyó las noticias esta mañana?
3. ¿Qué porcentaje durmió la siesta?
4. Según ustedes, ¿usaron bien el tiempo ayer? ¿Por qué?

Follow-up for 7-15. One student from each group tells the class what activities all of them did last Sunday.

Using visuals, ask *¿Qué hace/n esta/s persona/s?* Students respond: *El joven se afeita. La señora se peina.* Create a story about Rigoberto, or have students create a story using a series of visuals. Also recycle the present progressive: *El joven se está afeitando ahora. Él está afeitándose* (circle the syllable with the accent mark). You may review the rule of accentuation for *esdrújulas.*

G 7-15 El domingo pasado. Hagan una lista de las actividades que todos los miembros del grupo hicieron el domingo pasado. Después, comparen su lista con la de otro grupo. ¿En qué actividades coinciden?

4 7-16 Celebrando la victoria. Primera fase. Uno de los equipos de su universidad ganó un campeonato importante y ustedes decidieron organizar una fiesta en su honor. Explíquenle a otra pareja los siguientes detalles de la fiesta.

1. deporte y nombre del equipo que representó a la universidad
2. hora y lugar de la fiesta
3. número de personas que invitaron y cuántas asistieron
4. dinero que le pidieron a cada persona para los gastos de la fiesta
5. comida y bebida que sirvieron, y tipo de música que escucharon en la fiesta
6. regalos que les dieron a los jugadores

Suggestion. Remind students to use the expressions they have learned to accept invitations.

SITUACIONES

1. **Role A.** You had to work late last night and missed a very important basketball game at your college/university. Call a friend who went to the game and after greeting him/her a) explain why you did not go, b) ask as many questions as possible about the game, c) answer your friend's questions, and d) accept his/her invitation to go to another game next Saturday.

   Role B. A friend calls you to find out about last night's basketball game. Answer his/her questions giving as many details as possible. Then a) tell him/her that there is another game on Saturday, b) find out if he/she is free that evening, and d) if free, invite him/her to go with you.

2. One of you read in today's newspaper that a famous football player is going to be interviewed on TV tonight. The other should find out a) in which newspaper you read about the interview, b) the time of the interview, c) the channel (**el canal**), and d) who will do the interview.

3. Reflexive verbs and pronouns

	REFLEXIVES	
yo	me lavo	*I wash myself*
tú	te lavas	*you wash yourself*
Ud.	se lava	*you wash yourself*
él/ella	se lava	*he/she washes himself/herself*
nosotros/as	nos lavamos	*we wash ourselves*
vosotros/as	os laváis	*you wash yourselves*
Uds.	se lavan	*you wash yourselves*
ellos/ellas	se lavan	*they wash themselves*

VÍNCULOS

To practice reflexive verbs and pronouns
- SAM-OneKey: WB: 7-8, 7-9 / LM: 7-30, 7-31, 7-32
- Companion Website: AP 7-7
- *Gramática viva:* Grammar Point 45: Reflexive verbs
- IRCD: Chapter 7; pg. 255

- In *Lección 4*, you learned that true reflexive verbs express what people do *to* or *for* themselves. You also practiced the **yo, tú,** and **usted, él, ella** forms of some reflexive verbs, placing the reflexive pronouns before the conjugated verb. Now you will learn more about reflexives and practice other verb forms.

Alicia **se levanta** a las siete y media. *Alicia gets up at seven thirty.*
Nosotros **nos vestimos** rápidamente. *We get dressed quickly.*

- With verbs followed by an infinitive, place reflexive pronouns before the conjugated verb or attach them to the infinitive.

Yo **me** voy a acostar a las diez.⎫
Yo voy a acostar**me** a las diez.⎬ *I am going to go to bed at ten.*

ACENTOS

The verb form **maquillándose** has an accent mark. Do you know why?

- With the present progressive (**estar** + **-ndo**), place reflexive pronouns before the conjugated form of **estar** or attach them to the present participle. When attaching a pronoun, add a written accent mark to the stressed vowel (the vowel preceding **-ndo**) of the present participle.

Amelia **se** está maquillando ahora.⎫
Amelia está maquillándo**se** ahora.⎬ *Amelia is putting on makeup now.*

Suggestion. If possible, use visuals to review reflexive and nonreflexive verbs. For example, *La mamá peina a su hija. La mamá se peina. Roberto baña a su perro. Roberto se baña.* You may also create a story about a sports figure using a series of visuals. Also recycle the present progressive: *El joven se está bañando. El joven está bañándose* (circle the syllable with the accent mark). Demonstrate that certain verbs can be reflexive or nonreflexive: *Quito los libros de la mesa. Me quito el reloj. Pongo el reloj en la mesa. Me pongo el reloj.*

- When referring to parts of the body and articles of clothing, use definite articles rather than possessives with reflexive verbs.

Me lavo **los** dientes. *I brush my teeth.*
Me pongo **la** sudadera. *I put on my sweatshirt.*

- There are other Spanish verbs that use reflexive pronouns, but they do not necessarily convey the idea of doing something to or for oneself. These verbs normally convey the idea of mental or physical states.

María **se enfermó** la semana pasada, *María **got sick** last week and that*
y eso **nos preocupó** mucho. ***worried us** a lot.*

- Some verbs change meaning when used reflexively.

acostar	to put to bed	acostarse	to go to bed, to lie down
dormir	to sleep	dormirse	to fall asleep
ir	to go	irse	to go away, to leave (for)
levantar	to raise, to lift	levantarse	to get up
llamar	to call	llamarse	to be called
quitar	to take away	quitarse	to take off

¿Qué dice usted?

7-17 ¿Qué hacemos todos los días? Ponga estas actividades en el orden más lógico.

a. _6_ me duermo
b. _1_ me levanto
c. _4_ me voy a la universidad

d. _5_ me acuesto
e. _2_ me lavo la cara
f. _3_ me siento a desayunar

7-18 ¿Qué hacemos? Primera fase. Hablen sobre sus actividades diarias. ¿Sus horarios son similares o diferentes?

MODELO: E1: Yo me despierto a las siete.
　　　　　E2: Y yo (me despierto) a las ocho.

1. Yo me levanto....
2. Después me lavo....
3. Me visto....
4. Me siento a desayunar....

5. Me voy a la universidad....
6. Yo me baño....
7. Me acuesto....
8. Me duermo....

Segunda fase. Cambien de pareja y hablen sobre su propio horario y el de su compañero/a anterior. Comenten cuáles son sus horarios los fines de semana y compárenlos.

MODELO: E1: Juan y yo nos levantamos a las ocho. También nos bañamos por la tarde. ¿Y tú?
　　　　　E2: Yo me levanto a las siete.

7-19 Mis actividades de ayer. Haga una lista de todo lo que hizo ayer para cuidar de su salud. Después, compárela con la de su compañero/a.

Suggestion for 7-20. You may recycle the present progressive: *Son las 8:20. ¿Qué está haciendo Arturo? Son las 7:30. ¿Qué están haciendo Alicia y Berta? Hace mucho calor después del partido de fútbol; ¿qué están haciendo Alicia y Berta?*

7-20 Los horarios. Túrnense para hablar del horario de estos atletas. Háganse preguntas para compararlo con el horario de ustedes.

MODELO: acostarse / 11:00 / 10:30
　　　　　E1: Arturo se acuesta a las once.
　　　　　E2: Y Alicia y Berta se acuestan a las diez y media. ¿Y tú?
　　　　　E1: Yo me acuesto a _____.

	ARTURO	ALICIA Y BERTA	YO
despertarse	8:00	7:00	
levantarse	8:15	7:05	
bañarse	8:20	7:10	
vestirse	8:30	7:20	

7-21 ¿Qué hacen estas personas? Lean las siguientes situaciones y túrnense para hablar de lo que hacen y lo que van a hacer estas personas. Usen los verbos de la lista. Después, comparen sus opiniones con las de otros/as compañeros/as.

acostarse	afeitarse	bañarse	dormirse	irse	lavarse
levantarse	maquillarse	ponerse	quitarse	secarse	vestirse

MODELO: Bernardo está durmiendo y suena el despertador.
E1: Bernardo se despierta cuando oye el despertador. En tu opinión, ¿qué va a hacer después?
E2: Va a levantarse enseguida y después va a bañarse.

1. Teresa está enfrente del espejo y se prepara para ir a una fiesta muy elegante.
2. Juan y Tomás entran en el vestuario (*dressing room*) del gimnasio porque van a jugar al baloncesto con unos amigos.
3. Marisa y Sarita están en una playa de Punta del Este, en Uruguay.
4. Rogelio sale de la ducha y toma una toalla.
5. Son las once de la noche. Marta está en su cuarto y tiene mucho sueño.

7-22 Nuestra preparación para el campeonato. El mes pasado ustedes representaron a su universidad en un campeonato de tenis en Montevideo, Uruguay. Digan lo que hicieron...

■ para prepararse físicamente.

■ para prepararse mentalmente.

■ para cumplir (*to fulfill*) con las responsabilidades académicas.

Suggestion for 7-22. Personalize by asking any athletes in the class what they normally do to prepare for a game and what they did in their last important match or game.

SITUACIONES

1. **Role A.** You are a well-known sportsperson, highly admired by youngsters in your country. The reporter of a TV network is going to interview you to prepare a special about your life. Answer the reporter's questions as completely as possible. Remember that you are considered a role model by young people.

   Role B. You are a reporter for a major TV network. Today you are interviewing a well-respected and admired sports figure. After introducing yourself and greeting him/her, find out a) when he/she started to play, b) what school he/she went to, c) what his/her daily routine is, and d) the things he/she does daily to keep in shape (**estar en forma**).

2. **Role A.** You would like your younger brother to attend a summer camp. Ask the camp director questions to find out a) how many children there are per counselor (**consejero/a**), b) what time the children get up, c) what sports they play, d) what they eat, e) what they do in the evenings, and f) what time they go to bed.

   Role B. You are the director of the summer camp. Answer your prospective client's questions and add more information regarding the variety of activities.

VÍNCULOS

To practice pronouns after prepositions
- SAM-OneKey: WB: 7-10, 7-11 / LM: 7-33
- Companion Website: AP 7-8
- IRCD: Chapter 7; pg. 258

4. Pronouns after prepositions

Voy a la reunión del equipo ahora. ¿Quieres ir conmigo?

Sí, voy contigo.

- In *Lección 6*, you used **a** + **mí**, **ti**, and so on to clarify or emphasize the indirect object pronoun: **Le di el suéter a él.** These same pronouns are used after other prepositions, such as **de**, **para**, and **sin**.

Siempre habla **de ti**.	*He is always talking about you.*
El boleto es **para mí**.	*The ticket is for me.*
No quieren ir **sin nosotros**.	*They do not want to go without us.*

- In a few cases, Spanish does not use **mí** and **ti**. After **con**, use **conmigo** and **contigo**. After **entre**, use **tú y yo**.

¿Vas al partido **conmigo**?	*Are you going to the game with me?*
Sí, voy **contigo**.	*Yes, I am going with you.*
Pedro va a sentarse **entre tú y yo**.	*Pedro is going to sit between you and me.*

¿Qué dice usted?

7-23 Un amigo preguntón. Rosario habla con un amigo que hace muchas preguntas. Lea las preguntas en la columna de la izquierda y conéctelas con una respuesta o un comentario lógico de Rosario en la columna de la derecha.

1. ¿Con quién vas a ir al partido de tenis, Rosario? c
2. ¿Por qué no vemos las finales del campeonato con Sofía? f
3. Rosario, ¿para quién es esta raqueta de tenis? a
4. ¿Pueden mis amigos ir a la cancha con nosotros? b
5. En el partido de ayer hubo un accidente. ¿A quién le informaron primero del accidente? d
6. ¿De quién van a recibir el trofeo los ganadores? e

a. La compré para ti. ¿Te gusta?
b. Imposible. No podemos ir con ellos. Tengo sólo dos billetes (*tickets*).
c. Contigo, ¡por supuesto!
d. A la policía. Hay que informarles rápidamente.
e. De nosotros. De ti y de mí. ¡Qué emocionante!
f. Prefiero verlas sin ella. Habla mucho y no puedo concentrarme.

③ 7-24 Las prácticas de tenis. Identifíquense cada uno/a con un número y hagan preguntas para saber quién va a practicar tenis con quién. Contesten según la tabla.

MODELO: E1: ¿Con quién practica Jorge el sábado?
E3: Practica conmigo. (o E2: Practica con él/ella.)

LUNES	MARTES	MIÉRCOLES	JUEVES	VIERNES	SÁBADO
Pedro	Alicia	Carmen	Jorge	Carmen	Jorge
E1	E2	E3	E1	E2	E3

② 7-25 ¿Con quién va? Completen el siguiente diálogo, usando pronombres.

E1: Yo salgo ahora. ¿Vienes conmigo?
E2: No, no puedo ir _contigo_. Tengo que trabajar media hora más en la tienda.
E1: ¡Cuánto lo siento! Entonces, ¿vas a ir con Roberto?
E2: Sí, voy a ir con ___él___.
E1: Seguro que él no quiere ir sin ___ti___. Tú eres su mejor amigo/a.
E2: Sí, somos muy buenos amigos. ¿Y tú sabes dónde te vas a sentar?
E1: Sí, voy a sentarme entre _____ y _____. Answers may vary.

SITUACIONES

Role A. Your friend, the coach, gave you two tickets for today's football game, but you have no transportation. Call a friend and after greeting him/her, a) explain how you got the tickets for the game, b) invite him/her to go with you, and c) explain that you have no transportation.

Role B. A friend calls you to invite you to a football game. After exchanging greetings, a) thank him/her for the invitation, b) say that you would be delighted to go with him/her, c) that you can pick him/her up in your car, and d) agree on a time and place.

5. Some irregular preterits

Some irregular verbs do not stress the last syllable in the **yo,** and **usted, él, ella** preterit forms.

■ The verbs **hacer, querer,** and **venir** have an **i** in the preterit stem.

INFINITIVE	NEW STEM	PRETERIT FORMS
hacer	hic	hice, hiciste, hizo, hicimos, hicisteis, hicieron
querer[1]	quis	quise, quisiste, quiso, quisimos, quisisteis, quisieron
venir	vin	vine, viniste, vino, vinimos, vinisteis, vinieron

---

[1]The verb **querer** in the preterit followed by an infinitive normally means *to try (but fail) to do something.*

Quise hacerlo ayer. *I tried to do it yesterday.*

Follow-up for 7-24. Encourage students to vary questions. Give examples, if necessary: *¿Pedro y Jorge practican contigo? ¿Qué días practican contigo? ¿Te gusta practicar tenis con ellos?*

VÍNCULOS

To practice some irregular preterits
• SAM-OneKey: WB: 7-12, 7-13, 7-14 / LM: 7-34, 7-35, 7-36, 7-37
• Companion Website: AP 7-9
• *Gramática viva*: Grammar Point 38: Preterit tense of irregular verbs *ser, ir, tener, estar*
• IRCD: Chapter 7; pp. 259, 260, 261

Suggestion. Remind students that *¿Qué hiciste? ¿Qué hizo Ud.? ¿Qué hicieron Uds.?* are very common, information-gathering questions using the verb *hacer* that do not generally elicit a response using the verb *hacer*. Have students practice these questions by giving them two or three minutes to find out (and remember) what five other people did last night. Then ask students to report back to the class.

■ The verbs **decir**, **traer**, and all verbs ending in **-ducir** (e.g., **traducir**–*to translate*) have a **j** in the stem and use the ending **-eron** instead of **-ieron**. **Decir** also has an **i** in the stem.

INFINITIVE	NEW STEM	PRETERIT FORMS
decir	**dij**	dije, dijiste, dijo, dijimos, dijisteis, dijeron
traer	**traj**	traje, trajiste, trajo, trajimos, trajisteis, trajeron
traducir	**traduj**	traduje, tradujiste, tradujo, tradujimos, tradujisteis, tradujeron

■ The verbs **estar**, **tener**, **poder**, **poner**, and **saber** have a **u** in the preterit stem.

INFINITIVE	NEW STEM	PRETERIT FORMS
estar	**estuv**	estuve, estuviste, estuvo, estuvimos, estuvisteis, estuvieron
tener	**tuv**	tuve, tuviste, tuvo, tuvimos, tuvisteis, tuvieron
poder[1]	**pud**	pude, pudiste, pudo, pudimos, pudisteis, pudieron
poner	**pus**	puse, pusiste, puso, pusimos, pusisteis, pusieron
saber[2]	**sup**	supe, supiste, supo, supimos, supisteis, supieron

Suggestions. Relate a recent experience (or make one up) using visuals to introduce the preterit of these verbs and others: *El año pasado estuve en Miami. Estuve en un hotel de la playa y pude practicar español, porque en Miami viven muchos hispanos. Jugué a la lotería, pero no tuve suerte. No gané ni un centavo, pero pasé unos días muy agradables allí. Personalize: ¿Dónde estuvo Ud. el verano pasado? ¿Le gustó el lugar? ¿Tuvo la oportunidad de hablar español?*

¿Qué dice usted?

7-26 Un equipo indisciplinado. Después de las irregularidades en la práctica de ayer, el entrenador de la selección uruguaya de vóleibol se prepara para escribir un informe. Como el entrenador es de Inglaterra y su español no es perfecto, él revisa su texto. Para ayudarlo, haga un círculo alrededor de la expresión que corresponda en cada caso y escríbala en el espacio apropiado.

Les informo que durante la práctica de ayer, ocurrieron varios incidentes que me preocupan. Al comienzo, yo les (1) __dije__ (digo, dije, dijimos) a los jugadores que íbamos a practicar un poco más de tiempo. Ellos me (2) __dijeron__ (dijo, dijeron, dicen) que no podían quedarse más tiempo. Yo (3) __hice__ (hago, hice, hicieron) un gran esfuerzo para convencerlos de la importancia de prolongar un rato más la práctica, pero ellos no (4) __quisieron__ (quisieron, quieren, quiso) comprenderlo, y empezaron a protestar. Como no me escuchaban, mi asistente y el físicoterapeuta (5) __tuvieron__ (tuvieron, tenemos, tuvimos) que llamar al director de deportes de la universidad. Solamente él (6) __pudo__ (pudo, puede, pudieron) tranquilizarlos. El subdirector que (7) __vino__ (viene, vino, vinieron) con él les habló sobre sus obligaciones con la universidad, y todos juntos (8) __pusimos__ (pusieron, puso, pusimos) fin al problema. Después de unas horas, yo (9) __supe__ (sé, supe, supimos) que los jugadores escribieron una carta para pedir perdón.

---

[1]**Poder** used in the preterit usually means *to manage to do something*.

      Pude hacerlo esta mañana.   *I managed to do it this morning.*

[2]**Saber** in the preterit normally means *to learn* or *to find out*.

      Supe que llegaron anoche.   *I learned that you arrived last night.*

2 **7-27 ¿Qué hizo Ud. ayer?** Imagínese que ayer usted hizo una lista de cosas que tenía que hacer, pero sólo pudo hacer dos o tres. Marque lo que hizo y lo que no pudo hacer, y después conteste las preguntas de su compañero/a.

MODELO: comprar el trofeo para el campeonato
E1: ¿Compraste el trofeo para el campeonato?
E2: Quise comprarlo, pero no pude. o
Sí, pude comprarlo.
E1: ¿Por qué no pudiste comprarlo?
Porque tuve que regresar a una práctica en el laboratorio.

Follow-up for 7-27. Have students ask each other questions to try to find out what his/her partner really did yesterday.

	Sí	No
1. cambiar la chaqueta		
2. comprar los zapatos de tenis		
3. probarse el uniforme nuevo		
4. conocer al nuevo entrenador		
5. ver el video del último partido		
6. comentar las estrategias del próximo partido		

2 **7-28 ¿Qué ocurrió?** Expliquen qué le ocurrió a Javier el día de su cumpleaños. Den la mayor cantidad de información posible.

Suggestion for 7-28. You may use the Image Resource CD to teach students to construct orally a cohesive description/narration by presenting and modeling the following expressions: *pero, por eso/por esa razón, primero, después,* etc.

1.   2.   3.

4.   5.   6.

2 **7-29 Unos días de descanso.** Su compañero/a estuvo unos días en Argentina. Hágale preguntas sobre los siguientes puntos para saber más de su viaje.

1. lugares adonde fue
2. tiempo que estuvo fuera
3. cosas interesantes que hizo
4. los lugares que le gustaron más
5. si pudo hablar español y con quién(es)

Suggestion for 7-29. Students can consult the *Enfoque cultural* essay on Argentina, or make up details of their trip. They may also go to www.prenhall.com/mosaicos.

SITUACIONES

1. **Role A.** You won a contest **(concurso)** to attend the soccer World Cup **(la Copa Mundial).** Tell your friend that a) you won the contest and b) you went to the World Cup. Answer all his/her questions, giving as many details as possible.

   Role B. A friend tells you about the prize he/she won. Ask your friend a) how he/she found about the contest, b) how long he/she was away, c) how many games he/she attended, d) with whom he/she went, and e) details about the last game.

2. **Role A.** Imagine that yesterday you went to a sports event and had the opportunity to see and talk with your favorite sports star. Explain to a friend a) where you went, b) what happened and where, c) what you did when you saw this famous sports star, d) what he/she literally told you, and d) what happened finally.

   Role B. Your friend tells you that he/she saw a very famous sports star yesterday and that he/she had the opportunity to talk to him/her. Ask him/her questions about what happened and their conversation.

Suggestions. To clarify the concept, ask *¿Qué hora es?* Students reply *Es/Son las...* Then ask *¿Y a qué hora empezó esta clase?* Then conclude *La clase empezó hace... minutos.* Write the formula *hace + (minutos) + que + pretérito* on the board and give other examples.

You may write on the board several years and actions: *1990-llegar a San Antonio; 1992-empezar a estudiar; 1996-casarse; 2000-tener el primer hijo.* Then create a story and ask questions: *¿Cuándo llegó a San Antonio? Ah, hace... años que llegó a San Antonio. ¿Y cuántos años hace que empezó a estudiar? ¿Cuántos años hace que se casó? ¿Cuántos años hace que tuvo su primer hijo?* Personalize and encourage students to tell their partners about their own experiences.

 **ALGO MÁS**

Hace, meaning *ago*

■ To indicate the time that has passed since an action was completed, use **hace** + *length of time* + **que** + *preterit tense.* If you begin the sentence with the preterit tense of the verb, do not use **que.**

Hace dos horas que llegaron.⎫
Llegaron **hace** dos horas.⎭   *They arrived two hours ago.*

Hace una hora **que** empezó el partido.⎫
El partido empezó **hace** una hora.⎭   *The game started an hour ago.*

¿Qué dice usted?

7-30 ¿Cuánto tiempo hace...? Seleccione la pregunta más lógica para cada situación. Más de una respuesta correcta puede ser posible.

1. Usted observa que Jorge López, su entrenador, corre dos horas sin parar *(nonstop)* y no se cansa. Usted le pregunta:
   a. Sr. López, ¿cuánto tiempo hace que usted empezó a correr?
   b. ¿Cuánto tiempo hace que usted puede correr tanto *(so much)*, Sr. López?
   c. ¿Cuánto tiempo hace que no corre, Sr. López?

2. La semana pasada, usted vio un gran cambio en su ex compañero/a de cuarto. A diferencia del año pasado, ahora está más delgado/a y atlético/a, y parece más fuerte. Usted le pregunta:
   a. ¿Cuánto hace que comenzaste a practicar deportes?
   b. ¿Cuánto tiempo hace que no haces actividades físicas?
   c. ¿Cuánto tiempo hace que estás enfermo?

3. Isabel, una de las jugadoras de su equipo de baloncesto, hace un tiempo que no asiste a las prácticas. La entrenadora les pregunta a los miembros del equipo:
   a. ¿Cuándo fue la última vez que ustedes vieron a Isabel?
   b. ¿Cuánto tiempo hace que Isabel practicó por última vez?
   c. ¿Cuándo fue la última vez que nuestro equipo se reunió para practicar?

4. La persona que limpia el gimnasio desea limpiar los baños, pero no puede porque los jugadores todavía se están duchando. La persona le pregunta al primer jugador que sale del baño:
   a. ¿Cuánto tiempo hace que usted se duchó?
   b. ¿Cuánto tiempo hace que los jugadores empezaron a ducharse?
   c. ¿Cuánto tiempo hace que terminó el partido?

7-31 ¡A conocernos mejor! Para conocerlo/la mejor, su compañero/a quiere saber cuánto tiempo hace que usted hizo estas cosas. Responda con todos los detalles posibles.

MODELO: ganar el campeonato de tenis
   E1: ¿Cuánto tiempo hace que ganaste el campeonato de tenis?
   E2: Hace dos años. Fue un día extraordinario. Todos mis amigos me felicitaron, y después fuimos a un café a celebrar.

1. conocer a tu novio/a (esposo/a)
2. jugar al tenis, golf, etc. por primera vez
3. leer una buena revista de deportes
4. jugar vóleibol en la playa
5. ir a un estadio muy moderno
6. ver un partido de la Copa Mundial

7-32 Figuras del mundo de los deportes. Uno/a de ustedes va a hacer de reportero/a de una revista deportiva y otro/a va a escoger a uno/a de los deportistas de abajo. El/La reportero/a debe hacer por lo menos tres preguntas usando **hace**. El/La deportista debe contestar con los datos del/de la deportista que escogió. Depués, cambien de papel.

Suggestion for 7-32. You may wish to model this activity with a student first. Write on the board or a transparency, information about a sports figure (similar to what is presented in the activity), and play the role of the reporter. You may use the *usted* form of the verb since you and the student are playing imaginary roles. You may choose to have the students practice the *tú* form instead.

SANDRA ORDÓÑEZ

NACIONALIDAD: chilena
FECHA DE NACIMIENTO: 22 de febrero de 1979
RÉCORD DEPORTIVO:
1. Copa Nacional de Tenis, 1997 (cuarto lugar)
2. Copa Davis, 1998 (ganadora de la copa)
3. Torneo femenino de tenis en Chile, 1998 (segundo lugar)
4. Copa Davis, 1999 (tercer lugar)

JORGE PEDRERO

NACIONALIDAD: uruguayo
FECHA DE NACIMIENTO: 18 de abril de 1965
RÉCORD DEPORTIVO:
1. Capitán del equipo en el Torneo Nacional de Vóleibol de 1990 a 1995
2. Marcó 14 puntos en el partido entre la selección de vóleibol uruguaya y la argentina, 1994
3. Premio al deportista del año en Uruguay, 1993
4. Entrenador del equipo juvenil de vóleibol de Montevideo, 1988–1990

MÓNICA BERNINI

NACIONALIDAD: argentina
FECHA DE NACIMIENTO: 20 de diciembre de 1976
RÉCORD DEPORTIVO:
1. Primer lugar en las competencias de esquí de Bariloche, 1992
2. Segundo lugar en la Competencia de Esquí Chile-Argentina, 1995
3. Finalista del equipo argentino de las Olimpiadas de Invierno, 1996
4. Ganadora de la Competencia Nacional de Esquí, 2001

FELIPE JIMÉNEZ

NACIONALIDAD: boliviano
FECHA DE NACIMIENTO: 18 de junio de 1972
RÉCORD DEPORTIVO:
1. Jugador del Año, 1994
2. Representante de la Comisión Deportiva de Bolivia, 1996
3. Segundo lugar en el Campeonato Interamericano de Golf, 1998
4. Primer lugar en el Campeonato Nacional de Golf, 2001

MOSAICOS

Escuchar

VÍNCULOS

For materials related to the Mosaicos section, see
- SAM-OneKey: WB: 7-17, 7-18, 7-19, 7-20, 7-21, 7-22 / LM: 7-39
- IRCD: Chapter 7; pg. 266

Differentiating facts from opinions

When you talk to a person or watch a television report, you have to differentiate between factual information and personal opinion. You may hear someone say, "Today temperatures will rise to 40° Celsius, so avoid exercising outside." Facts indicate that the temperature will rise to 40° Celsius. The rest of the statement is a personal opinion.

Antes de escuchar

7-33 Los deportes. In activity **7-34,** you will listen to a conversation between Armando and Pablo, two soccer players, discussing the results of the game they just played. Before you listen, write down in Spanish one statement of factual information you think they will make and one opinion they will provide.

Información concreta: _____

Opinión personal: _____

A escuchar

Audioscript for 7-34. ARMANDO: [AUDIO] ¡Oye, Pablo! ¿Qué te pasó hoy? No jugaste como siempre. ¿Estás enfermo? PABLO: No, no estoy enfermo, pero sí sé que no jugué bien hoy. Hice lo que pude. Como no dormí muy bien anoche, estaba muy cansado. Pero tú sí hiciste dos goles. ¡Estuviste magnífico y ganamos! ARMANDO: ¡Gracias! Sí, ganamos tres a uno. ¡Felizmente! En el video del último partido, pude ver algunos de mis errores. Hoy traté de jugar bien. PABLO: ¿Cuándo es el próximo partido? ARMANDO: La próxima semana. Ahora voy a la reunión del equipo. ¿Quieres venir conmigo? Vamos a discutir las estrategias para el próximo partido. PABLO: Sí, por supuesto, pero no me va a ir muy bien. ARMANDO: No te preocupes. Es sólo un juego. Además tú eres un gran jugador.

7-34 Now, listen to the conversation between Armando and Pablo and write down in Spanish three facts and three opinions the soccer players provided.

Información concreta: _No dormí anoche, estaba cansado; hiciste dos goles; ganamos tres a uno; vi el video del último partido; el próximo partido es la próxima semana; voy a la reunión del equipo_

Opinión personal: _No jugaste como siempre; estuviste magnífico; eres un gran jugador._

Después de escuchar

7-35 ¿Y usted? Take turns asking and answering the following questions.

1. ¿Qué deportes practica la gente en su ciudad o región en el invierno? ¿Y en la primavera?
2. ¿Qué deportes practica usted en el invierno o la primavera? ¿Qué hace o no usted antes de practicar deportes? ¿Y después?
3. En su opinión, ¿cuál es el mejor equipo de fútbol americano? ¿Es su equipo favorito realmente un buen equipo?

Antes de escuchar

7-36 El atleta. In activity **7-37,** you will listen to a TV reporter interviewing Nicolás, an Argentinean skier, who discusses his recent stay in Bariloche. Before you listen, write down in Spanish one statement of factual information you think he will make about the slopes where the ski resort is located and one opinion about the people he may meet there.

Información concreta _____

Opinión personal _____

A escuchar

 7-37 Now listen to Nicolás' interview and write down in Spanish three statements of factual information and three opinions Nicolás offered about the place and/or the people.

Información concreta: *Cerro Catedral tiene 65 kilómetros de pistas para esquiar; nevó mucho, unos 30 centímetros de nieve; Cerro Catedral está a 20 kilómetros de Bariloche.*

Opinión personal: *Cerro Catedral es un lugar maravilloso; la ciudad es fantástica; la gente es muy amable.*

Después de escuchar

② **7-38 ¿Y usted?** Ask your partner questions to find out the following information.

1. deporte que practica y dónde lo practica
2. tiempo que hace que lo practica
3. atleta favorito/a en ese deporte y por qué

 # Conversar

Antes de conversar

Ⓖ **7-39 ¿Fanáticos del deporte?** Primero averigüen cuáles son los dos deportes favoritos de su grupo y, luego, completen la tabla con la información pertinente.

DEPORTE	INDIVIDUAL	EN GRUPO	LUGAR DONDE SE PRACTICA	CLIMA IDEAL PARA PRACTICARLO

Audioscript for 7-37: REPORTERO: Nicolás, bienvenido al Programa de Deportes. Sabemos que acabas de regresar de Bariloche, donde te entrenaste por algún tiempo. NICOLÁS: Sí, efectivamente. Estuve dos meses esquiando, junio y julio. Me encantó el lugar. Me gustó mucho Cerro Catedral; es un lugar maravilloso, con 65 kilómetros de pistas para esquiar. La ciudad de Bariloche es fantástica y la gente es muy amable. REPORTERO: ¿Fue tu primera visita a Bariloche? NICOLÁS: No. En mi infancia fui con mis padres varias veces. REPORTERO: ¿Y las pistas? ¿Estuvieron bien? NICOLÁS: Sí, estuvieron maravillosas, porque la primera semana de junio nevó mucho, unos 30 centímetros de nieve y pude esquiar muy bien. Al final llovió y no pude esquiar mucho. Por eso regresé a Buenos Aires. Pero me entrené muy bien y me siento muy bien. REPORTERO: ¡Qué bien! Y, dime, ¿a qué distancia está Cerro Catedral de Bariloche? NICOLÁS: Está muy cerca, a sólo 20 kilómetros. REPORTERO: ¿Y cuándo regresas a Bariloche? NICOLÁS: El próximo año. Voy a ir con unos amigos que quieren prepararse allí también. REPORTERO: Muy bien y buena suerte en la próxima competencia. NICOLÁS: Muchas gracias.

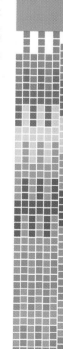

A conversar

G **7-40 Canal "Deportes para todos".** Imagínense que ustedes son reporteros de "Deportes para todos", una estación de televisión dedicada a los deportes. Con la información que aparece en el mapa, hagan lo siguiente:

- Preparen un informe del tiempo para la televisión en el que describen las condiciones del clima de hoy en cuatro ciudades hispanas en regiones diferentes: 1. en la costa del Atlántico, 2. en una zona de montañas, 3. en una región de clima muy frío, 4. en unas islas del Átlantico o del Pacífico. Indiquen para qué deportistas o aficionados es útil este informe del tiempo.

- Incluyan el pronóstico del tiempo (*weather forecast*) para mañana.

- Preséntenlo a la clase y contesten las preguntas de sus compañeros/as.

Suggestion for 7-40. To make students responsible for their own learning, every student in the group should present to the class the report on one of the cities of the group's choice. You may also consider making this assignment an out-of-class activity. Students who are computer literate may wish to present their weather report using Power Point or any other visual material. Since this is a speaking activity, weather reports should not be read. However, students may consult index cards.

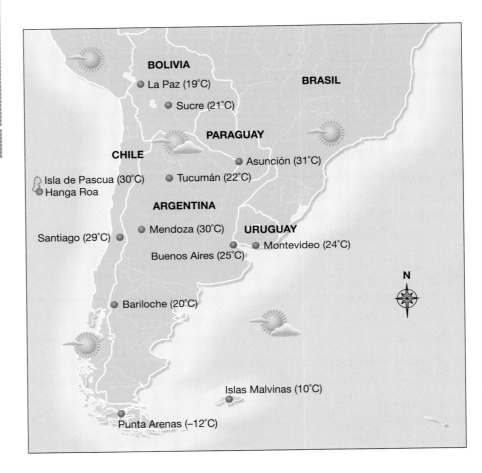

MODELO: Ahora canal "Deportes para todos" presenta el informe del tiempo para los aficionados al tenis. En este momento, en la ciudad de Tucumán, el cielo está un poco nublado y hace fresco. Los termómetros marcan 22 grados centígrados. Mañana va a estar despejado durante el día, con temperaturas entre los 24 y los 27 grados centígrados.

Después de conversar

(G) 7-41 Informe del tiempo en Internet. Ahora escriban el informe del tiempo que presentaron en la actividad **7-40** para los aficionados que consultan la página de Internet de "Deportes para todos". Pueden añadir imágenes si desean.

Suggestion for 7-41. If your class has a webpage, you may decide to offer a space for student (creative) writing. If so, students with computer skills may help you maintain that section of your webpage.

Antes de conversar

(G) 7-42 Historia de los deportes. En www.prenhall.com/mosaicos, busquen la siguiente información sobre uno de los deportes que se practican en Argentina, y tomen apuntes.

You may wish to remind students to fit the text to the medium of communication, a written weather forecast.

1. El nombre del deporte
2. Dos o tres datos históricos básicos sobre el deporte: a. cuándo empezó a practicarse, b. dónde empezó, c. algo interesante sobre los comienzos (*beginnings*) del deporte.
3. Un/a deportista argentino/a famoso/a en la historia de este deporte: a. nombre, fecha y lugar de nacimiento, b. datos sobre su carrera deportiva.

A conversar

(G) 7-43 Deportes y deportistas famosos. Hagan una presentación sobre el deporte que investigaron en la actividad **7-42** Usen la información que ya tienen u otra que deseen. Para hacer su presentación más interesante, pueden usar Internet o *Power Point*.

Después de conversar

7-44 Un/a deportista estrella (*star*). La revista *Deportes*, con la participación del público, va a seleccionar al deportista del año. Usted debe escribir la ficha (*personal history*) de uno de los deportistas nominados. Use la información de la actividad **7-42** y complete la ficha de este/a deportista famoso/a. Si quiere, puede incluir una foto.

Nombre: _____
Fecha de nacimiento: _____
Lugar de nacimiento: _____
Torneos/campeonatos en que participó:
_____
_____
Torneos/copas/campeonatos que ganó:
_____
_____
Dos razones para ser el/la deportista del año:
_____
_____

Suggestion for 7-42. Remind students of the importance of note taking while reading. As they research one of the sports provided on the webpage, they will find it useful to first skim the texts to get the gist, then do a second, more focused reading to get the specifics of what they need. Taking notes will be essential for the next phase of the activity (**7-43**). Once they have taken notes, it is important that students put the information in their own words. Processing the input in this fashion will help them better understand, organize the information, and recall it.

EN DIRECTO

To maintain the interest of listeners:

Hay hechos/ datos interesantes sobre...

La información que tengo/ tenemos sobre... es increíble.

¡Imagínense! Ganó el primer puesto en...

Este/a deportista juega (al...) como nadie.

Suggestion for 7-43. Since anything sports-related fascinates young people, your students may want to expand their presentation beyond their level of proficiency. Therefore, to avoid error making, we suggest that you not discourage them, but instead guide them in the preparation of their talk. Insist that students keep their presentation brief and express ideas in their own words with the help of visuals (pictures, video clips in Spanish, transparencies, Internet images, etc.). Advise them to organize the information well, to anticipate questions or comments from their classmates, and to be prepared to answer or react appropriately.

To make the best use of these presentations, we suggest that you keep the whole class involved. You may wish to ask that students in the audience: 1. write down at least two follow-up comments or questions for the presenters, 2. take notes of the most salient information in the presentation. To facilitate the students' note taking, you may wish to prepare a worksheet with the information they should jot down.

Leer

In this chapter, you will read a text in Spanish and differentiate facts from opinions. Remember to apply any other specific reading strategies you have learned so far to accomplish your goals.

Guía de prelectura

Look at the visuals, skim the text in activity **7-45**, and answer the questions.

1. Looking at the visuals, using your knowledge of the Spanish language, and keeping in mind the theme of this lesson, can you anticipate the main theme of this text?
   a. places where sports can be practiced in Uruguay
   b. sports people admired in Uruguay
   c. Uruguayans love sports

2. Now, use your background knowledge and your knowledge of Spanish to comprehend the text. On what did you base your answers to question 1?
   a. cognates in the title   b. visuals in the text   c. format of the text

3. Mark with a circle all the ideas that you anticipate will be covered in the text.
   a. sports frequently practiced in Uruguay
   b. sports originated in Uruguay
   c. places where sports may be practiced
   d. Uruguayan sports stars

Antes de leer

Suggestion for 7-45. As a warm-up, review and reinforce some key words in the activity by asking *¿Con qué palabras asocian ustedes los siguientes deportes, con agua, nieve o arena?* (Write words on the board.) 1. *el esquí*, 2. *la natación*, 3. *el vóleibol en la playa*, 4. *el surf*

7-45 ¿Qué se necesita para practicarlo? Primera fase. Clasifiquen cada palabra en la columna correspondiente.

fútbol	pelota	guantes	esquí
esquiar	montañas	correr	jugar
botas	pista	dunas	bicicleta
surf en la arena	cancha	ciclismo	saltar

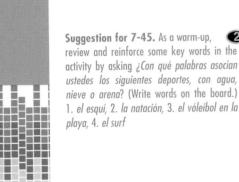

DEPORTE	MATERIAL DEPORTIVO	LUGAR DE PRÁCTICA	VERBO
fútbol	pelota	cancha	jugar
esquí	guantes	pista	esquiar
surf en la arena	botas	montañas	saltar
ciclismo	bicicleta	dunas	correr

Segunda fase. Ahora, respondan a estas preguntas.

1. ¿Les gustan los deportes individuales o prefieren los de equipo? ¿Por qué?
2. ¿Saben esquiar? ¿Esquían en la nieve o en el agua? ¿Esquían bien o regular?
3. ¿Hay buenos lugares donde se puede practicar surf acuático o en la arena en su país? ¿Dónde?

A leer

7-46 Primera mirada. Lea el siguiente artículo y, luego, siga las instrucciones.

Suggestion for 7-46. As a warm-up, have students brainstorm popular sports in the United States. For each sport, ask students where it is practiced, what equipment or clothing is needed, and what weather conditions favor its practice.

LOS DEPORTES: UNA PASIÓN URUGUAYA

El Uruguay es un país pequeño donde los deportes forman una parte integral de la vida de la mayor parte de sus habitantes.

Entre las grandes pasiones nacionales, desde luego, está el fútbol. Desde su infancia, muchos uruguayos acompañan fielmente a sus
5 equipos predilectos. En varias ocasiones, la selección nacional uruguaya ganó títulos y campeonatos importantes.

Pero los uruguayos son un pueblo inquieto, de una personalidad versátil que no limita su interés a un solo deporte. El basquetbol, el ciclismo, el fútbol de salón, el rugby, el boxeo y la pelota de
10 mano son otros deportes que tienen muchos aficionados.

Las hermosas y privilegiadas playas del Uruguay también favorecen los deportes acuáticos, como el surf, que, según los expertos, cuenta hoy con un gran número de aficionados. En 1993 en Uruguay se formó la Unión de Surf del Uruguay (USU). Ese
15 mismo año, el país envió a sus representantes a competir internacionalmente en el Primer Campeonato Panamericano de Surf en Isla Margarita, Venezuela. Hoy en día la USU promueve el surf, arbitra las competencias clasificatorias a nivel nacional, apoya a los competidores nacionales, representa a Uruguay en
20 competencias internacionales y compite en los Juegos Olímpicos con la Selección Uruguaya de Surf.

Sin duda, uno de los lugares predilectos de los uruguayos y turistas extranjeros para practicar el surf es Punta del Este. Ubicada al sureste del Uruguay, a 140 kilómetros de Montevideo, Punta del
25 Este es una hermosa península de enormes playas, con arenas finas y gruesas, rocas y un entorno de bosques y médanos[1].

Precisamente en estos médanos nació, en el siglo pasado, una variante del surf que está despertando grandes polémicas en el país: el surf en la arena o sandsurf. Los brasileños inventaron este deporte
30 en los años ochenta para no aburrirse cuando no había olas. La agradable temperatura de las playas uruguayas, la escasez de olas que a veces impide practicar el surf en el agua y la formación arenosa de algunas playas aumentaron considerablemente el número de personas que practican el surf en la arena. Por ejemplo, los médanos
35 de Valizas son los más grandes de Sudamérica y los terceros más grandes del mundo, algunos con 30 metros de altura y una longitud de bajada[2] de aproximadamente 125 metros. Sin embargo, las autoridades uruguayas están controlando e incluso prohibiendo la práctica de este deporte por el posible deterioro ecológico que ocasiona. No hay duda de que la prohibición del surf en la arena no
40 va a detener el espíritu activo de los uruguayos. Su creatividad los incentivará a buscar o inventar otras opciones para entretenerse.

[1] *dunes*   [2] *slope*

7-47 Opinión? Diga si las siguientes citas textuales (*quotations*) representan información concreta (C) o una opinión (O) del autor.

1. ___C___ "Desde su infancia, muchos uruguayos acompañan fielmente a sus equipos predilectos."

2. ___O___ "Pero los uruguayos son un pueblo inquieto, de una personalidad versátil que no limita su interés a un solo deporte."

3. ___C___ "En 1993 se formó la Unión de Surf del Uruguay (USU)."

4. ___C___ "Punta del Este es una hermosa península de enormes playas, con arenas finas y gruesas, rocas y un entorno de bosques y médanos."

5. ___O___ "La agradable temperatura de las playas uruguayas, la escasez de olas que a veces impide practicar el surf sobre el agua y la formación arenosa de algunas playas aumentaron considerablemente el número de adeptos al surf en la arena."

6. ___O___ "No hay duda de que la prohibición del surf en la arena no va a detener el espíritu activo de los uruguayos."

 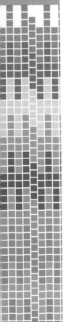

7-48 Segunda mirada. Lea el artículo otra vez y, según la información que aparece en él, haga lo siguiente:

1. Indique dos razones que explican la popularidad del fútbol en Uruguay.
2. Diga por qué los uruguayos tienen un carácter inquieto.
3. Nombre tres deportes que se juegan en equipo, dos que son principalmente deportes individuales, y uno que no requiere una pelota.
4. Dé dos razones para explicar por qué Punta del Este le ofrece al/a la surfista acuático/a un lugar ideal para practicar su deporte.
5. Explique dos hechos que provocaron el nacimiento del surf en la arena.
6. En su opinión, ¿deben prohibir el surf en la arena? ¿Por qué?

Después de leer

7-49 ¡Adivinen cuál es el deporte! Preparen una hoja descriptiva sobre el deporte favorito del grupo sin mencionar el nombre del deporte. Den la siguiente información e intercambien su hoja con otro grupo que debe adivinar cuál es el deporte.

1. Lugar donde se practica
2. Deporte individual o en grupo (número de personas en el equipo)
3. Clima ideal para practicarlo: Se practica en invierno/en... /cuando hace..., etc.
4. Un/a jugador/a famoso de este deporte
5. Su opinión sobre el/la jugador/a

 *Escribir*

Writing for a broader, impersonal audience about a specific subject requires special attention to the content about which you write, the amount of information you include, the use or avoidance of technical language, and the degree of objectivity and subjectivity of your text.

Readers of sports magazines are generally sports-oriented and knowledgeable about one or more sports. To write for such an audience of 'experts,' you should:

- Anticipate the kind of information your readers may know or may need.

- Use words specific to the sport.

- Use agile language that reflects the vitality of sports activities: action verbs, brief sentences, words that show intensity (adverbs), etc.

- Differentiate sports facts from people's opinions

7-50 Enfoque. Primera fase. Lea el siguiente informe deportivo y siga las instrucciones.

> 13 de abril
>
> Copa América: Argentina vence a Uruguay 4-2
>
> Argentina derrotó a Uruguay por 4-2 y se clasificó en la Copa América como segunda del Grupo B.
>
> Fabián Estoyanoff marcó sorpresivamente un gol para Uruguay a los 7 minutos. Pero a los 19 minutos, Cristián González, del cuadro argentino, marcó un gol de penal y luego, Luciano Figueroa marcó otro gol magistral a los 20 minutos. Vicente Sánchez igualó a los 37 minutos para el equipo uruguayo. Argentina definió el partido con los goles de Roberto Ayala, a los 80 minutos, y otra vez Figueroa, a los 89 minutos.
>
> El árbitro expulsó a un jugador uruguayo por mala conducta.
>
> El partido fue desordenado y rudo, pero muy emocionante. Unos 23.000 espectadores llegaron muy temprano al estadio "Miguel Grau" para acompañar a sus equipos. Rubén Selman arbitró impecablemente el partido.

Segunda fase. Answer the following questions, based on the sports report.

1. Mark with an *X* the main idea of the report.
   _____ Uruguay and Argentina were finalists in the World Soccer Cup.
   __X__ Argentina beat Uruguay in the Cup America.
   _____ Uruguay defeated Argentina in the Cup America.

2. Is this sports report effective? (Yes) No

3. Mark some possible reasons for your response to question 2.
   __X__ Reporter narrates the sports event chronologically.
   _____ There is no chronology in the report.
   _____ Reporter provides a detailed description of what went on during the game.
   __X__ Reporter uses words specific to soccer.
   __X__ The report uses action verbs, brief sentences, words that show intensity.
   __X__ The report is objective, that is, it informs the reader about facts of the game.

Antes de escribir

7-51 Preparación. Primera fase. En www.prenhall.com/mosaicos busque una noticia sobre un evento deportivo. Léala y anote lo siguiente:

1. el tipo de evento: un partido, un torneo, una competencia entre instituciones, un campeonato, una copa, etc.
2. dónde y cuándo ocurrió.
3. nombres de los/las deportistas, equipos, árbitros que participaron.
4. información concreta sobre el evento: ¿Quién ganó? ¿Cuál fue el puntaje (*score*)? ¿Batieron (*break*) un récord? ¿Quiénes fueron los deportistas sobresalientes (*outstanding*) en el evento?

Segunda fase. Prepárese para escribir un informe deportivo. Haga lo siguiente:

1. Haga una lista de palabras clave para su informe: nombres, verbos, adjetivos, adverbios, etc. Recuerde que debe usar palabras específicas del deporte.
2. Ordene cronológicamente los hechos del evento de la **Primera fase.**
3. Imagínese que usted fue uno de los espectadores. Escriba su opinión sobre el evento: ¿Le gustó el partido? ¿Le pareció sorprendente el puntaje? ¿Le gustó el árbitro? ¿Y los jugadores? ¿Cómo reaccionaron los aficionados?

A escribir

7-52 Manos a la obra. Usted es un/a periodista deportivo/a para la revista *Deportes del milenio*. Esta revista va a tener una página en la red, y usted va a ser la persona responsable de informar a los lectores sobre las noticias deportivas. Usando la información que recogió en **7-51, Segunda fase,** escriba su primer informe. Incluya lo siguiente:

1. información concreta sobre un evento deportivo en un país hispano
2. la reacción de los espectadores durante y después del evento
3. la opinión de los expertos o su opinión sobre el evento deportivo

Después de escribir

7-53 Revisión. Antes de presentar su proyecto, revise:

- la claridad y cantidad de información presentada. Recuerde que los informes deportivos por lo general son breves

- el vocabulario general y vocabulario especializado, la estructuras que utilizó para narrar cronológicamente el evento y la concordancia

- las expresiones para introducir su opinión o la de otras personas

- la ortografía y la acentuación

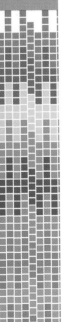

EN DIRECTO

To report factual information about a past sports event:

Los/las jugadores/as hicieron/marcaron/corrieron, etc.

En realidad, el árbitro, el/la entrenador/a, el/la jugador/a número... , etc.

Asistieron... personas.

To express an opinion about an event:

Según...

En mi opinión, ...

Me parece que...

Sin duda, ...

ENFOQUE CULTURAL

TEMAS: EL FÚTBOL Y LOS DEPORTES

Para pensar

¿Cuáles son algunos de los deportes favoritos en los Estados Unidos? ¿Qué deportes practica usted? ¿Y sus amigos/as? Piense en dos o tres deportes que se practican en su universidad.

El béisbol es uno de los deportes más populares del área del Caribe, especialmente en Cuba, Venezuela, la República Dominicana y Puerto Rico. Sammy Sosa es un famoso beisbolista dominicano.

El polo es otro deporte muy popular en Argentina y en Uruguay. El equipo nacional argentino ganó varios campeonatos mundiales. Uno de los jugadores de polo más conocidos es Nicolás Scortichini.

El deporte más popular de Latinoamérica es el fútbol. Los partidos de fútbol tienen siempre muchos aficionados que animan a sus equipos favoritos.

Para contestar

2 **Los deportes.** Conteste las siguientes preguntas.

1. ¿Qué deportes se practican más en España e Hispanoamérica? ¿Qué deportes piensa usted que no se practican? ¿Por qué?
2. ¿Cuáles son los deportes favoritos de los países hispanohablantes? ¿Dónde los practican?

G **Riqueza cultural.** Mencionen a dos famosos/as futbolistas, tenistas y beisbolistas españoles o hispanoamericanos. Digan de qué país son y, si es posible, en qué equipo(s) juegan.

Los españoles y los hispanoamericanos también disfrutan del ciclismo. Además de importantes competencias, hay muchas excursiones a lugares de interés turístico y ecológico organizadas para los aficionados de este deporte.

Para pensar

¿Qué sabe usted acerca de Argentina y Uruguay? ¿Sabe usted dónde están? ¿Qué lugares de interés hay en estos países?

VÍNCULOS

For materials related to the Enfoque cultural, see
- SAM-OneKey: WB: 7-23
- IRCD: Chapter 7; pg. 274

Argentina y Uruguay están en la costa oriental de América del Sur. Ambos países tienen una intensa vida intelectual y cultural.

Montevideo, la capital de Uruguay, es una ciudad moderna con un centro histórico que data de la época colonial. Precisamente, una de las ciudades más importantes del Uruguay se llama Colonia, y es famosa por su diseño y arquitectura. Montevideo, en cambio, está rodeada de hermosas playas.

En Montevideo se puede disfrutar de tiendas, museos, cafés, mercados y ferias. Por ejemplo, se puede visitar el Mercado del Puerto y la Avenida 18 de julio, donde hay muchas tiendas, teatros, museos y galerías de arte. De especial interés es el Museo del Gaucho, donde se puede apreciar todo lo relacionado con los gauchos, es decir, los vaqueros (cowboys) típicos de Uruguay y Argentina.

Expresiones uruguayas:

fenómeno	¡La pasé **fenómeno**!	*I had a great time!*
chiquilín/a	¡Mi **chiquilín** es muy tranquilo!	*My kid is very quiet!*
irse embalado	¡Se fue **embalado**!	*He/she left in a hurry!*
salvar/perder el examen	Mario **salvó el examen** de español, pero José lo **perdió**.	*Mario passed his Spanish exam, but José flunked it.*

Buenos Aires, la capital de Argentina, tiene un aire muy europeo, con amplios parques, anchas avenidas y altos edificios.

La amistad tiene gran importancia en la vida de los porteños, que es como se llama a las personas que nacieron en Buenos Aires. Por eso, los numerosos cafés de la ciudad están siempre llenos de personas que se reúnen a conversar mientras toman un delicioso cortado (café con crema) acompañado de una medialuna (un croissant pequeño).

Bariloche, a las orillas del lago Nahuel Huapi, es el lugar ideal para las personas a las que les gusta esquiar.

Expresiones argentinas:

ché	**Ché**, Martita, ¿dónde está mi camisa?	*Hey, Martita, where is my shirt?*
mandarse la parte	¡No te **mandes la parte**!	*Don't brag!*
laburo	Siempre salgo temprano para el **laburo**.	*I always leave early to go to my job.*
morocho/a	Isabel es **morocha**.	*Isabel is brunnette.*

Una de las características geográficas más distintivas de Argentina es la pampa. Estas enormes extensiones de tierra (land) llana y fértil constituyen una de las bases de la economía argentina.

Para contestar

En el mapa

1. Busque tres ciudades de Argentina y tres ciudades de Uruguay y diga dónde están situadas.
2. Diga qué países están al oeste, norte y este de Argentina.
3. Diga qué países están al este y norte de Uruguay.

Ahora diga...

1. por qué puede ser interesante ir a Montevideo o a Punta del Este.
2. qué lugar de interés le gustaría visitar en Argentina y por qué.

¿Qué dice Ud. si...

1. su amigo uruguayo sacó una mala nota en el examen final de biología.
2. Ud. no quiere ir a su trabajo hoy.
3. pasó momentos muy divertidos en una fiesta con sus compañeros/as.

Para investigar en Internet

Busque el nombre de dos equipos de fútbol de Uruguay y dos equipos de Argentina. Traiga esta información a clase y hable con sus compañeros/as sobre el último partido que jugaron, dónde jugaron, contra quién jugaron, quién ganó y cuál fue el puntaje.

¡Prepárese!

7-54 La honestidad. En el Episodio 7 aparece el tema de la honestidad o, mejor dicho, la falta de ella. Carlos está muy molesto por las acciones de Katie y empieza a dudar de su honestidad. La lista siguiente contiene algunas palabras importantes de este episodio. Indique sus equivalentes en inglés.

a. decepcionar
b. la mentira
c. la integridad
d. competitivo/a
e. el/la traidor/a

<u>e</u> *traitor*
<u>d</u> *competitive*
<u>a</u> *to deceive, cheat*
<u>b</u> *lie*
<u>c</u> *integrity*

Ángela no quiere perder su trabajo.

Katie y Carlos van al Museo Nacional de Antropología.

¡Sabrina y Efraín ganaron la primera fortuna!

Carlos tiene dudas sobre la honestidad de Katie.

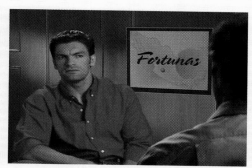

Carlos no quiere entrevistarse con Tito.

Ahora Ángela está muy contenta.

¡Responda!

7-55 Comparaciones. Usando las palabras de la lista en ejercicio 7-54, escriba oraciones completas en español, comparándose con los personajes de *Fortunas*. ¿Es usted como ellos o diferente?

MODELO: Katie dice mentiras y yo también. *o*
           Katie dice mentiras pero yo digo la verdad.

Suggestions 7-55. Point out to students that they may want to use another form of the words on the list, for example *traicionar* vs. *el/la traidor/a*. They may want to use antonyms or synonyms as well.

Esta canción moderna combina estilos musicales españoles y latinoamericanos como el flamenco, la salsa y la música tropical en un ritmo alegre y positivo.

¡Prepárese!

7-56 El título. ¿Puede adivinar lo que significa "Huracán", el título de la canción? En su opinión, ¿cuáles pueden ser algunos temas?

¡Escuche!

7-57 La letra. Mientras escucha la canción lea las palabras siguientes e indique sus equivalentes en inglés. Use un diccionario bilingüe si es necesario.

a. sentimiento   __d__ *kisses*
b. alma   __e__ *heaven*
c. fuego   __a__ *feeling*
d. besos   __c__ *fire*
e. cielo   __b__ *soul*

Ahora que conoce mejor la canción, ¿cuáles son sus ideas sobre el tema?

"Huracán"

Aunque digan lo que digan

No me importa el qué dirán
Sólo basta una mirada

Y desato un huracán

[...]
No me importa qué murmuren
Porque soy un huracán

¡Responda!

7-58 Las expresiones. Muchos países tienen expresiones populares que se usan coloquialmente y que pueden variar de país a país y de región a región. En "Huracán" la cantante dice que no le importa "el qué dirán", lo que dice la gente o el chisme (*gossip*). La lista siguiente contiene otras expresiones en español, léalas e indique sus equivalentes en inglés.

a. tener mala cara   __c__ *to keep one's word*
b. ser tal para cual   __e__ *to be sophisticated*
c. tener palabra   __b__ *two of a kind*
d. en un dos por tres   __a__ *to look bad*
e. tener mundo   __d__ *in a second/right away*

7-59 Más expresiones. Ahora indique los equivalentes en inglés de las siguientes expresiones en español.

a. ¡Salud!   __b__ *First rate!*
b. ¡Del uno!   __d__ *Nonsense!*
c. ¡Venga ya!   __e__ *All right!*
d. ¡Qué va!   __a__ *Cheers!*
e. ¡Vaya!   __c__ *Come off it!*

Suggestion 7-60. Talk about expressions, sayings, idioms and idiomatic phrases with your students and discuss why one cannot always translate literally from one language to another.

7-60 Ahora usted. Escriba una lista de expresiones populares de su país o región y luego intercambie su lista con la de un/a compañero/a. ¿Hay semejanzas? ¿Hay diferencias?

VOCABULARIO

`AUDIO` ## Deportes

el baloncesto/basquetbol	*basketball*
el béisbol	*baseball*
los bolos	*bowling*
el ciclismo	*cycling*
el esquí	*skiing, ski*
el fútbol	*soccer*
el tenis	*tennis*
el voleibol	*volleyball*

Equipo deportivo

el bate	*bat*
el/la cesto/a	*basket, hoop*
los palos	*golf clubs*
la pelota	*ball*
la raqueta	*racket*
la red	*net*

Eventos

el campeonato	*championship*
la carrera	*race*
el juego/partido	*game*
el torneo	*tournament*

Lugares

la cancha	*court, golf course*
el campo	*field*
la pista	*slope, court, track*

Personas

el/la aficionado/a	*fan*
el árbitro	*umpire, referee*
el campeón/la campeona	*champion*
el/la ciclista	*cyclist*
el/la entrenador/a	*coach*
el equipo	*team*
el/la jugador/a	*player*
el/la tenista	*tennis player*

Naturaleza

el árbol	*tree*
la atmósfera	*atmosphere*
la flor	*flower*
el lago	*lake*

Tiempo

despejado/a	*clear*
fresco/a	*cool*
el hielo	*ice*
la lluvia	*rain*
la nieve	*snow*
nublado/a	*cloudy*
el sol	*sun*
el viento	*wind*

Descripciones

contaminado/a	*polluted, contaminated*
contrario/a	*opposite, contrary*
emocionado/a	*excited*
mejor	*best*
mundial	*worldwide*

Verbos

acostar (ue)	*to put to bed*
acostar(se)	*to go to bed, to lie down*
afeitar(se)	*to shave*
aplaudir	*to applaud*
aprovechar	*to take advantage*
competir (i)	*to compete*
congelar(se)	*to freeze*
despertar(se) (ie)	*to wake up*
discutir	*to argue*
dormirse (ue)	*to fall asleep*
durar	*to last*
esquiar	*to ski*
ganar	*to win*
ir(se)	*to go away, to leave*
jugar a los bolos	*to bowl*
lavar(se) los dientes	*to brush one's teeth*
levantar	*to raise*
llover (ue)	*to rain*
maquillar(se)	*to put on makeup*
nevar (ie)	*to snow*
participar	*to participate*
patinar	*to skate*
perder (ie)	*to lose*
quitar	*to take away, to remove*
quitar(se)	*to take off*
representar	*to represent*
sentar(se) (ie)	*to sit down*
traducir (zc)	*to translate*

Palabras y expresiones útiles

cada	*each*
conmigo	*with me*
contigo	*with you* (familiar)
estar de acuerdo	*to agree*
el fin	*end*
Hace calor.	*It's hot.*
¿Qué tiempo hace?	*What's the weather like?*
sin	*without*

8

FIESTAS Y TRADICIONES

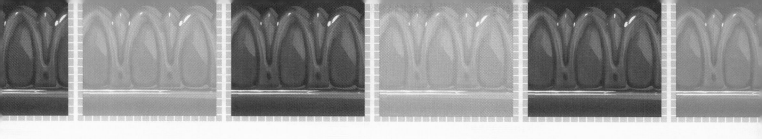

Objetivos comunicativos

- Talking about holiday activities
- Expressing ongoing actions in the past
- Extending, accepting, and declining invitations
- Making comparisons

Contenido

A primera vista
- Fiestas y tradiciones
- Otras celebraciones

Explicación y expansión
- The imperfect
- Imperfect of regular and irregular verbs
- The preterit and the imperfect
- Comparisons of inequality
- Comparisons of equality
- The superlative

Mosaicos
- Escuchar: Making inferences
- Conversar: Comparing experiences; narrating
- Leer: Identifying information stated in a text; making inferences
- Escribir: Narrating a real or an imaginary experience or event

Enfoque cultural
- Temas: La religión
- Vistas: México y Guatemala
          Para investigar en Internet
- Fortunas: Episodio 8
- Notas: El Chapo, *Los Originales de San Juan*

Vocabulario

A PRIMERA VISTA

Fiestas y tradiciones

Estas **carretas** adornadas "**hicieron el camino**" para llegar a El Rocío, un pequeño **pueblo** de la provincia de Huelva, en España, donde está la Ermita de la Virgen del Rocío. En el pueblo **se reúnen** cada año cerca de un millón de personas para celebrar la fiesta de la Virgen del Rocío.

El Día de los **Muertos**, también conocido como el Día de los Difuntos, se conmemora el 2 de noviembre y muchas familias van al **cementerio** ese día o el día anterior para recordar y llevarles **flores** a sus familiares o amigos **difuntos.** Especialmente en México, los preparativos para el día de los muertos **comienzan** con mucha anterioridad y hay familias que pasan la noche del primero al 2 de noviembre acompañando a sus muertos en el cementerio, como se ve en esta foto tomada en Pátzcuaro.

Las fiestas y los bailes que se celebran ayudan a mantener las **costumbres** de los **antepasados.** La diablada es uno de los festivales folclóricos con más colorido en Hispanoamérica. Se celebra durante el carnaval de Oruro en Bolivia y también en el norte de Chile y otros países, entre ellos, Perú.

La música, el baile y la **alegría** reinan en los **carnavales**. Hay **carrozas** y **comparsas** que bailan en las calles, muchas personas **se disfrazan** y todo el mundo **se divierte**. El último día de Carnaval es el martes **antes** del **comienzo** de la Cuaresma.

Point out that Holy Week is the week from Palm Sunday to Easter Sunday. The photograph shows an *hermandad*, religious brotherhood in Guatemala, whose members wear traditional outfits and carry floats of religious icons as an act of devotion, walking on beautiful *alfombras* made of flowers, seeds, and tinted sawdust.

You may talk about the *corridas*. Traditional of Spain and also held in some Hispanic countries, the *corridas* originated as ancient rituals in which men used to measure their strength and power over the bull. Although they are often criticized for their cruelty to animals, the *corridas* are still very popular, and experts agree that they are charged with symbolism and beauty. Many Hispanic cities have monumental *plazas* where the *corridas* take place. If possible, bring a video clip of a *corrida* and point out the colorful outfits of the *toreros* and *matadores*, the use of white handkerchiefs by the audience to comment on the bullfighter's performance, etc.

Note. Beginning with this lesson, cultural notes will be given in Spanish.

Ésta es una de las procesiones de Semana Santa en la Antigua Guatemala. Esta ciudad fue la **antigua** capital de Guatemala y es famosa por su arquitectura colonial y las **maravillosas** alfombras que se hacen con flores, semillas y aserrín para el paso de las procesiones.

CULTURA

Los hispanos y los norteamericanos tienen muchas fiestas y celebraciones diferentes. Por ejemplo, el Día de Acción de Gracias (*Thanksgiving*) no se celebra en los países hispanos y tampoco es tradicional el Día de las Brujas (*Halloween*), aunque se está comenzando a celebrar en algunas ciudades de Hispanoamérica. Por otro lado, debido a la importancia e influencia de la religión católica en los países hispanos, algunas fiestas religiosas se consideran también fiestas oficiales. Pero lo más importante es la gran diversidad de fiestas locales. Muchas personas trabajan todo el año para garantizar el éxito de estas celebraciones, en las que la gente baila y se divierte durante días enteros.

El día de **San Fermín**, el 7 de julio, se inicia la celebración de los **sanfermines** en Pamplona. Esta celebración, que dura del 7 al 14 de julio, es famosa mundialmente por **los** "encierros". Los jóvenes corren por las calles seguidos de los **toros**, hasta llegar a la **plaza** donde encierran a los toros y más tarde tienen lugar las corridas.

🔊AUDIO Días y fechas importantes

Follow-up. Use Image Resource CD to talk about festivities. Ask questions and personalize.

Note. *Pascuas* can refer to both Christmas and Easter: *la Pascua Florida* refers to Easter, *las Pascuas Navideñas* refers to Christmas.

In many countries, on New Year's Eve, people eat twelve grapes at the stroke of midnight to ensure good fortune in the New Year.

September 16 is Mexico's Independence Day. Remind students that the date of Independence Day varies from country to country, and have them research the date in several Latin American countries.

la Nochebuena

la Navidad

la Nochevieja

el Año Nuevo

el Día de la Independencia

la Pascua

el Día de la Madre

el Día del Padre

el Día de Acción de Gracias

el Día de las Brujas

el Día de los Enamorados/del Amor y la Amistad

¿Qué dice usted?

8-1 Asociaciones. Primera fase. Asocien las fechas de la izquierda con los días festivos de la derecha.

1. __h__ el 25 de diciembre
2. __g__ el 2 de noviembre
3. __f__ el 6 de enero
4. __a__ el 4 de julio
5. __c__ el 24 de diciembre
6. __d__ el 31 de diciembre
7. __e__ el 14 de febrero
8. __b__ el 31 de octubre

a. el Día de la Independencia de los Estados Unidos
b. el Día de las Brujas
c. la Nochebuena
d. la Nochevieja, el fin de año
e. el Día de los Enamorados, del Amor y la Amistad
f. el Día de los Reyes Magos
g. el Día de los Muertos
h. la Navidad

Segunda fase. En grupos pequeños, comenten:

- cuál(es) de estas fiestas celebra cada uno de ustedes.
- cuál es la predilecta de la mayoría de las personas del grupo, y por qué.

8-2 Festivales o desfiles. Piense en algunos festivales o desfiles (*parades*) importantes y complete el cuadro. Su compañero/a va a hacerle preguntas sobre ellos.

MODELO: E1: ¿En qué fiesta o desfile importante estás pensando?
E2: En el Cinco de Mayo
E1: ¿Dónde lo celebran?
E2: En México y en algunas ciudades de los Estados Unidos, como Austin, Texas.

FESTIVAL	FECHA	LUGAR	DESCRIPCIÓN	OPINIÓN

8-3 Unos días festivos. Hablen sobre cómo celebran ustedes estas fechas.

MODELO: E1: ¿Cómo celebras tu cumpleaños?
E2: Lo celebro con mi familia y mis amigos. Recibo regalos, y mi madre prepara mi comida favorita con pastel de chocolate de postre. Después escuchamos música, conversamos, y a veces bailamos.

1. la Nochevieja, el Fin de Año
2. la Navidad
3. el Día de Acción de Gracias
4. el Día de la Independencia
5. el Año Nuevo
6. el Día de la Madre

Suggestion for 8-1. As a preview, compare holiday traditions and celebrations, using comparative/superlative words ¿Qué costumbre es la más/menos importante de su familia? ¿Por qué tiene más/menos importancia ese día? Divide the class into groups of three or four.

VÍNCULOS
To practice vocabulario—Fiestas y tradiciones, Días y fechas importantes & Otras celebraciones
- SAM-OneKey: WB: 8-1, 8-2, 8-3, 8-4 / LM: 8-30, 8-31, 8-32, 8-33
- Companion Website: AP 8-1, AP 8-2, AP 8-3
- IRCD: Chapter 8; pp. 284, 286, 287, 288

Suggestions for 8-2. Talk about parades with which students are familiar and ask questions. You may also model the activity with a more proficient student. You may explain briefly the importance of *el Cinco de Mayo* as the day in which Mexicans defeated the French troops in Puebla in 1862 and/or encourage students to look for additional information.

Alternate for 8-3. Preview the imperfect by asking students questions regarding holiday celebrations as children: De niño/a, ¿cómo celebraba el día de las brujas? ¿Comía mucho el Día de Acción de Gracias? ¿Qué regalos le gustaba recibir el día de navidad?

Follow-up for 8-3. ¿Qué día festivo le gusta más? ¿Por qué? ¿A quién no le gustan los días festivos? ¿Por qué?

Suggestion for 8-4. You may assign students different research tasks based on the variety of festivities and celebrations that exist in the Hispanic world. For example, you may ask them to find out about the *Posadas* in Mexico, the *Fallas* in Valencia, Spain, etc. You may also ask students to do brief, structured presentations based on their research topic.

Alternate for 8-4. Recycle preterit usage by asking students to describe their last birthday, what they did last New Year's Eve, and so on: *¿Qué hizo Ud. el día de su cumpleaños el año pasado? ¿Cómo pasó la navidad su familia? ¿Fue a una fiesta para la nochevieja?*

8-4 Una celebración importante. Primera fase. Con su compañero/a escojan una celebración importante del mundo hispano (Carnaval, Semana Santa, Año Nuevo, La Diablada, Día de la Independencia, etc.) y busquen información en Internet sobre:

1. lugar
2. época del año
3. forma en que se celebra

Segunda fase. Imagínense que usted y su compañero/a estuvieron en un país hispano durante la celebración sobre la que investigaron en la **Primera fase.** Explíquenles a otros/as dos compañeros/as dónde estuvieron, qué fiesta celebraron y qué hicieron. Sus compañeros les van a hacer preguntas para obtener más información o aclarar algo que no comprendieron.

Otras celebraciones

AUDIO Una invitación a cenar

SRA. MENA: Pedro, tenemos que **invitar** a los Sosa a cenar.

SR. MENA: Es verdad. Ellos nos invitaron el mes pasado. ¿Por qué no los llamas ahora? Podemos reunirnos este fin de semana o el próximo.

(Unos minutos más tarde, las dos señoras hablan por teléfono.)

SRA. MENA: ¿Pueden cenar con nosotros el sábado?

SRA. SOSA: ¡Ay, María! Lo siento muchísimo, pero este sábado tenemos entradas para el **teatro.**

SRA. MENA: Ah, ¡**qué lástima**! ¿Y el sábado 15?

SRA. SOSA: **Encantados.** Tenemos muchos deseos de verlos.

SRA. MENA: Y nosotros también.

Warm-up for 8-5. Before students invite each other to attend events, model the activity with a more proficient student. Encourage students to use the expressions presented.

Note: *Será un placer* is used mainly in a formal context.

EN DIRECTO

To accept an invitation:
Gracias. Me encanta la idea.
Con mucho gusto.
Encantado/a.
Será un placer.

To apologize:
Me gustaría ir, pero...
¡Qué lástima/pena! Ese día tengo que...
No puedo, tengo un compromiso.

8-5 Una invitación. Primera fase. Completen el siguiente cuadro según la conversación de la señora Mena y la señora Sosa.

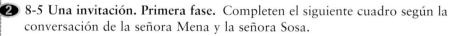

FECHAS DE LAS INVITACIONES	EXPRESIONES QUE USA LA SRA. SOSA
primera invitación:	para disculparse por no aceptar:
segunda invitación:	para aceptar la invitación:

Segunda fase. Ahora invite a su compañero/a a cenar, o a ir al teatro o a un partido importante. Después, su compañero/a va a invitarlo/la a usted. Además de las expresiones del diálogo, pueden usar las de la tabla.

Celebraciones personales

La boda del príncipe Felipe, en mayo de 2004, fue un gran acontecimiento histórico y social que millones de hispanos pudieron ver por televisión. En los países hispanos, el padrino de la boda es la persona que acompaña a la novia al altar y generalmente es su padre. La madrina está en el altar con el novio y normalmente es su madre.

2 **8-6 Una invitación de boda.** Lean la invitación de boda y la de la recepción, y contesten las preguntas. Luego preparen una lista con las diferencias que encuentran ustedes entre estas invitaciones y las de este país.

Pedro Martín Salda
Juana Montoya de Martín

Eduardo Calderón Solís
Elisa Noriega de Calderón

participan el matrimonio de sus hijos

Estelita
y
Alberto

y tienen el honor de invitarle a la ceremonia religiosa que se celebrará el viernes 9 de febrero, a las diecinueve treinta horas en el Convento de San Joaquín, Santa Cruz Cocalco N° 15, Legaria, dignándose impartir la bendición nupcial el R.P. José Ortuno S.J.
Ciudad de México, 2001

Agradecemos su presencia después de la ceremonia religiosa en el Club de Golf Chapultepec Av. Conscripto N° 425, Lomas Hipódromo

R.S.V.P.
529-99-43
520-16-85

Personal

1. ¿Cómo se llaman los padres de la novia? ¿Y los del novio?
2. ¿Cómo se llaman los novios?
3. ¿Qué día es la boda?
4. ¿A qué hora es?
5. ¿En qué país se celebra esta boda?
6. ¿Adónde van a ir los invitados después de la ceremonia?

CULTURA

La monarquía constitucional española es una de las más antiguas de Europa. Hoy en día la familia real es muy popular en el mundo hispano. El rey Juan Carlos I y la reina Sofía tienen tres hijos: Elena, Cristina y Felipe, Príncipe de Asturias y heredero del trono. Recientemente, el príncipe Felipe se casó con la periodista Letizia Ortiz.

Para obtener más información sobre los reyes de España vaya a www.prenhall.com/mosaicos.

Suggestion. You may want to point out that el *padrino* and la *madrina* are generally thought of as a part of Roman Catholic weddings/christenings.

Follow-up for 8-6. Discuss other events students have attended. You may wish to point out the abbreviations: *R.P. = reverendo padre* and *S.J. = Sociedad de Jesús.*

CULTURA

Los mariachis son grupos musicales de México que cantan y tocan violines, guitarras, guitarrones, trompetas y vihuelas. Muchos creen que la palabra "mariachi" viene del francés *mariage*, que significa "boda". En la época colonial, el novio contrataba estas bandas para festejar a la novia la noche de la boda. Otros opinan que "mariachi" proviene de una palabra indígena que designa la plataforma donde se paraban los músicos para tocar.

Suggestion for 8-7. Newspaper announcements, invitations, video clips of the celebration of a girl's fifteenth birthday, *la quinceañera,* prove useful to explain that custom. Point out that this event is not celebrated in all Hispanic countries.

8-7 Un día especial. Lean la invitación y contesten las preguntas.

Nuestro querido hijo

David

será llamado a la lectura de la Tora
con motivo de su Bar Mitzvah
el jueves 18 de noviembre de 2004
a las ocho de la mañana en la Sinagoga
Centro Hebreo, Avenida 13-15 Zona 9.

Nos sentiremos muy honrados en compartir
con ustedes tan memorable ocasión
y será un placer recibirles en el desayuno
que seguidamente ofreceremos en el
salón de fiestas de la sinagoga.

David y Ruth Bauman
Fax: (502) 238-2042
Ciudad de Guatemala, Guatemala

1. ¿Cuál es el motivo de la celebración?
2. ¿Qué día es la celebración? ¿A qué hora?
3. ¿Hay algo, además de la celebración religiosa?
4. ¿Quiénes son David y Ruth Bauman?
5. ¿En qué país tiene lugar esta celebración?

8-8 Una fiesta especial. Individualmente piensen en una celebración o fiesta en la que cada uno participó recientemente. Luego, explíquense cómo fue esa fiesta. Incluyan detalles sobre el número de invitados, el lugar, el menú, la música, cuánto costó todo, etc.

Warm-up for 8-9. As a prelistening activity, have students get in groups of four to share what their favorite holidays are and to narrate what they usually do on those days.

Audioscript for 8-9. Conversación 1. MUJER: ¿Por qué hay tantos niños en la calle? Y están disfrazados. HOMBRE: Hoy es una fiesta muy importante para los niños de Estados Unidos. MUJER: ¿Y qué hacen en la calle? HOMBRE: Les piden caramelos a los vecinos.

Conversación 2. MUJER: Ahora salgo para la iglesia y después voy al cementerio para llevarle flores a mi padre. HOMBRE: ¿Cuándo murió tu padre? MUJER: En el 91. HOMBRE: ¿Y haces esto todos los años? MUJER: Sí, todos los años, por supuesto.

Conversación 3. MUJER: ¿Qué le vas a regalar a tu novia mañana? HOMBRE: Todavía no sé. Quizás un perfume, un collar. MUJER: ¿Y van a salir por la noche? HOMBRE: Bueno, es un día muy especial para los novios. La voy a invitar a su restaurante favorito.

Conversación 4. MUJER: ¿Qué te trajeron anoche? NIÑO: Me trajeron una bicicleta. Yo les pedí muchas cosas, pero sólo me trajeron la bicicleta. MUJER: Es que hay muchos niños en el mundo y ellos tienen que llevarles regalos a todos.

AUDIO **8-9 Fiestas y tradiciones.** You will listen to four short dialogues about different holidays celebrated in the Hispanic world. Before you listen, write down the names of two holidays that you have studied or read about in this chapter.

_____

_____

Now, pay attention to the general idea of what is said. Then, as you listen, identify the holiday each conversation refers to by writing the appropriate conversation number next to it.

   _3_   el día del amor y la amistad, día de los enamorados

   _2_   el día de los muertos

   _4_   el día de los reyes magos

   _1_   el día de las brujas

1. The imperfect

Antes la música **era** más suave y romántica. **Tenía** más **melodía** y las **orquestas eran** magníficas.

Hoy en día no hay música; hay sólo **ruido,** y la gente se mueve mucho para bailar.

Y seguro que tu abuela decía lo mismo de los niños.

Antes las familias **hablaban** y **había** más **seguridad** en las calles.

Ahora es horrible. Hay mucha **violencia,** mucha **droga,** mucho **sexo,** y los niños no **respetan** a las personas mayores.

Suggestions. Use the Image Resource CD to describe the illustrations: *¿Cómo era la vida cuando la abuela era joven?* (Write *era* on the board or on a transparency.) *Según la abuela, la música era mejor porque tenía más melodía y era más suave y romántica. Ella cree que hoy no hay música, que hay sólo ruido.* Ask questions to check understanding.

You may talk and ask questions about the music and dances nowadays. Then compare them with the music in the 1960s or any other time that the students may be familiar with. Write imperfect forms and ask yes/no and either/or questions.

VÍNCULOS

To practice the imperfect
- SAM-OneKey: WB: 8-5 / LM: 8-34
- Companion Website: AP 8-4
- *Gramática viva*: Grammar Point 16: Imperfect tense of regular and irregular verbs
- IRCD: Chapter 8; pg. 289

■ So far you have seen two ways of talking about the past in Spanish: the preterit and the imperfect. In the preceding monolog, the grandmother used the imperfect because she was focusing on what used to happen when she was young. If she had been focusing on the fact that an action was completed, like something she did yesterday, she would have used the preterit. Generally, the imperfect is used to:

1. express habitual or repeated actions in the past.

Nosotros **íbamos** a la playa todos los días.   *We used to go to the beach every day.*

2. express an action or state that was in progress in the past.

Agustín **estaba** muy contento y **hablaba** de sus planes con su hermana.   *Agustín was very happy and was talking about his plans with his sister.*

Suggestions. Give examples of some uses of the imperfect: what you used to do while in college, descriptions of places or people, including age. You may wish to write some of the verb forms on the board and use visuals. Ask yes/no, either/or, and information questions to elicit the imperfect in answers.

3. describe characteristics and conditions in the past.

> La casa **era** blanca y **tenía** dos dormitorios.
>
> *The house was white and it had two bedrooms.*

4. tell time in the past.

> **Era** la una de la tarde; no **eran** las dos.
>
> *It was one in the afternoon; it was not two.*

5. tell age in the past.

> Ella **tenía** quince años entonces.
>
> *She was fifteen years old then.*

Note. Compare these time expressions to those related to the preterit: *ayer, una vez, la semana pasada, de repente.*

- Some time expressions that often accompany the imperfect to express ongoing or repeated actions or states in the past are **mientras, a veces, siempre, generalmente,** and **frecuentemente.**

2. Imperfect of regular and irregular verbs

Note. The *yo, él, ella, Ud.* forms are identical. Context will determine the meaning, but subject pronouns may be used for clarity.

Suggestions. Bring photos to class or ask students to bring photos to class and ask *¿Qué hacía / hacías / hacían cuando tomaron esta foto?* to preview imperfect/preterit contrast, or ask students to bring in photos. Allow students to guess what was happening in various photos before you tell them.

Remind students that *hay* and *había* are invariable. Provide additional examples.

REGULAR IMPERFECT			
	HABLAR	COMER	VIVIR
yo	hablaba	comía	vivía
tú	hablabas	comías	vivías
Ud., él, ella	hablaba	comía	vivía
nosotros/as	hablábamos	comíamos	vivíamos
vosotros/as	hablabais	comíais	vivíais
Uds., ellos/as	hablaban	comían	vivían

- Note that the endings for **-er** and **-ir** verbs are the same. All these forms have a written accent over the **í** of the ending: comía, vivías.

- The Spanish imperfect has several English equivalents.

VÍNCULOS

To practice imperfect of regular and irregular verbs
- SAM-OneKey: WB: 8-6, 8-7, 8-8 / LM: 8-35, 8-36, 8-37
- Companion Website: AP 8-5
- *Gramática viva*: Grammar Point 16: Imperfect tense of regular and irregular verbs
- IRCD: Chapter 8; pg. 290

> Mis amigos bailaban mucho.
>
> *My friends danced a lot.*
> *My friends were dancing a lot.*
> *My friends used to dance a lot.*
> *My friends would dance a lot.*
> (implying a repeated action)

- There are no stem changes in the imperfect.

> Ella no d**ue**rme bien ahora, pero antes d**o**rmía muy bien.
> *She does not sleep well now, but she used to sleep very well before.*

- Only three verbs are irregular in the imperfect.

> **ir** iba, ibas, iba, íbamos, ibais, iban
> **ser** era, eras, era, éramos, erais, eran
> **ver** veía, veías, veía, veíamos, veíais, veían

- The imperfect form of **hay** is **había** (*there was, there were, there used to be*). Both forms remain invariable.

> **Había** una invitación en el correo.
> *There was an invitation in the mail.*
> **Había** muchas personas en la fiesta.
> *There were many people at the party.*

¿Qué dice usted?

8-10 Cuando tenía cinco años. Primera fase. Marque cuáles eran sus actividades cuando usted tenía cinco años.

1. _____ Jugaba en el parque con mi perro.
2. _____ Ayudaba a mi mamá en la casa.
3. _____ Salía con mis padres los fines de semana.
4. _____ Iba a la playa en el verano.
5. _____ Miraba televisión hasta muy tarde.
6. _____ Celebraba el año nuevo con mis amigos.
7. _____ Asistía a las fiestas de la familia.
8. _____ ...

②Segunda fase. Comparen sus respuestas y, luego, respondan a estas preguntas.

1. ¿Quién de ustedes miraba más televisión?
2. ¿Quién de ustedes tenía una vida más activa? ¿Por qué?

②8-11 En la escuela secundaria. Primera fase. Marque en el cuadro la frecuencia con que usted y sus amigos/as hacían estas cosas. Después compare sus respuestas con las de su compañero/a.

MODELO: leer muchos libros
Siempre (frecuentemente/a veces/nunca) leíamos muchos libros.

ACTIVIDADES	SIEMPRE	FRECUENTEMENTE	A VECES	NUNCA
practicar deportes				
bailar mucho en las fiestas				
ir a los partidos de fútbol				
asistir a conciertos				
reunirse con amigos en el cine				

GSegunda fase. Formen pequeños grupos para hablar de lo siguiente:

1. ¿Cuál era la actividad que realizaban con menos frecuencia o nunca? ¿Por qué?
2. ¿Cuáles eran las dos actividades que realizaban con más frecuencia? ¿Por qué?

②8-12 Entrevista. Háganse las siguientes preguntas para saber cómo era la vida de cada uno/a cuando era pequeño/a.

1. ¿Dónde vivías, y con quién?
2. ¿A qué escuela ibas?
3. ¿Quién era tu mejor amigo/a? ¿Cómo era?
4. ¿Qué deportes practicabas?
5. ¿Qué programas de televisión veías?
6. ¿Qué te gustaba hacer en tu tiempo libre?

Follow-up for 8-10. In groups of four, students share information. One student reports to the class what activities they all used to do.

Suggestion for 8-11. While still working in groups, students should add to the chart an additional activity that they used to do very often and one that they hardly did.

Follow-up for 8-11. Find out what the activity was the whole class enjoyed the most and the least.

Suggestion for 8-12. Encourage students to listen carefully and ask follow-up questions to avoid a mechanical question/answer format. Model how to engage another person in conversation.

Follow-up for 8-12. Have students report to the class.

② 8-13 Mi casa. Descríbale a su compañero/a cómo era la casa o apartamento donde usted vivía cuando era niño/a. Después, su compañero/a debe hacer lo mismo.

② 8-14 Las fiestas infantiles. Comenten cómo eran las fiestas de cumpleaños y el día de las brujas cuando eran pequeños/as. Incluyan los siguientes puntos:

■ lugar de la celebración

■ horas (comienzo y final)

■ actividades

■ personas que participaban

■ comida y bebida que servían

■ ropa que llevaban

Ⓖ 8-15 Antes y ahora. En pequeños grupos, expliquen cómo era la vida antes y cómo es ahora con respecto a los siguientes temas:

■ la familia (tamaño, grado de movilidad, porcentaje de divorcios)

■ la mujer en la sociedad (participación en el mundo del trabajo/de la política, su independencia económica)

■ las ciudades (tamaño, los problemas ambientales (*environment*) como la contaminación, la delincuencia, el crimen)

SITUACIONES

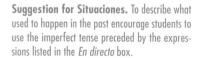

EN DIRECTO

To talk about how things used to be:

Entonces...

Por aquel entonces...

En aquellos tiempos...

1. **Role A.** You are a very famous public figure (a singer, a professor, a scientist, a sports person, etc.) who is going to be interviewed by a reporter from a major television station. The public is interested in knowing about your background. Give your interviewer as many details as possible as you talk about your past.

   Role B. You are interviewing a very famous person for a major television station. Ask your interviewee the following questions about his/her background: a) what the place he/she was born was like, b) how his/her family life and school days were, c) the type of music he/she used to listen to, d) the books he/she used to read, e) the holidays/ festivities he/she celebrated most and how he/she celebrated them, etc.

2. **Role A.** You are an exchange student and would like to find out about your host's weekend and holiday activities when he/she was in high school. Ask a) what he/she did on Saturday evenings, b) with whom, c) the time, and d) if the activities were the same during the summertime.

   Role B. You are the host of an exchange student. Answer his/her questions about your activities when you were in high school. Then explain that during a summer you went to a friend's house in Guadalajara, Mexico, and that while you were there you used to a) speak Spanish every day, b) go to the outdoor markets, c) listen to the mariachis, and d) eat excellent Mexican food everywhere (**en todas partes**).

3. The preterit and the imperfect

■ The preterit and the imperfect are not interchangeable.

■ Use the preterit:

1. to talk about the beginning or end of an event, action, or condition.

| Pepito **leyó** a los cinco años. | Pepito read (began reading) at age five. |

El niño **se enfermó** el sábado. — The child got sick (began feeling sick) on Saturday.

Pepito **leyó** el cuento. — Pepito read (finished) the story.

El niño **estuvo** enfermo ayer. — The child was sick (he is no longer sick) yesterday.

2. to talk about an event, action, or condition that occurred over a period of time with a definite beginning and end.

Vivieron en México por diez años. — They lived in Mexico for ten years.

3. to narrate a sequence of completed actions in the past (note that there is a forward movement of narrative time).

Oyeron un ruido, se **levantaron**, y **bajaron** las escaleras. — They heard a noise, got up, and went downstairs.

■ Use the imperfect:

1. to talk about customary or habitual actions, events, or conditions in the past.

Todos los días **llovía**, y por eso **leíamos** mucho. — It used to rain every day and that's why we read a lot.

2. to talk about an ongoing part of an event, action, or condition.

En ese momento **llovía** mucho y los niños **estaban** muy tristes. — At that moment it was raining a lot, and the children were very sad.

■ In a story, the imperfect provides the background information, whereas the preterit tells what happened. Note that an ongoing action expressed with the imperfect is often interrupted by a completed action expressed with the preterit.

Era navidad. Todos **dormíamos** cuando los niños **oyeron** un ruido en el techo. — It was Christmas. All of us were sleeping when the children heard a noise on the roof.

¿Qué dice usted?

8-16 ¡Qué día! Ayer iba a ser un día especial para Pedro, pero todos sus planes terminaron mal. Marque con un círculo las tres cosas que, en su opinión, probablemente le ocurrieron mientras trataba de realizar sus planes.

1. Mientras se bañaba temprano por la mañana, se cayó en el baño.
2. Mientras desayunaba tranquilamente, el teléfono sonó y no pudo terminar de comer.
3. Iba a la tienda para comprarle un anillo a su novia cuando alguien le robó el dinero.

Suggestion. Give examples of the use of both tenses either by narrating a personal experience or someone else's experience: *El verano pasado Juan y su hermano fueron a un lago en las montañas. El lugar era muy bonito. Había muchos árboles y el agua del lago era muy limpia. Estuvieron una semana allí y les gustó mucho. Todos los días se levantaban a las ocho más o menos, desayunaban y se iban al lago a nadar y a conversar con sus amigos. Por la tarde, montaban en bicicleta y se reunían con más amigos y a veces iban a un pueblo que estaba cerca. El último día fue muy triste para todos. Vieron a sus amigos, almorzaron con ellos y después volvieron a la casa para empacar. Fue un verano maravilloso para estos chicos.*

VÍNCULOS

To practice the preterit and the imperfect
● SAM-OneKey: WB: 8-9, 8-10, 8-11, 8-12 / LM: 8-38, 8-39
● Companion Website: AP 8-6
● *Gramática viva*: Grammar Points 40 and 41: Preterit vs. imperfect, Preterit vs. imperfect II

4. Mientras llamaba por teléfono a un restaurante para reservar una mesa, el restaurante se incendió.

5. Iba a proponerle matrimonio a su novia cuando su ex-novia lo llamó por teléfono.

6. Mientras preparaba una cena deliciosa para celebrar el cumpleaños de su novia, el perro se comió el pastel.

Suggestion for 8-17. Introduce *sentirse* using comprehensible input. You may say how you or someone else reacted to hearing some bad/good news: *Cuando escuché la noticia del accidente me sentí muy mal. Fue un accidente terrible y no pude dormir esa noche.* Then say how you were feeling later. *Por la mañana todavía me sentía mal y llamé a mi mejor amiga.*

8-17 La última vez. Túrnense para preguntarse cuándo fue la última vez que cada uno de ustedes hizo estas cosas y cómo se sentía mientras las hacía.

MODELO: correr en los sanfermines
           E1: ¿Cuándo fue la última vez que corriste en los sanfermines?
           E2: Corrí el año pasado.
           E1: ¿Y cómo te sentías mientras corrías?
           E2: Tenía mucho miedo.

1. participar en un campeonato   4. disfrazarse
2. ganar un premio   5. bailar en un carnaval
3. estar en un desfile   6. ...

8-18 ¿Pretérito o imperfecto? Completen esta narración usando el pretérito o el imperfecto.

En el mes de abril del año pasado mi familia y yo (1) _____fuimos_____ (ir) a Guatemala de vacaciones. Primero nosotros (2) _____estuvimos_____ (estar) en la ciudad de Guatemala, la capital. Allí (3) _____vimos_____ (ver) a unos parientes y (4) _____visitamos_____ (visitar) lugares muy interesantes, como el Museo Nacional de Arqueología y Etnología, donde (5) _____pudimos_____ (poder) admirar una excelente colección de objetos de la cultura maya, y el Mercado Central, donde mi mamá (6) _____compró_____ (comprar) unas blusas con unos diseños mayas preciosos.

En la mañana del tercer día, nosotros (7) _____nos fuimos_____ (irse) a Antigua, que está bastante cerca de la capital. (8) _____Hacía_____ (Hacer) un tiempo fabuloso. Como (9) _____era_____ (ser) primavera, muchos árboles y plantas (10) _____tenían_____ (tener) flores, y todo (11) _____estaba_____ (estar) muy verde. Nosotros (12) _____salimos_____ (salir) del hotel cerca de las cinco de la tarde y poco después (13) _____llegamos_____ (llegar) a una plaza donde había mucha gente. Allí (14) _____vimos_____ (ver) las procesiones de semana santa. El ambiente (15) _____era_____ (ser) impresionante; las personas (16) _____llevaban_____ (llevar) túnicas largas y (17) _____caminaban_____ (caminar) lentamente por la calle. ¡Nunca vamos a olvidar esa experiencia!

Warm-up for 8-19. Model this activity by describing an event and an unexpected occurrence, using visuals or gestures to facilitate comprehension: *El sábado pasado fui a una boda. La novia llevaba un velo muy largo. Después de la ceremonia fuimos a un hotel para el banquete. Todos estábamos muy contentos y bailábamos mientras la orquesta tocaba. Una pareja que se movía mucho mientras bailaba tropezó con la mesa donde estaban el pastel de boda y los platos de postre. ¡Total que el pastel se cayó al piso! La madre de la novia corrió hacia donde estaba el pastel y también se cayó. Los novios fueron adonde estaba la señora, pero ésta se levantó y dijo que estaba bien. La orquesta empezó a tocar y la fiesta continuó. Fue una boda inolvidable.*

8-19 Un evento inolvidable. Cuéntele a su compañero/a con todos los detalles algo inesperado (sorprendente) que le ocurrió durante una celebración, día festivo o evento especial el año pasado. Indique qué pasó, dónde, cuándo, etc. Describa la escena y los personajes. Su compañero/a debe hacerle preguntas para obtener más información.

SITUACIONES

1. **Role A.** Tell your friend about a festival, celebration or ceremony in which you participated recently. Answer his/her questions with as many details as you can.

   Role B. Your friend is going to tell you about an important event in which he/she participated. Ask him/her questions about where the event/festivity took place, the way people were dressed, how the place was decorated, etc. React appropriately to what you hear.

2. **Role A.** You have just come back from a Spanish-speaking country where you visited a town or city that was having a local festival. Explain to your friend what you saw and answer his/her questions.

   Role B. Your friend went to a festival in a Spanish-speaking country. Ask him/her: a) what the people were doing, b) what they were wearing, c) what they were eating, d) if there were open air markets, e) what people sold there, f) if he/she bought something etc.

Suggestion. Use the Image Resource CD to talk about the illustrations and ask questions: *¿Hay más personas en esta fiesta que en la otra? Y aquí en la clase, ¿hay menos personas que en la fiesta? ¿Qué fiesta es más alegre?* Write *más... que* and *menos... que* on the board. Compare yourself to a student or a famous person. Use visuals to elicit comparisons.

VÍNCULOS

To practice comparisons of inequality
- SAM-OneKey: WB: 8-13, 8-14, 8-15, 8-16 / LM: 8-40, 8-41, 8-42
- Companion Website: AP 8-7
- *Gramática viva*: Grammar Point 4: Comparatives and Superlatives
- IRCD: Chapter 8; pp. 295, 296

4. Comparisons of inequality

En esta fiesta hay **más** personas **que** en la otra.
Es **más** divertida **que** la otra.
Las personas bailan **más**.

En esta fiesta hay **menos** personas **que** en la otra.
Esta fiesta es **menos** alegre **que** la otra.
Las personas se divierten **menos**.

- Use **más... que** or **menos... que** to express comparisons of inequality with nouns, adjectives, and adverbs.

COMPARISONS OF INEQUALITY	
Cuando Alina era joven tenía { **más** / **menos** } amigos que Pepe.	*When Alina was young she had { more / fewer } friends than Pepe.*
Ella era { **más** / **menos** } activa que él.	*She was { more / less } active than he.*
Salía { **más** / **menos** } frecuentemente que él.	*She went out { more / less } frequently than he.*

- Use **de** instead of **que** before numbers.

   Había **más de** diez carrozas en el desfile. — *There were more than ten floats in the parade.*
   El año pasado vimos **menos de** diez. — *Last year we saw fewer than ten.*

■ The following adjectives have regular and irregular comparative forms.

bueno	más bueno o mejor	*better*
malo	más malo o peor[1]	*worse*
pequeño	más pequeño o menor	*smaller*
joven	más joven o menor	*younger*
grande	más grande o mayor	*bigger*
viejo	más viejo o mayor[2]	*older*

Esta banda es $\begin{Bmatrix} \text{mejor} \\ \text{peor} \end{Bmatrix}$ que aquélla. *This band is* $\begin{Bmatrix} better \\ worse \end{Bmatrix}$ *than that one.*

■ When **bien** and **mal** function as adverbs, they have the same irregular comparative forms as **bueno** and **malo**.

bien → mejor	Yo canto **mejor** que Héctor.	*I sing better than Héctor.*
mal → peor	Héctor canta **peor** que yo.	*Héctor sings worse than I.*

Suggestions for 8-20. Point to the location of these two Mexican cities on a map. You may mention that *Mérida* was chosen as the *Capital Americana de la Cultura* in 2000. Recycle weather expressions by asking students to guess what the weather is like in these cities. Ask them to compare the weather there and in their own city.

¿Qué dice usted?

❷ **8-20 Comparación de dos desfiles. Primera fase.** Lea la siguiente información sobre los desfiles de Veracruz y de Mérida en México. Después diga si las siguientes oraciones son correctas de acuerdo con la información de la tabla.

A INVESTIGAR

Busque la siguiente información antes de hacer la actividad **8-20:**

¿Quién fundó la ciudad de Veracruz?

¿Por qué es importante esta ciudad?

¿Qué ciudades mayas están cerca de Mérida?

	VERACRUZ	MÉRIDA
Habitantes	320.000	750.000
Público	8.000 personas	12.000 personas
Número de bandas	4	5

	Sí	No
1. Mérida tiene más habitantes que Veracruz.	X	
2. Menos personas asisten al desfile de Veracruz que al de Mérida.	X	
3. Hay más bandas en el desfile de Veracruz que en el de Mérida.		X
4. Hay más público en el desfile de Veracruz que en el de Mérida.	X	
5. Veracruz tiene menos habitantes que Mérida.	X	

❷ **Segunda fase.** Debido a los costos, la banda de su universidad sólo puede participar en uno de estos dos desfiles. Con la información que tienen de la Primera fase y la que aparece más abajo, decidan a cuál debe asistir y expliquen por qué.

	DESFILE DE VERACRUZ	DESFILE DE MERIDA
Transporte	30.000 pesos	30.500 pesos
Hotel	12.000 pesos	10.000 pesos
Comidas	2.000 pesos	3.000 pesos

[1]**Más bueno** and **más malo** are not used interchangeably with **mejor** and **peor**. **Más bueno** and **más malo** refer to a person's moral qualities.
[2]Use **mayor** to refer to a person's age. **Más viejo** is generally used with nouns other than people.

8-21 Personas famosas. Compare a las siguientes personas considerando su aspecto físico, su edad, el tipo de trabajo, dinero o popularidad.

1. Brad Pitt y Antonio Banderas
2. Penélope Cruz y Jennifer López
3. Tiger Woods y Sammy Sosa
4. el presidente y el vicepresidente

5. Comparisons of equality

COMPARISONS OF EQUALITY	
tan... como	as . . . as
tanto/a... como	as much . . . as
tantos/as... como	as many . . . as
tanto como	as much as

■ Use **tan... como** to express comparisons of equality with adjectives and adverbs.

| La boda fue **tan** elegante **como** la fiesta. | *The wedding was as elegant at the party.* |
| El padre bailó **tan** bien **como** su hija. | *The father danced as well as his daughter.* |

■ Use **tanto(s)/tanta(s)... como** to express comparisons of equality with nouns.

Había **tanto** ruido **como** en el carnaval.	*There was as much noise as a Mardi Gras.*
Había **tanta** alegría **como** en el carnaval.	*There was as much joy as at Mardi Gras.*
Había **tantos** desfiles **como** en el carnaval.	*There were as many parades as at Mardi Gras.*
Había **tantas** orquestas **como** en el carnaval.	*There were as many orchestras as at Mardi Gras.*

■ Use **tanto como** to express comparisons of equality with verbs.

Ellos bailaron **tanto como** nosotros. *They danced as much as we did.*

¿Qué dice usted?

8-22 Cuatro estudiantes guatemaltecos. Comparen a estos cuatro estudiantes.

MODELO: E1: Vilma tiene tantos hermanos como Marta.
E2: Sí, pero tiene más hermanos que Ricardo.

	PEDRO	VILMA	MARTA	RICARDO
Hermanos	2	3	3	2
Clases	5	5	4	6
Dinero	50 quetzales	80 quetzales	50 quetzales	80 quetzales
Discos	200	180	180	215
Videos	40	32	40	32

Suggestion for 8-22. Point out that the *quetzal*, which is a beautiful bird, is the symbol of Guatemala, similar to the American eagle in the United States. The *quetzal* is also the name of the monetary unit of Guatemala. You may ask students to find out the current rate of exchange on the Web or in a newspaper.

Follow-up for 8-22. Ask questions to summarize: *¿Pedro tiene tantas clases como Vilma? ¿Tiene Pedro tanto dinero como ella? Y, ¿Vilma tiene tantos hermanos como él?*

VÍNCULOS

To practice comparisons of equality
• SAM-OneKey: WB: 8-17, 8-18, 8-19 / LM: 8-43, 8-44, 8-45
• Companion Website: AP 8-8
• *Gramática viva*: Grammar Point 4: Comparatives and Superlatives
• IRCD: Chapter 8; pg. 297

2 **8-23 Opiniones.** Primero, den dos nombres de personas, desfiles, etc. Luego, expresen su opinión para compararlos. Pueden usar las palabras que aparecen entre paréntesis u otras de su elección.

MODELO: dos actores (bueno)
E1: Tom Cruise es tan buen actor como Johnny Depp.
E2: Sí, estoy de acuerdo/tienes razón. *o*
No, Johnny Depp es mejor actor que Tom Cruise.

1. dos actrices norteamericanas
(atractiva, alta, famosa, buena actriz...)
2. dos desfiles o celebraciones locales o nacionales
(número de personas, carrozas, divertido...)
3. dos películas nominadas para el Óscar
(actores, fotografía, acción, ...)
4. dos programas cómicos de la televisión
(cómico, malo, loco...)

G **8-24 Las diversiones. Primera fase.** Comparen las películas o los programas de televisión de antes con los de hoy en día, basándose en lo siguiente: los temas, los personajes, el uso de la tecnología, la violencia y el sexo.

Segunda fase. Ahora contesten las siguientes preguntas e intercambien opiniones con otros grupos.

1. ¿Creen ustedes que hoy en día hay más sexo y violencia en las películas y los programas de televisión que antes?
2. ¿Piensan ustedes que hoy hay más violencia social porque se ve más televisión, o porque los medios de comunicación tienen más influencia en los jóvenes que sus padres y la escuela?
3. ¿Piensan que el gobierno debe tener más control sobre los medios de comunicación y el arte?

SITUACIONES

1. One of you is in favor of small weddings and the other prefers big weddings. Compare both in regard to a) expenses (*gastos*), b) stress (*estrés*) for the bride and groom, c) work involved, and d) problems.

2. **Role A.** You are a student representative in charge of making a presentation before the Faculty Senate. You are to compare the graduation ceremony at your own university with the graduation ceremony at University X. Convince the faculty that the graduation ceremony at University X is better because it is: smaller, better organized, less expensive, there is better music and there are better speeches (*discursos*), etc.

   Role B. The rest of the class will represent the faculty senate and will ask questions to get a clear idea of the advantages of one type of ceremony over the other.

A conversar

2 **8-36 ¿Semejantes o diferentes?** Entreviste a su compañero/a usando las preguntas de 8-35 y tome notas de sus respuestas.

Después de conversar

2 **8-37 Almas gemelas** (*Identical souls*) **o mundos apartes** (*worlds apart*). Anónimamente, escriban un breve informe comparativo de su infancia y adolescencia. Otra pareja va a leer su informe y va a tratar de averigüar quiénes son ustedes. Sigan los siguientes modelos o combínenlos, de acuerdo a sus experiencias. Mantengan su identidad en secreto.

MODELOS:

Suggestions for 8-37. To prevent that students reading the reports recognize their classmates by their handwriting, you may ask that pairs type out their report. You may also ask that students share their report via e-mail. In that case, guesses as to who the people in the report are should be e-mailed to the instructor so he/she may remove e-mail addresses and/or names.

ALMAS GEMELAS

Somos dos almas gemelas. Tanto mi compañero/a como yo nacimos en...

MUNDOS APARTES

Somos dos mundos apartes. Uno/a de nosotros/as nació en..., el/la otro/a nació en...

Con respecto a los deportes...

La(s) fiesta(s) más importante(s)...

Durante/ Para... (nombre de la/s fiesta/s)...

Durante nuestra infancia/adolescencia...

Nuestras familias también tenían una/dos costumbre(s)

Mi compañero/a y yo tuvimos una niñez/adolescencia semejante/diferente.

Antes de conversar

8-38 Mi cumpleaños. Las siguientes palabras se relacionan con una fiesta de cumpleaños. Escríbalas en la columna apropiada.

pastel	comer	amigos	recibir regalos
bailar	auto	felicitar (*congratulate*)	familiares
ropa	joyas	divertirse	pasarlo bien
novio/a	colegas	sentirse contento/a	dinero

PERSONAS INVITADAS	ACTIVIDADES TÍPICAS	REGALOS	DESEOS DEL/DE LA CUMPLEAÑERO/A
amigos	comer	pastel	pasarlo bien
familiares	recibir regalos	ropa	sentirse contento/a
novio/a	bailar	joyas	divertirse
colegas	felicitar	auto	
		dinero	

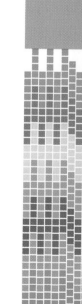

A conversar

Suggestion for 8-39. Depending on the level of proficiency of your students, you may wish to ask that students write down the questions in advance. You may provide them with some examples such as: *¿Querías celebrar tu cumpleaños solo/a o con amigos/con tu familia? ¿Querías hacer una fiesta en tu casa/ apartamento o querías salir a comer?*, etc.

❷ 8-39 Recuerdos de mi mejor/peor cumpleaños. Conversen sobre su mejor/peor cumpleaños. Averigüen lo siguiente.

1. Cómo lo quería celebrar cada uno/a y cómo lo celebró realmente
2. Quiénes lo/la llamaron o visitaron
3. Cómo lo pasó cada uno/a
4. Qué quería recibir de regalo cada uno/a y qué recibió realmente

Después de conversar

8-40 Querido diario (*diary*). Imagínese que usted tuvo un cumpleaños fabuloso o uno muy malo. Narre en su diario lo que le ocurrió.

EN DIRECTO

To show empathy:
¡Oh! ¡Qué lástima!
¡Cuánto lo siento! *How sad!*

To share someone's happiness:
¡Qué fabuloso/bueno!
¡Cuánto me alegro! *I'm happy to hear that!*

To thank someone for his/her empathy:
¡Oh, gracias!

Querido diario:

El día _____ (date) fue mi cumpleaños. Cumplí _____ años. _____ un día _____. (Say how the day was.)

Yo quería hacer lo siguiente el día de mi cumpleaños: _____, _____ y _____.

Afortunadamente/Desafortunadamente

_____

_____

(Say what you could actually do or you couldn't do because something happened. Explain what happened then describe how you felt about what you were able/unable to do. Explain why.)

_____

_____

En general, mi cumpleaños fue _____.

 Leer

In *Lección 8*, you will have the opportunity to further practice some strategies learned previously as well as focus on identifying information stated in a text and making inferences based on the information presented.

Guía de prelectura

Relying on the visuals, the text title, and cognates in activity **8-43**, answer these questions.

1. Thinking of the traditions and holidays celebrated in the Spanish-speaking world and of the ethnic diversity represented in the Hispanic cultures, what content areas do you expect the text will cover?
   a. The influence of the Spanish conquest on the indigenous cultures of America
   b. Some beliefs and customs of the indigenous people in America
   c. Cultures in contact in Spanish-speaking America

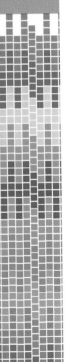

2. On what did you base your answers to question 1?
  (a.) The cognates in the title
  (b.) The photos in the text
  (c.) My personal knowledge of the topic

3. After reading the title, guess some of the information the reader will probably find in the text. Mark with an X all that may apply. You may verify your responses at a later time.
  (a.) _____ The geographic areas where the Maya empire settled and flourished
  (b.) _____ Some Mayans beliefs regarding life and death
  (c.) _____ Some rituals and practices of the Mayans
  d. _____ Some Mayan beliefs and practices that were affected by the Spanish Conquest

Antes de leer

8-41 Preparación. Las creencias (*beliefs*) sobre la muerte y las costumbres relacionadas con ella varían de una cultura a otra. Según sus conocimientos sobre el tema, indiquen si las siguientes prácticas se asocian con la cultura egipcia (**CE**), con alguna cultura indígena americana (**CI**), o con ambas (**A**).

1. __A__ Creían que había vida después de la muerte.
2. __A__ Construían pirámides para honrar a los muertos.
3. __CE__ Embalsamaban el cadáver para preservarlo.
4. __CE__ Rociaban (*Sprayed*) el cuerpo con perfumes.
5. __CI__ Vestían a los muertos con ropa funeraria especial.
6. __CI__ Preparaban comidas típicas de la región, y las ponían en las tumbas.
7. __CI__ Ponían una máscara sobre la cara del muerto.
8. __A__ Enterraban (*buried*) al muerto en las pirámides, en tumbas o sepulcros, de acuerdo al estatus social de la persona muerta.
9. __A__ La familia de la persona muerta depositaba joyas y objetos de valor en la tumba o pirámide.
10. __CI__ Rociaban el cadáver con un polvo de color rojo para simbolizar el renacimiento (*rebirth*).

8-42 Clasificación. Escriba cada palabra en la columna correspondiente.

anillo	carne	aretes
fruta	pulseras	copa
vegetales	cinturón	cuchillo de hueso

JOYAS	OTROS OBJETOS DE VALOR	COMIDA
anillo	copa	carne
aretes	cinturón	fruta
pulseras	cuchillo de hueso	vegetales

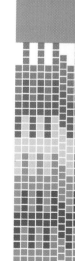

A leer

8-43 Primera mirada. Lea el siguiente texto y, luego, siga las instrucciones.

Creencias y costumbres mayas sobre la muerte

El origen de los mayas es incierto. Sin embargo, se sabe que esta civilización ocupó y se desarrolló en los actuales territorios de Guatemala, México, Belice, Honduras y El Salvador. Durante su período de mayor esplendor, los mayas construyeron ciudades y pirámides, donde enterraban a sus gobernantes y los veneraban después de muertos.

Los mayas compartían con otras culturas mesoamericanas algunas creencias y costumbres. Entre otras cosas, creían en la vida después de la muerte y en la interacción entre el mundo humano y el mundo espiritual. Creían que el destino de una persona después de la muerte dependía de la forma en que moría y no de su conducta mientras vivía. Los enterramientos[1] y los vestuarios funerarios confirman que los mayas creían que el espíritu se prolongaba más allá de la muerte. La mayoría de los muertos iba a Xibalbá, un lugar en el mundo de abajo.

Para llegar al inframundo había que superar numerosos peligros. El espíritu debía comer bien y cuidarse. Por eso, los mayas dejaban en la tumba un ajuar o vestimenta funeraria. También colocaban comida, agua y amuletos[2] protectores, de acuerdo con el estatus social del muerto.

Los mayas rociaban el cadáver con un polvo rojo que simbolizaba el

renacimiento. También lo adornaban con joyas, collares, pulseras y anillos de jade, hueso o concha[3] y un cinturón ceremonial. En muchos enterramientos ponían una máscara sobre la cara del muerto para ocultar su identidad. En la boca le ponían una cuenta[4] de jade, símbolo de lo precioso y lo perenne, para preservar su espíritu inmortal.

Algunas de estas creencias y costumbres todavía se conservan, con ciertas variaciones, en algunas comunidades de Guatemala, México y El Salvador.

[1]*graves*   [2]*amulets, charms*   [3]*shell*   [4]*bead*

Determine si las siguientes afirmaciones representan información explícita (**E**) en el texto o son inferencias (**I**) basadas en el contenido. Si es una inferencia, indique la(s) frase(s) en que se basa.

1. __E__ Los expertos no saben de dónde vinieron los mayas.
2. __I__ Los mayas crearon una gran civilización.
3. __I__ Las comunidades mayas tenían autoridades que los gobernaban.
4. __I__ Como los egipcios, los mayas construyeron edificios magníficos para honrar la memoria de personas de alto estatus en su comunidad.
5. __E__ Los mayas, como otros grupos indígenas, pensaban que la vida continuaba después de la muerte.
6. __E__ Para los mayas, el tipo de muerte determinaba el destino de una persona.
7. __I__ No todos los mayas iban al mismo destino después de la muerte.
8. __E__ La comida, el agua y los amuletos ayudaban al espíritu del muerto a llegar a su destino final.

8-44 Segunda mirada. Complete las siguientes ideas con información explícita en el texto.

1. Los mayas, como otras culturas indígenas de Mesoamérica, creían en...
   a. _____
   b. _____

2. Estas dos costumbres demuestran que los mayas tenían estas creencias...
   a. _____ b. _____

3. Para llegar a su destino final, el espíritu de los muertos tenía que...
   _____ y _____
4. Para indicar que el espíritu del muerto nacía otra vez, los mayas...
   _____

5. Para simbolizar la importancia y la inmortalidad del espíritu, los mayas...
   _____

Después de leer

8-45 Inferencias. Con un/a compañero/a, mencionen qué objetos probablemente ponían los mayas en la tumba o pirámide de un gobernante con las siguientes características:

1. era físicamente activo
2. le gustaba mucho el arte
3. estudiaba astronomía
4. le fascinaba la guerra

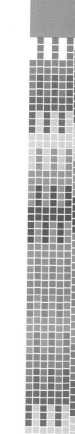

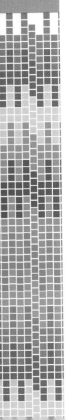

Escribir

In *this chapter* you will have the opportunity to review writing descriptions in the context of a narrative text.

In simple words, narrating is telling, recounting, reporting an event that may be real or imaginary following a sequence or order (from present to past, from past to present, or a combination of both). Furthermore, narration may serve a variety of purposes: to inform, to teach, to explain past or present actions or experiences, etc. However, how can we write narrative texts effectively?

The following tips will help you be a successful narrator:

1. Keep in mind the characters involved (their feelings, their physical and personality characteristics), the pace of action, the setting of your story (rural, cosmopolitan, mysterious, etc.), the time frame (present, past), the order (chronological, retrospective, etc.) in which the events unfold.

2. Determine the right perspective for your narration. Did you (and someone else) live the experience (protagonist/s)? Did you see how an event unfolded (eyewitness)?

3. Structure your narration as follows:

   ■ First introduce the character(s), describe the setting, and begin the action.

   ■ Then, present the unfolding of the action and describe the characters and the tensions caused by their actions or by the events around them.

   ■ Finally, present a closure to the tensions between/among characters or let the reader of your story imagine the end.

Antes de escribir

8-46 Enfoque. Primera fase. Lea la siguiente narración y siga las instrucciones.

Eran alrededor de las siete de la tarde del 24 de mayo cuando ocurrió lo que cambió nuestra vida por completo. Era una noche de otoño, y hacía viento. Empezaba a oscurecer. Era el cumpleaños de nuestra gran amiga Guadalupe Martínez.

Aunque tenía sólo viente años, Guadalupe era una chica excepcional. Estudiaba y también trabajaba para ayudar a su familia de ocho hermanos. Todos sus amigos la admirábamos por su generosidad, optimismo y alegría. Guadalupe era la hija, hermana y amiga que todos soñábamos tener.

El día de su cumpleaños por la mañana, Francisco y yo no la llamamos como de costumbre. Planeábamos darle una sorpresa para su cumpleaños. Después de todo, ¡sólo se cumplen veintiún años una vez en la vida! Primero, fuimos a un centro comercial y le buscamos un regalo especial. Caminamos varias horas hasta que encontramos un plato decorativo guatemalteco y un CD de su música favorita. Francisco también le compró un perfume, y yo agregué un buen libro al cesto de regalos. Finalmente, cerca de las cuatro de la tarde, volvimos a casa y envolvimos los regalos.

Después de un día muy ocupado, a las seis de la tarde Francisco y yo caminábamos a casa de Guadalupe. Estábamos a sólo unos 80 metros de su casa, cuando la ambulancia pasó a toda velocidad por la avenida en que caminábamos. Francisco y yo intuitivamente nos miramos y empezamos a caminar con más rapidez, pero en silencio. A sólo unos metros de su casa, supimos que algo pasaba en casa de Guadalupe. Francisco y yo corrimos. Cuando llegamos a la puerta de su cuarto, uno de los enfermeros nos dijo: "La señorita Martínez tuvo un accidente. Se quebró una pierna".

Francisco y yo sin decir una palabra llamamos al resto de nuestros amigos. Les dimos suficiente tiempo a los médicos y a las enfermeras para hacer su trabajo, pero a las 9:00 de la noche, todos los amigos de Guadalupe le celebramos su cumpleaños en el hospital. Fue un cumpleaños diferente a todos los anteriores, pero lo pasamos al lado de la cama de nuestra gran amiga.

Segunda fase. Answer the following questions, based on the story you just read.

1. Mark with an *X* the intended purpose of the story.
   __X__ To describe the life of a special person
   _____ To entertain readers
   __X__ To inform the reader about a sad experience
   _____ To teach a lesson

2. Based on its purpose, is the narration effective?   Yes   No

3. Mark some possible reasons for your response to question 2.
   __X__ The main character is described in an interesting manner to the reader.
   __X__ The pace of the story is good: the action moves quickly, and the amount of description is about right.
   _____ There is too much description, and the pace of the story is slow.
   __X__ There is enough information about the setting of the story.
   __X__ The experience is told in a chronological order.
   __X__ The narration has a clear organization: an introduction, a development, and a closure.
   __X__ The perspective (narrator) of the story makes it interesting and realistic to the reader.

8-47 Preparación. En la actividad **8-48,** usted va a narrar una historia o experiencia personal, real o imaginaria. Primero, haga lo siguiente:

■ Decida la base de su narración: ¿va a contar una experiencia real o una que es producto de su imaginación?

■ Determine el objetivo de su narración: ¿va a escribir usted para informar, relatar, entretener, enseñar?

■ Haga una lista del/de los protagonista(s) de su historia: ¿Cómo se llaman? ¿Cuántos hay? ¿Qué características físicas y de personalidad tienen los protagonistas?

■ Determine el tiempo y orden de su narración: ¿Va a relatar lo que ocurrió en el pasado o en el presente? ¿Va a narrar los hechos en orden cronológico (desde el pasado al presente o desde el presente al pasado)?

■ Escriba una lista de verbos que lo/la ayuden a describir el ambiente, y otros que cuenten la acción.

■ Organice la información de su narración: ¿Qué va a presentar en la introducción? ¿Cuál va a ser el conflicto? ¿Va a presentar la solución del problema o conflicto, o el lector va a imaginar el final?

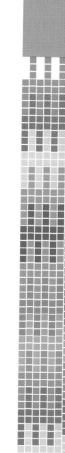

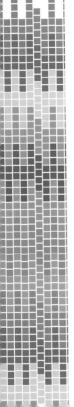

A escribir

8-48 Manos a la obra. Usando la información de la actividad anterior, escriba la narración. Las siguientes expresiones en *En directo* pueden resultarle muy útiles.

Después de escribir

8-49 Revisión. Ahora lea su narración, pensando en el lector. Verifique lo siguiente:

■ El contenido: ¿Incluyó usted toda la información necesaria o el lector todavía tiene preguntas? ¿Es interesante el contenido para el lector?

■ La organización: ¿Tiene su narración un orden que ayude al lector a seguir el flujo (*flow*) de la historia? ¿Presentó usted el conflicto o problema en la introducción? Desarrolló el conflicto en el cuerpo (*body*) del texto? ¿Hay una conclusión o resolución del conflicto al final de la historia o el lector debe imaginar el final?

■ La forma de su narración:

a. ¿Revisó la gramática de su narración? ¿Usó el vocabulario correcto, expresiones para indicar el orden cronológico, concordancia de tiempos (presente, pasado), etc.?

b. ¿Usó la puntuación y ortografía correctas?

Finalmente, comparta su narración con un/a compañero/a. Esto va a ayudar a mejorar algunas áreas débiles.

ENFOQUE CULTURAL

TEMAS: LA RELIGIÓN

Para pensar

¿Hay una religión oficial en los Estados Unidos? ¿Qué religiones hay en este país? ¿Qué fiestas religiosas se celebran aquí? ¿Cómo se celebran? ¿Participa usted en estas fiestas? ¿Qué hace?

La religión católica es la religión oficial en muchos países hispanos. Por eso hay muchas celebraciones de carácter religioso; por ejemplo, la procesión del día de la Virgen de Guadalupe en México.

En Guatemala, durante toda una semana a fines de noviembre, los hombres se preparan para celebrar la quema del diablo. Se visten de diablos y juegan a perseguir a los niños por las calles. Finalmente, el 7 de diciembre queman la figura de un diablo.

En Caracas, Venezuela, la fiesta religiosa más importante se celebra en la pascua de resurrección. Empieza con la bajada de palmeras el viernes antes del domingo de ramos, sigue con las procesiones el Jueves Santo y el Viernes Santo, y termina con la quema de Judas el domingo de pascua.

Para contestar

2 **Los feriados.** Contesten las siguientes preguntas.

1. Mencionen dos feriados religiosos que se celebran en el mundo hispano. ¿En qué países se celebran? ¿Cuándo se celebran?
2. Comenten cuándo y cómo se celebra una de las festividades mencionadas en el número 1.

G **Riqueza cultural.** En grupos de tres, escojan una fiesta religiosa y comparen cómo se celebra en los Estados Unidos y en el mundo hispano.

En la noche del 5 al 6 de enero, los Reyes Magos, montados en sus camellos, distribuyen regalos entre los niños. El día 6 hay una serie de procesiones de carrozas, orquestas y bailarines que recorren los pueblos y ciudades.

VÍNCULOS

For materials related to the Enfoque cultural, see
- SAM-OneKey: WB: 8-29
- IRCD: Chapter 8; pg. 312

Para pensar

¿Conoce usted a alguien de México o de Guatemala? ¿Sabe usted qué civilizaciones importantes se desarrollaron en esos países?

México y Guatemala son países vecinos que tienen una historia común.

La Ciudad de México es una de las ciudades más pobladas del planeta. Tiene hermosos parques, museos, galerías, iglesias, maravillosos restaurantes y una intensa vida nocturna.

En la península de Yucatán hay ruinas precolombinas extraordinarias, como la ciudad maya de Chichén Itza.

Guadalajara, la segunda ciudad de México en importancia, es conocida como la ciudad de los festivales. Tiene un encanto colonial, y es el lugar de origen de los mariachis y el tequila. En octubre, Guadalajara celebra el festival de los mariachis, con desfiles, misas cantadas por mariachis y bailes folclóricos.

Expresiones mexicanas:

cuate	¿Cómo está, **mi cuate**?	*How are you, my friend?*
se me hace	**Se me hace** que ese hombre es malo.	*It seems to me that that man is bad.*
qué tanto	¿**Qué tanto** te gusta él?	*How much do you like him?*
chaparra, güera	Ella es **chaparra y güera**.	*She is short and blond.*

Hay muchos lugares de interés en Guatemala. Por ejemplo, Santiago de Atitlán es famoso por sus maravillosos tejidos (weavings) y su hermosa iglesia construida en el siglo XVI.

Guatemala es un país de atractivos diversos que ofrece la posibilidad de explorar selvas tropicales, subir a la cima de volcanes, disfrutar de hermosas playas y también visitar innumerables restos arqueológicos.

Otro lugar fascinante es Chichicastenango, un auténtico pueblo indígena, donde todos los jueves y domingos se realiza el mercado de artesanías más famoso de América Latina.

Expresiones guatemaltecas:

baboso/a	No seas **baboso/a.**	*Don't be silly (a fool).*
patojo	**Los patojos** están jugando.	*The children are playing.*
pisto	Tengo poco **pisto.**	*I have little money.*

Para contestar

En el mapa

1. Diga qué ciudades mexicanas están cerca de la frontera de los Estados Unidos.
2. ¿Qué países están cerca de Guatemala?
3. Mencione dos diferencias geográficas entre México y Guatemala.

Ahora diga...

1. qué ciudades le gustaría visitar en México y en Guatemala.
2. en qué celebraciones de México y Guatemala le gustaría participar y por qué.

¿Qué dice Ud. si...

1. su amigo mexicano hace algo tonto.
2. su novio/a mexicano/a es bajo/a y rubio/a.
3. usted quiere decirle a un/una amigo/a de Guatemala que usted no tiene mucho dinero.

Para investigar en Internet

Busque información sobre la celebración de una de las siguientes fiestas religiosas, y presente un informe al resto de la clase. Explique cómo se celebra, quiénes participan, qué usa la gente que participa, qué comidas especiales se preparan, y cualquier otro detalle que le parezca interesante. Si es posible, traiga fotografías.

■ La semana santa en Sevilla, España, y en Antigua, Guatemala

■ La procesión del Señor de los Milagros en el Perú

■ El día de la Virgen del Carmen y el día de Corpus Christi en México.

■ El día de San Agustín en Puebla, México

Para los amantes de la cultura maya, Tikal es el lugar indicado.

¡Prepárese!

8-50 Mentiras. Aunque Katie está ganando la competencia, tanto los otros participantes como el público, tienen una opinión negativa de ella, especialmente Carlos, porque Katie le mintió. En su opinión, ¿cuándo es aceptable mentir y cuando no es aceptable? Escriba una lista de ocasiones aceptables y no aceptables, y después compare su lista con las de sus compañeros/as.

MODELO: Es aceptable mentir para proteger a otra persona.

8-51 Una mentirita (piadosa). Un equivalente en español de la expresión inglesa *white lie* es "una mentirita (piadosa)". Cuando usted era niño/a, ¿decía mentiras o "mentiritas piadosas"? ¿Conocía a alguien que lo hacía? Escriba oraciones en español usando el imperfecto o el pretérito para contar su experiencia. Use las palabras que aparecen en las tres columnas.

MODELO: Yo decía mentiras frecuentemente cuando era joven.
Una vez yo le dije una mentirita (piadosa) a mi maestra.

Yo	decir	una mentira
Mi mejor amigo/a		una mentirita (piadosa)
Mis hermanos		
Mi mamá		

El concurso es popular pero el público detesta a Katie.

¿Es posible el amor entre Katie y Carlos?

Carlos ya no tiene confianza en Katie.

Katie cree que es posible separar la relación y la competencia.

Según Carlos, no hay nada entre él y Katie.

Sabrina no está ganando pero está contenta; no le gusta lo que hizo Katie.

¡Responda!

8-52 Comparaciones. Imagínese que Tito, el periodista de *Fortunas*, quiere entrevistarlo/la para saber lo que piensa de los personajes del video. Compare a las siguientes personas para reflejar su opinión sobre ellas.

MODELO: Katie es más inteligente que Sabrina.

1. Katie y Carlos
2. Carlos y Efraín
3. Katie y Sabrina
4. Sabrina y Efraín
5. Angela y Manolo
6. Tito y Manolo

Suggestion for 8-52. Have students share their opinions/comparisons and then ask them to provide superlatives based on questions provided by you, such as: *¿Quién es el/la más inteligente del grupo?*, etc.

Esta canción es un ejemplo de corrido, una balada folclórica que expresa aspectos de la vida mexicana, sea en forma lírica, épica o narrativa. Este corrido es sobre la vida de El Chapo, un personaje, de fama local, originario de Michoacán.

¡Prepárese!

8-53 Comparaciones. En este curso usted ha tenido la oportunidad de escuchar varias canciones hispanas con estilos, influencias, instrumentos y temas diferentes. Escriba comparaciones de igualdad y de desigualdad con las palabras de la actividad para indicar sus opiniones personales sobre la música presentada.

MODELO: el piano / la trompeta
El piano es más difícil de tocar que la trompeta.

1. la música flamenca / la salsa
2. la quena andina / la marimba africana
3. la letra de "Cuéntame alegrías" / la letra de "Tu ausencia"
4. el rock español / el rock americano
5. bailar cumbia / bailar punta

¡Escuche!

8-54 Geografía. Los nombres de muchos lugares de México tienen origen indígena. Se mencionan algunos de éstos en "El Chapo". Mientras escucha la canción, llene los espacios en blanco con los nombres de la lista (uno de ellos se usa dos veces).

Apatzingán	Jalisco	Michoacán	Antúnez

Nació y creció entre los montes
Nunca lo podrá olvidar
El es de mérito <u>Antúnez</u>
Muy cerca de <u>Apatzingán</u>
Por su apodo conocido
El Chapo de <u>Michoacán</u>
…

Desciende de gente brava
De los famosos Arriola
Su hermano, el manchado es gallo
Que sabe usar la pistola
…

El Chapo sí que merece
Que le cante su corrido
El Chapo nació en <u>Jalisco</u>
Pero se crió en <u>Michoacán</u>

8-55 Sus orígenes. Ahora, conteste las siguientes preguntas personales.

1. ¿Dónde nació usted?
2. ¿Dónde se crió (raised)?
3. ¿Tenía algún apodo (nickname) cuando era niño/a?

¡Responda!

8-56 En México. Lea el relato de un viaje a México y llene los espacios en blanco con la forma correcta del pretérito o del imperfecto, según el caso.

Cuando mi mejor amigo, José, y yo (1) _____<u>hicimos</u>_____ (hacer) un viaje a México y a Guatemala, lo (2) _____<u>pasamos</u>_____ (pasar) muy bien. El viaje no (3) _____<u>fue</u>_____ (ir) sólo para diversión; también (4) __<u>aprendí/aprendimos</u>__ (aprender) mucho sobre la cultura de estos dos países.

En México nosotros (5) ___<u>nos quedamos</u>___ (quedarse) en la capital por tres días. (6) _____<u>Visitamos</u>_____ (visitar) muchos museos e iglesias que (7) _____<u>eran</u>_____ (ser) muy interesantes. Un día yo (8) _____<u>vi</u>_____ (ver) unas ruinas, y José (9) _____<u>anduvo</u>_____ (andar) por la ciudad. ¡(10) _____<u>Fueron</u>_____ (ser) unos días magníficos!

VOCABULARIO*

AUDIO ## Las fiestas

la alegría	joy
la boda	wedding
el carnaval	carnival, Mardi Gras
la carreta	cart, wagon
la carroza	float
la celebración	celebration
la comparsa	costumed group
la corrida (de toros)	bullfight
la costumbre	custom
el desfile	parade
la entrada	ticket for admission
la invitación	invitation
el preparativo	preparation
la procesión	procession
la tradición	tradition

Las personas

el antepasado	ancestor
la gente	people
el rey/la reina	king/queen

En el mundo moderno

la droga	drug
el ruido	noise
la seguridad	safety, security
el sexo	sex
la violencia	violence

La música

la melodía	melody
la orquesta	orchestra

Lugares

el camino	road, way
el cementerio	cemetery
la iglesia	church
la plaza (de toros)	bullring
el pueblo	town
el teatro	theater

Tiempo

antes	before
el comienzo	beginning
entonces	then
hoy en día	nowadays
mientras	while

Descripciones

antiguo/a	former, old
difunto/a, muerto/a	dead
maravilloso/a	marvelous
peor	worse, worst
suave	soft
último/a	last

Verbos

acompañar	to accompany
comenzar (ie)	to begin
disfrazarse	to wear a costume
divertirse (ie, i)	to have a good time
encerrar (ie)	to lock up
invitar	to invite
mantener (g, ie)	maintain
mover (ue)	to move
recordar (ue)	to remember
respetar	to respect
reunirse	to get together

Palabras y expresiones útiles

había	there was, there were
más... que	more . . . than, . . . -er than (e.g., shorter than)
menos... que	less than, fewer than
¡Qué pena!	What a pity!
tan... como	as . . . as
tanto/a como	as much . . . as
tantos/as como	as many as
tener deseos de + infinitivo	to feel like, to want

*See page 284 for holidays.

9

EL TRABAJO

Objetivos comunicativos

- Talking about the workplace and professions
- Discussing job skills and abilities
- Giving formal orders and instructions
- Expressing intention
- Avoiding repetition

Contenido

Las profesiones

AUDIO Carmen González, una **chef** de Coral Gables, FL muestra algunas de sus **especialidades.**

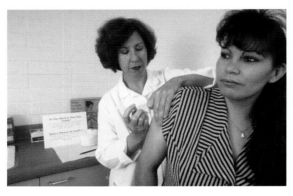

Una **médica** examina a un bebé en su **consultorio** en Santiago de Chile.

Dra. Alicia Gonica de Pérez

C A R D I Ó L O G A

Consultorio
La Concepción 81
Metro Pedro de Valdivia, Santiago
Teléfonos 264-2992 / 363-0690

Unos **bomberos apagan** un **incendio** en Ciudad de México.

Suggestions. Use visuals to introduce professions. Provide comprehensible input by asking questions about the photos. You may want to expand the activity by having students briefly describe the workers' job/task and the kind of preparation or education required. Point out some of the new professions for women. Personalize when possible: *¿Quién es la persona de la primera foto? ¿Dónde trabaja? Y Uds., ¿trabajan? ¿Dónde trabaja Ud.? ¿Sus padres trabajan? ¿Dónde? ¿Quién no trabaja?*

Follow-up. Working in pairs, have students ask each other about their jobs. (If students do not work, they may talk about an imaginary job.) Have them ask their partners what they do at work, if they are happy, what they like or do not like about their jobs.

Suggestions. Talk about the business cards and ask questions. Mention that in most industrialized countries employees get four to seven weeks of paid vacation: *En la mayoría de los países industrializados los empleados tienen de cuatro a siete semanas de vacaciones pagadas.* Ask students: *¿Piensan que en dos semanas de vacaciones hay tiempo para viajar, estar con la familia, descansar? ¿Cómo pueden los padres que tienen vacaciones cortas pasar más tiempo con sus familias y relajarse?*

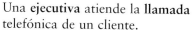
Una **ejecutiva** atiende la **llamada** telefónica de un cliente.

VÍNCULOS

To practice vocabulario—Las profesiones, Otras profesiones, oficios y ocupaciones & La entrevista profesional
- SAM-OneKey: WB: 9-1, 9-2, 9-3, 9-4 / LM: 9-26, 9-27, 9-28, 9-29
- Companion Website: AP 9-1 A, B
- IRCD: Chapter 9; pp. 320, 321, 322, 323, 327

Una **locutora** espera la **señal** para **comenzar** un programa de noticias en una estación de radio.

CULTURA

Uno de los hechos sociales más importantes de los países hispanos en los últimos años es el ingreso masivo de las mujeres al mercado laboral. Sin embargo, aún existen desigualdades evidentes. Por ejemplo, el desempleo entre las mujeres es mayor, y su representación en las empresas de alta productividad es mucho menor. Además, estudios recientes demuestran que, en general, los salarios de las mujeres son más bajos que los que reciben los hombres por el mismo tipo de trabajo.

Aunque se perciben algunos cambios, el trabajo doméstico no remunerado se continúa considerando una obligación que permanece asociada a las mujeres y niñas. No obstante, en muchos países hispanos ya se ofrecen programas educativos para combatir la discriminación.

Un **técnico** revisa los controles de una **compañía** petrolera.

Una **peluquera** le **corta** el pelo y peina a una de sus clientas.

Eduardo Salas González
Ingeniero de Fabricación

Orrego Luco 161
Providencia
Santiago, Chile

Tel. (56-2) 3346622
Fax (56-2) 3344919

Otras profesiones, oficios y ocupaciones

la juez

el abogado

el actor

el ama de casa

el policía

la bibliotecaria

la cajera

el chofer

el contador

la científica

la electricista

la enfermera

la mujer de negocios

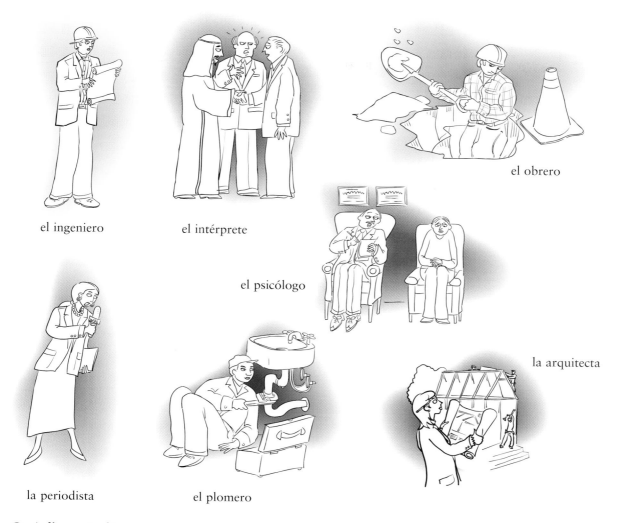

el ingeniero

el intérprete

el obrero

el psicólogo

la arquitecta

la periodista

el plomero

¿Qué dice usted?

2 **9-1 ¿Qué profesión debe tener?** Lean las siguientes descripciones y digan qué profesión u oficio de la lista deben tener las personas con estas características. ¡Ojo! A veces, más de una respuesta es posible.

científico/a	ingeniero/a	artista
sicólogo/a	mecánico/a	médico/a
abogado/a	actor/actriz	plomero/a

1. A Pablo le gusta observar y analizar el comportamiento (*behavior*) de las personas. sicólogo
2. Los hermanos Pedraza siempre resuelven los problemas del auto de su padre. Lo examinan y lo reparan a la perfección. mecánicos
3. Eva y Ana son lógicas y tienen facilidad para encontrar las causas de un problema y resolverlo. También pueden explicar la solución sin dificultad. abogadas/científicas
4. Al pequeño Jaimito le fascina desarmar (*disassemble*) aparatos electrónicos para estudiar cómo funcionan. ingeniero
5. Daniela es una chica muy sensible y una gran observadora. Le fascina expresar sus sentimientos y experiencias de manera artística. actriz/artista
6. Adela siempre lee libros sobre anatomía. Ella puede nombrar cada parte del cuerpo (*body*) humano. médico/a

Follow-up for 9-2. 7. *un/a ejecutivo/a*
8. *un/a mecánico/a*   9. *un/a cocinero/a*
10. *un/a abogado/a.*

❷ 9-2 Las profesiones y las características personales. Primera fase. Digan cómo deben ser estos/as profesionales.

MODELO: un piloto
           inteligente / serio / perezoso(a) /...
           Debe ser inteligente, serio y responsable. No debe ser perezoso.

1. un/a psiquiatra
   valiente / romántico(a) / irónico(a) / antipático(a) / inteligente /...
2. un actor/una actriz
   guapo(a) / atractivo(a) / simpático(a) / delgado(a) / alto(a)/...
3. un hombre/una mujer de negocios
   autoritario(a) / serio(a) / perezoso(a) / viejo(a) / responsable /...
4. un/a recepcionista...
5. un/a astronauta...
6. un ama de casa...

Segunda fase. Intercambien ideas sobre lo siguiente.

1. ¿Conoce a algún/a... (*profesión*)? ¿Cómo se llama? ¿Dónde trabaja?
2. ¿Qué características personales o especiales, en su opinión, lo/la ayudan en su profesión?

Suggestion. Recycle previously taught occupations and compare them with jobs here: *¿Un peluquero gana tanto dinero como un dentista? ¿Es mejor ser ingeniero o actor? ¿Un profesor trabaja más o menos que un médico?*

❷ 9-3 Asociaciones. Asocien una o más profesiones con los siguientes lugares de trabajo, y digan lo que hacen estas personas.

Note. Answers may vary but likely answers are included in column 2. Column 3 answers will, of course, depend on the students' answers for column 2.

LUGAR	PROFESIÓN	¿QUÉ HACE?
el hospital	enfermero/a	
el restaurante	chef	
la clase	profesor/a	
la estación de radio	locutor/a	
la tienda de ropa	dependiente/a (vendedor/a)	
el consultorio médico	doctor/a (médico/a)	
la peluquería	peluquero/a	
el banco	cajero/a	

Suggestions for 9-4. Rotate roles so that each one of the three students has the opportunity of identifying the profession and stating the advantages/disadvantages. Students may have some difficulty in expressing advantages/ disadvantages. In small groups, have students brainstorm at least three advantages and three disadvantages of specific jobs. Model the activity first: *¿Cuáles son las ventajas y desventajas de los siguientes trabajos: médico, enfermero, profesor, piloto?* Introduce the words *estrés* and *peligro* to talk about disadvantages. If desired, you may do only the identification part of the activity.

Ⓖ 9-4 ¿Cuál es la profesión? Primero identifiquen la ocupación o profesión, según la descripción. Luego, digan dos ventajas y dos desventajas de esta ocupación o profesión.

MODELO: Trabaja en la casa, limpia y lava los platos.
           E1: Es un ama de casa.
           E2: Una ventaja de ser ama de casa es que la mujer puede estar con los niños. Otra ventaja es que tiene un horario más flexible.
           E3: Una desventaja es que no gana dinero. Otra desventaja es que todos los días el ama de casa trabaja mucho.

1. Escribe artículos para el periódico. *periodista*
2. Presenta programas de televisión y a veces habla con el público. *locutor/a*
3. Traduce simultáneamente del inglés al español. *intérprete*
4. Mantiene el orden público. *policía*
5. Apaga incendios. *bombero*
6. Defiende o acusa a personas delante de un/a juez/a. *abogado/a*

Suggestion for 9-5. Have students report their partners' plans to the class. Ask questions to get students' opinions: *¿En qué trabajos... hay más estrés? ... se gana más dinero? ... dan más vacaciones?*

2 **9-5 Mi ocupación ideal para el futuro. Primera fase.** Piensen en su ocupación/ profesión ideal. Luego, sin mencionarla, pregúntele a su compañero/a lo que hacen las personas en esa profesión para averiguar cuál es.

Segunda fase. Haga una lista de tres requisitos de su trabajo ideal y compruebe si usted los tiene. Intercambie esta información con su compañero/a.

MODELO: Me gustaría ser actor/actriz. Un/a actor/actriz debe leer mucho; debe saber representar emociones y sentimientos y debe ser flexible para trabajar muchas horas. A mí me gusta leer y soy flexible, pero no puedo representar muy bien las emociones.

La entrevista

La entrevista de trabajo

SRA. ARCE: Buenos días, Sr. Solano. Soy Marcela Arce, presidenta de la compañía.

SR. SOLANO: Mucho gusto, señora.

SRA. ARCE: Siéntese, por favor. Usted **solicitó** el **puesto** de **gerente de ventas**, ¿verdad?

SR. SOLANO: Sí, señora. Leí en *El Mercurio* que había una **vacante.** Después pedí y llené una **solicitud.**

SRA. ARCE: Sí, aquí la tengo, y también su **currículum. Por cierto,** es excelente.

SR. SOLANO: Muchas gracias.

SRA. ARCE: **Actualmente** usted trabaja en la empresa Badosa. ¿Por qué quiere **dejar** su **puesto?**

SR. SOLANO: Bueno, **en realidad** yo estoy muy contento allí, pero a mí me gustaría trabajar en una compañía internacional y poder usar otras lenguas. Como usted ve en mi currículum, yo hablo español, inglés y francés.

SRA. ARCE: En su solicitud, usted **indica** que desea un **sueldo** de dos millones de pesos al mes. **Sin embargo,** en el puesto que tenemos, el sueldo que se **ofrece** es de un millón ochocientos mil pesos.

SR. SOLANO: Sí, lo sé, pero la diferencia no es tan importante. **Lo importante** es que aquí puedo tener la **oportunidad** de **comunicarme** con los **clientes** en su **propia** lengua. Yo creo que esto puede mejorar las ventas de Computel notablemente.

SRA. ARCE: Pues si le parece bien el sueldo, ¿por qué no pasamos a la oficina del director general para seguir hablando?

SR. SOLANO: **¡Cómo no!**

Suggestion for La entrevista. Have students role play this dialog, making the following changes: the job being offered, languages spoken, and salary (using currencies of other countries). *Pesos* are used in Chile. If possible, check the current exchange rate. This salary translates to approximately $3,000 dollars monthly.

Note: *El Mercurio* is one of the oldest Chilean newspapers. It was founded in Valparaíso in 1827, and in Santiago in 1900. You may wish to refer students to culture section for information about important cities in Chile.

LENGUA

In Spanish, **actualmente** can refer only to the present time. **Actualmente** yo trabajo en Valparaíso. (*At the present I work in Valparaíso.*) Therefore, **actualmente** is a false cognate of *actually.* The equivalents of *actually* in Spanish are **realmente** or **en realidad.** **Realmente/En realidad** yo sólo trabajé en Arica un mes. (*Actually I only worked in Arica for a month.*)

¿Qué dice usted?

② 9-6 Buscando información. Busquen la siguiente información en el diálogo anterior.

1. nombre de la presidenta de la compañía Marcela Arce
2. puesto que solicita el Sr. Solano gerente de ventas
3. nombre de la compañía donde trabaja el Sr. Solano Badosa
4. nombre de la compañía donde desea trabajar Computel
5. lenguas que habla español, inglés, francés
6. sueldo que desea el Sr. Solano dos millones de pesos
7. sueldo que se ofrece en el nuevo puesto 1.800.000 pesos
8. motivo para cambiar de puesto trabajar en una compañía internacional y usar otras lenguas

Follow-up for 9-7. Working in small groups, have students go through this process, step by step, actually seeking a job, either imaginary or taken from classified ads.

9-7 Buscando trabajo. Imagínese que usted está buscando trabajo. Diga en qué orden haría (*would do*) estas cosas.

    4   Me llaman de la Compañía Rosell para una entrevista.

    7   Les contesto que no, que se cerró el almacén.

    1   Leo los anuncios del periódico.

    3   Envío la solicitud al apartado postal de la Compañía Rosell.

    5   Voy a la compañía para la entrevista.

    6   Me preguntan si me despidieron (*fired*) del trabajo anterior.

    2   Preparo mi currículum y lleno la solicitud para la Compañía Rosell.

    8   Me ofrecen el puesto de vendedor/a.

Follow-up for 9-8. You may wish to ask pairs to share some of their recommendations with the class. The class as a whole may choose the best ones.

② 9-8 ¿Comportamiento apropiado o inapropiado? Preparen una lista de cuatro cosas que **se deben** o **no se deben hacer** antes de una entrevista y cuatro que se deben o no se deben hacer durante una entrevista. Después comparen su lista con la de otros/as compañeros/as.

(NO) SE DEBE HACER ANTES DE LA ENTREVISTA	(NO) SE DEBE HACER DURANTE LA ENTREVISTA

Warm-up for 9-9. Model the activity with one of your better students, using the transparency of an ad, if possible. Encourage students to answer giving as much information as possible.

Follow-up for 9-9. 7. *fecha en que puede empezar a trabajar* 8. *sueldo que desea ganar* 9. *habilidades especiales*

② 9-9 Entrevista para un trabajo. Ustedes están buscando trabajo y leen los siguientes anuncios en el periódico *La Tercera*. Cada uno/a debe escoger uno de los anuncios. Luego, como práctica para la entrevista, su compañero/a va a hacer el papel de jefe/a de personal de la empresa para obtener la siguiente información. Luego cambien de papel.

1. nombre de la persona que solicita el puesto
2. estudios que tiene
3. lenguas que habla
4. lugar donde trabaja y responsabilidades
5. experiencia anterior
6. razones para querer trabajar en esta compañía

INSTITUTO DE CIRUGÍA PLÁSTICA: CLÍNICA CÁRDENAS
Necesita Enfermera

Prótesis:
implantes faciales (Gorotex, silicona)
liposucción papada,
abdomen,
muslos

Informes:
Clinicasa, Apoquindo 4.100
Tel: 2062223/ 2129212

Llamar a secretaria: Marta

Hotel Galería Imperio
Necesita

RECEPCIONISTA
• Buena presencia
• Bilingüe español-inglés

CAMARERA
• Mín. 2 años experiencia
• Disponible trabajar por las mañanas y tardes

DIRIGIRSE AL HOTEL IMPERIO
Jefe de Personal
Alameda 237   Tel.: 2376419

EMPRESA EXPORTADORA DE FRUTAS
requiere

CONTADOR

Requisitos:
• Experiencia mínima de 5 años
• Graduado del Colegio de Contadores Públicos
• Para cita llamar a Curicó al 71-367801

EMPRESA MINERA
requiere
3 Ingenieros de Sistemas

REQUISITOS:
1. Mayor de 25 años
2. Experiencia en minas de cobre
3. Flexibilidad horaria
(incluidos fines de semana)

OFRECEMOS:
1. Ingreso superior a 2.000.000
2. Capacitación profesional
3. Bonos de participación

Interesados enviar currículum a:
Minería El Teniente

**Oficina de Personal
Agustinas 1892, Santiago**

9-10 Mi profesión. You will listen to Julieta Odriozola talking about her profession. Before you listen, write down the names of four professions that you associate with women.

_____

_____

Now, pay attention to the general idea of what is said. Then, as you listen mark the appropriate ending to each statement.

1. Julieta Odriozola es...
   _____ artista
   _____ política
   __X__ periodista

2. Julia tiene un horario...
   _____ de 9 a 5
   __X__ variable
   _____ de lunes a sábado

3. Julieta hace casi todo su trabajo en...
   _____ su auto
   _____ su casa
   __X__ diferentes lugares

4. Julieta trabaja básicamente con...
   _____ artistas jóvenes
   __X__ personas importantes
   _____ empleados de la comunidad

1. *Se* + verb constructions

■ Spanish uses the **se** + *verb* construction to emphasize the occurrence of an action rather than the person(s) responsible for that action. The noun (what is needed, sold, offered, etc.) usually follows the verb. The person(s) who sell(s), offer(s), etc. is not mentioned. This is normally done in English with the passive voice (is/are + *past participle*).

> **Se habla** español aquí.   *Spanish is spoken here.*

■ Use a singular verb with singular nouns and a plural verb with plural nouns.

> **Se necesita** un auto para ese trabajo.   *A car is needed for that job.*
> **Se venden** flores allí.   *Flowers are sold there.*

■ When the **se** + *verb* construction is followed not by a noun, but rather by an adverb, an infinitive, or a clause, use a singular verb. This is done in English with indefinite subjects such as *they, you, one, people*.

> **Se trabaja** mucho en esa oficina.   *They work a lot in that office.*
> **Se podía** hablar con el jefe a cualquier hora.   *You could talk to the boss any time.*
> **Se dice** que recibió un aumento.   *People say he/she/you got a raise.*

¿Qué dice usted?

9-11 Asociaciones. Primera fase. Asocie las actividades con los lugares donde ocurren.

1. __f__ Se cambian cheques en...   a. un almacén
2. __a__ Se vende ropa en...   b. un restaurante
3. __d__ Se toma el sol y se nada en...   c. un periódico
4. __b__ Se sirven comidas en...   d. una playa
5. __c__ Se dan noticias en...   e. un teatro
6. __e__ Se presentan comedias en...   f. un banco

2 **Segunda fase.** Piense en un edificio o lugar público que le gusta mucho. Luego dígale a su compañero/a qué se hace en ese lugar.

MODELO: Me gusta mucho la playa Reñaca, en Viña del Mar. Allí se camina por la playa, se participa en concursos durante el verano y se habla con chicos interesantes.

2 9-12 Organizando la oficina. Una compañía de limpieza sacó los muebles y otras cosas de su oficina para limpiar la alfombra. Para poner todo en su lugar, conteste las preguntas que le hacen los encargados de limpieza, de acuerdo con el dibujo.

MODELO: el sofá
        E1: ¿Dónde se pone el sofá?
        E2: Se pone entre las dos mesas pequeñas.

1. la mesa más larga
2. las revistas
3. la lámpara
4. las dos sillas
5. la computadora
6. la butaca grande
7. las plantas
8. el cesto

2 9-13 La oficina de antes y la de ahora. Primera fase. Decida qué cosas y/o servicios se necesitaban en una oficina hace treinta años y qué se necesita ahora. Compare sus respuestas con las de su compañero/a.

EQUIPO DE OFICINA	ANTES	AHORA
escritorio		
fotocopiadora		
computadora		
correo electrónico		
máquina de escribir		
teléfono		
calculadora		
fax		
escáner		

2 Segunda fase. Conversen sobre la oficina más moderna que cada uno/a de ustedes conoce. Expliquen cómo es.

2 9-14 Anuncios locos. Lean estos anuncios "locos". Luego, intercambien opiniones sobre cuáles les parecen más simpáticos. Finalmente, preparen juntos un anuncio "loco" para compartir con la clase.

1. Se necesitan ingenieros para diseñar y construir un puente desde Chile hasta China. Los interesados deben enviar su currículum en portugués.
2. Se necesita urgentemente un robot bilingüe para hacer todas las tareas de español.
3. Se busca un/a secretario/a para un ejecutivo muy desorganizado. Debe saber hablar y escribir en 40 lenguas.
4. Se compran monstruos para aterrorizar a los clientes de la compañía que nos hace la competencia. Se aceptan Dráculas o Frankensteins.
5. ¿?

Suggestion. A class or two before doing the situation, have students prepare in advance two ads in one of the following marketing areas: *ropa, maquillaje, computadoras.* When the situation day comes, have them use their ads.

Suggestions. Contrast the use of preterit and imperfect by giving examples: *El año pasado ustedes no estaban en mi clase de español. Yo no los conocía. Yo los conocí en septiembre cuando vinieron a mi clase. Yo no sabía entonces si eran buenos estudiantes, pero después de tener una o dos clases con ustedes supe que eran buenos.*

SITUACIONES

1. **Role A.** You are an advertising manager (*gerente de publicidad*) who is presenting a new campaign (*campaña*) to the president of a company. After showing the president two ads, a) ask him/her if he/she likes them, b) mention the magazines where the ads will appear, and c) explain the reasons why you chose those magazines. Then answer his/her questions.

   Role B. You are the president of an important company who has to decide about a new advertising campaign. After telling the ad manager that you like the ads and listening to his/her explanations, inquire a) about the cost of the campaign, and b) when it will begin.

2. One of you is conducting interviews for your company; the other is a prospective employee. The interviewer asks the candidate a) where he/she read the ad for the job, b) where he/she worked before, c) what he/she used to do there, d) where he/she is working now, and e) why he/she wants to change jobs and work for your company.

2. More on the preterit and the imperfect

- In *Lección 7* you practiced the preterit of **saber** with the meaning of finding out about something. You also practiced the preterit of **querer** with the meaning of wanting or trying to do something, but failing to accomplish it.

Supe que llegaron anoche.	*I found out that they arrived last night.*
Quise ir al aeropuerto, pero fue imposible.	*I wanted (and tried) to go to the airport, but it was impossible.*

  In the negative, the preterit of **querer** conveys the meaning of refusing to do something.

No quise ir.	*I refused to go.*

- Other verbs that convey a different meaning in English when the Spanish preterit is used follow:

IMPERFECT		PRETERIT	
Yo **conocía** a Ana.	*I knew Ana.*	**Conocí** a Ana.	*I met Ana.*
Podía hacerlo.	*I could do it. (was able)*	**Pude** hacerlo.	*I accomplished it. (managed to)*
No podía hacerlo.	*I couldn't do it. (wasn't able)*	**No pude** hacerlo.	*I couldn't do it. (tried and failed)*

- To express intentions in the past, use the imperfect of **ir + a +** *infinitive*.

Iba a salir, pero era muy tarde.	*I was going to go out, but it was very late.*

■ You have used the imperfect to express an action or event that was in progress in the past. You may also use the imperfect progressive when you want to emphasize the ongoing nature of the activity. Form the imperfect progressive with the imperfect of **estar** and the present participle (-**ndo**).

Pepe **estaba hablando** con el cajero cuando llegó el policía.

Pepe was talking to the cashier when the policeman arrived.

¿Qué dice usted?

2 **9-15 ¿Tiene usted buena memoria?** Anoche, el director del Hospital Providencia hizo una visita sorpresiva a la sala de emergencia. Desafortunadamente, cuando entró encontró muchas irregularidades, y se puso furioso. Marque las actividades que provocaron esta reacción del director del hospital.

1. _____ Las enfermeras estaban haciendo vida social entre ellas.
2. _____ Algunos médicos estaban mirando béisbol por televisión.
3. _____ Todos los asistentes de la sala de emergencia estaban trabajando.
4. _____ Una de las recepcionistas estaba hablando por teléfono con una paciente.
5. _____ Una empleada estaba hablando por teléfono con su esposo.
6. _____ Dos choferes estaban fumando en la recepción.
7. _____ Un chofer estaba saliendo del hospital para recoger a un paciente.
8. _____ El guardia estaba leyendo el periódico.

Possible answers for 9-15. Students may mark 1, 2, 5, 6, 8.

Suggestion for 9-15. Give some misinformation for students to disagree with:... *estaba cantando y bailando cuando yo entré. X y Y estaban haciendo la tarea. M estaba conversando con N.*

2 **9-16 Una oficina muy ocupada.** Ustedes visitaron la oficina que aparece en el dibujo. Túrnense para preguntar qué estaban haciendo las personas cuando cada uno/a de ustedes llegó.

MODELO: E1: ¿Qué estaba haciendo Alicia cuando tú llegaste a la oficina?
E2: Estaba conversando con un cliente.

Expansion for 9-17. *5. Un hombre miraba por un microscopio en un laboratorio donde había computadoras y diferentes productos químicos. (científico) 6. Una señora estaba enfrente de un micrófono en un estudio. Tenía unos papeles sobre un escritorio y observaba con mucha atención una señal para empezar a hablar. (locutora)*

② 9-17 A usar la imaginación. Estas descripciones indican lo que estaban haciendo varias personas ayer. Identifiquen cuál era el oficio o profesión de estas personas y qué iban a hacer después.

MODELO:　Un señor miraba los planos de un edificio y decía que ciertas cosas no estaban bien.
　　　　　E1:　Era el arquitecto del edificio.
　　　　　E2:　Iba a hacer unos cambios en los planos.

1. Un señor tenía un secador en la mano y le tocaba el pelo a una señora que estaba sentada enfrente de él. peluquero
2. Unos señores iban en un camión (*truck*) rojo con una sirena. El camión iba muy rápido y los autos y autobuses paraban al lado derecho de la calle. bomberos
3. Una joven que llevaba un vestido similar a los que se llevaban en la época de Cleopatra hablaba frente a una cámara. Estaba muy maquillada y tenía una línea negra alrededor de los ojos. actriz
4. Esta persona llevaba un traje espacial, guantes, botas muy grandes y un plástico transparente frente a los ojos para poder ver. astronauta

Suggestion for 9-18. *Encourage students to provide as many explanations as possible. Then, have pairs share their answers with the class.*

② 9-18 Una explicación lógica. Ayer ustedes tuvieron una reunión muy importante en su compañía para mostrarles unos productos nuevos a unas empresas extranjeras. Pero varias cosas salieron mal. Busquen una explicación lógica para lo que sucedió.

MODELO:　La secretaria no contestaba el teléfono.
　　　　　E1:　Estaba buscando un intérprete para la reunión.
　　　　　E2:　No, estaba buscando un salón más grande.

1. Varios empleados llegaron tarde.
2. El técnico no pudo arreglar una computadora que se necesitaba para la presentación.
3. Los periodistas no podían comprender lo que decía un director extranjero.
4. No les sirvieron café ni refrescos a los invitados.
5. Uno de los vendedores no quiso mostrar los productos nuevos.
6. No se pusieron anuncios en los periódicos.

SITUACIONES

Role A. One of your employees did not come to an important meeting at the office, so you call him/her to your office. Greet him/her and ask him/her why he was not at the meeting. After listening to his/her explanation, tell him/her a) that this is the second time this happens, and b) that you will not accept any more excuses in the future.

Role B. You are an employee who was supposed to attend an important meeting at the office, but could not make it. After greeting your boss, apologize and explain a) that your spouse got sick (*enfermarse*) and you had to take him/her to the hospital, and b) that you wanted to take a taxi to go to work, but all the taxis were occupied. Then, say that this will not happen again (*otra vez*).

3. Direct and indirect object pronouns

■ When direct and indirect object pronouns are used in the same sentence, the indirect object pronoun precedes the direct object pronoun. Place double object pronouns before conjugated verbs.

Ella me dio la solicitud.	*She gave me the application.*
Ella **me la** dio.	*She gave it to me.*

■ In compound verb constructions, you may place double object pronouns before the conjugated verb or attach them to the accompanying infinitive or present participle.

Él quiere darme el contrato.	*He wants to give me the contract.*
Él quiere dár**melo**.	*He wants to give it to me.*
Él **me lo** quiere dar.	
Te está diciendo la verdad.	*She is telling you the truth.*
Te la está diciendo.	*She is telling it to you.*
Está diciéndo**tela**.	

■ **Le** and **les** cannot be used with **lo**, **los**, **la**, or **las**. Change **le** or **les** to **se**.

Le dio el puesto a Berta.	*He gave the job to Berta.*
Se lo dio.	*He gave it to her.*
Les va a mostrar el anuncio.	*She is going to show them the ad.*
Se lo va a mostrar.	*She is going to show it to them.*

■ When a direct object pronoun and a reflexive pronoun are used together, the reflexive pronoun precedes the direct object pronoun.

Siempre me envío correos electrónicos para recordar lo que debo hacer.	*I always send myself e-mails to remember what I have to do.*
Siempre **me los** envío.	*I always send them to myself.*

¿Qué dice usted?

❷ 9-19 ¿Qué hace usted? La imparcialidad, la amabilidad y la confidencialidad son fundamentales en el trabajo. Lea las siguientes situaciones y seleccione lo que usted haría (*would do*) en cada una. Puede ser posible más de una respuesta correcta.

1. Un cliente le pide a usted el número de teléfono de la oficina del presidente de la compañía.
   a. __X__ Usted se lo da.   b. _____ Usted no se lo da.

2. Alguien le pide a usted que le permita leer un documento confidencial.
   a. _____ Usted se lo muestra.   b. __X__ Usted no se lo muestra.

3. La nueva jefa de personal le pide que le presente a todos los empleados de su oficina.
   a. __X__ Usted se los presenta.   b. _____ Usted no se los presenta.

4. Una empleada nueva le dice a usted que quiere vacaciones después de trabajar sólo tres meses.
   a. _____ Usted se las da.   b. __X__ Usted se las niega (*refuse*).

5. Un cliente bueno y uno malo le piden a usted una cita con el presidente de la compañía a la misma hora.
   a. __X__ Usted se la concede al buen cliente.
   b. __X__ Usted le pregunta al cliente malo si puede venir a otra hora.

VÍNCULOS

To practice direct and indirect object pronouns
- SAM-OneKey: WB: 9-12, 9-13, 9-14 / LM: 9-36, 9-37, 9-38
- Companion Website: AP 9-4
- *Gramática viva:* Grammar Point 10: Double-Object Pronouns; Object reflexive pronouns with command forms

Warm-up. Before introducing double object pronouns, review the direct and indirect objects as single objects. Students should recognize double object pronouns; some students can produce them correctly in controlled situations. However, it is very difficult for students to use them when speaking freely. Assure students, especially those who have more difficulty, that there will be ample opportunities to practice object pronouns throughout the course.

Note. *A* + noun or pronoun may be used to clarify the meaning of **se**: *Se lo da a ella. Se lo da a Ana.*

ACENTOS

You have learned that when the stress falls on the third syllable from the end, a written accent is required; therefore, you need to add one on the verb when double object pronouns are attached to an infinitive.

¿Va a darme la solicitud?
→ ¿Va a dármela?

When double object pronouns are attached to a present participle, the stress falls on the fourth syllable from the end, and a written accent is also required:

Se la está dando. →
Está dán do se la.
   4   3 2 1

2 **9-20 En ausencia del jefe.** En su función de gerente de la compañía, usted tuvo que viajar. Pero antes de salir, usted responsabilizó al jefe de publicidad de tratar con un empleado nuevo en la compañía. De regreso, usted conversa con el/la empleado/a nuevo/a para saber qué hizo el jefe de publicidad.

MODELO: darle el contrato (a usted)
E1: ¿Le dio el contrato?
E2: Sí, me lo dio.

1. explicar la campaña de publicidad
2. mostrar los anuncios
3. traer las revistas
4. pedir el cheque
5. dejar las fotos
6. describir a los/las modelos que se necesitan

3 **9-21 ¡El cliente siempre tiene la razón! Primera fase.** Dos de ustedes son clientes que cenaron en el restaurante de un hotel muy elegante y el tercero es el encargado del servicio del hotel. Este último les va a hacer preguntas y tomar notas para saber la opinión de ustedes sobre el servicio que recibieron.

1. ¿Cuándo les sirvieron el agua?
2. ¿Les mostraron la carta (*list*) de vinos enseguida?
3. ¿Les trajeron pan caliente a la mesa?
4. ¿Les dijo el camarero cuáles eran los platos especiales del día?
5. ¿Se los describió?
6. Después de que ustedes empezaron a comer, ¿les preguntó el camarero si la comida estaba bien?
7. ¿Les ofreció el camarero postres y café?
8. ¿Cómo fue el servicio en general?

Segunda fase. Los encargados del servicio del restaurante deben comparar sus notas para decidir qué áreas necesitan mejorar. Los clientes deben reunirse para comentar sus experiencias y compartir sus opiniones sobre el servicio del restaurante.

SITUACIONES

1. **Role A.** You are a reporter for *La Tercera,* a Santiago newspaper, and you have traveled to Valparaíso to cover a story. Since you left Santiago in a rush, you forgot your taperecorder and camera (*cámara*) in the taxi. Call a fellow reporter and a) tell him/her what happened, b) ask if he/she can lend you his/her car, taperecorder and camera, and c) explain that you need everything right away.

   Role B. You are a reporter for "Canal 5 de Playa Ancha" in Valparaíso. A colleague calls you to tell you about his/her ordeal. Ask him/her a) where it happened, and b) if he/she called the taxi company. Then say that he/she can come to your house to pick up what he/she needs.

2. One of you is an employee who has just returned from delivering a letter, the other is the boss. The boss will ask the employee questions to find out a) if he/she delivered the letter, b) to whom he/she gave the letter, c) when, and d) if the person signed a receipt (*recibo*).

4. Formal commands

Por favor, llene la solicitud y mándela por correo.

Suggestions. Remind students that they are already familiar with commands: some were introduced in *Bienvenidos* and have been used in activity directions, beginning in *Lección 4.* Review some: *escuche, levante la mano, abra el libro, lea la lección, levántese.*

Ask questions about the drawing.

VÍNCULOS
To practice formal commands
- SAM-OneKey: WB: 9-15, 9-16, 9-17, 9-18 / LM: 9-39, 9-40, 9-41, 9-42, 9-43
- Companion Website: AP 9-5
- *Gramática viva:* Grammar Point 12: Formal commands; formal commands vs. present indicative
- IRCD: Chapter 9; pg. 335

■ Commands (**los mandatos**) are the verb forms used to tell others to do something. Use formal commands with people you address as **usted** or **ustedes**. To form these commands, drop the final -o of the **yo** form of the present tense and add **-e(n)** for **-ar** verbs and **-a(n)** for **-er** and **-ir** verbs.

			USTED	USTEDES	
hablar	→	habl**o**	hable	hablen	*speak*
comer	→	com**o**	coma	coman	*eat*
escribir	→	escrib**o**	escriba	escriban	*write*

■ Verbs that are irregular in the **yo** form of the present tense maintain the same irregularity in the command form.

Suggestion. Point out the difference in stress between *hable* and *hablé.*

			USTED	USTEDES	
pensar	→	piens**o**	piense	piensen	*think*
dormir	→	duerm**o**	duerma	duerman	*sleep*
repetir	→	repit**o**	repita	repitan	*repeat*
poner	→	pong**o**	ponga	pongan	*put*

■ The use of *usted* and *ustedes* with command forms is optional. When used, they normally follow the command.

    Pase/Pase **usted.**   *Come in.*

■ To make a formal command negative, place **no** before the affirmative command.

    No salga ahora.   *Do not leave now.*

Suggestion. Remind students that they saw some of these orthographic changes while practicing the preterit in *Lección 6*.

■ Object and reflexive pronouns are attached to the end of affirmative commands (note the written accent over the stressed vowel). Object and reflexive pronouns precede negative commands and are not attached.

Cómpre**la**.	*Buy it.*
No **la** compre.	*Do not buy it.*
Háble**nle**.	*Talk to him/her.*
No **le** hablen.	*Do not talk to him/her.*
Siénte**se**.	*Sit down.*
No **se** siente.	*Do not sit down.*

■ The verbs **ir, ser,** and **saber** have irregular command forms.

ir: **vaya, vayan**   ser: **sea, sean**   saber: **sepa, sepan**

■ Verbs ending in **-car, -gar, -zar, -ger,** and **-guir** have spelling changes in command forms.

sacar	sac**o**	→	sa**que**, sa**quen**
jugar	jue**g**o	→	jue**gue**, jue**guen**
almorzar	almuer**z**o	→	almuer**ce**, almuer**cen**
recoger	reco**j**o	→	reco**ja**, reco**jan**
seguir	si**g**o	→	si**ga**, si**gan**

¿Qué dice usted?

❷ **9-22 ¿Dónde se dicen estas cosas?** Identifiquen el lugar donde se pueden escuchar o leer estas órdenes: en la sala de emergencia de un hospital (**E**), en un almacén (**A**), o en un estudio de televisión (**T**).

1. ___A___ Mande su solicitud para recibir la tarjeta de crédito por correo.
2. ___E___ No interrumpa a los médicos cuando hablan con los pacientes.
3. ___A___ Compren sus regalos de cumpleaños aquí.
4. ___A___ Pague en la caja.
5. ___E___ No haga visitas después de las nueve de la noche.
6. ___T___ Mueva el micrófono a la derecha.
7. ___E___ No traiga medicinas.
8. ___T___ Si hay luz roja, guarde silencio.

Note for 9-23. This is a good opportunity to show the location of the *Atacama* desert, *Viña del Mar, Valparaíso,* and *Santiago,* the capital. You may also mention that due to the topography of Chile—a narrow, long strip of land between the Andes and the Pacific Ocean—skiing, mountain climbing, and water sports such as sailing, surfing, fishing, and diving are popular sports among Chileans.

❷ **9-23 Preguntas de un/a estudiante.** Usted estuvo ausente en clase durante la semana dedicada a Chile y quiere saber qué tiene que hacer para ponerse al día. Su compañero/a, en el papel de profesor/a, contesta afirmativamente a sus preguntas. Después, cambien de papel.

MODELO: estudiar la Lección 9
                E1: ¿Estudio la Lección 9?
                E2: Sí, estúdiela.

1. contestar las preguntas sobre el desierto de Atacama
2. escuchar los discos del pianista chileno Claudio Arrau
3. escribir algunas expresiones chilenas
4. leer el Enfoque cultural sobre Chile
5. hacer la tarea sobre las culturas indígenas de Chile

9-24 En el hospital. Un/a enfermero/a entra en la habitación y le hace las siguientes preguntas al/a la paciente. Túrnense para hacer los papeles de enfermero/a y paciente.

MODELO: E1: ¿Le abro las cortinas?
E2: Sí, ábramelas, por favor. Quisiera leer.
No, no me las abra. Voy a dormir.

1. ¿Le pongo la televisión?
2. ¿Le traigo un jugo?
3. ¿Le pongo otra almohada?
4. ¿Me llevo estas flores?
5. ¿Le traigo el teléfono?
6. ...

Note for 9-24. To practice the use of pronouns with negative commands, you may tell students that the patient is a very negative person who will answer negatively all the nurse's questions.

9-25 Mandatos del entrenador de un equipo. Preparen una lista de sugerencias que el/la entrenador/a puede darles a los miembros de su equipo para lograr los objetivos siguientes. Comparen su lista con la de otros estudiantes.

MODELO: para mantenerse en buen estado físico
Practiquen todos los días. No se acuesten tarde.

1. para tener mejor rendimiento (*performance*)
2. para prepararse mentalmente para un partido difícil
3. para evitar problemas con el árbitro

9-26 ¿Qué deben hacer estas personas? Busquen una solución a los siguientes problemas y díganle a cada persona lo que debe hacer.

MODELO: El Sr. Álvarez no está contento en su trabajo.
E1: Busque otro trabajo inmediatamente.
E2: Hable con su jefe y explíquele la situación.

1. La Sra. Jiménez necesita más vendedores en su compañía.
2. El Sr. Jiménez es contador y tiene que terminar un informe, pero su computadora no funciona.
3. Unos hombres de negocios van a ir a Chile y no saben hablar español.
4. La Sra. Peña tuvo un accidente serio con su auto, y el otro chofer le dijo que iba a llamar a la policía.
5. La Sra. Hurtado entra en su apartamento y ve que hay agua en el piso de la cocina.
6. La cantante Mirta del Valle va a cantar en el Festival Internacional de la Canción en Viña del Mar, pero se siente bastante mal.

Suggestions for 9-26. Describe personal situations and elicit student advice: ¿*Qué debo hacer? No tengo dinero.* (*Trabaje. Pídales dinero a sus padres.*) *Tengo hambre.* (*Prepare algo. Coma.*) *Estoy triste.* (*Salga con nosotros. Practique deportes.*)

Give students five to ten minutes to write a *Querida Antonia* (Dear Abby) letter. Then collect the letters and redistribute them, so other students can act as Antonia, giving advice using commands.

SITUACIONES

1. **Role A.** You are going to be away for a series of job interviews. Tell your neighbor a) how long you will be away and b) ask him/her if he/she could do a few things for you while you are away. After he/she agrees, tell him/her to a) feed the cat every day, b) water the plants every (*cada*) three days, c) pick up the mail (*correspondencia*), and d) any other things that you may think of. Thank him/her for his/her help.

   Role B. Your neighbor tells you that he/she is going to be away and you agree to help him/her out. After he/she tells you what you will have to do, ask him/her a) whom should you call in case of an emergency (*emergencia*), and b) the telephone number of the veterinary.

2. **Role A.** You have moved to Concepción, Chile, and have opened a checking account (*cuenta corriente*) at Banco del Estado. Since you are not familiar with their system, ask an employee to help you. After he/she gives you all the details, a) thank him/her, and b) say that you are very happy with the service the bank provides the customers.

   Role B. You are an employee at the Banco del Estado. Using the check below, explain to the customer where a) to put the date, b) to write the payee's name, c) to write the amount (*cantidad*) in numbers, d) to write the amount in words, and e) sign (**firmar**) the check.

Alternate situation. Tell students they work in a bank and need to write concise instructions for new customers. Have them work in groups and then decide who wrote the most concise instructions.

MOSAICS

 ## *Escuchar*

Contextual guessing

Sometimes in the course of a conversation you might not understand a word or a phrase that you hear, but you can understand the message by using contextual cues, that is, by paying attention to the topic or to a part of the word that you don't understand. Also paying attention to the words that precede or follow what you did not understand will help.

Antes de escuchar

9-27. Profesiones diferentes. In activity **9-28**, you will listen to a conversation between two friends talking about their professions, what they do, and the advantages and disadvantages of their jobs. Before you listen, write down the name of two professions and an advantage and a disadvantage for each one.

PROFESIÓN	VENTAJA	DESVENTAJA
_____	_____	_____
_____	_____	_____

A escuchar

9-28. First, read the words in the left column and listen to the conversation between Estela and Susana. Then, state the probable meaning of each word based on the contextual cues you heard in the conversation. Finally, write down the cue words that helped you understand.

ESCUCHÉ...	POSIBLE SIGNIFICADO	ADIVINÉ EL SIGNIFICADO PORQUE...
neuróloga	neuroloigist	*neuralgias, nervios*
primordial	outmost	*relacionado a primer/o*
guardias	to be on duty	*quedarse en el hospital 24 horas, una vez a la semana*

VÍNCULOS

For materials related to the Mosaicos section, see
- SAM-OneKey: WB: 9-19, 9-20, 9-21, 9-22, 9-23, 9-24 / LM: 9-44
- IRCD: Chapter 9; pg. 341

Warm-up for 9-28. As a prelistening activity, have students get in groups of four and talk about the professions of five different people they know, what they do and what their personal characteristics are.

Audioscript for 9-28. ESTELA: Susana, te digo que me encanta ser una mujer de negocios. El sueldo es excelente y los beneficios sociales que recibo son estupendos. Imagínate, tengo un seguro médico maravilloso, cuatro semanas de vacaciones al año. Lo que no me gusta mucho es que tengo que viajar por lo menos treinta semanas al año y no tengo tiempo para estar mucho con mi familia. SUSANA: Me alegro de que te guste tu trabajo, Estela. A mí también me encanta el mío, pero es diferente, por supuesto. ESTELA: Sí, yo sé que eres neuróloga y ayudas a muchas personas. Eso debe ser maravilloso. Es horrible tener neuralgias o dolores de cabeza. ¡Tener un buen médico especialista si uno está mal de los nervios es primordial! SUSANA: Sí, me encanta ayudar a la gente. El único problema que tengo es que el horario es muy variable. Si alguien se enferma de noche, me tengo que levantar para ir a verlo al hospital si es necesario. También tengo guardias en el hospital una vez a la semana. Me tengo que quedar 24 horas en el hospital. ESTELA: Comprendo. No hay nada perfecto. SUSANA: No me quejo. Me gusta mi trabajo y gano un buen sueldo.

Después de escuchar

9-29 ¿Y usted? With a classmate, share your answers to the following questions.

1. ¿Cuáles son las ventajas y desventajas de ser médico, abogado o plomero?
2. En general, ¿qué profesión u ocupación le parece a usted que produce menos estrés?
3. ¿Qué profesión u ocupación, según usted, da más satisfacciones personales? ¿Por qué?

Antes de escuchar

9-30 El plomero y el electricista. In **9-31,** you will listen to a plumber and an electrician talking about their jobs. Before you listen, write down what you know about what they do, where they work, etc.

plomero _____
electricista _____

A escuchar

9-31. First, read the words in the left column and listen to the conversation. Then, state the probable meaning of each word, based on the contextual cues you heard in the conversation. Finally, write down the cue words that facilitated your comprehension.

ESCUCHÉ...	POSIBLE SIGNIFICADO	ADIVINÉ EL SIGNIFICADO PORQUE...
inundó	flooded	cognate: innundated
tubería	pipes	cognate: tube
ferretería	hardware store	-ía ending like *panadería*

Después de escuchar

9-32 ¿Y usted? With a classmate, share your answers to the following questions.

1. En su casa, ¿alguna vez tuvo que llamar a un plomero o a un electricista? ¿Por qué?
2. ¿Sabe usted hacer una instalación eléctrica? ¿Quién le enseñó?
3. ¿Cree usted que es importante saber arreglar las cosas en la casa? ¿Por qué?

Warm-up for 9-31. As a pre-listening activity, have students work in groups of four and imagine what they would be able to do around the house if they were plumbers and/or electricians.

Audioscript for 9-31:

RAFAEL: Rolando, te ves cansado. ¿Qué te pasa?

ROLANDO: Mi vecino me llamó anoche a medianoche porque tenía un problema serio en su casa. Imagínate que se le inundó la cocina. Había bastante agua debajo del fregadero, en el piso, en todas partes. Tuve que cerrar la llave muestra y esta mañana fui a arreglar todo. Cambié la tubería y le puse todo nuevo. Ahora ya no tiene problemas, pero fue mucho trabajo porque las tuberías eran viejas y estaban oxidadas y rotas.

RAFAEL: Bueno, pero ganaste mucho dinero, ¿no?

ROLANDO: Más o menos porque es mi vecino y tú sabes cómo son las cosas.

RAFAEL: Comprendo. A mí me pasó algo parecido. Mi vecina quería instalar una lámpara en su patio y tuve que ir a la ferretería a comprar todas las cosas: la lámpara, los cables.

ROLANDO: Y ¿por qué no fue ella a la ferretería?

RAFAEL: Bueno, es que es una persona mayor y no tiene auto. Es muy buena vecina y eso me dio oportunidad de ayudarla también.

Conversar

Antes de conversar

2 **9-33 ¿Qué requisitos se piden?** Completen la tabla con algunos requisitos que las compañías por lo general piden para los siguientes puestos.

PUESTOS	SE REQUIERE...	SE OFRECE(N)...
secretario/a	experiencia previa, capacidad de organización	sueldo compatible con experiencia, vacaciones pagadas
vendedor/a		
contador/a		
director/a de un instituto de idiomas extranjeros		

2 **9-34 Se ofrece y se busca trabajo.** Lea los siguientes anuncios con ofertas de trabajo, escoja un anuncio para un puesto que a usted le interese y prepare una lista de requisitos que, en su opinión, usted cumple (*meet*). Comparta su lista con su compañero/a.

INSTITUTO PRIVADO
necesita
DIRECTOR/A
Lugar de residencia, Región de los Lagos

Requisitos:
- Titulación adecuada al puesto
- Experiencia de 5 años en cargo similar
- Responsabilidad y constancia
- Capacidad de organización, coordinación y trabajo
- Relaciones públicas

Sueldo compatible con calificaciones

Interesados, enviar CV, con fotografía reciente a Casilla 934, Osorno, Chile   Se responderá por escrito

JEFE DE SERVICIO
necesita importante empresa
MANUFACTURERA DE PLÁSTICOS

Se requiere: Experiencia de 4 años en empresa del sector en puesto de similar responsabilidad. *Se ofrece:* Buenas perspectivas de avance profesional. Integración en empresa en expansión hacia el extranjero.

Interesados, enviar currículum y fotografía reciente, especificando pretensiones de sueldo, a Casilla 2568, Correo Santiago Centro, Santiago

EMPRESA DE EXPORTACIONES
necesita para Chile y el extranjero

VENDEDORES/AS REPRESENTANTES

Sueldo inicial 1,000.000
Comisión de ventas

Se requiere: Experiencia en ventas y representación. Buena presencia y deseos de superación. Mayor de 25 años. Buen dominio del inglés y/o francés; japonés y árabe deseables.

Se ofrece: Trabajo inmediato. Entrenamiento en la empresa. Promoción rápida. Sueldo negociable más comisión después del período de prueba.

Interesados, llamar a los teléfonos 2218765, 2169036 Lunes a viernes de 8:30 a 15:00 hrs.

BANCO O'HIGGINS
necesita
10 CONTADORES AUDITORES
Lugar de trabajo ideal: Viña del Mar

- Título universitario
- Mínimo 2 años de experiencia
- Flexibilidad horaria
- Deseo de viajar a otras regiones del país
- Capacidad de organización y trabajo

Sueldo atractivo

Interesados, enviar currículum, con fotografía a: Bco. O'Higgins, Casilla 1902-D, Viña del Mar

A conversar

9-35 Ahora escojan un papel: el de jefe de personal de las compañías representadas en los anuncios o el de una persona que busca un trabajo. Sigan las instrucciones para cada rol.

> **Jefe de personal:** Entreviste separadamente a dos personas que están interesadas en el puesto que ofrece su compañía. Pregúnteles sobre: a) su experiencia, b) sus estudios, c) sus preferencias de sueldo, etc. y decida cuál es la persona indicada para el puesto.
>
> **Persona que busca trabajo:** Escoja el anuncio con el trabajo que usted necesita. Responda a las preguntas del/de la jefe/a de personal de la manera más completa posible y haga preguntas si lo considera necesario.

Después de conversar

9-36 Expectativas y decisiones. Los jefes de personal y las personas que buscaban trabajo deben informar a la clase sobre lo siguiente:

> **Informe de las personas que buscaban trabajo:**
>
> 1. ¿Qué puesto buscaba usted? ¿Qué requisitos para el puesto cumple usted?
> 2. ¿Qué aspecto de la oferta de trabajo le pareció más atractivo?
> 3. ¿Cree usted que va a recibir la oferta de trabajo? ¿Por qué?

> **Informe de los jefes de personal:**
>
> 1. ¿Qué puesto ofrecía su compañía en el anuncio?
> 2. ¿Qué requisitos debía tener el/la candidato/a que buscaba su compañía?
> 3. ¿A qué candidato/a(s) va usted a contratar? ¿Por qué?

Antes de conversar

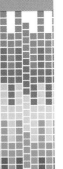 **9-37 Conflictos profesionales.** Lean las siguientes situaciones e identifiquen los problemas en cada una de ellas. Luego, escriban por los menos tres recomendaciones para cada caso.

1. Juan Miguel leyó un anuncio en Internet que ofrecía un trabajo de telemercado en la ciudad de Miami. Solicitó el puesto y lo llamaron a una entrevista. El día de la entrevista, Juan Miguel se puso los pantalones cortos que había comprado para la ocasión, zapatos de tenis, una camisa blanca y un par de aretes. Llegó a la entrevista puntualmente, esperó unos minutos hasta que alguien lo invitó a pasar a su oficina. Cuando entró a la oficina del entrevistador, éste lo miró con sorpresa. Nunca lo llamaron para ofrecerle el trabajo. Juan Miguel se pregunta por qué.

2. Consuelo es la secretaria personal del presidente de una gran compañía de productos tecnológicos. Su jefe siempre se reúne con personas importantes con quienes la compañía hace negocios. Por su trabajo, él comparte todo tipo de información con ella. Para no poner en riesgo a la compañía, Consuelo debe mantener esta información confidencial. Hace una semana, sin darse cuenta (*not realizing*), ella contestó unas preguntas de uno de sus amigos que era vendedor de otra compañía. De esa manera le dio información vital a su amigo. Consuelo pensó que su amigo vendedor no usaría la información para beneficiar a su propia compañía. En realidad, él no solamente usó la información sino que también provocó el fracaso (*failure*) de un proyecto importante para la compañía donde trabaja Consuelo. Ahora ella piensa que su jefe la va a despedir (*fire*) si descubre que ella es la responsable del fracaso.

A conversar

❷ **9-38 Consejos.** En el papel de Juan Miguel o de Consuelo, explíquenle al/a la consejero/a (su compañero/a) lo siguiente. El/La consejero/a va a hacerle preguntas y darle algunos consejos. Luego, cambien de papel.

1. Narre la experiencia que vive/vivió y diga cuáles son las complicaciones o consecuencias de sus acciones.
2. Hable de cómo se siente después de lo que ocurrió.
3. Tome notas de las mejores sugerencias que el/la consejero/a le dé.

Suggestions for 9-38. To prepare students to do activity **9-39,** every student should play the role of interviewer and interviewee.

Después de conversar

Ⓖ **9-39 Reflexiones.** Conversen sobre lo siguiente.

1. ¿Fue útil la conversación con el/la consejero/a? ¿Por qué?
2. ¿Qué sugerencias le parecieron mejores? ¿Qué recomendación o recomendaciones es/son la(s) más difícil(es) de seguir? ¿Por qué?

 # *Leer*

In *Lección 9*, you will practice identifying categories in the text and making inferences based on visuals, headlines, and subheadings.

Guía de prelectura

First, look at the photo and read the title and subhead of the article in **9-42.** Then, using the cues provided by the visuals and the headline and subheading, and relying on your knowledge of the topic, answer the following questions:

1. What ideas do you expect to find in this text?
   ⓐ The gap between men and women at work has disappeared in Chile.
   b. The work world in Chile is still a man's world.
   c. Women make the same salary as men in equal jobs.

2. On what did you base your answers to question 1? Circle the corresponding letter.
   ⓐ The headline and subheading only
   ⓑ The photos in the text
   ⓒ My personal knowledge of the topic

3. After reading the headline and subheading, can you guess some of the content of the text? Use your previously learned skills to anticipate the main topic of the text.

   The text will probably discuss the following ideas. Mark with an X all that may apply.
   a. ___X___ In the last decades, Chilean women have entered the work place in larger numbers.
   b. ___X___ Chilean women are discriminated against in the work place.
   c. _____ Women in Chile enjoy the same working conditions as men.
   d. ___X___ Although working women in Chile have made progress regarding their labor rights, they still have not been granted the same treatment at work that men enjoy.

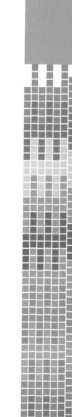

Antes de leer

9-40 Preparación. En general, la mujer en muchas partes del mundo no comenzó a trabajar fuera de casa hasta el siglo XX. Marque con una X las posibles razones de este fenómeno, según usted. Si tiene otra opción, agréguela.

1. ___X___ La mujeres antes del siglo XX tenían poca educación.
2. _____ Las mujeres decidieron trabajar fuera de casa porque no querían cuidar a sus hijos.
3. ___X___ Las economías de algunos países mejoraron y se presentaron más ofertas de trabajo para las mujeres.
4. _____ Los hombres se retiraron de sus trabajos para ayudar a las mujeres.
5. ___X___ Con más educación, las mujeres comenzaron a tener más confianza (*confidence*) en sí mismas.
6. ___X___ Por los cambios sociales, los jefes empezaron a valorar la capacidad de la mujer y las contribuciones que ésta podía hacer en el lugar de trabajo.
7. _____ ¿?

9-41 ¿Trabajos femeninos o masculinos? Primera fase. Algunas personas piensan que hay trabajos que las mujeres pueden hacer mejor que los hombres y viceversa. De la siguiente lista, indique cuáles áreas de trabajo se consideran en general más apropiadas para las mujeres (**M**) y cuáles para los hombres (**H**).

1. _____ educación
2. _____ enfermería
3. _____ gerencia (*management*)
4. _____ telemercado
5. _____ relaciones públicas
6. _____ economía
7. _____ medicina
8. _____ psicología
9. _____ mecánica
10. _____ limpieza (*cleaning*)

❷ **Segunda fase.** Comparen sus respuestas y respondan a estas preguntas.

1. Según ustedes, ¿hay realmente trabajos más apropiados para las mujeres que para los hombres? ¿Cuáles?
2. ¿Se basan las diferencias en la calidad de trabajo que hacen las personas de ese género (*gender*) o en otra cosa? Si su respuesta es afirmativa, explíquenla.

A leer

9-42 Primera mirada. Lea el siguiente artículo y haga lo que se indica.

¿Es justo el mundo laboral chileno?

Varias razones explican la creciente incorporación de la mujer chilena al mundo laboral. La bonanza financiera de los años 90 favoreció la creación de nuevos negocios y empresas, y un aumento de las ofertas de trabajo. Aunque la presencia femenina en la economía nacional es evidente, las chilenas aún no logran los niveles de participación de las argentinas y las colombianas.

Las estadísticas indican que la fuerza laboral femenina chilena aumentó de un 34% en 2002 a un 36% en 2004. No obstante, Colombia y Argentina superan a Chile con una tasa de un 45%. Según datos del Ministerio del Trabajo, entre febrero y abril de 2004, las empresarias chilenas aumentaron en un 50% y las mujeres que trabajan para otros en un 47%.

Según Fernanda Villegas, asesora laboral del Servicio Nacional de la Mujer (SERNAM), la mayor presencia femenina en el mundo laboral responde a un cambio generacional. Juan Pablo Swett, gerente del portal Trabajando.com, piensa que el incremento laboral femenino se debe a la mayor confianza de los jefes en la capacidad de la mujer.

Algunos sociólogos opinan que la tendencia al aumento de la presencia femenina en el mundo laboral es el resultado de cambios socioculturales, por eso, debería continuar, independientemente de las variaciones económicas. Sin embargo, algunos estudios muestran que la incorporación de la mujer al trabajo funciona por ciclos, es decir, cuando mejora la economía, la mujer participa en el desarrollo económico del país, pero deja de hacerlo cuando hay crisis. Afortunadamente, existen otros indicadores que prometen una participación más estable de la mujer en la economía: el continuo mejoramiento del nivel educativo femenino y la creación de pequeñas empresas dirigidas por mujeres.

Tipos y condiciones de trabajo para las mujeres

Las investigaciones indican que las mujeres chilenas en general trabajan en recursos humanos, mercadeo y relaciones públicas, áreas en que pueden hacer un mejor trabajo que el hombre.

Según expertos del Ministerio del Trabajo, aunque las mujeres pueden realizar ciertos trabajos desde casa, como el teletrabajo, las madres de familia que trabajan fuera de casa no siempre cuentan con las condiciones para hacerlo. Muchas de ellas no tienen acceso a guarderías para el cuidado de sus hijos, ni el apoyo del hombre en la casa. Además, afirma Alexandra Ruedas, del Ministerio del Trabajo, existen algunos mitos que las mujeres chilenas deben enfrentar. Muchos creen que las mujeres tienen menos años de estudio que los hombres. Pero las estadísticas indican que en promedio la mujer chilena tiene 11,7 años de estudios, mientras que el hombre estudia un promedio de 10,5 años.

A pesar de su mayor escolaridad, las chilenas ganan menos que los hombres en trabajos y especialidades iguales. Aunque estas diferencias están desapareciendo lentamente, algunas empresas prefieren contratar a un hombre y no a una mujer, especialmente durante los años de maternidad.

Sin duda, la entrada de la mujer en el mundo del trabajo marcó un momento histórico importante. Los avances que ésta ha hecho también son significativos, pero aún queda mucho camino por andar.

Indique cuáles de las siguientes afirmaciones son inferencias (I) basadas en el contenido del artículo. Si la afirmación es una inferencia (I), indique la(s) línea(s) donde está la información en que ésta se basa.

1. _____ El progreso de la economía es una de las causas del aumento de la presencia de la mujer en el trabajo.
2. ___I___ En comparación con Argentina, en Chile hay menos mujeres que trabajan.
3. _____ En el año 2002, hubo un incremento de la fuerza laboral femenina.
4. _____ En Colombia y Argentina el 45% de los trabajadores son mujeres.

5. ____ En 2004, era mayor el número de mujeres que participaban en el desarrollo económico de Chile.

6. ____ Los porcentajes indican que posiblemente más mujeres trabajan para sí mismas en casa.

7. _____ Se piensa que el aumento de trabajadoras en Chile responde a cambios sociales y culturales.

8. ____ Las mujeres tienen más capacidad que los hombres para vender y relacionarse con los clientes.

9. ____ Para las chilenas con hijos no es fácil trabajar fuera de casa.

10. ____ Las chilenas sufren de discriminación en el trabajo.

9-43 Segunda mirada. Las siguientes palabras aparecen en el artículo. Agrúpelas según el campo (*field*) con que se asocian.

tasa	teletrabajo	estadísticas	sociólogo
bonanza	tendencia	relaciones públicas	crisis
desarrollo	creación	empresarias	datos
aumento	asesora laboral	gerente	recursos humanos

1. Números o porcentaje: _tasa, datos, estadísticas_
2. Trabajos/profesiones: _empresarias, asesora laboral, sociólogo, gerente_
3. Áreas de trabajo: _recursos humanos, relaciones públicas, teletrabajo_
4. Condiciones económicas: _bonanza, crisis, desarrollo, creación, tendencia, aumento_

Después de leer

Suggestion for 9-44. To make this activity more interesting and intellectually challenging, once groups have finished writing their brief letter, you may wish to have two groups get together and compare responses orally. If time allows, you may have a whole class discussion to take a vote on the best suggestions given by the various groups.

9-44 Lluvia de ideas. El Ministerio de la Mujer de Chile pide la colaboración de las empresas para mejorar la situación laboral de las mujeres. El gerente de su compañía solicita que los jefes de personal identifiquen por lo menos **dos** problemas de las trabajadoras y den **tres** recomendaciones para cada problema. Respóndanle usando el documento que aparece a continuación. Usen los mandatos.

Para: Gerencia General

De: Jefes de Personal: _____ (nombres)

Estimado Sr. Gerente:

En respuesta a su petición sobre los problemas de las trabajadoras en nuestra compañía, los jefes de personal exponemos lo siguiente:

En nuestra opinión, las trabajadoras de nuestra empresa enfrentan estos problemas que requieren una pronta solución:

1. _____
2. _____

Para ayudar a resolverlos, sugerimos lo siguiente:
Para solucionar el primer problema, _____

Para solucionar el segundo problema, _____

Esperamos trabajar juntos con usted en beneficio de nuestras colegas.

Atentamente,

Jefes de Personal

Escribir

In today's world, getting the job you want may be difficult because of the job market. Therefore, answering a want ad takes as much skill as giving a good interview.

The following are some basic tips that may prove useful when answering a want ad in any language. Pay attention to . . .

a. the academic requirements of the job: Does it require a high school diploma or a college degree?

b. the worker profile the employer has in mind: Is experience required or not? If required, what kind and how much experience is required? What personality criteria will you need to meet to be considered for the job?

c. job-specific skills: Should you be a specialist in a field? What skills or dexterities should you possess? Should you be good at answering questions, speaking and/or writing in another language?, etc.

Antes de escribir

9-45 Preparación. Usted es un/a exitoso/a profesional chileno/a que hace un par de meses se divorció. Ahora debe cuidar a un hijo de cuatro años y a una hija de seis. Como necesita ayuda, usted escribió un anuncio en Internet para solicitar los servicios de una niñera (*nanny*). En preparación para la actividad **9-47**, lea el siguiente mensaje electrónico que una persona interesada le escribió en respuesta a su anuncio en Internet.

De: sofia.morales@entel.chile

Para: rruiz@ct.chile

Ref.:   Cuidado de sus hijos

Estimado/a señor/a Ruiz:

Mi nombre es Sofía Morales. Soy secretaria de profesión, pero por el momento estoy desempleada. Aunque no tengo mucha experiencia como niñera, pienso que puedo hacer un buen trabajo porque me fascinan los niños. Si me permite, me gustaría hacerle algunas preguntas preliminares para saber más sobre sus hijos.

Primero, con respecto al temperamento y gustos de los niños: ¿Son sociables? ¿Se adaptan fácilmente a personas desconocidas? ¿Lloran mucho cuando usted no está? ¿Qué se debe hacer para mantenerlos tranquilos y felices?

Segundo, en relación con los hábitos de ellos: ¿Se despiertan y se levantan temprano? ¿Duermen la siesta? ¿Se acuestan antes que usted regrese de su trabajo? ¿Cómo se divierten durante el día?

Tercero, con respecto a la comida: ¿Qué desayunan o almuerzan? ¿Debo prepararles el desayuno y el almuerzo? ¿Hay algo que deben o no deben comer o beber?

Finalmente, ¿a qué hora vuelve usted a casa? Yo debo regresar a mi casa antes de las 8:00 de la noche.

Tengo referencias que le puedo propocionar cuando usted las necesite.

Estaré encantada de conocer a sus hijos. Estoy segura de que si usted me da el trabajo, los niños y yo vamos a llevarnos muy bien.

Atentamente,

Sofía Morales

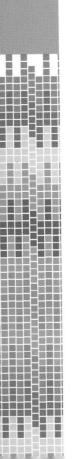

9-46 ¡Las prioridades deciden! A usted le gusta la candidata que le escribió. Puesto que necesita pronto su servicio escríbale una carta inmediatemente.

1. Para la introducción de su carta, puede agradecer así: "Muchas gracias por responder al anuncio de niñera que puse en Internet". Ahora, escriba otra manera de agradecerle a la persona que respondió a su anuncio.

   _____

2. Para contestar las preguntas de la candidata, lea con cuidado la lista de preguntas que recibió y responda a cada una de ellas. Recuerde que en general, los mandatos van a ser muy útiles para indicarle a la candidata lo que debe hacer. Por ejemplo, "Mándeme sus referencias por correo".

3. Para terminar su carta, informe a la candidata sobre la posible fecha y hora de la entrevista y cuándo va a saber la decisión final que usted tomó. Por ejemplo, "Por favor, llámeme por teléfono el lunes por la mañana para hablar sobre fecha y hora de la entrevista".

A escribir

9-47 Manos a la obra. Respóndale —con la mayor cantidad de detalles posible— el mensaje electrónico a su futura niñera. Use la información de la actividad **9-46.**

Después de escribir

9-48 Revisión. Ahora lea su mensaje electrónico, pensando en su lectora. Verifique lo siguiente:

- El contenido: ¿Respondió usted a todas las preguntas de la candidata? ¿Le dio los detalles necesarios?

- La organización: ¿Tiene su correo electrónico una organización clara, es decir, una introducción, un cuerpo y un cierre?

- La forma de su mensaje:
  a. ¿Revisó la gramática: el vocabulario correcto, algunas expresiones de cortesía y de despedida, la concordancia, el tiempo (presente, pasado), el uso de los mandatos, etc.?
  b. ¿Usó la puntuación y la ortografía correctas?

Finalmente, comparta su mensaje electrónico con un/a compañero/a. Esto puede darle la perspectiva de un lector potencial.

ENFOQUE CULTURAL

TEMAS: LA ECONOMÍA

Para pensar

Generalmente, ¿es fácil conseguir trabajo después de graduarse de la universidad? ¿Hay mucho desempleo en los Estados Unidos? ¿Ganan mucho dinero los profesionales jóvenes y con poca experiencia? ¿Existen aún diferencias notables entre las oportunidades y la remuneración que perciben los hombres y las mujeres por un trabajo similar?

Muchos niños y jóvenes de las clases más pobres trabajan desde pequeños limpiando zapatos, vendiendo periódicos o dulces en la calle, y aun como empleados domésticos.

Hay países hispanos con problemas económicos y pocas posibilidades de empleo en el sector privado y en el público.

Los sueldos bajos traen una serie de consecuencias sociales: los jóvenes tienen que permanecer en la casa de sus padres y deben conseguir dos y hasta tres empleos para sobrevivir.

Para contestar

2 Los trabajos. Respondan a las siguientes preguntas.

1. Mencionen algunos trabajos que los jóvenes de las clases más pobres tienen en algunos países hispanos.
2. ¿Cuáles son algunas consecuencias de una economía en crisis?

G Riqueza cultural. En grupos de tres, identifiquen lo siguiente y compartan luego esta información con la clase.

a. Las zonas de los Estados Unidos que tienen un mayor desarrollo económico
b. Dos países hispanos que muestran desarrollo en algunas áreas de la economía

Cerca de Santiago, se encuentran las grandes industrias del vino con sus viñedos. Concha y Toro, Santa Rita y Macul exportan sus vinos a muchos países del mundo. La fruta constituye también una de las industrias más prósperas de Chile. Éstas se exportan a varios continentes en todas las estaciones del año.

VÍNCULOS

For materials related to the Enfoque cultural, see
- SAM-OneKey: WB: 9-25
- IRCD: Chapter 9; pg. 350

Chile está en el suroeste de América del Sur y tiene una larga costa en el Océano Pacífico. La capital de Chile es Santiago.

Para pensar

¿Sabe usted dónde está Chile? ¿Sabe usted qué productos chilenos se consumen mucho en los Estados Unidos? ¿Conoce usted a alguna persona chilena famosa?

La economía chilena ha mejorado mucho en los últimos años. La producción agrícola, mineral e industrial es muy importante y ha contribuido a mejorar la economía del país. Varias compañías que se nacionalizaron en los años 70 ahora son privadas.

Viña del Mar es el principal balneario en el centro del país. En esta ciudad se lleva a cabo el famoso Festival Internacional de la Canción.

Algunos de los lugares favoritos para ir a esquiar en la nieve, especialmente de junio a octubre, son Portillo, Farellones, La Parva y Valle Nevado.

Valparaíso es el principal puerto de Chile. La ciudad de Valparaíso es un lugar turístico y cultural muy interesante. Allí se encuentra la casa museo del poeta Pablo Neruda, ganador del Premio Nobel de Literatura en 1971.

Expresiones chilenas:

pololo/a	María, te presento a mi pololo.	*María, this is my boyfriend.*
planchado/sin chaucha	Está planchado/sin chaucha.	*He is broke.*
tinca	Me tinca que hizo algo malo.	*I have the feeling that he/she did something wrong.*
el descueve	Mi jefe es el descueve.	*My boss is far out.*

Para contestar

En el mapa

1. Diga qué ciudades chilenas están cerca de la frontera con Perú.
2. ¿Qué países están cerca de Chile?
3. Mencione una característica geográfica de Chile.

Ahora diga...

1. si le gustaría visitar Santiago y por qué.
2. qué lugar visitaría en Valparaíso.

¿Qué dice Ud. si...

1. tiene una fuerte impresión de que su amigo fue a una entrevista y le ofrecieron el trabajo.
2. tiene planes de ir al cine con la persona a quien ama.
3. se da cuenta de que no tiene dinero.
4. piensa que la nueva gerente de su compañía es excepcional.

Para investigar en Internet

Busque en la página de un periódico chileno qué trabajos se ofrecen, qué sueldos pagan y cuáles son los requisitos necesarios para obtenerlos, etc. Compare los puestos que ofrecen estos avisos en Chile con los puestos que se ofrecen en avisos semejantes en los periódicos de los Estados Unidos. Comente las semejanzas y diferencias con sus compañeros/as de clase.

¡Prepárese!

9-49 Misterios y pistas. ¿Qué relaciones hay entre las palabras clave de las pistas del Misterio 4? ¿Con qué las asocia? ¿Qué cree que simbolizan? ¿Cómo se pueden relacionar estas cosas con el misterio, "Un lugar estratégico"?

1. La **fuente** de la **civilización**
2. La **flor** de la **civilización**
3. El **manantial** del **romance**
4. El **barco** de la **vida**

Con un/a compañero/a, indique lo siguiente:

	RELACIÓN CON	SÍMBOLO DE
fuente		
civilización		
flor		
manantial		
romance		
barco		
vida		

Manolo quiere que el concurso tenga un tono más personal.

Aunque cuestiona su amistad, Carlos quizás perdone a Katie.

Katie y Efraín forman una alianza.

Katie y Efraín comparten sus pistas.

Tito le pregunta a Sabrina si ella está celosa.

Sabrina quiere ganar y dice que va a ganar.

¡Responda!

9-50 ¿Qué deben hacer? Carlos está decepcionado de Katie; Efraín quiere formar una alianza con Katie; Sabrina quiere ganar el concurso. ¿Qué les puede decir a los participantes para ayudarlos en sus planes? Use los mandatos formales para darles instrucciones y consejos sobre lo que ocurre en este episodio.

MODELO: Carlos   No perdone a Katie porque ella lo decepcionó.

PARTICIPANTE	SU CONSEJO
Carlos	_____
Katie	_____
Efraín	_____
Sabrina	_____

La música de Violeta Parra se reconoce por altó contenido social y es representativa de la Nueva Canción, una forma artística musical de Latinoamérica en la cual el autor expresa sus opiniones políticas y la importancia de la cultura autóctona.

¡Prepárese!

Suggestion for 9-51. Point out that the word *luceros* (stars) in the first stanza symbolizes eyes.

9-51 El simbolismo. Lea esta lista de palabras que se usan en "Gracias a la vida" y exprese lo que pueden simbolizar, según su experiencia personal.

PALABRA	PUEDE SIMBOLIZAR...
luceros	_____
el abecedario	_____
el oído	_____
la risa	_____
el llanto	_____

¡Escuche!

9-52 La canción. Lea parte de la letra de "Gracias a la vida". Después de escuchar la canción conteste las preguntas.

Gracias a la vida que me ha dado tanto
me dio dos luceros que cuando los abro
perfecto distingo lo negro del blanco
y en el alto cielo su fondo estrellado
y en las multitudes el hombre que yo amo.
[...]
me ha dado el oído que en todo su ancho
graba noche y día grillos y canarios
[...]
me ha dado el sonido y el abecedario
con él las palabras que pienso y declaro
[...]

me ha dado la marcha de mis pies cansados
con ellos anduve ciudades y charcos
[...]
me dio el corazón que agita su marco
cuando miro el fruto del cerebro humano,
cuando miro al bueno tan lejos del malo,
[...]
me ha dado la risa y me ha dado el llanto,
así yo distingo dicha de quebranto
los dos materiales que forman mi canto
y el canto de ustedes que es el mismo canto
y que el canto de todos que es mi propio canto.

1. En su opinión, ¿cuáles son los temas de "Gracias a la vida"?
2. ¿Cuáles son algunos de los mensajes de la canción?
3. ¿A quién cree que se dirige la cantautora?
4. ¿Qué palabras puede usar para describir esta canción?

¡Responda!

Suggestion for 9-53. Ask for volunteers to read their work aloud to the class.

9-53 El pasado. La autora de "Gracias a la vida" recuerda cosas y actividades importantes de su vida. Piense en las cosas y actividades de su niñez o del lugar donde vivía antes de estudiar en la universidad que eran importantes para usted. Escriba una breve composición sobre este tema, usando los tiempos pasados para contar lo que hacía y cómo era su vida entonces.

MODELO: Cuando yo era niño/a...

VOCABULARIO

AUDIO ## Profesiones, oficios y ocupaciones

el/la abogado/a	*lawyer*
el actor/la actriz	*actor/actress*
el ama de casa	*housewife, homemaker*
el/la arquitecto/a	*architect*
el/la bibliotecario/a	*librarian*
el/la bombero/a	*firefighter*
el/la cajero/a	*cashier*
el/la chofer	*driver*
el/la científico/a	*scientist*
el/la contador/a	*accountant*
el/la ejecutivo/a	*executive*
el/la electricista	*electrician*
el/la empleado/a	*employee*
el/la enfermero/a	*nurse*
el/la gerente (de ventas)	*(sales) manager*
el hombre/la mujer de negocios	*businessman/woman*
el/la ingeniero/a	*engineer*
el/la intérprete	*interpreter*
el/la jefe/jefa	*boss*
el/la juez	*judge*
el/la locutor/a	*radio announcer*
el/la médico/a	*medical doctor*
el/la obrero/a	*worker*
el/la peluquero/a	*hairdresser*
el/la periodista	*journalist*
el/la plomero/a	*plumber*
el policía/la (mujer) policía	*policeman, policewoman*
el/la (p)sicólogo/a	*psychologist*
el/la técnico/a	*technician*
el/la vendedor/a	*salesman, saleswoman*

Lugares

el banco	*bank*
la compañía/empresa	*company*
el consultorio	*doctor's office*
la peluquería	*beauty salon, barbershop*

Trabajo

el anuncio	*ad (advertisement)*
el/la cliente/a	*client*
el currículum	*résumé*
la entrevista	*interview*
la experiencia	*experience*
el incendio	*fire*
la llamada	*call*
el puesto	*position*
la oportunidad	*opportunity*
la solicitud	*application*
el sueldo	*salary*
la vacante	*opening*
las ventas	*sales*

Verbos

apagar	*to extinguish, to turn off*
atender (ie)	*to answer, to attend*
comenzar (ie)	*to begin*
comunicar(se)	*to communicate*
cortar	*to cut*
dejar	*to leave*
enviar	*to send*
esperar	*to wait for*
indicar	*to indicate*
llenar	*to fill (out)*
mandar	*to send*
mejorar	*to improve*
ofrecer (zc)	*to offer*
solicitar	*to apply (for)*

Palabras y expresiones útiles

actualmente	*at the present time*
¡Cómo no!	*Of course!*
lo importante	*the important thing*
por cierto	*by the way*
por correo	*by mail*
propio/a	*own*
en realidad/realmente	*in fact, really*
la señal	*signal*
sin embargo	*nevertheless*

10

LA COMIDA Y LA NUTRICIÓN

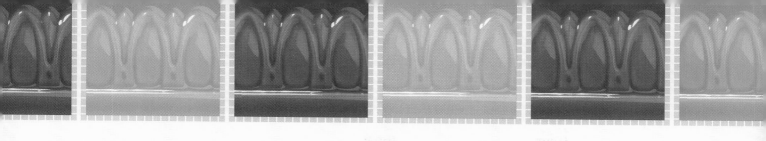

Objetivos comunicativos

- Discussing food, shopping, and planning menus
- Expressing wishes and hope
- Making requests and expressing opinions

- Expressing doubt
- Giving advice

Contenido

VÍNCULOS

To practice vocabulario—En el supermercado
- SAM-OneKey: WB: 10-1, 10-2, 10-3, 10-4, 10-5 / LM: 10-22, 10-23, 10-24, 10-25, 10-26
- Companion Website: AP 10-1 A, B, C
- IRCD: Chapter 10; pp. 358, 359, 361, 363

Suggestions. Using the Image Resource CD, present the foods by talking about your likes and dislikes: *A mí me gustan mucho las zanahorias. Tienen mucha vitamina A. Yo como zanahorias dos o tres veces a la semana. También me gustan las espinacas. Popeye* (write name on board) *come espinacas y por eso es muy fuerte. Y a Ud., ¿le gustan las espinacas? ¿Le gustan las zanahorias? Y a Bugs Bunny, ¿le gustan las espinacas o las zanahorias?*

After you have introduced several items, re-describe some and have students identify them. Then have students, working in pairs or groups: a) describe items, b) categorize them in groups, or c) put together balanced meals.

With the help of the Image Resouce CD, introduce other food items.

Point out the difference between Spanish and Mexican *tortillas.* Have students identify certain items: *Se venden en McDonald's con las hamburguesas. Se usa para cocinar.* Bring in menus from Hispanic restaurants to talk about Hispanic cuisine and the differences among countries and regions.

Have students discuss in groups of two or three what items they like or dislike. Emphasize use of the definite article: *Me gustan los frijoles.* Have students describe meals during a typical day at home.

Discuss the pros and cons of vegetarianism.

Have students prepare a list of what they buy and eat in a typical week.

En el supermercado

Frutas y verduras

Productos lácteos

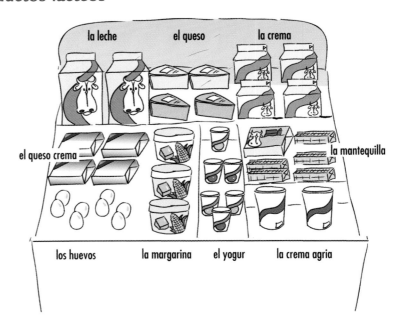

Pescado y Mariscos

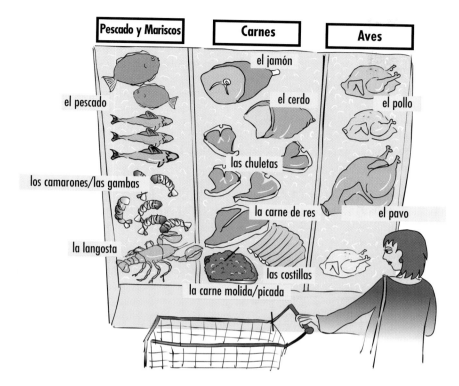

Pescado y Mariscos
- el pescado
- los camarones/las gambas
- la langosta

Carnes
- el jamón
- el cerdo
- las chuletas
- la carne de res
- las costillas
- la carne molida/picada

Aves
- el pollo
- el pavo

LENGUA

Names of certain food products vary by country. For example, **aguacate** is known as **palta** in some countries in South America; **maíz** is known as **elote** in Mexico and some Central American countries, and **choclo** in parts of South America; **pavo** is **guajolote** in Mexico; and **camarones** is **gambas** in Spain.

Los condimentos

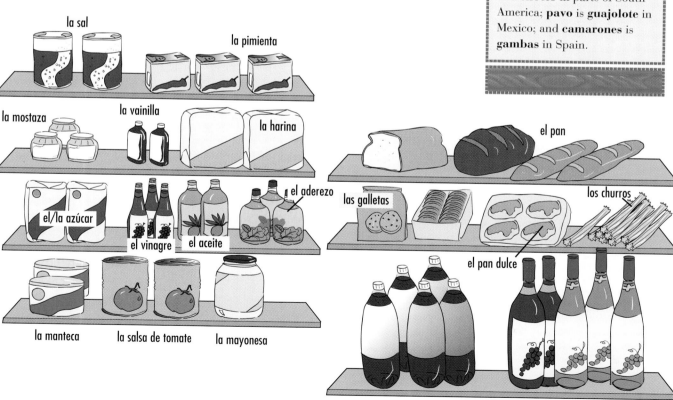

- la sal
- la pimienta
- la mostaza
- la vainilla
- la harina
- el/la azúcar
- el vinagre
- el aceite
- el aderezo
- la manteca
- la salsa de tomate
- la mayonesa
- el pan
- las galletas
- los churros
- el pan dulce
- los refrescos
- el vino tinto
- el vino blanco

¿Qué dice usted?

Warm-up for 10-1. Select other foods presented and ask students if they like them, how they prepare them, etc.

❷ **10-1 Asociaciones.** Después de asociar cada explicación con la palabra adecuada, comenten entre ustedes si les gustan o no estos alimentos.

1. ___d___ Se toma mucho en el verano, cuando hace calor.
2. ___e___ Se pone en la ensalada.
3. ___b___ Se usan para hacer vino.
4. ___a___ Se come en el desayuno con huevos fritos.
5. ___f___ Se prepara para el Día de Acción de Gracias.
6. ___c___ Se usa para preparar la ensalada de atún o de pollo.

a. el jamón
b. las uvas
c. la mayonesa
d. el helado
e. el aderezo
f. el pavo

Follow-up for 10-2. Present additional vocabulary related to the nutritional value of food: *vitaminas, calcio, fibra, proteínas, sin aditivos, calorías, grasa, colesterol.* Discuss preparation methods: *crudo, asado, al horno, hervido, al vapor.*

❷ **10-2 Dietas diferentes. Primera fase.** Completen la tabla con comidas adecuadas para estas dietas. Luego, discutan entre ustedes por qué se debe o no se debe comer cada cosa.

DIETA	SE DEBE COMER	NO SE DEBE COMER
vegetariana		
para diabéticos		
para engordar (*gain weight*)		
para bajar de peso (*lose weight*)		

EN DIRECTO

To give some general advice:
Deben + *infinitive* (comer/beber/ etc...)
Para bajar de peso, recomendamos + *noun* (las verduras, el agua, etc.)
Para obtener calcio/proteínas/fibra es bueno + *infinitive* (comer/beber/ etc.)

Segunda fase. Completen las siguientes ideas con sus recomendaciones para cada una de estas personas. Digan por qué.

1. Pedro, que es vegetariano, debe comer...
2. Mi padre, que es diabético,...
3. Luisa está muy delgada y...
4. Joaquín y Fabricio quieren bajar de peso. Por lo tanto...

Note for 10-3. Spanish uses the definite article to express "per:" *20 centavos la libra, 44 centavos el kilo.* Practice conversion from kilos to pounds and vice versa, stressing that a kilo equals 2.2 pounds. Tell students that you also say body weight in kilos, as in ¡*Después de mi dieta, peso sólo 50 kilos!* Beginning in the year 2000, Ecuador started using the US dollar as its currency. Use this exercise as an opportunity to explore exchange rates of currencies of several Spanish-speaking countries: *¿Qué otras monedas conoce Ud.? ¿Cuál es la moneda oficial de Bolivia? ¿Y de Chile?* Students can look up exchange rates on the Internet.

❷ **10-3 ¿Qué necesitamos?** Ustedes son estudiantes de intercambio en Ecuador. Le quieren preparar una cena a la familia con la que viven, pero no tienen todos los ingredientes necesarios. ¿Qué necesitan y cuánto cuestan estos ingredientes?

MODELO: E1: Vamos a preparar hamburguesas. Necesitamos un kilo de carne molida.
E2: Eso cuesta tres dólares el kilo.

Ⓖ **10-4 Los estudiantes y la comida. Primera fase.** En pequeños grupos, hablen de las comidas típicas de los estudiantes de su universidad. ¿Qué comen? ¿Cuándo comen?

Segunda fase. Hagan una lista de recomendaciones para una dieta estudiantil más saludable (*healthy*) y compártanla con el resto de la clase. Piensen en el desayuno, el almuerzo y la cena.

Suggestion for 10-4. Students can use the expressions in the **En directo** box, such as *deber* or *recomendar* + infinitive. If you wish to preview the use of the subjunctive with *recomendar*, you may also do so.

La mesa

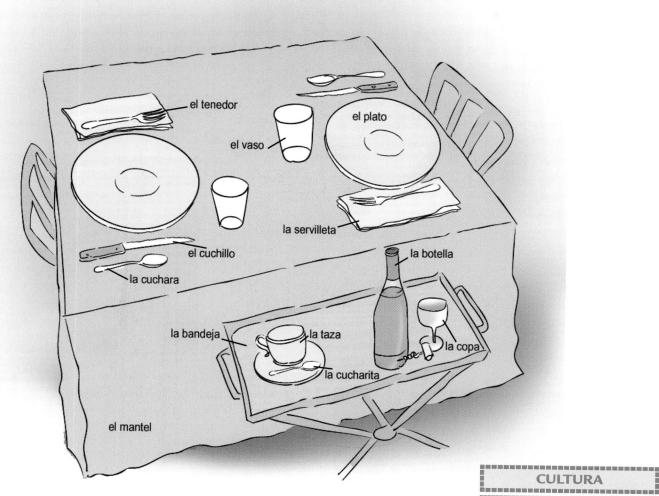

el tenedor

el plato

el vaso

la servilleta

el cuchillo

la cuchara

la botella

la bandeja la taza

la copa

la cucharita

el mantel

¿Qué dice usted?

❷ 10-5 Entrenamiento de un/a camarero/a. Usted y su compañero/a son camareros/as en un restaurante y uno/a de ustedes es nuevo/a en el puesto. Dígale a su nuevo/a compañero/a dónde debe poner cada cosa de acuerdo con el dibujo. Después cambien de papel.

MODELO: E1: Ponga el cuchillo a la derecha del plato.
           E2: Muy bien. ¿Y dónde pongo la copa?
           E1: _____.

Follow-up for 10-5. Students may recycle formal commands or expressions in this activity with *se: el cuchillo se pone a la derecha.* Ask students what they need to eat/drink certain types of food/beverages. You may introduce *cubiertos: ¿Qué (cubiertos) necesita usted para comer un bistec? ¿Y para tomar sopa? ¿Y para comer una ensalada? ¿Necesita usted un plato o una copa para beber vino? Y para beber café, ¿qué necesita?*

¿Dónde se compra?

AUDIO

En el área del Caribe, se consumen muchas frutas tropicales, como los plátanos, los mangos, las piñas y las papayas. En Estados Unidos, durante el invierno, se importan muchas frutas de Chile y otros países del hemisferio sur. Ecuador cultiva mucha fruta —sobre todo piña, limón, melón, papaya y maracuyá— y la exporta a los países europeos y a Estados Unidos.

En Bolivia, como en todos los países hispanos, hay buenas **pastelerías** donde se venden los **dulces** típicos de la región.

El pescado y los mariscos son muy importantes en la dieta de algunos países hispanoamericanos como Chile, Perú y Ecuador. En la provincia de Esmeraldas, en Ecuador, uno de los platos típicos es el encocado, pescado que se cocina con leche de coco.

La **artesanía** de Paraguay —especialmente los tejidos y los cestos— es muy apreciada en todo el mundo.

¿Qué dice usted?

② 10-6 La compra y los preparativos. Primero preparen un menú y luego una lista de lo que tienen que comprar para una cena. Después háganle preguntas a otra pareja para obtener la siguiente información:

1. menú
2. ingredientes
3. número de invitados
4. costo de la cena
5. división del trabajo
6. limpieza

Suggestion for 10-6. Recycle verbs dealing with cleaning the house.

② 10-7 Una cena. Usted estuvo muy ocupado/a ayer porque tuvo invitados a cenar. Dígale a su compañero/a todas las cosas que hizo. Su compañero/a le va a preguntar dónde hizo la compra, a quién invitó, qué sirvió, y si lo pasaron bien (*had fun*). Después cambien de papel.

EN DIRECTO

To express that you had a good time:

Lo pasamos muy bien.

Fue estupendo.

Estuvo muy divertido.

EMPANADAS
salteñas bolivianas

MASA

6 tazas de harina	6 cucharadas de manteca
2 yemas de huevo	$\frac{1}{2}$ taza de leche
1 cucharada de azúcar	$1\frac{1}{2}$ tazas de agua tibia
1 cucharadita de sal	

Prepare la masa el día anterior. Mezcle todos los ingredientes para la masa. Amase bastante y envuelva la masa en una servilleta húmeda. Déjela en el refrigerador toda la noche.

RELLENO

3 cucharadas de manteca	1 taza de cebolla blanca picada
1 taza de cebolla verde picada	$1\frac{1}{2}$ cucharada de gelatina sin sabor disuelta en $\frac{1}{2}$ taza de agua
$\frac{1}{2}$ taza de ají colorado	sal y azúcar al gusto
comino y orégano al gusto	1 libra de carne de res picada
1 taza de arvejas cocinadas	1 taza de papas a medio cocinar en cubitos
$\frac{1}{2}$ taza de pasas	2 huevos duros, cortados
6 aceitunas negras, cortadas y sin pepa	

Prepare el relleno también el día anterior. Fría la cebolla en la manteca y agregue el ají, la sal, el azúcar, el comino y el orégano. Añada la carne y cocínela ligeramente. Retire el relleno del fuego y deje que se enfríe un poco. Añada la gelatina, las arvejas y la papa. Deje el relleno en el refrigerador toda la noche.

Para hacer las empanadas, haga unos círculos con la masa de 7 a 10 centímetros de diámetro y $\frac{1}{4}$ centímetro de grosor. Ponga encima de cada círculo un poco del relleno y añádale las pasas, el huevo duro y las aceitunas. Doble y haga pequeños pliegues en el borde de la masa para que no se salga el relleno. Pase un poco de leche o de huevo batido por el borde. Ponga las empanadas sobre moldes de horno enharinados. Póngales un poco de leche o huevo por encima a cada una para que tomen color.

Hornear a 400 grados por 20 a 30 minutos.

Follow-up for recipe. You may explain that *empanadas* are very popular in the Hispanic world and that there are variations according to the country. You may also talk about the great variety of *ajíes/chiles* (for example, *ají colorado*) and that *colorado* is a synonym of *rojo*.

Introduce some of the new words in the recipe, using visuals and comprehensible input: *masa, tibio, relleno, sabor,* and so on. For example: *El agua no debe estar ni caliente ni fría; debe estar tibia.*

LENGUA

Al dar una receta en español, normalmente se usan mandatos (**cocine el arroz, añada la sal**), la construcción **se + verbo** (**se cocina el arroz, se añade la sal**), o el infinitivo (**cocinar el arroz, añadir la sal**).

Follow-up for 10-8. Have students present few of their own recipes.

2 **10-8 Mi receta favorita.** Escojan una receta simple. Escriban los ingredientes y después explíquenle a otra pareja cómo se prepara el plato. Las siguientes palabras pueden facilitarles la explicación: **batir** (*to beat*), **hervir** (**ie**) (*to boil*), **freír** (**i**) (*to fry*), **cortar** (*to cut*).

AUDIO **10-9 Una cena perfecta.** You will listen to a married couple talking about their plans for dinner tonight. Before you listen, make a list of four ingredients you would need to prepare a salad and an entrée.

ensalada ——————————————————
plato principal ——————————————————

Now, pay attention to the general idea of what is said. Then, as you listen mark the appropriate ending to each statement.

1. Rodolfo es...
   __X__ un buen cocinero.
   _____ muy perezoso.
   __X__ el esposo de Manuela.
2. Manuela va a...
   _____ cocinar ceviche.
   __X__ poner la mesa.
   _____ llamar a los invitados.
3. Rodolfo va a comprar...
   __X__ pescado y maíz.
   _____ limón y camarones.
   _____ espinacas y aguacates.
4. Manuela tiene...
   _____ todos los ingredientes.
   _____ muchos vegetales y frutas.
   __X__ casi todos los ingredientes.

Audioscript for 10-9:
MANUELA: Rodolfo, esta noche tenemos invitados. Como ellos son americanos, quiero que prepares un ceviche de pescado al estilo del Hotel Colón de Quito. ¿Qué te parece?
RODOLFO: Lo que tú digas, Manuela. Tú sabes que a mí me gusta cocinar y, según tú, soy un cocinero excelente. Dime, ¿tenemos todos los ingredientes para el ceviche?
MANUELA: Sí, creo que tenemos todo. Sólo hay que comprar el pescado porque en casa tenemos todo lo demás: cebollas, tomates, limón, lechuga.
RODOLFO: ¿Tenemos maíz?
MANUELA: ¡Ay! No, no tenemos. ¿Puedes comprar maíz, por favor?
RODOLFO: Muy bien. Entonces tú pones la mesa y yo hago todo lo demás.
MANUELA: ¡Qué maravilloso es no tener que trabajar ni cocinar cuando hay invitados!
RODOLFO: Bueno, me voy al supermercado. Si se te ocurre otra cosa me llamas al celular.
MANUELA: Gracias, Rodolfo.

Antes de seguir...

The indicative and the subjunctive

In previous lessons, you used the indicative mood to state facts (what is happening, what regularly happens, or what has happened) and to talk about what you are certain will occur. Thus, in the sentence *Yo sé que Pepe siempre come en ese restaurante*, the speaker is stating the facts as he or she knows them to be true: Pepe always eats at that restaurant. The indicative is used to talk about actions, events, or states the speaker sees as real.

In this chapter, you will learn about the subjunctive, a verbal mood used for anticipated or hypothetical actions, events, or states. You already know and have used two forms of the subjunctive when you practiced the formal commands in *Lección 9*. With a command, you are trying to impose your will on someone else since you are expressing what you want that person to do: *Venga temprano* is equivalent to saying *Quiero que venga temprano*. Note that the arrival has not happened yet, in fact, it may not happen at all; therefore, it is an unrealized action and the subjunctive is needed.

In this chapter, you will learn about the use of the subjunctive to talk about what you want, hope, or doubt will happen.

1. The present subjunctive

Suggestion. Mention that English also has the subjunctive, although it is not so highly developed as in Spanish: It is important that you be on time. It is urgent that he pay the bill.

Give examples of the indicative and the subjunctive in context: *Yo cocino todos los días. Generalmente preparo comida boliviana. Esta noche mi esposo/a quiere que cocine comida española y que prepare una paella.* As you speak, write the indicative verb forms on the board. When you say the subjunctive verb forms, cross out the final *-o* and write the appropriate ending. Point out the similarity of the *usted* command and the subjunctive.

VÍNCULOS

To practice the present subjunctive
- SAM-OneKey: WB: 10-6, 10-7 /
  LM: 10-27, 10-28
- Companion Website: AP 10-2
- *Gramática viva:* Grammar Points 35 and 36: Present subjunctive: irregular verbs; Present subjunctive: regular verbs
- IRCD: Chapter 10; pg. 365

Follow-up. After going over the dialog, ask questions to check comprehension. Personalize: *¿Cuándo va Ud. al supermercado? ¿A qué supermercado va? ¿Le gusta ir? ¿Qué compra Ud. generalmente?* Then, have students role-play the dialog. Encourage them to ask for other vegetables and meats.

Suggestion. Review the present tense of irregular verbs. Use contextually and contrast with the subjunctive in appropriate situations: *Cuando llego a mi casa después del supermercado, yo pongo las verduras en la cocina, pero hoy tenemos invitados y mi esposo/a quiere que las ponga en el refrigerador. Yo deseo salir después, pero mi esposo/a no quiere que salga. Necesita que lo/la ayude a cocinar.*

SR. MENA: ¿Qué traigo del supermercado?

SRA. MENA: Necesito que traigas un kilo de camarones frescos y también lechuga y tomate para la ensalada.

SR. MENA: ¿Eso es todo?

SRA. MENA: Sí, y espero que vuelvas rápido y que me puedas ayudar. Tengo mil cosas que hacer.

■ To form the present subjunctive, use the **yo** form of the present indicative, drop the final **-o,** and add the subjunctive ending. Notice that as with **usted/ ustedes** commands, -ar verbs change the -a to -e, while -er and -ir verbs change the e and the i to **a.**

	HABLAR	**COMER**	**VIVIR**
yo	habl**e**	com**a**	viv**a**
tú	habl**es**	com**as**	viv**as**
Ud., él, ella	habl**e**	com**a**	viv**a**
nosotros/as	habl**emos**	com**amos**	viv**amos**
vosotros/as	habl**éis**	com**áis**	viv**áis**
Uds., ellos/as	habl**en**	com**an**	viv**an**

■ The present subjunctive of the following verbs with irregular indicative **yo** forms is as follows:

conocer:	conozca, conozcas...	salir:	salga, salgas...
decir:	diga, digas...	tener:	tenga, tengas...
hacer:	haga, hagas...	traer:	traiga, traigas...
oír:	oiga, oigas...	venir:	venga, vengas...
poner:	ponga, pongas...	ver:	vea, veas...

■ The present subjunctive of **hay** is **haya**. The following verbs also have irregular subjunctive forms:

ir:	**vaya, vayas...**	saber:	**sepa, sepas...**
ser:	**sea, seas...**		

■ Stem-changing **-ar** and **-er** verbs follow the same pattern as the present indicative.

pensar: **piense, pienses, piense, pensemos, penséis, piensen**
volver: **vuelva, vuelvas, vuelva, volvamos, volváis, vuelvan**

■ Stem-changing **-ir** verbs follow the same pattern as the present indicative but have an additional change in the **nosotros** and **vosotros** forms.

preferir: **prefiera, prefieras, prefiera, prefiramos, prefiráis, prefieran**
dormir: **duerma, duermas, duerma, durmamos, durmáis, duerman**

■ Verbs ending in **-car, -gar, -ger, -zar,** and **-guir** have spelling changes.

sacar: **saque, saques, saque, saquemos, saquéis, saquen**
jugar: **juegue, juegues, juegue, juguemos, juguéis, jueguen**
recoger: **recoja, recojas, recoja, recojamos, recojáis, recojan**
almorzar: **almuerce, almuerces, almuerce, almorcemos, almorcéis, almuercen**
seguir: **siga, sigas, siga, sigamos, sigáis, sigan**

LENGUA

Remember that you have seen these same orthographic changes in the formal commands:
Saque los platos.
No jueguen ahora.

¿Qué dice usted?

10-10 En la cocina. Escoja la forma verbal correcta para completar lo que le dice un chef a su nuevo asistente.

1. Yo sé que tú __quieres__ (quieres, quieras) ser un buen cocinero.
2. El secreto de la buena cocina __es__ (es, sea) usar ingredientes de primera calidad.
3. Debes saber que nosotros __compramos__ (compramos, compremos) vegetales frescos todos los días.
4. Quiero que tú __estés__ (estás, estés) aquí temprano para lavar y preparar los vegetales.
5. Los primeros días quiero que __mires__ (miras, mires) cómo cortan los vegetales para aprender a hacerlo bien.
6. Aquí traen los mariscos y el pescado fresco por la mañana, y quiero que __llegues__ (llegas, llegues) antes de las 10 para recibir el pescado y enseñarte a reconocerlo.

G **10-11 Excursión a las islas Galápagos. Primera fase.** Su clase está planeando una excursión a las islas Galápagos, en Ecuador. Primero, busquen en Internet la siguiente información sobre estas islas y coméntenla entre ustedes.

1. localización
2. clima
3. lugares de interés
4. tipo de alojamiento (*accomodation*)
5. tipo de transporte para llegar allí

Segunda fase. Ahora escriban una lista de todas las cosas que hay que hacer para preparar la excursión.

MODELO: E1: Hay que reservar los pasajes.
                    E2: Sí, y necesitamos comprar unas mochilas.

Tercera fase. Por último, decidan qué quieren ustedes que haga cada persona de su grupo y compártanlo con la clase.

MODELO: reservar los pasajes
                    Queremos que Juan reserve los pasajes

2. Subjunctive to express wishes and hope

■ Notice in the examples below that there are two clauses, each with a different subject. When the verb of the main clause expresses a wish or hope, use a subjunctive verb form in the dependent clause.

MAIN CLAUSE	DEPENDENT CLAUSE
La mamá **quiere**	que Alfredo **ponga** la mesa.
The mother wants	*Alfredo to set the table.*
Yo **espero**	que él **termine** temprano.
I hope	*he finishes early.*

■ When there is only one subject, use the infinitive instead of the subjunctive.

Los niños **necesitan almorzar** temprano para ir al gimnasio.	*The children need to have lunch early to go to the gym.*
El mayor **quiere prepararse** un sándwich.	*The older one wants to make himself a sandwich.*
El menor **desea tomar** leche con galletas.	*The younger one wants to have milk and cookies.*

■ With the verb **decir,** use the subjunctive in the dependent clause when expressing a wish or an order. Use the indicative when reporting information.

Dice que los niños **duermen.** (reporting information)	*She says (that) the children are sleeping.*
Dice que los niños **duerman.** (expressing an order)	*She says (that) the children should sleep.*

Follow-up for 10-11. You may create groups of five and assign one research item to each student. Once they exchange the information they have obtained, encourage them to brainstorm on the things that they will need or they will have to do to prepare for the excursion. Recycle vocabulary of clothes and weather expressions and vocabulary of clothes: *¿Qué necesitas llevar para protegerte del sol? ¿Qué ropa es más cómoda para caminar mucho?*

VÍNCULOS

To practice the subjunctive used to express wishes and hope
● SAM-OneKey: WB: 10-8, 10-9, 10-10, 10-11 / LM: 10-29, 10-30
● Companion Website: AP 10-3
● *Gramática viva:* Grammar Points 52 and 53: Subjunctive after impersonal expressions; Subjunctive with expressions of advice and recommendation
● IRCD: Chapter 10; pg. 369

Suggestions. To clarify the change in subject, have students say and do one thing they would like to do and one thing they want a classmate to do: *Quiero cerrar la puerta. Quiero que Clara cierre la puerta.*

Point out that the construction in English "I want you to do this" has no direct parallel in Spanish and can cause confusion. Once reworded into "I want that you do this," however, it makes sense and it is similar to English constructions, such as "I hope/prefer/recommend that you do this."

Ask students to tell you what they want you to do. Write *Quiero que Ud...* on the board.

Act like a small child and have the students be your parents. You say *No quiero comer;* students respond *Quiero (Espero) que comas.* Other examples: *No quiero salir, correr, escuchar, trabajar, practicar, bañarme, ir, acostarme, venir, sentarme.* You may also use direct and indirect objects in your sentences, for which students must supply the pronouns in their response: *No quiero comer este taco. Quiero que lo comas.*

■ Some common verbs that express want and hope are **desear, esperar, necesitar, preferir,** and **querer.**

> Quieren/Desean que **compres** mariscos.
> *They want you to buy seafood.*

Suggestions. Using visuals showing people performing various activities, give examples using the verbs *permitir* and *prohibir* followed by the subjunctive and then the infinitive: *El doctor le permite que camine. El doctor le permite caminar. Le prohíbe que juegue al béisbol. Le prohíbe jugar al béisbol.*

Ask students to list things that they would like to have happen in the future, using *ojalá: Ojalá que yo pueda ser feliz toda mi vida.*

Give examples using the present tense of *necesitar* followed by a clause with a verb in the subjunctive: *Necesito que limpien la cocina. También necesito que preparen la ensalada.* Then, change *necesito* to *es necesario.* You may use a transparency with the first two sentences as a first layer, then on the second layer hide *necesito* and write *es necesario.*

■ Verbs which express an intention to influence the actions of others (**aconsejar, pedir, permitir, prohibir, recomendar**) also require the subjunctive. With these verbs, Spanish speakers often use an indirect object.

> **Les** permite que **salgan** esta noche.
> *She allows them to go out tonight.*

■ The expression **ojalá (que)** (*I/we hope*), which comes from Arabic, originally meaning *May Allah grant that . . .* , is always followed by the subjunctive.

> Ojalá (que) ellos **vengan** temprano.
> *I hope they will come early.*
>
> Ojalá (que) **puedas** ir al supermercado.
> *I hope you can go to the supermarket.*

■ You may also try to impose your will or express your influence, wishes, and hope through some impersonal expressions such as **es necesario, es importante, es bueno,** and **es mejor.**

> Es necesario que ellos **vengan** temprano.
> *It is necessary that they come early.*
>
> Es mejor que **comas** pescado.
> *It is better that you eat fish.*

■ If you are not addressing or speaking about someone in particular, use the infinitive.

> Es mejor **comer** pescado.
> *It is better to eat fish.*

¿Qué dice usted?

Answers for 10-12. Answers may vary.

❷ 10-12 Comentarios y deseos. El Club de Español va a dar una fiesta mañana. Marque los comentarios o deseos de los estudiantes.

1. ___X___ Esperamos que la fiesta empiece puntualmente.
2. _____ Ojalá que no sirvan comida.
3. ___X___ Esperamos que pongan música ecuatoriana.
4. _____ Queremos que también inviten a los estudiantes de francés.
5. _____ Ojalá que la fiesta termine temprano.
6. ___X___ Deseamos que los profesores traigan mucha comida.

❷ 10-13 Una fiesta de aniversario. Primera fase. Los hijos de los señores Sánchez están muy ocupados preparando la fiesta de aniversario de sus padres, quienes cumplen cincuenta años de casados. ¿Qué quiere, necesita o espera la persona responsable de la fiesta que hagan estas personas?

Pedro, Carlos y Mirta

Ana

César

Lola

Jorge y Roberto

Hilda y Ramiro

② **Segunda fase.** Aparte de la decoración y la comida, ¿qué es importante, necesario o imprescindible que los hijos hagan para hacer felices a sus padres? Escriban una lista de cuatro cosas más como mínimo.

② **10-14 Unos invitados para el fin de semana.** Prepare una lista de las cosas que usted necesita hacer y otra lista con lo que espera que hagan sus invitados. Después, compare sus listas con las de un/a compañero/a.

MODELO: E1: Necesito limpiar la sala el viernes.
E2: Yo también necesito limpiarla./Yo no, la sala está limpia. Yo necesito comprar leche y jugo.
E1: Espero que mis invitados lleguen temprano.
E2: Y yo espero que a mis invitados les gusten los platos que voy a servir.

LO QUE USTED NECESITA HACER

_____

_____

_____

_____

LO QUE ESPERA QUE HAGAN SUS INVITADOS

_____

_____

_____

_____

Suggestion for 10-14: Encourage students to use impersonal expressions in the exchange:
E1: *Necesito poner la mesa.*
E2: *Sí, es mejor poner/que pongas la mesa temprano.*

10-15 Un trabajo complicado. Primera fase. Usted trabaja en un supermercado. Marque las actividades que se prohíben, las que se permiten y las que se recomiendan durante las horas de trabajo.

	SE PROHÍBE	SE PERMITE	SE RECOMIENDA
1. fumar			
2. comer frutas			
3. hablar por teléfono			
4. descansar 15 minutos			
5. ayudar a los clientes a encontrar los productos			
6. usar el baño			

2 Segunda fase. Ustedes descubrieron que ambos/as trabajan en supermercados. Por eso, cada uno/a de ustedes tiene curiosidad por saber cuáles son las obligaciones y condiciones de trabajo del/de la otro/a. Háganse preguntas usando los verbos **pedir, prohibir, permitir, decir, recomendar.**

MODELO: E1: ¿Qué te prohíbe tu jefe en el trabajo?
E2: Me prohíbe que hable por teléfono con mis amigos.
E1: ¿Qué te recomiendan tus compañeros de trabajo?
E2: Me recomiendan que sea amable con los clientes.

1. llevar un uniforme limpio
2. cambiar las verduras que no están frescas
3. usar el celular mientras trabajo
4. llegar temprano al trabajo
5. revisar las fechas de la leche y los quesos
6. atender a los clientes en la caja
7. saber dónde están los diferentes productos
8. …

Warm-up for 10-16. Encourage students to use their imagination. Explain that you are opening the restaurant and that you have to decide what silverware (*cubiertos*) you should buy (clarify the meaning of *cubiertos* by saying *cuchillos, tenedores, cucharas*) and wether you should use authentic pottery or normal plates. Ask them for ideas about the decorations, the publicity, the music, etc. Write *Es importante/bueno/mejor que…* on the board and ask for students' suggestions. Divide the class in small groups to offer you advice.

G 10-16 Consejos y sugerencias. Usted está organizando un nuevo restaurante de comida boliviana y ecuatoriana, y tiene algunos problemas en ciertas áreas. Explíqueles a dos de sus compañeros/as cuáles son los problemas. Ellos/as deben decirle qué debe hacer.

MODELO: cocineros
E1: Los cocineros que tengo no son nativos de esos países.
E2: Es importante que pongas anuncios en los periódicos para conseguir cocineros nativos.
E3: Y también es bueno que algunos camareros sean de Ecuador o de Bolivia.

1. productos de comida
2. cervezas y otras bebidas
3. decoración del lugar
4. música ambiental
5. ingredientes para las empanadas salteñas
6. publicidad

SITUACIONES

Role A. You are unable to go to the market this week because you are sick (*enfermo/a*). Call a friend to explain your predicament, and ask him/her to go for you. Answer his/her questions and a) say what you need him/her to buy for you (chicken, some vegetables, fruit, bread, and so on), b) give him advice about the shops where he/she can get those items, c) explain that you will pay him/her when he/she comes to your house, and d) thank him/her.

Role B. When a friend of yours calls to ask for a favor, a) say that you will be happy to do his/her shopping, and b) ask what he/she needs. After writing down the list, say that it is important that he/she rest and that you will be at his/her house around 11:00 a.m.

3. Subjunctive with verbs and expressions of doubt

- When the verb in the main clause expresses doubt or uncertainty, use a subjunctive verb form in the dependent clause.

    Dudo que **vendan** pescado fresco.   *I doubt (that) they sell fresh fish.*

- When the verbs **creer** and **pensar** are used in the negative and doubt is implied, the subjunctive is used. In questions with these verbs, the subjunctive may be used to express uncertainty or to anticipate a negative response. If the question simply seeks information, use the indicative.

    SUBJUNCTIVE

    Hace sol; no creo que **llueva** hoy.   *It is sunny out; I do not think it will rain.*

    ¿Crees que **haga** frío en La Paz?   *Do you think it will be cold in La Paz? (I am not sure.)*

    INDICATIVE

    ¿Crees que **hace** frío en La Paz?   *Do you think it is/will be cold in La Paz? (Should I wear a coat?)*

- Use the subjunctive with impersonal expressions that denote doubt or uncertainty, such as **es dudoso que, es difícil que, es probable que,** and **es posible que.**

    Es dudoso que **encontremos** frutas tropicales allí.   *It is doubtful that we will find tropical fruits there.*
    Es posible que **vendan** uvas.   *It is possible that they sell grapes.*

VÍNCULOS

To practice the subjunctive with verbs and expressions of doubt
- SAM-OneKey: WB: 10-12, 10-13, 10-14 / LM: 10-31, 10-32, 10-33
- Companion Website: AP 10-4
- *Gramática viva:* Grammar Point 55: Subjunctive with expressions of opinion or doubt

Suggestions. Tell students about important people that are friends of yours and the fabulous trips you take. Students react by using *Dudo que...*

Make statements about personalities, activities, the university, and so on to elicit opinions from students: *La comida de la cafetería es excelente.* Students answer, *Sí, creo que...* or *Dudo que...*

Give examples of impersonal expressions followed by the indicative to describe your class: *Es verdad que mis alumnos hablan español. Es obvio que hablan bien. Es seguro que estudian y practican mucho.* Write the impersonal expressions either in a column on the board or on a transparency. Then give related examples of impersonal expressions followed by the subjunctive: *Es probable que estudien los domingos. Es posible que practiquen dos o tres horas todos los días.*

■ Use the indicative with impersonal expressions that denote certainty: **es cierto/verdad que, es seguro que,** and **es obvio que.**

> Es verdad/cierto que el vino **es** muy bueno.
>
> *It is true that the wine is very good.*

■ Since the expressions **tal vez** and **quizá(s)** convey uncertainty, the subjunctive is normally used.

> Tal vez
> Quizá(s) } ella **pruebe** el postre.
>
> *Perhaps she will try the dessert.*

¿Qué dice usted?

Follow-up for 10-17: Check how many students agreed or disagreed with the statements. Have them explain.

10-17 ¿Están de acuerdo? Primera fase. Lean las siguientes opiniones y marquen si están de acuerdo o no con ellas.

	Sí	No
1. Yo creo que el aceite de oliva es bueno para la salud.	_____	_____
2. Yo dudo que el yogur con frutas tenga muchas calorías.	_____	_____
3. Creo que el agua que se bebe en las ciudades de este país es muy buena.	_____	_____
4. Es posible que los dulces tengan más calorías que el queso.	_____	_____
5. Es obvio que el pescado es mejor que la carne para la salud.	_____	_____
6. No creo que la comida afecte nuestra personalidad.	_____	_____

Segunda fase. Ahora intercambien opiniones basándose en lo que marcaron en la **Primera fase.**

MODELO: E1: Yo creo que el aceite de oliva es bueno para la salud, y debemos usarlo en ensaladas y para cocinar.

E2: Tal vez/Quizá(s) sea mejor que otros aceites, pero debemos usar poco.

10-18 Opiniones. Intercambien opiniones sobre los siguientes temas. Después, comparen sus opiniones con las de otros/as compañeros/as y compartan el resultado con la clase. Pueden usar algunas de estas expresiones si lo desean.

caloría	grasa
proteína	vitamina
sano/a	peligroso/a (*dangerous*)

MODELO: la carne de cerdo

E1: Creo que una porción de carne de cerdo tiene menos grasa que un bistec.

E2: Estoy de acuerdo, pero dudo que tenga menos grasa que el pescado.

1. las bebidas alcohólicas
2. el pescado y los camarones
3. las frutas y las verduras
4. la vida sedentaria

EN DIRECTO

To report agreement:

Todos creemos/pensamos que…

Nosotros estamos de acuerdo con que…

To report different opinions:

No hay consenso entre nosotros/ellos. Unos piensan que…, otros creen que…

2 **10-19 Una cena con alguien famoso. Primera fase.** Ustedes ganaron un concurso, y el premio es una cena con la persona que ustedes admiran más. Escojan a la persona admirada y después hagan una lista de tres cosas que esperan que pasen y tres cosas que dudan que pasen en la cena. Expliquen por qué.

MODELO: Persona admirada: Marc Anthony
              E1: Esperamos que Marc Anthony pague la cena porque él tiene
                   mucho dinero.
              E2: Dudo que Marc Anthony cante durante la cena porque no va a
                   querer que lo reconozcan.

Segunda fase. Reúnanse con otra pareja y explíquenle a quién escogieron ustedes y por qué. Infórmenle sobre sus esperanzas (*hopes*) y dudas con respecto a la situación. Comenten si están de acuerdo o no con lo que dicen sus compañeros/as.

SITUACIONES

You have to give a class presentation about food from Ecuador, Bolivia or Paraguay. Go to your local market, find the section where Hispanic foods are sold or search for information on the Internet. During the next class meeting, interview a classmate about the following topics. Then exchange roles.

- Three items of produce or products typical of the country

- Prices of these produce items or products if bought in the United States

- The recipe of a dish in which the items are used, including ingredients and manner of preparation

- Your main source of information

EN DIRECTO

To show interest in someone else's work:

¿Cómo va tu presentación/ proyecto/trabajo?

¿Cómo vas con…?

¡Genial!

MOSAICS

VÍNCULOS

For materials related to the Mosaicos section, see
- SAM-OneKey: WB: 10-15, 10-16, 10-17, 10-18, 10-19, 10-20 / LM: 10-34

 ## Escuchar

Recording detail

Sometimes you need to recognize specific information from a list of various possibilities. For example, if you have a list of all the groceries that you usually buy, but somebody tells you specifically what to buy, you write a check mark only next to those you are being told to buy and disregard the others.

Antes de escuchar

10-20 ¡Un lío! (*A mess*). In **10-21,** you will listen to a list of groceries that Andrea, Carolina, Roberto, and Darío bought. Before you listen, write down a list of the groceries you regularly buy, and those you buy on special occasions.

regularmente _____

en ocasiones especiales _____

A escuchar

Audioscript for 10-21.

Andrea compró pollo, zanahoria, aguacates, papas y camarones.
Carolina compró ajos, cebollas, espinacas, maíz y pollo.
Roberto compró langosta, sal, pimienta y aguacates.
Darío compró jamón, papas, aderezo, y pimientos verdes.
Todos compraron carne molida.

AUDIO **10-21.** Now, listen to the list of groceries that Andrea, Carolina, Roberto and Darío bought. As you listen, mark A, C, R or D next to each product to identify who bought what.

__D__	aderezo	_____	cerdo	_____	pepinos
__A, R__	aguacates	__C__	espinacas	__R__	pimienta
__C__	ajos	__D__	jamón	__D__	pimientos verdes
__A__	camarones	__R__	langosta	__A, C__	pollo
__A, C, R, D__	carne molida	__C__	maíz	__R__	sal
__C__	cebollas	__A, D__	papas	__A__	zanahorias

Después de escuchar

❷ **10-22 ¿Y usted?** With a classmate, share your answers to the following questions.

1. ¿Cuál es su plato favorito?
2. ¿Qué productos compra usted para preparar su plato favorito?
3. ¿Con quién comparte generalmente su plato favorito y por qué?

Antes de escuchar

10-23 Productos típicos. In **10-24,** you will listen to a conversation between Isabel and Raimundo regarding the origin of various products. Before you listen, write down the Spanish names of four fruits and four vegetables you like.

Frutas: _____

Vegetales: _____

A escuchar

 10-24. Now, listen to the conversation between Isabel y Raimundo. As you listen, mark all products that are originally from America (**A**) and those that are not (**NA**).

__A__ aguacate	__A__ chocolate	__A__ papa
__NA__ arroz	__A__ maíz	__NA__ té
__NA__ café	__NA__ naranja	__A__ tomate

Después de escuchar

10-25 ¿Y usted? With a classmate, share your answers to the following questions.

1. ¿Cuáles son las frutas y vegetales típicos de América que le gustan? ¿Cuáles no le gustan?
2. ¿Puede usted conseguir esos productos siempre en su ciudad? ¿Dónde los compra? ¿Son caros o baratos?
3. ¿Cuándo come usted estos productos? ¿Cómo los come: crudos, cocinados, fritos, en ensaladas, en sopas, etc.?

Conversar

Antes de conversar

10-26 ¿Más o menos saludable? Primera fase. Clasifiquen los siguientes productos o alimentos en la columna correspondiente, según su opinión.

los camarones	las papas	el pollo
las espinacas	el vino	el queso
el jamón	la fruta	la carne de res
las legumbres	el helado	las bebidas con gas
la cerveza	el pan blanco	las bebidas alcohólicas

MÁS SALUDABLES:	MENOS SALUDABLES:
las espinacas, las legumbres	el jamón, el queso
las papas, los camarones	el helado, las bebidas con gas
la fruta, la carne de res	la cerveza
el pollo	el pan blanco
el vino	las bebidas alcohólicas

Audioscript for 10-24:

RAIMUNDO: ¿Dices que en Europa no conocían las papas en el siglo XVI? ¡Eso es imposible!

ISABEL: Sí, es verdad. No las conocían. Las papas son originarias de América y como no había contacto entre los dos continentes, los europeos no sabían que existían.

RAIMUNDO: Pues yo no tenía ni idea. ¿Y el arroz?

ISABEL: No, el arroz no es de este continente, pero el tomate sí es de aquí.

RAIMUNDO: ¡No me digas, Isabel! ¿Y qué otros productos no conocían en Europa?

ISABEL: Bueno, pues no conocían el maíz.

RAIMUNDO: Es difícil pensar que cosas tan comunes como la papa, el tomate y el maíz no existían en aquella época en Europa.

ISABEL: Ni tampoco el chocolate.

RAIMUNDO: ¡Ah, por favor, estás exagerando! ¿El chocolate no es europeo?

ISABEL: No, no lo es y por mucho tiempo los españoles eran los únicos que tenían el secreto de la preparación del chocolate, y así lo podían exportar a otros países.

RAIMUNDO: Ahora me vas a decir que el café y el té son también americanos.

ISABEL: No, el café es originario de África y el té de la China.

RAIMUNDO: ¿Y el aguacate y las naranjas?

ISABEL: El aguacate es americano. Las naranjas no. Los árabes las llevaron a España y de allí pasaron a América.

RAIMUNDO: Bueno, muchas gracias por la lección. He aprendido mucho hoy.

Possible answers for 10-26, Primera fase. Answers may vary. Accept any response that is well supported.

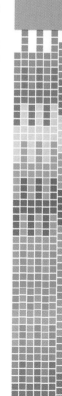

G **Segunda fase.** Escriban en la tabla los productos o alimentos de la **Primera fase** que en general producen los siguientes efectos.

ENGORDAN	AYUDAN A ADELGAZAR	DAN ENERGÍA	AUMENTAN EL COLESTEROL

A conversar

G **10-27 ¿Qué hábitos de comida tienes?** Averigüen las preferencias de comida de los miembros del grupo en las siguientes categorías. Después, sumen los números en las columnas para saber qué comida les gusta más y cuál les gusta menos.

MODELO: los mariscos
E1: ¿Te gustan los mariscos?
E2: Me encantan. ¿Y a ti?
E1: A mí no me gustan.

ALIMENTO	ENCANTAR	GUSTAR MUCHO	GUSTAR	NO GUSTAR
la fruta				
las verduras				
la carne				
los mariscos				
los productos lácteos				
los dulces				

Después de conversar

G **10-28 Reflexiones.** Comparen los resultados de **10-27** para determinar las categorías de alimentos que se consumen más en la clase. Luego, respondan a estas preguntas.

1. ¿Qué tipos de comida se comen más en su clase?
2. En general, ¿ustedes se alimentan bien o mal? ¿Por qué?
3. ¿Deben ustedes mejorar su dieta? ¿Qué es importante que hagan?

Antes de conversar

2 **10-29 ¡A pasarlo bien!** Determinen si las siguientes son preocupaciones de los organizadores (**O**) de una fiesta, de los invitados (**I**) o de ambos (**A**).

1. __A__ el grado de formalidad de la fiesta
2. __O__ hacer la lista de invitados
3. __A__ la ropa que se va a llevar
4. __O__ la música que se va a tocar

5. ___0___ la comida que se va a servir
6. ___0___ el horario de la fiesta
7. ___0___ la limpieza y la decoración
8. ___I___ el transporte
9. ___A___ el permiso o la prohibición de bebidas alcohólicas
10. ___I___ dar disculpas por no poder ir

Suggestion for 10-30. If circumstances allow, you may wish to plan a real end-of-the-term party/gathering. If so, explain to students that all plans will be voted and that the best two ones will be chosen. Therefore, give each group the opportunity to present their plan in the most attractive way possible. They may do an electronic presentation, for example.

A conversar

G 10-30 Mil decisiones. Éste es un momento especial del año y ustedes van a dar una fiesta diferente de otras. Va a ser una fiesta con comida nutritiva y saludable. Preparen un plan y traten de convencer al resto de la clase sobre su plan con buenas ideas y material visual si es necesario.

1. el tipo de fiesta que van a dar (formal o informal), el lugar, la fecha y la hora
2. los invitados. ¿A quiénes van a invitar? ¿Cuántas personas son?
3. la comida, las bebidas, etc. ¿Qué comida se va a servir? ¿Es necesario que haya algo para los vegetarianos? ¿Y para las personas que no beben alcohol?
4. las actividades, la música. ¿Cómo van a divertirse? ¿Es importante que haya juegos para las personas que no bailan?

EN DIRECTO

To influence someone's decision:
Es mejor/menos dañino (*harmful*) que... + subjuntivo
¿No te/le(s) parece más saludable que + subjuntivo...?
¿Qué te/le(s) parece si + indicativo...?

Después de conversar

G 10-31 Nuestra votación. Ahora discutan cuál es el plan presentado por los grupos durante la actividad **10-30** que ustedes van a escoger. Explíquenle a la clase por qué.

Leer

In *Lección 10*, you will review some previous strategies and will discover new meanings by identifying words that are related semantically (in meaning) or linguistically (in grammatical form). This strategy may also help you expand your vocabulary.

Guía de prelectura

Use the cues provided by the visuals, the headline, and the subheading in activity **10-34,** and your personal knowledge to answer the following questions:

1. What information will you likely find in this article?
   a. A brand new diet born in the Mediterranean countries
      Yes (No)
   b. A diet that the Mediterranean peoples have followed for centuries
      (Yes) No
   c. A balanced diet based on the foods grown or produced in the Mediterranean countries
      (Yes) No
   d. The effect of food and life style on the lives of Mediterranean peoples
      (Yes) No

EN DIRECTO

To explain the reason behind a decision:
Votamos por el plan... porque...
Nos gustó/convenció el plan... por el valor nutritivo de la comida/el costo/la variedad de..., etc.
Nuestra decisión se basa en lo siguiente: ...

Answers for Guía de prelectura. Students may have a difference of opinion. Therefore, accept any response that is logically supported.

2. What helped you answer question 1? Circle the corresponding letter.
   (a.) The headline, subheading and photo
   b. Only the visuals in the text
   (c.) My personal knowledge of diets

3. Now, can you hypothesize about some content of the text? Anticipate the main ideas of the text. Mark with a circle all that may apply.
   (a.) Health quality and longevity are dependent on people's eating habits and life style.
   (b.) Certain produce grown in the Mediterranean countries helps people maintain a balanced diet.
   (c.) Diets that are rich in carbohydrates, fruit, white meats, and grains are healthful.
   (d.) Certain produce and foods help prevent, among others, some heart-related diseases that kill millions in other parts of the world.
   (e.) A healthy life is more than the food people eat. It is also a lifestyle.

Antes de leer

Answers for 10-32. Answers may vary. Accept any response that is logically supported.

Possible answers: Mediterráneo: Más: 1, 2, 4, 5, 6, 8 Igual: 6 Nuestro país: Más: 3

(G) 10-32 Preparación. Considerando el clima de cada región, indiquen si los siguientes alimentos se consumen más (+) o igual (=) en el Mediterráneo o en su país.

	MEDITERRÁNEO	NUESTRO PAÍS
1. el aceite de oliva	+	
2. las frutas	+	
3. el pan		+
4. las carnes blancas	+	
5. los frutos secos	+	
6. el vino	+	
7. las verduras	=	=
8. el pescado	+	

Possible answers for 10-33. Answers may vary. Accept any response that is logically supported.

(2) 10-33 Hábitos y comidas saludables. ¿Qué alimentos y actividades son saludables para el organismo humano? Marquen los que correspondan, según ustedes.

1. _____ el pan y las pastas
2. _____ caminar al aire libre
3. _____ las legumbres
4. _____ la leche sin grasa
5. _____ beber alcohol
6. _____ las verduras
7. _____ la crema de leche
8. _____ tomar vino en la cena
9. _____ las carnes rojas
10. _____ los pescados y mariscos

A leer

10-34 Primera mirada. Lea el siguiente artículo sobre una dieta y, luego, siga las instrucciones.

La dieta mediterránea: ¿una nueva moda o un nuevo modo de vivir?

Los europeos que viven en las costas del mediterráneo tienen una calidad de vida mejor que en muchos otros países del mundo, viven más años y tienen mejor salud. La explicación de este fenómeno, según los expertos, está en la dieta mediterránea.

La dieta del Mediterráneo se basa en alimentos ricos en hidratos de carbono como el pan y la pasta, el aceite de oliva, moderadas cantidades de vino durante las comidas, verduras, vegetales, frutas, frutos secos y legumbres, que le dan al organismo humano fibra y antioxidantes. Además, se consumen menos carnes rojas y grasas animales y mayor cantidad de carnes blancas y pescado, productos lácteos y huevos, de donde se obtienen las proteínas.

¿Por qué se la considera una dieta saludable?

Varios estudios realizados en Grecia sabrayaron la eficacia de esta dieta. Los científicos observaron que los habitantes del Mediterráneo sufrían menos de enfermedades cardiovasculares, arteriosclerosis y enfermedades degenerativas. Por eso, tenían una expectativa de vida superior a la de las personas de otras regiones del globo.

Así entre 1958 y 1964, se estudiaron los hábitos dietéticos de siete países, cuatro no mediterráneos: Estados Unidos, Japón, Finlandia y Holanda, y tres mediterráneos: Yugoslavia, Italia y Grecia.

¿En qué consiste la dieta mediterránea?

Los expertos observaron que la dieta de los países del Mediterráneo tenía ciertas características comunes: gran consumo de pescado y carnes blancas, cereales y legumbres, frutas y verduras, poca carne roja, consumo moderado de vino con el almuerzo o la cena, además del uso del aceite de oliva para cocinar. Todo lo anterior coincidía con una baja incidencia de enfermedades coronarias y menos colesterol entre los habitantes de estos países en comparación con los de otros.

Una dieta y un estilo de vida

Aunque el clima, los cultivos y la comida varían de región a región en el mundo, es posible construir una pirámide de alimentos que incluya los nutrientes necesarios para una buena alimentación.

Los estudios y los expertos concluyen que para mantener una buena nutrición y una vida sana nuestra dieta debe incluir lo siguiente:

- muchas verduras y cereales, pan y papas
- fruta fresca
- legumbres al menos dos veces a la semana
- alimentos frescos de temporada
- aceite de oliva
- leche, yogures y quesos bajos en grasa para obtener calcio
- pescado tres o cuatro veces por semana
- carne sin grasa dos o tres veces por semana y carnes rojas una vez al mes
- poca sal, pero condimentos como el ajo, la cebolla, el vinagre, el limón o las hierbas aromáticas
- unos dos litros de agua al día
- pocos dulces
- poco o nada de alcohol, excepto el vino a la hora de las comidas
- caminar y hacer ejercicio al aire libre
- dormir unas siete u ocho horas

Answers for 10-34. Cierto: 1, 2, 6, 7, 10
Falso: 3. *alimentos ricos en hidratos de carbono*, 4. *obtiene proteínas de las carne blancas y pescado, productos lácteos y huevos*, 5. *pocas cantidades*, 8. *en cualquier lugar del mundo*, 9. *alimentación y actividad física al aire libre*

Según el contenido del artículo, ¿son las siguientes afirmaciones ciertas (**C**) o falsas (**F**)? Si la afirmación es falsa, dé la información correcta.

1. _____ El artículo afirma que la alimentación mediterránea es más sana para el cuerpo humano que la de otros lugares del mundo.
2. _____ La dieta mediterránea prolonga la vida las personas.
3. _____ Los seguidores de esta dieta deben eliminar los hidratos de carbono.
4. _____ Para mantenerse sana, la gente del mediterráneo evita las proteínas.
5. _____ Las carnes rojas se consumen en grandes cantidades.
6. _____ Los estudiosos afirman que esta dieta previene (*prevents*) algunas enfermedades.
7. _____ Esta dieta ayuda a controlar mejor el colesterol.
8. _____ Solamente en el mediterráneo se puede seguir esta dieta.
9. _____ Los expertos sugieren que para ser sanas, las personas sólo deben preocuparse de su alimentación.
10. _____ Según los científicos, una dieta equilibrada y la actividad física ayudan a tener buena salud y vivir más años.

10-35 Segunda mirada. Busque en el artículo palabras que se asocien con lo siguiente.

1. hidratos de carbono: ___ pan, pasta ___
2. fibras y antioxidantes: ___ hortalizas, frutas, frutos secos, legumbres ___
3. proteínas: ___ carnes, pescado, productos lácteos, huevos ___
4. grasa: ___ aceite de oliva ___
5. algunos países mediterráneos: ___ Yugoslavia, Italia, Grecia ___
6. actividades que afectan positivamente la salud: ___ caminar, hacer ejercicio, dormir ___

10-36 Una raíz (*root*) común. Busque en el artículo los sustantivos o adjetivos asociados con los siguientes verbos. Escríbalos en la línea correspondiente.

VERBOS	SUSTANTIVOS
1. explicar:	explicación
2. nacer:	nacimiento
3. consumir:	consumo
4. incidir:	incidencia
5. enfermarse:	enfermedad
6. habitar:	habitantes
7. alimentar:	alimentación
8. nutrir:	nutrición
	ADJETIVOS
9. moderar:	moderadas/moderado
10. degenerar:	degenerativas

Después de leer

10-37 Aplicación. Una nutricionista norteamericana le pide ayuda para preparar un panfleto (*flyer*) en español. Su objetivo es convencer a la comunidad hispana de que mejore su dieta para vivir más y mejor. Ayúdela en las áreas donde tiene duda. Marque la alternativa correcta.

¿Alguna vez pensó que su dieta puede acortar su vida?

Coma bien y viva sin (1) __enfermedades__ (enfermedades/enfermos). Su
(2) __alimentación__ (alimento/alimentación) puede (3) __influir__ (influir, influencia) positiva o negativamente en su salud. Imite a los (4) __habitantes__ (habitados/habitantes) de los países mediterráneos. Consuma hidratos de carbono y vino con (5) __moderación__ (moderadas/moderación). Cocine legumbres y coma frutas y carnes blancas en cantidades ilimitadas. No olvide que las enfermedades (6) __degenerativas__ (degeneradas/degenerativas) ocurren por falta de proteínas, hidratos de carbono, calcio, etcétera. Cuide su salud y la de su familia con una buena (7) __nutrición__ (nutritiva/nutrición).

 *Escribir*

We are often confronted with situations, conflicts, and dilemmas in which our input or advice is needed or required. At work or at home, we must tell others what to do; with friends, we may act as confidants and, as such, give them advice. Overall, advice and guidance constitute social, communicative tasks that we accomplish with or for others.

In Spanish, giving advice or telling others what to do requires the following:

- special attention to the degree of intimacy or familiarity with the person you are addressing: is he/she a friend or a stranger? Are you giving directions or advice to someone younger or older than you? Is the person your superior at work or someone under your supervision? etc.

- the use of expressions that signal the degree of familiarity or intimacy with the person to whom you are talking or writing. In Spanish this is indicated, among other ways, with the personal pronouns **tú** and **usted**.

In *Lección 10* you will have the opportunity to correspond with someone and give guidance and advice.

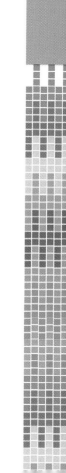

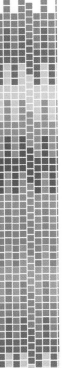

Antes de escribir

10-38 Análisis. Primera fase. Usted acaba de recibir esta carta de uno de sus buenos amigos. Léala y siga las instrucciones.

Querido/a amigo/a,

Te pido disculpas por no escribirte antes, pero te explico las razones a continuación. Desde hace tiempo, siempre me siento fatigado. Aunque estoy trabajando sólo seis horas por día, a las 3:00 de la tarde ya quiero irme a casa a descansar. Como no tengo apetito, cocino poco. Generalmente preparo algo rápido y fácil: una sopa enlatada o huevos fritos con tocino. De vez en cuando cocino una hamburguesa y, a veces, cuando me canso de la carne, tomo una buena porción de helados con galletas. ¡Ah, claro, mis amigos siempre me encuentran en los cafés de la universidad bebiendo un expreso o un capuchino! Necesito la cafeína para tener energía y hacer mi trabajo. El único problema es que el café me llena de energía y entusiasmo de día, pero no puedo dormir de noche. Las mañanas son una verdadera tortura. Generalmente me levanto tarde, falto a clases a veces y no me alcanza el tiempo para hacer mi trabajo.

Creo que debo buscar ayuda. Quisiera ver un médico, pero no tengo dinero ahora. ¿Qué te parece? Estoy pobre y enfermo.

Bueno, escríbeme para saber de ti. Te contestaré tan pronto pueda. Cuídate mucho.

Un fuerte abrazo,

Tomás

Segunda fase. Answer the following questions, based on the letter in **Primera fase.**

1. Mark with an X the likely purpose(s) of the letter:
   (a.) To restart communication with someone close after some period of silence
   (b.) To apologize and explain something
   (c.) To tell a friend how things are going
   d. To arouse compassion

2. Based on its purpose(s), is the letter effective?
   ___X___ Yes　　　　　_____ No

3. Mark some possible reasons for your response to question 2.
    a. Tomás describes in detail what he does on a daily basis.
    (b.) Tomás provides his friend with credible reasons for his silence.
    (c.) Tomás explains the cause for not writing and acknowledges he
        needs help.
    (d.) The tone of Tomás's letter is intimate.

4. Write down some expressions in the letter that signal the degree of familiarity
   or intimacy Tomás has with the person to whom he is writing.

   Querido/a, te, escríbeme para saber qué tal te va a ti. Cuídate mucho, Un fuerte abrazo.

10-39 Preparación. Primera fase. En la actividad **10-40,** usted va a responder
la carta de Tomás. Pero antes, escriba tres problemas de su amigo en la
primera columna y en la otra, algunas ideas para ayudarlo a resolver cada
problema.

PROBLEMAS DE TOMÁS:	ALGUNAS POSIBLES SOLUCIONES:
1.	1.
2.	2.
3.	3.

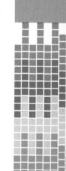

EN DIRECTO

**To express concern or
sympathy:**
Me preocupa (mucho) que…
Siento que…

**To suggest or tell a friend
what to do:**
Te recomiendo/sugiero/
aconsejo que…
Es importante/necesario/
urgente que…

Suggestions for En directo. Provide examples for _Me preocupa que…_ and _Siento que…_
followed by the subjunctive. These expressions
are presented here as a preview and to help students communicate better in Spanish. The use of
subjunctive with expressions of emotions is presented in _Lección 11._

Segunda fase. Ahora…

1. escriba algunas formas gramaticales que se usan para dar sugerencias. ¿Son
   formas personales o impersonales?

2. escriba algunas ideas (deseos, peticiones, sugerencias) que usted va a incluir
   en el párrafo de cierre (*closing*).

   MODELO: Espero que sigas mis consejos.

A escribir

10-40 Manos a la obra. Respóndale a la carta a su amigo. Use la información
que preparó en la actividad **10-39.** No se olvide de usar un tono amistoso en
su carta.

Después de escribir

10-41 Revisión. Antes de darle la carta a su compañero/a editor/a, léala y verifique lo siguiente, pensando en Tomás:

■ El contenido. ¿Le demostró interés o preocupación por su situación a Tomás? ¿Le indicó los problemas más serios, en su opinión? ¿Le dio algunas posibles soluciones?

■ La organización. ¿Tiene la carta una introducción, un cuerpo, un párrafo de cierre y una despedida?

■ La gramática. ¿Usó el vocabulario correcto, algunas expresiones de cohesión, la concordancia, el tiempo (presente, pasado), las formas para recomendar, etc.?

■ La puntuación y la ortografía. ¿Usó comas, puntos, etc. donde eran necesarios?

Finalmente, comparta su carta con su compañero/a.

ENFOQUE CULTURAL

Para pensar

¿Dónde se puede comprar artesanía en los Estados Unidos?
¿Hay algún lugar cerca de donde usted vive? ¿Qué se puede
comprar ahí? ¿Cómo son los precios? Generalmente, ¿qué tipo
de artesanía se vende: de cerámica, metal, madera, cuero?

*En estos mercados se
pueden encontrar
artículos de lana y
alpaca como suéteres,
ponchos, sombreros,
guantes, alfombras.
Uno de los mercados
más conocidos es el
mercado de Otavalo
en Ecuador.*

*Los mercados artesanales son muy comunes en
muchos países hispanos, especialmente en aquellos
con una población indígena grande, como Bolivia,
Ecuador, Paraguay.*

Para contestar

2 **Los mercados.** Respondan a las siguientes preguntas.

1. ¿Han visitado alguna vez un mercado artesanal o
   un mercado al aire libre en los Estados Unidos?
   ¿Y en el extranjero?
2. ¿Qué productos pueden comprar en un mercado
   artesanal? ¿Y en un mercado al aire libre?
3. Imagínense que ustedes van a ir al Ecuador. Digan a
   qué famoso mercado les gustaría ir y qué quisieran
   comprar.

*También en los mercados al aire libre se puede comprar
todo tipo de frutas frescas, verduras, hierbas, etc.*

G **Riqueza cultural.** En grupos de tres, comenten:

a. Las ventajas y desventajas de comprar productos en un mercado artesanal en
   vez de una tienda.
b. Las ventajas y desventajas de comprar verduras y frutas en un mercado al
   aire libre en vez de supermercados.

Luego, presenten a la clase sus conclusiones.

VÍNCULOS

For materials related to the Enfoque cultural, see
- SAM-OneKey: WB: 10-21
- IRCD: Chapter 10; pg. 386

Bolivia y Paraguay son los dos países de América del Sur que no tienen salida al mar.

Para pensar

¿Sabe usted dónde están Ecuador, Bolivia y Paraguay? ¿Sabe usted qué famoso archipiélago está frente a las costas del Ecuador? ¿Sabe usted cómo se llama el lago que comparten Bolivia y Perú? ¿Alguna vez oyó el arpa paraguaya?

Frente a las costas del Ecuador está el Archipiélago de las Islas Galápagos. Ahí se encuentran especies únicas como la famosa tortuga gigante, llamada galápago.

Expresiones ecuatorianas:

un cuaje de risa	Me dio **un cuaje de risa**.	*I laughed a lot.*
buena nota	Ella es una **buena nota**.	*She's a nice person.*
creer ocho veces	Sí, sí, te **creo ocho veces**.	*Yeah, sure, I believe you (said with disbelief).*

Bolivia comparte con Perú el lago Titicaca, el lago navegable más alto del mundo. Bolivia tien una gran riqueza minera. Es uno de los más grandes productores mundiales de estaño (tin), cobre y plata.

Muchos misioneros jesuitas fueron al Paraguay durante la época de la colonia. Ellos les enseñaron español a los indígenas, pero también aprendieron su lengua, el guaraní.

Expresiones bolivianas:

gallo tuerto	Es tan desconfiado/a como **gallo tuerto**.	*He/she distrusts everybody.*
samba canuta	Te voy a dar una **samba canuta**.	*I am going to spank you.*

Expresiones paraguayas:

caigue	No seas **caigue**.	*Do not be lazy.*
salame	Es un **salame**.	*He is a fool.*

Para contestar

En el mapa

1. Diga cuáles son las ciudades capitales del Ecuador, Bolivia y Paraguay.
2. ¿Qué países están al sur/norte de Bolivia? ¿Y de Ecuador?
3. Mencione una diferencia geográfica muy importante entre Ecuador y Bolivia y Ecuador y Paraguay.

Ahora diga...

1. si le gustaría visitar las Islas Galápagos y por qué.
2. qué lugar de Bolivia o Paraguay le gustaría visitar.

¿Qué dice usted si...

1. usted cree que su hermano/a no está diciendo la verdad.
2. su compañero/a no quiere ayudarlo a arreglar su departamento/casa.
3. alguien lo/la hace reír mucho.

Paraguay tiene una rica tradición folclórica expresada en su música (la polka y la guaranía), sus hermosos tejidos (weavings) y su comida variada.

Para investigar en Internet

Busque información acerca de los mercados artesanales en Bolivia, Ecuador, Paraguay. Diga dónde están, qué tipo de productos venden y, si es posible, traiga a clase una ilustración de los productos que ofrecen. Vaya a www.prenhall.com/mosaicos.

¡Prepárese!

10-42 Opiniones. En este episodio hay sorpresas y cambios. Efraín se muestra atraído por Katie, Katie piensa todavía en Carlos y Sabrina revela que ella y Katie están trabajando juntas. En su opinión, ¿quién es honesto y quién no? ¿Es posible saberlo con seguridad? Indique sus opiniones.

En mi opinión…

1. … Katie es / no es honesta porque _____.
2. … Efraín es / no es honesto porque _____.
3. … Sabrina es / no es honesta porque _____.
4. … Carlos es / no es honesto porque _____.

¿Tienen las mismas opiniones sus compañeros de clase? ¿Por qué?

Ángela y Manolo no están seguros de quién va a ganar el concurso.

Katie y Efraín están en Xochimilco para buscar la solución al cuarto Misterio.

Katie entendió las pistas porque leyó sobre la historia de Xochimilco.

Parece que a Efraín le gusta mucho Katie.

¡Katie y Efraín solucionaron el misterio!

Sabrina dice que ella y Katie están
concentradas para ganar.

¡Responda!

10-43 Más opiniones. Complete las oraciones siguientes de una manera lógica
con la forma correcta de un verbo en el presente de subjuntivo o de indicativo.

1. Le recomiendo a Katie que...
2. Ojalá que Katie y Sabrina...
3. Efraín espera que Katie...
4. Es bueno que Carlos y Katie...
5. Es verdad que el concurso...
6. El público cree que Carlos...
7. Yo dudo que Efraín...
8. Es importante que el concurso...
9. ...

Esta canción es un ejemplo de la música taquirari, original de Bolivia y una combinación de tradiciones musicales indígenas y españolas. Aunque un tema típico de taquirari es el amor, "Sol de primavera" es una canción instrumental.

¡Prepárese!

10-44 Preferencias. ¿Qué tipo de música prefieren sus compañeros y Ud.? Hable con otros cinco estudiantes para averiguar sus preferencias. Luego compare su información con la del resto de la clase.

MÚSICA	NOMBRE	LE GUSTA PORQUE…
instrumental	_____	_____
clásica	_____	_____
rock	_____	_____
ska	_____	_____
latina	_____	_____
otra	_____	_____

¡Escuche!

10-45 Asociaciones. Lea las siguientes oraciones Luego, escuche la canción y llene los espacios en blanco, según su opinión.

1. "Sol de primavera" me hace pensar en _____.
2. La canción me hace sentir _____.
3. Cuando escucho esta canción tengo deseos de _____.
4. Una buena ocasión para escuchar esta canción o este estilo de música es _____.
5. La guitarra y la quena (una flauta andina) son _____.

¡Responda!

2 10-46 Temas. Escriba por lo menos cinco temas posibles para "Sol de primavera" y compártalos con un/a compañero/a. Túrnense usando el presente de subjuntivo para dar sus opiniones sobre los diferentes temas. Pueden usar los verbos y expresiones de la lista.

MODELO: E1: Un tema posible es el amor.
         E2: Yo dudo que el tema **sea** el amor.

dudar   negar   no creer   no estar seguro/a de   tal vez   quizás

VOCABULARIO

Comida

el aceite	oil
el aderezo	salad dressing
el aguacate	avocado
el ajo	garlic
las aves	poultry, foul
el/la azúcar	sugar
el camarón	shrimp
la carne	meat
molida/picada	ground beef
de res	beef/steak
la cebolla	onion
el cerdo	pork
la cereza	cherry
la chuleta	chop
la costilla	rib
la crema	cream
el dulce	candy/sweets
las espinacas	spinach
la fresa	strawberry
la galleta	cookie
la gelatina	gelatin
la harina	flour
la langosta	lobster
el limón	lemon
el maíz/elote	corn
la mantequilla	butter
la manzana	apple
la margarina	margarine
los mariscos	shellfish
la masa	dough
la mayonesa	mayonnaise
la mostaza	mustard
la pastelería	pastry shop
el pavo	turkey
el pepino	cucumber
la pera	pear
la pimienta	pepper
el pimiento verde	green pepper
la piña	pineapple
el plátano/la banana	banana
la receta	recipe
la sal	salt
la salsa de tomate	tomato sauce
la toronja/el pomelo	grapefruit
la uva	grape
la vainilla	vanilla
la verdura	vegetable
el vinagre	vinegar
el vino (tinto)	(red) wine
el yogur	yogurt
la zanahoria	carrot

En la mesa

la bandeja	tray
la botella	bottle
la copa	(stemmed) glass
la cuchara	spoon
la cucharita	teaspoon
el cuchillo	knife
el mantel	tablecloth
el plato	plate, dish
la servilleta	napkin
la taza	cup
el tenedor	fork
el vaso	glass

Verbos

aconsejar	to advise
añadir	to add
batir	to beat
dudar	to doubt
esperar	to hope, to expect
freír (i)	to fry
hervir (ie, i)	to boil
permitir	to permit, to allow
prohibir	to prohibit, to forbid
recomendar	to recommend

Descripciones

agrio/a	sour
lácteo/a	dairy (product), milky
sano/a	healthy

Palabras y expresiones útiles

la artesanía	handicraft
ojalá	I/we hope
quizá(s)/tal vez	maybe

*For impersonal expressions requiring the subjunctive and the indicative see pages 368, 371 and 372.

11

LA SALUD Y LOS MÉDICOS

Objetivos comunicativos

- Talking about the body
- Describing health conditions and medical treatments
- Expressing emotions, opinions, and attitudes
- Expressing expectations and wishes
- Giving informal orders and instructions
- Expressing goals and purposes

Contenido

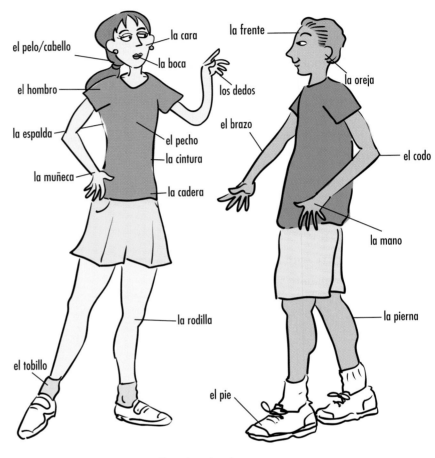

A PRIMERA VISTA

Las partes del cuerpo

Suggestions. Present body parts by pointing to your own body or using the Image Resource CD. Personalize and use gestures to facilitate comprehension: *A mí me gusta esquiar, pero tengo problemas con las rodillas. También tengo problemas con este hombro. El año pasado me caí y por eso tengo problemas con el hombro. Mi amigo Pedro también esquía. Él esquía muy bien, pero el sábado pasado se cayó y se fracturó el brazo. El médico dice que no debe mover el brazo porque tiene un hueso fracturado. Él está muy aburrido porque no puede esquiar.* Ask questions to check comprehension.

Mention parts of the body and have students point to them.

Give commands using parts of the body; present *derecho/a* and *izquierdo/a* to make the commands more challenging: *Ponga la mano derecha sobre la cabeza. Ponga la mano izquierda sobre el hombro derecho.*

In groups, have students give commands to one another.

VÍNCULOS

To practice vocabulary—Las partes del cuerpo
- SAM-OneKey: WB: 11-1, 11-2, 11-3, 11-4, 11-5 / LM: 11-27, 11-28, 11-29, 11-30
- Companion Website: AP 11-1
- IRCD: Chapter 11; pp. 394, 395, 396, 398, 400

el pelo/cabello · la cara · la boca · el hombro · la espalda · los dedos · el pecho · la cintura · la muñeca · la cadera · la rodilla · el tobillo · el pie

la frente · la oreja · el brazo · el codo · la mano · la pierna

Note. You may present additional words such as *lengua, talón, nalgas, piel, costilla, hígado, riñones.*

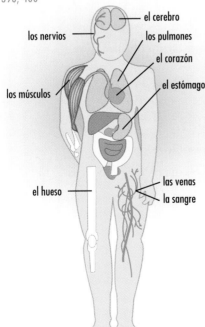

el cerebro · los nervios · los pulmones · el corazón · los músculos · el estómago · el hueso · las venas · la sangre

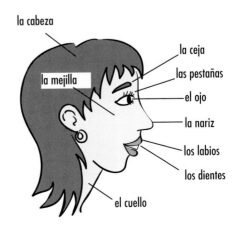

la cabeza · la mejilla · la ceja · las pestañas · el ojo · la nariz · los labios · los dientes · el cuello

La salud

¿Qué les pasa a estas personas?

Tiene **catarro. Estornuda** y tiene mucha **tos.**

Se torció el tobillo.

¿Qué dice usted?

11-1 Asociación. Primera fase. Decidan en qué parte del cuerpo se ponen estos accesorios y esta ropa.

1. los calcetines   g   a. la muñeca
2. el anillo   b   b. el dedo
3. los guantes   h   c. la cintura
4. el cinturón   c   d. las orejas
5. el collar   e   e. el cuello
6. los aretes   d   f. la cabeza
7. el reloj   a   g. los pies
8. el sombrero   f   h. las manos

Segunda fase. Digan qué accesorios de la lista no tienen ustedes y mencionen tres que consideren absolutamente indispensables en su vida. ¿Por qué? Comparen sus respuestas.

Se cayó y **se fracturó** el brazo.

11-2 ¿Para qué sirve/n? Asocien la explicación de la derecha con la parte del cuerpo correspondiente. Después, ustedes deben decir para qué sirven estas partes del cuerpo.

MODELO: los dedos
               Hay cinco en cada mano.
               Sirven para tocar el piano.

1. las manos   g   a. Unen las manos con el cuerpo.
2. la sangre   d   b. Permiten que las personas vean.
3. los pulmones   c   c. Toman el oxígeno del aire y lo pasan a la sangre.
4. los brazos   a   d. Es un líquido rojo que circula por el cuerpo.
5. los ojos   b   e. Unen el cuerpo con los pies.
6. las piernas   e   f. Se deben lavar después de comer.
7. los dientes   f   g. Están al final de los brazos.
8. el cerebro   h   h. Le da órdenes al cuerpo.

Suggestions. Talk about the first drawing to familiarize students with the vocabulary; write on the board some of the words, especially if you are going to use them later when personalizing. Use gestures: *Jorgito no está bien. Está enfermo. Fíjense en la cara de Jorgito. Tiene mala cara, y se siente muy mal. Tiene dolor de garganta y tose. Su mamá está muy preocupada y quiere saber si Jorgito tiene fiebre y le pone el termómetro. Jorgito tiene 39 grados. Recuerden que en los países hispanos no se usa el sistema Fahrenheit (39° centígrados es más o menos 102° Fahrenheit). Ella está más preocupada ahora y quiere que Jorgito tome una aspirina. Además, ella va a llamar al médico.*

Ask yes/no questions to check understanding: *¿La mamá está enferma? ¿Jorgito tiene dolor de espalda? ¿Jorgito tiene dolor de garganta? ¿Jorgito tiene fiebre?* Point to yourself and say, *Tengo 37°. ¿Tengo fiebre?* Emphasize that 37° is normal (98.6°F). Ask additional questions based on temperature: *Si una persona tiene 40°, ¿tiene fiebre? ¿Y si tiene 38°? ¿Cuál es el equivalente de 102° Fahrenheit en centígrados?*

Suggestions. Follow a similar procedure and personalize: *¿Cuándo va usted al médico? ¿Qué hace Ud. cuando le duele la garganta? ¿Es usted alérgico/a a los antibióticos? ¿Para qué son los antibióticos? ¿Qué le receta el médico cuando tiene fiebre?*

Review parts of the body. Then expand by acting as if you had various aches and pains, complaining, *Me duele/n...* To have students practice these expressions, say *¿Tengo dolor de... ?* Students respond with *Sí, le duele/n...* Remind students that the verb *doler* is conjugated like *gustar.*

Jorgito está enfermo

AUDIO

SRA. VILLA: Jorgito, **tienes muy mala cara.** ¿Estás **enfermo?**

JORGITO: **Me siento** muy mal y **tengo dolor de garganta.** Anoche tosí mucho.

SRA. VILLA: (Le pone el termómetro.) Tienes una **fiebre** de 39 grados. Te voy a dar una **aspirina** y enseguida llamo al Dr. Bosque.

DOCTOR: Vamos a ver, Jorgito. Cuéntame cómo te sientes.

JORGITO: Ahora **me duele** la cabeza y también me duelen los **oídos.**

DOCTOR: Vamos a **examinarte** los **oídos** y la garganta. Abre bien la boca y di "Ah". Tienes una **infección.** No es **seria,** pero es necesario que **te cuides.**

JORGITO: Doctor, no quiero que me ponga una **inyección.**

DOCTOR: ¡No, qué va! Te voy a **recetar** unas **pastillas.** Debes tomarlas **cada cuatro horas.**

JORGITO: Está bien, doctor.

DOCTOR: **Además,** tienes **gripe.** Debes descansar y beber mucho líquido. Aquí está la **receta,** señora.

SRA. VILLA: Gracias, doctor.

¿Qué dice usted?

2 **11-3 La enfermedad de Jorgito.** Completen la tabla con la información correcta.

Síntomas:	
Recomendaciones:	
Nombre del médico:	

2 **11-4 Usted es el/la doctor/a.** ¿Qué recomienda en estos casos? Primero, escoja la mejor recomendación. Luego compare sus repuestas con las de su compañero/a, y juntos piensen en otras dos sugerencias para el mismo problema.

1. Su paciente tiene una infección en los ojos. Le recomiendo que...
   a. nade en la piscina.
   b. tome antibióticos.
   c. lea mucho.
   d. ...

2. Su paciente tiene fiebre y le duele el cuerpo. Le aconsejo que...
   a. descanse y tome aspirinas.
   b. coma mucho y camine.
   c. vaya a su trabajo.
   d. ...

3. A su paciente le duelen mucho una rodilla y un pie. Le pido que...
   a. corra todos los días.
   b. tome clases de baile.
   c. descanse y no camine.
   d. ...

4. A su paciente le duele la garganta y tiene tos. Le digo que es importante que...
   a. hable poco y no salga.
   b. vaya a esquiar.
   c. cante en el concierto.
   d. ...

2 **11-5 En el consultorio.** Usted tiene un catarro terrible y va a ver a su médico/a. Dígale cómo se siente y pregúntele qué debe hacer. El/La médico/a debe hacerle alguna recomendación y contestar sus preguntas.

MODELO: E1: Me siento.../Tengo...
               E2: Creo que...
               E1: ¿Es/No es bueno comer muchas frutas y verduras?
               E2: Es excelente comer frutas y verduras porque tienen muchas vitaminas.

RECOMENDACIONES

1. tomar vitaminas, especialmente vitamina C
2. comer carne frecuentemente
3. beber ocho vasos de agua todos los días
4. hacer ejercicio cada día
5. ...

Suggestions for 11-4. Set up other situations, asking groups to come up with recommendations and then sharing each group's suggestions with the class.

Suggestions for 11-5. Before this activity, brainstorm with students the most common symptoms of a strong cold.

CULTURA

In some Spanish-speaking countries, the word **sanatorio** is used instead of **hospital;** in others, **sanatorio** has the connotation of a hospital specializing in the pulmonary and respiratory fields. The word **clínica** is used in some countries when referring to a private hospital; **hospital** may refer to a government- or religious-run hospital, which provides medical care at no charge.

Suggestions for 11-6. You may preview informal commands: *Llama a la Dra. Corona López.* Encourage students to list other symptoms for themselves or family members.

Before doing *Segunda fase,* review with students proper salutations and ways of addressing a doctor and a patient during an office visit. Make sure students use *usted* to address each other.

❷ 11-6 ¿A quién debo llamar? Primera fase. Explíquele a su compañero/a sus síntomas o lo que usted necesita. Su compañero/a le va a decir a quién debe llamar de acuerdo con los anuncios de abajo.

MODELO: necesitar un examen médico para un nuevo trabajo
          E1: Necesito un examen médico para un nuevo trabajo.
          E2: Debes llamar a la Dra. Corona López.

LENGUA

Traditionally, because professions such as lawyers or doctors were associated with men, only the masculine form was used in Spanish: **el médico, el abogado.** However, as more women started to get degrees in these professions, the feminine article is used before a masculine noun: **la médico, la abogado, la juez.** This is still common in some places. Thus, the feminine forms of these nouns are becoming more popular: **la médica, la abogada, la jueza.**

Dr. Fco. Javier Amador Cumplido *Cirugía y enfermedades de los ojos* **86-43-57** Consultorio 204	**Dra. Silvia Corona López** *Medicina Interna* **86-51-49**	**Clínica de Asma y Alergias** *Dr. Rubén Shturman* Amsterdam 219-A 2° piso **294-3866** **584-0153**
Dr. Héctor Molina Oviedo *Psiquiatra* **86-51-49** Consultorio 402	**Dr. Jaime A. Rodríguez Peláez** *Pediatra* Niños y Adolescentes **86-17-15**	**Dra. Gabriela Jacobo de Alcaraz** Cirujano Dentista **86-48-44** Consultorio 314

DR. RAÚL ELGUEZÁBAL R.
Medicina Familiar y Cirugía
86-34-73 EU.
428-4846
Consultorio 309

1. dolerle la cabeza cuando lee o mira televisión   Dr. Amador Cumplido
2. sentirse triste y deprimido/a   Dr. Molina Oviedo
3. estar enfermo/a y tener fiebre   Dra. Corona López/Dr. Elguezábal
4. buscar un médico para un sobrino de cinco años   Dr. Rodríguez Peláez
5. no poder respirar bien y tener la piel (*skin*) irritada   Dr. Shturman
6. dolerle los dientes cuando come   Dra. Jacobo de Alcaraz
7. no poder dormir   Dra. Corona López/Dr. Elguezábal/Dr. Molina Oviedo
8. ...

Segunda fase. Escojan dos de los problemas mencionados. Uno/a de ustedes es el/la enfermo/a y otro/a el/la médico/a elegido/a. El/La enfermo/a debe explicar los síntomas y detalles de su enfermedad. El/La médico/a debe hacer recomendaciones y sugerencias al/a la enfermo/a. Después cambien de papel.

Médicos, farmacias y hospitales

Suggestions. Present vocabulary in context, describing scenes. Ask questions about the illustrations. Play doctor, asking students how they feel. Prescribe accordingly; then have students do the same, working in pairs. Students play the roles of doctor and patient: *"Todavía me duelen mucho los ojos. No sé qué tengo". "Pues, tiene una infección. Le voy a recetar unos antibióticos".*

AUDIO

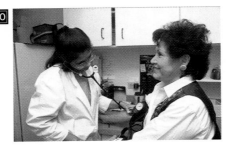

*Una enfermera le toma **la tensión arterial** a una paciente en un hospital.*

En muchos países hispanos, los médicos recién graduados tienen que trabajar en zonas rurales o muy pobres, como una forma de servicio social, antes de establecer su propio **consultorio** o trabajar en un hospital.

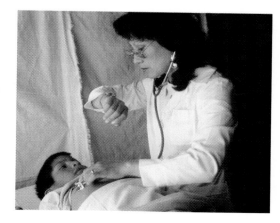

En varios países hispanos la restricción sobre la venta de medicinas es similar a la de los Estados Unidos. Los antibióticos y somníferos, por ejemplo, ya no se venden sin receta. Sin embargo, en otros países, hay menos restricciones sobre las medicinas, y se pueden obtener muchas de ellas sin receta médica. En casos que no son graves, los clientes siguen los consejos del **farmacéutico**, estableciéndose de esta forma una relación personal entre ellos. Los farmacéuticos también ponen inyecciones y toman la tensión arterial.

¿Qué dice usted?

2 11-7 Una emergencia. Primera fase. Usted y su amigo/a están de viaje en la República Dominicana, y su amigo/a tiene un problema de salud. En un cibercafé de Santo Domingo, han encontrado la información en la página 400 sobre médicos y farmacias de turno. Decidan cuál es el número más apropiado para llamar, basándose en el problema médico de su amigo/a.

Segunda fase. Haga la llamada, describa la enfermedad y pida la dirección de la consulta o la farmacia. Después el/la farmacéutico/a o el/la médico/a le debe hacer preguntas y sugerir el remedio adecuado.

Suggestions for 11-7. Explain that there is a night and holiday rotation duty: *farmacias de guardia/de turno* appear in local newspapers. Have students do this activity in pairs and report to the class.

11-8 Me duele mucho. You will listen to a young man talking to his father about how he feels after twisting his ankle. Before you listen, list two symptoms you think he has.

Now, pay attention to the general idea of what is said. Then, as you listen circle the letter that indicates the appropriate ending to each statement.

1. Esteban tiene...
   a. una infección en el tobillo.
   b. mucho dolor.
   c. fiebre.

2. El padre de Esteban quiere...
   a. que Esteban descanse y se cuide.
   b. llevar a Esteban al hospital.
   c. que Esteban tome una aspirina.

3. El padre de Esteban le dice que...
   a. lo ayuda a caminar para llevarlo al hospital.
   b. decida si prefiere descansar o ir al hospital.
   c. el médico puede verlo esa tarde.

4. Esteban decide...
   a. no escuchar a su padre.
   b. jugar al fútbol al día siguiente.
   c. ir al hospital con su padre.

1. The subjunctive with expressions of emotion

Me molesta que fumen

VÍNCULOS

To practice the subjunctive with expressions of emotion
- SAM-OneKey: WB: 11-6, 11-7, 11-8 / LM: 11-31, 11-32
- Companion Website: AP 11-2
- *Gramática viva*: Grammar Point 54: Subjunctive with expressions of emotion
- IRCD: Chapter 11; pg. 401

■ When the verb of the main clause expresses emotion (e.g., fear, happiness, sorrow), use a subjunctive verb form in the dependent clause.

Sentimos mucho que el niño **tenga** fiebre.	*We are very sorry (that) the child has a fever.*
Me alegro de que **estés** con él.	*I am glad (that) you are with him.*

■ Some common verbs that express emotion are **alegrarse (de)**, **sentir**, **gustar**, **encantar**, **molestar**, and **temer** (to fear).

■ Impersonal expressions and other expressions that show emotion are also followed by the subjunctive.

Es triste que el niño **esté** enfermo.	*It is sad that the child is sick.*
¡Qué lástima que no **pueda** ir a la fiesta!	*What a shame that he cannot go to the party!*

¿Qué dice usted?

11-9 Un amigo enfermo. Asocie cada comentario sobre la enfermedad de su amigo con la reacción adecuada.

1. Pedro está muy enfermo. __b__
2. Sus padres llegan hoy para estar con él. __a__
3. Creo que el doctor Pérez lo va a operar. __c__
4. Dicen que es una operación seria. __e__
5. No va a poder participar en el campeonato. __d__

a. Me alegro de que vengan.
b. Siento mucho que esté tan mal.
c. ¡Qué bueno que sea ése el médico!
d. Es una lástima que no pueda jugar.
e. Ojalá que no tenga complicaciones.

Suggestions. Introduce the verb *molestar,* give examples, and clarify that it does not have any sexual connotations.

Give examples using expressions of emotion: *Me alegro de que estén todos aquí. A mí me gusta que todos lleguen temprano y practiquen español con sus compañeros. Siento que no tengamos películas en español para hoy.*

Ask students to finish the following introductory clauses: *Me alegro de que tú... Siento que tú... No me gusta que tú...*

EN DIRECTO

To express empathy:

Siento que...

Me alegro de que...

Temo que...

Espero que...

No me gusta que...

¡Qué agradable que...

11-10 Una visita a un/a amigo/a. Han operado a su amigo/a de la rodilla. Usted va a visitarlo/la a la clínica. A continuación está lo que su amigo/a le dice. Usted debe escoger entre las expresiones de **En directo** para responderle.

1. Me duele bastante la rodilla.
2. Tengo fiebre y dolor de cabeza.
3. Tengo dolor de estómago porque las medicinas son muy fuertes.
4. Tengo náuseas por los efectos de la anestesia.
5. Detesto estar acostado tanto tiempo.
6. La comida del hospital es buenísima.
7. Las enfermeras vienen a verme cada media hora.
8. La cirujana que me operó es muy simpática.

11-11 Reacciones. María Luisa y Rafael trabajan en un hospital. Su compañero/a le va a decir lo que ellos piensan hacer la semana próxima. Reaccione usando las expresiones de **En directo**. Después cambien de papel.

PERSONAS	LUNES	MIÉRCOLES	VIERNES	DOMINGO
María Luisa	empezar una dieta	ir al gimnasio	hacer ejercicio en su casa	caminar 2 Km.
Rafael	trabajar en el hospital todo el día	salir del hospital temprano para ir al cine	quedarse en su casa	reunirse con sus amigos

Follow-up for 11-12. Students list what they like others to do, and they share their lists with partners.

11-12 ¿Qué me molesta? Primera fase. Haga una lista de los hábitos de otras personas que le molestan. Compare su lista con la de su compañero/a.

MODELO: Me molesta que mis amigos lleguen tarde.

Segunda fase. En pequeños grupos, comparen sus listas y escojan los seis hábitos que les molestan más a todos en el grupo. Digan por qué. Compartan sus resultados con el resto de la clase.

SITUACIONES

1. **Role 1.** Recently you decided to change your lifestyle and to join an aerobics class (*clase de ejercicios aeróbicos*). You are also following a healthful diet and feel much better. You run into a friend whom you have not seen for some time. Answer your friend's questions. Convince him/her to join you in your exercise class.

   Role 2. You run into a friend whom you have not seen for some time. Tell him/her a) that he/she looks (*verse*) great, and b) ask what he/she is doing. After listening to his/her explanation, a) inquire how many times a week he/she goes to the gym, b) at what time, c) how much the classes cost, and d) what he/she eats and drinks. He/She will try to persuade you to join the program.

2. One of you is a doctor and the other is a patient. The patient should describe all his/her symptoms and his/her lifestyle (*vida activa, vida sedentaria*). While the patient is talking, the doctor should ask pertinent questions and approve or disapprove of his/her lifestyle. As a final step, the doctor should give some advice or prescribe some medication for the patient.

2. Informal commands

Consejos para una vida sana

Respira por la nariz; no respires por la boca.
Relájate para evitar el estrés.
Empieza un programa de ejercicios.
Cuídate, y no te canses mucho los primeros días.
Come muchas frutas y verduras.
No comas mucha grasa.

VÍNCULOS
To practice informal commands
- SAM-OneKey: WB: 11-9, 11-10, 11-11, 11-12 / LM: 11-33, 11-34, 11-35, 11-36
- Companion Website: AP 11-3
- *Gramática viva*: Grammar Point 21: Informal commands; Informal commands vs. present indicative
- IRCD: Chapter 11; pg. 403

■ Use informal commands with those whom you address as **tú**. To form the affirmative **tú** command, use the present indicative **tú** form without the final **-s**.

Suggestions. Write the *tú* form of some verbs (*cocinas, bebes, escribes*) on the board and erase the final *-s*. Do TPR using informal commands.

Model several *tú* commands, going from the negative to the affirmative (*no leas/lee; no llames/llama*). Then give the negative and have students supply the affirmative. Give the affirmative command and have students give the negative.

	PRESENT INDICATIVE	AFFIRMATIVE *TÚ* COMMAND
llamar:	llamas	**llama**
leer:	lees	**lee**
escribir:	escribes	**escribe**

■ For the negative **tú** command, use the **tú** subjunctive form.

No llames.
No leas.
No escribas.

■ Placement of object and reflexive pronouns with **tú** commands is the same as with **usted** commands.

AFFIRMATIVE COMMAND	NEGATIVE *TÚ* COMMAND
Bébela.	No **la** bebas.
Háblale.	No **le** hables.
Siéntate.	No **te** sientes.

■ The plural of **tú** commands in Spanish-speaking America is the **ustedes** command.

Escribe (tú).   **Escriban** (ustedes).

Note. See presentation of the *vosotros* commands in *Expansión gramatical*, pp. A1–A2.

■ Some **-er** and **-ir** verbs have shortened affirmative **tú** commands, but their negative command takes the subjunctive form like other verbs.

	AFFIRMATIVE	NEGATIVE
poner:	**pon**	**no pongas**
salir:	**sal**	**no salgas**
tener:	**ten**	**no tengas**
venir:	**ven**	**no vengas**
hacer:	**haz**	**no hagas**
decir:	**di**	**no digas**
ir:	**ve**	**no vayas**
ser:	**sé**	**no seas**

Follow-up for 11-13. Have students think of sentences requesting advice: *¿Debo caminar todos los días? ¿Debo salir por la mañana o por la tarde?* Then ask other students to give their advice using a *tú* command. Ask if classmates agree with the advice given; if not, they should provide their own advice.

```
A INVESTIGAR
```

Haga una investigación sobre una de estas tres ciudades: Santo Domingo, La Habana o San Juan. Averigüe lo siguiente:

- Ubicación y tamaño
- Tres lugares de interés
- Dos platos típicos
- El nombre y la dirección de un hospital
- Un dato que le parezca interesante

Escriba un breve párrafo para informar a la clase.

Suggestions for 11-14. Encourage students to give additional advice, using affirmative and negative commands.

You may explain that *mofongo* is a typical Puerto Rican dish made of green plantains, fried pork meat, and garlic.

You may bring a cassette or a CD of the *bomba* and the *plena*, typical music of Puerto Rico.

¿Qué dice usted?

11-13 Consejos. Escoja los consejos más adecuados para cada situación.

1. Su compañero se torció el tobillo y le duele mucho.
   a. Mira más programas de televisión.
   b. Llama al médico.
   c. Ve al cine con tu novio/a.
   d. Camina una hora esta tarde.
   e. Practica en el laboratorio.
   f. Quédate en cama.

2. Su hermana está embarazada (*pregnant*).
   a. No comas hamburguesas.
   b. No hagas ejercicios fuertes.
   c. No bebas té.
   d. No fumes.
   e. No bebas vino ni cerveza.
   f. No consumas cafeína.

3. Su amiga tiene mucho catarro.
   a. Ve al cine por la noche.
   b. Bebe mucho líquido.
   c. Escucha los casetes de español.
   d. No tomes aspirinas.
   e. Camina por el campo.
   f. Toma sopa de pollo.

4. A su mamá le duele el estómago.
   a. Evita (*avoid*) la grasa.
   b. Toma muchos helados.
   c. No comas mucho.
   d. Compra papas fritas.
   e. Acuéstate y descansa.
   f. Si no te sientes mejor, llama al médico.

5. Su amigo quiere preparar unas empanadas salteñas.
   a. Corta las papas en cuadritos.
   b. Compra más tomates y lechuga.
   c. Hierve los huevos durante un minuto.
   d. Prepara la masa el día anterior.
   e. No le pongas carne al relleno.
   f. Ponle pasas y aceitunas.

6. Su primo quiere visitar Cuba este verano.
   a. Lleva un abrigo de invierno.
   b. Prueba las frutas tropicales.
   c. Camina por la parte antigua de La Habana.
   d. Visita la playa de Varadero.
   e. Practica español antes de ir.
   f. Compra varios mapas.

11-14 Una cura de reposo. Su amigo/a estuvo muy enfermo, y su médico le recomendó pasar dos semanas de descanso total en Puerto Rico. Usted está de acuerdo con el médico, y le dice a su amigo/a lo que debe hacer allí. Después cambien de papel.

MODELO: visitar el parque nacional de El Yunque / no pensar en los negocios
           Visita el parque nacional de El Yunque. / No pienses en los negocios.

1. disfrutar de las playas de Isla Verde
2. respirar aire puro y descansar
3. no llamar a tu oficina
4. caminar por la parte histórica de San Juan
5. probar una comida típica, como el mofongo
6. salir por las noches y aprender a bailar la bomba y la plena

G **11-15 Una vida sana.** Ustedes están preocupados por el estilo de vida de uno/a de sus amigos/as. En grupos, lean lo que hace en un día típico e identifiquen los problemas que tiene. Después, hagan una lista de cinco actividades que él/ella debe hacer y cinco que no debe hacer para cambiar su estilo de vida. Comparen su lista con las de otros grupos.

Warm-up for 11-15. Give examples of attitudes and activities of a healthy and an unhealthy lifestyle. Students respond: *es sano, no es sano.*

> Se levanta tarde todos los días. Tan pronto se levanta, se sienta a comer su desayuno favorito: tres huevos fritos con tostadas y dos tazas de café cubano con bastante azúcar. Luego lee el periódico en su dormitorio, mira televisión unas cuatro horas y habla con amigos por teléfono. Como no le gusta cocinar, llama por teléfono al restaurante de la esquina y pide el almuerzo. Generalmente come hamburguesas o bistec con papas fritas y toma una o dos cervezas. Por la tarde, duerme una siesta larga, se levanta y prepara su bebida favorita: un Cuba Libre. Por la noche, les escribe cartas a sus amigos, ve las noticias, se sienta en el balcón de su casa a mirar a la gente que pasa por la calle y se acuesta a las 10:00 de la noche.

Note for 11-16. You may point out that the word *fisioterapeuta* is also used.

Suggestion for 11-16. You may wish to set the following contexts for students to give orders to one another: in the classroom, in the language lab, in the doctor's office, in a dentist office, in the hospital, etc.

Alternate for 11-16. You may also mention specific health problems for which students may give advice: *Su mejor amigo se torció un tobillo. A su compañero le duele la espalda.*

Suggestions for 11-17. Introduce the new words *enamorarse* and *casarse* through comprehensible input.

Encourage students to use informal commands whenever possible. With the class as a whole, students share the advice given and choose the best one(s).

G **11-16 En la consulta de un/a fisioterapista** (*physical therapist*). En grupos, túrnense para representar a un/a fisioterapista y a sus pacientes. Cada integrante del grupo debe darle una orden a otro/a estudiante. Este/a estudiante debe hacer lo que le indicaron. Además de los verbos que conocen, los siguientes verbos pueden ser útiles para sus órdenes: **estirar** (*to stretch*), **doblar** (*to bend*), **cruzar** (*to cross*).

MODELO: Levántate rápidamente, camina un poco y siéntate enseguida.

2 **11-17 El correo sentimental.** Ustedes están a cargo del correo sentimental de un periódico y tienen que contestar las cartas que se reciben. ¿Qué consejos le van a dar a "Un enamorado"?

Querida Violeta:

Estoy desesperado y no sé con quién debo hablar ni qué debo hacer. Soy estudiante universitario y estoy en el último año de mi carrera. Hace poco conocí a una muchacha muy bonita y simpática en una de mis clases. Yo me enamoré de ella y empezamos a salir. Ella me decía que me quería mucho y que debíamos casarnos después de terminar los estudios. Yo también la quería mucho, pero un día le dije que era mejor esperar un poco antes de tomar una decisión tan seria como el matrimonio. Ella lo comprendió y me dijo que estaba de acuerdo conmigo.

Poco después empecé a notar que cada vez que venía a mi apartamento, faltaban cosas. Un día fue un cuchillo, otro día fue un tenedor, más adelante fue mi cámara, la semana pasada desaparecieron unos antibióticos del baño, etc. La otra noche fuimos a un restaurante a comer y vi que ponía dos cucharitas en su bolsa y que tomaba unas pastillas blancas muy pequeñas.

¿Qué debo hacer? Ella es una muchacha de una familia muy decente y no necesita estas cosas. Me siento culpable, pues no sé si esto es la consecuencia de nuestra conversación sobre el matrimonio o si es una enfermedad psicológica. Estoy totalmente confundido. Aconséjeme, por favor.

Un enamorado

Tomás

SITUACIONES

1. **Role A.** Your friend is not feeling well, and you go to his/her apartment to offer help. Ask how he/she is feeling. Then tell him/her to a) have some chicken soup, b) go to bed, and c) call the doctor. Offer to go out to get some chicken soup and help with house chores.

   Role B. You are not feeling well and a friend has come to help you. Explain a) that you have a sore throat and fever, and b) that you coughed a lot last night. After listening to your friend's advice and thanking him/her, say a) that you are not hungry now, b) that you already called your doctor and left a message (*mensaje*), and c) that you are going to rest while you wait for the doctor's call.

2. **Role A.** Call a friend and tell him/her the bad news that your mutual friend Roberto broke an ankle and he is at the hospital. Answer your friend's questions by saying a) that Roberto is doing fine and b) that you are planning to visit him this afternoon. Then ask your friend if he/she would like to come along, and agree to pick him/her up at five.

   Role B. A friend calls to tell you about Roberto's accident. Ask him/her a) how Roberto is, and b) say that you would like to see him. Then ask your friend if he/she is planning to visit him at the hospital. Use the expressions in the *En directo* box to express your reaction.

3. *Por* and *para* (review)

In previous lessons, you have used **por** in expressions such as **por favor, por ejemplo,** and **por ciento.** You have also used **por** and **para** to express the following meanings:

POR	PARA
MOVEMENT	
■ through or by a place	■ toward a destination
Caminaron **por** el hospital. *They walked through the hospital.*	Caminaron **para** el hospital. *They walked toward the hospital.*
TIME	
■ duration of an event	■ action deadline
Estuvo con el médico **por** una hora. *He was with the doctor for an hour.*	Necesita el antibiótico **para** el martes. *He needs the antibiotic by Tuesday.*
ACTION	
■ reason or motive of an action	■ for whom something is intended or done
Ana fue al consultorio **por** el dolor de garganta. *Ana went to the doctor's office because of a sore throat.*	Compró el antibiótico **para** Ana. *He bought the antibiotic for Ana.*

4. Other uses of *por* and *para*

Use **por** to:

- indicate exchange or substitution

    Irma pagó $120 **por** la medicina.
    Cambió estas pastillas **por** ésas.

    Irma paid $120 for the medicine.
    She changed these pills for those.

- express unit or rate

    Yo camino 5 kilómetros **por** hora.
    El interés es (el) diez **por** ciento.

    I walk 5 kilometers per hour.
    The interest is ten per cent.

- express means of transportation

    Lo mandaron **por** avión.
    Prefieren ir **por** tren.

    They sent it by plane.
    They'd rather go by train.

- express the object of an errand

    Fue **por** las aspirinas.
    Pasamos **por** ti a las 5:00.

    He went for the aspirins.
    We'll come by for you at 5:00.

Use **para** to...

- express judgment or point of view.

    Para nosotros, esta es la mejor farmacia.

    For us, this is the best drugstore.

    Es un caso difícil **para** un médico joven.

    It is a difficult case for a young doctor.

- indicate intention or purpose, when followed by an infinitive.

    Fueron **para** comprar aspirinas.
    Salió **para** ayudar a los enfermos.

    They went to buy aspirin.
    He left to help the sick people.

Suggestion. Mention "in order to" as an English equivalent of *para* and provide examples.

¿Qué dice usted?

11-18 ¿Por o para? Casi todas las oraciones siguientes pueden completarse con **por** o **para**, pero sólo una de estas preposiciones refleja lo que quiere decir la persona. Trace un círculo alrededor de la preposición que debe usarse.

1. Toward a destination
   Salimos **por**/**para** el consultorio del médico a las nueve de la mañana.
2. Through
   Fuimos **por**/**para** el túnel para llegar más rápido.
3. Reason or motive of an action
   Ana fue a ver al médico **por**/**para** su dolor de garganta.
4. For whom something is intended or done
   El médico escribió la receta de un antibiótico **por**/**para** Ana.
5. The object of an errand
   Yo fui a la farmacia **por**/**para** el antibiótico.
6. Indicate exchange or substitution
   Pagué veinte pesos **por**/**para** el antibiótico.

❷ **11-19 ¿Por dónde y para dónde van?** Túrnense para hacer y contestar preguntas según los siguientes dibujos.

MODELO: E1: ¿Por dónde va el alumno?
E2: Va por el pasillo.
E1: ¿Para dónde va?
E2: Va para su clase de español.

1.

2.

3.

4.

❷ **11-20 En el laboratorio.** Túrnense para averiguar cuándo van a estar listos los resultados de los análisis (*tests*) de unos pacientes. Consulten la tabla para obtener la información correcta.

MODELO: Alfredo Benítez   un análisis   2:00 de la tarde
E1: ¿Cuándo va a estar listo el análisis del Sr. Benítez?
E2: Va a estar listo para las dos (de la tarde).

PACIENTE	ANÁLISIS	RESULTADOS
Hilda Corvalán	1	11:00 de la mañana
Alfonso González	2	esta tarde
Jorge Pérez Robles	3	3:15 de la tarde
Aleida Miranda	1	mañana por la mañana
César Gómez Villegas	4	martes
Irene Santa Cruz	1	...

2 **11-21 ¿Para qué fueron?** Túrnense y pregúntense para qué fueron las personas a estos lugares. Deben usar su imaginación para contestar y dar detalles adicionales.

MODELO: Pablo fue al supermercado.
          E1: ¿Para qué fue al supermercado?
          E2: Fue para comprar leche y huevos.
               Quiere hacer un postre.

1. Jorge fue al hospital.
2. Ignacio fue a la farmacia.
3. Sara y Gloria fueron al gimnasio.
4. La Sra. Méndez fue al centro comercial.
5. Alejandro y Martín fueron a Cuba el 24 de diciembre.
6. Carlos fue a ver al psicólogo.

11-22 La graduación de un nuevo médico. Complete estos párrafos sobre la graduación de Fernando con **por** o **para,** según el contexto.

El 14 de junio es la graduación de Fernando en la Facultad de Medicina de la Universidad Católica Madre y Maestra de Santiago de los Caballeros. Sus padres, los señores Rovira, viven en Puerto Plata, pero van a ir (1) __para__ la graduación y quieren llevarle un regalo a Fernando. El lunes pasado fueron a una tienda y pagaron $100 (2) __por__ un regalo muy bonito (3) __para__ Fernando. Graciela, su hermana gemela, vive en Miami y no puede ir (4) __por__ su trabajo. Ella también le compró un regalo y se lo envió (5) __por__ avión porque quiere que llegue (6) __para__ el día de la graduación.

El día 14 (7) __por__ la mañana, los padres de Fernando salieron (8) __para__ la universidad. Estaba lloviendo, y (9) __por__ eso salieron temprano. Normalmente, ellos pueden estar en la universidad en una hora más o menos, pero (10) __por__ la lluvia, el viaje duró casi dos horas. (11) __Para__ ellos, que son mayores, el viaje fue un poco largo, pero al final pudieron pasar ese día con su hijo.

SITUACIONES

Role A. You are stressed out and need to rest. Following doctor's orders you are planning to rent a furnished apartment at the beach. You found one in the classified ads. Call the landlord and tell him/her a) when you will need the apartment, and b) for how long. Ask how much the rent is and inquire about the size of the rooms and other facilities. Answer his/her question(s) and then make an appointment to see it.

Role B. You are a landlord who is renting an apartment at the beach. A prospective renter calls you. Answer his/her questions and ask him/her how many people will be staying at the apartment. Agree on a date and time to show the property.

VÍNCULOS

To practice relative pronouns
- SAM-OneKey: WB: 11-17, 11-18, 11-19 / LM: 11-41, 11-42
- Companion Website: AP 11-5
- *Gramática viva*: Grammar Point 46: Relatives

5. Relative pronouns

■ The relative pronouns **que** and **quien(es)** combine two clauses into one sentence.

Los médicos trabajan en ese hospital.	*The doctors work at that hospital.*
Los médicos son excelentes.	*The doctors are excellent.*
Los médicos **que** trabajan en ese hospital son excelentes.	*The doctors who work at that hospital are excellent.*

■ **Que** is the most commonly used relative pronoun. It introduces a dependent clause, and it may refer to persons or things.

Las vitaminas **que** yo tomo son muy caras.	*The vitamins that I take are very expensive.*
Ése es el médico **que** me receta las vitaminas.	*That is the doctor who prescribes the vitamins.*

■ **Quien(es)** refers only to persons and may replace **que** in a clause set off by commas.

Los Márquez, **quienes/que** viven en la ciudad, prefieren el campo.	*The Márquezes, who live in the city, prefer the country.*

■ Use **quien(es)** after a preposition (**a, con, de, por, para,** etc.) when referring to people.

Allí está el enfermero **con quien** hablé esta mañana.	*There is the nurse with whom I spoke this morning.*
Ésos son los señores **a quienes** les debes dar la receta.	*Those are the gentlemen to whom you should give the prescription.*

Suggestions. Point out that the use of relative pronouns makes conversation more interesting, concise, and adultlike—it is a sign of a more advanced speaker.

Use visuals, pretending you are related to the people portrayed. *La chica que está jugando al vóleibol es mi hermana.*

Suggestion for 11-23. Have students work in pairs.

¿Qué dice usted?

11-23 Una telenovela dominicana. Joaquín está enfermo hoy, y por eso empezó a mirar una telenovela en uno de los canales de la televisión. Le gustó tanto que le mandó un correo electrónico a un amigo, contándole detalles de la telenovela. Complete el correo electrónico de Joaquín con **que** o **quien**.

Mi corazón es una telenovela dominicana (1) __que__ tiene mucho público. El actor principal es Agustín Montalvo. Él es el actor de (2) __quien__ todos hablan. La crítica cree que este año va a ganar el premio Talía, (3) __que__ es el equivalente del Óscar norteamericano. El 90 por ciento de las chicas dicen que Agustín es el actor con (4) __quien__ les gustaría salir. En la telenovela, Agustín hace el papel del médico (5) __que__ quiere salvar la vida de Silvina del Bosque, la actriz principal, (6) __quien/que__ tuvo un accidente terrible y está inconsciente. Agustín es el hombre (7) __que__ ella quiere, pero Agustín está enamorado de Esmeralda del Valle, una mujer a (8) __quien__ sólo le interesa el dinero de Agustín. La telenovela es muy melodramática y siempre hay problemas (9) __que__ mantienen el interés del público.

② **11-24 Un accidente.** Completen esta conversación con el nombre de una persona y los pronombres **que** o **quien.**

E1: ¿Qué haces aquí en el hospital? ¿A quién viniste a ver?

E2: A __(nombre)__, el/la chico/a con __quien__ estoy saliendo.

E1: ¿Y cómo está?

E2: Bastante bien, gracias a Dios. Tuvimos un accidente bastante serio con el carro __que__ su padre le regaló.

E1: ¡Qué horror! ¿Y llamaste a alguien?

E2: No tuve tiempo. Enseguida llegó la policía. Bueno, te hablo después. Allí viene la doctora __que__ nos atendió, y quiero hacerle unas preguntas.

② **11-25 Mi médico/a o dentista.** Descríbale su médico/a o dentista a su compañero/a. Mencione por lo menos tres características.

MODELO: Mi médico/a es... Es un/a médico/a que...

SITUACIONES

Role A. A close relative of yours (husband, wife, son, daughter) has recently had surgery (*una operación*), and you need some information in order to fill out an insurance form. You call the hospital and ask a) the name of the doctor who performed surgery on your relative, b) the amount of time that the surgery took, c) the prescriptions that the doctor gave him/her, d) the number of days that he/she will have to stay at the hospital.

Role B. You work answering the phone at a local hospital. A relative of one of the patients calls to find out some information he/she needs in order to fill out an insurance form. Identify yourself and answer his/her questions.

MOSAICOS

Escuchar

VÍNCULOS

For materials related to the Mosaicos section, see
- SAM-OneKey: WB: 11-20, 11-21, 11-22, 11-23, 11-24, 11-25 / LM:11-43

Summarizing information

Sometimes when you listen to a conversation, a news report, or a lecture you need to summarize what was said for someone who was not present. To that end, you will give the general information of what was said and, when asked for or needed, will include some details to make your summary clearer. Needless to say, note taking is of paramount importance when summarizing. Therefore, jot down key information (ideas, words, concepts, data, etc.) in the order in which it appears in a listening text (a conversation, a lecture, etc.). Those notes will serve as the basis for your summary.

Antes de escuchar

11-26 ¿Cómo está Sebastián? In activity **11-27**, you will listen to a conversation between two friends regarding Sebastian's health. Before you listen, write down the Spanish names for three health professionals, three symptoms patients might experience, and three different types of treatments they might receive.

profesionales de la salud _____

síntomas _____

tratamientos _____

Audioscript for 11-27:

ROSINA: ¿Dices que Sebastián está muy enfermo? ¡Eso no puede ser! Yo lo vi hace dos semanas y estaba muy bien.

DIANA: Sí, es verdad, pero ahora Sebastián está en el hospital. La semana pasada tuvo un dolor de estómago muy fuerte, náuseas y fiebre muy alta. Tuvo que llamar a la ambulancia porque no podía manejar y, como vive solo, no tenía otra alternativa.

ROSINA: ¡Ay! ¡Cuánto lo siento! ¡Qué lástima! La próxima semana es su cumpleaños, y no va a poder celebrarlo con nosotros.

DIANA: No, no lo creo. El Dr. Méndez lo examinó y le recetó unos antibióticos. Parece que tiene una fuerte infección intestinal.

ROSINA: ¡Pobre! Seguro que le dieron una dieta especial también, ¿no?

DIANA: Sí, parece que la semana pasada fue a un restaurante y comió algo que no estaba fresco. Ahora en el hospital puede comer sólo cosas muy sanas. Claro, tú sabes, la comida del hospital no es buena. Afortunadamente, sus padres han llegado hoy para estar con él, y le van a preparar platos especiales.

ROSINA: ¡Qué bien! Ojalá que no tenga complicaciones y que salga pronto del hospital.

DIANA: Bueno, eso esperamos todos. ¿Por qué no vamos a visitarlo?

ROSINA: ¡Buena idea! Vamos esta tarde, si quieres.

A escuchar

11-27. Now, read the following statements. Then, listen to the conversation between two friends regarding Sebastian's health. Finally, circle the statement that better summarizes what you have heard.

1. Los padres y amigos de Sebastián están preocupados porque Sebastián está enfermo y no va a poder celebrar su cumpleaños la próxima semana.

2. Sebastián está en el hospital con una infección intestinal. Antes de ir, él tenía dolor de estómago, náuseas y fiebre. Ahora toma antibióticos y tiene una dieta especial.

3. Sebastián vive solo. Por eso, siempre come en un restaurante, y la semana pasada comió algo que no estaba fresco. Ahora, sus padres han venido a cuidarlo y a prepararle comida especial.

4. El Dr. Méndez es un excelente médico y dice que Sebastián va a salir del hospital pronto, pero tiene que empezar una dieta y cuidarse mucho.

Después de escuchar

11-28 ¿Y usted? Share your answers to the following questions:

1. ¿Tiene usted una dieta sana? ¿Qué come típicamente para el almuerzo o la cena?
2. ¿Come usted en restaurantes frecuentemente? ¿Por qué?
3. ¿Qué cree usted que debe hacer para mantener o mejorar su salud?

La salud y los médicos   413

Antes de escuchar

11-29 Consejos de la nutricionista. In 11-30, you will listen to a conversation between a nutritionist and a group of college students. Before you listen, write down a list of four suggestions you think the nutritionist will make and two questions the students will probably ask her.

consejos. _____

_____

posibles preguntas _____

_____

A escuchar

AUDIO **11-30 Consejos de la nutricionista.** Now, read the following statements and, then, listen to the advice a nutritionist gives a group of college students. Finally, circle the statement that best summarizes what you have heard.

1. La nutricionista les recomienda a los estudiantes que vean al médico una vez por mes.
2. La nutricionista les aconseja que hagan mucho ejercicio y coman comida con poca sal.
3. La nutricionista les sugiere que coman comida rápida y beban alcohol sólo los fines de semana.
4. La nutricionista aconseja la moderación en la comida, bebida y ejercicios para mantener una vida saludable.

Después de escuchar

11-31 ¿Y usted? With a classmate, share your answers to the following questions.

1. ¿Cuál es su rutina diaria con respecto a su comida y actividades?
2. ¿Qué hace usted para mantener una vida saludable?
3. ¿Qué aspecto de su vida piensa usted que puede cambiar para mejorar su estado físico?

 ## Conversar

Antes de conversar

11-32 ¿Quiere vivir más? Primera fase. Marque los hábitos o condiciones que, según usted, ayudan a prolongar la vida de las personas.

1. _____ hacer ejercicio físico regularmente
2. _____ trabajar poco
3. _____ tener mucho estrés
4. _____ comer regularmente carne roja
5. _____ ser vegetariano/a
6. _____ consumir carne blanca
7. _____ beber vino con el almuerzo o la cena
8. _____ pasar muchas horas inactivo
9. _____ usar la medicina alternativa
10. _____ usar muchos condimentos
11. _____ ponerle mucha sal a la comida

Audioscript for 11-30. NUTRICIONISTA: Como ustedes saben, es necesario mantener una dieta sana y balanceada para evitar enfermedades y mantener un peso ideal. En primer lugar, es necesario hacerse un examen médico anual, no fumar ni consumir mucho alcohol.

FABIÁN: Pero aquí en la universidad todos salimos los fines de semana y tomamos cerveza para relajarnos y divertirnos. ¿Qué tiene eso de malo?

NUTRICIONISTA: En realidad tomar cerveza o vino tinto no es malo, siempre que sea en cantidades moderadas. Todo es cuestión de moderación. La sal, por ejemplo, es buena, pero en altas cantidades puede ser dañina.

FABIOLA: ¿Y la carne roja?

NUTRICIONISTA: Es necesario limitar el consumo de grasas animales para evitar el aumento del colesterol en la sangre el pescado y el pollo tienen menos grasa.

FABIÁN: En mi casa mis padres comen muchas frutas y verduras, pero a mí no me gustan mucho.

NUTRICIONISTA: Es una lástima, porque las frutas y verduras tienen muchos minerales y vitaminas. Además, tienen fibra, y la fibra es buena para la salud.

FABIOLA: Yo quiero bajar de peso. ¿Qué debo hacer?

NUTRICIONISTA: Mantén una dieta balanceada y haz ejercicios regularmente, por lo menos veinte minutos, tres veces a la semana. No es conveniente bajar mucho de peso rápidamente; es preferible bajar poco a poco y cambiar los hábitos de comida y ejercicios. Así se puede mantener el peso ideal, mejorar la salud y la apariencia física.

FABIOLA: Bien, voy a ver si puedo hacer lo que usted dice. Suena fácil, pero debo tener mucha disciplina.

FABIÁN: Sí, es verdad, sobre todo los fines de semana.

NUTRICIONISTA: Recuerden, todo con moderación. Incluso hacer mucho ejercicio puede hacer daño. Buena suerte, y si necesitan más información pueden venir a verme en el hospital.

Possible answers for 11-32. Answers may vary, but students may check the following responses: 1, 5, 6, 7, 10.

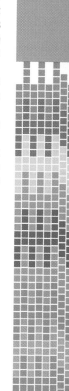

Suggestion for 11-32. Segunda fase. Since students will use the questionnaire in activity 11-33, you may want to prepare only one version for the whole class to use. To that end, have groups share with the class their questions in every specific area. Have students vote on the better (more interesting, more suitable) questions, and have a couple of students prepare the final questionnaire for the class for extra credit.

Ⓖ **Segunda fase.** Primero, comparen sus respuestas a las preguntas de la **Primera fase** y, luego, escriban un cuestionario para determinar si las personas hacen o no lo necesario para vivir más años. Consideren las siguientes áreas en su cuestionario.

TEMAS	EJEMPLOS
1. actividades/hábitos	¿Se mantiene usted activo/a?
2. comida	¿Consume verduras regularmente?
3. bebidas	¿Bebe alcohol? ¿Con qué frecuencia?

A conversar

❷ **11-33 ¿Te cuidas para vivir más?** Usen el cuestionario de la actividad **11-32**, **Segunda fase** para entrevistarse entre ustedes. Tomen notas de la información adicional importante que mencione su compañero/a durante la conversación. Esto los/las puede ayudar a determinar si cada uno de ustedes realmente se cuida o no para vivir más.

Después de conversar

11-34 Para reflexionar. Use la información que le dio su compañero/a en **11-33** y converse con él/ella sobre lo siguiente:

1. Mencione las actividades de su compañero/a que, según usted, van a contribuir a una vida más larga. Felicítelo/la (*Congratulate him/her*).
2. También indique los buenos hábitos de alimentación (comida, bebida) de su compañero/a que prolongarán la vida de él/ella.
3. Si es necesario, dele consejos o recomendaciones para mejorar sus hábitos.

Antes de conversar

❷ **11-35 Las enfermedades del siglo XXI. Primera fase.** Marquen los tipos de enfermedades que probablemente se asocian con este siglo.

1. _____ cardiovasculares
2. _____ respiratorias
3. _____ mentales
4. _____ nerviosas

Segunda fase. Escriban por lo menos dos ejemplos de enfermedades específicas en cada grupo.

1. cardiovasculares _____
2. respiratorias _____
3. mentales _____
4. nerviosas _____

EN DIRECTO

To congratulate or praise someone:

Felicitaciones por + [*verb, noun*].

Te felicito. Te alimentas muy bien.

¡Qué bien, [*name*]! Vas a vivir muchos años.

To express happiness or satisfaction at someone's success:

Me alegro de que + [*subjunctive*].

¡Qué fabuloso que + [*subjunctive*]!

Suggestion for 11-34. You may wish to ask students to prepare in advance (outside of class) for this activity by organizing the information they gathered and writing out some thoughts.

A conversar

2 **11-36 ¿Qué es bueno hacer?** Averigüen si alguien que ustedes conocen (familiar, amigo o conocido) sufre de alguna de las enfermedades mencionadas en actividad **11-35**. Luego, den una recomendación general y otra específica para los pacientes con estas enfermedades.

ENFERMEDAD ESPECÍFICA	PACIENTE	RECOMENDACIÓN GENERAL	RECOMENDACIÓN ESPECÍFICA
Cardiovascular: _____			
Respiratoria: _____			
Mental: _____			
Nerviosa: _____			

Después de conversar

G **11-37 ¿Qué debemos saber y hacer?** Preparen una breve presentación de una enfermedad del siglo XXI que a ustedes les interese para compartir con la clase. Hagan lo siguiente:

1. Den el nombre de la enfermedad e indiquen los órganos o partes del cuerpo afectados.
2. Indiquen los síntomas básicos de la enfermedad.
3. Mencionen algunos tratamientos médicos.
4. Den dos recomendaciones generales y dos específicas para los pacientes.

Para que su presentación sea más clara e interesante, usen material visual, como fotos, videos, afiches, etc.

 ## Leer

Identifying what information is relevant in a text and disregarding what is irrelevant are time-saving strategies. They help you become not only a more fluent reader, but also a more focused one. By filtering information (identifying what's important and letting go of what is not), you also become a more accurate reader. The following cues may help you identify what is important:

- Read the title and subtitle of the text.

- Brainstorm its possible content by using your knowledge of the topic or theme.

- Take notes of key information or ideas that, in your view, the text should include.

Guía de prelectura

Look at the visuals, the title, and the subheads in activity **11-40** and then answer the following questions. Use the cues provided by the headline and subheading and your personal knowledge to answer. Do not worry if your attempts to anticipate the content of the text are incorrect. You will be able to correct your responses later.

Suggestions for 11-36. You may wish to ask students to do some brief research on the some website addresses. Here students go to **www.prenhall.com.** Remind them to take notes, they can also save information (facts, pictures, website addresses, etc.) for future reference.

Suggestions for 11-37. Should technology be available, you may encourage students to do a PowerPoint presentation. The Web has plenty of information and visual material for student use. However, you may wish to limit sources to Spanish.

EN DIRECTO

To make a general recommendation:
Es importante/bueno/ conveniente/aconsejable + [*infinitive*].

To make a recommendation to someone specific:
Es importante que + [*name*(s)] + [*subjunctive*].

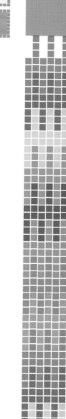

1. What key information (concepts, ideas, etc.) will this article likely contain?
   a. Diseases unknown to man appear because of the opening of new economic markets around the world.
   (b.) Diseases that experts thought had disappeared emerge again due to environmental changes around the world.
   (c.) Infectious, killer diseases that travel across the oceans are on the rise.
   (d.) Poor, developing nations export their diseases as their citizens migrate to developed countries.

Note. Answers for question 2 may vary.

2. How did you figure out the answers to question 1? Circle the corresponding letter.
   (a.) The title, subtitle, and photo
   b. The visuals in the text
   (c.) Knowledge of the topic
   (d.) Some research I did before reading the article

3. Now, can you hypothesize about the probable content of the text? The article will probably present the following content. Circle all that apply:
   (a.) The names of some of the diseases more commonly associated with globalization.
   (b.) Key geographical areas around the world where some infectious diseases were born.
   (c.) Explanation for the emergence of some diseases that were previously eliminated.
   (d.) Some measures the governments are taking to prevent the spread of such infectious disease.
   e. An analysis of how globalization is responsible for the spread of certain diseases.

Antes de leer

2 **11-38 Preparación. Primera fase.** ¿Cuáles de las siguientes enfermedades se consideran enfermedades tropicales? Márquenlas.

1. _____ la gripe
2. __X__ la tuberculosis
3. __X__ el dengue
4. __X__ el virus del Nilo
5. _____ la fiebre del pollo (*SARS*)
6. __X__ la malaria
7. __X__ la viruela (*smallpox*)
8. _____ la neumonía

Answers for 11-38. Segunda fase.
1: *la tuberculosis, el dengue, el virus del Nilo*;
2: 2, 3, 4, 5, 6, 7.

2 **Segunda fase.** Determinen lo siguiente:
1. ¿Cuál(es) de las enfermedades de la **Primera fase** ya está(n) presentes en su país?
2. ¿Cuál(es) de las enfermedades de la **Primera fase** es/son contagiosa(s)?

Suggestions for 11-39. You may provide students with web addresses—so they can do their research. Send them to www.prenhall.com for links. Encourage them to use visuals in their presentations.

G **11-39 ¿Cuáles son las causas y síntomas?** Hagan una breve investigación para averiguar las causas y síntomas de **dos** de estas enfermedades: la malaria, la fiebre del pollo, la tuberculosis, el dengue. Luego, compartan la información con la clase. El siguiente plan les puede ser útil.

1. lugar de origen y causa de la enfermedad
2. síntomas
3. posibles tratamientos

A leer

11-40 Primera mirada. Lea el siguiente artículo y, luego, siga las instrucciones.

Las enfermedades y la globalización

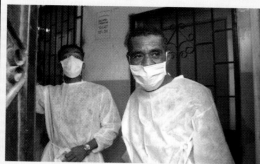

Enfermedades tropicales como el dengue, la viruela, la malaria, la tuberculosis, la enfermedad del sueño que, según muchos, ya no existían, reaparecen y se extienden por todo el mundo. Las causas de su reaparición son evidentes: cambios en el medio ambiente y el constante movimiento de personas entre los continentes. Los turistas y los trabajadores migratorios transportan estos virus e infecciones. De la misma manera, los cambios climáticos facilitan la adaptación de los virus a nuevos ambientes y los hacen resistentes.

Desafíos y prevención

Un claro ejemplo del nivel de adaptabilidad de estas enfermedades infecciosas es la tuberculosis. Los científicos pensaban que ésta estaba controlada en los países desarrollados. Sin embargo, los hechos nos muestran que esta enfermedad ha evolucionado de tal manera que en países desarrollados como Alemania, Italia o España, por ejemplo, hay pacientes con tuberculosis porque las bacterias no reaccionan a los medicamentos tradicionales. Se piensa que alrededor de un 32% de la población del mundo sufre y morirá de esta enfermedad.

La Organización Mundial de la Salud (OMS) expresa gran preocupación por la malaria. Según los expertos, el mosquito que la provoca puede sobrevivir largos viajes interoceánicos. Por eso, hay personas enfermas de malaria en muchas partes del mundo. Sin duda, la malaria es peligrosa si no se detecta a tiempo. Sus síntomas son semejantes a los de la gripe; por lo tanto un médico sin experiencia en este tipo de enfermedades la puede confundir con la gripe y tratarla con medicamentos inadecuados.

El virus del Nilo constituye otra de las enfermedades turistas. Esta enfermedad mató por lo menos a 125 norteamericanos en el año 2002 y alarmó a varios países europeos.

Sorpresa y medidas

A fines del siglo XX, gracias a una campaña mundial contra la viruela, casi toda la población mundial fue inmunizada contra esta enfermedad. Sin embargo, en la actualidad, la viruela de los monos, una variedad típica de la selva de algunos países africanos, ya se reproduce en otros lugares del globo, como los Estados Unidos. En este país se están volviendo a fabricar vacunas contra esta enfermedad que no se producían desde hacía años.

El dengue es indudablemente la enfermedad más extendida en los últimos años. Los expertos afirman que es posible que dos quintas partes de la población del mundo contraigan esta mortal fiebre endémica. Geográficamente, el dengue nació en el suroeste asiático, pero rápidamente pasó al Caribe y Centro y Sudamérica. En los últimos años, se han detectado casos incluso en España.

Las migraciones en masa, causadas por las guerras, y la falta de fondos en los ministerios de salud han provocado el retorno de la enfermedad del sueño en África. Los estudios indican que más de 100.000 individuos están infectados en el África subsahariana. Este fenómeno se repite en países como Sudán y Uganda.

La lista de enfermedades que surgen de nuevo por la movilidad de la población del mundo actual es larga, pero los fondos mundiales para realizar investigaciones sobre las enfermedades que causan el 90 por ciento de las muertes en el mundo son mínimos y limitados. Sin duda, la globalización ha resuelto algunos problemas, pero ha creado otros.

De las siguientes afirmaciones, indique cuáles representan ideas principales (**P**) del artículo y cuáles son ideas secundarias (**S**).

1. ___P___ La reaparición de algunas enfermedades es causada por la interconexión de los mercados del mundo.
2. ___P___ La gran movilidad de las personas por razones económicas causa la reaparición de enfermedades tropicales que en algún momento desaparecieron.
3. ___P___ Los cambios de clima, provocados por los cambios en el medio ambiente (*environment*), ayudan a que algunos virus sean más resistentes.
4. ___S___ Las enfermedades turistas mataron a norteamericanos y europeos.
5. ___P___ Algunas enfermedades que nacieron en un punto específico del mundo se expanden a otros continentes.
6. ___S___ Los países desarrollados como los Estados Unidos están fabricando vacunas para combatir algunas enfermedades contagiosas.

11-41 Segunda mirada. Según el contenido del artículo, subraye las expresiones que se relacionan con estos temas:

1. Enfermedades tropicales: las infecciones, <u>la viruela</u>, <u>el virus del Nilo</u>, <u>la tuberculosis</u>, <u>la enfermedad del sueño</u>
2. Desafíos de las enfermedades para los expertos: la infección, <u>la adaptabilidad</u>, el desarrollo, <u>la evolución</u>, <u>la resistencia</u>
3. Medidas que los gobiernos toman para enfrentar estas enfermedades: <u>campañas</u>, <u>inmunización</u>, reproducción, <u>vacunas</u>, <u>prevención</u>

Después de leer

11-42 Ampliación. Primera fase. Busque en el artículo la palabra que se asocia con los verbos de la lista. Luego clasifíquela en la columna apropiada. Subraye la terminación de la palabra. ¿Qué género tiene, femenino o masculino?

VERBO	SUSTANTIVO	GÉNERO
1. enfermarse	enferme<u>dad</u>	femenino
2. reaparecer	reapari<u>ción</u>	femenino
3. mover	movim<u>iento</u>	masculino
4. adaptar	adapta<u>ción</u>	femenino
5. prevenir	preven<u>ción</u>	femenino
6. migrar	migra<u>ción</u>	femenino
7. retornar	retorn<u>o</u>	masculino
8. globalizar	globaliza<u>ción</u>	femenino

Segunda fase. Complete el siguiente texto con un verbo o sustantivo de la **Primera fase.**

La interconexión del mundo actual

Muchos piensan que los efectos de la (1) ___globalización___ siempre son positivos. Sin embargo, hay un gran número de personas en todo el mundo que cree lo contrario. Según ellos, es triste ver que muchas de las (2) ___enfermedades___ que ya se creían eliminadas (3) ___reaparecen___ con mucha fuerza y amenazan matar a millones de víctimas inocentes en todos los continentes. Piensan que los países desarrollados y más ricos pueden tomar medidas para (4) ___prevenir___ la propagación de estas enfermedades mortales. No obstante, la realidad indica que el (5) ___movimiento___ masivo de inmigrantes entre los continentes inevitablemente facilita el (6) ___retorno___ de éstas.

Escribir

In our daily lives, we regularly share information by summarizing what we hear, see, or read. The focus of a good summary is on the main issues or facts upon which the story, event, or experience is based. When we summarize, we progressively reduce the original text by eliminating secondary ideas, redundancies, repetitions, etc.

A good written summary has, among others, the following features:

a. It presents the main ideas or characteristics of the object being summarized
b. It sums up all the parts of what is being recapitulated
c. It has a cohesive and coherent organization

Therefore, to write a good summary, keep in mind the following:

a. Read a text or observe carefully. Identify the theme of your summary, the time frame when what you are summarizing exists or takes place, the reasons for its existence or why it happened, who is responsible for its existence or occurrence, what the consequences are (when applicable), etc.
b. Collect all the relevant information and organize it. Distinguish main ideas or information from secondary ones. Underline them.
c. Find a method or system that will help you remember. Taking notes, diagramming, outlining may work for you.
d. Be brief; that is, avoid details.

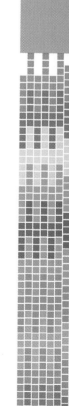

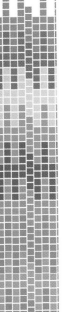

Antes de escribir

11-43 Preparación. Primera fase. El siguiente es un resumen de un evento histórico relacionado con la salud. Léalo y, luego, siga las instrucciones.

Según algunos, el año 1526 marca un evento trágico para los indígenas de América. Ocurre la primera epidemia de viruela que mata a miles de indios en los Andes. Esta nueva enfermedad contagiosa que llegó con los europeos al continente americano encontró a los nativos sin defensas para enfrentarla.

Sin embargo, la historia nos indica que fueron los indígenas del Caribe los primeros contagiados por las enfermedades europeas. Se piensa que el 9 de diciembre de 1493, la influenza tocó las puertas de América cuando 1.500 hombres y animales domésticos desembarcaron en Santo Domingo. Al día siguiente de su llegada, los pasajeros del barco Isabela empezaron a presentar síntomas evidentes de influeza: alta fiebre e intenso dolor en el cuerpo al punto de la postración. Éstos contagiaron a los indígenas, quienes murieron por miles.

Aunque varias enfermedades cruzaron los océanos para llegar a América, la que causó mayor desolación y muerte entre la población indígena fue la viruela. Nuevamente, los indios de Santo Domingo fueron las primeras víctimas en 1518 y 1519. Según los datos históricos, sólo un millón de ellos lograron sobrevivir la mortal epidemia.

Segunda fase. Answer the following questions, based on the summary in the **Primera fase.**

1. Circle the theme of the summary:
   a. Indigenous people of America infected the helpless conquistadors with their infectious diseases.
   b. Conquistadors brought unknown, contagious diseases that killed large numbers of indigenous people in America.
   c. Animals brought by conquistadors killed only American Indians with whom they came into contact.

2. Is there a time frame for this historical event?   Yes   No

3. If yes, indicate a time frame when the event happened.
   a. The beginning of the sixteenth century
   b. The end of the fifteenth and the beginning of the sixteenth centuries

4. Mark some possible reasons that explain this event.
   a. The Spaniards wanted to kill as many Indians as possible to take over their land.
   b.) The animals the conquistadors brought along spread the infectious disease among the ship crew who, in turn, passed it on to the American Indians with whom they came into contact.
   c.) The American Indians' immune systems were defenseless and unprepared to fight these diseases.

5. Identify the consequences of this event.
   a. Everyone infected survived.
   b.) Probably some of the Spaniards survived, but many American Indians died.
   c. Everyone died.

11-44 Antes de resumir. Primera fase. En la actividad **11-45**, usted va a resumir un texto sobre un tema de salud de su elección. Pero antes, lea la siguiente lista de posibles temas y seleccione uno que le interese. Escriba algunas ideas que lo/la ayuden a enfocar su atención en el tema que escogió.

1. la viruela
2. la fiebre del pollo
3. la enfermedad del sueño
4. el dengue
5. la malaria
6. la hepatitis

ENFERMEDAD	LUGAR DE ORIGEN	CAUSAS	SÍNTOMAS BÁSICOS
• _____	• _____	• _____	• _____
		• _____	• _____
		• _____	• _____

Segunda fase. Ahora haga lo siguiente.

1. Lea el/los artículo(s) del tema que seleccionó.
2. Identifique el tema del texto, el tiempo en que se sitúa o existe, las razones de su existencia, el/los responsable(s), las consecuencias, etc.
3. Separe la información (ideas, conceptos, datos, etc.) más importante de la secundaria y tome notas.
4. Haga una lista de palabras que le van a ser útiles para darle cohesión a su texto.

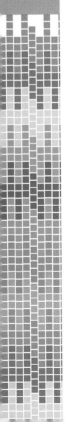

A escribir

11-45 Manos a la obra. Escriba el resumen del texto que leyó en **11-44, Segunda fase.** Use la información que preparó en la actividad **11-44, Segunda fase.** No olvide que su resumen debe ser breve y conciso.

Después de escribir

11-46 Revisión. Antes de darle el resumen a su compañero/a editor/a, léalo y verifique lo siguiente, pensando en su lector.

- El contenido. En su resumen, ¿se concentró en el tema central del artículo? ¿Incluyó toda la información importante? ¿Puso el evento/la experiencia/el fenómeno dentro de un marco de tiempo? ¿Dio las razones que lo explican?

- La organización. ¿Tiene su resumen un orden y organización claros?

- La gramática. ¿Usó el vocabulario correcto, algunas expresiones de cohesión, la concordancia, el tiempo (presente, pasado) y modos (indicativo, subjuntivo), etc.?

- La puntuación y ortografía. ¿Usó comas, puntos, etc. donde eran necesarios?

Finalmente, comparta su resumen con su compañero/a.

ENFOQUE CULTURAL

TEMAS: LAS FARMACIAS Y LA MEDICINA NO TRADICIONAL

Para pensar

Cuando usted necesita una operación o tiene un accidente, ¿adónde va? ¿Tiene que pagar o no? Cuando usted está enfermo/a y necesita medicinas, ¿adónde va a comprarlas? ¿Qué necesita para comprarlas?

En la mayor parte de los países hispanos existen hospitales y centros de salud financiados por el gobierno donde las personas pueden ir sin tener que pagar absolutamente nada por los servicios o medicinas que reciben.

En muchos países, especialmente en los caribeños, algunas personas van a ver a los curanderos, quienes, según la creencia popular, tienen poderes especiales para curar todo tipo de enfermedad.

En el mundo hispano, las farmacias están en locales separados y venden todo tipo de remedios y artículos de belleza. Al igual que en los Estados Unidos, en muchos lugares se necesita tener receta médica para comprar antibióticos. Muchas veces los clientes de la farmacia le preguntan al/a la farmacéutico/a qué remedio o antibiótico deben comprar para curar o tratar su enfermedad.

Para contestar

2 **El sistema de salud.** Respondan a las siguientes preguntas.

1. ¿Qué saben ustedes del sistema de salud público y privado en algunos países hispanos?
2. ¿Cómo son las farmacias en los países hispanos? ¿Qué venden?
3. Además de las medicinas tradicionales, ¿qué otro tipo de medicinas toman algunas personas en los países hispanos? Nombren dos o tres medicinas y digan para qué sirven.

G **Riqueza cultural.** En grupos de tres, discutan las ventajas y desventajas de consultar a un curandero (especialista en yerbas medicinales) o algún otro especialista en medicina alternativa como un acupunturista o un reflexólogo. Luego, presenten a la clase sus conclusiones.

Muchas personas prefieren curarse con yerbas medicinales. Por ejemplo, para el dolor de estómago se recomienda tomar un té de manzanilla (camomille), o un té de ruda (rue). Otra yerba medicinal muy conocida es la uña de gato (cat's claw), que se considera buena para el tratamiento del cáncer.

VÍNCULOS

For materials related to the Enfoque cultural, see
- SAM-OneKey: WB: 11-26
- IRCD: Chapter 11; pg. 424

Cuba, La República Dominicana y Puerto Rico se encuentran en el Mar Caribe.

Para pensar

¿Sabe usted dónde quedan Cuba, Puerto Rico y la República Dominicana?
¿Sabe usted que Santo Domingo es la ciudad más antigua de las Américas?
¿Conoce usted a algún deportista o artista famoso de estos países?

En La Habana existen edificios de gran belleza y valor histórico, como el Castillo del Morro y la Fortaleza de la Cabaña.

La industria del tabaco es muy importante en Cuba. Se dice que el mejor tabaco del mundo se cultiva en Vuelta Abajo, en Pinar del Río, en el oeste de Cuba.

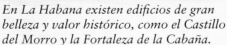

El Viejo San Juan es una hermosa zona de Puerto Rico donde hay tiendas de diferentes tipos, hermosas plazas, cafés al aire libre, museos, galerías de arte e interesantes edificios que datan de los siglos XVI y XVII. Al lado del Viejo San Juan está el San Juan moderno.

Expresiones cubanas:

la guagua	Ahí viene la **guagua**.	*The bus is coming.*
despeluzar	La quiere **despeluzar**.	*He wants to take all her money.*
fula	No tiene **fulas**.	*He does not have dollars.*

En el bosque tropical El Yunque se puede caminar por diferentes senderos, explorar hermosas caídas de agua y admirar diferentes especies de aves y una gran variedad de plantas, como las orquídeas y los helechos.

Santo Domingo, la capital, tiene una hermosa zona colonial con edificios que datan del siglo XVI. Entre ellos están la Catedral Primada de América, el Alcázar de Colón, las ruinas de San Francisco, el Museo de las Casas Reales y muchos más.

Expresiones puertorriqueñas:

macacoa	Yo no compro la lotería porque tengo una **macacoa** terrible.	*I do not buy the lottery because I have horrible bad luck.*
revolú	Se formó el **revolú**.	*Things got messy.*
bendito	¡Ay, **bendito**!	*Oh, my!*

Expresiones dominicanas:

varado	Me tiene **varado/a**.	*He/she keeps me from succeeding.*
aceitado	Está **aceitado/a**.	*He/she is ready to comply.*
se aflojó	Ya **se aflojó**.	*He/she chickened out.*

Para contestar

En el mapa

1. Diga dónde están Cuba, Puerto Rico y la República Dominicana y cuáles son sus capitales.
2. ¿Qué países están cerca de la República Dominicana?

En la República Dominicana hay muchos lagos y hermosos parques nacionales. Uno de los más conocidos es el Lago Enriquillo. En el centro de este lago se encuentra el Parque Nacional Isla Cabritos.

Ahora diga...

1. si le gustaría visitar La Habana, San Juan o Santo Domingo y por qué.
2. qué lugar de San Juan o de La Habana le interesaría visitar.

¿Qué dice usted si...

1. su amigo/a tiene miedo de hacer lo que pensaba hacer.
2. su amigo/a tiene mala suerte.
3. alguien le quiere quitar su dinero.

Para investigar en Internet

Busque información *www.prenhall.com/mosaicos* acerca de la medicina no tradicional en Cuba, Puerto Rico o la República Dominicana. Diga quiénes la practican, qué remedios, yerbas o productos usan, y qué personas recurren a ellos.

¡Prepárese!

11-47 Por y Para. Llene los espacios en blanco con **por** o **para.**

1. Ángela y Manolo trabajan ___por___ muchas horas en el concurso cada día.
2. Carlos perdona a Katie ___para___ llevarse mejor con ella.
3. Carlos mira el papel en la mochila de Katie ___para___ saber qué pista tiene ella.
4. ___Por___ sus acciones, Katie piensa que Carlos y Efraín tienen una alianza.
5. ___Para___ Efraín, la relación entre Katie y Carlos no es importante.
6. Efraín opina que la confianza es importante ___para___ tener éxito en el amor.

A Ángela no le gustan las acciones de Katie aunque ella está ganando.

Parece que Carlos ha perdonado a Katie.

Carlos mira el papel que está en la mochila de Katie.

Efraín admite que tiene una alianza con Carlos.

A Tito le interesa la relación entre Carlos y Katie, pero a Efraín no le importa.

Según Efraín, la falta de confianza no es buena para el amor.

¡Responda!

11-48 Asociaciones. Imagínese que es uno de los concursantes. Haga una asociación de palabras entre el Misterio 5 y las cuatro pistas. Después compare su lista con la de un/a compañero/a.

Misterio 5
Un lugar sagrado: _____

Pistas

1. Cerro sagrado: _____
2. Enseñanza militar: _____
3. Residencia presidencial: _____
4. Manantial y acueducto: _____

11-49 Soluciones. Al comparar su lista con la de su compañero/a, ¿qué ideas tienen para tratar de solucionar este misterio?

_____
_____
_____

En el Caribe el pregonero iba de casa en casa vendiendo muchos productos, especialmente frutas y vegetales. En esta canción Tito Nieves, cantante puertorriqueño conocido como el Pavarotti de la salsa, canta sobre el trabajo y los productos típicos del pregonero.

¡Prepárese!

Suggestion for 11-50. Discuss the difference in vocabulary and types of native fruits between Caribbean and other Spanish-speaking countries; for example, *quenepa*: a sour fruit with a hard skin, *guineitos*: bananas.

11-50 Los productos. Lea la lista de productos que vende el pregonero y trate de rellenar los espacios en blanco mientras escucha la canción.

quenepa	piña	guayaba	caña	tamarindo	guineitos
mango	naranja	coco	pomarrosas	toronja	

Ay, casera,
llevo la _____ fresca,
la _____ madura,
llevo la _____ dulce
Y el _____ seco, cáscara dura.
...

De Ponce le traigo la _____,
de Mayagüez el _____,
para rebajar la _____,
refresco de _____.

Venga y cómpreme caserita
porque yo soy pregonero

del río traigo _____,
del cañaveral caña dulce,
de mi bella playa coco seco
para ponerla dura la _____
para la desilusión corazones
de mi guineal _____

Salsa

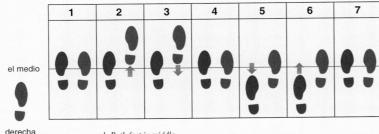

el medio

izquierda   derecha
(left)   (right)

1. Both feet in middle
2. Right foot forward; left foot in middle
3. Step in place with left foot, then move right foot back to middle
4. Both feet in middle
5. Left foot back; right foot in middle
6. Step in place with right foot, then move left foot back to middle
7. Both feet in middle

¡Escuche!

11-51 ¡Vamos a bailar salsa! "El pregonero" es un ejemplo de música **salsa,** un estilo musical bailable muy popular en las islas hispánicas del Caribe. Su ritmo es muy alegre y vivo; sus temas pueden ser serios o muy alegres. No importa el tema; a todos les gusta bailar salsa. Mire el diagrama de abajo y trate de seguir los pasos de salsa con sus compañeros de clase mientras escuchan la canción.

¡Responda!

11-52 El pregonero y la casera. La casera usa mandatos informales para hablar con el pregonero mientras él usa mandatos formales. Complete el diálogo.

PREGONERO: ¡(1) _Compre_ (Comprar) frutas y vegetales! ¡(2) _Mire_ (Mirar) lo que tengo aquí!

CASERA: (3) _Ven_ (Venir) acá; (4) _enséñame_ (enseñarme) las frutas más frescas que tienes.

PREGONERO: Tengo naranjas y piñas dulces. Tengo cocos buenísimos y también guíneos.

CASERA: (5) _Dame_ (Darme) una piña, tres naranjas y dos cocos, por favor. ¿Cuánto es?

PREGONERO: (6) _Págueme_ (Pagarme) dos dólares, por favor.

CASERA: ¿Tienes cambio?

PREGONERO: Sí, señora.

CASERA: Está bien. Gracias.

VOCABULARIO

AUDIO ## El cuerpo humano

la boca	mouth
el brazo	arm
el cabello	hair
la cabeza	head
la cadera	hip
la cara	face
la ceja	eyebrow
el cerebro	brain
la cintura	waist
el codo	elbow
el corazón	heart
el cuello	neck
el dedo	finger
el diente	tooth
la espalda	back
el estómago	stomach
la frente	forehead
la garganta	throat
el hombro	shoulder
el hueso	bone
el labio	lip
la mano	hand
la mejilla	cheek
la muñeca	wrist
el músculo	muscle
la nariz	nose
el nervio	nerve
el oído	(inner) ear
la oreja	(outer) ear
el pecho	chest
la pestaña	eyelash
el pie	foot
la pierna	leg
el pulmón	lung
la rodilla	knee
la sangre	blood
el tobillo	ankle
la vena	vein

Tratamientos médicos

la aspirina	aspirin
la inyección	injection
la pastilla	pill
la receta	prescription
el termómetro	thermometer

La salud

el catarro	cold
la enfermedad	illness
el/la farmacéutico/a	pharmacist
la fiebre	fever
la gripe	flu
la infección	infection
el síntoma	symptom
la tensión (arterial)	(blood) pressure
la tos	cough

Verbos

alegrarse (de)	to be glad (about)
caer(se)	to fall
cuidar(se)	to take care of
doler (ue)	to hurt
enfermarse	to become sick
estornudar	to sneeze
examinar	to examine
fracturar(se)	to fracture, break
fumar	to smoke
molestar	to bother, be bothered by
recetar	to prescribe
respirar	to breathe
sentir (ie, i)	to be sorry
sentirse (ie, i)	to feel
temer	to fear
torcer(se) (ue)	to twist
toser	to cough

Descripciones

deprimido/a	depressed
enfermo/a	sick
serio/a	serious

Palabras y expresiones útiles

cada... horas	every . . . hours
el consultorio	doctor's office
¿Qué te/le(s) pasa?	What's wrong (with you)?
tener dolor de...	to have a(n) . . . ache
tener mala cara	to look terrible

12

LAS VACACIONES Y LOS VIAJES

Objetivos comunicativos

- Making travel arrangements
- Asking about and discussing itineraries
- Describing and getting hotel accommodations
- Expressing denial and uncertainty
- Expressing possession (emphatically)
- Talking about the future

Contenido

A primera vista

- Los medios de transporte
- Las reservaciones y el hotel

Explicación y expansión

- Affirmative and negative expressions
- Indicative and subjunctive in adjective clauses
- Stressed possessive adjectives
- Possessive pronouns
- The future tense

Mosaicos

- Escuchar: Reporting what was said
- Conversar: Finding out people's plans and reporting them; giving advice
- Leer: Summarizing a text
- Escribir: Stating facts and giving advice

Enfoque cultural

- Temas: La música y el baile
- Vistas: Panamá y Costa Rica
  Para investigar en Internet
- Fortunas: Episodio 12
- Notas: "Ligia Elena", *Rubén Blades*

Vocabulario

A PRIMERA VISTA

Los medios de transporte

Mucha gente usa el transporte público. Los **autobuses** son populares en las ciudades y también para **viajar** largas distancias. Son la solución para las personas que no tienen **carro,** o a quienes simplemente no les gusta **manejar** en las **carreteras** y **autopistas.** El **metro** es otra forma de transporte eficiente en los centros urbanos, como Madrid, Barcelona, Santiago, Buenos Aires, Caracas y la Ciudad de México.

AVE, el **tren** español de alta velocidad entre Madrid y otras grandes ciudades españolas, viaja a unos 300 kilómetros por hora. La RENFE (Red Nacional de Ferrocarriles Españoles) es tan importante en España, un país relativamente pequeño, como las **líneas aéreas** en los Estados Unidos.

Un **crucero** es otra forma de **viajar.** En **barcos** modernos con una capacidad de 400 hasta más de 2.000 **pasajeros,** se puede hacer de todo. En las **escalas** en los diferentes puertos hay excursiones organizadas y oportunidades para ir de compras. De noche, la diversión continúa en la discoteca, el casino y el teatro. Un crucero es un medio de transporte y un lugar para pasar las vacaciones.

En un avión

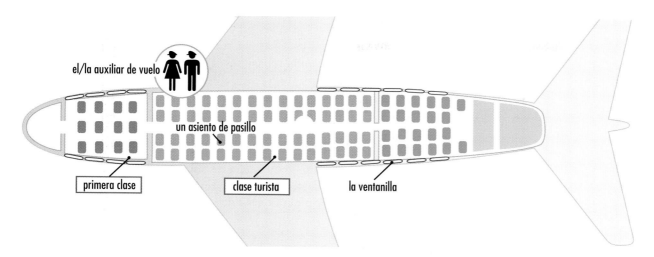

el/la auxiliar de vuelo

un asiento de pasillo

primera clase

clase turista

la ventanilla

El **avión** es la solución, aunque más cara, para viajar rápidamente de un lugar a otro, especialmente en zonas donde es difícil construir carreteras por la geografía o el clima, como en las selvas y en las montañas.

En el aeropuerto

Los pasajeros **hacen cola** frente al mostrador de la **aerolínea** para **facturar** el **equipaje,** pedir un **asiento** y conseguir la **tarjeta de embarque.**

el inspector de aduana

la aduana

el mostrador

VUELO: 190
DESTINO: SAN JOSÉ
SALIDA: 9:30

SALA DE ESPERA

la maleta

el equipaje

el maletín

VÍNCULOS

To practice vocabulario—Los medios de transporte

- SAM-OneKey: WB: 12-1, 12-2, 12-3, 12-4, 12-5 / LM: 12-28, 12-29, 12-30, 12-31, 12-32, 12-33
- Companion Website: AP 12-1 A, B
- IRCD: Chapter 12; pp. 433, 434, 435, 436, 438

Suggestions. Mention *azafata* as another word for la *auxiliar de vuelo*, especially in Spain; *aeromozo/a* is another variant.

Introduce the phrases *pasaje/boleto de ida y vuelta* and *pasaje/boleto de ida*.

Use the Image Resource CD to talk about a plane and recycle comparisons by asking students to compare first-class and tourist class.

In groups, students decide which is their favorite means of transportation and why. Then, they share their conclusions with the whole class.

Suggestions. Use the Image Resource CD and introduce vocabulary by talking about the illustration. Ask where the people are, what they are doing, what luggage they have, and so on. You may want to bring a packed suitcase or backpack to discuss what one should take on a trip. Have students plan a one-year trip. How much would such a trip cost? What would they take? What arrangements would be necessary in advance? Where would they go?

En el mostrador de la línea aérea

Suggestions. As a warm-up, talk about the dialog to practice vocabulary. Ask questions to check comprehension. Have students role-play the dialog.

Note. In Spain *billete* is used instead of *boleto/pasaje*.

EMPLEADA: Buenos días. Su **pasaporte** y su **boleto,** por favor.

VIAJERO: Aquí están. Y si es posible, prefiero un asiento cerca de una **salida de emergencia.**

EMPLEADA: Muy bien. ¿**Ventanilla** o pasillo?

VIAJERO: Pasillo, por favor. Señorita, ¿usted sabe si se venden **cheques de viajero** aquí en el **aeropuerto**?

EMPLEADA: Sí, hay una oficina de American Express enfrente a la derecha.

VIAJERO: Gracias. ¿Me acreditó los kilómetros a mi programa de viajero frecuente?

EMPLEADA: Sí, y su **pasaje** es **de ida y vuelta,** así que va a tener bastantes kilómetros. Su asiento a San José es el 10F. Aquí tiene su tarjeta de embarque. La puerta de salida es la 80. ¡Que tenga un buen viaje!

Suggestions. Ask questions regarding the arrival and departure times of the flights in the illustration. One student plays the role of an airline agent; a second student wants to find out the departure time and gate of a flight.

El avión para San José sale a las tres y media por la puerta 1A. ¿A qué hora sale el **vuelo** para Panamá?

SALIDA DEPARTURE DESTINATION	ABORDAR BOARDING	SALA LOUNGE	PUERTA GATE	DESTINO DESTINATION
3:30	3:00	B	1A	SAN JOSÉ
3:50	3:20	B	4	MANAGUA
4:10	3:40	B	6	GUATEMALA
4:25	3:55	B	10	PANAMÁ
4:45	4:15	B	8	LIMÓN
5:10	4:40	B	5	MÉXICO D.F.
6:00	5:30	D	5	KINGSTON

¿Qué dice usted?

Note for 12-1. You may point out that both *viajar por* and *viajar en* are used.

12-1 Asociaciones. Primera fase. Asocie cada palabra con su descripción. Luego, compare sus respuestas con las de un/a compañero/a.

1. ___d___ tren de alta velocidad
2. ___h___ viaje en un barco grande
3. ___a___ persona que sirve la comida en un vuelo
4. ___e___ transporte subterráneo
5. ___f___ inspección al llegar a otro país
6. ___b___ documento de identificación necesario para viajar al extranjero
7. ___g___ pasaje para ir de Quito a San José y volver a Quito
8. ___c___ se viaja en un asiento cómodo y se come bien

a. el/la auxiliar de vuelo
b. pasaporte
c. primera clase
d. AVE
e. metro
f. aduana
g. boleto de ida y vuelta
h. crucero

② Segunda fase. Hablen de su último viaje. Especifiquen:

- medio de transporte

- tipo de boleto

- comodidad (primera clase, turista, etc.)

- necesidad de pasaporte, pasar por aduana, etc.

② 12-2 Solicitud del cliente. Usted es un/a agente de viajes y su compañero/a es su cliente/a. Hágale preguntas a su cliente/a para llenar el siguiente formulario (*form*) y después hágale algunas recomendaciones para el viaje.

Suggestions for 12-2. Before doing this activity, you may wish to have students brainstorm the type of information a travel agent may request from a prospective client. Later, they may write down the questions they will ask.

NOMBRE: _____
Nº de pasaporte: _____
Fecha/s de viaje: _____
Medio de transporte: _____
Destino: _____

② 12-3 En una agencia de viajes. Primera fase. Busquen en Internet la siguiente información para planear un viaje turístico a Costa Rica:

- itinerario posible

- hoteles

- medios de transporte

- actividades y visitas

- precios de las distintas opciones

Segunda fase. Ahora túrnense para hacer el papel de agente de viaje y cliente/a. El/La cliente/a debe decirle al/a la agente de viajes que quiere viajar a Costa Rica. El/La agente debe recomendarle un viaje de acuerdo con los datos que obtuvo en la *Primera fase*.

Alternate for 12-3. As an alternative to the Internet, you may ask students to bring ads from the travel sections of newspapers or magazines and describe the trip they plan to take according to the information in the ad.

Ask students to give you the list of things they need for the trip by using the subjunctive: *Es necesario que yo/usted presente el pasaporte, tenga cheques de viajero, haga reservaciones para el vuelo,* etc. Discuss the travel plans in the class by reporting trip plans.

Follow-up for 12-4. Expand the car vocabulary by using newspaper or magazine ads. Ask yes/no and either/or questions to review and reinforce vocabulary. Discuss cars with students by talking about *carros/coches pequeños/grandes, consumo de gasolina, contaminación,* etc.   **AUDIO**

Suggest that students write an ad that advises on how to avoid accidents. The ad must have a title, tell what group or company sponsors it, and offer three original suggestions for avoiding accidents.

After students have studied car vocabulary, give half the class the picture of a car without the parts identified. The other students say the part of the car, and the first group must label it correctly.

Suggestion for 12-5. Students form groups to find out which car is the favorite. Then, they take a poll to find out which one is the favorite for the entire class.

Viajando en coche

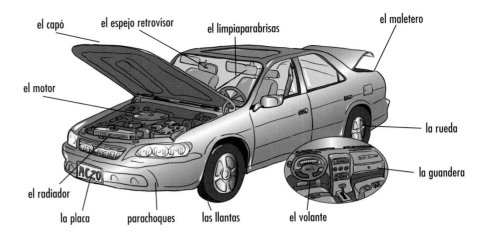

el capó — el espejo retrovisor — el limpiaparabrisas — el maletero — el motor — la rueda — el radiador — la guandera — la placa — parachoques — las llantas — el volante

¿Qué dice usted?

12-4 ¿Qué es? Busquen en el dibujo la palabra que corresponda a las siguientes descripciones. Después, den una descripción de las otras partes del coche indicadas en el dibujo para ver si otra pareja sabe qué son.

1. Es para poner el equipaje.   el maletero
2. Permite ver bien cuando llueve.   el limpiaparabrisas
3. Son negras y llevan aire por dentro.   las llantas
4. Controla la dirección del coche.   el volante
5. Hay que ponerle agua si no queremos   el radiador
   que se caliente el motor.

12-5 Mi auto favorito. Primero, averigüen qué medio de transporte usa cada uno de ustedes con más frecuencia. Después, pregúntense cuál es el auto favorito de cada uno y por qué. Cada uno debe dar cuatro razones para explicar por qué le gusta más.

Las reservaciones y el hotel

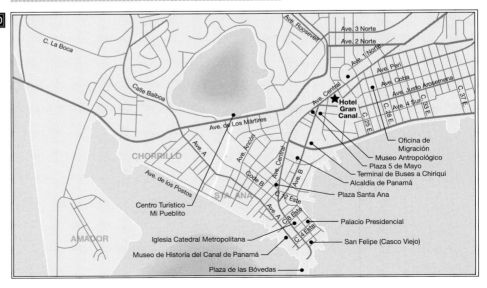

EMPLEADO: Buenas tardes. ¿En qué le puedo servir?

SRA. LOAIZA: Buenas tardes. Tenemos dos **habitaciones** reservadas a nuestro nombre, señores Loaiza.

EMPLEADO: Sí, señora. Tengo **una doble** y **una sencilla**.

SRA. LOAIZA: Muy bien. Una es para nosotros y otra para nuestro hijo. Quisiera dejar algunos cheques de viajero en un lugar seguro. ¿Podría usted…?

EMPLEADO: ¿Por qué no los deja en la **caja fuerte** de su habitación.

SRA. LOAIZA: Muy bien.

EMPLEADO: Bueno, aquí tiene las **llaves**. Enseguida les subirán las **maletas**. Sus habitaciones están en el segundo piso.

(*Más tarde.*)

SR. LOAIZA: Por favor, ¿nos puede indicar cómo llegar a la Plaza 5 de Mayo?

CONSERJE: Sí, cómo no. Mire, sigan derecho por esta calle hasta la próxima **esquina**. Allí, **doblen a la izquierda** y caminen una cuadra hasta la plaza que está **a la derecha**. No se pueden **perder**.

SR. LOAIZA: Muchísimas gracias.

¿Qué dice usted?

2 12-6 Estamos perdidos. Use el plano que aparece en la página 446 y pregúntele a su compañero/a cómo ir a ciertos lugares. Su compañero/a le debe explicar cómo llegar.

USTED ESTÁ EN:	USTED DESEA IR:
la Plaza 5 de Mayo	al Palacio Presidencial
la Avenida Ancón y la Avenida A	al Casco Viejo
el Museo de Historia del Canal de Panamá	al Centro Turístico Mi Pueblito

2 12-7 El hotel. Primera fase. Busquen en www.prenhall.com/mosaicos la siguiente información sobre el hotel de Costa Rica Selva Bananito Lodge y compártanla entre ustedes.

1. localización
2. instrucciones para llegar
3. servicios que ofrece el hotel
4. atracciones más interesantes en su opinión

Suggestions. Have students role-play seeking accommodations: One student plays the part of the registration desk clerk, the other is the guest. You may wish to provide additional vocabulary: *ascensor, taxista, inscribirse*. A variation: Each group must find lodging in its price range (*casa de huéspedes, albergue, pensión, posada, parador, hotel, hotel de lujo*). Tell students that in lower-price range establishments, it is often wise to ask to see the room before registering. Remind students of the polite use of *quisiera*. You say rudely *Quiero una habitación;* students correct you, *Quisiera una habitación*.

Variation. Have students work in pairs to role-play the following: You have just won a two-month trip anywhere in the Spanish-speaking world. Discuss with your partner where you would like to go; be specific about the places, dates, travel mode, and activities. Your partner will ask questions to get additional information about your plans.

Warm-up for 12-6. Model the activity and practice phrases for giving directions.

Suggestion. Introduce and practice phrases for giving directions by drawing a simple map of the university campus on the chalkboard or a transparency. Tell how to get from one place to the other: *Para ir a la biblioteca, salgo de este edificio y sigo derecho hasta la Facultad de Ciencias. Allí doblo a la izquierda y enseguida veo la biblioteca.* Then give directions to go to various buildings. If students have maps of the campus, they can follow the directions by drawing a dotted line. For additional practice with directions, use a map of your town or city and have students work in pairs, asking and giving directions.

Segunda fase. Usted sabe que el hotel *Selva Bananito Lodge* acepta guías voluntarios para los turistas que hablan inglés. Hable con el/la jefe/a de personal —otro/a compañero/a— para ofrecer sus servicios y obtener la siguiente información sobre el trabajo.

1. obligaciones y horarios
2. beneficios que reciben (comidas, alojamiento, etc.)
3. número de semanas o meses que dura el trabajo
4. fecha en que comienza el trabajo
5. forma más conveniente de llegar al hotel

Suggestions. Present the steps involved in sending a letter or a postcard. Then see if students can recall them (additional vocabulary: *estampilla, timbre, correo aéreo, correo ordinario, declarar, llenar un formulario*). You may wish to mention that stamps are also sold at tobacco shops in Spain. Recycle indirect object pronouns: *¿A quién... le escribe usted? ... le manda postales cuando está de vacaciones? ... le envía paquetes?*

El correo y la correspondencia

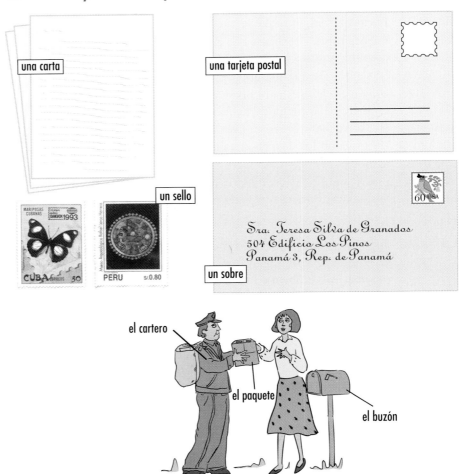

una carta

una tarjeta postal

un sello

un sobre

Sra. Teresa Silva de Granados
504 Edificio Los Pinos
Panamá 3, Rep. de Panamá

el cartero

el paquete

el buzón

A INVESTIGAR

La construcción del Canal de Panamá, que une el Océano Atlántico con el Océano Pacífico, hizo realidad un sueño de más de tres siglos. Requirió la participación de varios países y es una de las iniciativas internacionales que más positivamente ha influido en la economía mundial. Busque en Internet al menos tres datos sobre la historia del canal.

¿Qué dice usted?

12-8 La correspondencia. Primera fase. Completen las oraciones con la palabra adecuada y escriban la letra correspondiente.

1. __b__ El lugar donde se recoge la correspondencia y se compran sellos es el...
2. __a__ La persona que reparte cartas y tarjetas es el...
3. __f__ El depósito donde ponemos las cartas que queremos enviar es el...
4. __d__ Para mandar una carta la ponemos dentro de un...

a. cartero
b. correo
c. sello
d. sobre
e. paquete
f. buzón

5. ___e___ Si queremos mandar un regalo de una ciudad a otra, tenemos que preparar un…

6. ___c___ No se puede mandar una carta sin escribir la dirección y ponerle un…

2 **Segunda fase.** Respondan a las siguientes preguntas.

1. ¿Cuándo fue la última vez que usted fue al correo?
2. ¿Para qué fue? ¿Para comprar sellos o un sobre o para enviar un paquete?
3. ¿Es el correo electrónico un medio de comunicación más eficaz que el correo postal? ¿Por qué?

12-9 Un correo electrónico nostálgico. Primera fase. Envíele un mensaje electrónico o una postal a su compañero/a favorito/a. Cuéntele algunos aspectos especiales de sus últimas vacaciones:

■ lugar(es) que visitó

■ personas que conoció

■ experiencias interesantes o divertidas que vivió

■ otras experiencias que recuerda con nostalgia

Su compañero/a le responderá por escrito, reaccionará a sus comentarios y le hará preguntas para obtener más detalles.

12-10 Antes de viajar. You will listen to a young man who is checking in at the airport. Before you listen, list two questions you think the airline employee might ask him and the answers that you think the young man might provide.

_____

_____

Now, pay attention to the general idea of what is said. Then, as you listen mark the appropriate ending to each statement.

1. El viajero va a facturar…
   a. tres maletas
   b. un maletín de mano
   c. dos maletas

2. El viajero prefiere un asiento…
   a. al lado de ventanilla
   b. en el pasillo
   c. en la parte posterior del avión

3. El agente le puede conseguir un asiento…
   a. de pasillo, el 28C
   b. en el centro, entre la ventanilla y el pasillo
   c. en la ventanilla en primera clase

4. La empleada le dice al pasajero que…
   a. tiene tiempo para llamar por teléfono
   b. puede llamar desde el avión
   c. no tiene que pasar por seguridad

Note for 12-9. You may explain that in some countries the word *emilio* is used when referring to e-mail. In others, the word *emiliano* or *e-mail* is used.

Warm-up for 12-10. As a pre-listening activity, have students get in groups of four and discuss if they have traveled abroad and where, what documents they had to get before they traveled and what inconveniences they had to face.

Audioscript for 12-10:

AGENTE: Buenas tardes, señor. Su pasaje y pasaporte, por favor.

VIAJERO: Buenas tardes. Aquí están.

AGENTE: Muy bien. ¿Cuántas maletas va a facturar?

VIAJERO: Dos. Llevo también un maletín de mano, pero no lo voy a facturar.

AGENTE: Muy bien. Ponga las maletas aquí, por favor. Ahora dígame, ¿prefiere ventanilla, pasillo o en el centro?

VIAJERO: En el pasillo, por favor. Y quisiera uno de los primeros asientos.

AGENTE: Lo siento, pero sólo quedan asientos después de la fila 27. Le puedo dar el 28 C.

VIAJERO: Bueno, está bien.

AGENTE: La puerta de salida es el número 8. Aquí tiene su pasaporte y tarjeta de embarque. Ahora, pase por seguridad y luego diríjase a la puerta de salida.

VIAJERO: Gracias, señor. ¿Tengo tiempo para hacer una llamada?

AGENTE: Sí, el avión sale en 45 minutos. No se preocupe. Que tenga un buen vuelo.

EXPLICACIÓN Y EXPANSIÓN

VÍNCULOS

To practice affirmative and negative expressions

- SAM-OneKey: WB: 12-6, 12-7, 12-8, 12-9 / LM: 12-34, 12-35, 12-36, 12-37
- Companion Website: AP 12-2
- *Gramática viva*: Grammar Point 24: Negatives
- IRCD: Chapter 12, pg. 440

1. Affirmative and negative expressions

AGENTE: Lo siento, ese **vuelo** está **lleno.** No hay ningún asiento disponible.

RICARDO: ¿Y el de la tarde?

AGENTE: Hay algunos asientos **vacíos,** pero el vuelo **hace escala** en San José.

MARISELA: ¿Y no hay otro vuelo directo?

AGENTE: No, es el único; pero, ¿por qué no reservan en el vuelo de la tarde y los pongo en la **lista de espera** para el otro?

RICARDO: Está bien. Siempre hay alguien que **cancela.**

Note. *Nunca* and *jamás* may be used interchangeably, although *jamás* is more emphatic. For dramatic emphasis, you may wish to use them together: *Nunca jamás voy a viajar en esa aerolínea.*

AFFIRMATIVE		NEGATIVE	
todo	*everything*	nada	*nothing*
algo	*something, anything*		
todos	*everybody, all*	nadie	*no one, nobody*
alguien	*someone, anyone*		
algún, alguno/a (-os, -as)	*some, any, several*	ningún, ninguno/a	*no, not any, none*
o... o	*either . . . or*	ni... ni	*neither . . . nor*
siempre	*always*	nunca	*never, (not) ever*
una vez	*once*		
alguna vez	*sometime, ever*	jamás	*never, (not) ever*
algunas veces	*sometimes*		
a veces	*at times*		
también	*also, too*	tampoco	*neither, not*

■ Negative words may precede or follow the verb. If they follow the verb, use the word **no** before the verb.

> **Nadie** vive aquí.   *No one/Nobody lives here.*
> **No** vive **nadie** aquí.

■ **Alguno** and **ninguno** shorten to **algún** and **ningún** before masculine singular nouns.

> ¿Ves **algún** coche?   *Do you see any cars?*
> **No** veo **ningún** coche.   *I do not see any car.*

■ Use the personal **a** when **alguno/a/os/as** and **ninguno/a** refer to persons and are the direct object of the verb. Use it also with **alguien** and **nadie** since they always refer to people. Notice that in the negative only the singular forms **ninguno** and **ninguna** are used.

> ¿Conoces a **alguno** de los chicos?   *Do you know any of the boys?*
> **No**, no conozco **a ninguno**.   *No, I do not know any.*
> ¿Conoces **alguno** de los libros?   *Do you know any of the books?*
> No, **no** conozco **ninguno**.   *No, I do not know any.*

> **LENGUA**
>
> In Spanish, **ningunos/as** is used only with plural nouns that do not have a singular form; for example, **víveres** (*food, provisions*): **No trajeron ningunos víveres.**

¿Qué dice usted?

12-11 Nada de nada. Asocie cada pregunta con sus probables respuestas.

1. __e__ ¿Visitó usted Costa Rica alguna vez?
2. __d__ ¿Conoce a alguien en Panamá?
3. __b__ ¿Baila alguno de los bailes típicos de la región?
4. __c__ ¿Alguien sabe dónde está el volcán Irazú?
5. __f__ ¿Hay muchos estudiantes que viajaron a Panamá?
6. __a__ ¿Conoce alguna canción de Rubén Blades?

a. No, ninguna.
b. No, ninguno.
c. Nadie lo sabe.
d. No, a nadie.
e. No, nunca.
f. Sólo fueron algunos.

❷ 12-12 ¿Con qué frecuencia? Complete la siguiente tabla, indicando la frecuencia con que usted participa en las siguientes actividades, y diga por qué las hace. Después pregúntele a su compañero/a y anote la información obtenida.

MODELO: viajar a California
> E1: Yo viajo a California dos veces al año para visitar a mis padres. ¿Y tú?
> E2: Yo no viajo nunca porque mis padres viven en mi ciudad./Yo los llamo por teléfono todos los días porque los quiero mucho.

Follow-up for 12-12. Have students change partners and share with the new partner the information they obtained from the previous one.

ACTIVIDAD	YO	RAZÓN	MI COMPAÑERO/A	RAZÓN
ver programas sobre la naturaleza				
practicar el ciclismo				
comer en restaurantes hispanos				
dormir la siesta				
ir de vacaciones al Caribe				
viajar en tren				
usar el transporte público				

Warm-up for 12-13. Ask questions such as *¿Sirven bebidas alcohólicas? ¿Hay música?* Ask proficient students to answer negatively.

❷ **12-13 Un restaurante malo.** Usted está de viaje con un/a compañero/a y quiere ir a un restaurante que está cerca del hotel. Su compañero/a, que ya conoce el restaurante, va a contestar sus preguntas negativamente.

MODELO: servir platos típicos
          E1: ¿Sirven platos típicos?
          E2: No, no sirven ningún plato típico.

1. preparar platos de dieta
2. tener ensaladas buenas
3. servir pescado fresco
4. tener vinos de la región
5. aceptar tarjetas de crédito
6. …

❷ **12-14 ¡La negatividad es contagiosa!** Después de pasar el día con un amigo/a muy negativo/a, usted se siente influenciado/a y contesta a todo negativamente.

MODELO: llamar a alguien
          E1: ¿Vas a llamar a alguien?
          E2: No, no voy a llamar a nadie.

1. visitar Panamá alguna vez
2. ver alguna película esta noche
3. leer o escuchar música
4. salir con algún amigo
5. mandarle a alguien un correo electrónico
6. …

Warm-up for 12-15. Have students tell you what they want to do: *Quiero pasar una semana en la playa.* You agree: *Yo también.* Then have students tell you what they do not want to do: *No quiero llevar mucha ropa...* You agree: *Yo tampoco.*

❷ **12-15 Planeando un viaje. Primera fase.** Ustedes quieren hacer ecoturismo en Costa Rica. Primero comenten qué van o no van a hacer antes de llegar a su destino.

MODELO: comprar el pasaje dos semanas antes
          E1: Yo quiero comprar el pasaje dos semanas antes.
          E2: Yo también./Pues yo no. Es más barato comprarlo un mes antes.
          no llevar cheques de viajero
          E1: Yo no voy a llevar cheques de viajero.
          E2: Yo tampoco./Yo voy a llevar algunos y también mi tarjeta de crédito.

1. buscar información sobre Costa Rica
2. comprar zapatos cómodos para caminar
3. pedir un asiento de pasillo
4. no llevar mucha ropa
5. facturar el equipaje
6. no gastar mucho dinero
7. …
8. …

❷ **Segunda fase.** Conversen sobre todo lo que van a hacer después de llegar a su destino. Después, reúnanse con otra pareja y explíquenle tres de sus planes. Sus compañeros/as deben hacerles preguntas para averiguar detalles adicionales.

SITUACIONES

1. **Role A:** You are a flight attendant in business class. Ask one of your passengers if he/she would like to a) drink something, b) eat, and c) watch the film. Then a) answer his/her questions on the time of landing, b) tell him/her there are no magazines in Spanish, and c) offer him/her a blanket and pillow.

   Role B: You are a passenger in business class. Answer the flight attendant's questions negatively. Then a) ask him/her at what time the flight is scheduled to arrive in Panama, b) ask for a magazine in Spanish, and c) thank him/her.

2. One of you is a passenger, the other is a customs officer. The customs officer asks you, the passenger, if you are carrying a) any plants or seeds (*semillas*), b) fruit, and c) more than $10,000. Answer the questions in the negative. The customs officer will then ask you to open your luggage so that he/she can check it.

2. Indicative and subjunctive in adjective clauses

- An adjective clause is a dependent clause that is used as an adjective.

ADJECTIVE

Vamos a ir a un hotel muy **moderno.**

ADJECTIVE CLAUSE

Vamos a ir a un hotel **que es muy moderno.**

- Use the indicative in an adjective clause that refers to a person, place, or thing (antecedent) that exists or is known.

  > Hay un hotel que **queda** cerca de la estación.
  > *There is a hotel that is near the station.*

  > Quiero viajar en el tren que **sale** por la mañana.
  > *I want to travel on the train that leaves in the morning.*
  > (You know there is such a train.)

- Use the subjunctive in an adjective clause that refers to a person, place, or thing that does not exist or whose existence is unknown or in question.

  > No hay ningún hotel que **quede** cerca de la estación.
  > *There is not any hotel that is near the station.*

  > Quiero viajar en un tren que **salga** por la mañana.
  > *I want to travel on a train that leaves in the morning.*
  > (Any train, as long as it leaves in the morning.)

- When the antecedent is a specific person and functions as a direct object, use the indicative and the personal **a.** If the antecedent is not a specific person, use the subjunctive and do not use the personal **a.**

  > Busco **a** la/una auxiliar que **va** en ese vuelo.
  > *I am looking for the/a flight attendant that goes on that flight.*
  > (A specific flight attendant that I know is on that flight.)

  > Busco una auxiliar que **vaya** en ese vuelo.
  > *I am looking for a flight attendant that goes on that flight.*
  > (Any flight attendant as long as she goes on that flight.)

VÍNCULOS

To practice indicative and subjunctive in adjective clauses
- SAM-OneKey: WB: 12-10, 12-11, 12-12, 12-13 / LM: 12-38, 12-39, 12-40
- Companion Website: AP 12-3
- IRCD: Chapter 12; pg. 445

Suggestions. Use visuals to illustrate existent versus nonexistent antecedents. For example, a beach scene: *Hay personas que juegan al voleibol. Hay personas que están tomando helados, pero no hay nadie que escuche la radio. No hay nadie que esté nadando.* Present comparisons: *Sí, hay alguien que entiende esto.* (Existent.) *No, no hay nadie que lo entienda.* (Nonexistent.)

Suggestion. Ask questions with *hay,* using the indicative and the subjunctive: *¿Hay una clase que termina/termine a las cuatro?* Point out that when a person is not sure or has no knowledge of the existence of the antecedent, he/she uses the subjunctive.

■ In questions, you may use the indicative or the subjunctive according to the degree of certainty you have about the matter.

> ¿Hay alguien aquí que **sale** en ese vuelo?
> *Is there anyone here leaving on that flight?*
> (I do not know, but assume there may be.)

> ¿Hay alguien aquí que **salga** en ese vuelo?
> *Is there anyone here leaving on that flight?*
> (I do not know, but I doubt it.)

¿Qué dice usted?

12-16 ¿Cuál es la respuesta correcta? Marque la forma verbal (indicativo o subjuntivo) para completar correctamente cada grupo de oraciones.

1. Hay un vuelo que ___a___ por la mañana.	a. sale
2. No hay ningún vuelo que ___b___ por la noche.	b. salga

3. Me interesa un hotel (*any hotel*) que ___b___ cerca del centro.	a. queda
4. Hay un hotel que no es muy caro y ___a___ en el centro.	b. quede

5. Busco al empleado que ___a___ inglés.	a. habla
6. Busco un empleado (*any employee*) que ___b___ inglés.	b. hable

Warm up for 12-17. You may practice the use of the indicative and the subjunctive with *hay alguien* and *no hay nadie* before doing the activity: *—¿Hay alguien en esta clase que viaje en avión con frecuencia? —Sí, hay alguien que viaja... —¿Quién es? —Es... —¿Hay alguien que haga viajes largos en auto por lo menos una vez al año? —No, no hay nadie que haga... /Sí, hay alguien que hace...*

Suggestion for 12-17. Encourage students to make up additional questions using the sibjunctive. You may practice the use of *ningún* and *ninguna* when doing this activity.

❷ 12-17 ¡Ni idea! Usted no tiene ni idea sobre algunos aspectos de la vida de sus compañeros/as de la clase de español. Túrnense para hacerse preguntas. Si la respuesta es afirmativa, deben decir quién es esa persona y dar información adicional.

MODELO: usar vaqueros cuando viaja
E1: ¿Hay alguien que use vaqueros cuando viaja?
E2: Sí, hay alguien que siempre usa vaqueros cuando viaja.
E1: ¿Quién es?
E2: Es Marta. Sé que le gustan los vaqueros y siempre se los pone.
E1: ¿Hay alguien que sea costarricense?
E2: No, no hay nadie que sea costarricense.

1. tenerles fobia a los aviones
2. usar mucho su diccionario en los viajes
3. conocer una de las siete maravillas del mundo
4. saber pilotear un avión
5. ir a esquiar en sus vacaciones de invierno
6. viajar a Panamá este año

❷ 12-18 Emergencia. Dos empleados de la aerolínea costarricense Travelair se enfermaron, y hay mucho trabajo inconcluso en el aeropuerto. Túrnense para hacer los papeles de gerente y de ayudante de la aerolínea. El/La gerente necesita que se hagan ciertas cosas; su ayudante debe informarle si hay o no alguien que pueda hacerlas. Si no hay nadie, el/la gerente debe ofrecer soluciones.

MODELO: programar la computadora
            E1: Necesito a alguien que programe la computadora para los
                itinerarios.
            E2: Hay un empleado/alguien en el aeropuerto que puede hacerlo. *o*
                No hay nadie en el aeropuerto que la pueda programar.
            E1: Es indispensable buscar/que busquemos a alguien que lo haga.

1. hablar inglés, japonés y español en el vuelo a Tamarindo
2. recibir el vuelo que viene de Puerto Jiménez
3. darles esta información a los pasajeros del vuelo 562
4. llevar a los pasajeros a inmigración
5. poder trabajar este fin de semana
6. …

2 12-19 Un lugar para descansar. Primera fase. Túrnense para hacerse preguntas
sobre un lugar de descanso. Deben contestar según la información de la tabla.

MODELO: hotel / tener piscina para niños
            E1: ¿Hay un hotel que tenga piscina para niños?
            E2: Sí, hay un hotel que tiene piscina para niños. *o* No, no hay
                ningún hotel que tenga piscina para niños.

HAY	NO HAY
tiendas / vender ropa para esquiar	autobús / llegar por la mañana
cines / dar películas españolas	cafetería / servir comida vegetariana
lugares / aceptar cheques de viajero	lugares / aceptar cheques personales

Segunda fase. Ahora ustedes deben describir cómo desean que sea su lugar
ideal de descanso, explicando su localización, ambiente y atracciones. Después,
intercambien ideas con otra pareja.

2 12-20 Agencia *Viaje ahora.* Usted piensa viajar al extranjero, pero no conoce
ninguna buena agencia de viajes. Dígale a su compañero/a adónde quiere ir y
pídale información sobre una agencia. Su compañero/a le va a dar información
basándose en el anuncio de la agencia Viaje Ahora. Usted debe hacerle por lo
menos tres preguntas adicionales.

Note for 12-19. You may point out that when referring to theaters and films, the verbs *poner* and *pasar* are also used: *En ese cine ponen/ pasan películas extranjeras*

Suggestion for 12-19. Segunda fase. Before doing *Segunda fase,* have students brainstorm in small groups basic requirements they look for in a vacation spot. You may wish to classify the information as follows: *1. comodidades/ atracciones en los hoteles; 2. lugares de interés en la ciudad/ pueblo; 3. actividades interesantes en el lugar; 4. medios de transporte público; 5. tipo de tiendas; 6. características de los restaurantes/ bares, etc.*

Warm-up for 12-20. Have students skim the ad and ask some questions to check understanding: *¿Cómo se llama la agencia? ¿Dónde está la agencia?* After each answer, rephrase it by using an adjective clause: *Es una agencia que se llama Viaje Ahora. Es una agencia que está en Panamá.*

TURISMO
Viaje ahora
Servicio de viajes
Le planeamos su viaje a cualquier parte
de Panamá y del extranjero.
Boletos de avión, de barco; alquiler de autos;
reservaciones de hoteles; excursiones
20 años sirviendo al público
TELÉFONOS: 270-2040   270-3230
Calle 50 #134

Suggestion. Have students look for information on Panama in the Internet by going to www.pa/informacion.html. You may also wish to refer them to the culture section at the end of this chapter.

SITUACIONES

Role A. You want to visit Panama. Call your travel agent to find out: a) the cost of the trip, b) the flight schedule, and c) if you need a visa. Once you have the answers, explain to your travel agent the class of hotel you would like to stay in (area, approximate price range, etc.).

Role B. You are a travel agent. Answer your customer's questions and give him/her a) the prices of economy- and business-class tickets, b) the departure time. Ask for his/her nationality to know whether he/she needs a visa. Regarding hotels, give him/her information on two different rates and explain what each rate offers. You must also tell him/her what he/she should visit in Panama (the Canal, the old part of the city, the San Blas Islands, Darién, etc.).

VÍNCULOS

To practice stressed possessive adjectives & possessive pronouns
- SAM-OneKey: WB: 12-14, 12-15, 12-16, 12-17 / LM: 12-41, 12-42, 12-43, 12-44
- Companion Website: AP 12-4, AP 12-5
- *Gramática viva*: Grammar Point 31: Possessives
- IRCD: Chapter 12; pp. 446, 447

Suggestion. Before introducing stressed possessive adjectives, review short-form possessives: *mi, mis, tu, tus,* etc. Then compare *mis llaves* with *las llaves mías.* Have students practice using a few nouns with possessives.

3. Stressed possessive adjectives

SINGULAR		PLURAL		
MASCULINE	FEMININE	MASCULINE	FEMININE	
mío	**mía**	**míos**	**mías**	*my, (of) mine*
tuyo	**tuya**	**tuyos**	**tuyas**	*your (familiar), (of) yours*
suyo	**suya**	**suyos**	**suyas**	*your (formal), his, her, its, their, (of) yours, his, hers, theirs*
nuestro	**nuestra**	**nuestros**	**nuestras**	*our, (of) ours*
vuestro	**vuestra**	**vuestros**	**vuestras**	*your (familiar), (of) yours*

- Stressed possessive adjectives follow the noun they modify and agree with it in gender and number. An article or demonstrative adjective usually precedes the noun. Use stressed possessives for emphasis.

El cuarto **mío** es grandísimo.	*My room is very big.*
La maleta **mía** está en la recepción.	*My suitcase is at the front desk.*
Esos primos **míos** llegan hoy.	*Those cousins of mine arrive today.*
Las llaves **mías** están en la puerta.	*My keys are in the door.*

4. Possessive pronouns

SINGULAR				PLURAL			
MASCULINE		FEMININE		MASCULINE		FEMININE	
el	mío tuyo suyo nuestro vuestro	la	mía tuya suya nuestra vuestra	los	míos tuyos suyos nuestros vuestros	las	mías tuyas suyas nuestras vuestras

Suggestions. 1. Remind students that pronouns are used to avoid repetition of the noun. Provide examples: *¿Tienes tu mochila? ¿Dónde está la mía?* 2. Practice possessive pronoun forms by holding up items that belong to various students and saying: *¿Es mi mochila? No, es la suya,* etc.

- Possessive pronouns have the same form as stressed possessive adjectives.

- The definite article precedes the possessive pronoun, and they both agree in gender and number with the noun to which they refer.

¿Tienes la mochila suya?	*Do you have his backpack?*
Sí, tengo **la suya.**	*Yes, I have his.*

- After the verb **ser,** the article is usually omitted.

Esa maleta es **mía.**	*That suitcase is mine.*

- To be clearer and more specific, the following structures may be used to replace any corresponding form of **el/la suyo/a.**

la de usted	*yours* (singular)
la de él	*his*
la de ella	*hers*

la mochila suya → **la suya** *or*

la de ustedes	*yours* (plural)
la de ellos	*theirs* (masculine, plural)
la de ellas	*theirs* (feminine, plural)

¿Qué dice usted?

12-21 ¿De quién(es) son estas cosas? Escoja la repuesta correcta para cada una de las preguntas y escriba la letra correspondiente en la columna de la izquierda.

1. ¿Es ésta tu mochila? ___a___   a. Sí, es la mía.   b. Sí, es la tuya.
2. ¿Son éstas las llaves de Pedro? ___a___   a. Sí, son las suyas. b. Sí, son las mías.
3. ¿Es éste el maletín de Alicia? ___b___   a. No, es la tuya.   b. No, no es el suyo.
4. ¿Es éste su asiento? ___b___   a. Sí, es la mía.   b. Sí, es el mío.
5. ¿Son éstos los boletos nuestros? ___a___   a. Sí, son los suyos. b. Sí, son las suyas.

② **12-22 Las posesiones.** Es el fin del año escolar, y usted y su compañero/a están poniendo sus cosas y las de otro/a compañero/a en dos coches. Háganse preguntas para averiguar de quién es cada cosa.

MODELO: esta lámpara
E1: ¿De quién es esta lámpara?
E2: Es suya. Va en su coche. o Es mía. Va en mi coche.

1. esos casetes
2. esta maleta
3. este maletín
4. estos discos

5. las revistas
6. el radio
7. la bicicleta
8. esta mochila

② **12-23 Preparándose para un viaje.** Ustedes van a hacer un viaje en auto, y deben tomar varias decisiones antes de salir. Háganse preguntas para decidir lo que van a hacer, y den una razón.

MODELO: usar mi coche/tu coche
E1: ¿Vamos a usar mi coche o el tuyo?
E2: Prefiero usar el tuyo/mío porque es mejor/más nuevo.

1. hablar con mi agente/tu agente
2. llevar tus maletas/las de mi hermano
3. usar mis mapas/tus mapas

4. llevar tu cámara/mi cámara
5. llevar tu celular/el de mi madre
6. …

② **12-24 Unas vacaciones en un crucero.** Usted y un/a amigo/a tomaron un crucero durante las vacaciones. Su compañero/a tomó otro crucero. Intercambien sus experiencias en las áreas siguientes.

MODELO: el barco
E1: Nuestro barco era nuevo y grandísimo.
E2: El nuestro era pequeño, pero muy cómodo. o
El nuestro era muy grande también.

1. el camarote (*cabin*)
2. los compañeros de mesa
3. la comida

4. el/la guía
5. las excursiones
6. …

Suggestions. Encourage students to ask more questions to ensure that the wallet belongs to the person claiming it.

Students should boast about their condos. You may wish to model the activity with a proficient student. Use the expressions in the *En directo* box.

EN DIRECTO

To boast about something:
No te lo puedes ni imaginar.
You could not even imagine.
¡Es increíble!
Lo que te diga es poco.
I cannot tell you enough.

SITUACIONES

1. **Role A:** Yesterday you lost your wallet (black, new, with $20, some photos, and a credit card inside) in a San Jose hotel. Answer all the questions the employee at the Lost and Found desk asks you. Then show him/her an identification document and thank him/her.

   Role B: You work at the Lost and Found desk of a hotel in San José, and you are helping a customer who lost a wallet. Get the following information: a) the name of the person, b) the description of the wallet, c) the date it was lost, and d) a list of what was in the wallet. You must then ask him/her for some identification and return the wallet back to him/her.

2. Each of you has a condominium in an exclusive summer resort and wants to impress the other. Speak of your condominium, giving the most information possible.

5. The future tense

You have been using the present tense and **ir + a +** *infinitive* to express future plans. Spanish also has a future tense. Although you have these other ways to express a future action, event, or state, you should be able to recognize the future tense in reading and in listening.

- The future tense is formed by adding the future endings **-é, -ás, -á, -emos, -éis,** and **-án** to the infinitive. These endings are the same for **-ar, -er,** and **-ir** verbs.

FUTURE TENSE			
	HABLAR	COMER	VIVIR
yo	hablaré	comeré	viviré
tú	hablarás	comerás	vivirás
Ud., él, ella	hablará	comerá	vivirá
nosotros/as	hablaremos	comeremos	viviremos
vosotros/as	hablaréis	comeréis	viviréis
Uds., ellos/as	hablarán	comerán	vivirán

- A few verbs have irregular stems in the future tense and can be grouped into three categories. The first group drops the **e** from the infinitive ending.

IRREGULAR FUTURE—GROUP 1		
INFINITIVE	NEW STEM	FUTURE FORMS
poder	**podr-**	podré, podrás, podrá, podremos, podréis, podrán
querer	**querr-**	querré, querrás, querrá, querremos, querréis, querrán
saber	**sabr-**	sabré, sabrás, sabrá, sabremos, sabréis, sabrán

- The second group replaces the **e** or **i** of the infinitive ending with a **d.**

IRREGULAR FUTURE—GROUP 2		
INFINITIVE	NEW STEM	FUTURE FORMS
poner	**pondr-**	pondré, pondrás, pondrá, pondremos, pondréis, pondrán
tener	**tendr-**	tendré, tendrás, tendrá, tendremos, tendréis, tendrán
salir	**saldr-**	saldré, saldrás, saldrá, saldremos, saldréis, saldrán
venir	**vendr-**	vendré, vendrás, vendrá, vendremos, vendréis, vendrán

- The third group consists of two verbs (**decir, hacer**) that have completely different stems in the future tense.

IRREGULAR FUTURE—GROUP 3		
INFINITIVE	NEW STEM	FUTURE FORMS
decir	**dir-**	diré, dirás, dirá, diremos, diréis, dirán
hacer	**har-**	haré, harás, hará, haremos, haréis, harán

Suggestion. Show and narrate visuals in context. For example: *La semana próxima Rafael va a ir en viaje de negocios a Costa Rica. Estará dos días en San José, donde tendrá varias reuniones de negocios. Su secretaria le hará una reservación en un hotel que le recomendaron. En Costa Rica, visitará algunas plantaciones de banano en la costa del Pacífico. Después de regresar a los Estados Unidos, se pondrá en contacto con algunas compañías que quieran importar bananos de Costa Rica.* Ask yes/no questions using the future to check comprehension. Follow up with information questions, using the visuals.

Note. The *ir a +* infinitive construction is commonly used to express future action; allow students to answer using either construction.

VÍNCULOS

To practice the future tense
- SAM-OneKey: WB: 12-18, 12-19, 12-20 / LM: 12-45, 12-46
- Companion Website: AP 12-6
- *Gramática viva:* Grammar Points 13 and 14: Future irregular; Future regular
- IRCD: Chapter 12; pg. 449

■ In addition to referring to future actions, the Spanish future tense can also be used to express probability in the present.

Todavía no están en el hotel.	*They still are not at the hotel.*
El vuelo **estará** atrasado, ¿no?	*The flight is probably/must be late, right?*
Dice que va a ver la telenovela, así que **serán** las nueve.	*He says he is going to watch the soap opera, so it must be nine.*

■ The future of **hay** is **habrá**.

Habrá muchos pasajeros en el vuelo.	*There will be many passengers on the flight.*

Note. *Haber* as an auxiliary verb is presented in *Lección 13.* At this point, use only *habrá* as the future of *hay.*

¿Qué dice usted?

Note for 12-25. You may point out that el Casco Viejo is the old section of Panama City. You may also show the location of the San Blas Islands near the north coast of Panama.

12-25 ¿Qué lugares de Panamá van a visitar los miembros de esta familia? Complete las oraciones de la izquierda con la forma correcta del verbo.

1. La abuela ___c___ a una prima que vive en Panamá.
2. La madre y su hija ___e___ la Catedral Metropolitana.
3. Mi padre y yo ___d___ el Canal.
4. Tú ___b___ las Islas San Blas.
5. Yo ___a___ el Casco Viejo.

a. visitaré
b. visitarás
c. visitará
d. visitaremos
e. visitarán

12-26 Intercambio: Un viaje a Panamá. Ramiro va a la Ciudad de Panamá a visitar a su familia. Háganse preguntas y contesten de acuerdo con la agenda que Ramiro preparó.

MODELO: E1: ¿Qué hará Ramiro el miércoles por la noche?
E2: Cenará con unos amigos.
E1: ¿Cuándo irá al cine con los primos?
E2: Irá al cine con los primos el martes.

LUNES	MARTES	MIÉRCOLES	JUEVES	VIERNES
salir para Panamá	visitar el Casco Viejo	salir de compras	visitar las Islas San Blas	preparar las maletas
comer con los tíos	conocer a otros familiares	ir a un museo	comprar artesanías	almorzar con su tío
acostarse temprano	ir al cine con los primos	cenar con unos amigos	ir a un concierto	ir a una discoteca

Suggestions for 12-27. Before doing the activity, on a map show the route the cruise will follow. Ask questions regarding Cozumel, the Panama Canal, and Acapulco. If time allows, talk about these places, show photos, etc. This may also be a good opportunity to have students give brief, guided presentations on these places: location, economic importance in the region, things they can offer the tourist, etc.

12-27 Un crucero inolvidable. Los Almagro viven en Miami, y van a tomar un crucero que atravesará el Canal de Panamá y llegará hasta Acapulco. De allí regresarán a Miami en avión. Primero, digan qué harán los miembros de la familia, usando los verbos entre paréntesis. Después, pongan las acciones en orden cronológico y comparen sus respuestas con las de otros/as compañeros/as.

___5___ Los Almagro _llegarán_ (llegar) a Acapulco.

___3___ El crucero _hará_ (hacer) escala en Cozumel, y los pasajeros _disfrutarán_ (disfrutar) de un día en la playa.

___1___ La señora de Almagro _irá_ (ir) a la agencia de viajes para comprar los pasajes.

___6___ Por la mañana del primer día en Acapulco, la familia _irá_ (ir) al mercado para comprar artesanías.

___8___ En el aeropuerto, los agentes de aduana _revisarán_ (revisar) el equipaje, y la familia Almagro _regresará_ (regresar) a su casa.

___7___ Sus hijos _pasarán_ (pasar) la tarde en la playa porque saben que es el último día de sus vacaciones.

___2___ Los señores Almagro y sus hijos Mauro y Gloria _tomarán_ (tomar) el barco en Miami.

___4___ De allí, el crucero _seguirá_ (seguir) a Panamá y _cruzará_ (cruzar) el Canal.

2 12-28 ¿Por qué lo harán? Cada uno tiene diferentes motivos para hacer lo que hace. Piensen en dos motivos probables para cada una de las situaciones siguientes.

MODELO: Los Rivas van a Europa todos los años.
             E1: Tendrán mucho dinero, ¿no?
             E2: Tendrán familiares allá.

1. Pedro siempre viaja con poco equipaje.
2. Los Pérez nunca están los fines de semana en la ciudad.
3. Rosa no contesta el teléfono hace dos días.
4. Pilar no llama a sus parientes cuando viene a la ciudad.
5. Los Gómez están en el aeropuerto.
6. El vuelo va a salir una hora más tarde.
7. Pedro siempre saca muy buenas notas en sus clases.
8. El señor López toma el tren para ir a trabajar.

2 12-29 Planes futuros. Hablen del futuro en relación con los siguientes puntos y luego compartan sus planes con otra pareja.

MODELO: su graduación
             E1: Dentro de 2 años terminaremos la universidad.
             E2: No, yo no terminaré todavía. Tendré que estudiar un semestre más.

1. sus estudios
2. su vivienda
3. sus amistades

4. su vida profesional
5. sus planes de viaje
6. …

G 12-30 El horóscopo. Escriban su nombre en un papel. Luego, pongan el papel en una caja o en otro lugar designado por su profesor/a. Mezclen bien los papeles. Luego, cada estudiante debe sacar un papel al azar (*at random*). Después, preparen el horóscopo de esa persona para leerlo en la próxima clase. Los demás estudiantes tratarán de averiguar de quién es el horóscopo.

SITUACIONES

One of you is about to spend a few days' holiday in your favorite place. The other is very curious and will ask questions to find out: a) where, how, with whom, and for how long the other one is going, and b) where he/she will be staying.

Warm-up for 12-32. As a pre-listening activity, have students get in groups of four and discuss where they would like to travel, why they would like to go to that place, and what they would like to do there.

Audioscript for 12-32:

AGENTE: Agencia Costamar, buenas tardes. ¿En qué puedo servirle?

SILVANA: Buenas tardes. Habla Silvana Valdivieso. Ayer llamé para pedir información acerca de dos viajes, uno para Panamá y el otro para México. Me dijeron que llamara hoy.

AGENTE: Muy bien. Espere un minuto, por favor, mientras consigo su información. A ver, a ver... sí, aquí está.

SILVANA: ¡Qué bien! Dígame.

AGENTE: La oferta para México es para un viaje de diez días. La de Panamá es para un viaje de siete días.

SILVANA: Seguro que la de México es más cara, ¿no?

AGENTE: Bueno, sí, pero la diferencia no es mucha. Sólo 350 dólares más

SILVANA: Está bien. Y, ¿qué incluye?

AGENTE: Bueno, incluye estadía en un hotel en el Distrito Federal por tres días, luego, un viaje a Cancún por tres días, con estadía en un hotel en la playa. Además dos excursiones: una a las ruinas mayas de Chichen Itza y otra a la isla de Cozumel. Con los pasajes, los hoteles y las excursiones, el precio es $1.850,00.

SILVANA: ¿Y el viaje a Panamá?

AGENTE: Bueno, éste incluye dos días en la Ciudad de Panamá, un viaje en barco para cruzar el canal y un viaje a la playa por tres días. Todos los hoteles son de cinco estrellas, y el precio es de $1.500. Tanto en México como en Panamá va a tener oportunidad de ir a la playa y descansar bastante.

SILVANA: Bueno, creo que prefiero ir a Panamá. Hace mucho tiempo que quiero conocer el Canal de Panamá. ¿Me hace la reservación, por favor?

AGENTE: Por supuesto. ¿Me da la tarjeta de crédito, por favor?

SILVANA: Sí, es VISA, 444-8888-999, fecha de vencimiento, 12/12/2009.

AGENTE: Muy bien. Le envío los pasajes y la información de los hoteles por correo electrónico inmediatamente. Si tiene cualquier otra pregunta, por favor, me llama por teléfono, que estamos para servirle.

SILVANA: Muchas gracias, entonces. Hasta luego.

AGENTE: Hasta luego.

 ## *Escuchar*

Reporting What was Said

When you report what somebody said, most of the time you do not remember the exact words that were used. Instead, you retell what was said, using the third person. For example, in Spanish you may say, "Pedro dice que este verano él va a ir a Puerto Rico," or "Ellos dicen que ese carro es suyo."

Antes de escuchar

12-31 Un viaje. In activity **12-32** you will listen to a conversation between a travel agent and a client, Silvana, who wants to buy a vacation package to Latin America. Before you listen, write down the information you think Silvana will need before choosing the right package.

_____

_____

_____

A escuchar

12-32 Read the report statements below. Then, listen to the conversation between Silvana and the travel agent about the two different vacation packages she had inquired about. As you listen, circle the statements that best report what was said.

(1.) Silvana habla con el agente de viajes y le pregunta las diferentes posibilidades que tiene para viajar a México y a Panamá.

2. Silvana dice que prefiere ir a Panamá porque siempre quiso conocer ese país.

(3.) El agente de viajes le dice a Silvana que el viaje a México es por más tiempo y un poco más caro que el viaje a Panamá.

4. El agente de viajes le dice a Silvana que le enviará los pasajes y la información sobre los hoteles por correo regular ese mismo día.

Después de escuchar

12-33 ¿Y usted? With a classmate, share your answers to the following questions.

1. ¿Alguna vez viajó usted a México, Panamá o algún otro país hispano? ¿Qué lugares visitó?

2. ¿Por qué cree usted que debe ser interesante cruzar el Canal de Panamá?

3. ¿Qué otro país hispano quisiera conocer? ¿Por qué?

Antes de escuchar

12-34 Buscando un hotel. In activity **12-35** you will listen to a conversation between Mr. Hernández, who is looking for a good hotel in San José, Costa Rica, and a travel agent. Before you listen, write down a list of four questions you think Mr. Hernández will ask.

_____

_____

A escuchar

 12-35 Read the report statements below. Then, listen to the conversation between Mr. Hernández and the travel agent. As you listen, circle the statements that best report what was said.

1. El Sr. Hernández dice que quiere un hotel económico que esté cerca del centro de la ciudad.
2. La agente le dice que tiene varias posibilidades y le describe tres hoteles para que él escoja.
3. El Sr. Hernández dice que él prefiere que sus hijos y esposa estén cómodos aunque (*even though*) él tenga que tomar un taxi o manejar mucho.
4. La agente le dice al cliente que la elección que ha hecho no es buena porque el hotel es muy caro y está muy lejos del centro de la ciudad.

Después de escuchar

 12-36 ¿Y usted? With a classmate, share your answers to the following questions.

1. Cuando usted busca un hotel, ¿es importante que el hotel sea económico o que sea de lujo?
2. ¿Qué servicios o comodidades prefiere usted que ofrezca un hotel?
3. ¿Cuál es su hotel favorito? ¿Por qué?

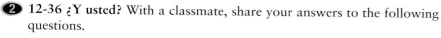

Conversar

Antes de conversar

 12-37 Viaje de trabajo. Primera fase. Algunos profesionales viajan a otros países para hacer negocios o investigaciones relacionadas con su profesión. Primero seleccionen a **uno** de los siguientes profesionales:

1. bióloga que hará investigación en Costa Rica sobre reservas forestales
2. etnólogo que realizará una investigación sobre los indígenas panameños
3. gerente de una compañía estadounidense que piensa hacer negocios en Costa Rica
4. publicista norteamericano que desea promocionar productos de su país en Costa Rica y Panamá

VÍNCULOS

For materials related to the Mosaicos section see
- SAM-OneKey: WB: 12-21, 12-22, 12-23, 12-24, 12-25, 12-26 / LM: 12-47

Warm-up for 12-35. As a pre-listening activity, have students get in groups of four and discuss what they look for in a hotel when they travel out of town or abroad.

Audioscript for 12-35. ARMANDO: Señorita, habla el señor Hernández. Viajo a San José dentro de un mes, y estoy buscando un hotel que esté en el centro de la ciudad, pero que tenga una piscina, ya que viajo con mi esposa y mis hijos.

AGENTE: Mire, señor, le voy a dar varias posibilidades. El Hotel Grano de Oro es un hotel pequeño cerca del centro, y tiene un servicio extraordinario. Tiene algunas habitaciones grandes hasta para cuatro personas, con jacuzzi.

ARMANDO: ¡Uhm! ¡Qué bien! ¿Qué más tiene?

AGENTE: Bueno, tenemos el hotel Buganvilla. Tiene habitaciones bastante grandes, excelente servicio y un restaurante de primera categoría. Además, tiene unos jardines muy bonitos y una piscina muy grande también.

ARMANDO: Bueno, bueno...

AGENTE: También tenemos otro hotel que es maravilloso, pero está a 45 minutos de San José y es más caro. Tiene una piscina para mayores y otra para niños y unos jardines espectaculares. También se pueden alquilar bicicletas.

ARMANDO: ¡Qué bien! Claro que la única desventaja es que no está en el centro, pero creo que es mejor que haga la reservación en este hotel. Mi esposa e hijos van a estar más contentos, y yo puedo alquilar un carro o tomar un taxi.

AGENTE: Muy buena selección, señor Hernández.

ARMANDO: Sí, creo que sí. Muchas gracias por su ayuda. Hágame la reservación entonces para la última semana de enero.

AGENTE: Muy bien, señor Hernández.

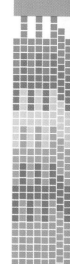

Ahora preparen un plan de trabajo básico para la persona que escogieron en el país que visitará. Cubran los siguientes puntos:

1. explicación del plan de trabajo
2. cuándo y cómo lo va realizar
3. con quién(es) se va a reunir

Segunda fase. Basándose en el plan del/de la profesional que escogieron en la **Primera fase,** completen la tabla con las posibles necesidades de este/a profesional.

PROFESIONAL	NECESIDADES
_____ bióloga	alojamiento: _____
	_____
_____ etnólogo	transporte: _____
	_____
_____ gerente	actividades de tiempo libre: _____
	_____
_____ publicista	_____
	_____

A conversar

2 12-38 Planes. Usted es el/la profesional de la actividad **12-37.** Hoy debe ponerse en contacto con un/a ejecutivo/a o profesional en el país que visitará. Llámelo/la por teléfono para informarle sobre sus planes. Dele la siguiente información:

1. la fecha y hora de llegada a la ciudad de destino
2. la aerolínea y el número de vuelo en que viajará
3. las actividades profesionales que hará durante su estancia
4. algunas actividades de tiempo libre que le gustaría hacer; pídale información si es necesario

Después de conversar

12-39 ¡A informar a los superiores! Usted es el ejecutivo que recibió la llamada. Escríbale un correo electrónico a su jefe/a para informarle sobre los planes de la persona con quien usted conversó. Dele la siguiente información:

1. la fecha de llegada de esta persona
2. las actividades de negocio o profesionales durante su estancia
3. algunas actividades de tiempo libre que usted le recomendó

Antes de conversar

G 12-40 ¿Quién lo merece (deserves)? Después de estudiar español juntos por un año, ustedes deben separarse de sus compañeros con quienes compartieron muchas experiencias en el salón de clase. Por eso, decidieron premiar (reward) a una persona del grupo con unas vacaciones inolvidables. Hagan lo siguiente:

a. Escojan a una persona de la clase, quien, en su opinión, merece unas vacaciones inolvidables. Den tres razones para justificar su elección.

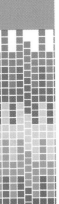

EN DIRECTO

To ask questions about plans:
¿Qué planes tiene?
¿Qué/Dónde/Con quién piensa + *infinitive*?

To inform someone about plans:
Quisiera informarle que…
Me gustaría darle información sobre…

To suggest some ideas:
¿Qué le parece…?
¿Por qué no…?

b. Luego, indiquen…

- una ciudad hispana adonde ustedes quieren que él/ella vaya.

- el medio de transporte en que viajará.

- la cantidad de dinero (moneda nacional del país) que ustedes le darán a esta persona y algunas recomendaciones de cómo gastarlo.

c. Den un mínimo de cinco sugerencias de actividades a realizar (qué comprar, adónde ir, qué comer o beber, qué ver, etc.).

A conversar

 12-41 Nuestro/a candidato/a y nuestro plan. Informen detalladamente a la clase sobre lo siguiente:

a. la persona a quien escogieron y las razones de su elección.
b. la ciudad hispana adonde ustedes quieren que él/ella vaya, el transporte que usará, la cantidad de dinero que ustedes le darán y algunas sugerencias de cómo gastarlo.
c. cinco actividades que ustedes le sugieren a esta persona para hacer. Finalmente, la clase votará por el mejor plan de vacaciones.

Después de conversar

12-42 ¡Qué viaje tan inolvidable! Usted es el/la estudiante que recibió el premio. Después de pasar la primera semana de sus vacaciones inolvidables, quiere compartir con sus compañeros/as sus impresiones, experiencias y aventuras en el lugar adonde viajó. Escríbales una carta para contarles los detalles de su viaje. También incluya algunos planes detallados para los días de vacaciones que le quedan.

Leer

In this chapter, however, you will practice summarizing a newspaper article whose content is not presented in a chronological order. Therefore, summarizing a text of this nature requires a different approach. You need to discern what pieces of information are important to represent the text as a whole. The following considerations may help you summarize a text like this:

- First, read the title or headline and subtitles or subheadings, when appropriate.

- Using your knowledge of the topic, anticipate some potential content of the text.

- Underline the main ideas in each paragraph.

- Look for the content relationship between and among paragraphs. This will help you see how individual pieces (each paragraph) fit in the whole (text).

- Take notes of key information and ideas.

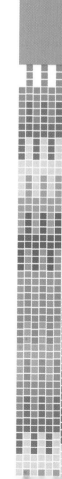

Guía de prelectura

Use the cues provided by the visuals, the headline, and subheading in activity **12-44** and your personal knowledge to answer these questions. Try making educated guesses about the content of the text. You will be able to verify your answers later.

1. What key information will this article probably tackle?
   a. Bad weather conditions may scare flyers.
   b. Many people prefer means of transportation other than airplanes.
   c. Fear may negatively affect frequent business flyers.
   d. Panic of flying is treatable.

2. How did you figure out the answers to question 1? Circle the appropriate letter.
   a. The headline, subheading, and visuals
   b. Your personal travel experience

3. Now, can you hypothesize about the probable content of the text? Anticipate some of the secondary ideas.

   The article will probably include this content. Circle all that apply.
   a. Some data to convince aerophobic people that the fear of flying is groundless
   b. Examples of drawbacks caused by the fear of flying
   c. Airline losses caused by the fear of traveling by plane
   d. Classes aerophobic people can take to cope with their problem
   e. Step-by-step methods to combat aerophobia
   f. Alternative means of transportation for aerophobic people

Antes de leer

12-43 Preparación. Primera fase. Marque con una X las oraciones que reflejan su opinión sobre los viajes.

1. _____ Prefiero viajar por tierra porque los autobuses y los carros son más seguros.
2. _____ Me encantan los viajes por avión porque son más rápidos.
3. _____ Cuando viajo por avión, me pongo nervioso/a porque pienso que el avión tendrá un accidente.
4. _____ Al subir al avión, pienso que podemos chocar (*crash*) en el aire.
5. _____ Es mejor beber alcohol para relajarse durante un viaje en avión.
6. _____ El estar encerrado en el avión me produce asfixia (*suffocation*).
7. _____ No como en el avión porque pienso que voy a atragantarme (*choke*).
8. _____ Creo que soy aviofóbico/a; es decir, tengo pánico de viajar por avión.

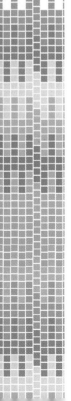

❷ Segunda fase. Ahora comparen sus respuestas y respondan a las siguientes preguntas.

1. ¿Es alguno de ustedes aviofóbico/a?
2. ¿Necesitan ustedes relajarse durante un vuelo? ¿Cómo lo hacen?
3. ¿Creen ustedes que la fobia a viajar en avión se puede curar? ¿Cómo?

A leer

12-44 Primera mirada. Lea el artículo y siga las indicaciones.

El cielo puede esperar

CÓMO PERDER EL MIEDO AL AVIÓN

Hay más probabilidades de que ganes la lotería dos semanas seguidas que de que se caiga un aeroplano. Según las estadísticas, en Estados Unidos, por cada víctima de accidente aéreo, mueren 210 conductores de autos, hay 110 asesinatos, 65 caídas fatales, 15 asfixiados por atragantarse y cuatro que mueren simplemente por caerles objetos encima cuando caminan por la calle.

Sin embargo, el avión es el medio de transporte que despierta mayor pánico entre los viajeros: uno de cuatro españoles experimenta esa alergia al vuelo; algunos superan sus problemas a base de coraje, tranquilizantes o alcohol, pero ésta no es una buena solución, como afirma Enrique Gil Ángel, siquiatra y profesor del cursillo *Miedo a volar.*

Para los profesionales que deben viajar frecuentemente en avión, el asunto puede convertirse en algo muy serio: oportunidades de negocio perdidas, puestos de trabajo a los que no se puede aspirar sólo por el miedo a volar… Sacrificarse y viajar por aire a pesar de la fobia tampoco sirve de nada: el ejecutivo que llega a una reunión de trabajo con estrés, ansiedad y falta de concentración por culpa del calvario de un viaje por aire no responde satisfactoriamente y, en muchos casos, llega a la conclusión de que es mejor no hacerlo.

En España, desde hace cinco años, la empresa Grupo Especial Directivos de Iberia ofrece el seminario *Cómo perder el miedo al avión.* El cursillo propone que el miedo a volar puede superarse con información directa sobre la seguridad aérea, apoyo psicológico específico y experiencia real de vuelo en un ambiente adecuado.

Los aviofóbicos tienen dos miedos:

- Miedo técnico: piensan que el avión puede caerse, porque no son capaces de asimilar que vuele un artefacto como ése.
- Miedo psicológico: angustia ante la expectativa de estar encerrados en el aire.

Durante el seminario, Javier del Campo desmonta las teorías catastrofistas de los asistentes con argumentos técnicos y explica exhaustivamente las severas pruebas de seguridad que pasan los aparatos y las frecuentes revisiones periódicas a que obliga la ley. "Todo está previsto en la aviación; por ejemplo, poca gente sabe que para probar la resistencia de los cristales se lanzan pollos con un cañón de artillería, de manera que chocan a unos 300 kilómetros por hora contra el avión, que es la velocidad a la que puede impactar un ave en vuelo real."

Del Campo asegura que después de asistir al cursillo, los participantes no tienen la más mínima duda sobre la seguridad en los aviones: sólo les queda "la parte irracional del problema".

De esta materia se encarga el doctor Gil Nagel, quien trata cada caso individualmente, enseña técnicas de autocontrol, y vigila las reacciones emocionales de los asistentes para liberarlos del problema. Nagel utiliza también terapia de grupo y un método denominado *desensibilización sistemática,* que consiste en enfrentar al paciente con la causa de su miedo.

Tanto el comandante del Campo como el doctor Nagel coinciden en que las personas con aviofobia generalmente son algo más inteligentes que la persona media, tratan siempre de tenerlo todo bajo control y son muy creativas.

Marque la afirmación que resume mejor el contenido del artículo.

1. _____ Por razones lógicas, algunas personas sienten un miedo horrible de viajar en avión; según los científicos, este pánico, que afecta solamente a la víctima que la sufre, no tiene cura. Así lo demostraron, los intentos que hicieron los psiquíatras y expertos en aviación en España.

2. ___X___ La fobia de muchas personas a viajar por avión no es racional ni fundamentada. En la mayoría de los casos, las víctimas de la aviofobia no poseen información técnica sobre el control de calidad que realizan las compañías que construyen los aviones. Los problemas psicológicos, económicos y laborales causados por este miedo extremo se pueden evitar con información científica y tratamiento, como lo demuestran algunos tratamientos realizados en España.

3. _____ El pánico de algunas personas a volar se basa en la gran cantidad de accidentes de aviación. Aunque los técnicos y científicos digan lo contrario, las estadísticas de accidentes indican que la mayor cantidad de muertes ocurren en la industria de la aviación. Algunos expertos en aeronáutica y psicólogos españoles han tratado de ayudar a los aviofóbicos con cursos especialmente diseñados para ellos, pero no han tenido ningún éxito.

12-45 Segunda mirada. Basándose en la información del artículo, ordene las siguientes causas de muerte de 1 a 5 (5, más significativa; 1, menos significativa), según el número de víctimas que ocasionan.

___5___ accidentes automovilísticos   ___3___ caídas mortales
___2___ asfixias   ___4___ asesinatos
___1___ accidentes de aviación

12-46 Una mirada más. Busque en el artículo la siguiente información.

1. Tres maneras tradicionales que los viajeros utilizan para controlar el miedo al avión antes de tomar el cursillo: _coraje, tranquilizantes, alcohol_
2. Tres efectos psicológicos que sufren los aviofóbicos: _estrés, ansiedad, falta de concentración_
3. Las estrategias que se utilizan en el cursillo para ayudar a superar...
   a. el miedo técnico: _desmonta las teorías catastrofistas de los asistentes con argumentos técnicos y explica exhaustivamente las severas pruebas de seguridad que pasan los aparatos y las frecuentes revisiones periódicas a que obliga la ley_
   b. el miedo psicológico: _técnicas de autocontrol, desensibilización sistemática_

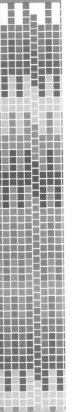

Después de leer

12-47 Ampliación. Primera fase. ¿Qué palabras del artículo están asociadas por su significado con las siguientes?

1. aéreo: <u>aeroplano, avión, aviofóbico, aviofobia</u>
2. muertos: <u>víctima, mueren, asesinatos, fatal</u>
3. miedo: <u>pánico, aviofóbico, aviofobia</u>
4. chocar: <u>accidente</u>

Segunda fase. Complete el siguiente texto con un verbo o sustantivo de la **Primera fase.**

La persona que es (1) <u>víctima</u> del pánico a volar, o (2) <u>aviofobia</u>, cree que cuando viaja en un (3) <u>avión</u>, éste va a sufrir un (4) <u>accidente</u> fatal y va a morir. Sin embargo, las estadísticas indican que es más probable que una persona muera en un (5) <u>asesinato</u> que en un choque de aviones, por ejemplo. Usando información real, los expertos tratan de curar el miedo infundado del (6) <u>aviofóbico</u>.

 Escribir

In academic life, you are often faced with tasks that require presenting factual information. Facts are considered objective, neutral, impartial measures or representations of reality. Therefore, to maintain objectivity, you should provide reliable data such as statistics, opinions and statements made by experts, etc.

Facts also serve as the basis to support a personal view on an issue. A psychologist, for example, may recommend a class instead of medication to an aerophobic person based on the fact that certain fears are better cured by confronting them.

Therefore, to take an objective position on a particular issue or problem.

- inform yourself by reading and/or consulting sources
- make statements based on the information you collected
- acknowledge the sources as you present facts

Antes de escribir

12-48 Preparación. Su amigo, Sebastián, ganó en un concurso un pasaje de ida y vuelta a San José, Costa Rica. Quiere devolver el premio porque les tiene pánico a los aviones y le escribió a usted para pedirle consejo. Para escribirle una carta objetiva y ayudarlo a superar su enfermedad, haga lo siguiente:

a. Lea uno o dos artículo(s) sobre el tema y subraye las ideas, los conceptos, los datos concretos.
b. Tome nota de los datos objetivos más relevantes sobre la aviación que puedan ayudar a su amigo. Puede usar la información de "El cielo puede esperar", otro texto o el conocimiento de los expertos.
c. Haga una lista de palabras que le van a ser útiles para darle cohesión a su texto.
d. Seleccione algunos ejemplos que lo/la puedan ayudar a demostrar su posición o razonamiento (*reasoning*) sobre la aviofobia.
e. Finalmente, escriba algunas formas lingüísticas que lo/la ayudarán a expresar información concreta y dar sugerencias a su amigo.

Suggestion for 12-48. Depending on your students' level of proficiency and interests, you may wish to expand the scope of this writing task. For example, you may ask that students anonymously write down a phobia they may have or pretend they have. Doing so may give individual students the opportunity to carry out research in an area of personal interest and use the information to write a letter and help someone. You may also opt for providing students with your own choices: *fobia a las ratas, a las serpientes, a la oscuridad,* etc.

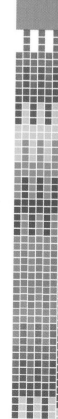

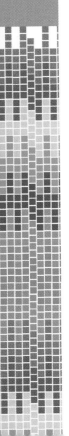

A escribir

12-49 Manos a la obra. Contéstele a Sebastián. Incluya los datos objetivos y concretos que preparó en la actividad **12-48**. Además, recuerde darle buenos consejos para que su amigo olvide su fobia de volar.

Después de escribir

12-50 Revisión. Antes de enviar su carta, léala y verifique lo siguiente, pensando en su lector/a.

- El contenido: ¿Se concentró en las fobias en su carta? ¿Hizo afirmaciones basadas en datos concretos o en la opinión de los expertos?

- La organización: ¿Está su carta bien organizada? ¿Sigue un orden claro?

- La gramática. ¿Usó conceptos relevantes al tema, expresiones de cohesión, la concordancia correcta, el tiempo (presente, pasado, futuro) y modos (indicativo, subjuntivo, etc.) apropiados?

- La puntuación y ortografía. ¿Utilizó las comas, puntos, etc. necesarios? Finalmente, comparta su carta con su compañero/a editor/a.

ENFOQUE CULTURAL

TEMAS: LA MÚSICA Y EL BAILE

Para pensar

¿Cuál es su música favorita? ¿Qué tipo de música puede usted escuchar en la radio? ¿Hay algún tipo de música que sea típicamente estadounidense? ¿Cuál es?

La música hispana contemporánea es muy variada y refleja la variedad étnica de los diferentes países.

En los países con una población indígena significativa (México, Guatemala, Perú, Bolivia, Ecuador), se escucha mucha música indígena. Ésta puede ser triste y melancólica, o rápida y alegre. Un ejemplo de música indígena es el huayno peruano.

VÍNCULOS

For materials related to the Enfoque cultural see
• SAM-OneKey: WB: 12-27
• IRCD: Chaper 12; pg. 462

En todos los países hispanos se escucha y se baila música de origen africano, que se caracteriza por ser rápida, alegre y vibrante. La cumbia, el merengue, la salsa y la rumba son ejemplos de esta música tan popular.

Para contestar

2 La música hispana. Respondan a las siguientes preguntas.

1. ¿Por qué se dice que la música hispana contemporánea es muy variada? Expliquen.
2. Cada país tiene su música típica. Mencione la música típica de Chile, Venezuela y Panamá.
3. ¿Cuáles son algunos cantantes hispanos famosos?

G Riqueza cultural. En grupos de tres, comparen los diferentes tipos de música que ustedes escuchan generalmente con algunos de los ritmos hispanos mencionados arriba.

Hay muchísimos cantantes famosos en el mundo hispano. Por ejemplo, Celia Cruz (de Cuba), llamada la reina de la salsa, Thalía (de México), Enrique Iglesias (de España), José Luis Rodríguez (de Venezuela), Rubén Blades (de Panamá), Gloria Estefan de Cuba y los Estados Unidos.

Para pensar

¿Sabe usted dónde queda Panamá? ¿Tiene usted idea de cuándo se construyó el Canal de Panamá y cuál es su importancia? ¿Sabe usted dónde está Costa Rica? ¿Conoce usted algún político, cantante, deportista o persona famosa de estos países?

Panamá y Costa Rica se encuentran en la América Central y tienen costas en el Océano Pacífico y en el Mar Caribe.

Hay muchos lugares de interés que se pueden visitar en el Casco Viejo de la Ciudad de Panamá, como el Museo de Arte Colonial Religioso. Pero también siempre hay algo que hacer para divertirse, como ir a un festival de jazz, a las exposiciones de arte, a las competencias deportivas, etc.

El folclore panameño es muy rico e interesante. Al norte de Panamá, todos los años se celebra la Fiesta de la Pollera, en la cual se pueden apreciar bailes regionales tradicionales como la Danza de los Toros y la Danza de los Diablos.

Cerca de la Ciudad de Panamá se encuentra el famoso Canal de Panamá que conecta el Océano Pacífico con el Mar Caribe.

Expresiones panameñas:

desorejado/a	Es una **desorejada**.	She is tone deaf.
embolatar	Él la **embolató y no** se casó con ella.	He lied and made false promises and did not marry her.
pachocha	¡Apúrense! ¡Ustedes tienen una **pachocha**!	Hurry up! You are so slow!

La marimba y la guitarra son importantes instrumentos en la música de los "ticos" —nombre con el que se conoce a los costarricenses—. La guitarra se usa especialmente en danzas típicas como el punto guanacasteco, el baile nacional.

Costa Rica es un país ideal para hacer ecoturismo y para practicar una serie de deportes como windsurfing, ciclismo o tabla hawaiana.

Expresiones costarricenses:

upe	¡Upe!	(Type of greeting)
chunche	Pásame ese **chunche**.	Give me that thing.
maje	El es un **maje**.	He is a fool.
paltó	No tengo **paltó**.	I do not have a jacket.
fajarse	Me **fajé**, pero terminé el trabajo.	I put a lot of effort, but finished the job.

Para contestar

En el mapa

1. Diga dónde está Panamá y cuál es su capital. ¿Y Costa Rica?
2. ¿Qué países están cerca de Panamá? ¿Y de Costa Rica?
3. Mencione una semejanza geográfica entre Panamá y Costa Rica.

Ahora diga...

1. si le gustaría visitar Panamá o Costa Rica, y por qué.
2. qué lugar de Panamá le interesaría visitar.
3. si le gustaría visitar Sarchi, y por qué.

¿Qué dice usted si...

1. su amigo no sabe ni puede cantar.
2. su compañero siempre llega tarde a todas partes.
3. usted estudió mucho.

No muy lejos de San José está el pueblito de Sarchí, famoso por sus hermosas carretas pintadas de brillantes colores y carteras de cuero.

Para investigar en Internet

Busque información acerca de dos conjuntos panameños de música popular y dos conjuntos de música folclórica de algún otro país latinoamericano. Para cada conjunto, diga cómo se llama, qué tipo de música toca, qué instrumentos usa, etc. Traiga esta información a clase para hacer una presentación de lo que averiguó, y diga qué conjunto le gusta más y por qué. Si puede, traiga una grabación del conjunto y toque la música en clase.

¡Prepárese!

② **12-51 Predicciones.** Ahora que ha visto once episodios de *Fortunas*, haga predicciones sobre lo que pasará en el Episodio 12. Recuerde que en este episodio los participantes están tratando de solucionar el quinto misterio y ganar la segunda fortuna. Use el tiempo futuro y escriba oraciones completas para los sujetos de la lista siguiente. Intercambie sus predicciones con las de un/a compañero/a.

1. Katie...
2. Efraín...
3. Sabrina...
4. Carlos...
5. La segunda fortuna...
6. Los cuatro participantes...
7. El público...
8. ...

Ángela y Manolo comentan el engaño y la falta de integridad de los participantes.

Carlos y Efraín formaron una alianza.

Carlos y Efraín solucionan el quinto misterio y ganan la segunda fortuna.

Efraín se entera de que él y Carlos tienen que compartir el misterio y la fortuna con Katie.

Katie formó alianzas con Carlos y con
Sabrina, pero todavía está en primer lugar.

Sabrina está muy enfadada por las acciones
de Katie.

12-52 Resultados. Lea las predicciones que le dio su compañero/a. Sus
predicciones para el Episodio 12 ¿eran correctas? ¿Y las suyas?

¡Responda!

12-53 Los participantes. ¿Quién quiere que gane el concurso? ¿Por qué?
Imagínese que es el/la ganador/a y escriba un breve informe que explique lo que
va a hacer después de ganar *Fortunas*. Su informe debe tener por lo menos cinco
oraciones completas. Use el tiempo futuro y/o la estructura *ir + a + infinitivo*.

Suggestion for 12-53. Have students
exchange *informes* with a partner. After reading
his/her partner's work each student should write
three questions to ask the author. Solicit volunteers to read their work, have their partners ask
the prepared questions and answer the questions
in front of the class.

Rubén Blades, de Panamá, es conocido no sólo por su música sino también por su talento como actor y su activismo social. Frecuentemente comenta temas sociales en sus canciones y *Ligia Elena* no es una excepción ya que trata del tema de un amor prohibido por diferencias raciales y socioeconómicas.

¡Prepárese!

2 **12-54 La canción.** Túrnense para formular y contestar negativamente las siguientes preguntas sobre el tema, la letra y el artista de "Ligia Elena."

1. ¿Conoces alguna canción de Rubén Blades?
2. ¿Sabes la letra de "Ligia Elena"?
3. ¿Alguna vez fuiste a un concierto de música latina?
4. ¿Alguien te compró un disco compacto de este artista?
5. ¿Escuchas música con temas sociales?
6. ¿A todos los estudiantes les gusta la canción?

¡Escuche!

Note. You may clarify the following words/expressions: *se ha fugado* (has eloped) *regaños* (scoldings), and *na'* (nada).

12-55 Reacciones y opiniones. Mientras escucha "Ligia Elena" complete la siguiente tabla con adjetivos u otras palabras o expresiones que reflejen sus reacciones y opiniones sobre la canción. Parte de la letra está incluida aquí.

ELEMENTOS	ES.../SON...
El ritmo	_____
La letra	_____
El tema	_____
La vocalización	_____
Los instrumentos	_____

LIGIA ELENA

Ligia Elena la cándida niña de la sociedad
se ha fugado con un trompetista de la vecindad.
El padre la busca afanosamente,
lo está comentando toda la gente
y la madre angustiada pregunta ¿en dónde estará?

De nada sirvieron regaños ni viajes ni monjas,
ni las promesas de amor que le hicieran los niños de bien.
Fue tan buena la nota que dio aquel humilde trompeta
que entre acordes de cariño eterno se fue ella con él.

Pudo más el amor que el dinero, señor.
¡Qué buena la nota que dio aquel trompeta!
Eso del racismo, *brother*, no está en na'.
Deja que la agarre nos jura el papá.

Ligia Elena está llena de felicidad.

¡Responda!

12-56 ¿Qué hará Rubén Blades? Imagínese que es reportero/a para Univisión, el canal hispano, y que va a entrevistar a Rubén Blades sobre su carrera. Use el tiempo futuro para hacerle cinco preguntas sobre sus planes.

2 **12-57 Entrevista.** Intercambie sus preguntas con un/a compañero/a y túrnese con él/ella para hacer los papeles de reportero/a y de Rubén Blades. Después hagan sus entrevistas frente a la clase.

VOCABULARIO*

AUDIO ## Medios de transporte

el auto(móvil)/coche/carro	car
el autobús/bus	bus
el avión	plane
el barco	ship/boat
el metro	subway
el tren	train

En el aeropuerto

la aduana	customs
la aerolínea	airline
el mostrador	counter
la puerta (de salida)	gate
el vuelo	flight

En un avión

el asiento	seat
de pasillo/ventanilla	aisle/window seat
la ventanilla	window

El correo

el buzón	mailbox
la carta	letter
el paquete	package
el sello	stamp
el sobre	envelope
la tarjeta postal	post card

Personas

el/la agente de viajes	travel agent
el/la auxiliar de vuelo	flight attendant
el/la cartero/a	letter carrier
el/la conserje	concierge
el/la empleado/a	employee
el/la pasajero/a	passenger

Partes de un coche

la batería/el acumulador	battery
el capó	hood
el espejo retrovisor	rearview mirror
la guantera	glove compartment
el limpiaparabrisas	windshield wiper
la llanta	tire
el maletero	trunk
el parabrisas	windshield
el parachoques	bumper
la placa	plates
el radiador	radiator
la rueda	wheel
el volante	steering wheel

Viajes

la agencia de viajes	travel agency
la autopista	freeway
el boleto/pasaje	ticket
la carretera	highway
el cheque de viajero	traveler's check
el crucero	cruise
el destino	destination
el equipaje	luggage
la hora de llegada/salida	arrival/departure time
la lista de espera	waiting list
la maleta	suitcase
el maletín	briefcase
el pasaporte	passport
la tarjeta de embarque	boarding pass
la velocidad	speed

En el hotel

la caja fuerte	safe box
la habitación doble/sencilla	double/single room
la llave	key
la recepción	front desk

Lugares

la cuadra	city block
la esquina	corner

Descripciones

lleno/a	full
vacío/a	empty

Verbos

cancelar	to cancel
doblar	to turn
facturar	to check in (luggage)
manejar	to drive
perderse (ie)	to get lost
reservar	to make a reservation
revisar	to inspect
viajar	to travel
volar (ue)	to fly

Palabras y expresiones útiles

a la izquierda/derecha	to the left/right
de ida y vuelta	round trip
hacer cola	to stand in line
hacer escala	to make a stopover
seguir (i) derecho	to go straight ahead
una vez	once

*For a list of affirmative and negative expressions, see pages 450–451. For a list of stressed possessive adjectives and pronouns, see pages 456–457.

13

LA CULTURA Y EL ARTE

Objetivos comunicativos

- Stating facts in the present and the past
- Giving opinions
- Describing states and conditions
- Talking about the past from a present-time perspective
- Hypothesizing about the future

Contenido

A primera vista
- Caras de hoy
- La literatura, la pintura, la música
- El español en el mundo

Explicación y expansión
- The conditional
- The past participle and the present perfect
- Past participles used as adjectives
- Reciprocal verbs and pronouns

Mosaicos
- Escuchar: Identifying the speaker
- Conversar: Stating facts about a public figure; giving an opinion and supporting it
- Leer: Identifying the narrator and protagonist of a story; differentiating facts from hypotheses about the future in a literary text
- Escribir: Reporting biographical information; writing to spark interest

Enfoque cultural
- Temas: Escritores y artistas de España e Hispanoamérica

  Para investigar en Internet
- Fortunas: Episodio 13
- Notas: El sentimiento del latino en Nueva York, *Ángel Canales*

Vocabulario

Caras de hoy

CULTURA

El flamenco es un tipo de música que se originó en Andalucía, en el sur de España, hacia el **siglo** XV. Inicialmente eran canciones **breves,** sin acompañamiento instrumental, que los gitanos (*gypsies*) cantaban para lamentarse de sus malas condiciones de vida. A través de los siglos, el flamenco ha continuado su desarrollo y ha añadido instrumentos musicales, principalmente la guitarra. A partir del siglo XVIII adquirió gran popularidad el baile flamenco, que es uno de los más emocionantes y variados del mundo.

Suggestion. Expand each area by mentioning some of the following prominent literary figures: Carlos Fuentes or Elena Garro, from Mexico; Álvaro Mutis, from Colombia; Blanca Varela, from Peru; the Chicanas Sandra Cisneros and Ana Castillo; and the Dominican Junot Díaz. You may also mention some figures of popular culture like Rubén Blades, Enrique Iglesias, Jennifer López, or Edward James Olmos. Artists such as the Cubans Ernesto Pujol and Mará Martínez-Cañas and the Mexican Arturo Elizondo, enrich this presentation. If available, consult *Review: Latin American Literature and Arts,* a publication of the Americas Society.

Gabriel García Márquez, colombiano, es considerado uno de los mejores **escritores** de hoy en día. **A través de** sus **novelas** y **cuentos** ha sabido recrear un **mundo** mítico de gran riqueza humana. En su novela *Cien años de soledad* (1967) narra en tono épico la historia de una familia y la **fundación** y **desarrollo** de Macondo, un pueblo creado en su imaginación. En 1982 este autor recibió el **Premio** Nobel de Literatura.

El español Paco de Lucía es uno de los **guitarristas** más famosos de la actualidad. Ha sabido **popularizar** la música del flamenco al combinarla con otros tipos de música, como el jazz y la música latina, abriendo grandes posibilidades para las nuevas generaciones de músicos flamencos. Sus conciertos son inolvidables por su indiscutible arte flamenco, su destreza y su profesionalismo.

Considerada una **estrella** en Argentina, su país natal, Cecilia Roth vivió como **exiliada** política en España durante los años 1970 y principios de los 1980. Allí **actuó** en algunas películas conocidas y se hizo muy famosa al protagonizar *Todo sobre mi madre,* dirigida por Pedro Almodóvar.

La danza latinoamericana tiene una larga tradición, tanto en su manifestación clásica como contemporánea. Alicia Alonso, de Cuba, Julio Bocca, de Argentina, y la bailarina mexicana Laura Rocha, quien dirige su compañía, Barro Rojo, se han presentado en muchos países de América Latina, en Estados Unidos y en Europa.

El escultor y pintor colombiano Fernando Botero es conocido por sus voluminosas figuras humanas que se exponen en todos los museos del mundo. Botero reconoce la influencia artística de los grandes **pintores** españoles Velázquez y Goya, así como la de los **muralistas** mexicanos. En su obra, Botero critica con humor una sociedad infantilizada o inmadura en la que abundan los símbolos de la autoridad y del poder: clérigos, presidentes, burgueses, etc.

A INVESTIGAR

Busque información en Internet sobre los muralistas mexicanos. ¿Quiénes son? ¿Qué tipo de pintura hacen? ¿Cuáles son algunos de sus temas? Traiga a clase alguna reproducción de estos murales para describirla.

¿Qué dice usted?

2 **13-1 Una nueva generación. Primera fase.** Llenen la tabla con la información que obtuvieron sobre ciertos hispanos prominentes.

NOMBRE	PROFESIÓN	LUGAR DE ORIGEN	DATOS INTERESANTES
Paco de Lucía	músico	España	toca la guitarra
Laura Rocha	bailarina	México	dirige su propia compañía de danza
Fernando Botero	escultor	Colombia	su obra tiene mucho humor
Cecilia Roth	actriz	Argentina	se exilió en España
Gabriel García Márquez	escritor	Colombia	ganó el Premio Nobel

G **Segunda fase.** Comparen su tabla con la de otra pareja, y entre todos hagan una lista de otros artistas o escritores hispanos famosos. Pueden pensar en el cine, la música, la pintura, el periodismo, etc. Incluyan el nombre y cubran los siguientes puntos:

1. profesión
2. lugar de origen
3. algunos datos interesantes de su carrera

VÍNCULOS

To practice vocabulario—La cultura y el arte & El español en el mundo
- SAM-OneKey: WB: 13-1, 13-2, 13-3, 13-4 / LM: 13-24, 13-25, 13-26, 13-27
- Companion Website: AP 13-1 A, B
- IRCD: Chapter 13; pg. 471

Note. Answers may vary: *escultor/pintor, se exilió en España/trabajó con Almodóvar,* etc. Accept answers as long as they reflect the information given.

Suggestions for 13-1. Turn this into a class discussion, writing names on the board and listing professions and nationalities. Have students locate the countries of origin on a map. Assign students a particular figure to look up on the Internet, reporting back to the class.

13-2 Biografías. Usen la información que obtuvieron en Internet sobre una figura hispana para preparar un breve informe que cubra los siguientes puntos:

1. fecha y lugar de nacimiento
2. obra(s) y méritos artísticos
3. reconocimientos o premios importantes
4. una anécdota o algún acontecimiento interesante de su vida

La literatura, la pintura, la música

La lengua española ha producido algunas de las obras más importantes de la literatura universal. *Don Quijote de La Mancha*, del español Miguel de Cervantes, es una obra **maestra** del siglo XVII, donde se cuentan las aventuras de un caballero y su ayudante. En Hispanoamérica, la lista de escritores excelentes es interminable. No hay más que pensar en los argentinos Jorge Luis Borges o Julio Cortázar, los chilenos Pablo Neruda y Gabriela Mistral, o los mexicanos Octavio Paz, Carlos Fuentes, Elena Garro o Elena Poniatowska. Durante los años 1970, el llamado "boom" latinoamericano, trajo un renacimiento de la novela. En casi todos los países de Hispanoamérica se escribieron obras maestras que renovaron las técnicas narrativas y que le aseguraron a esta literatura el reconocimiento mundial.

El Museo del Prado tiene una excelente colección de cuadros de pintores españoles, como Velázquez, del siglo XVII, y Goya, del XVIII. Los grandes pintores de nuestra época, Picasso y Dalí, también son españoles. ¿Y quién no conoce a los pintores mexicanos, como Diego Rivera o Frida Khalo?

La variedad de la música hispanomericana, que cubre desde la música afrocaribeña, con sus tambores y trompetas, hasta las melodías de los Andes, con sus quenas y charangos, es impresionante. Entre todas estas formas musicales, el tango siempre se ha distinguido por la riqueza de las voces de sus más notables intérpretes, como Carlos Gardel. El tango surgió entre los europeos que se trasladaron a Argentina a comienzos del siglo XX, en busca de una vida mejor.

El español en el mundo

AUDIO

Población de habla hispana en el mundo

El español, también conocido como castellano porque se originó en Castilla, una región del centro de España, también se habla en toda América Central y del Sur, excepto en Brasil y las Guayanas. También se habla español en Guinea Ecuatorial, el Sahara, y parte de los Estados Unidos y Filipinas. Considerando el número de hablantes, el español es la cuarta lengua en el mundo, ya que lo hablan aproximadamente 330 millones de personas.

CONCENTRACIÓN DE HISPANOHABLANTES EN LOS ESTADOS UNIDOS

- Más de 1 millón de hispanos
- Más de 250 mil hispanos
- Más de 100 mil hispanos
- Menos de 100 mil hispanos

¿Qué dice usted?

2 **13-3 ¿Dónde viven?** Uno/a de ustedes es un/a periodista que busca datos sobre la población de habla hispana en los Estados Unidos y en el resto del mundo. El/La otro/a trabaja en un Centro de Estadística y le puede dar los datos que usted necesita. Consulten la información que se presenta.

Ciudades con el mayor número de hispanohablantes

1. Los Ángeles	4.780.000
2. Nueva York	2.780.000
3. Miami	1.100.000
4. San Francisco	970.000
5. Chicago	890.000
6. Houston	770.000
7. Dallas	520.000
8. Phoenix	345.000
9. Denver	226.000
10. Washington, D.C.	225.000

Origen de los inmigrantes

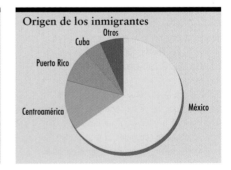

MODELO: E1: ¿Sabe usted/Me puede decir cuáles son las regiones o países africanos donde se habla español?

E2: Sí, son Guinea Ecuatorial y el Sahara.

1. países de Asia donde se habla español
2. país americano con mayor número de hispanohablantes
3. ciudades de Estados Unidos con mayor número de hispanos
4. país de origen de la mayoría de hispanos que viven en Estados Unidos
5. estados con más de 250.000 hispanos
6. ...

Warm-up for 13-4. Guide students in their search by mentioning the many areas in which we see Hispanic influence. Each possible career ties into at least one impact area, including architecture, agriculture, the food industry, history, politics, military service, law, law enforcement, medicine, literature, art, entertainment, sports, education, and media. Encourage students' continued study of Spanish by pointing out additional job opportunities and possible increased income available to those who can successfully communicate with this vast customer base and demonstrate cultural awareness. Cite the need for marketing and advertising in Spanish. Discuss the significant voting power of Hispanics, and mention NAFTA and other international agreements involving Spanish-speaking countries.

Suggestion for 13-5. Give students the names of Hispanic magazines that are easily available: *People en español, Latina, Vanidades,* etc. They may find also magazines and newspapers in the Internet. You may mention the following newspapers on line: *El Universal* y *El Nacional* (from Caracas), *Clarín, Página 12* y *La Nación* (from Buenos Aires), *El Peruano* (from Lima), *El País* (from Madrid).

Warm-up for 13-6. As a pre-listening activity, have students get in groups of four and discuss some cultural events they like to attend when they are back in their hometown and/or when they are in school.

Audioscript for 13-6:
ALBERTO: Josefina, mi amor, ¿adónde quieres ir esta noche?
JOSEFINA: Mira, yo quisiera ir al Centro de Arte de América Latina. Hoy va a tocar la Orquesta Sinfónica de Puerto Rico. ¿Qué te parece? Empieza a las 8 de la noche y la entrada cuesta 25 pesos.
ALBERTO: Un poco caro, pero bueno, vale la pena. Hay que ver si hay entradas. Llama por teléfono o ve a Internet. Si no tienen entradas para el concierto, podemos ir a la lectura de poemas de los Nuyorican Poets. Va a ser en el mismo centro, pero en otra sala. Va a incluir a Martín Espada, Sandra Maria Esteves y Naomi Ayala. ¿Qué piensas?
JOSEFINA: ¡Me parece excelente! Y, ¿a qué hora empieza?
ALBERTO: A las siete y media. Las entradas cuestan 10 pesos.
JOSEFINA: Bueno, voy a ver. Si no conseguimos entradas para ninguna de las dos cosas, ¿qué te parece si vamos al Museo de Arte Latinoamericano? Siempre tienen exposiciones interesantes y la ventaja es que podemos ir ahora mismo sin tener que esperar hasta más tarde. Las entradas son más baratas también.
ALBERTO: Bueno, decide tú. Me gustan todas las posibilidades.
JOSEFINA: Voy a llamar a todos los lugares y luego decidimos, pero yo prefiero ir al concierto de la orquesta sinfónica.
ALBERTO: Bueno, bueno. Avísame, entonces.

2 **13-4 El español en el trabajo. Primera fase.** Hagan una lista de cinco carreras en los Estados Unidos que requieran comunicarse con personas hispanohablantes. Luego comparen su lista con la de otra pareja.

Segunda fase. Comenten lo siguiente.

1. ¿En qué áreas geográficas de los Estados Unidos se pueden conseguir estos trabajos con más facilidad?
2. ¿En qué contextos será una ventaja saber hablar, leer y escribir en español?

13-5 Los medios de comunicación en español. Primera fase. En una revista o un periódico en español escoja un artículo que le interese, léalo y resúmalo.

Segunda fase. Comparta con la clase el contenido del artículo que leyó en la **Primera fase.** Puede incluir la siguiente información en su presentación:

1. ¿Cómo se llama la revista o el periódico de donde obtuvo el artículo?
2. ¿Quién lo escribió?
3. ¿Cuál es el tema del artículo?
4. ¿Cuáles son las ideas centrales que se presentan?
5. ¿Por qué decidió usted leer específicamente este artículo? ¿Cuál es su opinión sobre el contenido (la opinión, los datos, la información, etc.) del artículo?

AUDIO **13-6 ¿Adónde vamos?** You will listen to a young, married couple trying to decide where to go on a Sunday evening. Before you listen, list three places where you think they might want to go.

_____

_____

Now, pay attention to the general idea of what is said. Then, as you listen circle the appropriate ending for each statement.

1. Entre los eventos culturales a los que Alberto y Josefina consideran ir está...
   a. una exposición de arte precolombino
   b. una lectura de poemas
   c. un concierto de música popular

2. Josefina prefiere ir al...
   a. concierto de la orquesta sinfónica
   b. museo de arte latinoamericano
   c. lugar que sea más barato

3. Para averiguar si hay entradas, Josefina va a...
   a. usar Internet
   b. llamar por teléfono a todos los lugares
   c. ir personalmente al centro

4. Según esta conversación podemos ver que...
   a. Alberto siempre decide a qué lugar van a ir y no escucha a nadie
   b. Josefina no acepta ninguna sugerencia e impone su voluntad
   c. Alberto y Josefina discuten las posibilidades y deciden juntos

1. The conditional

In *Lección 6*, you began to use the expression **me gustaría...** to express what you would like. **Gustaría** is a form of the conditional.

VÍNCULOS

To practice the conditional
- SAM-OneKey: WB: 13-5, 13-6, 13-7 / LM: 13-28, 13-29
- Companion Website: AP 13-2
- *Gramática viva:* Grammar Point 5: Conditional
- IRCD: Chapter 13; pg. 475

■ The use of the conditional in Spanish is similar to the use of the construction *would + verb* in English when hypothesizing about a situation that does not form part of the speaker's reality.

> Yo **saldría** temprano para el concierto. — *I would leave early for the concert.*

■ When English *would* implies *used to*, the imperfect is used.

> Cuando era chica, **salía** temprano para la escuela. — *When I was young, I would (used to) leave early for school.*

■ Spanish also uses the conditional to express probability in the past.

> Estaba tomando café. **Serían** las diez de la mañana. — *I was having coffee. It was probably ten in the morning.*

■ The conditional is easy to recognize. It is formed by adding the endings **-ía, -ías, -ía, -íamos, -íais, -ían** to the infinitive.

CONDITIONAL			
	HABLAR	COMER	VIVIR
yo	hablaría	comería	viviría
tú	hablarías	comerías	vivirías
Ud., él, ella	hablaría	comería	viviría
nosotros/as	hablaríamos	comeríamos	viviríamos
vosotros/as	hablaríais	comeríais	viviríais
Uds., ellos/as	hablarían	comerían	vivirían

■ Verbs that have an irregular stem in the future have that same stem in the conditional.

IRREGULAR CONDITIONAL VERBS		
INFINITIVE	NEW STEM	CONDITIONAL FORMS
haber	**habr-**	habría, habrías, habría...
poder	**podr-**	podría, podrías, podría...
querer	**querr-**	querría, querrías, querría...
saber	**sabr-**	sabría, sabrías, sabría...
poner	**pondr-**	pondría, pondrías, pondría...
tener	**tendr-**	tendría, tendrías, tendría...
salir	**saldr-**	saldría, saldrías, saldría...
venir	**vendr-**	vendría, vendrías, vendría...
decir	**dir-**	diría, dirías, diría...
hacer	**har-**	haría, harías, haría...

Suggestions. Review the future tense before introducing the conditional; then compare the two. Use conditional forms in questions: *¿Podría Ud. saludar en español a otra persona? ¿Qué le diría? Y Ud., ¿iría a la playa en traje de baño? ¿Y vendría a la universidad en traje de baño?* If possible, use transparencies or visuals to elicit answers.

You may point out that the conditional is also used to soften requests and statements: *Me gustaría visitar el museo. ¿Podría darme la dirección?*

Suggestions. You may wish to explain that *haber* is the infinite of *hay, había,* etc. The use of *haber* with perfect tenses will be presented in this lesson, as well as in lessons 14 and 15.

Suggestion for 13-7. Review the cultural material presented in *A primera vista* by talking about it and asking some questions. For example, *García Márquez es uno de los grandes escritores de la lengua española. ¿Sabe Ud. de dónde es? ¿Cuál es su novela más conocida? ¿Qué premio importante ganó en 1982? ¿Qué instrumento musical toca Paco de Lucía? ¿Ha escuchado algunos de sus discos? ¿Le han gustado?*

Note. All answers are possible. You may wish to have students explain why they chose their answers.

¿Qué dice usted?

13-7 ¿Qué haría usted en estas situaciones? Primera fase. Lea las siguientes situaciones y marque con un círculo lo que usted probablemente haría.

1. Es el cumpleaños de su mejor amigo, quien sigue cursos avanzados de español, y usted le quiere regalar un libro.
   a. Le compraría una novela breve de García Márquez.
   b. Le regalaría *El Quijote* de Cervantes.
   c. Le daría un buen diccionario.

2. Paco de Lucía va a dar un concierto en su ciudad este fin de semana.
   a. Invitaría a mi novio/a al concierto.
   b. Llamaría a mis amigos para ir al concierto.
   c. Compraría algunos de sus discos antes de ir al concierto.

3. Van a estrenar (*show for the first time*) una nueva película de Cecilia Roth.
   a. La iría a ver lo antes posible.
   b. Leería las reseñas (*reviews*) antes de ir a verla.
   c. Hablaría con mis amigos para ver si quieren ir.

4. Hay una exposición de esculturas de Botero en el museo de arte de su ciudad.
   a. Iría a Internet para saber más sobre su obra.
   b. Compraría boletos rápidamente para no perder la oportunidad de verla.
   c. Se lo diría a mi amigo/a para ir juntos.

5. Usted va a pasar unos días en Madrid. ¿Qué haría en el Museo del Prado?
   a. Visitaría las salas donde están las pinturas de Velázquez.
   b. Vería los cuadros de Goya primero.
   c. Pasaría una o dos horas en el museo para conocerlo.

❷ Segunda fase. Compare sus respuestas con las de su compañero/a y después digan qué es lo que ustedes harían realmente en esas situaciones.

13-8 La lotería. Primera fase. Usted participó en un concurso (*contest*) literario internacional importante y ganó el primer premio y quinientos mil dólares. Diga lo que haría usted con el dinero y por qué. Como usted es generoso/a, considere lo siguiente:

- lo que haría por un familiar o amigo/a

- lo que haría para alguna organización cultural

- lo que haría para animar a los jóvenes a escribir

Ⓖ Segunda fase. En grupo, comenten sus planes. Luego, seleccionen el mejor plan, expliquen por qué lo escogieron y compartan esta información con la clase.

❷ 13-9 ¿Qué harían ustedes? Primero digan qué harían en las siguientes situaciones. Después comparen sus respuestas con las de otros estudiantes.

1. Usted entra en un museo donde se muestran obras de pintores famosos y ve que en una de las salas, que está vacía, hay un ladrón (*thief*) tratando de robar un cuadro.
2. Usted pudo conseguir las dos últimas entradas para un concierto de Paco de Lucía e invitó a una persona importante, pero ahora no encuentra las entradas.
3. Usted descubre que alguien de su universidad o su trabajo está vendiendo entradas falsas y muy baratas para un concierto de música folclórica de Colombia.
4. Usted descubre de casualidad (*by chance*) que su mejor amigo/a se presentó a un concurso literario con un cuento escrito por otra persona.

2 **13-10 ¿Qué le pasaría a Miguel? Primera fase.** Aparentemente Miguel se levantó ayer con el pie izquierdo (*off to a bad start*). Seleccionen una explicación hipotética de todo que le pasó a Miguel.

1. Miguel fue al aeropuerto a buscar a un amigo puertorriqueño, pero no lo encontró.
   a. Probablemente Miguel no sabría bien la hora de llegada del avión.
   b. El amigo de Miguel no podría salir del aeropuerto a tiempo porque tendría problemas con la aduana.
   c. El amigo de Miguel llegaría tarde al aeropuerto de su ciudad y perdería el vuelo.

2. Cuando llegó al lugar donde estaba su auto, Miguel no encontró el suéter nuevo que tenía sobre el asiento.
   a. Miguel dejaría el auto abierto, y alguien le robaría el suéter.
   b. Miguel pensaría que llevó el suéter, pero seguramente lo dejó en casa.
   c. La novia de Miguel se lo llevaría.

3. Un policía se acercó al auto de Miguel y le puso una multa (*ticket*).
   a. Miguel no tendría permiso para conducir.
   b. Miguel no estacionaría el auto en el lugar apropiado.
   c. El policía detestaría a Miguel.

2 **Segunda fase.** Cuando Miguel llegó a su casa, le ocurrieron otras cosas. ¿Podrían explicar por qué le ocurrirían esas cosas a Miguel?

1. Cuando Miguel llegó a su casa, no pudo abrir la puerta.
2. Finalmente, cuando entró en su casa, encendió la computadora, pero no pudo ver nada en la pantalla (*screen*).

G **13-11 ¡Agenda presidencial! Primera fase.** Usted es uno/a de los/as candidatos/as a la presidencia de su país, y lo/la han invitado a dar un discurso en un club de escritores e intelectuales hispanos. Prepare una lista de lo que usted haría como presidente/a del país en las siguientes áreas:

- inmigración
- empleo
- salud
- cultura

Segunda fase. Pronuncie el discurso justificando su agenda política. Luego, los intelectuales (sus compañeros/as) le harán preguntas. Respóndalas.

SITUACIONES

Role A: You need advice and decide to speak to your best friend. Explain that a) you have written a novel that you would like to publish, b) that you would like to know about literary contests in your area, and c) that you would like to find a publisher (*casa editorial*). Then answer your partner's questions.

Role B: You would like to give your friend good advice but need more information. Ask him/her a) what the novel is about, b) when he/she wrote it, and c) how long it is. Tell your friend that you would love to read the novel, and a) that he/she should ask your literature teacher for professional advice, b) that perhaps he/she should consider finding a literary agent, and c) that you have a friend who works at one of the major publishing companies who might be interested in reading his/her work.

VÍNCULOS

To practice the past participle and the present perfect
- SAM-OneKey: WB: 13-8, 13-9, 13-10, 13-11 / LM: 13-30, 13-31, 13-32
- Companion Website: AP 13-3
- *Gramática viva:* Grammar Point 27: Past participle and the present perfect
- IRCD: Chapter 13; pg. 478

2. The past participle and the present perfect

- Both Spanish and English have perfect tenses that are used to refer to past actions, events, and conditions. Both languages use an auxiliary verb (**haber** in Spanish, *to have* in English) and a past participle. In English, past participles are often formed with the endings *-ed* and *-en*; for example, *finished, eaten.*

- Use the present perfect to refer to a past event, action, or condition that has some relation to the present.

Victoria, ¿ya **has leído** el libro?	*Victoria, have you read the book yet?*
No, no lo **he leído** todavía.	*No, I have not read it yet.*

- Place object and reflexive pronouns before the auxiliary **haber.** Do not place any word between **haber** and the past participle.

¿**Le has dado** el libro de Borges?	*Have you given her Borges' book?*
No, todavía no **se lo** he dado.	*No, I have not given it to her yet.*

- All past participles of -ar verbs end in **-ado,** whereas past participles of **-er** and **-ir** verbs generally end in **-ido.** If the stem of an **-er** or **-ir** verb ends in a vowel, use a written accent on the **i** of **-ido** (leer → leído).

Suggestion. Provide comprehensible input: *Yo he visitado Miami dos veces. He comido comida cubana muchas veces. Nunca he ido a San Antonio. Tampoco he ido a San Diego.* Write the verb forms *visitar → he visitado, comer → he comido, ir → he ido* on the board as you say them. Ask questions: *Y usted, ¿ha visitado Miami? ¿Cuántas veces? ¿Ha comido comida cubana? ¿Ha ido a San Antonio? ¿Ha comido fajitas/comida mexicana en San Antonio?* Then have students work in pairs to find out what countries or cities they have visited and how many times.

Alternate. Give commands: *Hable con el dependiente. Compre ese disco. Pague la cuenta.* Students answer: *Ya he...*

Suggestion. Review *tener que* + infinitive. Give examples contrasting its use with that of *haber* + past participle: *Juan no ha terminado el proyecto porque está muy ocupado. Tiene que terminar el proyecto esta noche.*

Suggestion. Introduce *romper, cubrir, morir* through comprehensible input. Use visuals, if possible. You may explain that compounds of verbs whose past participles are irregular have the same irregularity: *escribir → escrito; describir → descrito.*

PRESENT TENSE HABER		+	PAST PARTICIPLE
yo	he		
tú	has		
Ud., él, ella	ha		hablado
nosotros/as	hemos		comido
vosotros/as	habéis		vivido
Uds., ellos/as	han		

- Form the present perfect of the indicative by using the present tense of **haber** as an auxiliary verb with the past participle of the main verb. **Tener** is never used as the auxiliary verb to form the perfect tense.

Han trabajado mucho para comprar la casa.	*They have worked a lot to buy the house.*
Algunos músicos hispanos **han obtenido** muchos premios.	*Some Hispanic musicians have obtained many awards.*

- Some -er and -ir verbs have irregular past participles. Here are some of the more common ones:

IRREGULAR PAST PARTICIPLES			
hacer	**hecho**	abrir	**abierto**
poner	**puesto**	escribir	**escrito**
romper	**roto**	cubrir	**cubierto**
ver	**visto**	decir	**dicho**
volver	**vuelto**	morir	**muerto**

- The present perfect of **hay** is **ha habido.**

Ha habido más trabajo últimamente.	*There has been more work lately.*

- Use the present tense of **acabar + de +** *infinitive*, not the present perfect, to state that something has just happened.

Acabo de oír las noticias.	*I have just heard the news.*

¿Qué dice usted?

13-12 Lo que no he hecho. Usted y su compañero/a deben decir las cosas que no han hecho de cada lista. Después, comparen sus respuestas con las de otros estudiantes.

1. Yo nunca he estado en...
   a. Colombia
   b. Filipinas
   c. España

2. Yo nunca he visto...
   a. un espectáculo de flamenco
   b. una película mexicana
   c. a una persona bailar el tango

3. Yo nunca he ido a...
   a. un país donde se hable español
   b. un café-teatro
   c. un concierto de Paco de Lucía

4. Yo nunca he escrito...
   a. una novela
   b. una carta de negocios
   c. un poema

5. Yo nunca he roto...
   a. un plato
   b. un vaso
   c. un disco

6. Yo nunca he dicho...
   a. una mala palabra
   b. una mentira (*lie*)
   c. no a un amigo

13-13 Confesiones. Túrnense para decir si cada uno de ustedes ha hecho o no las siguientes cosas. Su compañero/a no le va a creer y le va a pedir detalles.

MODELO: conocer a Elena Poniatowska
           E1: Yo he conocido a Elena Poniatowska.
           E2: ¡Vamos! Tú no has conocido a Elena Poniatowska.
           E1: Yo sí la he conocido.
           E2: ...

1. ver el Desfile de las Rosas en Pasadena
2. conocer personalmente a la actriz Salma Hayek
3. nunca hablar mal de mis amigos
4. visitar muchos países hispanos
5. enamorarse de un/a artista
6. ...

13-14 Un/a hispano/a famoso/a. Primera fase. Piensen en un/a hispano/a famoso/a y preparen una lista de cinco cosas que ustedes creen que él/ella ha hecho para tener éxito. Después comparen su lista con la de otra pareja y háganse preguntas.

MODELO: Julio Bocca es un bailarín excelente.
           Ha bailado en las principales ciudades del mundo.

Segunda fase. Digan *tres* cosas que ustedes han hecho que los/las ha ayudado a tener éxito en su vida personal, académica o profesional.

13-15 Preparativos para un viaje a California. Usted y su compañero/a van a hacer un viaje a California para observar de cerca la influencia hispana en ese estado. Háganse preguntas para ver qué preparativos ha hecho cada uno/a para el viaje.

MODELO: pedir información a la Cámara de Comercio
           E1: ¿Has pedido información a la Cámara de Comercio?
           E2: No, no la he pedido todavía. *o* Sí, ya la pedí.

1. llamar a la línea aérea
2. ir a la agencia de viajes
3. hacer las reservaciones

4. leer artículos sobre las misiones
5. buscar hoteles en Internet
6. obtener mapas para ir a Santa Bárbara

Follow-up for 13-12. Have students share information with the class: *Mi compañero/a nunca ha estado en... Nunca ha hecho...* Then take a poll to find out what students have never done.

Note for 13-13. Practice other expressions that may be used to express disbelief: *¡Por favor! No te creo.*

Alternate for 13-13. Have students tell interesting things that they have done.

LENGUA

Spanish speakers add **sí** when they wish to emphasize a verbal expression: **Yo sí conozco/conocí/he conocido a Antonio Banderas.**

Suggestion for 13-15. Through brainstorming, have students generate five or more preparations they need to make before the trip. Have students share their ideas with the whole class. Encourage students to produce both negative and affirmative responses.

Warm-up for 13-16. Practice by having students list five things that they have just done. Or ask questions: *¿Tiene hambre? (No, acabo de comer.) ¿Tiene sueño? ¿Quiere bailar? ¿Quiere nadar? ¿Tiene sed?*

13-16 Justo ahora. Con su compañero/a, digan qué acaban de hacer estas personas. Den la mayor información posible.

MODELO: Juan y Ramiro salen del estadio.
Acaban de ver un partido de béisbol muy importante.
Fueron a ver a Alex Rodríguez porque es su jugador favorito.

1. Maricarmen y sus amigos salen de un concierto de guitarra.
2. Pedro y Alina salen de una tienda donde se alquilan películas.
3. Mercedes y Paula traen palomitas de maíz para todo el grupo.
4. Un hombre sale corriendo de una tienda de artesanías.
5. Jorge y Rubén salen de una joyería (*jewelry store*).
6. Frente a todos sus amigos, Rubén le da una sorpresa a su novia.

13-17 ¿Cómo han contribuido los inmigrantes? Por diversas razones, las personas de algunas comunidades étnicas han emigrado a muchas partes del mundo. Piensen en una comunidad de inmigrantes en su país y hagan lo siguiente:

■ Primero, identifiquen un grupo étnico que ha inmigrado a su país.

■ Luego, escojan una o más áreas en las que este grupo de inmigrantes ha contribuido al país: negocios, arquitectura, música, arte, moda, ciencia, literatura, etc.

■ Finalmente, preparen una breve presentación oral explicando cómo han contribuido estas personas a la sociedad. Den ejemplos concretos.

13-18 Los problemas de las minorías. Primera fase. Con su compañero/a, prepare una lista de *tres* problemas que existen en una de las comunidades hispanas de este país. Consideren las siguientes áreas:

1. la salud
2. el trabajo
3. la educación
4. la vivienda (*housing*)

Segunda fase. Ahora, comenten qué se ha hecho para superar esos problemas. Luego preparen otra lista de cosas que no se han hecho, pero que, según ustedes, deberían hacerse. Compartan su lista con la clase.

SITUACIONES

1. One of you is a journalist and the other is a famous Hispanic author living in the United States. The reporter would like to know: a) the number of novels the author has written, b) their dates of publication, c) how long the author has been living in the United States, d) the prizes the author has won, e) which is the author's favorite novel, and f) why.

2. Each of you must choose one of the famous personalities presented at the beginning of the lesson. Do not mention his/her name, but ask questions to find out whom your partner has chosen. Each one of you must then say what this person has accomplished to become famous.

3. Past participles used as adjectives

■ When a past participle is used as an adjective, it agrees with the noun it modifies.

un cantante **conocido**	*a well-known singer*
una puerta **cerrada**	*a closed door*
los libros **abiertos**	*the open books*
unas películas **alquiladas**	*some rented films*

■ Spanish uses **estar** + *past participle* to express a state or condition resulting from a prior action.

ACTION	RESULT
Ella terminó el trabajo.	El trabajo **está terminado.**
Magdalena se sentó.	Magdalena **está sentada.**
Reservaron las habitaciones.	Las habitaciones **están reservadas**

¿Qué dice usted?

13-19 La opinión del profesor. Complete la siguiente conversación entre Arturo y su profesor de pintura, con la forma correcta del participio usado como adjetivo.

ARTURO: Profesor, el cuadro no está (1) ___terminado___ (terminado, terminada), pero quisiera saber su opinión.

PROFESOR: Me gustan los colores, pero cambiaría un poco los detalles de la casa. Por ejemplo, tendría la puerta y una ventana (2) ___abiertas___ (abiertos, abiertas) para ver algo del interior.

ARTURO: Buena idea. ¿Y las personas que aparecen en el cuadro?

PROFESOR: Me parece que están bien, excepto la niña que está (3) ___sentada___ (sentado, sentada) al lado del perro en el jardín. Parece más una mujer pequeña que una niña. El perro está muy bien (4) ___pintado___ (pintado, pintada). En general, me parece que la composición del cuadro es muy buena.

ARTURO: Así es que le parecen bien las flores y los árboles a la derecha.

PROFESOR: Sí, están muy bien, y la idea de poner al perro (5) ___acostado___ (acostado, acostada) al lado de las flores es muy buena. El contraste de los colores es excelente.

Ⓖ **13-20 ¿Un robo o un cuarto desordenado? Primera fase.** Su compañero/a de cuarto y usted entraron en su habitación y vieron que estaba muy desordenada y que faltaban algunas cosas. Túrnense para describirle a la policía lo que vio cada uno, usando las palabras de abajo. Hagan las modificaciones necesarias.

MODELO: ventana / abierto
Cuando entré, la ventana (no) estaba abierta.

roto	colgado	encendido	tendido
abierto	cerrado	cubierto	destruido
apagado	descubierto	quebrado	pintado

VÍNCULOS

To practice past participles used as adjectives
• SAM-OneKey: WB: 13-12, 13-13, 13-14 / LM: 13-33, 13-34
• Companion Website: AP 13-4

Suggestion. Illustrate action and result by performing tasks in class. Close the text and say, *He cerrado el libro. Ahora el libro está cerrado.* Open the door and say, *He abierto la puerta. La puerta está abierta.*

ESTUDIANTE 1

1. el espejo del armario ___estaba roto___
2. la cama ___estaba tendida___
3. los libros ___estaban abiertos___
4. la computadora ___estaba cubierta___

ESTUDIANTE 2

1. la ropa ___estaba colgada___
2. el televisor ___estaba encendido___
3. las ventanas ___estaban cerradas___
4. la lámpara ___estaba rota___

Segunda fase. Después de escuchar el relato de ustedes, uno/a de los/las policías hará lo siguiente:

1. Les hará preguntas si necesita más información.
2. Les dirá **tres** cosas que él/ella haría en la situación de ustedes.

13-21 Una noche muy especial. El siguiente párrafo cuenta algo que le ocurrió a Rosalía. Para saber lo que le pasó, llene los blancos con la forma correcta del participio pasado de los verbos entre paréntesis.

Rosalía del Corral entró en el teatro, caminó por el pasillo y se sentó. Su mejor amiga estaba (1) ___sentada___ (sentar) a su lado. Era una noche muy especial porque iban a anunciar qué actores hispanos eran los ganadores del premio de excelencia por su actuación y todos estaban muy (2) ___emocionados___ (emocionar). El presentador habló unos minutos sobre la importancia del acto, la orquesta tocó algunas canciones (3) ___conocidas___ (conocer) y otras personas hablaron hasta que llegó el momento (4) ___esperado___ (esperar). Una chica le entregó dos sobres (5) ___cerrados___ (cerrar) al presentador. Éste abrió el primero y con el sobre (6) ___abierto___ (abrir) en la mano, dijo el nombre de la ganadora. Rosalía no podía creerlo. Sólo repetía en su mente: "¡He (7) ___ganado___ (ganar)! ¡He (8) ___recibido___ (recibir) el premio!" Sin saber cómo, se levantó del asiento para ir al escenario. Se sentía muy (9) ___confundida___ (confundir), y en ese mismo momento se despertó y vio que estaba (10) ___acostada___ (acostar) en su cuarto. ¡Todo era un sueño!

SITUACIONES

Role A. You are a reporter for *The New Herald,* a Miami newspaper, and are going to interview one of the people in a shelter as a result of a hurricane in the area. Ask him/her about a) the time of his/her arrival at the shelter and the means of transportation he/she used to get there, b) why he/she abandoned his/her house, c) if he/she knows anyone in the shelter, and d) ask him/her to describe the state of his/her neighborhood.

Role B. You live in Little Havana, an area in Miami where a hurricane has caused a lot of damage. You are currently in a Red Cross shelter and a reporter is going to interview you about what has happened. Answer his/her questions telling him/her that a) your house has been badly damaged b) that other houses in the neighborhood have also been destroyed c) that you have lost personal belongings, and d) that some friends have helped you.

4. Reciprocal verbs and pronouns

VÍNCULOS

To practice reciprocal verbs and pronouns
- SAM-OneKey: WB: 13-15, 13-16 / LM: 13-35, 13-36
- Companion Website: AP 13-5
- IRCD: Chapter 13; pg. 483

Están enamorados, y se quieren mucho.

Se besan y se abrazan.

Se llevan muy mal.

No se ven, ni se llaman por teléfono.

Se odian, y se pelean todo el tiempo.

■ Use plural reflexive pronouns (**nos, os, se**) to express reciprocal actions. In English, reciprocal actions are usually expressed with *each other* or *one another.*

> Muchos hispanos **se abrazan** cuando **se saludan.**
>
> Nosotros **nos vemos** todas las semanas.
>
> En mi familia **nos llevamos** muy bien.

> *Many Hispanics embrace when they greet each other.*
>
> *We see each other every week.*
>
> *In our family we get along very well.*

Suggestions. Introduce reciprocal verbs and pronouns by talking about the illustrations and/or members of your class. For example, look at a student and say: *Yo miro a Pedro. Pedro me mira a mí.* (use hand gesture) *Pedro y yo nos miramos. Él y yo nos respetamos. Nos hablamos en la clase y a veces nos vemos en la cafetería o en un pasillo y nos saludamos.* Practice *llevarse bien/mal.* You may introduce additional vocabulary and expressions such as *darse la mano, extrañarse/echarse de menos.*

¿Qué dice usted?

13-22 Indicaciones de reciprocidad. Escoja las ideas de la columna de la derecha que mejor completen las oraciones de la izquierda.

1. Cuando Pedro y su amigo Juan se ven en alguna reunión, ellos ___b___.
2. El perro y el gato de María se pelean todo el tiempo. Ellos ___d___.
3. Alberto y yo somos muy buenos amigos, pero vivimos en ciudades diferentes. No hablamos mucho por teléfono, pero ___a___.
4. Alicia y Pepe son novios y se quieren mucho. Cuando se despiden por la noche, ellos se abrazan y ___e___.
5. Mis abuelos dicen que el secreto de su matrimonio tan feliz es que ellos se quieren mucho y ___c___.

> a. nos mandamos correos electrónicos
> b. se dan la mano o se abrazan
> c. se respetan
> d. se odian
> e. se besan

13-23 ¿Qué hacen los buenos amigos? Primera fase. En grupos pequeños, hagan lo siguiente:

1. Preparen una lista de las actitudes que ustedes consideran importantes para mantener una buena amistad.
2. Escojan las cuatro más importantes.
3. Comparen su lista con la de otros grupos.
4. Finalmente, si consideran que hay otras actitudes o valores que no han sido escogidas, incorpórenlas en su lista.

Suggestion for 13-23. You may give examples of what students could say when comparing their lists: *Para nosotros, la generosidad es importante en una buena amistad.*

2 Segunda fase. Primero, determine si los buenos amigos hacen o no hacen estas cosas, y bajo qué circunstancias. Después, comparta sus ideas con su compañero/a.

MODELO: mandarse mensajes electrónicos
E1: (Yo creo que) los buenos amigos se mandan mensajes electrónicos si viven lejos.
E2: Yo también, pero creo que no se mandan muchos mensajes si se ven frecuentemente.

1. _____ llamarse todos los días
2. _____ comprenderse
3. _____ ayudarse cuando tienen problemas
4. _____ insultarse y pelearse
5. _____ regalarse cosas
6. _____ darse consejos cuando los necesitan
7. _____ quererse
8. _____ criticarse continuamente

2 13-24 Consejos. Identifiquen el (los) problema(s) de las siguientes personas. Luego, búsquenles una solución.

1. Rafael y Josefina son novios, pero no se ven con mucha frecuencia. Él vive en Monterrey, México, y ella vive en Los Ángeles. Tienen una relación a distancia.
2. Catalina y Raquel son compañeras de cuarto. A veces cuando Catalina quiere estudiar, llega al cuarto y encuentra a Raquel escuchando música de Ricky Martin o Gloria Estefan con sus amigos.
3. Los estudiantes de historia tienen miedo de expresar sus opiniones en clase porque el profesor no parece interesarse por lo que dicen. A veces los estudiantes no prestan atención en clase.

2 13-25 Mis relaciones con... Piense en una persona importante en su vida (padre/madre, novio/a, pariente, un/a amigo/a, etc.) y dígale a su compañero/a cómo son las relaciones entre ustedes. Las preguntas de más abajo pueden serle útiles.

MODELO: Mis relaciones con mi hermano son muy buenas.
Nosotros nos queremos. A veces...

1. ¿Se respetan?
2. ¿Se quieren?
3. ¿Se detestan?
4. ¿Se comunican?
5. ¿Se pelean?
6. ...

EN DIRECTO

To complain about something or someone:
Tengo una queja.
I have a complaint.
Quisiera quejarme de...
I would like to complain about . . .
Quisiera hablar con usted sobre un problema que tengo con...
I would like to discuss with you a problem that I have with . . .

 **SITUACIONES**

Role A: You have problems with a colleague at work, so go to see your boss. Explain to your boss that your colleague does not treat you well. Then answer your boss's questions and tell him/her that in addition to this, your colleague, a) reads the documents on your desk whenever you are away and b) speaks badly of you with other employees. Answer your boss's questions and agree to a meeting.

Role B: You are the curator of a museum in Mexico City. Listen to one of your employees' complaints. Ask him/her questions to find out a) if there are negative attitudes from both persons involved in the problem. If there are, ask him/her a) to explain why, b) if he/she can remember a specific discussion, and c) since when he/she has noticed this attitude from his/her colleague. Then ask him/her a) to what documents he/she is referring, b) if there are witnesses (**testigos**), and c) if you should call a meeting among the three of you.

MOSAICOS

 Escuchar

Identifying the speaker

When you listen to a radio announcement or a voice message, you frequently know who is speaking from the content of the message. For example, if you hear a recording in your voice mail saying "Do you need money to pay for your college tuition? We can give you a loan right now. Just call us at 555-555-555!," you immediately know the caller is somebody working for a bank or a credit card, even if you had never heard that voice before.

Antes de escuchar

13-26 Los horarios. In **13-27**, you will listen to a series of recordings from places you have called to ask for information. Before you listen, write down the names of three places or institutions that usually have recordings of their schedule for callers.

_____

_____

_____

A escuchar

13-27 Now, listen to the recordings. As you listen, identify the origin of the recording and write next to it the number corresponding to the order in which the information was given.

    __4__ teatro local

    __3__ sala de conciertos

    __1__ cine

    __2__ museo

Después de escuchar

13-28 ¿Y usted? With a classmate, share your answers to the following questions.

1. ¿Ha ido usted a un museo o a un concierto últimamente? ¿Qué museo visitó o a qué concierto fue?
2. ¿Cree usted que es importante visitar museos o ir a conciertos de música clásica? ¿Por qué?
3. ¿Qué otra actividad cultural le interesa a usted? ¿Por qué?

VÍNCULOS

For materials related to the Mosaicos section, see
- SAM-OneKey: WB: 13-17, 13-18, 13-19, 13-20, 13-21, 13-22 / LM: 13-37

Warm-up for 13-27. As a pre-listening activity, have students work in groups of four and discuss if they know when museums are open, what time the movie theaters show the films, and when there are concerts in the concert hall.

Audioscript for 13-27. 1. MALE VOICE: El Festival de Cine argentino empieza el 28 de agosto a las 10 de la mañana en el cine Metro. Las entradas estarán a la venta en el cine a partir de las 8 de la mañana. 2. FEMALE VOICE: La exposición de artistas latinoamericanos empieza el día lunes 23 de octubre. Las salas del museo abrirán a las 10 de la mañana y estarán abiertas hasta las 4 de la tarde. 3. MALE VOICE: El concierto de guitarra clásica española ha sido cancelado el día de hoy. 4. FEMALE VOICE: La presentación de la obra *Nuestra Señora de las Nubes* por el grupo de teatro Malayerba se llevará a cabo el miércoles 26 de junio a las 8 de la noche.

Audioscript for 13-30. 1. A mí me encantan las comedias y los dramas. Aunque por lo general sólo tengo que leer algunas escenas de las obras para mis clase de literatura, yo busco el tiempo para leer toda la obra. Este año vamos a tener otro festival de teatro español, donde se presentarán dramas y comedias clásicas y algunas obras de los mejores autores del siglo XX. El año pasado no pude ir y lo sentí muchísimo, pero este año voy a ir de todas maneras. **2.** Estudio arte en la universidad. Pienso hacer mis estudios de posgrado aquí para poder enseñar después de mi graduación. A mí me interesa mucho el arte moderno y he hecho investigaciones sobre algunos escultores contemporáneos de varios países hispanoamericanos. Este mes tenemos la suerte de tener una exposición de escultores peruanos aquí en el Museo de Arte de la universidad y algunos de ellos vendrán para hablar de su arte y dar sus ideas. He hablado con dos de mis compañeros y pensamos ir a la exposición juntos. **3.** Me encanta tocar el piano. Empecé mis clases de piano en la escuela primaria y las seguí durante la escuela secundaria. Ahora voy a casa de mi profesora una o dos veces al mes para escuchar sus comentarios y mantener la técnica necesaria para las piezas que me gusta tocar. Hago esto porque me gusta, y no pienso ser una concertista profesional. Cada vez que tengo la oportunidad de asistir a conciertos, lo hago. Este sábado pienso ir a escuchar a la pianista cubana Martha Marchena. Va a dar un concierto con la orquesta sinfónica de El Salvador. **4.** Pinto desde hace varios años. Mi profesor cree que puedo llegar a ser un buen pintor. A mí me gustan las pinturas de Velázquez, Goya y el Greco, pero en realidad, prefiero las de los pintores mexicanos. Hoy quiero ir a una exposición de arte mexicano. Sé que exhiben las obras de Kamilo Almanza y José Baray. No me la puedo perder.

Warm-up for 13-30. As a prelistening activity, have students get together in groups of four and discuss what their favorite cultural activities are and if they have a chance to do them often.

Antes de escuchar

13-29 Actividades culturales. In **13-30**, you will listen to four students talk about the type of cultural activities they like or plan to do. Before you listen, write down a list of three cultural activities that, in your view, might interest them.

_____

_____

A escuchar

13-30 Now, listen to the students. As you listen, write the number of the passage next to each statement associated with the student who probably uttered it.

___2___ María Cecilia prefiere la escultura. Ella se especializa en arte moderno.

___4___ A Joaquín le gusta más la pintura mexicana. Él es pintor.

___1___ A Rosa María le gusta el teatro. Ella es artista.

___3___ Eugenia prefiere la música. Ella es pianista.

Después de escuchar

13-31 ¿Y usted? Share your answers to the following questions with a classmate.

1. ¿Es importante para usted ir a exposiciones de arte, a conciertos de música clásica o al teatro? ¿Por qué?
2. ¿Qué prefiere usted, la música o la pintura?
3. ¿Cuál es su pintor o músico favorito? ¿Por qué le gusta?

 # Conversar

Antes de conversar

13-32 La vida de los famosos. Escojan a una de las personas de la lista. Luego, busquen la información sobre él/ella mencionada en la tabla u otra de interés para ustedes.

| Frida Khalo | Pablo Casals | Violeta Parra | Pablo Picasso |
| Plácido Domingo | Elena Poniatowska | Carlos Gardel | Francisco Goya |

NOMBRE	DATOS PERSONALES	PROFESIÓN	LOGROS
_____	Fecha de nacimiento:		Premios:
	Lugar de nacimiento/ muerte:		Reconocimientos:

A conversar

② 13-33 La escalera a la fama. Hagan una breve presentación sobre la persona escogida en **13-32.** Sus compañeros/as tomarán notas y les harán preguntas. Incluyan la mayor información posible en su presentación.

Después de conversar

Ⓖ 13-34 ¡Nos quitamos el sombrero (*We take our hats off*)! Decidan a cuál de las figuras famosas de la actividad **13-33** elegirían ustedes como la persona más admirable. Expliquen por qué.

Antes de conversar

Ⓖ 13-35 Comunidad en peligro de desaparición. Imagínense que su comunidad está en peligro de desaparecer a causa de un fenómeno natural. El gobierno de su país ha pedido que cada organización piense en algunos productos u objetos culturales o artísticos que salvaría para dar información a las generaciones futuras. Lean las preguntas del gobierno y discutan las respuestas. Tomen notas para compartir sus ideas con la clase.

1. ¿Qué texto impreso (*printed*) de su comunidad salvarían ustedes: un libro, una revista, un periódico, un anuncio publicitario, etc.? ¿Por qué? ¿Quién lo escribió o creó? ¿Cómo lo salvarían: en papel, en formato electrónico o digital, en piedra, en una cápsula, etc.?
2. Con respecto a la creación artística de su comunidad, ¿qué salvarían ustedes: un cuadro, una escultura, una pieza musical (canción, CD, obra musical, etc.)? ¿Por qué? ¿Cómo lo/la salvarían?
3. Para dar información sobre los adelantos tecnológicos de su comunidad, ¿qué aparato o sistema científico guardarían ustedes? ¿Por qué?

A conversar

Ⓖ 13-36 ¿Qué salvaríamos y cómo? Compartan con el resto de la clase sus respuestas a la actividad **13-35.** Apoyen (*support*) cada selección con argumentos lógicos dados por el grupo. Prepárense para defender su posición. Sus compañeros/as tomarán notas sobre la propuesta de cada grupo.

Después de conversar

Ⓖ 13-37 Informe al gobierno. Imagínense que ustedes son responsables de informar al gobierno sobre la propuesta de su comunidad. Comparen su propuesta con las de otros grupos, y hagan lo siguiente.

1. Evalúen las propuestas. ¿Cuál de ellas tiene más sentido o es más factible (*feasible*)? ¿Por qué? Tomen nota de los fundamentos que apoyan la propuesta que ustedes eligieron.
2. Escriban el informe para el gobierno en nombre de su comunidad.

Suggestion for 13-33. You may wish to ask students in the audience to take notes and ask follow-up questions that will fill an information gap.

Alternate for 13-33. Ask students in the audience to think of three questions they would ask of this famous personality, if they had the chance to meet her/him in person. Presenters may pretend they are this famous person and answer their classmates' questions.

Suggestions for 13-36. You may defer this activity one class period and, thus, give students some extra time to look for visual materials for their presentation and refine their notes and arguments. Extra time will raise their confidence—they will prepare better—and may result in a more interesting debate as students use their background knowledge in the various fields to respond and present their views.

Suggestions for 13-37. You may ask students to share their report with other groups via e-mail. This task will give students the chance to practice presenting and defending their views in writing.

EN DIRECTO

To acknowledge not having requested some information:
Lamentablemente, no tengo/tenemos esa información.
Unfortunately, I/we do not have that information.
Lo siento/sentimos, pero no sé/sabemos...
I am/We are sorry, but I/we do not know . . .

To acknowledge you had not thought of something, but will look into it:
La verdad es que no pensé/pensamos en eso, pero lo averiguaré/averiguaremos.
The truth is that I/we did not think of it, but I/we will find out.

To support a decision:
Hemos elegido a... porque...
We have chosen . . . because . . .
Lo que más influyó en nuestra decisión fue/fueron [cualidades, valores].
What influenced our decision the most was/were [qualities, values].

To present a response from a group:
Con respecto a..., nosotros pensamos que...
In regards to . . . , we think that . . .
La decisión final no fue fácil, pero llegamos a la siguiente conclusión:...
The final decision was not easy, but we arrived at the following conclusion:

To support the view or choice of a group:
Nuestra decisión/selección está basada en lo siguiente...
Our decisión/choice is based on the following . . .

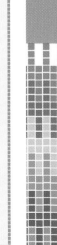

📖 *Leer*

When we read a narrative of any kind, we often try to make sense of its content (concepts or experiences) by relying on our knowledge of human experience, or by associating it with our own cultural or personal experience.

Some general considerations about narration

At the organizational level, a narrative piece generally has some basic features.

1. It relates an event in which a number of characters—who possess some physical and emotional characteristics—interact in a setting within a time frame (present, past). Occurrences within the story have an order (chronological, retrospective, etc.).
2. Traditionally one may expect to see the presentation of a conflict at the beginning of the story, followed by actions through which characters display their weaknesses and/or strengths, thus creating escalating tensions among them. Finally, the conflict created by the narrator is either solved (fixed end) or the reader is left with the task of imagining the solution to the conflict (open end).
3. An event or experience may be told from at least two perspectives: that of a protagonist (I, we) or that of a witness (he/she, they).

Guía de prelectura

Look at the title of the story in activity **13-40.** Then, answer these questions, using your knowledge of the human experience and your personal knowledge of the topic.

1. What may be the main theme of this narration? Circle all that may apply, in your view.
   (a.) the life of an ethnographer as he/she studies a community
   (b.) the love affairs of an ethnographer while on the field
   c. a description of the members of an indigenous group and their habitat

2. How did you guess the answer(s) to question 1?
   (a.) Personal experience
   (b.) Knowledge of what ethnographic research entails
   (c.) Consultation of some sources (dictionary, encyclopedia, experts, etc.).

3. Now, can you hypothesize about the probable organization of the text? Write a check mark next to all that apply:
   (a.) It may start with a flashback in which the narrator presents the problem.
   (b.) The main character(s) will be introduced in the first part of the story.
   (c.) Characters will start revealing their inner feelings through the actions that follow their introduction in the setting.
   (d.) The conflict will reach a climax.
   e. The story will have no end.

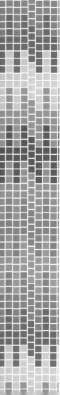

Antes de leer

13-38 Preparación. La vivienda (*housing*) puede variar de lugar a lugar y de cultura a cultura. Lea las siguientes descripciones y marque las que usted asocia con una vivienda indígena.

1. Los indígenas viven a la intemperie, es decir, al aire libre.
2. Los indígenas viven en casas de materiales naturales como madera, bambú, etc.
3. Las casas de los indígenas son de construcción sólida.
4. Las casas tienen toldos (*awnings*) de materiales resistentes como el cuero.
5. Generalmente las viviendas indígenas están construidas en la pradera (*prairie*).

13-39 ¿Qué costumbres tienen? Indique si es probable (**P**) o improbable (**I**) que un/a etnógrafo/a haga las siguientes afirmaciones después de vivir en una comunidad indígena.

	PROBABLE	IMPROBABLE
1. Existen brujos (*sorcerers*) que revelan sus secretos sólo a los iniciados (*novices*) que quieren aprender.	P	
2. Los indígenas hablan mi lengua mejor que yo.		I
3. Me levantaba al alba, es decir, antes de la salida del sol.	P	
4. Me cubría el cuerpo con ropas extrañas.	P	
5. Me encantaba comer sus comidas ásperas, desagradables.		I
6. Cuando recién llegué, tomaba notas sigilosamente (*discreetly*) para evitar las sospechas de los indígenas.	P	
7. Al clarear el día (*dawn*), siempre tenía sueños extraños.		I
8. Viví tanto tiempo entre los indígenas que comencé a pensar como ellos.	P	

A leer

13-40 Primera mirada. Lea el siguiente cuento y siga las indicaciones.

El Etnógrafo

de Jorge Luis Borges

El caso me lo refirieron en Texas, pero había acontecido en otro estado. Cuenta con un solo protagonista, salvo que en toda historia los protagonistas son miles, visibles e invisibles, vivos y muertos. Se llamaba, creo, Fred Murdock. Era alto a la manera americana, ni rubio ni moreno, de perfil de hacha,[1] de muy pocas palabras. Nada singular había en él, ni siquiera esa fingida singularidad que es propia de los jóvenes. Naturalmente respetuoso, no descreía de los libros ni de quienes escriben los libros. Era suya esa edad en que el hombre no sabe aún quién es y está listo para entregarse a lo que le propone el azar,[2] la mística del persa o el desconocido origen del húngaro, las aventuras de la guerra o del álgebra, el puritanismo o la orgía. En la universidad le aconsejaron el estudio de las lenguas indígenas. Hay ritos esotéricos que perduran en ciertas tribus

[1]*axe* [2]*chance*

del oeste; su profesor, un hombre entrado en años, le propuso que hiciera su habitación en una toldería,[3] que observara los ritos y que descubriera el secreto que los brujos revelan al iniciado. A su vuelta, redactaría una tesis que las autoridades del instituto darían a la imprenta.[4] Murdock aceptó con alacridad.[5] Uno de sus mayores había muerto en las guerras de la frontera; esa antigua discordia de sus estirpes era un vínculo ahora. Previó, sin duda, las dificultades que lo aguardaban; tenía que lograr que los hombres rojos lo aceptaran como uno de los suyos. Emprendió la larga aventura. Más de dos años habitó en la pradera, bajo toldos de cuero o a la intemperie. Se levantaba antes del alba, se acostaba al anochecer, llegó a soñar en un idioma que no era el de sus padres. Acostumbró su paladar a sabores ásperos, se cubrió con ropas extrañas, olvidó los amigos y la ciudad, llegó a pensar de una manera que su lógica rechazaba. Durante los primeros meses de aprendizaje tomaba notas sigilosas, que rompería después, acaso para no despertar la suspicacia de los otros, acaso porque ya no las precisaba. Al término de un plazo prefijado por ciertos ejercicios, de índole moral y de índole física, el sacerdote le ordenó que fuera recordando sus sueños y que se los confiara al clarear el día. Comprobó que en las noches de luna llena soñaba con bisontes. Confió estos sueños repetidos a su maestro; éste acabó por revelarle su doctrina secreta. Una mañana, sin haberse despedido de nadie, Murdock se fue.

En la ciudad, sintió la nostalgia de aquellas tardes iniciales de la pradera en que había sentido, hace tiempo, la nostalgia de la ciudad. Se encaminó al despacho del profesor y le dijo que sabía el secreto y que había resuelto no publicarlo.

—¿Lo ata[6] su juramento? —preguntó el otro.

—No es ésa mi razón —dijo Murdock—. En esas lejanías aprendí algo que no puedo decir.

—¿Acaso el idioma inglés es insuficiente? —observaría el otro.

—Nada de eso, señor. Ahora que poseo el secreto, podría enunciarlo de cien modos distintos y aun contradictorios. No sé muy bien cómo decirle que el secreto es precioso y que ahora la ciencia, nuestra ciencia, me parece una mera frivolidad.

Agregó al cabo de una pausa:

—El secreto, por lo demás, no vale lo que valen los caminos que me condujeron a él. Esos caminos hay que andarlos.

El profesor le dijo con frialdad:

—Comunicaré su decisión al Concejo.[7] ¿Usted piensa vivir entre los indios?

Murdock le contestó:

—No. Tal vez no vuelva a la pradera. Lo que me enseñaron sus hombres vale para cualquier lugar y para cualquier circunstancia.

Tal fue, en esencia, el diálogo.

Fred se casó, se divorció y es ahora uno de los bibliotecarios de Yale.

[3]*indian dwellings with leather sunshades*   [4]*printing house*   [5]*with ease, quickly*   [6]*paralyze*   [7]*council*

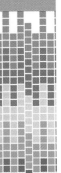

Marque con un círculo la información relacionada con el narrador del cuento.

1. El narrador del cuento es Fred Murdock.
2. No sabemos cómo se llama el narrador.
3. El narrador escuchó lo que le ocurrió al protagonista del cuento.

Marque con un círculo la información relacionada con el/la protagonista y la trama (*plot*) de esta historia.

4. El protagonista era una persona que físicamente llamaba la atención porque era muy distinto/a de los demás.
5. Por su edad, el protagonista no había decidido qué quería hacer profesionalmente.
6. Las experiencias que el protagonista vivió no lo afectaron para nada.
7. Al hablar con una persona importante de la comunidad donde vivía, el protagonista experimentó un cambio significativo en su vida.
8. El descubrimiento de un secreto cambió la vida del protagonista.

13-41 Segunda mirada. Reconstruya el cuento en el orden cronológico apropiado. La primera situación ya está marcada.

_____1_____ Alguien en la universidad le sugirió a Murdock que estudiara una lengua indígena.

_____7_____ Entre los indios, se acostumbró a comer su comida, a hablar la lengua de ellos, a vestirse y a pensar como ellos.

_____4_____ Fred aceptó la oferta.

_____13_____ Murdock se casó y ahora trabaja en la biblioteca de la universidad de Yale.

_____2_____ Su profesor le propuso que viviera entre los indígenas para aprender sobre sus ritos y descubrir un secreto.

_____11_____ El joven etnógrafo salió de la comunidad indígena sin decirle adiós a nadie.

_____5_____ Antes de tomar una decisión, pensó en los problemas que tendría al vivir en una cultura diferente a la suya.

_____8_____ Al principio, tomaba notas secretamente, las cuales probablemente rompería más tarde.

_____10_____ El gran maestro espiritual le contó el gran secreto.

_____3_____ El profesor le dijo que probablemente, a su regreso, se publicaría su tesis.

_____6_____ Empezó su aventura y se fue a vivir entre los indios por un periodo de dos años.

_____9_____ Después de algunos ejercicios morales y físicos, Murdock tuvo que recordar sus sueños y contárselos a su guía espiritual.

_____12_____ El protagonista fue a la oficina de su profesor y le dijo que había aprendido el secreto, pero que no podía compartirlo con nadie.

13-42 Una mirada más. Lea las siguientes citas tomadas de _El etnógrafo_ e indique si cada una de ellas es un acontecimiento (_happening_), (**A**) o una hipótesis (**H**) sobre el futuro.

1. ___A___ ... había acontecido en otro estado.
2. ___A___ En la universidad le aconsejaron el estudio de las lenguas indígenas.
3. ___H___ A su vuelta, redactaría una tesis.
4. ___A___ Una mañana, sin haberse despedido de nadie, Murdock se fue.
5. ___H___ ... las autoridades del instituto darían a la imprenta.
6. ___A___ Lo que me enseñaron sus hombres vale para cualquier lugar y para cualquier circunstancia.
7. ___H___ ... podría enunciarlo de cien modos distintos y aun contradictorios.
8. ___A___ Fred se casó, se divorció y es ahora uno de los bibliotecarios de Yale.

Después de leer

G **13-43 Ampliación.** Comenten las siguientes preguntas y prepárense para compartir las respuestas con la clase.

Sobre la vida de Murdock en las tolderías:

1. ¿Qué cambios en su vida diaria tendría que hacer Murdock para adaptarse a la comunidad indígena?
2. ¿Qué harían los indígenas para aceptar a Murdock entre ellos?
3. ¿Qué dirían las notas que tomaba Fred Murdock?

Sobre el secreto que Murdock descubrió:

4. ¿Qué secreto descubriría el etnógrafo? ¿Por qué no podría compartirlo con nadie?
5. ¿Por qué decidiría el protagonista trabajar de bibliotecario en la universidad de Yale?

Suggestions for 13-43. Encourage students to be responsible for their own learning by asking that each member of the group take notes of the answer to each question. When the class gets together to share responses, each student should be able to report the views of his/her group.

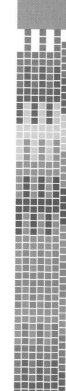

Escribir

People write biographies for various reasons. Depending on the intended purpose, biography reports may require a particular focus on one or various aspects of a person's life such as work and accomplishments, historical events and cultural factors that may have influenced his/her work and so on.

In general, when writing a biography, keep the following in mind.

1. Provide the person's basic information: date and place of birth. If relevant to your purpose for writing this text, you may mention the person's family information.
2. Present his/her educational background: studies, degrees, occupation, etc. If you are writing about someone older, you may consider including an anecdote of his/her youth to spark your reader's interest. Indicate this individual's major life and professional accomplishments (trials, struggles, challenges overcome, awards, etc.).
3. Include information on his/her community (religious, ethnic, geographic, cultural, etc.). Mention the most outstanding contributions this person (has) made in his/her lifetime. Demonstrate the effect of this person's actions on his/her community.

Antes de escribir

13-44 Enfoque. Primera fase. Lea el siguiente informe biográfico y siga las instrucciones.

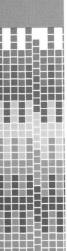

Letizia Ortiz Rocasolano, la periodista que se convirtió en princesa

Leticia nació el 15 de septiembre de 1972 en Oviedo, España. Hija de Paloma Rocasolano, enfermera, y de Jesús Ortiz, periodista fundador y director de Antena 3 Radio (hasta 1987) en el Principado de Oviedo. Menchu Álvarez del Valle, la esposa de su abuelo paterno, José Luis Ortiz, fue quien probablemente influyó más en la pasión de Letizia por el periodismo.

Letizia hizo sus estudios primarios en el colegio público Gesta, de Oviedo, junto con sus hermanas Telma y Erika. Después cursó sus estudios secundarios en el instituto Alfonso II, donde tomó clases de ballet tres días por semana. Por razones de trabajo del padre, Letizia y su familia se mudaron a Madrid cuando ella tenía quince años. En Madrid continuó sus estudios en el instituto Ramiro de Maeztu, donde se graduó. Después de un largo noviazgo, Letizia se casó con un profesor de literatura, Alonso Guerrero Pérez, en agosto de 1998. A sólo doce meses de casados, ambos decidieron divorciarse.

A los dieciocho años, Letizia había entrado en la Universidad Complutense, donde se diplomó en periodismo. Mientras estudiaba, comenzó a colaborar en el periódico *ABC* y con la agencia Efe. Entre 1992 y 1993 recibió una beca para hacer sus prácticas —en las áreas de economía, televisión y espectáculos— en el periódico *La Nueva España* de Oviedo. Más tarde obtuvo un máster en información audiovisual y se trasladó a México. Allí hizo sus estudios de doctorado y trabajó en el diario *Público de Guadalajara* (Jalisco), aunque nunca escribió su tesis doctoral.

Su incursión en el mundo de la televisión comenzó en la cadena de noticias CNN. Allí trabajó dos años en el turno matinal. En el año 2000, inició su trabajo en Televisión Española en el programa Informe Semanal.

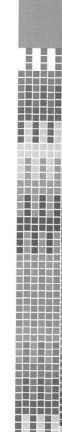

En septiembre de 2003, con cuatro millones de espectadores en el Telediario de las nueve de la noche, Letizia asumió otras labores periodísticas como enviada especial en Nueva York para cubrir los atentados del 11 de septiembre y, más tarde, la guerra de Iraq y otros eventos mundiales. Fue en la ceremonia de entrega de los Premios Príncipe de Asturias, en octubre de 2003, cuando el mundo se enteró de su compromiso con el príncipe Felipe de Borbón.

Felipe y Letizia se conocieron en 2002, durante una cena en casa del director de Documentos TV, Pedro Erquicia. El príncipe y Letizia se enamoraron. La relación se consolidó aún más cuando el príncipe pidió su mano el 6 de noviembre de 2003. "Me da muchísima alegría manifestar lo enamorado que estoy de Letizia. Es la mujer con la que quiero casarme, y reúne todos los requisitos para asumir las responsabilidades de princesa de Asturias y próxima reina de España".

Los españoles aceptaron la elección del príncipe, y en mayo de 2004, Felipe de Borbón hizo a Letizia su princesa al contraer matrimonio con ella en una ceremonia transmitida por televisión a todo el mundo.

Segunda fase. Answer the following questions, based on the biography you just read.

1. Circle the intended purpose of the report.
   a. to give a brief account of the life of a prominent person
   b. to entertain readers
   c. to describe a well-known public figure

2. Based on its purpose, is the biography report effective?
   Yes   No

3. Mark some possible reasons for your response.
   a. The public figure is described in an interesting manner.
   b. The average person can comprehend the experiences of the central figure because they belong to the realm of human experience, regardless of cultural background.
   c. There is extremely detailed information.
   d. The events in the lifetime of this figure are told in a backward manner, from present to past.
   e. The biography report has a clear organization: an introduction, a forward movement in time, and a closure.

13-45 Preparación. Primera fase. En *www.prenhall.com/mosaicos*, busque información biográfica sobre una persona hispana que a usted le interese en uno de estos campos: los deportes, el arte (música, baile, pintura, arquitectura, escultura, etc.), la ciencia, la política, etc. Obtenga la siguiente información y tome notas.

1. Nombre, fecha y lugar de nacimiento: ¿Cuándo y dónde nació?
2. Información familiar: ¿Es soltero/a, casado/a, divorciado/a, separado/a? ¿Tiene hijos? ¿Cuántos?
3. Estudios y formación profesional: ¿Cuáles son los mayores logros personales y/o profesionales de esta persona a través de su vida? ¿Qué barreras ha superado (*overcome*)? ¿Cómo las superó?
4. Su comunidad: ¿En qué área se destaca (*stands out*): religiosa, étnica, profesional, científica, artística, deportiva, etc.? ¿Cómo se ha beneficiado la comunidad de sus éxitos?

Segunda fase. Ahora seleccione la información que va a ayudarlo/la a escribir un informe biográfico eficaz. Haga lo siguiente:

1. Seleccione los logros más significativos de la persona que usted escogió en la **Primera fase.** Tome nota de las fechas en que esta persona recibió algún premio o reconocimiento, por ejemplo. Recuerde que para despertar el interés de su lector, debe incluir hechos datos (*facts*) importantes sobre la vida de la persona escogida.
2. Escriba algunas formas lingüísticas que lo/la ayudarán a expresar información concreta (hechos) y destacar la figura de esta persona.

A escribir

13-46 Manos a la obra. Su comunidad ha decidido empezar una campaña para incentivar a los jóvenes a encauzar (*channel*) mejor sus vidas en un mundo en crisis. Usted es uno/a de los responsables de presentarles a una personalidad del mundo hispano que, en su opinión, representa un excelente ejemplo. Escriba un informe biográfico para una revista electrónica, usando la información obtenida en la actividad **13-45, Segunda fase.** El propósito de su informe es despertar la curiosidad de los jóvenes por conocer qué sacrificios han hecho los famosos para tener éxito.

Después de escribir

13-47 Revisión. Su compañero/a editor/a va a ayudarle a expresar mejor sus ideas para que sus lectores jóvenes se beneficien de las experiencias reales de otros. No se olvide de verificar que:

■ el informe biográfico tenga información interesante para su lector/a.

■ las ideas estén bien organizadas.

■ haya conexión dentro de los párrafos y entre ellos (use conectores para hacer transiciones).

■ el vocabulario sea variado e interesante.

■ la ortografía, puntuación, acentuación, etc. sean apropiadas.

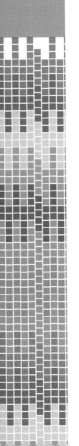

ENFOQUE CULTURAL

Para pensar

¿Conoce usted a algún pintor o escultor hispano famoso? ¿A quién? ¿Ha visto usted alguna de sus obras? ¿Conoce usted a algún escritor hispano? ¿Ha leído usted alguna novela española o hispanoamericana en español o en traducción al inglés? ¿Cuál?

Miguel de Cervantes y Saavedra (1547–1616) es considerado el más grande escritor español. Su famosa novela, Don Quijote de la Mancha, *ha sido traducida a casi todas las lenguas del mundo. Las contribuciones de los escritores latinoamericanos a la literatura universal también han sido inmensas. Gabriela Mistral y Pablo Neruda, fotos abajo, dos grandes poetas chilenos, ganaron el premio Nobel de Literatura, Mistral en 1945 y Neruda en 1971.*

Hay muchos artistas españoles e hispanoamericanos de renombre mundial. Picasso y Dalí, nacidos en España, son dos de los más grandes. Aquí tenemos una obra de Frida Kahlo (1907–54). Fue una famosa pintora mexicana que sigue teniendo mucha influencia en el arte latinoamericano. Su trabajo consistió mayormente en autorretratos que reflejaban su historia y su percepción del mundo.

Pedro Almodóvar es uno de los cineastas más famosos de España. En 1988 su película Mujeres al borde de un ataque de nervios *fue nominada la mejor película extranjera y es la película española que ha tenido más éxito. Años después,* Todo sobre mi madre *ganó el Óscar a la mejor película de habla no inglesa y* Hable con ella *ganó el Óscar al mejor guión.*

Para contestar

2 Cultura y arte. Respondan a las siguientes preguntas.

1. ¿Qué dos pintores españoles famosos conoce? ¿Y latinoamericanos?
2. ¿Cuáles son algunos escritores españoles o hispanoamericanos que han recibido premios y reconocimiento mundial?

G Riqueza cultural. En grupos de tres, hablen de la trascendencia del Premio Nobel de Literatura y digan por qué es importante.

Para investigar en Internet

Busque el nombre de un pintor, un escultor, un músico o un escritor hispano que no haya sido mencionado en este capítulo. Obtenga información sobre esta persona y preséntele a la clase lo que averiguó acerca de él/ella y de su trabajo. Sus compañeros/as, divididos/as en grupos, le darán su opinión sobre la obra de este/a famoso/a, basándose únicamente en lo que usted presentó.

VÍNCULOS

For materials related to the Enfoque cultural, see
- SAM-OneKey: WB: 13-23

¡Prepárese!

13-48 ¿Qué haría? Imagínese lo que están pensando los participantes de *Fortunas* (Katie, Carlos, Efraín y Sabrina). Si usted fuera uno de ellos, ¿qué haría? Escriba una oración desde el punto de vista de cada participante, usando el tiempo condicional.

MODELO: yo
           Para ganar *Fortunas* yo no haría alianzas con Katie.

1. Katie: _____
2. Carlos: _____
3. Efraín: _____
4. Sabrina: _____

Ángela tiene dudas sobre las alianzas y la posible cooperación entre los participantes.

Todos consideran cooperar y compartir sus pistas para solucionar la última fortuna.

Katie trata de convencer a Sabrina de que es buena idea compartir las pistas.

Efraín piensa que Katie tiene razón, aunque no le gusta admitirlo.

Todos leen y comparten sus pistas.

Sabrina piensa que es un error ayudar a Katie, aunque todos tendrán el mismo número de puntos.

¡Responda!

13-49 La cooperación. Evidentemente los cuatro participantes han decidido cooperar y compartir sus pistas para solucionar la última fortuna. Complete las oraciones siguientes con la forma correcta de **haber** y el participio pasado del verbo entre paréntesis.

Todos (1) ___se han reunido___ (reunirse) para hablar de la cooperación. Sabrina (2) ___ha tenido___ (tener) muchas dudas sobre las alianzas y las mentiras. Por su parte, Katie (3) ___ha tratado___ (tratar) de convencer a Sabrina de que la cooperación es una buena idea. Los cuatro (4) ___han abierto___ (abrir) los sobres y (5) ___han leído___ (leer) sus pistas. Por último, Sabrina le (6) ___ha dicho___ (decir) a Tito que no está satisfecha con los eventos de hoy.

NOTAS: "EL SENTIMIENTO DEL LATINO EN NUEVA YORK", ÁNGEL CANALES

Esta canción habla del sentimiento y el orgullo del inmigrante latino en la ciudad de Nueva York y de lo importante que es la música en su vida. La letra se refiere a diferentes instrumentos, estilos musicales y países.

¡Prepárese!

Suggestion for 13-50. Present this exercise as a competition. Divide the class into groups to compose their lists and then check to see who came up with the most countries.

13-50 Los países hispanos. El título de la canción, "El sentimiento del latino en Nueva York", se refiere a la inmigración hispana en esa ciudad. Según lo que ha aprendido hasta ahora, haga una lista de los países hispanos que están representados en los Estados Unidos. ¿Cuáles de ellos cree que se mencionarán en la canción?

¡Escuche!

13-51 Los instrumentos. Mientras escucha "El sentimiento del latino en Nueva York" complete los espacios en blanco con las palabras de la lista siguiente. Todos son instrumentos musicales.

> la trompeta   la conga   la clave   el timbal
> el trombón   el (saxofón) barítono   el bongó

Se oye el repique del (1) _timbal_, de la (2) _conga_
y del (3) _bongó_
en los barrios de Manhattan, de Brooklyn y del Bronx
en las calles neoyorquinas vibran nuestras alegrías
sufrimiento y expresión del latino con sabor
Escuchan la (4) _trompeta_, el (5) _trombón_ y el
(6) _(saxofón) barítono_
Y la (7) _clave_ aunque escondida
Ay pero siempre cargando el sabor
El sonero ya se inspira y nos canta con fervor
Y mi pueblo está gozando en las calles de Nueva York
Pero oye, pueblo lindo, lo que hoy te canto yo.
Es el sonido que el americano oye y no entiende
el sentimiento del latino en Nueva York

Ay, pero que la bomba y la plena del puertorro
es su identificación y el merengue apambichao
es la del tigre dominicano
Ay, pero la cumbia es sentimiento colombiano,
la guajira y el son montuno es el sentimiento
cubano.
Es el sonido que el americano oye y no
entiende.

¡Responda!

Suggestion for 13-52. Students can refer to previous *Notas* sections for clues.

13-52 ¿Música y baile. El autor de esta canción se refiere a diferentes estilos musicales y a los países donde son populares. Use el condicional y forme oraciones completas indicando qué tipo de música tocaría, bailaría o cantaría en cada uno de los países siguientes.

MODELO: España
          Yo bailaría flamenco.

1. Puerto Rico
2. México
3. Nicaragua
4. Bolivia
5. Cuba

6. Panamá
7. Perú
8. Colombia
9. Estados Unidos
10. La República Dominicana

VOCABULARIO

Personas

el/la bailarín/bailarina	*dancer*
el/la emigrante	*emigrant*
el/la escritor/a	*writer*
el/la escultor/a	*sculptor*
el/la guitarrista	*guitar player*
el/la hispanohablante	*Spanish speaker*
el/la inmigrante	*immigrant*
el/la novelista	*novelist*
el/la pintor/a	*painter*

El país

el área	*area*
el comercio	*commerce*
el gobierno	*government*
el idioma	*language*
la obra	*work*
obra maestra	*masterpiece*
la población	*population*
la política	*politics*
la sociedad	*society*

Manifestaciones culturales

el cuento	*story*
la novela	*novel*
la pintura	*painting*

Verbos

abrazar(se) (c)	*to embrace*
acabar	*to finish*
aceptar	*to accept*
actuar	*to act*
besar	*to kiss*
contar (ue)	*to tell, count*
cubrir	*to cover*
emigrar	*to emigrate*
haber	*to have* (auxiliary verb)
llevarse bien	*to get along well*
llevarse mal	*not to get along*
morir (ue)	*to die*
nacer (zc)	*to be born*
odiar	*to hate*
pelear	*to fight*
romper	*to break*
saludar(se)	*to greet*

Palabras y expresiones útiles

a través de	*through*
acabar de + infinitivo	*to have just + past participle*
desde	*since*
en la actualidad	*at the present time*
estar enamorado/a	*to be in love*
el premio	*award/prize*
según	*according to*
tener éxito	*to be successful*
todavía	*still, yet*
ya	*already*

14

CAMBIOS DE LA SOCIEDAD

Objetivos comunicativos

- Describing and discussing demographics
- Describing social conditions
- Projecting conditions, goals, and purposes
- Expressing conjecture
- Talking about the past from a past perspective

Contenido

Las sociedades de hoy

VÍNCULOS

To practice vocabulary—Las sociedades de hoy, El papel de la mujer & Temas de hoy
- SAM-OneKey: WB: 14-1, 14-2, 14-3, 14-4 / LM: 14-24, 14-25, 14-26, 14-27
- Companion Website: AP 14-1
- IRCD: Chapter 14; pp. 502, 503, 505, 506

Suggestion. Prepare students to better understand these charts by discussing changes in society such as birth, illiteracy, child mortality, unemployment rates, etc. Ask questions such as *¿Cuál es el promedio de hijos que las familias tienen en su país? ¿Tienen más o menos hijos que antes? ¿Sabe usted si hay muchas personas analfabetas, es decir, que no saben leer ni escribir, en su país? En general, ¿cree usted que hay más analfabetas o analfabetos en el mundo? Si una persona es analfabeta, ¿puede encontrar trabajo fácilmente? ¿Hay mucho desempleo en su ciudad?, etc.* Also discuss issues related to family structure, divorce rate, number of children, career choices for women and men, and so on in the last 50 years, using questions such as *¿La familia de hoy es diferente a la de sus abuelos? ¿Cómo ha cambiado? ¿Tiene la mujer más oportunidades profesionales fuera de la casa ahora? ¿Ud. cree que el número promedio de hijos de cada familia ha subido o bajado?*

AUDIO Estos **datos** proceden del Centro de Derechos Reproductivos, una ONG (Organización No Gubernamental) dedicada a promover la **igualdad** de la mujer en todo el mundo y a garantizar sus **derechos** reproductivos y humanos. La organización también se asegura de que todas las mujeres tengan acceso a los servicios básicos de salud.

1997-2000	Argentina	Bolivia	Colombia	Guatemala
Población	36.577.000	8.142.000	41.564.000	11.090.000
Tasa de crecimiento annual	1.3 %	2.4 %	1.9 %	2.7 %
Población rural	10 %	37 %	2 %	60 %
Población urbana	90 %	63 %	74 %	40 %
Porcentaje de mujeres	50 %	50.3 %	50.6 %	49.6 %
Tasa de fertilidad	2.6 hijos por mujer	4.2 hijos por mujer	2.7 hijos por mujer	4.8 hijos por mujer
Analfabetismo entre los hombres	3.1 %	7.9 %	8.2 %	23.8 %
Analfabetismo entre las mujeres	3.2 %	20.6 %	8.2 %	38.7 %
La tasa de desempleo	14.9 %	11.4 %	12.6 %	5.2 %
Mortalidad infantil	19 por cada mil nacimientos	60 por cada mil nacimientos	23 por cada mil nacimientos	42 por cada mil nacimientos

Si consideramos el tamaño del país, ¿cuál de estos países está más poblado? ¿Cuál tiene menos **habitantes**? ¿Qué país tiene una población más rural? ¿Qué porcentaje de personas vive en la ciudad en Argentina? ¿De dónde son las mujeres que tienen más hijos? ¿Se relaciona esto con la vida en el campo? ¿Por qué? ¿Dónde hay más **analfabetos** probablemente, en el campo o en las ciudades? ¿Dónde hay más **desempleo**? ¿En qué país se mueren más niños al nacer?

¿Cómo son el español y la española de hoy? ¿Dónde viven? ¿Cómo estudian? ¿**Se casan** o se divorcian? ¿Dejan el **hogar** o **continúan,** ya adultos, viviendo con los padres? Estos datos, sacados de 160.000 personas, proceden de una encuesta hecha en España.

El Instituto Nacional de Estadística contrató a 4.000 personas para hacer entrevistas y sacar el perfil de 34 millones de españoles mayores de diez años de edad.

Según la encuesta, el español típico está casado y tiene un hijo o dos. La familia tradicional, de tres o más generaciones, es ya historia porque en la mayoría de los hogares el **promedio** de hijos es de 1,5. Tal es el caso en el 23 **por ciento** de los 11.836.320 hogares en España.

A diferencia de sus vecinos en el resto de Europa, los jóvenes españoles no viven **solos** o independientes. Los que sí viven solos tienen más de 65 años, son **viudos** y son en su **mayoría** mujeres.

Actualmente, la edad **promedio** del español es de 36,2 años. Sin embargo, contando solamente a los mayores de 10 años, la edad promedio salta a los 40,3 años.

La española

Hay 17.385.890 de españolas mayores de 10 años

Mis Padres

Viven con sus padres (%)
Sí 35
No 64,8

Se van de casa
Hasta los años 80 . . . . 25,5 años
Década de los 90 . . . . 27,7 años

Siguen en casa
El 55,1 por ciento de las que tienen entre 23 y 32 años
El 86,3 por ciento de las solteras

Vuelven a casa
El 24 por ciento de las separadas y divorciadas

Mis Estudios

Elementales 51,9%
Medios 11,3%
Superiores 7,5%

Carecen de Estudios (%)
Mayores de 70 años 29,4
Entre 10 y 19 años 0,5

Analfabetismo (%)
Mayores de 70 años 20
Entre 10 y 19 años 0,3

Mi familia

Casadas 51,4%
Solteras 47,7%

Número de hijos 1,5

Diferencia de edad
Con el marido . . . . 1–2 años
Con el hijo mayor . . . 25–29 años

El español

Hay 16.541.720 de españoles mayores de 10 años

Mis Padres

Viven con sus padres (%)
Sí 40,1
No 59,8

Se van de casa
Hasta los años 80 . . . . 26,5 años
Década de los 90 . . . . 28,5 años

Siguen en casa
El 69,2 por ciento de los que tienen entre 23 y 32 años
El 90 por ciento de los solteros

Vuelven a casa
El 37,9 por ciento de los separados y divorciados

Mis Estudios

Elementales 52,4%
Medios 6,1%
Superiores 8,8%

Carecen de Estudios (%)
Mayores de 70 años 20,4
Entre 10 y 19 años 0,5

Analfabetismo (%)
Mayores de 70 años 8,9
Entre 10 y 19 años 0,2

Mi familia

Casados 54,6%
Solteros 44,4%

Número de hijos 1,4

Diferencia de edad
Con la esposa . . . . 1–2 años
Con el hijo mayor 25–29

CULTURA

El índice de natalidad en los países hispanos ha descendido de manera espectacular en los últimos treinta años. A pesar de las circunstancias particulares de cada país, ésta parece ser la tendencia general. En Perú y Bolivia, por ejemplo, los gobiernos han apoyado campañas para mostrar las **ventajas** de los planes familiares y el control de la natalidad. En Venezuela, sin embargo, el promedio de hijos ha bajado en treinta años de 6,7 a 2,7 sin campañas por parte del gobierno. Esto se debe a varios factores, como la crisis económica, la escasez de vivienda y el mayor acceso de las mujeres al trabajo y a la educación. Pero tal vez el caso más extremo de esta tendencia es el de España, que ha pasado de ser el país de Europa con más hijos por pareja en los años 1960, a ser, junto con Italia, el país con el índice de natalidad más bajo.

¿Qué dice usted?

❷ 14-1 ¿Cómo es la sociedad en Hispanoamérica? Determinen si las siguientes afirmaciones son ciertas (**C**) o falsas (**F**). En caso de que sean falsas, den la información correcta.

1. ___C___ En Guatemala viven menos mujeres que hombres.
2. ___F___ En Bolivia hay menos mujeres analfabetas que hombres.
3. ___C___ Bolivia tiene menos habitantes que Guatemala.
4. ___F___ Las argentinas tienen más hijos que las guatemaltecas.
5. ___F___ En Colombia se mueren más niños que en Bolivia.

❷ 14-2 Las encuestas. Primera fase. Busquen en el artículo y en las tablas la información necesaria para contestar las siguientes preguntas. Después comparen sus respuestas con las de otros/as compañeros/as.

1. De los 16.541.720 españoles mayores de 10 años, ¿qué porcentaje vive con los padres? 40,1%
2. ¿Cuál es la edad promedio a la que se van de casa los hombres? ¿Y las mujeres? 28,5/27,7
3. ¿Qué porcentaje de los solteros sigue viviendo con sus padres? 90%
4. Después de una separación o un divorcio, ¿qué porcentaje de mujeres vuelve a la casa de sus padres? 24%
5. ¿Cuál es el índice (porcentaje) de analfabetismo entre las mujeres mayores de 70 años? ¿Entre los hombres? ¿Es grande la diferencia? 20%/8,9%/sí
6. ¿Quiénes realizan más estudios a nivel de educación media, los hombres o las mujeres? las mujeres
7. ¿Cuántos años de diferencia hay entre el hijo mayor y su padre? 25–29 años
8. ¿Quiénes constituyen la mayoría en España, los hombres o las mujeres? las mujeres
9. Según la información que ustedes tienen, ¿hay algunos datos que pueden compararse con datos similares de Estados Unidos? ¿Cuáles? Answers will vary.

Segunda fase. Piense en diez familias que usted conoce y haga un cálculo, basándose en los siguientes puntos. Después compare sus resultados con los de su compañero/a.

1. porcentaje de jóvenes entre 10 y 18 años que viven con sus padres
2. edad promedio en la que se casan las personas
3. edad promedio en la que tienen hijos
4. promedio de hijos por pareja

❷ 14-3 Nuestras cifras. Primera fase. Háganse preguntas para obtener los siguientes datos sobre sus respectivas familias.

1. número de personas que forman la familia nuclear
2. número de hombres y de mujeres
3. edad promedio de los miembros de la familia
4. número de personas que estudian
5. número de personas que trabajan

Ⓖ Segunda fase. Formen grupos y recopilen (*compile*) la información obtenida. Con esta información, preparen una tabla que indique el porcentaje de familias que hay:

1. con menos de tres miembros o más de tres miembros
2. con mayoría de mujeres o mayoría de hombres
3. con edad promedio de 40 años más o menos
4. con más o menos de dos personas con estudios universitarios
5. donde trabajan más o menos de dos miembros

El papel de la mujer

El papel de la mujer ha cambiado mucho en España en los últimos años. Hoy en día, el nuevo gobierno español incluye tantas mujeres como hombres.

Note: You may point out that *Dinero* is a well-known Colombian magazine.

Suggestions. Discuss jobs seen traditionally as either "men's work" or "women's work." Personalize and ask students if there are student jobs that are considered typical of one gender or the other.

Ask students about gender roles in their everyday lives. Do they get different treatment for being male or female? *¿Tienen sus padres las mismas aspiraciones para los hijos que para las hijas? En nuestra sociedad, ¿qué actividades se consideran adecuadas o inadecuadas para un hombre o una mujer? ¿Sufren o han sufrido discriminación alguna vez por ser hombre o mujer? ¿En qué circunstancias? ¿En el trabajo? ¿En los estudios?*

■ (FEMPRESS) En un reciente estudio realizado en 553 empresas colombianas, Luz Gabriela Arango encontró que sólo el 23,7% de las directivas están constituidas por mujeres. Con todo, el estudio muestra que en este terreno, así como en otros, ha habido enormes cambios. En los años 1950, por ejemplo, todas las sucursales bancarias tenían un varón como gerente. En los años 1990, una alta proporción era dirigida por mujeres.

La encuesta "clase empresarial", realizada a ejecutivos, señala que la confianza en el desempeño profesional de la mujer es mayor que en el del hombre. De hecho, el 96,8% de los entrevistados le dio la más alta calificación a su honestidad; el 80% a la calidad de su trabajo; el 81,6% en materia de confiabilidad; el 79,2% lo dio a su cumplimiento.

En cuanto al manejo de la autoridad, las ejecutivas entrevistadas por *Dinero* consideran que mientras se valora a un hombre por ser enérgico, cuando una mujer asume posiciones fuertes puede causar rechazo. En cuanto al poder, se sienten menos ambiciosas y le dan menor prioridad que los hombres.

Las gerencias administrativas y de recursos industriales en manos de mujeres están aumentando. En algunas entrevistas de *Dinero*, se destaca y se apoya la participación de las mujeres en la empresa pues las consideran más responsables, más comprometidas, más honestas, se ausentan menos del trabajo que los hombres, demuestran mayor eficiencia en el manejo del tiempo y son más transparentes en el trabajo.

Es interesante ver, dice CIDER (Centro Interdisciplinario do Estudios Regionales), las áreas en las cuales se ha concentrado la presencia femenina. Éstas son, en sectores financieros y de servicios en el caso de la empresa privada, y en instituciones de servicio y manejo de relaciones públicas en el sector público, como son los ministerios de salud, educación, trabajo y relaciones exteriores. La mayor concentración de fuerza laboral femenina en un alto nivel se ubica en las labores ejecutivas, mientras que sólo el 8,2% de los funcionarios hombres está en ese nivel no directivo.

A INVESTIGAR

Investigue los siguientes temas relacionados con la situación de la mujer en el mundo de habla hispana y en los Estados Unidos.

■ Diferencias salariales entre el hombre y la mujer

■ La educación de la mujer

■ Las mujeres en la política

Follow-up for 14-4. Ask students to make comparisons between the role of women in Colombia and women's role in the United States.

Follow-up for 14-5. Discuss the role of women in society. Depending on your group, you may wish to provide students with the names of female public figures they are familiar with, such as: Rosa Parks, Oprah Winfrey, Hillary Clinton, etc. Personalize by asking: *¿Cuántas mujeres hay en su familia? ¿Cuántas de ellas trabajan fuera de casa? ¿Qué trabajo hacen? ¿Fue fácil o difícil para ellas conseguir el puesto que tienen? ¿Ha sufrido discriminación alguien de su familia o entre sus amigos?*

Follow-up for 14-6. Have each group provide at least one example from their list. Encourage a final summary of predictions for this century.

Warm-up. Introduce the theme of this newspaper article by asking students the role that computers have in their lives. *¿Usan ustedes la computadora todos los días? ¿Para qué la usan? ¿Leen las noticias en Internet? ¿Qué tipo de noticias? ¿Usan Internet para comprar? ¿Para hacer investigación?*

Suggestion for the newspaper cliping. Have students read the newspaper cliping in preparation for activity 14-7. You may wish to ask comprehension questions to provide students with model questions they may use in 14-7: *Los jóvenes españoles usan Internet para planificar sus vacaciones. Compran billetes o reservan hoteles, por ejemplo. ¿Planifica usted sus vacaciones en Internet también?*

¿Qué dice usted?

14-4 La mujer de hoy. Prepare un informe sobre la situación de la mujer en el mundo hispanohablante, utilizando la información que leyó en las estadísticas y las citas (*quotes*) de más arriba. Compare su informe con el de su compañero/a.

14-5 Mujeres ejecutivas. Primera fase. Cada uno/a de ustedes debe hacer una lista de cinco mujeres que ocupan puestos importantes en países hispanos o en su país. Hablen sobre estas mujeres, basándose en los siguientes puntos:

■ puesto que ocupan y responsabilidades que tienen

■ su personalidad y rasgos (*traits*) de carácter

■ barreras que cada una ha tenido que superar en su área de trabajo

Segunda fase. Ahora, comenten lo siguiente.

1. ¿Qué tipo de personalidad y rasgos de carácter tienen en común estas mujeres?
2. ¿Realizan estas mujeres trabajos tradicionalmente femeninos, o han incursionado en el mundo laboral típicamente masculino?
3. ¿Hay semejanzas entre las barreras que estas mujeres han tenido que superar? ¿Cuáles son? ¿Cómo han logrado superarlas?

14-6 Hacia un nuevo siglo. Conversen sobre los logros de la mujer en este siglo y el pasado. Hagan una lista de los cambios que han afectado a la mujer en las siguientes áreas en los últimos 50 años.

■ la familia   ■ la casa   ■ la educación

■ el trabajo   ■ el gobierno/la política

Temas de hoy

Unos 2,5 millones de españoles han usado Internet para preparar sus vacaciones

La mitad de los españoles que viajan, mantienen o han tenido algún contacto con la red

EFE, Madrid
ELPAIS.es, 09-07-2004

Unos 2,5 millones de españoles han usado Internet para organizar sus vacaciones, comprar billetes de avión o de tren y reservar hotel o paquetes turísticos, según el informe del Observatorio Español de Internet (OEI), que cifra en 500 millones de euros el gasto que han supuesto estas compras por la red.

Francesc Canals, presidente del Observatorio, ha explicado que Internet está cambiando la forma de operar a la hora de organizar las vacaciones por la gratuidad del medio y la facilidad de uso, hasta el punto de que la mitad de los españoles que viajan, mantienen o han tenido algún contacto con Internet, aunque sólo sea de paso como turistas virtuales.

Según Canals, se estima que en España, uno de los países con más vacaciones del mundo, el 75% de la población (unos 36 millones) hace vacaciones, y de estos el 75% (unos 27

millones) las disfrutan en segundas residencias. El resto, entre 9 y 9,5 millones, se dedica a viajar, aunque sólo la mitad lo hace fuera del territorio nacional.

La explosión del turismo en Internet se refleja en el hecho de que en un año se ha pasado de 250 portales de viajes a más de 700, y a ello ha contribuido la puesta en marcha de operadores de vuelos baratos que permiten viajar a partir de 10 euros. En verano, según Canals, las compras turísticas han ganado a los vídeos, DVD, CD y otros soportes informáticos que siempre han sido los líderes de venta.

El 35% de las ventas en la red corresponden a billetes de avión, el 25% a paquetes turísticos completos y otro 25% a reservas de hoteles; con el resto se adquieren servicios turísticos complementarios como coches o guías de viaje.

¿Qué dice usted?

2 **14-7 Entrevista. Primera fase.** Vuelvan a leer el artículo anterior. Túrnense en los papeles de periodista y estudiante para entrevistarse sobre la organización de vacaciones por Internet.

PERIODISTA: ¿Usas Internet para organizar tus vacaciones?
ESTUDIANTE: Sí, siempre hago mis reservaciones por Internet.
PERIODISTA: ¿Cuáles son las ventajas de usar este medio para reservar vuelos y hoteles?
ESTUDIANTE: ...

G **Segunda fase.** Hagan entre todos una encuesta para averiguar los siguientes datos de toda la clase:

1. número de estudiantes que organizan sus vacaciones por Internet
2. portales visitados por los estudiantes
3. objetivos turísticos más comunes entre los estudiantes

UDIO **14-8 La mujer en los países hispanos.** You will listen to a conversation between a reporter and a female lawyer about the status of women in the Hispanic world. Before you listen, list two questions you think the reporter might ask the lawyer and the answers that you think she might provide.

_____

_____

Now, pay attention to the general idea of what is said. Then, as you listen, circle the appropriate ending to each statement.

1. La doctora Gómez dice que la situación de la mujer ha mejorado porque...
   a. más mujeres son jefas de empresas.
   b. ahora hay más leyes que las protegen.
   c. hay muchas mujeres que no tienen hijos.

2. Según la doctora Gómez, en comparación con los hombres, las mujeres...
   a. no tienen que trabajar tanto.
   b. tienen que estar mejor preparadas.
   c. no estudian tanto.

3. Las mujeres hispanas ganan...
   a. más dinero que los hombres.
   b. tanto dinero como los hombres.
   c. menos dinero que los hombres.

4. En los hogares hispanos, el trabajo de la casa y la crianza de los hijos...
   a. está principalmente en manos de las mujeres.
   b. es compartido por todos los miembros de la familia.
   c. es la responsabilidad de los empleados domésticos.

Warm-up for 14-7. You may also ask that students write down the questions in advance.

Audioscript for 14-8.

REPORTERO: Buenas tardes, Dra. Gómez. Muchas gracias por acceder a esta entrevista para Radio América. Queremos que nos diga algo sobre la situación de la mujer en los países hispanos.

DRA. GÓMEZ: Gracias por invitarme. Será un placer.

REPORTERO: Dígame, Dra. Gómez, ¿cuál es la situación de la mujer en los países hispanos en la actualidad?

DRA. GÓMEZ: Bueno, la situación de la mujer ha cambiado mucho en los últimos años, pero sólo en el aspecto legal.

REPORTERO: ¿Qué quiere decir?

DRA. GÓMEZ: Bueno, lo que sucede es que las nuevas leyes protegen a la mujer, pero así y todo es más difícil para la mujer conseguir trabajo que para el hombre.

REPORTERO: Sí, pero hay muchas mujeres que trabajan hoy en día.

DRA. GÓMEZ: Sí, es verdad. Sin embargo, a las mujeres se les exige más preparación que a los hombres. Además, a las mujeres no se les paga lo mismo que a los hombres.

REPORTERO: ¿Y ha mejorado la situación de la mujer en el hogar?

DRA. GÓMEZ: Muy poco. Algunos hombres colaboran con las labores domésticas y en la crianza de los niños, pero en la mayor parte de los hogares hispanos es la mujer la encargada de la casa. Tenemos entonces una situación donde la mujer tiene dos trabajos, uno fuera de casa por el que le pagan muy poco, y otro en la casa donde no se le paga absolutamente nada.

REPORTERO: ¿Usted. cree que hay alguna esperanza de que esto cambie?

DRA. GÓMEZ: Bueno, poco a poco las cosas van cambiando. Hay más mujeres que estudian y esperan un poco más antes de casarse. Las mujeres ahora quieren estudiar, trabajar y ser independientes económicamente. Yo tengo esperanza de que esta situación cambie en un corto plazo, ya que habrá más mujeres como jefas de empresas, profesoras universitarias, ministras, médicas, abogadas, economistas. Poco a poco irán mejorando las cosas y habrá que seguir adelante.

REPORTERO: Bueno, Dra. Gómez, muchas gracias por compartir su opinión con nosotros.

DRA. GÓMEZ: Gracias a usted.

VÍNCULOS

To practice adverbial conjunctions that always require the subjunctive
- SAM-OneKey: WB: 14-5, 14-6, 14-7 / LM: 14-28, 14-29
- Companion Website: AP 14-2

Suggestions. Review uses of the subjunctive in noun (who, what) and adjective (which, what kind) clauses.

Since the structures presented in this section are complex, you may want to stress only recognition; tell students you do not expect them to be able to produce the structure right away. Review the functions of adverbs (when, where, how) and of adverbial clauses. A mnemonic device to remember the conjunctions that take the subjunctive is CASPA (dandruff): *con tal de que, antes de que, sin que, para que, a menos que.*

Note. *En caso de que* is not presented in the lesson; it may be introduced for recognition only.

Suggestion. A mnemonic device to remember those conjunctions that can take either the subjunctive or the indicative is MATCHED CDS, which stands for:

m	ientras	**c**	omo
a	unque	**d**	onde
t	an pronto como	**s**	egún
c	uando		
h	asta que		
e	n cuanto		
d	espués de que		

VÍNCULOS

To practice adverbial conjunctions: Subjunctive or indicative
- SAM-OneKey: WB: 14-8, 14-9, 14-10 / LM: 14-30, 14-31
- Companion Website: AP 14-3
- *Gramática viva* 1st Yr Review: Grammar Point 20: Indirect style: Indicative and Subjunctive

1. Adverbial conjunctions that always require the subjunctive

a menos que	*unless*	**para que**	*so that*
antes (de) que	*before*	**sin que**	*without*
con tal (de) que	*provided that*		

These conjunctions always require the subjunctive when followed by a dependent clause.

Los empleados tienen una reunión **antes de que** su representante **hable** con el director.
The employees are having a meeting before their representative speaks with the director.

Ellos aceptan el mismo sueldo, **con tal de que mejore** el plan de hospitalización.
They accept the same salary, provided that the hospitalization plan improves.

El representante habla con el director **para que** los empleados **tengan** más beneficios.
The representative speaks with the director so that the employees may have more benefits.

2. Adverbial conjunctions: Subjunctive or indicative

aunque	*although, even though, even if*	**en cuanto**	*as soon as*
		hasta que	*until*
como	*as, how, however*	**mientras**	*while*
cuando	*when*	**según**	*according to, as*
después (de) que	*after*	**tan pronto (como)**	*as soon as*
donde	*where, wherever*		

■ These conjunctions require the subjunctive when the event in the adverbial clause has not yet occurred. Note that the main clause expresses future time.

Va a luchar **hasta que** la compañía **tenga** un programa de entrenamiento.
She is going to fight until the company starts a training program.

Nos reuniremos **después que comiencen** el programa.
We will meet after they start the program.

Me llamará **tan pronto reciba** la aprobación del programa.
She will call me as soon as she receives the approval of the program.

- These conjunctions require the indicative when the event in the adverbial clause has taken place, is taking place, or usually takes place.

> Siempre apoya a los empleados **hasta que comienza** el programa de entrenamiento.
> *She always provides support to the employees until the training program starts.*

> Nos reunimos **después que comenzaron** el programa.
> *We met after they started the program.*

> Me llamó **tan pronto recibió** la aprobación del programa.
> *She called me as soon as she received the approval for the program.*

- **Como, donde,** and **según** require the indicative when they refer to something definite or known, and the subjunctive when they refer to something indefinite or unknown.

> Van a organizar el programa **como sugiere** el consejero.
> *They are going to organize the program as the adviser suggests.*

> Van a organizar el programa **como sugiera** el consejero.
> *They are going to organize the program as the adviser may suggest.*

> Vamos a reunirnos **donde** ella **dice.**
> *We are going to meet where she says.*

> Vamos a reunirnos **donde** ella **diga.**
> *We are going to meet wherever she says.*

> Llena el formulario **según dice** el consejero.
> *Fill the form according to what the adviser says.*

> Llena el formulario **según diga** el consejero.
> *Fill the form according to whatever the adviser says.*

- **Aunque** also requires the subjunctive when it introduces a condition not regarded as fact.

> Lo compro **aunque es** caro. *I will buy it although it is expensive.*
> Lo compro **aunque sea** caro. *I will buy it although it may be expensive.*

LENGUA

You learned that in Spanish, the subject is normally placed after the verb when asking a question: **¿La llamó el consejero?** (*Did the adviser call her?*) You may also postpone the subject in statements, especially when you wish to emphasize the subject: **La llamó el consejero.** (*The adviser called her.*)

¿Qué dice usted?

14-9 ¿Cuáles serán los cambios? Escoja la letra de la forma verbal correcta para completar las siguientes afirmaciones.

1. __b__ No es probable que una mujer sea presidenta de este país a menos de que (a. cambian, b. cambien) mucho las cosas.
2. __a__ Las leyes de los impuestos cambiaron según lo (a. pidieron, b. pidan) los miembros de la comisión.
3. __a__ Las familias que tenían pocos hijos protestaron cuando (a. se aprobaron, b. se aprueben) las nuevas leyes.
4. __b__ Como resultado, el gobierno disminuyó los impuestos a las familias numerosas para que las mujeres (a. tienen, b. tengan) más hijos y aumente así la natalidad en el país.
5. __b__ Muchas personas dicen que no creerán en esta disminución de los impuestos hasta que no la (a. ven, b. vean).
6. __b__ Otras personas creen que existen muchos problemas en las escuelas y que a menos que (a. se toman, b. se tomen) medidas drásticas, los problemas aumentarán en el futuro.

Alternate for 14-10. You are a parent listing conditions under which your child can borrow the car: *No puedes usar el auto a menos que...* or *Puedes usarlo con tal que...* Your partner plays the part of the child and answers accordingly.

❷ 14-10 ¿Acepto o no acepto? A usted le han ofrecido un puesto en otra ciudad y está considerando la posibilidad de aceptarlo. Complete la oración "(No) Acepto..." usando las expresiones adverbiales de la izquierda y las selecciones apropiadas de la derecha. Su compañero/a debe decirle lo que piensa, escogiendo otras expresiones o selecciones.

MODELO:　a menos que suban el sueldo aquí / (no) paguen la mudanza
　　　　　E1: Lo acepto a menos que me suban el sueldo aquí.
　　　　　E2: No lo aceptes a menos que te paguen la mudanza. o Acéptalo
　　　　　　　a menos que no te paguen la mudanza.

a menos que	esta semana termine
para que	(no) venda la casa
con tal (de) que	los alquileres no sean altos
sin que	mi familia conozca el lugar
antes (de) que	haya oportunidades de ascenso
	mi esposo(a)/amigo(a) consiga un trabajo allí
	la compañía pague el seguro de hospitalización
	tengan un buen plan de retiro (*retirement*)
	mi familia pueda vivir mejor
	...

❷ 14-11 El trabajo a distancia. Usted y su compañero/a trabajan desde su casa en un proyecto para una compañía en otra ciudad. Todo lo hacen en la computadora y se comunican por correo electrónico, fax y teléfono. Digan lo que van a hacer, usando las expresiones de la izquierda y una frase apropiada de la columna de la derecha.

MODELO:　Yo voy a trabajar en la computadora hasta que... empezar las
　　　　　noticias / ser la hora de cenar
　　　　　E1: Voy a trabajar en la computadora hasta que empiecen las
　　　　　　　noticias.
　　　　　E2: Y yo voy a trabajar hasta que sea la hora de cenar.

1. Voy a enviarles un fax en cuanto...	leer los mensajes electrónicos
2. Comeré después de que...	tener tiempo
3. Voy a comprobar estos números tan pronto como...	hablar con el jefe de ventas
	ser muy tarde
4. No me acostaré hasta que...	ser las 12:00
5. Voy a trabajar esta noche aunque...	tener mucho sueño
6. Te mandaré mi sección antes de que...	recibir la información
	terminar el proyecto

❷ 14-12 Después de que termine el año escolar. Primera fase. Usted quiere descansar y divertirse después de que terminen las clases, pero también quiere hacer algo por su comunidad. Complete tres de las opciones que le interesen en cada columna y añada una más para expresar sus propias ideas. Después comparta sus planes con su compañero/a.

DIVERSIÓN DURANTE
LAS VACACIONES

1. Quiero dormir hasta que...
2. No voy a abrir los libros aunque...
3. Haré un crucero por... tan pronto como...
4. Iré a la playa todos los días a menos que...
5. ...

AYUDA COMUNITARIA DURANTE
LAS VACACIONES

1. Trabajaré de voluntario donde...
2. Ayudaré en la biblioteca después de que...
3. Les serviré comida a los desamparados (*homeless*) mientras...
4. Organizaré juegos infantiles en el parque para que...
5. ...

Ⓖ Segunda fase. Preparen un plan para ayudar a su comunidad. En su plan deben indicar lo siguiente:

■ sector de la comunidad

■ tipo de ayuda

■ frecuencia

■ medios que van a usar

■ resultados que esperan obtener

❷ 14-13 El hombre y la mujer en la sociedad. Primero, indique su opinión con una X en la columna apropiada. Después compare sus respuestas con las de un/a compañero/a. Si la respuesta es negativa, defiendan su opinión y expliquen cuándo o bajo qué condiciones ocurrirán los cambios necesarios.

MODELO: ocupan más o menos el mismo número de puestos importantes. No, los hombres ocupan la mayoría de los puestos importantes en las compañías y en el gobierno. Esto va a cambiar cuando las generaciones jóvenes puedan tomar más decisiones.

Follow-up for 14-13. In small groups, students share their answers regarding when the changes will occur, under what conditions, and so on: *Va a haber una división justa de las tareas domésticas cuando los hombres colaboren en el trabajo de la casa.*

LOS HOMBRES Y LAS MUJERES...	SÍ	NO
reciben la misma educación.		
son tratados de la misma forma en el trabajo.		
ganan el mismo sueldo por el mismo trabajo.		
tienen las mismas oportunidades.		
hacen las mismas tareas domésticas.		
tienen los mismos derechos en un divorcio.		

SITUACIONES

1. **Role A.** You are the employees' representative in your company. Many employees have young children and can't find appropriate day care for them. In one of the company's buildings there is a vacant lounge that could be converted into a day-care center. Talk to the company president and explain: a) the employees' needs, b) the fact that a vacant lounge exists, and c) the advantages that a day-care center would bring to the company and its employees. Answer questions of the president based on the following information: there would be 25 children between the ages of one and four; it would require 20,000 pesos and three additional employees.

   Role B. You are the president of a company and the employees' representative comes to see you. Listen to his/her explanation and ask for the following information: a) the number and ages of the children that would benefit, b) the cost of turning the lounge into a day-care center, and c) the number of extra personnel needed. Then tell him/her that you will talk to the company Board of Directors **(Junta Directiva)** and will inform him/her of your decision.

2. You and your partner have just won 10 million dollars in the lottery and have decided to make donations to three institutions: your university, a hospital, and a museum. Decide a) how much you will give to each institution, b) how you want them to use the money, and c) under what conditions they should use it.

Suggestions. Present the past perfect in the same manner as the present perfect. You may wish to contrast the use of the two tenses: *Gracias por invitarme, pero ya he comido. Cuando Luis me invitó a cenar, ya yo había comido.*

3. The past perfect

■ Form the past perfect with the imperfect tense of **haber** and the past participle of the main verb.

IMPERFECT *HABER*		PAST PARTICIPLE
yo	había	
tú	habías	
Ud., él, ella	había	hablado
nosotros/s	habíamos	comido
vosotros/as	habíais	vivido
Uds., ellos/as	habían	

■ Use the past perfect to refer to a past event or action that occurred prior to another past event or action.

Los legisladores **habían buscado** la información en los archivos antes de escribir el informe.	*The legislators had looked for the information in the archives before writing the paper.*
Todos **habían terminado** a las dos.	*Everyone had finished at two.*

¿Qué dice usted?

② 14-14 ¡Recuerdos! Primera fase. Primero, marque con una *X* las opciones que representen su realidad y la de sus parientes o amigos en diferentes momentos de su vida. Luego compare sus respuestas con las de un/a compañero/a.

1. _____ Cuando yo tenía diez años, ya había escuchado discusiones políticas en mi casa.

2. _____ Cuando cumplimos diecisiete años, mis amigos y yo ya nos habíamos inscrito en un partido político.

3. _____ Cuando terminé la escuela secundaria, mis padres ya me habían comprado un carro.

4. _____ Cuando empecé la universidad, yo ya había trabajado por lo menos en dos lugares y había ahorrado (*saved*) algún dinero.

5. _____ Cuando pasó el primer mes de clases en la universidad, yo ya me había acostumbrado a todo el trabajo que tenía que hacer.

6. _____ Cuando visité a mi familia después de algunos meses, ellos ya sospechaban que yo me había hecho más independiente.

Segunda fase. Ahora hable con su compañero/a de un miembro de su familia o de un/a amigo/a con respecto a lo siguiente:

■ una experiencia divertida, triste o increíble que había tenido antes de graduarse de la escuela secundaria

■ dos logros —económicos, académicos, o personales— que había conseguido antes de entrar a la universidad o antes de los 18 años

■ algo positivo que le había ocurrido en su vida sentimental antes de cumplir los 22 años

② 14-15 ¡Qué familia tan colaboradora! La Sra. Jiménez, vicepresidenta de una multinacional, salió muy temprano de casa hoy y volvió tarde. Al salir de prisa por la mañana, había dejado mucho trabajo doméstico sin hacer. Pero al regresar, se dio cuenta de que todos los miembros de su familia habían ayudado con las tareas domésticas. Túrnense para decir qué había hecho cada uno.

MODELO: Cuando iba a salir, le dijo a su esposo que probablemente llegaría un poco tarde.

              Al volver, vio que su esposo había cocinado para toda la familia.

1. Después del desayuno dejó los platos sucios en la lavadora de platos.
2. Antes de irse a la oficina, vio que había muchas hojas secas en el jardín.
3. Cuando salía de casa notó que el garaje estaba sucio.
4. Los dormitorios de sus hijos estaban desordenados y había ropa en el piso.
5. Como tenía prisa, dejó en su casa unas cuentas importantes que quería mandar por correo.
6. No llevó una ropa que quería dejar en la tintorería (*dry cleaner*).

Warm-up for 14-15. Tell students what had happened to you before you came to class. Then ask the students questions based on what you said; encourage them to use their imagination.

14-16 Un día terrible y un día maravilloso. Cada uno de ustedes trabaja en empresas que dependen mucho de los adelantos de la nueva tecnología. Ayer fue un día terrible para usted en el trabajo y un día maravilloso para su compañero/a. Cada uno/a va a contar todas las cosas que le habían pasado antes de terminar el día. No se olvide de reaccionar apropiadamente al contenido de la historia y de hacer preguntas cuando sea necesario.

MODELO: E1: Ayer fue un día terrible. Cuando llegué a mi oficina, alguien había usado mi computadora y había perdido unos documentos importantes. Un compañero...

E2: Fue un día maravilloso para mí. Cuando llegué al trabajo, mi jefe me dijo que habían comprado computadoras nuevas para todos los empleados. Yo...

14-17 Una encuesta. Primera fase. Marque sus respuestas en la columna correspondiente y dígale a su compañero/a si usted u otros miembros de su familia ya habían hecho estas cosas antes del nuevo siglo.

MODELO: buscar trabajo por Internet
E1: Mi hermano y yo ya habíamos buscado trabajo por Internet.
E2: Yo nunca había usado Internet para buscar trabajo.

LENGUA

The letter **o** changes to **u** when it precedes a word beginning with **o** or **ho**:

usted o su familia →
usted **u** otro miembro de su familia
horas o minutos →
minutos **u** horas

	SÍ	NO	QUIÉNES
1. manejar un carro que funciona con hidrógeno			
2. hacer trabajo voluntario en la comunidad			
3. votar en las elecciones presidenciales			
4. leer periódicos extranjeros en Internet			
5. encontrar amigos por medio del correo electrónico			
6. comprar un televisor de alta definición			

Segunda fase. Averigüen cuáles son las tres actividades de la lista que marcaron más personas del grupo y qué miembros de la familia las hicieron. ¿Eran hombres o mujeres? Después comparen sus resultados con los de otros grupos.

SITUACIONES

Role A. You are an important businessman/woman who founded a survey company. Answer the questions that a reporter is going to ask you. Give him/her detailed information on how you think surveys will be undertaken in the future.

Role B. You are a reporter interviewing an important businessman/woman who founded a survey company. Ask him/her questions to find out: a) the date he/she opened the company, b) what he/she had done before starting the company (studies, positions held, places of residence, etc.) and c) his/her opinion on how surveys will be undertaken in the future.

4. Infinitive as subject of a sentence and as object of a preposition

- The infinitive is the only verb form that may be used as the subject of a sentence. As the subject it corresponds to the English *-ing* form.

Dialogar es necesario para lograr cambios.	*Talking is necessary for changes to occur.*
Hacer comentarios negativos no es bueno para las relaciones laborales.	*Making negative pronouncements is not good for work relations.*

- Use an infinitive after a preposition.

Llama **antes de ir.**	*Call before going.*
No llegues **sin avisarles.**	*Do not arrive without letting them know.*

- **Al** + *infinitive* is the equivalent of **cuando** + *verb*.

Al llegar, llamó al director.	*Upon arriving, he called the director.*
Cuando llegó, llamó al director.	*When he arrived, he called the director.*

¿Qué dice usted?

14-18 ¿Qué hay que hacer? Asocie las frases en la columna de la derecha con las de la izquierda.

1. __b__ Educarse...
2. __c__ Estudiar idiomas...
3. __a__ Votar en las elecciones...
4. __e__ Aceptar a los inmigrantes...
5. __d__ Reciclar los periódicos...
6. __f__ Participar en la vida política y económica...

a. es importante para mantener la democracia.
b. es vital para conseguir un buen trabajo.
c. es la mejor manera de aprender sobre otras culturas.
d. es necesario para proteger el medio ambiente.
e. es indispensable para una convivencia sana dentro de una comunidad.
f. es un derecho de todas la mujeres como ciudadanas de un país.

VÍNCULOS

To practice infinitive as subject of a sentence and as object of a preposition
- SAM-OneKey: WB: 14-14, 14-15, 14-16 / LM: 14-34, 14-35
- Companion Website: AP 14-5
- IRCD: Chapter 14; pg. 515

Suggestion. Use the Image Resource CD or bring international signs (e.g., a lighted cigarette crossed by a diagonal line) and give the Spanish equivalents.

Suggestion for 14-19. Primera fase. Use comprehensible input to introduce the words *tirar, disminuir,* and *casco* before doing the activity.

② **14-19 Los letreros en nuestra sociedad. Primera fase.** Todos estamos acostumbrados a ver letreros o avisos (*signs*) en muchos lugares. Digan dónde se ven avisos como éstos.

MODELO: No correr.
　　　　E1: En el pasillo de una escuela.
　　　　E2: En el área/la zona de una piscina.

1. Usar el cinturón de seguridad.
2. No tirar basura.
3. Disminuir la velocidad.
4. No traer vasos de cristal.
5. Usar cascos en esta área.
6. No abrir esta puerta.
7. No fumar.
8. Hablar en voz baja.

Segunda fase. Ahora, preparen un letrero para mostrárselo a otra pareja. Ellos/as tienen que decir dónde sería bueno ponerlo y por qué. Después, compartan sus letreros con la clase.

② **14-20 Opiniones.** Primero, marque con una X el casillero correspondiente en la tabla de acuerdo a su opinión. Después, compare sus respuestas con las de su compañero/a y añadan comentarios adicionales.

MODELO: dormir ocho horas
　　　　E1: Para mí, es necesario dormir ocho horas.
　　　　E2: Pues, para mí, dormir ocho horas es difícil. Trabajo mucho y generalmente, duermo seis.

ACTIVIDAD	IMPORTANTE	NECESARIO	DIVERTIDO	ABURRIDO	TERRIBLE	DIFÍCIL
mejorar el sistema educativo						
mantener las tradiciones familiares						
saber lo que pasa en el mundo						
usar el correo electrónico						
entender la televisión hispana						
conocer otras culturas						
luchar por una sociedad justa						
discriminar a los hombres/las mujeres						
ser madre/padre en estos tiempos						

14-21 Reacciones diferentes. Primera fase. Averigüe qué hace su compañero/a en los siguientes casos.

MODELO: antes de viajar en avión
        E1: ¿Qué haces antes de viajar en avión?
        E2: Antes de viajar en avión, normalmente compro unas revistas o pongo un buen libro en mi mochila.

1. antes de hacer un viaje largo en auto
2. antes de preparar un informe
3. después de leer las noticias en Internet
4. después de asistir a un partido de fútbol
5. antes de dormir
6. antes de ir a una entrevista para un trabajo

Segunda fase. Ahora, comparta la información que obtuvo en la **Primera fase** con otro/a estudiante diferente. ¿Reaccionan sus compañeros del mismo modo?

MODELO: E1: Antes de viajar en avión, X siempre va al banco y retira dinero. ¿Tú haces lo mismo?
        E2: Yo hago algo diferente. Generalmente rezo (*pray*) porque tengo pánico de viajar en avión.

14-22 ¡Viva la independencia! Al convertirse en una empresaria muy exitosa, la señora Suárez ya tiene un buen capital; por lo tanto desea hacer otras cosas interesantes. ¿Qué resultados van a tener sus planes?

MODELO: E1: Piensa trabajar menos horas.
        E2: Al trabajar menos tiempo, va a levantarse un poco más tarde.
        E1: Y al levantarse más tarde va a sentirse más relajada.

1. Le gustaría viajar por América Latina.
2. Quiere aprender a esquiar.
3. Desea tomar clases de pintura con un discípulo de Picasso.
4. Piensa pasar más tiempo con amigos.
5. Quiere contratar a dos empleados para que hagan su trabajo.
6. Como es divorciada, le gustaría conocer a alguien que sea compatible con ella.

14-23 Unos avisos. Preparen dos avisos que se relacionen con algún problema o preocupación social. Compártanlos con la clase y digan dónde se deben poner.

Suggestion for 14-22. This activity can be used to review the present subjunctive following *cuando*. Students can make a statement using *cuando + subjunctive*, and their partners can reply using *al + infinitive*, such as the following: *E1: María quiere aprender a jugar tenis cuando termine el semestre.* Or *Cuando termine el semestre, María va a tomar clases de tenis dos veces a la semana. E2: ¡Qué bueno! Al terminar el semestre va a tener más tiempo para practicar.*

SITUACIONES

The Students' Association in your university/college would like to publish a document on student rights and obligations. They have asked you and your partner to collaborate. Write a list of five fundamental rights and responsibilities that are representative of university students in today's society. Share your list with the class. After all the lists have been presented, the class should decide on the five most relevant rights and responsibilities.

Escuchar

Identifying the speaker's point of view

When you listen to politicians, scientists, or lawyers being interviewed you notice that they frequently present their point of view about the situation or topic being discussed with the intention of convincing the listener of their position. It is important for you, as a listener, to identify their point of view to understand their position on an issue.

Antes de escuchar

14-24 Los cambios en la familia. In **14-25,** you will listen to a conversation between two women discussing the changes the Hispanic family has undergone. Before you listen, anticipate and write down some of the changes they will probably mention in reference to responsibilities in childrearing and house chores.

A escuchar

14-25. First read the statements below and, then, listen to the conversation between Sonia and Vilma regarding the changes in the Hispanic family they have witnessed during their lifetimes. As you listen, circle the statements that reflect Sonia's (**S**) point of view and those that represent Vilma's (**V**).

1. (S) V Los cambios que han ocurrido en la sociedad han tenido un efecto positivo.
2. S (V) La estructura de la familia ha cambiado, y ahora nadie se ocupa de la casa.
3. (S) V No era bueno el papel secundario que tenía la mujer en la casa.
4. S (V) Los abuelos han perdido el papel importante que tenían en la familia.
5. (S) V La mujer debe desarrollarse profesional e intelectualmente.

Después de escuchar

(G) 14-26 ¿Y usted? Working in a small group, share your answers to the following questions.

1. ¿Piensa que los padres deben continuar trabajando fuera de la casa cuando tengan hijos pequeños?
2. ¿Le parece a usted que es importante que tanto el padre como la madre contribuyan a la economía del hogar? ¿Por qué?
3. ¿Cómo cree usted que se podría mejorar la situación de la familia en el mundo actual?

Warm-up for 14-25. As a prelistening activity, have students work in groups of four and discuss the advantages and disadvantages of having both parents working outside the house.

Audioscript for 14-25:

VILMA: Mira, Sonia, en los últimos años han ocurrido demasiados cambios en la sociedad, y estos cambios se han reflejado en la familia.
SONIA: Sí, es verdad, pero los cambios son positivos, ¿no crees?
VILMA: No sé qué decirte, Sonia. Antes las labores estaban bien definidas y cada uno sabía lo que tenía que hacer. La responsabilidad del padre era mantener económicamente a la familia, mientras que la madre se ocupaba de las labores domésticas y de la educación de los niños. Ahora, parece que nadie se ocupa de la casa.
SONIA: Bueno, pero acuérdate que siempre la última palabra la tenía el padre y él era el rey del hogar. La mujer tenía un papel secundario. Yo prefiero los cambios que han ocurrido porque hoy la mujer tiene un papel más importante tanto en la familia como en la sociedad.
VILMA: Pero, ¿a qué costo? Antes los abuelos ayudaban a cuidar a los niños y todos los miembros de la familia les mostraban cariño. Ahora, los niños están en las guarderías y los abuelos en las residencias de la tercera edad.
SONIA: Sí, eso sí es triste. Aunque el papel de la mujer en la sociedad sea mejor ahora, no me gusta que los niños pasen tantas horas del día separados de sus padres y abuelos. Debería haber más equilibrio para que la mujer no se sacrifique y deje de crecer intelectualmente y profesionalmente.
VILMA: Tú eres más moderna que yo, Sonia. Yo prefiero los tiempos de antes cuando todo era más sencillo.
SONIA: Yo no. Yo prefiero ver a la mujer desarrollarse igual que el hombre.

Antes de escuchar

14-27 Problemas de familia. In **14-28,** you will listen to a lecture given in a local library by a sociologist, Dr. Angulo. Before you listen, write down a list of four problems that modern families are facing.

A escuchar

14-28. First, read the statements below and, then, listen to part of Dr. Angulo's lecture. As you listen, circle the statements that best reflect Dr. Angulo's point of view.

1. El cuidado de los niños es responsabilidad de la sociedad.
2. Los hombres y las mujeres deben tener las mismas oportunidades y responsabilidades.
3. La falta de supervisión puede traer como consecuencia que los niños se relacionen con personas que no son buenas.
4. La violencia es causada por el alto número de familias que tienen sólo un padre o una madre.

Después de escuchar

14-29 ¿Y usted? Working in a small group, share your answers to the following questions.

1. ¿Qué programas hay en su comunidad que sirven de apoyo a las familias donde no hay una figura materna o una figura paterna?
2. ¿Ha trabajado usted en alguno de esos programas? ¿Cómo ha cooperado usted? Si no lo ha hecho, ¿cómo piensa usted que podría cooperar?
3. ¿Qué programa(s) adicional(es) piensa usted que podría haber en su comunidad para ayudar a los niños y a los jóvenes?

 *Conversar*

Antes de conversar

14-30 Los cambios de la sociedad. Lea la siguiente noticia publicada en un periódico español. Marque las ideas centrales.

VÍNCULOS

For materials related to the Mosaicos section, see
• SAM-OneKey: WB: 14-17, 14-18, 14-19, 14-20, 14-21, 14-22 / LM: 14-36

Warm-up for 14-28. As a prelistening activity, have students get together in groups of four and discuss the problems that single parents face in our society.

Audioscript for 14-28. DRA. ANGULO: Buenas tardes, señoras y señores. Muchas gracias por haberme invitado a hablar con ustedes sobre este tema que nos toca a todos, hombres, mujeres, jóvenes, ancianos. Hoy en día la familia moderna está atravesando una situación muy difícil.

Por un lado está la importancia de lograr la igualdad entre el hombre y la mujer en el campo profesional, pero por otro está la importancia de lograr la igualdad de responsabilidades entre ellos en el hogar y en particular en la crianza y educación de los niños. Frecuentemente vemos que los niños y adolescentes no tienen mucha supervisión porque los padres están muy ocupados o agotados de tanto trabajo. Si a esto se añade el alto índice de divorcio, muchos niños se crían en hogares con un solo padre. Para compensar la ausencia de uno de los padres, los niños muchas veces se refugian en las amistades que consiguen en la calle, en las escuelas, en los parques, sin que los padres sepan quiénes son realmente esas personas.

Otro de los problemas serios de nuestra sociedad es el consumo de drogas entre la gente joven. Las drogas traen violencia; por eso, en muchos barrios de nuestra ciudad, muchas personas no quieren salir de noche por la falta de seguridad en la calle.

Hago un llamado entonces a los hombres y mujeres para que pensemos no sólo en nuestro futuro, sino en el de nuestra sociedad. Es necesario construir una sociedad de igualdad de oportunidades pero también de responsabilidades.

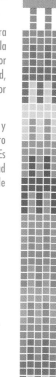

Las mujeres hacen historia en España

El nuevo Primer Ministro español, José Luis Rodríguez Zapatero, cumplió la promesa que había hecho durante su campaña, de darles a las españolas el lugar que se merecen en la importante labor de gobernar España.

Entre los dieciséis ministerios, ocho son ocupados por mujeres y ocho por hombres.

Una de las nuevas figuras femeninas del gabinete español es María Teresa Fernández de la Vega, la primera mujer Vicepresidenta de España y ministra de la Presidencia. Gran conocedora del sistema legal español, la nueva Vicepresidenta ha participado en importantes proyectos de democratización posteriores a la dictadura de Francisco Franco.

Las proyecciones futuras del trabajo de Fernández de la Vega son inmensas, ya que tendrá la responsabilidad de coordinar todos los ministerios, excepto el de economía. Ella y sus colegas ministras, Carmen Calvo (Ministra de Cultura), María Jesús Sansegundo (Ministra de Educación), Magdalena Álvarez (Ministra de Infraestructuras), María Antonia Trujillo (Ministra de Vivienda), Cristina Narbona (Ministra de Medio Ambiente), Elena Espinosa (Ministra de Agricultura y Pesca) y Elena Salgado (Ministra de Sanidad)[1], tendrán un papel protagónico en la vida política de la España del siglo XXI.

[1]*health*

A conversar

G **14-31 Problemas y soluciones.** Al asumir la Vicepresidencia, María Fernández de la Vega encontró los problemas mencionados en la tabla, pero ella desea solucionarlos pronto. Léanlos y luego indiquen cuál de las ministras del gabinete español tendrá la responsabilidad de resolver cada problema y cómo creen ustedes que lo hará.

PROBLEMAS	¿QUÉ MINISTRA?	¿CÓMO LO HARÁ?
La atención en los hospitales rurales es deficiente. Debe mejorarse.		
Hay demasiados alumnos en los salones de clase.		
El aire de muchas ciudades españolas está contaminado.		
Muchas especies marinas están desapareciendo.		
A causa de la llegada de un gran número de inmigrantes de África, no hay suficientes viviendas.		

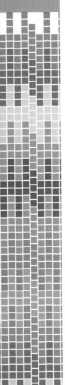

Después de conversar

G **14-32 ¿Qué condiciones deben darse (*occur*)?** Ustedes son consejeros de la nueva vicepresidenta y deben ayudarla a resolver los problemas que enfrenta el país. Discutan qué condiciones deberán darse y qué efecto esperan ustedes que estas soluciones tengan en la población o el lugar. Lean el ejemplo. Finalmente, prepárense para compartir sus ideas con la clase.

PROBLEMA	CONDICIÓN/CONDICIONES PARA RESOLVERLO	EFECTO EN LA CIUDAD/CIUDADANOS
Situación económica de los inmigrantes	*A menos que* la sociedad les dé oportunidades para mejorar su condición económica, su situación no va a cambiar. *o Con tal de que* mejoren su estatus de vida, ellos deben tener la oportunidad de conseguir un trabajo.	La educación será vital *para que* los inmigrantes obtengan trabajos mejor pagados.
Desempleo		
Condiciones de los hospitales rurales		
Contaminación		
Extinción de algunas especies marinas		
Convivencia entre los españoles y los nuevos inmigrantes		

Antes de conversar

2 **14-33 ¡Nuestros problemas!** Indiquen y expliquen por lo menos un problema (local, nacional o mundial) en las siguientes áreas.

MODELO: **Área:** seguridad

Problema: terrorismo

Explicación del problema: Hoy existen grupos terroristas que atacan y crean caos en el mundo. Nadie se siente seguro.

ÁREA

1. economía
2. igualdad
3. armas
4. salud

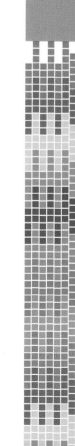

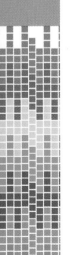

EN DIRECTO

To present a group's conclusion:

Después de discutir sobre el tema, llegamos/hemos llegado a la siguiente conclusión.

Nuestro grupo cree/piensa que...

A nuestro grupo le parece que...

Para nosotros, el problema más serio es...

To support a group's view or position:

No tenemos duda de que sea... el problema más serio porque...

Si miramos/observamos... nos damos cuenta de que...

Las estadísticas/ La opinión de los expertos apoyan nuestra conclusión.

Note for 14-35. Translation of expressions in the *En directo* box has not been provided this time because by now learners should be familiar with these expressions.

Suggestion for 14-35. Before students present their report, you may wish to exemplify presenting and defending a personal or a group position in regards to a controversial issue.

(G) 14-34 ¿Qué problema es más serio? Conversen sobre los problemas mencionados en **14-33**. Hagan lo siguiente:

1. Digan cuál de los problemas mencionados en **14-33** piensan que es más serio. Expliquen por qué.
2. Luego, háganse preguntas relacionadas con el problema más serio. Utilicen en sus respuestas las expresiones indicadas en *En directo* y tomen notas de las respuestas del grupo.

> MODELO:　la falta de seguridad en las escuelas
> 　　　　　E1: ¿Creen/Les parece/Piensan que podamos terminar con la falta de seguridad en las escuelas?
> 　　　　　E2: Sí, cuando haya más disciplina y eduquemos mejor a los niños.

3. Lleguen a una conclusión entre todos sobre cuándo se solucionará el problema. Usen las siguientes expresiones:
> 　　　después de que　tan pronto como　en cuanto　cuando

Después de conversar

(G) 14-35 ¡A compartir! Preséntenle a la clase la información y conclusión a la que llegaron en la actividad **14-34**. Prepárense para presentar y defender su posición.

 Leer

Identifying the tone of a text

Have you ever heard a song or read a poem or a narrative, and had the sensation that a happy, sad, or funny feeling invaded you? Most likely the explanation to such an experience lies in the words chosen by the author to describe feelings, the setting, to create a special atmosphere in the poem. Likewise, a narrator will choose words and arrange events or occurrences in a particular manner to bring a story to life and cause a particular effect on the reader: suspense, tension, anger, frustration, excitement, etc.

Explained in very simple words, the tone of a text is that peculiar manner or style used by the speaker or writer—based on the content he/she is presenting—that creates a particular mood or reaction on the listener or reader.

In *Lección 14*, you will have the opportunity to determine the tone of a poem in Spanish.

Guía de prelectura

Look at the picture and the title of the poem in activity **14-38** and answer the following questions, using your personal experience, or your knowledge of love relations.

1. What may the central idea of this poem be? Circle all that may apply, in your view.
   a. A person falls in love with a dwarf.
   (b.) A woman thinks her beloved husband is lovely like a pet.
   (c.) A woman feels she is a prisoner of a man who keeps her caged like a bird.

2. How did you guess the answer(s) to question 1?
   (a.) personal experience
   (b.) knowledge of love relationships
   (c.) reading of poems about love relationships

Antes de leer

14-36 Preparación. De la siguiente lista de palabras o símbolos, ¿cuáles asocian ustedes con la relación de una pareja? Márquenlos con una equis (**X**) y prepárense para justificar su selección.

1. _____ una paloma (*dove*)
2. _____ el corazón
3. _____ querer, amar
4. _____ odiar, detestar
5. _____ un canario
6. _____ atrapar
7. _____ una jaula donde viven pájaros
8. _____ comprensión
9. _____ liberar
10. _____ dar

Suggestion for 14-36. Allow any response as long as it is supported logically. Encourage students to support their choice by either explaining or exemplifying.

14-37 Vivencias. Lean las siguientes afirmaciones. Luego comenten si alguna vez ustedes mismos han dicho estas palabras, las han leído o escuchado. ¿En qué circunstancias dijeron o escucharon estas afirmaciones? ¿Dónde las leyeron? ¿En qué circunstancias diferentes podrían usar estas expresiones?

1. Me siento como un/a prisionero/a.
2. Por favor, déjame vivir mi vida.
3. Te amo.
4. No me pidas que te comprenda.
5. El problema es que tú no me entiendes.
6. Quiero volar como un pájaro.
7. Vivo sin libertad, como un pájaro en una jaula.
8. Suéltame. Déjame tranquilo/a.

Suggestion for 14-37. You may wish to model the activity as follows: *Una vez tuve una pareja que quería controlarme. Yo me sentía como un/a prisionero/a en una jaula. Yo quería liberarme de él/ella y volar libre como un pájaro. Una vez cuando él/ella me mintió, le dije: "No me pidas que te comprenda." Por fin, rompimos y ahora soy feliz con mi actual pareja. Él/Ella siempre me dice: "Te amo."*

Suggestion for 14-38. Since this may be the first poem students read in Spanish, do not expect them to verbalize possible interpretations of it. Allow them to answer by quoting directly from the poem, if necessary.

Answers for 14-38. 1. I: tono triste; 2. I: una mujer; 3: C; 4. I: la hace infeliz; 5. I: ni ahora ni nunca; 6. I: no se refiere al aspecto físico; 7. I: quiere escapar; 8. I: ya no lo ama.

A leer

14-38 Primera mirada. Lea el siguiente poema y, luego, siga las instrucciones.

Hombre pequeñito
de Alfonsina Storni

Hombre pequeñito, hombre pequeñito,
Suelta a tu canario, que quiere volar...
Yo soy el canario, hombre pequeñito,
Déjame saltar.
Estuve en tu jaula, hombre pequeñito,
Hombre pequeñito que jaula me das,
Digo pequeñito porque no me entiendes,
Ni me entenderás.
Tampoco te entiendo, pero mientras tanto
Ábreme la jaula que quiero escapar;
Hombre pequeñito, te amé media hora.
No me pidas más.

Indique si las siguientes afirmaciones son interpretaciones correctas (**C**) o incorrectas (**I**) del poema. Si son incorrectas explique por qué.

1. _____ El poema tiene un tono alegre.
2. _____ La persona que habla en este poema es un hombre.
3. _____ La voz del poema siente que la persona con quien conversa es un/a opresor/a.
4. _____ La persona con quien la voz dialoga lo/la trata bien y lo/la hace feliz.
5. _____ La persona piensa que su pareja no la comprende ahora, pero lo hará en el futuro.
6. _____ La expresión "pequeñito" en este poema significa que la persona es de baja estatura.
7. _____ La voz del poema quiere continuar viviendo con su compañero/a.
8. _____ El/La narrador/a del poema desea darle amor a su pareja.

Después de leer

14-39 Segunda mirada. Marque el tono de cada una de las siguientes citas según el contexto del poema: tono irónico (**TI**), tono de seguridad (**TS**), tono de ruego (*pleading*) o súplica (**TR**), tono de desesperanza (**TD**).

1. __TI__ Hombre pequeñito, hombre pequeñito.
2. __TR__ Suelta a tu canario.
3. __TS/TD__ Digo pequeñito porque no me entiendes.
4. __TS/TD__ Ni me entenderás.
5. __TS__ Tampoco te entiendo...
6. __TR__ Ábreme la jaula...
7. __TR/TS__ ...quiero escapar
8. __TS__ No me pidas más.

 *Escribir*

Writing poetry is a unique artistic expression that allows human beings to convey concepts and feelings such as justice, heroism, beauty, love, sadness, loneliness, and to celebrate a special event, to mourn the death of a loved one, etc.

A poem undoubtedly affects a reader's mood not only by its content, but also by the manner in which its content is presented. Effects may range from feelings of happiness to sadness, and comfort, for example.

Overall, we must remember that poetry is a reflection of human experience, and in that sense, anyone can write poetry.

Antes de escribir

14-40 Preparación. Primera fase. Prepárese para escribir su propio poema, siguiendo el modelo del poema de la actividad **14-38.** Haga lo siguiente:

1. Decida para quién va a escribir el poema: ¿para una mujer o para un hombre?
2. Escriba una o dos palabras que describan a esta persona:
   _____ _____
3. Escoja un objeto, un animal, u otro elemento que represente sus sentimientos sobre la relación que tiene con esa persona: _____
4. Escriba tres o cuatro cosas que usted le pediría a la persona que haga por usted:
   _____   _____   _____   _____
5. Indique un lugar que usted asocia con esta relación: _____
6. Mencione una o dos cosas que usted le pediría a la persona que no haga.
   _____   _____

A escribir

14-41 Manos a la obra. Ahora, complete su poema, siguiendo el poema en **14-38.** Puede darle un tono alegre, triste, nostálgico, etc. No se olvide de darle un título.

Título: _____

Autor: _____

_____, _____,

_____ a tu _____, que quiere _____

Yo soy _____, _____,

_____.

_____, _____,

_____ que _____ me das.

Digo _____ porque no _____,

Ni _____.

Tampoco te _____, pero mientras tanto

_____ que quiero _____;

_____, te _____ media hora.

No me _____ más.

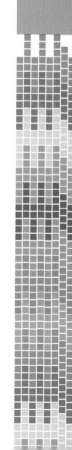

Después de escribir

14-42 Revisión. Lea su poema una vez más y responda a estas preguntas.

1. ¿Está usted satisfecho/a con el mensaje que le da a la persona a quien usted se lo escribe?
2. ¿Son comprensibles y coherentes las ideas?
3. ¿Siente usted que el poema tendrá el efecto que usted quiere?

Ahora, revise si...

- el vocabulario que usted usó es apropiado para describir a esta persona y los sentimientos que usted tiene por él/ella.

- la ortografía, puntuación, acentuación, etc. son apropiadas.

Finalmente, déle el poema a un/a compañero/a para que lo lea y lo disfrute.

ENFOQUE CULTURAL

Para pensar

¿Qué tipo de gobierno tiene los Estados Unidos? ¿Y los países hispanos? ¿Hay algún país hispano que tenga una monarquía? ¿Cuál? ¿Hay algún país hispano con un gobierno dictatorial en este momento?¿Cuál? Casi todos los países hispanos tienen un gobierno democrático.

A causa de las grandes desigualdades sociales y a la multitud de problemas económicos, en algunos países hispanos, como Colombia, Perú, México, por ejemplo, han surgido grupos guerrilleros o revolucionarios.

Para contestar

2 **La democracia.** Respondan a las siguientes preguntas.

1. ¿Qué grupos amenazan a la democracia en los países hispanos?
2. ¿Cuáles, en su opinión, son los problemas que afectan más seriamente a la democracia en Hispanoamérica?
3. ¿Le parece a usted que los jóvenes deben mantenerse activos en la política? ¿Por qué?

En algunos países existen traficantes de drogas que también amenazan la paz y la democracia.

En España, después del regreso al trono del Rey Juan Carlos I se inició el camino a la democracia. En junio de 1977 se llevaron a cabo las primeras elecciones después de 40 años de dictadura de Francisco Franco.

G **Riqueza cultural.** En grupos de tres, discutan uno de los siguientes temas, mencionando sus causas y sus consecuencias. Si es necesario, investiguen sobre el tema.

- la revolución cubana
- el narcotráfico en Colombia
- el movimiento guerrillero en México (Chiapas)
- las dictaduras de los años 1970 (Chile, Uruguay, Argentina)

Para investigar en Internet

Busque el nombre y afiliación política de los presidentes de 5 países hispanos (dos de Sudamérica, dos de Centroamérica y uno de Norteamérica). Diga si son conservadores o liberales, qué reformas han hecho en su país, etc. Traiga esta información a clase y haga una presentación acerca de lo que averiguó. Sus compañeros/as, divididos/as en grupos, escogerán a uno de esos presidentes y darán su opinión sobre su labor, basándose únicamente en lo que usted presentó.

VÍNCULOS

For materials related to the Enfoque cultural, see
- SAM-OneKey: WB: 14-23

¡Prepárese!

Suggestion for 14-43. This exercise can be modified if the students will be watching *Fortunas* outside of class. In class they can discuss whether or not they were correct when they worked on their own.

G

14-43 El arte. El Misterio 7, "Casa de belleza", tiene que ver con unos artistas mexicanos. Hagan una lista de todo lo que saben sobre el arte y/o los artistas mexicanos. Después, compartan su lista con las de otros grupos. Aquí están las pistas:

1. Accidente famoso
2. La bella y la bestia
3. Matrimonio tumultuoso
4. Vestidos de Tehuana

¿Pudieron adivinar a qué o a quién se refiere "Casa de belleza"? Miren ahora el Episodio 14 para ver si tenían razón.

Ángela y Manolo hablan de quién va a ganar el concurso. ¿Será Katie?

Katie pasea por las calles de Coyoacán.

Katie pudo solucionar la pista, "Vestidos de Tehuana" por sus conocimientos de arte mexicano.

Katie y Sabrina formaron una alianza para solucionar este misterio.

Carlos no entiende bien sus sentimientos por Katie.

Carlos le dice a Tito que le importa más ganar en la vida que ganar el juego.

¡Responda!

14-44 Acciones. Combine los infinitivos de la columna de la izquierda con las frases de la columna de la derecha para formar oraciones lógicas en las que el infinitivo sea el sujeto.

1. __b__ Mentir...
2. __d__ Competir...
3. __e__ Hacer...
4. __c__ Cooperar...
5. __a__ Enamorarse...

  a. de una competidora puede traer problemas de amor.
  b. a los amigos causa falta de confianza.
  c. con todos es una buena idea porque así todos ganan puntos.
  d. con los otros participantes puede ser difícil.
  e. alianzas es bueno porque dos personas pueden compartir los resultados.

Esta canción es un ejemplo del ritmo cubano "son montuno" y trata de un guajiro (campesino) que vive una vida humilde. El guajiro de la canción es un vendedor ambulante de frutas frescas, como el mamey, y está tratando de vender lo suficiente como para comprarle un traje de moda a su "guajira".

¡Prepárese!

Suggestion for 14-45. You may want to ask students to use a bilingual dictionary for this exercise.

14-45 Otros tiempos. Lea la letra de "Trabajador guajiro" y preste especial atención a las siguientes palabras: cosechar, maíz, buey y carreta. ¿Qué significan? ¿Qué tipo de vida representan?

Trabajador guajiro

El trabajador guajiro
sí que vive bien feliz,
porque tiene a su guajira
y cosecha su maíz.

Por la mañana temprano
enyugando bien los bueyes
que van a halar la carreta
cargadita de mameyes.

Y ahora se va para la ciudad
a vender mamey
y después comprar.

Y ahora se va para la ciudad
a vender mamey
y después comprar
un traje bien lindo
que sea de la moda
para su guajira
que es su reina mora.

A vender mamey, guajiro,
con el rocío de la mañana sale a la ciudad.

Un traje a su jibarita le quiere comprar
y los bueyes la carreta comienzan a arrastrar
y alegre el jibarito va cantando así.

¡Escuche!

14-46 Los instrumentos. Mientras escucha la canción complete las palabras siguientes para ver qué instrumentos se usan en esta canción. Todos son cognados.

1. la t <u>r</u> om <u>pe</u> t a
2. el <u>p i a n</u> o
3. el <u>t</u> r o m b <u>ó</u> n
4. el b <u>o n</u> g <u>ó</u>
5. la f <u>l</u> a u <u>ta</u>
6. el v <u>i</u> o <u>lí</u> n

¡Responda!

14-47 La vida campesina. Complete los espacios en blanco con una conjunción adverbial de la lista según la letra de la canción.

despúes de que a menos que para que con tal de que cuando donde aunque

1. El guajiro no le comprará un traje de moda a su guajira <u>a menos que</u> venda suficiente fruta en la ciudad.
2. A él no le importa trabajar mucho <u>con tal de que</u> le compren las frutas.
3. <u>Aunque</u> su vida es sencilla y humilde, el guajiro vive feliz.
4. Los bueyes arrastrarán la carreta <u>para que</u> el guajiro llegue a la ciudad.
5. El guajiro está alegre <u>cuando</u> trabaja.

VOCABULARIO*

La sociedad

la confianza	trust
el derecho	right
el divorcio	divorce
la eficiencia	efficiency
el hogar	home
la honestidad	honesty
la igualdad	equality
el ministerio	ministry
la separación	separation
la ventaja	advantage

Encuestas

los datos	data
la estadística	statistic
la mayoría	majority
la mitad	half
el perfil	profile
el promedio	average
el porcentaje	percentage

Personas

el/la habitante	inhabitant
el/la vecino/a	neighbor
la viuda	widow
el viudo	widower

Descripción

analfabeto/a	illiterate
actual	present, current
adulto/a	adult
enérgico/a	energetic
fiable	trustworthy
financiero	financial
notable	notable, noteworthy
solo/a	alone

Verbos

casarse	to get married
continuar	to continue
divorciarse	to divorce
encontrar (ue)	to find
proceder (de)	to come from
realizar (c)	to carry out
saltar	to jump

Palabras y expresiones útiles

el nivel	level
la sucursal	branch (business)

*For a list of adverbial conjunctions, see pages 508–509.

15

LA CIENCIA Y LA TECNOLOGÍA

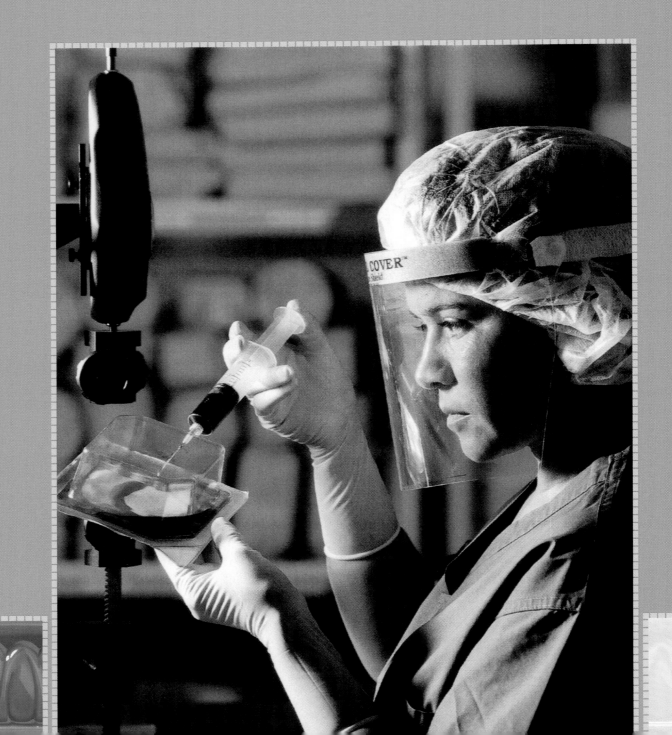

Objetivos comunicativos

- Talking about advances in science and technology
- Giving opinions and making suggestions
- Hypothesizing about the present and the future
- Softening requests and statements
- Expressing unexpected occurrences
- Expressing contrary-to-fact conditions in the present

Contenido

A PRIMERA VISTA

AUDIO *La conservación del medio ambiente*

Suggestion. Ask students to mention ecological problems in the world, such as destruction of the ozone layer, pollution, acid rain, overpopulation, destruction of the rain forest. Provide any vocabulary they may need. Move the discussion into speculation about the future. In the field of medicine, will there be a cure for cancer, heart disease, AIDS?

VÍNCULOS

To practice vocabulario—La conservación del medio ambiente, ¿Qué nos espera en el futuro? & Nuevas fronteras
- SAM-OneKey: WB: 15-1, 15-2, 15-3, 15-4 / LM: 15-22, 15-23, 15-24, 15-25
- Companion Website: AP 15-1 A, B
- IRCD: Chapter 15; pp. 534, 536

¡AÚN ES TIEMPO!

La reserva de la biosfera es nuestra oportunidad

La reserva de la biosfera del alto Golfo de California y del delta del río Colorado puede ser la salvación de nuestra cultura pesquera. Juntos vamos a desarrollar un plan que nos permita manejar la reproducción y recuperación de los recursos naturales y de esta manera, asegurar nuestro bienestar y el de nuestros hijos.

¡El éxito depende de su participación!

A INVESTIGAR

Busque información en Internet sobre organizaciones como Greenpeace o el Club Sierra, cuyo propósito es la protección del medio ambiente. Escoja una de esas organizaciones y prepare un breve informe oral con la siguiente información:

- ¿Qué objetivos tiene la organización?
- ¿Cómo se financia?
- ¿Quiénes trabajan en ella?
- ¿Cuál fue una de sus campañas recientes?
- ¿Qué objetivos tenía? ¿Cómo la realizaron?

La **cuenca** del río Amazonas cubre un área de más de 7 millones de kilómetros cuadrados, región comparable en extensión a dos terceras partes del territorio de los Estados Unidos. Debido a su densa vegetación selvática, esta área es conocida como el "pulmón" del **planeta**. Hoy en día, miles de **campesinos** llegan a la **selva** en busca de **tierra** para cultivar. La **deforestación** de nuestros **bosques** se considera una pérdida irreparable para el **medio ambiente** del planeta.

¿Qué dice usted?

② **15-1 Amigos de la tierra.** Completen la siguiente tabla de acuerdo con la información presentada. Después, hablen de la gravedad de cada situación y den ideas para mejorarla.

Follow-up for 15-1. Compare the strategies of various pairs, emphasizing the variety of ideas presented to solve current ecological problems.

TEMA	PROBLEMA	ESTRATEGIA
la industria pesquera		
los bosques tropicales		

② **15-2 El futuro.** Primero, haga una lista de tres adelantos científicos y tres cambios sociales que espera que se realicen en el siglo XXI. Luego, compare su lista con la de su compañero/a.

ADELANTOS CIENTÍFICOS

_____

_____

_____

CAMBIOS SOCIALES

_____

_____

_____

Suggestion for 15-2. One student could write on the board the advances and changes that students included in their lists. The class could try to reach a consensus as to the feasibility of such progress.

Ⓖ **15-3 El problema más serio de hoy.** Preparen un informe oral sobre su preocupación principal en cuanto al futuro del mundo y del ser humano. Incluyan soluciones posibles. Presenten sus ideas a la clase.

Follow-up for 15-3. Have students present their primary concern to the class as a whole. Rank problems by the number of students concerned about the same issue.

La ciudad del futuro

1 LAS CIUDADES

- Se construirán ciudades verticales con edificios climatizados por medio de energía solar. Algunas se construirán sobre el mar.
- El 90% de la población vivirá en las ciudades.
- Las basuras urbanas serán recicladas.

2 LA ATMÓSFERA

- La atmósfera sufrirá un calentamiento que hará subir el nivel del mar por los deshielos, causando inundaciones.
- La contaminación de los mares provocará la extinción de los bancos de peces.
- El agujero de la capa de ozono hará aumentar el número de enfermos de cáncer de piel.
- Se cultivarán plantas que mejoren la calidad del aire.

3 LAS VIVIENDAS

- Todos los hogares estarán conectados a Internet. Las compras de alimentos se harán virtualmente.
- Las puertas y los aparatos electrónicos serán activados por la voz.
- Habrá robots que se ocuparán de hacer la limpieza.

④ EL TRANSPORTE

- Los trenes de alta velocidad conectarán las grandes ciudades y circularán por rieles suspendidos a la altura de los edificios.
- Los coches combinarán la energía eléctrica y la energía solar. Serán pequeñas cápsulas voladoras que podrán despegar y aterrizar verticalmente.
- El tráfico aéreo será controlado por satélite.

⑤ LA CIENCIA Y LA TECNOLOGÍA

- Habrá clonaciones de animales extinguidos.
- Los embriones humanos se seleccionarán genéticamente.
- Todos los teléfonos móviles tendrán una computadora incorporada.
- Los pacientes serán tratados en sus casas mediante la telemedicina.

¿Qué dice usted?

② 15-4 Un futuro mejor. Primera fase. Comparen las ciudades de hoy con las del futuro basándose en las ilustraciones anteriores. Consideren por lo menos dos de los siguientes temas: uso de ciencia-tecnología, medio ambiente, transporte, calidad de vida, criminalidad, delincuencia, consumismo, salud.

Segunda fase. Ahora hablen sobre dos problemas específicos que existen en la ciudad del presente. Hagan una lista de dos aspectos de cada problema que les gustaría mejorar. Luego, compartan sus ideas con el resto de la clase.

MODELO: En la ciudad contemporánea hay poca seguridad física. Cualquier persona puede tener una arma y matar a quien quiera. Nos gustaría proponer una ley para limitar el uso de las armas de fuego.

G 15-5 Un mundo de tecnología. Piense en el impacto de la tecnología en su vida. Anote tres actividades diarias en las cuales usted usa una forma de telecomunicación o una computadora. Compare sus notas con las de sus compañeros/as. Según ustedes, ¿es optativo u obligatorio el uso de la tecnología hoy en día?

G 15-6 ¡El futuro es hoy! Primero, individualmente hagan una lista de cinco cosas que existen hoy y que no existían cuando sus padres tenían su edad. Luego, comparen su lista entre ustedes y expliquen el impacto y las consecuencias de estas nuevas cosas en sus vidas.

G 15-7 Los OVNIS (Objetos Voladores No Identificados). Imagínense que han visto una nave espacial de otro planeta. Describan todo lo que vieron, comentando las semejanzas y las diferencias entre ustedes y los vecinos desconocidos.

Suggestions for 15-4. Have students review comparatives before doing **Primera fase.** When doing **Segunda fase,** encourage them to express their concerns about current problems and to speculate about possible solutions.

Suggestion for 15-7. There are many opinions as to the existence of UFOs and life on other planets. What do students think? Have them debate the issue.

Nuevas fronteras

Una astronauta hispana

Ellen Ochoa es la primera mujer hispana astronauta. En 1990 fue seleccionada por la NASA y poco después cumplió su primera misión espacial. A bordo del *Discovery*, fue en 1999 a la estación espacial internacional para llevar equipo y repuestos.

Alcanzando las estrellas

Cuando tenía 9 años, Franklin Chang Díaz construyó su propia nave espacial usando una silla de la cocina y una caja de cartón. A los 15 años, diseñó un cohete mecánico y lo disparó hacia el cielo con un pobre ratoncito en la cabina, ¡y el ratón regresó a la tierra sano y salvo gracias a un paracaídas!

Más tarde Chang Díaz diseñó un motor de cohete para transportar a seres humanos al planeta Marte.

Originalmente de Costa Rica, Chang Díaz es el astronauta hispanoamericano más destacado de la NASA y el primer director latino del Laboratorio de Propulsión Avanzada de la NASA en Houston. En 1986, Chang Díaz llegó a ser el primer hispanoamericano que viajó en el transbordador espacial. En 1998 cumplió una misión en el *Discovery* y en el 2002 en el Endeavour.

¿Qué dice usted?

Warm-up for 15-8. Have students research current NASA information regarding the exploration of Mars. Encourage conversation related to our future in space—will we eventually live there?

❷ 15-8 ¿Vamos al planeta Marte? ¿Creen ustedes que, durante su vida, será posible viajar al planeta Marte? Planeen el viaje y expliquen con quiénes irán, qué llevarán, cuánto tiempo tardarán en llegar, qué verán allí y cómo se sentirán física y emocionalmente en este nuevo ambiente. Compartan su plan con otros "astronautas" para formular el mejor plan posible.

AUDIO 15-9 El problema de la alimentación. You will listen to a short talk about the problem of feeding the world population. Before you listen, list two problems you think the speaker will mention and two solutions you think she might provide.

_____

_____

First, read the following incomplete ideas; then, pay attention to the general idea of what is said. Mark the appropriate ending to each statement as you listen.

1. Los gobiernos tienen que solucionar este problema:
   _____ el atraso de la agricultura
   ___X___ la falta de alimentos para la población
   _____ las pocas variedades de productos

2. La tecnología y los científicos...
   ___X___ pueden ayudar a solucionar este problema
   _____ trabajan en las Islas Filipinas
   _____ desarrollan computadoras de mucha utilidad

3. Si se aumenta la producción del arroz, los gobiernos pueden...
   _____ exportarlo y ganar más dinero
   ___X___ alimentar a más personas
   _____ obtener variedades más nutritivas

4. Hay que aprovechar los avances de la tecnología, pero también es necesario...
   _____ aumentar la productividad en un 70 por ciento
   _____ conseguir alimentos básicos
   ___X___ cambiar los métodos de cultivo

Warm-up for 15-9. As a prelistening activity, have students work in groups of four and discuss the role of governments in the development of agriculture.

Audioscript for 15-9.
Uno de los problemas que tienen que resolver los gobiernos del mundo es el de la alimentación de sus pueblos. Este problema se hace mayor cuando se toma en consideración el crecimiento de la población. ¿Cómo se va a poder alimentar a una población que crece año tras año? La tecnología y los científicos que trabajan en diferentes centros de estudios en el mundo son los que pueden dar una respuesta.

Muchos de estos centros de estudio están en países del Tercer Mundo, que son los que se ven más afectados por el crecimiento de la población y la falta de alimentos. En las Islas Filipinas se encuentra el Instituto Internacional para la Investigación del Arroz, uno de los alimentos básicos en muchas regiones del planeta, especialmente en Asia.

Hoy en día, a través de la ingeniería genética, se han conseguido variedades de arroz que resultan mucho más productivas. Con ellas, la producción de arroz podría aumentar en un 70 por ciento y alimentar a un mayor número de personas. Los métodos de cultivo también tendrán que cambiar. Si se usan las mismas técnicas que se han usado a través de los siglos, la productividad sólo podrá aumentar en un 1 por ciento, más o menos. Con las nuevas técnicas, la producción podría aumentar en un 10 por ciento.

La ingeniería genética, unida a nuevos métodos de cultivo, puede ser la respuesta a los problemas que tenemos hoy y que tendremos que resolver en este siglo.

1. The imperfect subjunctive

In previous chapters, you studied the forms and uses of the present subjunctive. Now you will study the past subjunctive, which is also called the imperfect subjunctive. All regular and irregular past subjunctive verb forms are based on the **ustedes, ellos/as** form of the preterit. Drop the **-on** preterit ending and substitute the past subjunctive endings. The following chart will help you see how the past subjunctive is formed. Note the written accent on the **nosotros** forms.

VÍNCULOS

To practice the imperfect subjunctive
- SAM-OneKey: WB: 15-5, 15-6, 15-7 / LM: 15-26, 15-27, 15-28
- Companion Website: AP 15-2
- IRCD: Chapter 15; pg. 539

PAST OR IMPERFECT SUBJUNCTIVE				
	HABLAR (hablar~~on~~)	COMER (comier~~on~~)	VIVIR (vivier~~on~~)	ESTAR (estuvier~~on~~)
yo	hablara	comiera	viviera	estuviera
tú	hablaras	comieras	vivieras	estuvieras
Ud., él, ella	hablara	comiera	viviera	estuviera
nosotros/as	habláramos	comiéramos	viviéramos	estuviéramos
vosotros/as	hablarais	comierais	vivierais	estuvierais
Uds., ellos/as	hablaran	comieran	vivieran	estuvieran

Suggestions. You may wish to review the *Uds., ellos/as* forms of the preterit before introducing the past subjunctive. Do a quick question/answer activity: *¿Salieron Uds. anoche? ¿Adónde fueron? ¿Y qué hicieron allí?* Use related questions to simulate natural conversation and spontaneity. Remind students that they have used the imperfect subjunctive of *querer* for polite requests: *Quisiera comprar un regalo para una chica.*

- The present subjunctive is oriented to the present or future, whereas the past subjunctive focuses on the past. In general, the same rules that determine the use of the present subjunctive also apply to the past subjunctive.

  HOY → PRESENT SUBJUNCTIVE

  Los astronautas quieren que los trajes espaciales **sean** más ligeros.
  The astronauts want the spacesuits to be lighter.

  Van a cambiar los trajes espaciales para que **sean** más ligeros.
  They are going to change the spacesuits so they will be lighter.

  AYER → PAST SUBJUNCTIVE

  Los astronautas querían que los trajes espaciales **fueran** más ligeros.
  The astronauts wanted the spacesuits to be lighter.

  Cambiaron los trajes espaciales para que **fueran** más ligeros.
  They changed the space suits so they would be lighter.

- Use the past subjunctive after the expression **como si** (*as if, as though*). The verb in the main clause may be in the present or in the past.

  Gastan dinero en aparatos electrónicos **como si fueran** ricos.
  They spend money on electronic gadgets as though they were rich.

  Hablaba con el científico **como si entendiera** el problema.
  He talked with the scientist as if he understood the problem.

¿Qué dice usted?

2 15-10 Cuando era niño/a. Primera fase. Individualmente marquen con un círculo lo que sus padres querían o no querían que ustedes hicieran cuando eran niños/as. Después comparen sus respuestas.

1. Querían que comiera muchos vegetales y frutas.
2. Querían que estudiara ciencias.
3. No querían que viera programas violentos en la televisión.
4. Querían que cuidara el medio ambiente.
5. Querían que leyera sobre el programa espacial y los astronautas.
6. No querían que estuviera sin hacer nada.

Segunda fase. Ahora, individualmente marquen con un círculo lo que cada uno de ustedes quería que sus padres hicieran cuando ustedes eran niños. Luego, comparen sus respuestas. Añadan otra opción, si es necesario.

1. Para divertirme con la tecnología...
   a. yo quería que me llevaran a ver una nave espacial
   b. deseaba que me permitieran jugar videojuegos muchas horas

2. Para estar con mis amigos...
   a. yo quería que me llevaran al parque los fines de semana
   b. les pedía que me permitieran jugar en las casas de ellos

3. Para pasarlo bien los fines de semana...
   a. yo quería que me dieran más dinero
   b. insistía en que me permitieran tener fiestas en casa

4. Para celebrar mi cumpleaños...
   a. siempre quería que me regalaran juguetes electrónicos
   b. prefería que me compraran ropa

2 15-11 En el laboratorio. Pedro es muy inteligente, pero muy distraído. Hoy hizo unos experimentos con un científico en el laboratorio. ¿Qué le dijo el científico en estas situaciones? Túrnense para dar respuestas lógicas.

MODELO: Pedro no se puso los guantes para hacer el experimento.
          (El científico) Le dijo que se pusiera los guantes.

1. Llegó tarde al laboratorio.
2. Escuchaba música mientras hacía un experimento.
3. Dejó una botella de alcohol cerca de una estufa.
4. No esterilizó unos instrumentos.
5. Recibió una llamada en su celular.
6. La mesa donde Pedro trabajaba estaba muy desordenada.

2 15-12 Alguien que no nos cae bien. Primera fase. Imagínense que ustedes conocen a una persona arrogante que cree que es mejor que nadie. Digan cómo se comporta esta persona en cada uno de los siguientes aspectos. Pueden usar los verbos que aparecen más abajo u otros.

MODELO: hablar
          Habla como si fuera más inteligente que sus amigos.

| manejar | vivir | usar | gastar |
| discutir | cambiar | vestirse | caminar |

1. su dinero/sus finanzas
2. su estilo de vestir
3. sus conversaciones con otras personas
4. la manera en que maneja su automóvil

2 **Segunda fase.** Ahora respondan a las siguientes preguntas.

1. ¿Conoce usted a alguna persona que sea arrogante?
2. ¿Qué hábito o comportamiento de esa persona le molesta a usted? ¿Por qué?
3. ¿Le gustaría a usted que esta persona cambiara? Si es así, ¿qué costumbre o comportamiento le gustaría que cambiara?

G **15-13 Un tren de alta velocidad.** El mes pasado comenzó a prestar servicio un tren de alta velocidad que conecta diferentes ciudades en la zona donde usted vive. Hablen de la situación actual del tren y compárenla con la situación de antes. Compartan sus opiniones con las de otros grupos. ¿En qué está de acuerdo toda la clase?

SITUACIONES

Role A. You are very concerned about the pollution and deterioration of the environment and have therefore joined an ecological group that wants to improve the situation. Talk with your partner and explain: a) what the purpose of creating the group was, b) who the members of the group are, and c) what the group has accomplished up to this point. Answer your partner's questions and explain how you feel as a member of the group.

Role B. Your partner gives you information about an ecological group to which he/she belongs. After listening to him/her, ask questions to get more information (members' duties, meetings, etc.). Then: a) tell him/her that you are interested in joining, and b) find out the date and time of the next meeting.

2. *If*-clauses

■ Use the present or future indicative in the main clause and present indicative in the *if*-clause to express what happens or will happen if certain conditions are met.

> **Puedes** obtener información sobre el Amazonas si la **buscas** en Internet.
> *You can get information on the Amazon if you look for it on the Internet.*

> Los bosques van a desaparecer si **continuamos** cortando árboles.
> *Forests will disappear if we continue cutting down trees.*

> Si **cuidamos** los recursos naturales, las generaciones futuras **tendrán** una vida mejor.
> *If we take care of the natural resources, future generations will have a better life.*

■ Use the imperfect subjunctive in the *if*-clause to express a condition that is unlikely or contrary-to-fact. Use the conditional in the main clause.

> Si le **dieran** más dinero al aeropuerto, el tráfico aéreo **podría** mejorar.
> *If the airport were to get more money, air traffic could improve.*

> Si **usáramos** la energía solar en las casas, **ahorraríamos** mucho petróleo.
> *If we used solar energy in our homes, we would save a lot of oil.*

VÍNCULOS

To practice *if*-clauses
● SAM-OneKey: WB: 15-8, 15-9, 15-10 / LM: 15-29, 15-30
● Companion Website: AP 15-3

Suggestion. Provide a situation and say what you would do: *Si yo me ganara la lotería, compraría una casa más grande.* Give other examples. Then, ask questions to find out what students would do. Explain that the order of the clauses is often reversed: *Iría a España si me ganara la lotería.*

¿Qué dice usted?

Follow-up for 15-14. Students discuss some of these problems, provide other possible completions, and share them with the class.

② **15-14 El mundo que todos queremos.** Completen las ideas de la izquierda con una de las conclusiones de la derecha. En algunos casos, puede haber más de una respuesta lógica.

1. _b, e_ Si tuviéramos más disciplina en las escuelas,...
2. _e_ Si hubiera menos violencia en la televisión,...
3. _a, d_ Si cuidáramos más nuestro planeta,...
4. _c_ Tendríamos un mundo mejor...
5. _d_ Si hubiera trenes de alta velocidad...
6. _f_ Gastaríamos menos gasolina...

a. no contaminaríamos tanto el medio ambiente.
b. los alumnos aprenderían más.
c. si todos nos respetáramos más.
d. las personas manejarían menos en las carreteras.
e. habría menos problemas en la sociedad.
f. si usáramos el transporte público.

② **15-15 ¿Qué pasa si...?** Túrnense para decir qué resultados se pueden obtener si se hacen ciertas cosas.

MODELO: leer los periódicos
Si leen los periódicos regularmente, sabrán qué está pasando en el mundo.

1. aprender otra lengua
2. reciclar plásticos y papel
3. proteger los recursos naturales
4. decir que "no" a las drogas
5. comunicarse solamente por correo electrónico
6. construir estaciones espaciales

② **15-16 ¿Cómo sería el mundo?** Den sus razones para explicar cómo sería el mundo si se dieran las siguientes circunstancias. Después, compartan sus ideas con otros/as estudiantes.

1. si no hubiera televisión
2. si viviéramos 150 años
3. si la clonación fuera legal
4. si no hubiera fronteras entre los países
5. si pudiéramos viajar en autos supersónicos a todas partes
6. ...

Follow-up for 15-17. Get students' input to add another area to the activity. You may divide the class in small groups and assign an area to each group. After groups have reached some conclusions, they share them with the rest of the class.

Ⓖ **15-17 Cambios.** Digan qué harían ustedes en las siguientes áreas, si pudieran hacer cambios para mejorar las condiciones de vida en el país.

1. la falta de seguridad en las calles
2. las leyes de inmigración
3. la contaminación
4. los guetos (*ghettos*)
5. el fraude en Internet
6. ...

SITUACIONES

Your university has received a large sum of money to set up a recycling program on condition that students participate and organize parts of the program. Your partner and you would like to take part in this project. Talk in detail about: a) how you will participate in the project, b) what should be recycled and where, c) the staff needed and the costs, etc.

3. *Se* for unplanned occurrences

■ Use **se** + *indirect object* + *verb* to express unplanned or accidental events. This construction emphasizes the event in order to imply that no one is directly responsible.

Se **les apagaron** las luces. — *Their lights went out.*
A él **se le acabó** el dinero. — *He ran out of money.*
Se **nos olvidó** el número. — *We forgot the number.*
A los Álvarez se **les descompuso** la computadora. — *The Alvarez's computer broke down on them.*
Se **te rompió** la chaqueta. — *Your jacket got torn.*

■ Use an indirect object pronoun (**me, te, le, nos, os, les**) to indicate whom the unplanned or accidental event affects. Place the pronoun between **se** and the verb. If what is lost, forgotten, and so on, is plural, the verb also must be plural.

Se **me quedó** el dinero en el hotel. — *I left the money in the hotel.*
Se **me quedaron** los boletos en casa. — *I left the tickets at home.*

¿Qué dice usted?

② 15-18 ¿Qué les pasó? Complete lógicamente las oraciones de la columna de la izquierda, usando las oraciones de la columna de la derecha.

1. ___e___ Hablaron con el plomero porque
2. ___a___ Tuve que usar la tarjeta de crédito porque...
3. ___c___ No pude llamarte por el celular porque...
4. ___f___ Tuvieron que llamar al electricista porque...
5. ___b___ Llamamos al técnico porque
6. ___d___ Llegué tarde a casa de mi novia porque...

a. se me quedó el dinero en casa.
b. se nos descompuso la computadora.
c. se me olvidó tu nuevo número de teléfono.
d. se me perdió la llave del coche.
e. se les inundó el baño.
f. se les apagaron las luces en la casa.

15-19 Problemas. Usted trabaja en el laboratorio de ingeniería genética. Ayer hubo muchos problemas. Explique qué pasó usando las sugerencias entre paréntesis.

MODELO: El investigador no pudo completar el experimento.
(olvidarse la fórmula)
Se le olvidó la fórmula.

1. Los técnicos estaban preocupados. (romperse el microscopio)
2. El director no fue a trabajar. (enfermarse un hijo)
3. Los ayudantes llegaron tarde. (acabarse la gasolina)
4. La doctora Milán no pudo entrar en el laboratorio. (perderse las llaves)
5. El subdirector no recibió su correo electrónico. (descomponerse la computadora)
6. Un técnico estaba histérico. (perderse unos datos importantes)

Suggestions. Pretend to accidentally drop your keys, then deliberately drop them: *Se me cayeron las llaves./Dejé caer las llaves.*

Have one individual and a group drop, break, or tear one object, then several objects in order to demonstrate the difference between *Se le(s)* and *cayó/cayeron.* Ask, *¿Qué le(s) pasó?*

VÍNCULOS
To practice *se* for unplanned occurrences
• SAM-OneKey: WB: 15-11, 15-12, 15-13, 15-14 / LM:15-31, 15-32, 15-33
• Companion Website: AP 15-4
• IRCD: Chapters 15; pg. 544

Follow-up for 15-18. Show visuals and ask *¿Qué le(s) pasó?* Visuals may show someone with a broken leg, a baseball catcher missing the ball, a groom who forgot the ring. Be imaginative!

Answers for 15-19. 1. *se les rompió*, 2. *se le enfermó*, 3. *se les acabó*, 4. *se le perdieron*, 5. *se le descompuso*, 6. *se le perdieron*

2 **15-20 ¿Qué pasó?** Túrnense para describir lo que ven en los dibujos y después digan qué les pasó a las personas.

MODELO: María no se sentía bien y decidió llamar al médico. Cuando encontró un teléfono público para llamarlo, se le olvidó el número.

a.

b.

c.

SITUACIONES

Role A. You are driving through a school zone and a police officer stops you and asks you several questions because he/she suspects you are driving over the speed limit. Answer the police officer's questions and explain that you do not have your license with you. Try to convince him/her that you are a good driver and that you do not go over the speed limit.

Role B. You are a police officer. It is the end of the school day, and you are making sure that drivers are respecting the speed limit in the school zone while the children come out. You decided to stop a driver who seemed to be driving over the speed limit. To confirm your suspicions, do the following: a) ask him/her what speed must be maintained in a school zone, b) at what speed he/she was driving, and c) ask to see his/her driving license. Finally tell him/her that it is illegal to drive without a license and that you are going to give him/her a fine.

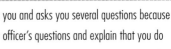

MOSAICOS

 Escuchar

VÍNCULOS

For materials related to the Mosaicos section, see
- SAM-OneKey: WB: 15-15, 15-16, 15-17, 15-18, 15-19, 15-20 / LM: 15-34
- IRCD: Chapter 15; pp. 547, 550

Identifying main idea, specific information, and the speaker's intention

In your daily interactions with others, you do more than simply listen to recognize main ideas, recall information, or identify the speaker's intention. You need to process (analyze, decipher, decode, discriminate, etc.) information on the spot.

In the following listening tasks, you will have to identify and write in Spanish the speaker's intention. You may do it as follows:

- *X quiere que Y* + subjunctive (Pablo quiere que sus padres le den dinero.)

- *X quiere* + infinitive (Pablo quiere conseguir dinero de sus padres.)

- *Que le den dinero* (elliptical version of *Pablo quiere que...*)

Antes de escuchar

15-22 ¿Qué les pasó? In **15-23**, you will listen to Ignacio and Lidia talking about the problems they have had today. Before you listen, write down three things that may go wrong when you are in a hurry.

_____

_____

A escuchar

15-23 First read the statements below and then listen to Ignacio, Lidia, and Agustín. As you listen, mark the statements that reflect the main problem each of them had and the specific details supporting your choice. Finally, write each speaker's intention for sharing this information.

1. Ignacio
   Problema principal: a. No se pudo bañar ni cambiar de ropa.
   　　　　　　　　　　　　ⓑ Llegó tarde a la cita con su novia.
   Detalles:　　　　　　　a. Fue a sus clases en la universidad.
   　　　　　　　　　　　　ⓑ Se le perdió la llave de su casa.
   Intención:　　　　　　　*Desea que su novia lo perdone.*

2. Lidia
   Problema principal:　ⓐ Su auto no funciona.
   　　　　　　　　　　　　b. No tiene mucho dinero.
   Detalles:　　　　　　　a. El mecánico le va a cobrar mucho dinero.
   　　　　　　　　　　　　ⓑ Oyó un ruido raro.
   Intención:　　　　　　　*Quiere que su madre le dé dinero.*

Warm-up for 15-23. As a prelistening activity, have students work in groups of four and discuss what happened to them last weekend that ruined or might have ruined their plans.

Audioscript for 15-23. 1. IGNACIO: Mira, Mariela, yo quería llegar a tiempo a nuestra cita pero tuve muchos problemas. Después de mis clases fui a mi casa para bañarme y cambiarme de ropa, pero cuando busqué mi llave para abrir la puerta, me di cuenta de que no la tenía. La había dejado en la universidad. Tuve que regresar a la universidad a buscarla. Te ruego que me disculpes, no fue mi intención, yo te quiero mucho. 2. LIDIA: Mamá, estoy preocupadísima. Esta mañana salí en el auto, pero después de manejar unos minutos, noté un ruido raro y vi que el motor estaba caliente. De repente el auto dejó de funcionar y me tuve que ir a trabajar en taxi. Ahora necesito que alguien me lleve a recoger el carro. ¡Ay, Dios mío! ¿Cómo le voy a pagar al mecánico si no tengo dinero?

Después de escuchar

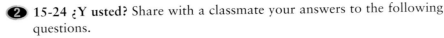

15-24 ¿Y usted? Share with a classmate your answers to the following questions.

1. ¿Cómo ha pasado el día de hoy? ¿Ha tenido algún problema?
2. ¿A quién llama usted generalmente cuando tiene un problema? ¿Por qué?
3. ¿Qué haría usted si tuviera los problemas que tuvieron Ignacio y Lidia?

Antes de escuchar

AUDIO **15-25 Avances en la medicina.** In **15-26** you will listen to a presentation about technology and medicine and what is expected to happen in the future. Before you listen, write down a list of two technological or medical advances you are aware of and how they help patients.

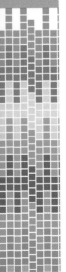

Warm-up for 15-26. As a prelistening activity, have students work in groups of four and discuss what they know about the use of computers and technology in medicine.

Audioscript for 15-26. La tecnología se usa cada día más para tratar a los enfermos y a las personas que han sufrido accidentes.

El médico norteamericano Paul Soll implantó el primer marcapasos, un pequeño generador electrónico que regula los latidos del corazón, en 1952. Desde entonces, el marcapasos ha salvado de la muerte a infinidad de enfermos del corazón y los adelantos en los implantes continúan multiplicándose.

Otro adelanto es un implante, mejor dicho una microcomputadora, que se coloca en el oído interno. Con este implante, los sordos pueden oír, pero los sonidos que reciben son diferentes, como si se tratara de una lengua extranjera. Pronto los sordos podrán escuchar los sonidos exactamente como se producen.

En la actualidad se están haciendo investigaciones en diferentes áreas; por ejemplo, se están haciendo grandes esfuerzos para crear un implante que funcione como un ojo artificial para que los ciegos puedan ver. También se está trabajando en la posibilidad de diseñar implantes que envíen corrientes eléctricas a los músculos para que los parapléjicos puedan caminar.

A escuchar

15-26. First read the statements below and then listen to the presentation. As you listen, mark the statements that reflect the main idea, the specific details supporting the main idea, and each speaker's intention for sharing this information.

1. El marcapasos...
   a. se usa para ayudar a los corredores
   b. les ha salvado la vida a muchas personas

   Detalles: a. Regula los latidos del corazón de los pacientes
             b. Se inventó hace 10 años
   Intención: _____ informar al público. _____

2. Con el implante en el oído...
   a. los sonidos suenan como una lengua extranjera
   b. los sordos pueden oír muy pocos sonidos

   Detalles: a. El aparato se coloca en el oído interno
             b. El aparato aumenta el volumen de los sonidos
   Intención: _____ informar al público. _____

3. En la actualidad se están haciendo...
   a. máquinas eléctricas que ayudan a los enfermos.
   b. implantes para ayudar a los ciegos y a los parapléjicos.

   Detalles: Uno de los avances...
             a. es como un ojo artificial.
             b. es un músculo artificial.
   Intención: _____ informar al público. _____

Después de escuchar

15-27 ¿Y usted? With a classmate, share your answers to the following questions.

1. Según usted, ¿de qué otra forma la tecnología puede ayudar a la medicina?
2. ¿Conoce usted a alguien que se haya beneficiado de la tecnología en el tratamiento de su salud?
3. ¿En qué otras áreas, además de la medicina, puede ayudar la tecnología? Explique.

Conversar

Antes de conversar

15-28 Anécdotas. Primera fase. Lea las siguientes anécdotas que les ocurrieron a dos celebridades y luego, siga las instrucciones.

> Hace unos años, cuando comenzaba mi carrera, invité a comer a una amiga un sábado por la noche. Recuerdo que fuimos a un restaurante francés muy elegante y caro de San Francisco, donde yo vivía entonces. Después de que habíamos comido y bebido el mejor champán, me trajeron la cuenta. Llevé la mano al bolsillo de mi chaqueta y, con horror, me di cuenta de que se me había olvidado la billetera en casa. Llamé al camarero y le expliqué la situación. Incluso le dije quién era. Con una mirada y tono irónicos el camarero me dijo: Si usted es..., yo soy Brad Pitt. Por favor, no me cuente historias.

> Lo recuerdo como si fuera hoy. Una tarde de invierno, mi esposo y yo decidimos ir de incógnito a Manhattan. Nos pusimos los vaqueros, tomamos nuestros abrigos y salimos. Íbamos a pasar unas horas comprando en las tiendas chinas, y luego íbamos a ver una película. Después de manejar y conversar animadamente unos 20 minutos por las carreteras, se nos descompuso el Ferrari. ¡Qué horrible! Tanto mi esposo como yo nos bajamos del carro para ver qué había pasado. Aparentemente no había ningún problema mecánico en el coche. Volvimos al carro y, de repente, mi esposo se dio cuenta de que se nos había descompuesto el marcador de gasolina y que se nos había olvidado llenar el tanque. Como estábamos bloqueando una ruta muy transitada, llegó la policía y nos preguntó qué nos había ocurrido. Le contamos la historia, pero no nos creyó y nos puso una multa.

Segunda fase. Ahora piense en una experiencia semejante —trágica, cómica, tragicómica— a los relatos de la **Primera fase.** Tome nota de los siguientes detalles para compartir con un/a compañero/a.

- Quién(es) estaba(n) presente(s) en la situación.
- Cuándo y dónde ocurrió. Escriba algunas palabras (adjetivos, verbos, adverbios) que describan el escenario.
- Qué ocurrió, qué hicieron y cómo reaccionaron usted y la(s) otra(s) persona(s).
- Cómo terminó la situación.

En el recuadro en la proxima página, hay algunas ideas que pueden ayudar.

Se le quedó algo importante en un lugar que ya había cerrado.
Se le olvidó algo importante en un lugar público o inapropiado.
Se le rompió algo de mucho valor: una joya, un jarrón de cristal, un espejo fino...
Al regresar de un viaje, ve que se le quedó algo indispensable en el hotel.
Se lo/la quedó la tarea en la casa de sus padres, a 400 millas de la universidad.

A conversar

G **15-29 Increíble!** Compartan la experiencia para la que se prepararon en la actividad **15-28**. Cada miembro del grupo debe reaccionar mientras escucha el relato de los otros y hacer preguntas. Finalmente, el grupo debe elegir la experiencia que les pareció mas interesante.

Después de conversar

G **15-30 La anécdota más increíble de todas.** Un miembro de cada grupo de la actividad anterior debe compartir con la clase la anécdota más increíble de su grupo. Al final, la clase entera votará por la anécdota más increíble de todas. Finalmente, la persona que tuvo esta experiencia responderá a las preguntas o reaccionará a los comentarios de sus compañeros/as.

Alternate for 15-30. You may want to ask that each group share their most incredible anecdote with the rest of the class in writing via e-mail. Every student in the class should read everyone else's anecdote and send their vote to you by e-mail.

Antes de conversar

2 **15-31 La tecnología en la rutina diaria.** Hagan una lista de algunos usos de la tecnología que son imprescindibles en la vida diaria, en las siguientes áreas. Pueden añadir otra área, si es necesario.

ESTUDIOS	CASA	TRABAJO	TRANSPORTE	SALUD	RELACIONES INTERPERSONALES	¿OTRA?

Suggestion for 15-32. Remind students if necessary that each member of the group should take notes of his/her group's conclusions to be able to share them later with the rest of the class.

A conversar

G **15-32 ¿Es la tecnología una ayuda o una limitación?** Comparen las listas que prepararon en **15-31** y, luego hagan lo siguiente.

1. Escojan los dos aparatos tecnológicos más imprescindibles en cada área.
2. Comenten **una** manera en que el uso de estos aparatos los/las ha afectado positiva o negativamente en cada una de las áreas indicadas en **15-31**.
3. Prepárense para compartir sus conclusiones con la clase. Tomen apuntes.

MODELO: E1: Yo no podría vivir sin café; por eso, la cafetera es imprescindible en mi casa. Definitivamente la invención de la cafetera me ha afectado positivamente.

E2: Yo tampoco podría vivir sin tomar café. Así que estoy de acuerdo contigo. *o* Yo no estoy de acuerdo. Me parece que la cafetera ha afectado negativamente nuestra salud.

E3: Yo también. Bueno, entonces todos pensamos que la invención de la cafetera ha sido positiva para nosotros. *o* Bueno, entonces parece que hay una minoría en nuestro grupo que piensa que la cafetera no nos ha beneficiado.

Después de conversar

G **15-33 Conclusiones.** Ahora compartan con la clase las conclusiones a las que llegaron en la actividad **15-32.** Justifiquen su posición.

 *Leer*

Identifying the perspective of the story and recognizing affixes

A narrative is told by a narrator from one of two perspectives: that of a protagonist (someone who tells his/her own experiences: I, we) or that of a witness (someone who tells what he/she sees or witnesses: he, she, they). Therefore, to identify the perspective of a story, the following questions will help you: Who witnesses the event? Who is speaking? Who is responding?

Guía de prelectura

Look at the picture and the title of the story in activities **15-35** and **15-36**, and answer these questions, using your knowledge of the world and of technology.

1. Anticipate the content of the story by its title. What ideas or concepts do you associate with the word "apocalypse"? Circle all that apply, in your view.
   a. birth
   b. death
   c. destruction
   d. life

2. What may be the central idea of this story? Circle all that may apply, in your opinion.
   a. A scientist uses technology to destroy himself.
   b. Human beings use technology to make their lives easier.
   c. There are two sides to the use of technology: one constructive, another destructive.

3. How did you guess the answers to questions 1 and 2?
   a. what I have read about the topic
   b. personal view of the topic
   c. what experts think of the topic
   d. the visual material used

4. Now, skim the text on page 550 and find at least two words that support your answers to questions 1 and 2. extinción/desapareciendo/reducido/se extinguieron.

Antes de leer

2 **15-34. Preparación.** De la siguiente lista, marquen con un círculo las máquinas, aparatos o servicios que ustedes esperarían encontrar en una sociedad donde se usa una tecnología avanzada. Luego, compartan sus respuestas con la clase.

1. teléfonos inalámbricos
2. automóviles voladores
3. relojes digitales
4. servicio postal automatizado
5. computadoras compactas
6. impresoras electrónicas
7. aviones sin pilotos
8. luces activadas por la voz humana

LENGUA

Hay numerosas expresiones con **se** que forman parte del lenguaje diario de las personas de habla hispana.

Lea las siguientes expresiones y piense en qué situaciones se podrían usar.
- Se me pone la piel de gallina (*goosebumps*).
- Se me fue el alma a los pies (*heart sank*).
- Se me va la lengua (*gave myself away*).
- Se me congela la pantalla (*freezes on me*).

Answers for Guía de prelectura, number 3: d, but you may accept any well-supported answer.

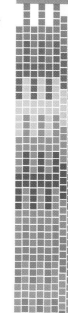

2 **15-35 ¿Qué ven ustedes?** Contesten las siguientes preguntas, basándose en el dibujo.

a. ¿Qué tipo de lugar es éste?
b. ¿Hay algún aparato en el dibujo que pueda hacer el trabajo mejor que un ser humano? ¿Cuál?
c. ¿Cómo se imaginan ustedes la vida del profesional que aparece en el dibujo: su rutina diaria, sus intereses, sus pasatiempos, sus relaciones interpersonales, etc.?

Note for 15-36. New words: *alfileres, décuplo, ademán, tropezarse*

Suggestion for 15-36. Point out the use of *hombres* as "human beings." Explain that currently *seres humanos* is more widely used. As a warm-up activity, you may wish to divide the class into groups of four and have them list five elements they associate with modern life. You may guide them by saying: *El teléfono es un aparato que yo asocio con la vida moderna.* Before reading, explain to students that *quedase means quedara,* and *aumentase means aumentara.*

A leer

15-36 Primera mirada. Lea el siguiente microcuento escrito por Marco Denevi, un conocido escritor argentino, y luego siga las instrucciones.

Apocalipsis I

La extinción de la raza de los hombres se sitúa aproximadamente a fines del siglo XXXI. La cosa sucedió así: las máquinas habían alcanzado tal perfección que los hombres no necesitaban comer, ni dormir, ni leer, ni escribir, ni siquiera pensar. Les bastaba apretar botones y las máquinas lo hacían todo por ellos.

Gradualmente fueron desapareciendo las mesas, los teléfonos, los Leonardo da Vinci, las rosas de té, las tiendas de antigüedades, los discos con las nueve sinfonías de Beethoven, el vino de Burdeos[1], las golondrinas, los cuadros de Salvador Dalí[2], los relojes, los sellos postales, los alfileres[3], el Museo del Prado, la sopa de cebolla, los transatlánticos, las pirámides de Egipto, las Obras Completas de don Benito Pérez Galdós.[4] Sólo había máquinas.

Después los hombres empezaron a notar que ellos mismos iban desapareciendo paulatinamente[5] y que en cambio las máquinas se multiplicaban. Bastó poco tiempo para que el número de los hombres quedase reducido a la mitad y el de las máquinas aumentase al doble y luego al décuplo.[6] Las máquinas terminaron por ocupar todo el espacio disponible. Nadie podía dar un paso, hacer un simple ademán[7] sin tropezarse[8] con una de ellas. Finalmente los hombres se extinguieron.

Como el último se olvidó de desconectar las máquinas, desde entonces seguimos funcionando.

---

[1]región de Francia famosa por sus vinos   [2]famoso pintor y diseñador español conocido por su estilo surrealista y su excentricidad   [3]*pins*
[4]famoso novelista español (1843–1920)   [5]*gradualmente*   [6]*tenfold*   [7]*gesture*   [8]*stumble*

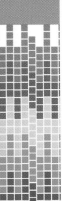

Marque con un círculo la información relacionada con la perspectiva del narrador.

1. _____ El narrador de la historia es un científico que vive la experiencia.
2. _____ No se puede saber quién es el narrador porque no hay diálogo entre las máquinas.
3. __X__ Quien vive la experiencia es quien la relata.

Marque con una X la información relacionada con el narrador.

4. __X__ Al fin de la historia descubrimos quién es el narrador.
5. __X__ El narrador habla desde la perspectiva del tiempo futuro.
6. _____ El protagonista de la historia es un ser humano.
7. __X__ El narrador es una máquina.

Marque con una *X* la información relacionada con la trama de esta historia.

8. ___X___ Según el narrador, las máquinas evolucionaron tanto que lograron alcanzar la perfección del ser humano.

9. _____ El ser humano, según el narrador, se dio cuenta de que las máquinas lo estaban controlando, y las destruyó.

10. ___X___ Al fin de la historia, la mayor parte del espacio lo ocupaban las máquinas porque había menos seres humanos.

Después de leer

15-37 Ampliación. Busque en el texto el antónimo de las siguientes palabras y escríbalo en los espacios en blanco. Cuando sea necesario, agregue uno de los siguientes prefijos para formar el antónimo: **in-, im-, des-**.

1. aparecer   desaparecer

2. completas   incompletas

3. empezar   terminar

4. aumentar   reducir/disminuir

5. perfección   imperfección

6. conectar   desconectar

Escribir

In works of fiction there seems to be no limits as to how events and characters are represented. In fact anything may happen or become a reality in the writer's eyes. Therefore, through fantasy, characters' behaviors and views are exaggerated to impact the reader. In that sense, history may also be also considered fiction when courageous, extraordinary actions turn individuals into heroes.

In general, fiction is one way of presenting reality. It represents the dreams of human beings. Fiction is like daydreaming. It helps us deal with our present and speculate about our future.

Antes de escribir

15-38 Preparación. Imagínese que usted es una de las máquinas que quedaron funcionando después de la desaparición de los seres humanos. Usted siente que su existencia ha cambiado desde que ellos se extinguieron. Prepárese para escribir sobre el pasado y el futuro de las computadoras en "Apocalipsis I."

1. Escriba algunas ideas que describan la existencia de las máquinas después de la desaparición del ser humano: ¿Es su vida actual (rutina, costumbres, creencias, etc.) semejante o diferente a la del pasado? ¿Qué hacían las computadoras antes que ya no hacen hoy o viceversa?

2. Indique dos actividades o condiciones que usted extraña (*miss*) cuando piensa en su vida con los seres humanos:

   a. la interacción diaria

   MODELO: Si pudiéramos escuchar las divertidas conversaciones de los seres humanos, no nos sentiríamos tan solas.

   b. el trabajo cotidiano

   MODELO: Si los seres humanos vivieran, no tendríamos que hacer todo el trabajo sin su ayuda.

3. Mencione tres errores cometidos por el ser humano que, según usted, tuvieron relación directa con su desaparición y explique por qué.

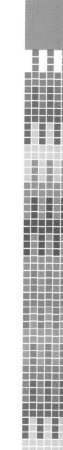

A escribir

15-39 Manos a la obra. Ahora, en el papel de una de las máquinas que sobrevivió la desaparición del ser humano, escriba un cibertexto. Use la información que preparó en **15-38** para hacer lo siguiente:

- Describa su existencia antes y después de la desaparición de los seres humanos.

- Indique las cosas que usted extraña con nostalgia de su interacción diaria y su trabajo cotidiano con los humanos.

- Especule sobre algunos errores que, según usted, provocaron la extinción de la raza humana.

Después de escribir

15-40 Revisión. Lea su cibertexto. Recuerde que éste va a ser leído por otras máquinas de inteligencia superior a la humana que no toleran errores ni imprecisiones de ningún tipo.

- El contenido. En su cibertexto, ¿usó ideas originales e interesantes? ¿Resaltó las características positivas y/o negativas del ser humano? ¿Fluyen las ideas?

- La organización. ¿Hay un orden lógico y claro en la presentación de las ideas?

- La forma de su cibertexto.

   a. La gramática. ¿Usó vocabulario apropiado al tema y expresiones de cohesión? ¿Revisó la concordancia, el tiempo (presente, pasado, futuro, condicional) y los modos (indicativo, subjuntivo)?
   b. La puntuación y ortografía. ¿Utilizó las comas, puntos, etc. necesarios?

Finalmente, comparta su cibertexto con su compañero/a editor.

ENFOQUE CULTURAL

TEMAS: LA ECONOMÍA, LA INDUSTRIA Y LA TECNOLOGÍA EN LOS PAÍSES HISPANOS

Para pensar

¿Cuáles son algunas de las industrias más importantes en los Estados Unidos? ¿Qué avances tecnológicos se han llevado a cabo en los últimos años? ¿Cómo han influido estos avances en la vida diaria de los ciudadanos? ¿Sabe usted qué industrias se han desarrollado más en los países hispanos en las últimas décadas?

Todos los países hispanos están haciendo grandes avances industriales y tecnológicos.

Existe una serie de acuerdos entre los diferentes países para integrar sus economías y eliminar las barreras de exportación. En América del Sur están, entre otros, el Grupo de los Tres, formado por México, Venezuela y Colombia; y el Mercado Común del Cono Sur, integrado por Argentina, Brasil, Paraguay y Uruguay. Además existe el Tratado de Libre Comercio, formado por México, Canadá y los Estados Unidos, al cual se ha incorporado Chile.

Venezuela y México han desarrollado su industria petrolera y mineral. España ha mantenido y modernizado algunas de sus industrias tradicionales, como la textil, la siderúrgica, la química y la automotriz. También ha desarrollado otras, como la industria de la cerámica, el calzado, etc.

América Central ha empezado últimamente un movimiento hacia el desarrollo industrial y se han establecido fábricas que producen pintura, detergentes, fertilizantes e insecticidas. Al mismo tiempo, muchas multinacionales se han instalado en América Central para aprovechar una mano de obra más barata que la de los países desarrollados.

La economía del Perú está sólidamente basada en la agricultura, minería y pesca. Los principales productos agrícolas son la papa, la caña de azúcar, el maíz, el café y el trigo (wheat). En cuanto a la minería, el Perú es uno de los más grandes productores mundiales de cobre, plata y zinc.

Bolivia es el primer productor mundial de aluminio, pero también produce zinc, plomo, plata y estaño, entre otros minerales. Como otros países hispanos, Bolivia también ha desarrollado la industria del procesamiento de alimentos, la del tabaco y la artesanal.

Chile tiene una gran industria agrícola y minera, además de su fuerte industria pesquera. Entre los principales productos agrícolas se encuentran las frutas y los excelentes vinos chilenos. Chile es uno de los más grandes productores mundiales de cobre y el mayor productor de acero en América del Sur.

Argentina y Uruguay son mundialmente famosos por su industria agrícola y ganadera. Su industria manufacturera y minera también están creciendo. En Uruguay, por ejemplo, se manufacturan productos de lana, algodón y rayón. Paraguay es un país principalmente agrícola y su industria manufacturera está íntimamente ligada a los productos agrícolas, como por ejemplo productos de madera, alimenticios y químicos.

Para contestar

2 **Las industrias del mundo hispano.** Respondan a lo siguiente.

1. Mencionen algunas asociaciones de comercio internacional que han formado los países hispanos. ¿Qué ventajas tiene, en la opinión de ustedes, pertenecer a estos organismos?
2. ¿Qué países hispanos tienen una fuerte industria agrícola? ¿Cuáles son algunos de sus productos?

G **Riqueza cultural.** En grupos de tres, discutan las ventajas y desventajas de tener una economía basada en la agricultura. Luego, presenten sus conclusiones a la clase.

Para investigar en Internet

Busque información acerca de oportunidades comerciales en los países hispanos. Traiga la información a la clase y comente con sus compañeros/as las ventajas o desventajas de esas oportunidades para los países hispanos y para los países que tienen fuertes relaciones comerciales con los países hispanos. Defienda sus opiniones.

VÍNCULOS

For materials related to the Enfoque cultural, see
• SAM-OneKey: WB: 15-21

¡Prepárese!

(G) **15-41 ¿Quién ganó?** Antes de saber quién ganó *Fortunas* —Efraín, Katie, Carlos o Sabrina— traten de adivinar quién fue el/la ganador/a. Después comparen sus opiniones con el resto de la clase. Luego miren el Episodio 15 para ver cuál fue el resultado.

Todos esperan con mucha anticipación saber el resultado final.

Carlos lee los resultados primero, antes que los demás.

Efraín y Sabrina están muy impacientes por saber quién ganó.

¡Ganó Katie!

Katie siente verdadero amor por Carlos.

Katie está contenta no sólo por ganar *Fortunas*, sino porque también ganó en el amor.

¡Responda!

15-42 Los resultados. ¿Cuántos de ustedes adivinaron correctamente? En su opinión, ¿por qué ganó Katie?

15-43 En conclusión. Ahora que ha terminado el concurso y que usted ha podido participar como parte del público, conteste las siguientes preguntas para expresar su opinión sobre *Fortunas*.

1. ¿Lo/La sorprendió que Katie ganara el concurso? ¿Por qué?
2. De los cuatro participantes, ¿a quién le gustaría tener como amigo/a? ¿Por qué?
3. ¿Es bueno formar alianzas en un concurso de este tipo, o es mejor trabajar solo/a?
4. Si tuviera la oportunidad de participar en un concurso como *Fortunas*, ¿lo haría? ¿Por qué?
5. Si estuviera encargado/a del concurso, ¿qué cambiaría y por qué?

NOTAS: "HACIENDO TIEMPO", MILLO TORRES Y EL TERCER PLANETA

En la *Lección 15,* usted leyó sobre algunos científicos a quienes les interesa la ciencia y la tecnología. Pero también existen artistas, como Millo Torres y su grupo musical El Tercer Planeta que se dedican a explorar el presente y el futuro a través de la música. Al mezclar ritmos caribeños con el reggae y el ska, ellos han logrado un sonido moderno y atractivo.

¡Prepárese!

Answers for 15-44. tiempo, años, días, vida, mañana, ahora, anoche

Haciendo tiempo in this context means "doing time in jail."

15-44 El tiempo. Lea la letra de "Haciendo tiempo" e identifique las palabras que se refieren al tiempo: al tiempo en general, al presente, al pasado y al futuro.

Haciendo tiempo

Me siento en silencio y meditación
buscando salida a esta situación
y como cuesta trabajo tomar decisión
yo sigo haciendo tiempo en esta prisión.

Pasaron los años, los días dirán
si el latir de mi vida se arrepentirá.
Me habré enloquecido o quizás me perdí
pero mañana ya es tarde y ahora vivo sin ti.

Me quedo en la cama recostado del tiempo
si es que la herida sana o se lastima por dentro
si estaba dormido, lo que anoche soñé
pesadilla que yo siento, porque no desperté.
Me asomo a la puerta, se escucha una voz,
el aullido del viento ya me confesó,
busca en los rincones de tu corazón
escondido tras la espera está la solución.

¡Escuche!

15-45 ¿Qué haría usted? El autor dice que está "haciendo tiempo en esta prisión". Mientras escucha la canción, haga una lista de situaciones en las cuales usted se ha sentido como el compositor de la canción. Después, use el imperfecto del subjuntivo para indicar lo que haría en cada situación si las circunstancias fueran diferentes.

MODELO: Situación: el trabajo / Si no necesitara el dinero, no trabajaría.

¡Responda!

15-46 Expresiones. A continuación hay expresiones sobre el tema del tiempo en las que donde se emplea **se + complemento indirecto + verbo,** una estructura presentada en esta lección. Indique lo que significan en inglés.

1. __a__ Se me voló el tiempo.
2. __d__ Se le hizo corto el tiempo.
3. __c__ Se les volaron los años.
4. __b__ Se nos acabó el tiempo.

a. *The time flew.*
b. *Time ran out.*
c. *The years flew by.*
d. *Time was short.*

VOCABULARIO

El universo

la biosfera	*biosphere*
el cielo	*sky*
el planeta	*planet*

El mundo

el bosque tropical	*rain forest*
la conservación	*preservation*
la cuenca	*river basin*
la deforestación	*deforestation*
el medio ambiente	*environment*
la pérdida	*loss*
los recursos	*resources*
la reserva	*reserve*
la selva	*jungle*
la tierra	*land, soil*
la vida	*life*

Comunicaciones electrónicas

el correo electrónico	*e-mail*
el ratón	*mouse*

Viajes espaciales

el cohete	*rocket*
la nave espacial	*space ship*
el paracaídas	*parachute*
el transbordador espacial	*space shuttle*

Personas

el/la astronauta	*astronaut*
el/la campesino/a	*peasant*
el ser humano	*human being*

Descripciones

destacado/a	*outstanding, distinguished*
dispuesto/a	*ready*
liberado/a	*released*
portátil	*portable*

Verbos

amenazar (c)	*to threaten, to menace*
apagar	*to turn off the lights*
construir (y)	*to build*
descomponer	*to break down*
diseñar	*to design*
manejar	*to manage, to handle*
olvidar	*to forget*
romper	*to tear*

Palabras y expresiones útiles

(de) cartón	*cardboard*
debido a	*due to*
en busca de	*in search of*
sano/a y salvo/a	*safe and sound*

EXPANSIÓN GRAMATICAL

This special grammatical supplement includes structures considered optional for the introductory level by instructors emphasizing proficiency, except for the *vosotros* command forms. The *vosotros* forms are included in this section for the instructors who use them to address their students. The other functions and structures presented here are normally beyond the level of performance of first-year students, therefore most instructors would present them for recognition only.

The explanation and activities in this section use the same format as grammatical material throughout *Mosaicos* in order to facilitate their incorporation into the core lessons of the program or their addition as another chapter in the book.

Objetivos comunicativos

Giving informal orders or commands to two or more people (in Spain)
Expressing an indirect wish so that a third party do something
Suggesting that someone and the speaker do something
Reacting to a past occurrence or event
Hypothesizing about an occurrence or event in the past
Expressing contrary-to-fact conditions in the past
Emphasizing a fact resulting from the action of someone or something

Estructuras

■ *Vosotros* commands

■ Indirect commands

■ The Spanish equivalents of English *let's*

■ The present perfect subjunctive

■ The conditional perfect and the pluperfect subjunctive

■ *If*-clauses (using the perfect tense)

■ The passive voice

1. Vosotros commands

	AFFIRMATIVE	NEGATIVE
hablar	hablad	no habléis
comer	comed	no comáis
escribir	escribid	no escribáis

- To use the affirmative **vosotros** command, change the final **-r** of the infinitive to **-d**.

- Use the **vosotros** form of the present subjunctive for the **vosotros** negative command.

- For the affirmative **vosotros** command of reflexive verbs, drop the final **-d** and add the pronoun **os**: **levantad + os = levantaos.** The verb **irse** is an exception: **idos.**

¿Qué dice usted?

EG-1 Buenos consejos. Usted quiere que sus mejores amigos cambien sus hábitos y vivan una vida más sana. Dígales qué deben hacer.

MODELO: caminar dos kilómetros todos los días
           Caminad dos kilómetros todos los días.

1. comer muchas frutas y vegetales
2. empezar un programa de ejercicios
3. no respirar por la boca
4. no cansarse mucho los primeros días
5. relajarse para evitar el estrés
6. dormir no menos de ocho horas

G **EG-2 Órdenes en grupo.** Cada uno/a de ustedes va a hacer el papel de profesor/a de educación física y le va a dar una orden a los otros estudiantes del grupo. Los estudiantes deben hacer lo que el/la profesor/a les indica.

MODELO: *Levantad los brazos y las piernas.*

SITUACIONES

You and your partner have rented a cabin in the mountains for a month. Some of your friends are going to use the cabin part of the time and you would like to give them some rules to make sure they leave everything in order. Write the rules and then compare them with those of another couple.

2. Indirect commands

You have used commands directly to tell others to do something: **Salga/Salgan ahora.** Now you are going to use indirect commands to say what someone else should do: **Que salga Berta.** Note that this indirect command is equivalent to saying **Quiero que Berta salga,** but without expressing the main verb **quiero.**

- The word **que** introduces the indirect command. The subject, if stated, normally follows the verb.

     Que cocine Roberto.   *Let Roberto cook.*
     Que descanse María.   *Let María rest.*

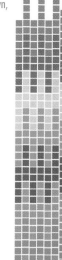

Suggestion. Mention several chores that have to be done: *Hay que limpiar el garaje. También hay que lavar las copas*. Then, assign the chores to various students, using indirect commands; *Que lo limpie Amanda. Que las lave Agustín.*

■ Reflexive and object pronouns always precede the verb.

Que **se siente** a la mesa.	*Let him sit at the table.*
Que **le sirvan** la cena.	*Let them serve him dinner.*
Que **se la sirvan** ahora.	*Let them serve it to him now.*

Suggestion for EG-3. Each student should cover one of the lists.

❷ EG-3 Una clase de cocina. Un chef muy conocido ha accedido a dar una clase de cocina con el fin de recaudar (*raise*) dinero para una obra social. Usted y su compañero/a forman parte del comité que organiza la clase. Su compañero/a tiene la lista de las personas que desean ayudar y usted tiene la lista de las tareas pendientes. Háganse preguntas y contéstense con la información que cada uno/a tiene.

MODELO: *Eduardo, Alicia y Pedro preparar los anuncios, comprar los refrescos*
E1: *¿Quién va a preparar los anuncios?*
E2: *Que los preparen Alicia y Pedro. ¿Y qué va a hacer Eduardo?*
E1: *Que compre los refrescos.*

Personas

Beatriz
Alberto y Rubén
Miguel
Elena y Amanda
Ana María
Emilio
Un camarero

Tareas

traer los platos
tener los ingredientes listos
buscar las sillas
copiar las recetas
servir el vino
recibir a las personas
ayudar al chef

Suggestion for EG-4. Encourage students to use indirect commands when assigning responsibilities to the various members of the group.

❷ EG-4 Una fiesta hispana. Primera fase. Para celebrar el final de curso ustedes han decidido organizar una fiesta en el departamento de español. Hagan una lista de todo lo que necesitan y otra lista de todas las personas que van a invitar, además de sus compañeros/as de clase.

Segunda fase. Decidan qué otras personas de la clase pueden encargarse de cada sección y por qué. Su compañero/a, que está de acuerdo con usted, le dará algunas ideas.

MODELO: E1: *Que se encargue Juan de comprar las invitaciones porque tiene que ir al supermercado esta tarde.*
E2: *Sí, pero que las escriban María y Pedro que escriben mejor.*

SITUACIONES

Role A. You are a new manager for the Student Union who wants to improve the food and the service at the cafeteria. In a meeting with the cafeteria manager, say a) that it is important that students receive a better service, b) inform the manager of the type of food you would like to find in the cafeteria and of the ways in which the service could be improved, and c) say that you hope the prices will not increase **(subir)** this semester.

Role B. You are the cafeteria manager. Agree with the Student Union manager and tell him/her a) that you have a good team and you want everyone to do a good job, b) that you will be happy to meet with a student committee and have students suggest **(sugerir)** menus, and c) that you will do your best **(hacer lo posible)** to convince your team to incorporate your suggestions.

3. The Spanish equivalents of English *let's*

In Spanish, you may suggest that two or more people, including yourself, do something together in the following ways.

■ **Vamos + a +** *infinitive* is commonly used in Spanish to express English *let's + verb*.

> **Vamos a llamar** al doctor.   *Let's call the doctor.*

■ Use **vamos** by itself to mean *let's go*. The negative *let's not go* is **no vayamos**.

> **Vamos** al hospital.   *Let's go to the hospital.*
> **No vayamos** al hospital.   *Let's not go to the hospital.*

■ Another equivalent for *let's + verb* is the **nosotros** form of the present subjunctive.

> **Hablemos** con el médico.   *Let's talk to the doctor.*
> **No hablemos** con la enfermera.   *Let's not talk to the nurse.*

■ The final **-s** of reflexive affirmative commands is dropped when the pronoun **nos** is attached. Note the additional written accent.

> **Levantemos + nos**   →   **Levantémonos.**
> **Sirvamos + nos**   →   **Sirvámonos.**

■ Placement of object and reflexive pronouns is the same as with **usted(es)** commands.

> **Comprémosla.**   *Let's buy it.*
> **No la compremos.**   *Let's not buy it.*

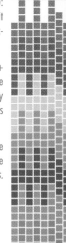

¿Qué dice usted?

EG-5 ¿Qué debemos hacer? Usted está estudiando con un/a compañero/a y cuidando al mismo tiempo a su hermanito. El niño les dice que se siente mal. Cada uno/a de ustedes debe escoger tres de las siguientes opciones y decirle a su compañero/a lo que deben o no deben hacer.

MODELO: llevarlo a su cuarto   llamar a tus padres
         E1: *Llevémoslo a su cuarto.*   E2: *Llamemos a tus padres.*

1. darle agua
2. llevarlo al parque
3. comprarle juguetes
4. ponerle el termómetro
5. llamar al médico
6. preguntarle qué le duele
7. prepararle una hamburguesa
8. explicarle los síntomas al doctor
9. ponerle la televisión
10. acostarlo

EG-6 Resoluciones. Usted y su compañero/a deciden llevar una vida más sana. Túrnense para decir lo que piensan hacer. Su compañero/a va a decirle si está de acuerdo o no con su sugerencia.

MODELO: comer más verduras
         E1: *Vamos a comer más verduras.*
         E2: *Sí, comamos más verduras./No,(no comamos más verduras,)*
             comamos más frutas.

1. tomar vitaminas y minerales
2. caminar tres kilómetros diariamente
3. beber ocho vasos de agua todos los días
4. acostarse más temprano
5. dormir ocho horas todas las noches
6. ...

EG-7 Los preparativos para un beneficio. En pequeños grupos, decidan qué actividades van a hacer para recaudar (*collect*) fondos a beneficio de un hospital. Deben mencionar cinco actividades.

MODELO: Organicemos un partido del equipo de basquetbol.

SITUACIONES

You and your partner are planning to visit a classmate who is in the hospital. Decide a) when you will visit him/her, b) what you are going to take him/her, and c) what you can do for your classmate after he/she leaves the hospital. Then, exchange this information with another pair of students.

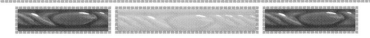

4. The present perfect subjunctive

Use the present perfect subjunctive to react to a past occurrence, event or condition. The present perfect subjunctive is formed with the present subjunctive of the verb **haber** + *past participle.*

Suggestion. Contrast present subjunctive and present perfect subjunctive: *Mañana tienen un examen. Espero que estudien esta noche. Hoy tienen un examen. Espero que hayan estudiado ayer.* Write pairs of sentences on the board, circle the dependent clause with the present subjunctive and draw an arrow pointing to the right to show that the action/state has not happened yet. Then, circle the dependent clause with the perfect subjunctive and draw an arrow pointing to the left to show that the action/state happened or was supposed to have happened before what is stated in the main clause.

PRESENT SUBJUNCTIVE OF *HABER* + *PAST PARTICIPLE*		
yo	haya	
yú	hayas	
Ud., él/ella	haya	hablado
nosotros/as	hayamos	comido
vosotros/as	hayáis	vivido
Uds., ellos/as	hayan	

Note that the dependent clause using the present perfect subjunctive describes what has happened before the time expressed or implied in the main clause, which is the present. Its English equivalent is normally *has/have* + *past participle,* but it may vary according to the context.

Your friend tells you:	Your reaction to this past event:
Mis hijos volvieron de sus vacaciones.	Me alegro de que **hayan llegado.** *I'm glad they arrived early.*
Your secretary informs you:	Your reaction to this past news:
El gerente de ventas no vino a trabajar ayer.	Es posible que **haya estado** enfermo. *It's possible that he may have been sick.*

¿Qué dice usted?

2 **EG-8 ¿Qué espera usted?** Escoja la oración que complete lógicamente las siguientes Situaciones. Compare sus respuestas con las de su compañero/a.

1. Su computadora no estaba funcionando bien y usted se la dio a un técnico para que la reparara. Usted espera que...
   a. la haya vendido.
   b. haya destruido sus programas.
   (c.) haya encontrado el problema.

2. Su amigo acaba de regresar de Puerto Rico, donde fue a pasar sus vacaciones. Usted le dice: "Espero que...
   (a.) hayas visitado el Viejo San Juan".
   b. te hayas aburrido mucho".
   c. hayas perdido todo tu dinero".

3. Uno de sus compañeros ha estado muy grave en el hospital, pero ya está en la casa. Usted le habla y le dice: "Siento mucho que...
   a. hayas vendido la casa".
   (b.) hayas estado tan mal".
   c. hayas salido del hospital".

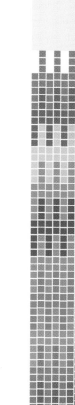

4. Usted llama por teléfono a un amigo para invitarlo a cenar, pero nadie contesta el teléfono. Es probable que su amigo...
   a. haya cenado ya.
   b. haya salido de su casa.
   c. haya cambiado su teléfono.

5. Uno de sus parientes dijo una mentira (*lie*). Como es natural, a usted le molesta mucho que no...
   a. haya dicho la verdad.
   b. haya dicho nada.
   c. haya hablado con sus parientes.

Warm-up for EG-9. This is a good opportunity to recycle what was mentioned in *Lección 2* regarding Hispanic influence in Los Angeles.

Note for EG-9. The Huntington Library, built in a 200 acre garden, houses a Guttenberg Bible and original Shakespearean works.

2 EG-9 Un viaje. Uno de sus amigos pasó un semestre en Los Ángeles. Túrnese con su compañero/a para decirle lo que esperan que haya hecho en su visita.

MODELO: ir a Beverly Hills / visitar la Biblioteca Huntington
           E1: *Espero que hayas ido a Beverly Hills.*
           E2: *Y yo espero que hayas visitado la Biblioteca Huntington.*

1. ver las Torres de Watts
2. ir a los Estudios Universal
3. caminar por la calle Olvera
4. comer comida mexicana
5. manejar hasta el observatorio del Monte Wilson
6. asistir al Desfile de las Rosas

2 EG-10 Los adelantos científicos. Usted y su compañero/a trabajan con otros científicos en un laboratorio de ingeniería genética. Háganse preguntas para saber qué han o no han logrado en sus investigaciones.

MODELO: aislar el nuevo virus / es posible que
           E1: *¿Han aislado el nuevo virus?*
           E2: *Es posible que lo hayamos / hayan aislado.*

1. cambiar la estructura de la célula / dudar
2. no hacer implantes nuevos / es una lástima
3. duplicar órganos / no creer que
4. regular el ritmo del corazón / esperar
5. reactivar los músculos atrofiados / es probable que
6. modificar los genes / es importante que

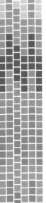

EN DIRECTO

To express that you remember or recognize someone in a photo:
Mira, mira, ésta/éste es...
Look, this is . . .
Te equivocas
You are wrong.
Pero, ¿no ves que es.../
Tiene/lleva...
But, don't you see it is . . .
(a person's name)
¿Has visto a...?

SITUACIONES

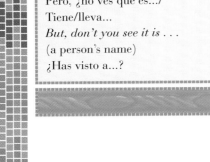

You and your classmate graduated years ago and are remembering the times when you were at the university. You have found a group photo of your Spanish class. Talk about each of your classmates saying a) what you know they have done in their lives, b) what you hope they have done, and c) what you doubt they have done. Use your imagination and the expressions in the box to sound more natural.

5. The conditional perfect and the pluperfect subjunctive

In this section you will study two new verb tenses: the conditional perfect and the pluperfect subjunctive. Use this tense to hypothesize about an occurrence or event in the past.

- Use the conditional of **haber** + *past participle* to form the conditional perfect.

CONDITIONAL PERFECT		
yo	habría	
tú	habrías	
Ud., él, ella	habría	hablado
nosotros/as	habríamos	comido
vosotros/as	habríais	vivido
Uds., ellos/as	habrían	

- The conditional perfect usually corresponds to English *would have + past participle*.

> Sé que le **habría gustado** esta casa.　*I know you/he/she would have liked this house.*

- Use the past subjunctive of **haber** + *past participle* to form the pluperfect subjunctive.

PLUPERFECT SUBJUNCTIVE		
yo	hubiera	
tú	hubieras	
Ud., él, ella	hubiera	hablado
nosotros/as	hubiéramos	comido
vosotros/as	hubierais	vivido
Uds., ellos/as	hubieran	

- The pluperfect subjunctive corresponds to English *might have, would have,* or *had + past participle*. It is used in constructions where the subjunctive is normally required.

> Dudaba que **hubiera venido** temprano. 　*I doubted that he had/would have come early.*
>
> Esperaba que **hubieran comido** en casa. 　*I was hoping that they would have eaten at home.*
>
> Ojalá que **hubieran visto** ese letrero. 　*I wish they had seen that sign.*

¿Qué dice usted?

2 EG-11 ¿Qué habría hecho en estas Situaciones? Primera fase. Digan qué habría hecho cada uno/a de ustedes en las siguientes situaciones. Después escojan la respuesta que les parezca mejor para cada situación.

MODELO:　Usted recibió una invitación para una recepción en la Casa Blanca.
　　　　E1: *Se lo habría dicho a todos mis compañeros.*
　　　　E2: *Habría leído la invitación varias veces porque habría pensado que era una broma.*

Suggestion. Contrast present perfect subjunctive and pluperfect subjunctive. Write *Hoy* and *Ayer* on the board/ a transparency. Under *Hoy*, write *Espero* and under *Ayer, que hayan estudiado.* Ask questions so students can say what they wish happened yesterday. Then write *La semana pasada* to the right of *Ayer.* Write *Esperaba* under *Ayer* and *que hubieran estudiado* under *La semana pasada.* Say what you wished had happened last week.

Note. The verb forms presented in this sections are rather complex; an average first-year student may be able to recognize them in reading, but will definitely have difficulty producing them orally and/or in writing.

1. En el aeropuerto le dijeron que podía viajar en primera clase todo el año sin pagar.
2. Le pidieron sugerencias para mejorar la situación de los vuelos y los aeropuertos.
3. La NASA lo/la llamó para ver si le interesaba vivir tres meses en una estación espacial.
4. Le dijeron que organizara la fiesta de fin de curso de su clase.
5. Le pidieron que revisara los programas en su universidad y sugiriera los cambios necesarios.

Segunda fase. Comparen las respuestas que escogieron con las de otra pareja y decidan cuál es la mejor. Después compartan sus respuestas con el resto de la clase.

② EG-12 Nuestras esperanzas. Usted y su compañero/a esperaban que el nuevo gobierno hiciera muchas cosas en beneficio de la sociedad. Se lograron algunas cosas, pero otras no. Túrnense para decir qué esperaban que el nuevo gobierno y su gabinete hubieran hecho y si lo han hecho o no.

MODELO: subir el sueldo mínimo / mejorar el sistema de educación
E1: *Esperaba que hubieran subido el sueldo mínimo y (no) lo han hecho.*
E2: *Y yo esperaba que hubieran mejorado el sistema de educación (no) lo han hecho.*

1. bajar los impuestos (*taxes*)
2. mejorar el transporte público
3. terminar con la corrupción
4. construir viviendas (*housing*) para familias pobres
5. ofrecer mejores planes de salud
6. proteger el medio ambiente
7. ...
8. ...

SITUACIONES

Role A. You had an argument **(pelea)** with your significant other. Explain to your best friend what happened and ask him/her what he/she would have done in your place. Then tell him/her what you intend to do.

Role B. Your best friend explains to you that he/she had an argument with his/her significant other. Ask questions to obtain some details. Then a) tell him/her what you would have done in the same situation, b) ask him/her what he/she intends to do and c) give him/her your advice.

6. *If*-clauses (using the perfect tenses)

The conditional perfect and pluperfect subjunctive are used in contrary-to-fact if-statements which refer to actions, events, experiences related to the past.

Si **hubieras venido**, te **habría gustado** la conferencia.

If you had come (which you did not), you would have liked the lecture.

Note. Hypothesizing about the past is a more appropriate function for students with a higher degree of proficiency. You may wish to present this section for recognition only or to satisfy the needs and/or curiosity of more motivated students.

¿Qué dice usted?

2 EG-13 La vida sería diferente. Con su compañero/a, diga cuáles habrían sido las consecuencias si...

MODELO: no se hubieran inventado los aviones
E1: *Habríamos viajado en barco, en tren o en autobús.*
E2: *Habríamos contaminado menos la atmósfera.*

1. no se hubiera inventado la bomba atómica
2. no se hubieran deforestado los bosques
3. los ingleses hubieran descubierto América
4. las mujeres hubieran tenido siempre las mismas oportunidades que los hombres
5. no se hubieran creado las vacunas (*vaccination*)
6. los jóvenes hubieran gobernado el mundo

2 EG-14 Unas excusas. ¿Qué excusas darían ustedes en las siguientes Situaciones?

MODELO: Un amigo le pidió que participara en un experimento.
E1: *Si mis padres me lo hubieran permitido, habría participado.*
E2: *Si hubiera tenido tiempo, habría participado.*

1. Una organización quería que usted donara botellas y papeles para reciclar.
2. Le pidieron su coche para llevar unas ratas al laboratorio.
3. Lo/La necesitaban de voluntario/a para probar una vacuna contra el catarro.
4. Un/a compañero/a quería venderle su computadora portátil.
5. Una compañía necesitaba probar unos paracaídas y buscaba personas interesadas en las pruebas.
6. Alquilaban un robot para que hiciera las tareas domésticas.

2 EG-15 Volver a vivir. Piense en una experiencia negativa que usted haya tenido. Cuéntele a su compañero/a qué le pasó y dígale qué habría hecho si hubiera sabido en ese momento lo que sabe hoy. Después, su compañero/a debe hacer lo mismo.

SITUACIONES

Role A. You attended a conference/lecture about the city of the future. Tell your classmate a) where and when the conference/lecture took place, b) that he/she would have found it very interesting, and c) the things that he/she would have learned if he/she had attended.

Role B. Your classmate has attended a conference/lecture about the city of the future. Ask him/her questions to find out more about the things he/she learned.

7. The passive voice

The passive voice emphasizes a fact resulting from the action of someone or something.

■ The passive voice in Spanish is formed with the verb **ser** + *past participle;* the passive voice is most commonly used in the preterit, though at times you may see it used in other tenses.

> La planta nuclear **fue construida** en 1980.
>
> *The nuclear plant was built in 1980.*

■ Use the preposition **por** when indicating who or what performs the action.

> El bosque **fue destruido.** (Who or what did it is not expressed.)
>
> *The forest was destroyed.*
>
> El bosque **fue destruido por** el fuego. (The fire id it.)
>
> *The forest was destroyed by the fire.*

■ The past participle functions as an adjective and therefore agrees in gender and number with the subject.

> Los árboles fueron **destruidos** por la lluvia ácida.
>
> *The trees were destroyed by the acid rain.*
>
> La cura fue **descubierta** el año pasado.
>
> *The cure was discovered last year.*

■ You'll most often find the passive voice in written Spanish, especially in newspapers and formal writing. However, in conversation, Spanish speakers normally use two different constructions that you have already studied—a third person plural verb or a **se** construction.

> **Vendieron** el laboratorio.
>
> *They sold the laboratory.*
>
> **Se vendió** el edificio.
>
> *The building was sold.*

¿Qué dice usted?

2 **EG-16 La comunicación oral.** Túrnese con su compañero/a para decir lo que pasó en una reunión del presidente y los ministros. ¿Cómo lo dirían los periódicos? ¿Cómo lo dirían ustedes en una conversación?

MODELO: ministros / recibir / el presidente
           E1: *Los ministros fueron recibidos por el presidente.*
           E2: *El presidente recibió a los ministros.*

1. la agenda / preparar / el secretario *fue preparada/preparó*
2. la agenda / aprobar / todos *fue aprobada/aprobaron*
3. el proyecto para disminuir la contaminación / escribir / el Sr. Sosa *fue escrito/escribió*
4. el proyecto / presentar / la Ministra de Salud *fue presentado/presentó*
5. unos comentarios / leer / el presidente *fueron leídos/leyó*
6. las preguntas / contestar / el ministro *fueron contestados/contestó*

❷ EG-17 Dos reporteros. Túrnese con su compañero/a para decir cómo escribirían las siguientes noticias para un periódico.

MODELO: la lluvia ácida dañó las cosechas
Las cosechas fueron dañadas por la lluvia ácida.

1. La zona del Amazonas se conoce como el "pulmón" del planeta. *es conocido*
2. Los campesinos deforestaron la selva. *fue deforestada*
3. Los campesinos cultivaron la tierra. *fue cultivada*
4. Estos grupos cortaron muchos árboles. *fueron cortados*
5. La invasión de los seres humanos exterminó muchas especies de animales. *fueron examinados*
6. El gobierno plantará mil árboles para mejorar la situación. *serán plantados*

SITUACIONES

You and your classmate are TV newscasters. You must write and give a piece of news to your viewers on a great discovery. Inform them that a) some very secret plans have been discovered by the CIA, b) that important security measures have been taken, c) that politicians are now deliberating on how to respond to a possible threat **(peligro)** to the population, d) that public transport has been interrupted in major cities, e) that the situation is under control and f) that nobody should be afraid.

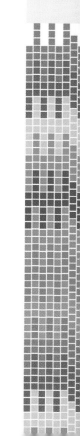

APÉNDICE 1

Composition correction codes

As part of the process of developing good writing skills in Spanish, you will be exchanging compositions with a classmate. The following correction codes can be very helpful as you critique each other's work.

Code	Interpretation
C	Conjugation of a verb, or an error in some derived verb form, for example **la puerta estaba *abrida.**
Cog	False cognate, for example **sopa** for **jabón,** or **ropa** for **soga.**
D	Dictionary error, for example **banco** for **orilla,** or even **morderse las uñas** for **comerse las uñas.**
F	Form (often a "regularized" adjective, such as **una niña muy *jóvena**).
G	Incorrect gender assignment to a noun, for example **la programa** for **el programa.**
Mode	Mode confusion (if subjunctive, change to indicative and vice versa).
Nag	Noun agreements (gender, number) with adjectives and other noun-centered forms such as pronouns, demonstratives, possessives.
NE	**No existe.** Use this code to signal a made-up word or expression that does not exist in Spanish, for example ***en facto** for **en realidad.**
Prim	Preterite/imperfect confusion (if preterite, change to imperfect and vice versa).
R	Rewrite successfully completed.
Ref	Reflexive. Use this code to signal that a reflexive verb/construction is needed.
Sag	Subject-verb agreement error, for example ***Juan querías salir.**
S/E	**Ser/estar** confusion (if **ser,** change to **estar** and vice versa).
Sp	Spelling error. Use this code to signal errors in spelling. Note that written accent marks are considered part of a word's spelling in Spanish.
T	Tense. Use this code to signal any non-Prim (see above) tense error.
X	Any basic grammatical error not covered by some other symbol, but which the student should reasonably know, such as **después de *yendo** for **después de ir.**
Wo	Word order error, for example, ***es no grande** for **no es grande.**
+	Use this code to signal any especially nice touch in the student's writing.
?	Use this code to signal that the reader could not make any sense of the word, clause, sentence, or paragraph.

Adapted from Higgs, 1979

Word formation in Spanish

Recognizing certain patterns in Spanish word formation can be a big help in deciphering meaning. Use the following information about word formation to help you as you read.

- **Prefixes.** Spanish and English share a number of prefixes that shade the meaning of the word to which they are attached: **inter-** (between, among); **intro/a-** (within); **ex-** (former, toward the outside); **en-/em-** (the state of becoming); **in-/a-** (not, without), among others.

inter-	interdisciplinario, interacción
intro/a-	introvertido, introspección
ex-	ex-esposo, exponer *(expose)*
en-/em-	enrojecer *(to turn red)*, empobrecer *(to become poor)*
in-/a-	inmoral, incompleto, amoral, asexual

- **Suffixes.** Suffixes and, in general, word endings will help you identify various aspects of words such as part of speech, gender, meaning, degree, etc. Common Spanish suffixes are **-ría, -za, -miento, -dad/tad, -ura, -oso/a, -izo/a, -(c)ito/a,** and **-mente.**

-ría	place where something is made and/or bought: **panadería, zapatería** *(shoe store)*, **librería.**
-za	feminine, abstract noun: **pobreza** *(poverty)*, **riqueza** *(wealth, richness)*.
-miento	masculine, abstract noun: **empobrecimiento** *(impoverishment)*, **entrenamiento** *(training)*.
-dad/tad	feminine noun: **ciudad** *(city)*, **libertad** *(liberty, freedom)*
-ura	feminine noun: **verdura, locura** *(craziness)*.
-oso/a	adjective meaning having the characteristics of the noun to which it's attached: **montañoso, lluvioso** *(rainy)*.
-izo/a	adjective meaning having the characteristics of the noun to which it's attached: **rojizo** *(reddish)*, **enfermizo** *(sickly)*.
-(c)ito/a	diminutive form of noun or adjective: **Juanito, mesita** *(little table)*, **Carmencita.**
-mente	attached to the feminine form of adjective to form an adverb: **rápidamente, felizmente** *(happily)*.

- **Compounds.** Compounds are made up of two words (e.g., *mailman*), each of which has meaning in and of itself: **tocadiscos** *(record player)* from **tocar** and **disco; sacacorchos** *(cork screw)* from **sacar** and **corcho.** Your knowledge of the root words will help you recognize the compound; and likewise, learning compounds can help you to learn the root words. What do you think **sacar** means?

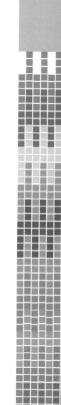

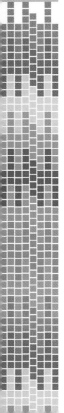

■ **Spanish-English associations.** Learning to associate aspects of word formation in Spanish with aspects of word formation in English can be very helpful. Look at the associations below.

SPANISH	ENGLISH
es/ex + consonant	*s* + consonant
esclerosis, extraño	*sclerosis, strange*
gu-	*w-*
guerra, Guillermo	*war, William*
-tad/dad	*-ty*
libertad, calidad	*liberty, quality*
-sión/-ción	*-sion/-tion*
tensión, emoción	*tension, emotion*

Stress and written accents in Spanish

In Spanish, normal word stress falls on the second-to-last syllable of words ending in a vowel, **-n**, or **-s**, and on the last syllable of words ending in other consonants.

hablo	clase	amiga	libros
escuchan	comer	universidad	venir

When a word does not follow this pattern, a written accent is used to signal where the word is stressed. Below are examples of words that do not follow the pattern.

1. Words accented on the third-to-last syllable:

física	sábado	simpático
catástrofe	gramática	matemáticas

2. Words that are accented on the last syllable despite ending in a vowel, **-n** or **-s**.

hablé	comí	están	estás
alemán	Belén	inglés	conversación

3. Words that are accented on the second-to-last syllable despite ending in a consonant other than **-n** or **-s**.

lápiz	útil	débil	mártir
Félix	cárcel	módem	fácil

Diphthongs

The combination of an unstressed **i** or **u** with another vowel forms a single syllable which is called a diphthong. When the diphthong is in the accented syllable of a word and a written accent is required, it is written over the other vowel, not over the **i** or **u**.

Dios	adiós	bien	también
seis	dieciséis	continuo	continuó

When a stressed **i** or **u** appears with another vowel, two syllables are formed, and a written accent mark is used over the **i** or **u**.

cafetería	país	Raúl	frío
continúa	río	leíste	economía

Interrogative and monosyllabic words

Some words in Spanish follow normal stress patterns but use written accents for other reasons. For example, interrogative and exclamatory words always use a written accent on the stressed vowel: **¿Dónde viven ellos?, ¿Cuántas clases tienes?, ¡Qué bueno!** Many one-syllable (monosyllabic) words carry a written accent to distinguish them from other words with the same spelling but different meanings.

dé	*give* (formal command)	de	*of*
él	*he*	el	*the*
más	*more*	mas	*but*
mí	*me*	mi	*my*
sé	*I know, be* (formal command)	se	*him/herself, (to)him/her/them*
sí	*yes*	si	*if*
té	*tea*	te	*(to) you*
tú	*you*	tu	*your*

Verb Charts

REGULAR VERBS: SIMPLE TENSES

Infinitive Present Participle Past Participle	Indicative						Subjunctive		Imperative
	Present	Imperfect	Preterit	Future	Conditional	Present	Imperfect	
hablar hablando hablado	hablo hablas habla hablamos habláis hablan	hablaba hablabas hablaba hablábamos hablabais hablaban	hablé hablaste habló hablamos hablasteis hablaron	hablaré hablarás hablará hablaremos hablaréis hablarán	hablaría hablarías hablaría hablaríamos hablaríais hablarían	hable hables hable hablemos habléis hablen	hablara hablaras hablara habláramos hablarais hablaran	habla tú, no hables hable usted hablemos hablen Uds.
comer comiendo comido	como comes come comemos coméis comen	comía comías comía comíamos comíais comían	comí comiste comió comimos comisteis comieron	comeré comerás comerá comeremos comeréis comerán	comería comerías comería comeríamos comeríais comerían	coma comas coma comamos comáis coman	comiera comieras comiera comiéramos comierais comieran	come tú, no comas coma usted comamos coman Uds.
vivir viviendo vivido	vivo vives vive vivimos vivís viven	vivía vivías vivía vivíamos vivíais vivían	viví viviste vivió vivimos vivisteis vivieron	viviré vivirás vivirá viviremos viviréis vivirán	viviría vivirías viviría viviríamos viviríais vivirían	viva vivas viva vivamos viváis vivan	viviera vivieras viviera viviéramos vivierais vivieran	vive tú, no vivas viva usted vivamos vivan Uds.

Vosotros Commands

hablar	comer	vivir
hablad, no habléis	comed, no comáis	vivid, no viváis

REGULAR VERBS: PERFECT TENSES

Indicative										Subjunctive		
Present Perfect		Past Perfect		Preterit Perfect		Future Perfect		Conditional Perfect		Present Perfect		Past Perfect
he has ha hemos habéis han	hablado comido vivido	había habías había habíamos habíais habían	hablado comido vivido	hube hubiste hubo hubimos hubisteis hubieron	hablado comido vivido	habré habrás habrá habremos habréis habrán	hablado comido vivido	habría habrías habría habríamos habríais habrían	hablado comido vivido	haya hayas haya hayamos hayáis hayan	hablado comido vivido	hubiera hablado hubieras comido hubiera vivido hubiéramos hubierais hubieran

IRREGULAR VERBS

Infinitive Present Participle Past Participle	Indicative					Subjunctive		Imperative
	Present	Imperfect	Preterit	Future	Conditional	Present	Imperfect	
andar andando andado	ando andas anda andamos andáis andan	andaba andabas andaba andábamos andabais andaban	anduve anduviste anduvo anduvimos anduvisteis anduvieron	andaré andarás andará andaremos andaréis andarán	andaría andarías andaría andaríamos andaríais andarían	ande andes ande andemos andéis anden	anduviera anduvieras anduviera anduviéramos anduvierais anduvieran	anda tú, no andes ande usted andemos anden Uds.
caer cayendo caído	caigo caes cae caemos caéis caen	caía caías caía caíamos caíais caían	caí caíste cayó caímos caísteis cayeron	caeré caerás caerá caeremos caeréis caerán	caería caerías caería caeríamos caeríais caerían	caiga caigas caiga caigamos caigáis caigan	cayera cayeras cayera cayéramos cayerais cayeran	cae tú, no caigas caiga usted caigamos caigan Uds.
dar dando dado	doy das da damos dais dan	daba dabas daba dábamos dabais daban	di diste dio dimos disteis dieron	daré darás dará daremos daréis darán	daría darías daría daríamos daríais darían	dé des dé demos deis den	diera dieras diera diéramos dierais dieran	da tú, no des dé usted demos den Uds.

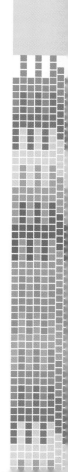

IRREGULAR VERBS (CONTINUED)

Infinitive Present Participle Past Participle	Indicative					Subjunctive		Imperative
	Present	Imperfect	Preterit	Future	Conditional	Present	Imperfect	
decir diciendo dicho	digo dices dice decimos decís dicen	decía decías decía decíamos decíais decían	dije dijiste dijo dijimos dijisteis dijeron	diré dirás dirá diremos diréis dirán	diría dirías diría diríamos diríais dirían	diga digas diga digamos digáis digan	dijera dijeras dijera dijéramos dijerais dijeran	di tú, no digas diga usted digamos decid vosotros, no digáis digan Uds.
estar estando estado	estoy estás está estamos estáis están	estaba estabas estaba estábamos estabais estaban	estuve estuviste estuvo estuvimos estuvisteis estuvieron	estaré estarás estará estaremos estaréis estarán	estaría estarías estaría estaríamos estaríais estarían	esté estés esté estemos estéis estén	estuviera estuvieras estuviera estuviéramos estuvierais estuvieran	está tú, no estés esté usted estemos estad vosotros, no estéis estén Uds.
haber habiendo habido	he has ha hemos habéis han	había habías había habíamos habíais habían	hube hubiste hubo hubimos hubisteis hubieron	habré habrás habrá habremos habréis habrán	habría habrías habría habríamos habríais habrían	haya hayas haya hayamos hayáis hayan	hubiera hubieras hubiera hubiéramos hubierais hubieran	
hacer haciendo hecho	hago haces hace hacemos hacéis hacen	hacía hacías hacía hacíamos hacíais hacían	hice hiciste hizo hicimos hicisteis hicieron	haré harás hará haremos haréis harán	haría harías haría haríamos haríais harían	haga hagas haga hagamos hagáis hagan	hiciera hicieras hiciera hiciéramos hicierais hicieran	haz tú, no hagas haga usted hagamos haced vosotros, no hagáis hagan Uds.
ir yendo ido	voy vas va vamos vais van	iba ibas iba íbamos ibais iban	fui fuiste fue fuimos fuisteis fueron	iré irás irá iremos iréis irán	iría irías iría iríamos iríais irían	vaya vayas vaya vayamos vayáis vayan	fuera fueras fuera fuéramos fuerais fueran	ve tú, no vayas vaya usted vamos, no vayamos id vosotros, no vayáis vayan Uds.

IRREGULAR VERBS (CONTINUED)

Infinitive Present Participle Past Participle	Indicative					Subjunctive		Imperative
	Present	Imperfect	Preterit	Future	Conditional	Present	Imperfect	
oír oyendo oído	oigo oyes oye oímos oís oyen	oía oías oía oíamos oíais oían	oí oíste oyó oímos oísteis oyeron	oiré oirás oirá oiremos oiréis oirán	oiría oirías oiría oiríamos oiríais oirían	oiga oigas oiga oigamos oigáis oigan	oyera oyeras oyera oyéramos oyerais oyeran	oye tú, no oigas oiga usted oigamos oigan Uds.
poder pudiendo podido	puedo puedes puede podemos podéis pueden	podía podías podía podíamos podíais podían	pude pudiste pudo pudimos pudisteis pudieron	podré podrás podrá podremos podréis podrán	podría podrías podría podríamos podríais podrían	pueda puedas pueda podamos podáis puedan	pudiera pudieras pudiera pudiéramos pudierais pudieran	
poner poniendo puesto	pongo pones pone ponemos ponéis ponen	ponía ponías ponía poníamos poníais ponían	puse pusiste puso pusimos pusisteis pusieron	pondré pondrás pondrá pondremos pondréis pondrán	pondría pondrías pondría pondríamos pondríais pondrían	ponga pongas ponga pongamos pongáis pongan	pusiera pusieras pusiera pusiéramos pusierais pusieran	pon tú, no pongas ponga usted pongamos pongan Uds.
querer queriendo querido	quiero quieres quiere queremos queréis quieren	quería querías quería queríamos queríais querían	quise quisiste quiso quisimos quisisteis quisieron	querré querrás querrá querremos querréis querrán	querría querrías querría querríamos querríais querrían	quiera quieras quiera queramos queráis quieran	quisiera quisieras quisiera quisiéramos quisierais quisieran	quiere tú, no quieras quiera usted queramos quieran Uds.
saber sabiendo sabido	sé sabes sabe sabemos sabéis saben	sabía sabías sabía sabíamos sabíais sabían	supe supiste supo supimos supisteis supieron	sabré sabrás sabrá sabremos sabréis sabrán	sabría sabrías sabría sabríamos sabríais sabrían	sepa sepas sepa sepamos sepáis sepan	supiera supieras supiera supiéramos supiérais supieran	sabe tú, no sepas sepa usted sepamos sepan Uds.
salir saliendo salido	salgo sales sale salimos salís salen	salía salías salía salíamos salíais salían	salí saliste salió salimos salisteis salieron	saldré saldrás saldrá saldremos saldréis saldrán	saldría saldrías saldría saldríamos saldríais saldrían	salga salgas salga salgamos salgáis salgan	saliera salieras saliera saliéramos salierais salieran	sal tú, no salgas salga usted salgamos salgan Uds.

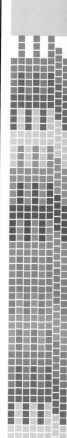

IRREGULAR VERBS (CONTINUED)

Infinitive Present Participle Past Participle	Indicative					Subjunctive		Imperative
	Present	Imperfect	Preterit	Future	Conditional	Present	Imperfect	
ser siendo sido	soy eres es somos sois son	era eras era éramos erais eran	fui fuiste fue fuimos fuisteis fueron	seré serás será seremos seréis serán	sería serías sería seríamos seríais serían	sea seas sea seamos seáis sean	fuera fueras fuera fuéramos fuerais fueran	sé tú, no seas sea usted seamos sed vosotros, no seáis sean Uds.
tener teniendo tenido	tengo tienes tiene tenemos tenéis tienen	tenía tenías tenía teníamos teníais tenían	tuve tuviste tuvo tuvimos tuvisteis tuvieron	tendré tendrás tendrá tendremos tendréis tendrán	tendría tendrías tendría tendríamos tendríais tendrían	tenga tengas tenga tengamos tengáis tengan	tuviera tuvieras tuviera tuviéramos tuvierais tuvieran	ten tú, no tengas tenga usted tengamos tened vosotros, no tengáis tengan Uds.
traer trayendo traído	traigo traes trae traemos traéis traen	traía traías traía traíamos traíais traían	traje trajiste trajo trajimos trajisteis trajeron	traeré traerás traerá traeremos traeréis traerán	traería traerías traería traeríamos traeríais traerían	traiga traigas traiga traigamos traigáis traigan	trajera trajeras trajera trajéramos trajerais trajeran	trae tú, no traigas traiga usted traigamos traed vosotros, no traigáis traigan Uds.
venir viniendo venido	vengo vienes viene venimos venís vienen	venía venías venía veníamos veníais venían	vine viniste vino vinimos vinisteis vinieron	vendré vendrás vendrá vendremos vendréis vendrán	vendría vendrías vendría vendríamos vendríais vendrían	venga vengas venga vengamos vengáis vengan	viniera vinieras viniera viniéramos vinierais vinieran	ven tú, no vengas venga usted vengamos venid vosotros, no vengáis vengan Uds.
ver viendo visto	veo ves ve vemos véis ven	veía veías veía veíamos veíais veían	vi viste vio vimos visteis vieron	veré verás verá veremos veréis verán	vería verías vería veríamos veríais verían	vea veas vea veamos veáis vean	viera vieras viera viéramos vierais vieran	ve tú, no veas vea usted veamos ved vosotros, no veáis vean Uds.

STEM-CHANGING AND ORTHOGRAPHIC-CHANGING VERBS

Infinitive Present Participle Past Participle	Indicative					Subjunctive		Imperative
	Present	Imperfect	Preterit	Future	Conditional	Present	Imperfect	
dormir (ue, u) durmiendo dormido	duermo duermes duerme dormimos dormís duermen	dormía dormías dormía dormíamos dormíais dormían	dormí dormiste durmió dormimos dormisteis durmieron	dormiré dormirás dormirá dormiremos dormiréis dormirán	dormiría dormirías dormiría dormiríamos dormiríais dormirían	duerma duermas duerma durmamos durmáis duerman	durmiera durmieras durmiera durmiéramos durmierais durmieran	duerme tú, no duermas duerma usted durmamos dormid vosotros, no durmáis duerman Uds.
incluir (y) incluyendo incluido	incluyo incluyes incluye incluimos incluís incluyen	incluía incluías incluía incluíamos incluíais incluían	incluí incluiste incluyó incluimos incluisteis incluyeron	incluiré incluirás incluirá incluiremos incluiréis incluirán	incluiría incluirías incluiría incluiríamos incluiríais incluirían	incluya incluyas incluya incluyamos incluyáis incluyan	incluyera incluyeras incluyera incluyéramos incluyerais incluyeran	incluye tú, no incluyas incluya usted incluyamos incluid vosotros, no incluyáis incluyan Uds.
pedir (i, i) pidiendo pedido	pido pides pide pedimos pedís piden	pedía pedías pedía pedíamos pedíais pedían	pedí pediste pidió pedimos pedisteis pidieron	pediré pedirás pedirá pediremos pediréis pedirán	pediría pedirías pediría pediríamos pediríais pedirían	pida pidas pida pidamos pidáis pidan	pidiera pidieras pidiera pidiéramos pidierais pidieran	pide tú, no pidas pida usted pidamos pedid vosotros, no pidáis pidan Uds.
pensar (ie) pensando pensado	pienso piensas piensa pensamos pensáis piensan	pensaba pensabas pensaba pensábamos pensabais pensaban	pensé pensaste pensó pensamos pensasteis pensaron	pensaré pensarás pensará pensaremos pensaréis pensarán	pensaría pensarías pensaría pensaríamos pensaríais pensarían	piense pienses piense pensemos penséis piensen	pensara pensaras pensara pensáramos pensarais pensaran	piensa tú, no pienses piense usted pensemos pensad vosotros, no penséis piensen Uds.

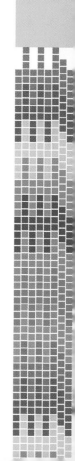

STEM-CHANGING AND ORTHOGRAPHIC-CHANGING VERBS (CONTINUED)

Infinitive Present Participle Past Participle	Indicative Present	Imperfect	Preterit	Future	Conditional	Subjunctive Present	Imperfect	Imperative
producir (zc) produciendo producido	produzco produces produce producimos producís producen	producía producías producía producíamos producíais producían	produje produjiste produjo produjimos produjisteis produjeron	produciré producirás producirá produciremos produciréis producirán	produciría producirías produciría produciríamos produciríais producirían	produzca produzcas produzca produzcamos produzcáis produzcan	produjera produjeras produjera produjéramos produjerais produjeran	produce tú, no produzcas produzca usted produzcamos pruducid vosotros, no produzcáis produzcan Uds.
reír (i, i) riendo reído	río ríes ríe reímos reís ríen	reía reías reía reíamos reíais reían	reí reíste rio reímos reísteis rieron	reiré reirás reirá reiremos reiréis reirán	reiría reirías reiría reiríamos reiríais reirían	ría rías ría riamos riáis rían	riera rieras riera riéramos rierais rieran	ríe tú, no rías ría usted riamos reíd vosotros, no riáis rían Uds.
seguir (i, i) (ga) siguiendo seguido	sigo sigues sigue seguimos seguís siguen	seguía seguías seguía seguíamos seguíais seguían	seguí seguiste siguió seguimos seguisteis siguieron	seguiré seguirás seguirá seguiremos seguiréis seguirán	seguiría seguirías seguiría seguiríamos seguiríais seguirían	siga sigas siga sigamos sigáis sigan	siguiera siguieras siguiera siguiéramos siguierais siguieran	sigue tú, no sigas siga usted sigamos seguid vosotros, no sigáis sigan Uds.
sentir (ie, i) sintiendo sentido	siento sientes siente sentimos sentís sienten	sentía sentías sentía sentíamos sentiais sentían	sentí sentiste sintió sentimos sentisteis sintieron	sentiré sentirás sentirá sentiremos sentiréis sentirán	sentiría sentirías sentiría sentiríamos sentiríais sentirían	sienta sientas sienta sintamos sintáis sientan	sintiera sintieras sintiera sintiéramos sintierais sintieran	siente tú, no sientas sienta usted sintamos sentid vosotros, no sintáis sientan Uds.
volver (ue) volviendo vuelto	vuelvo vuelves vuelve volvemos volvéis vuelven	volvía volvías volvía volvíamos volvíais volvían	volví volviste volvió volvimos volvisteis volvieron	volveré volverás volverá volveremos volveréis volverán	volvería volverías volvería volveríamos volveríais volverían	vuelva vuelvas vuelva volvamos volváis vuelvan	volviera volvieras volviera volviéramos volvierais volvieran	vuelve tú, no vuelvas vuelva usted volvamos volved vosotros, no volváis vuelvan Uds.

SPANISH TO ENGLISH VOCABULARY

This vocabulary includes all words presented in the text, except for proper nouns spelled the same in English and Spanish, diminutives with a literal meaning, typical expressions of the Hispanic countries presented in the **Enfoque cultural**, and cardinal numbers (found on pages 14 and 15). Other cognates and words easily recognized because of the context are not included either.

The number following each entry corresponds to the **lección** in which the word was first introduced. Numbers in italics followed by *r* signal that the item was presented for recognition rather than as active vocabulary.

A

a   *at, to* P
abajo   *below 4r*
el/la abogado/a   *lawyer 9*
abrazar(se)   (c) *to embrace 13*
el abrigo   *coat 6*
la abuela   *grandmother 4*
el abuelo   *grandfather 4*
aburrido/a   *boring 1*
aburrirse   *to be bored 7r*
acabar   *to finish 13*
acabar de +   inf. *to have just + past participle 13*
acceder   *to agree 10r; to access 14r*
el acceso   *access 9r*
el accidente   *accident 9r*
la acción   *action 8r*
el aceite   *oil 10*
la aceituna   *olive 10r*
aceptar   *to accept 8r, 13*
aclarar   *to clarify 8r*
acompañar   *to accompany 8*
aconsejable   *advisable 12r*
aconsejar   *to give advice 5r, 10*
acostar(se)   *to go to bed, to lie down 7*
acostar (ue)   *to put to bed 7*
acostumbrado/a   *used to 10r; accustomed 14r*
la actitud   *attitude 5r*
la actividad   *activity 1r*
el actor/la actriz   *actor/actress 3r; 9*
actual   *present, current 14*
la actualidad   *present time 4r*
actualmente   *at the present time 9*
actuar   *to act 13*
acuático/a   adj. *water 7r*

adecuado/a   *appropriate 4r*
adelante   *forward 9r;* más adelante *later on 11r*
adelgazar   (c) *to lose weight 10r*
el ademán   *gesture 15r*
adepto/a   *follower 7r*
el aderezo   *salad dressing 10*
adicional   *additional 4r*
administrativo/a   *administrative 5r*
el/la adolescente   *adolescent 4r*
¿Adónde?   *Where (to)? 3*
adornado/a   *decorated 8r*
la aduana   *customs 12*
adulto/a   *adult 3r, 14*
la aerolínea   *airline 12*
afeitar(se)   *to shave 7*
el/la aficionado/a   *fan 7*
afirmativamente   *in the affirmative 5r*
las afueras   *outskirts 5*
la agencia de viajes   *travel agency 12*
la agenda   *agenda 3r*
el/la agente   *agent 5r*
el/la agente de viajes   *travel agent 12*
agradable   *nice 2*
agrícola   *agricultural 9r*
agrio/a   *sour 10*
el agua   *water 3*
el aguacate   *avocado 10*
el agujero   *hole 14r*
ahí   *there 1r*
el/la ahijado/a   *godchild 4*
ahora   *now 2*
ahorrar   *to save 6r*
el aire acondicionado   *air conditioning 5*
al aire libre   *outdoors 3*
el ají   *pepper 10r*
el ajiaco   *type of soup 4r*

el ajo   *garlic 10*
al   *to the (contraction of a + el) 3*
la alarma   *alarm 5r*
alcohólico/a   *alcoholic 10r*
alegrarse (de)   *to be glad (about) 11*
alegre   *happy, glad 2*
la alegría   *joy 8*
el alfabeto   *alphabet Pr*
el alfiler   *pin 15r*
la alfombra   *carpet, rug 5*
el alga   *seaweed 10r*
algo   *something 1*
el algodón   *cotton 6*
algunos/as   *any, some 5r*
la alimentación   *diet 10r*
alimentar   *to feed 10r*
el alimento   *food 5r*
allá   *over there 5*
allí   *there 1r, 3r, 5*
el almacén   *department store 6*
la almohada   *pillow 5*
almorzar (ue)   *to have lunch 4*
¿Aló?   *Hello 3*
el almuerzo   *lunch Pr, 3*
el alojamiento   *lodging 12r*
alquilar   *to rent 3*
el alquiler   *rent 5r*
el altar   *altar 8r*
alto/a   *tall 2*
el/la alumno/a   *student 1*
el ama de casa   *housewife, homemaker 9*
el/la amante   *lover 8r*
amar   *to love 14r*
amazónico/a   *Amazonian 6r*
ambicioso/a   *ambitious Pr*
ambiental   *environmental 8r*
amenazar (c)   *to threaten, to menace 15*

americano/a   *American* 3r
el/la amigo/a   *friend* P
la ampliación   *enlargement, expansion* 1r
amueblado/a   *furnished* 5r
añadir   *to add* 6r, 10
el analfabetismo   *illiteracy* 14r
analfabeto/a   *illiterate* 14
ancho/a   *wide* 6
andino/a   *Andean* 6r
la angustia   *anguish* 12r
el anillo   *ring* 6
el anisado   *anisette (licor)* 3r
el aniversario   *anniversary* Pr
anotar   *to jot down* 6r
el año   *year* P
el antepasado   *ancestor* 8
anterioridad: con anterioridad   *in advance* 8r
antes   *adv. in advance, before* 1r; 8
el antibiótico   *antibiotic* 11r
antiguo/a   *former, old* 8
antipático/a   *unpleasant* 2
la antropología   *anthropology* 1
anual   *annual* 7r
el anuncio   *ad (advertisement)* 9
apagar   *to extinguish, to turn off* 9; *to turn off the lights* 15
el apartado postal (de correos)   *P.O. box* 9r
el apartamento   *apartment* 1r, 5
el apetito   *appetite* 10r
aplaudir   *to applaud* 7
el apoyo   *support* 9r
aprender   *to learn* 1r
apretar (ie)   *to press* 15r
la aprobación   *approval* 14r
apropiado/a   *appropriate* 4r
aprovechar   *to take advantage* 7
aquí   *here* 5
el árbitro   *umpire, referee* 7
el árbol   *tree* 4r, 7
el área   *area* 13
la arena   *sand* 7r
arenoso/a   *sandy* 7r
el arete   *earring* 6
argentino/a   *Argentinean* 2
el argumento   *argument* 12r
el armario   *closet, armoire* 5
la arqueología   *archaeology* 8r
arqueológico/a   *archaelogical* 8r
el/la arquitecto/a   *architect* 9
arquitectura   *architecture* 1
arreglar   *to fix, to repair* 9r
arriba   *above* 5r
arrogante   *arrogant* Pr
el arroz   *rice* 3
artesanal   *adj. handicrafts* 10r
la artesanía   *handicraft* 10
la arveja   *pea* 10r

el ascensor   *elevator* 5r
el aserrín   *sawdust* 8r
el asesinato   *assassination, murder* 12r
la asfixia   *asphyxia* 12r
así   *this way* 6
el asiento   *seat* 12
la asistencia   *attendance* 7r
el aspecto   *appearance* 8r
la aspiradora   *vacuum cleaner* 5
la aspirina   *aspirin* 11
el/la astronauta   *astronaut* 9r, 15
la atención   *attention, service* 3r
atender (ie)   *to answer, to attend* 9
aterrizar (c)   *to land* 15r
aterrorizar (c)   *to terrorize* 9r
el/la atleta   *athlete* 7r
atlético/a   *athletic* Pr
la atmósfera   *atmosphere* 7
el atractivo   *attraction* 8r; *adj. attractive* Pr
atrapar   *to catch* 14r
atrasado/a   *late* 12r
aun   *even* 9r
aún   *still* 9r
la ausencia   *absence* 9r
auténtico/a   *authentic* 8r
el auto(móvil)/coche/carro   *car* 12
el autobús/bus   *bus* 12
la autopista   *freeway* 12
el/la autor/a   *author* 5r
la autoridad   *authority* 7r
autoritario/a   *authoritarian* 9r
el/la auxiliar de vuelo   *flight attendant* 12
el avance   *advance* 9r
la avenida   *avenue* Pr
las aves   *poultry, foul* 10
el avión   *plane* 12
la ayuda   *help* 4r
ayudar   *to help* 5
azar: el azar   *at random* 12r
el/la azúcar   *sugar* 10
el azulejo   *tile* 5r

B

bailar   *to dance* 1
el/la bailarín/bailarina   *dancer* 13
el baile   *dance* 1r
la bajada   *slope* 7r
bajar   *to get off, to come down* 7r; bajar de peso *to lose weight* 3r
bajo/a   *short (in stature)* 2
el balboa   *monetary unit of Panamá* 1r
el balcón   *balcony* 5r
el baloncesto/basquetbol   *basketball* 7

la bañadera   *tub* 5
bañar(se)   *to take a bath, to bathe* 4
el banco   *bank* 9
la banda   *band* 8r
la bandeja   *tray* 10
el baño   *bathroom* 5
el banquete   *banquet* Pr
el bar   *bar* 4r
barato/a   *inexpensive, cheap* 6
la barbacoa   *barbecue* 5
el barco   *ship/boat* 12
barrer   *to sweep* 5
el barrio   *neighborhood* 5
básicamente   *basically* 4r
bastante bien   *a lot* 10r
bastar   *to be enough* 15r
la basura   *garbage, trash* 5
la bata   *robe* 6
el bate   *bat* 7
la batería/el acumulador   *battery* 12
batir   *to beat* 10
el bautizo   *baptism, christening* 4
beber   *to drink* 3
la bebida   *drink* 3
el béisbol   *baseball* 7
el beneficio   *benefit* 5r
besar   *to kiss* 13
la biblioteca   *library* 1
el/la bibliotecario/a   *librarian* 9
los bienes   *goods* 9r; bienes raíces *real estate* 5r
bilingüe   *bilingual* 2
el billete   *ticket* 3r
la billetera   *wallet* 6
la biología   *biology* 1r
la biosfera   *biosphere* 15
el bistec   *steak* 3
la blusa   *blouse* 6
la boca   *mouth* 11
la boda   *wedding* 8
el boleto/pasaje   *ticket* 12
el bolígrafo   *ballpoint pen* P
el bolívar   *monetary unit of Venezuela* 1r
el boliviano   *monetary unit of Bolivia* 1r
los bolos   *bowling* 7
la bolsa   *purse* 6
el/la bombero/a   *firefighter* 9
bonito/a   *pretty* 2
el borde   *edge* 10r
el borrador   *eraser* P
el bosque   *forest* 5r; bosque tropical *rain forest* 5r
la bota   *boot* 6
el bote   *boat* 10r
la botella   *bottle* 10
brasileño/a   *Brazilian* 7r
el brazo   *arm* 11
buena suerte   *good luck* 1

la bufanda *scarf 6*
busca: en busca de *in search of 9r*
buscar *to look for 1*
la butaca *armchair 5*
el buzón *mailbox 12*

C

el cabello *hair 11*
la cabeza *head 11*
la cabina *cabin, cockpit 15r*
cada *adj. each, every 1r; each 7*
cada... horas *every . . . hours 11*
la cadera *hip 11*
caer bien *to like 6r*
caer(se) *to fall 11*
café *brown eyes 2*
el café *coffee 1r; plus café after dinner drink 3r*
el café *coffee house 1; coffee 3*
la cafetería *cafeteria 1*
la caída *drop 6r*
la caja *cash register 9r; box 12r*
la caja fuerte *safe box 12*
el/la cajero/a *cashier 9*
el calcetín *sock 6*
el calcio *calcium 10r*
la calculadora *calculator P*
el cálculo *calculus 1r*
la calefacción *heating 5*
el calentamiento *warming 15r*
la calidad *quality 5r*
caliente *hot 3*
callado/a *quiet 2*
la calle *street P*
el calor: hacer calor *to be hot (weather) 4r*
la caloría *calorie 10r*
el calzoncillo *boxer shorts 6*
la cama *bed 5*
el camarón *shrimp 10*
el camarote *cabin (on boat) 12r*
cambiar *to change, to exchange 6*
el camello *camel 8r*
el/la caminante *walker 3r*
caminar *to walk 1*
la caminata *walk 10r*
el camino *road, way 8*
el camión *truck 9r*
la camisa *shirt 6*
la camiseta *T-shirt 6*
el camisón *nightgown 6*
el campamento *camp 6r*
la campaña *campaign 9r*
el campeón/la campeona *champion 7*
el campeonato *championship 7*
el/la campesino/a *peasant 15*
el campo *field 7*
el canal *channel 7r; canal 12r*

cancelar *to cancel 12*
el cáncer *cancer 3r*
la cancha *court, golf course 7*
la canción *song 3*
cansado/a *tired 2*
el/la cantante *singer 3r*
cantar *to sing 3*
la cantidad *quantity, amount 4r*
cantonés/cantonesa *Cantonese 3r*
la capa *layer 15r*
la capital *capital 1r*
el capitán/la capitana *captain 7r*
el capó *hood 12*
la cara *face 11*
el carácter *character 8r*
caribeño/a *from the Caribbean 6r*
el cariño *affection, love 5r, 14r*
el carnaval *carnival, Mardi Gras 8*
la carne *meat 10*
caro/a *expensive 6*
la carrera *career 1r; race 7*
la carreta *cart, wagon 8*
la carretera *highway 12*
la carroza *float 8*
la carta *menu 3r; letter 12*
el/la cartero/a *letter carrier 12*
(de) cartón *cardboard 15*
la casa *house, home 1*
casado/a *married 2*
casarse *to get married 4r, 4, 14*
casero/a *adj. house 11r*
el casillero *pigeonhole 5r*
el caso *case 9r*
el catarro *cold 11*
católico/a *Catholic 8r*
la causa *cause 12r*
la cebolla *onion 5r, 10*
la ceja *eyebrow 11*
la celebración *celebration 8*
celebrar *to celebrate 3*
el celular *cellular phone 10r*
el cementerio *cemetery 8*
la cena *dinner, supper 3*
cenar *to have dinner 3*
centrar(se) *to center 10r*
el centro *downtown, center 1r, 5; centro comercial shopping center 5r, 6*
cerca (de) *near (close to) 5*
el cerdo *pork 10*
el cerebro *brain 11*
la ceremonia *ceremony 6r*
la cereza *cherry 10*
la cerveza *beer 3*
el césped *lawn 5*
el/la cesto/a *basket, hoop 7*
el cesto *wastepaper basket P*
[S.L.1]el ceviche *raw fish dish 3*
el champaña *champagne 4r*
la chaqueta *jacket 6*

el cheque de viajero *traveler's check 12; el cheque check 6r*
la chica *girl P*
el chico *boy P*
chileno/a *Chilean 2*
la chimenea *fireplace 5*
chocar (qu) *to crash 12r*
el chocolate *chocolate 3r*
el/la chofer *driver 9*
la chuleta *chop 10*
el churro *deep fried batter 10r*
el ciclismo *cycling 7*
el/la ciclista *cyclist 7*
ciego/a *blind 15r*
el cielo *sky 12r, 15*
ciencias *sciences 1; las ciencias políticas political science 1*
el/la científico/a *scientist 9*
cierto *adv. true, certain 1r*
la cifra *figure 14r*
la cima *summit, top 8r*
el cine *movies 3*
la cintura *waist 11*
el cinturón *belt 6*
la circunstancia *circumstance 5r*
el/la cirujano/a *surgeon 11r*
la ciudad *city 1r, 3*
la civilización *civilization 4r*
¡Claro! *of course 5*
el/la cliente/a *client 6r, 9*
climatizado/a *air conditioned 15r*
la clínica *clinic, hospital 11r*
la cocina *kitchen 5*
cocinado/a *cooked 10r*
cocinar *to cook 5*
el coco *coconut 4r*
el codo *elbow 11*
el cognado *cognate Pr*
la coherencia *coherence 4r*
el cohete *rocket 15*
la colección *collection 4r*
el collar *necklace 6*
colombiano/a *Colombian 2*
el colón *monetary unit of Costa Rica and El Salvador 1r*
de color entero *solid color 6*
el colorido *color 8r; colorful 8r*
la columna *column 4r*
el comedor *dining room 5*
comentar *to comment, to discuss 6r*
comenzar (ie) *to begin 8, 9*
comer *to eat 1r, 3*
el comercio *commerce 13*
cómico/a *comic, funny Pr*
la comida *dinner, supper 3*
el comienzo *beginning 8*
el comino *cumin 10r*
la comisión *commission 7r*
como *adv. as, like 1r*
¿Cómo es? *What is he/she/it like? P*

la cómoda   *dresser* 5
cómodo/a   *comfortable* 3r
¡Cómo no!   *Of course!* 9
¿Cómo se llama usted?   *What's your name? (formal)* P
¿Cómo te llamas?   *What's your name? (familiar)* P
¿Cómo te va?   *How is it going?* 1
el/la compañero/a   *partner, classmate* Pr, 1
la compañía/empresa   *company* 9
la comparación   *comparison* 8r
comparar   *to compare* 4r
la comparsa   *costumed group* 8
la compensación   *compensation* 5r
la competencia   *competition* 1r
competir (i)   *to compete* 7
complicado/a   *complex* 10r
el comportamiento   *behavior* 9r
composición   *composition* 1r
comprar   *to buy* 1
la computadora   *computer* P
comunicar(se) (qu)   *to communicate* 3r, 9
la comunidad   *community* 4r
con   *with* 1
el concierto   *concert* Pr
la concordancia   *agreement* 4r
el concurso   *contest* 1r
la condición   *condition* 10r
el condimento   *condiment* 10r
el condominio   *condominium* 1r
la conferencia   *lecture* 1r
la confianza   *trust* 14
congelar(se)   *to freeze* 7
el congreso   *congress, convention* 5r
el conjunto   *set, group* 12r; *adj. joint* 9r
conmigo   *with me* 7
conocer (zc)   *to know, to meet* 5
el/la consejero/a   *counselor, adviser* 9r
el consejo   *advice* 11r
el/la conserje   *concierge* 12
la conservación   *preservation* 15
conservado/a   *kept, preserved* 5r
considerablemente   *considerably* 7r
la construcción   *construction* 5r
construir (y)   *to build* 15
el consultorio   *doctor's office* 9, 11
la contabilidad   *accounting* 1r
el/la contador/a   *accountant* 9
el contagio   *contagion, spreading of a disease* 11r
la contaminación   *contamination* 8r
contaminado/a   *polluted, contaminated* 7
contar (ue)   *to tell* 8r; *to tell, count* 13
contener (g, ie)   *to contain* 10r

el contenido   *n. contents* 4r; *contenido adj. controlled* 11r
contento/a   *happy, glad* 2
contestar   *to answer* 6
contigo   *with you (familiar)* 7
continuación: a continuación   *below* 10r
continuar   *to continue* 14
contra   *against* 7r
contrario/a   *opposite, contrary* 7
el contraste   *contrast* 4r
contratar   *to hire* 14r
el contrato   *contract* 9r
la conversación   *conversation* Pr
conversador/a   *talkative* 2
conversar   *to talk, to converse* 1
la copa   *drink* 3r; *(stemmed) glass* 10
la copia   *copy* 6r
copiar   *to copy* 1r
el coraje   *courage* 12r
el corazón   *heart* 11
la corbata   *tie* 6
el córdoba   *monetary unit of Nicaragua* 1r
correcto/a   *correct* 4r
el correo electrónico   *e-mail* 15
correr   *to run* 3
correspondiente   *corresponding* 7r
la corrida (de toros)   *bullfight* 1r, 8
cortar   *to cut* 5r, 9
la cortesía   *courtesy* Pr
la cortina   *curtain* 5
corto/a   *short (in length)* 2
la cosa   *thing* 1r
el cosmético   *cosmetic* 6r
cosmopolita   *cosmopolitan* 6r
costar (ue)   *to cost* 4
la costilla   *rib* 10
la costumbre   *custom* 8
crear   *to create* 4r
creativo/a   *creative* Pr
el crecimiento   *growth* 15r
creer   *to believe* 5
la crema   *cream* 10
el crimen   *crime* 8r
criollo/a   *adj. Spanish American* 3r
la crisis   *crisis* 14r
el crucero   *cruise* 6r, 12
el cuaderno   *notebook* P
la cuadra   *city block* 12
cuadrado/a   *square* 15r
el cuadro   *picture* 5
de cuadros   *plaid* 6
cuando   *adv. when* 1r
¿Cuánto cuesta?   *How much is it?* 1
cuarto   *quarter* P
el cuarto/dormitorio   *bedroom* 5
cubano/a   *Cuban* 2
el cubo: en cubitos   *in cubes* 10r
cubrir   *to cover* 13

la cucharada   *spoon(full)* 10r
la cucharadita   *teaspoon* 10r
la cuchara   *spoon* 10
la cucharita   *teaspoon* 10
el cuchillo   *knife* 10
la cueca   *typical Chilean music* 12r
el cuello   *neck* 11
la cuenca   *river basin* 15
la cuenta: cuenta corriente   *checking account* 9r
el cuento   *story* 13
de cuero   *leather* 6
cuidar(se)   *to take care of* 5r, 11
el cultivo   *cultivation* 15r
la cumbia   *Colombian music and dance* 4r
el cumpleaños   *birthday* Pr, 3
el/la curandero/a   *quack doctor* 11r
la curiosidad   *curiosity* 1r
curioso/a   *curious* 5r
el currículum   *résumé* 9
el cursillo   *short course of studies* 12r
el curso   *course* 1r

D

dar   *to give, to hand* 6
los datos   *data* 14
de   *of, from* 2
debajo (de)   *under* P
deber   *ought to, should* 3
debido a   *due to* 15
débil   *weak* 2
decir (g, i)   *to say, tell* 4
el décuplo   *decuple, tenfold* 15r
el dedo   *finger* 11
la defensa   *defense* 11r
la deforestación   *deforestation* 15
dejar   *to leave (behind)* 5r; *to leave* 9
delante de   *in front of* 9r
delgado/a   *thin* 2
la delincuencia   *delinquency* 8r
del   *of the (contraction of de + el)* 1r, 2
el demostrativo   *demonstrative* 5r
denso/a   *dense* 15r
el/la dentista   *dentist* 11r
dentro   *inside, in* 4r
el departamento   *department* 1r
el/la dependiente/a   *salesperson* 1
el/la deportista   *sportsman/woman* 7r
deportivo/a   *adj. sport* 1r
deprimido/a   *depressed* 11
la derecha   *right* 4r
el derecho   *right* 14
[S.L.2]desayunar   *to have breakfast* 4
el desayuno   *breakfast* 3
descansar   *to rest* 3
el descanso   *rest* 7r

descomponer   *to break down* 15
desconocido/a   *unknown* 9r
describir   *describe* 1r
la descripción   *description* Pr
el descuento   *discount* 6r
desde   *since* 13
desde luego   *of course* 7r
desear   *to wish, to want* 2
desempleado/a   *unemployed* 9r
el desfile   *parade* 8
desfile de moda   *fashion show* 6r
el deshielo   *thaw* 15r
el desierto   *desert* 3r
desorganizado/a   *disorganized* 9r
despacio   *slowly* Pr
la despedida   *farewell* Pr
despegar   *to take off* 15r
despejado/a   *clear* 7
el despertador   *alarm clock* 7r
despertar(se) (ie)   *to wake up* 7
después   *after, later* 1r; *then* 4r
destacado/a   *outstanding,
   distinguished* 15
el destino   *destination* 3r, 12
detener (g, ie)   *to stop* 7r
el deterioro   *damage* 7r
determinado/a   *specific* 6r
detrás (de)   *behind* P
el día   *day* P
el/la diabético/a   *diabetic* 10r
el diablo   *devil* 8r
el diálogo   *dialog* 5r
el diámetro   *diameter* 10r
el dibujo   *drawing* 4r
el diccionario   *dictionary* 1
el diente   *tooth* 11
la diferencia   *difference* 3r
diferente   *different* 1r
difícil   *difficult* 1
difunto/a, muerto/a   *dead* 8
dinámico/a   *dynamic* Pr
el dinero   *money* 3r, 6
Dios   *God* 8r
la dirección   *address* P; *direction* 12r
la directiva   *board of directors* 14r
el directorio   *directory* 5r
la discoteca   *dance club* 1
la discriminación   *discrimination* 14r
discutir   *to argue* 7
el/la diseñador/a   *designer* 5r
diseñar   *to design* 9r, 15
el diseño   *design* 1r
el disfraz   *costume* 8r
disfrazarse   *to wear a costume* 8
dispuesto/a   *ready* 15
la distancia   *distance* 12r
disuelto/a   *dissolved* 10r
la diversión   *entertainment* 3r
diverso   *diverse, different* 5r
divertido/a   *funny, amusing* 2

divertirse (ie, i)   *to have a good
   time* 8; *to have a good time/fun* 3r
divorciado/a   *divorced* 4
divorciarse   *to divorce* 14
el divorcio   *divorce* 14
doblar   *to fold* 5; *to bend* 11r;
   to turn 12
doble   *double* 5r
el/la doctor/a   *doctor* Pr
doler (ue)   *to hurt* 11
doméstico/a   *domestic* 4r
el/la dominicano/a   *Dominican* 2,
   11r
dónde   *interrog. where* 1r
¿Dónde está...?   *Where is . . . ?* P
[S.L.3]dormir (ue)   *to sleep* 4; **dormir la
   siesta**   *to take a nap* 4
dormirse (ue)   *to fall asleep* 7
la droga   *drug* 8
la ducha   *shower* 5
dudar   *to doubt* 10
el dulce   *candy/sweets* 10
durante   *during* 1r
durar   *to last* 7
duro/a   *hard* 10r
el/la camarero/a   *waiter/waitress* 3

E

ecológico/a   *ecological* 7r
la economía   *economics* 1;
   economy 2r; *inexpensive* [S.L.4]5r
ecuatoriano/a   *Ecuadorian* 10r
el edificio   *building* 1r, 5
educado/a   *educated* 5r
el efecto   *effect* 10r
la eficiencia   *efficiency* 14
eficiente   *efficient* Pr
el/la ejecutivo/a   *executive* 9
el ejemplo   *example* 1r
el ejercicio   *exercise* 4r
él   *he* P
el/la electricista   *electrician* 9
eléctrico/a   *electric* 3r
electrónico/a   *electronic* 3r
elegante   *elegant* Pr
eliminar   *to eliminate* 10r
ella   *she* P
ellos/ellas   *they* 1
embarazada   *pregnant* 11r
la emergencia   *emergency* 9r
el/la emigrante   *emigrant* 13
emigrar   *to emigrate* 13
emocionado/a   *excited* 7
la empanada   *small meat pie* 10r;
   empanadas salteñas *typical
   Bolivian meat pies* 10r **empezar
   (ie, c)**   *to begin, start* 3r; *to begin,
   to start* 4

el/la empleado/a   *employee* 9, 12
en   *in* P
en busca de   *in search of* 15
en efectivo   *cash* 6
en la actualidad   *at the present
   time* 13
en punto   *sharp* P
en realidad/realmente   *in fact, really* 9
enamorarse   *to fall in love* 11r
encantado/a   *delighted* P
encantar   *to delight, to love* 6
el encanto   *charm* 1r
encerrado/a   *locked up* 12r
encerrar (ie)   *to lock up* 8
el encierro (de los toros)   *penning
   (of bulls)* 8r
encima   *on top* 10r
encontrar (ue)   *to find* 6, 14
la energía   *energy* 1r
enérgico/a   *energetic* 14
enfermarse   *to become sick* 11
la enfermedad   *illness* 11
el/la enfermero/a   *nurse* 9
enfermo/a   *adj. sick* 3r; *sick* 11
enfrente (de)   *in front of* P
enfriar   *to cool down* 10r
engordar   *to gain weight* 10r
enharinado/a   *lightly covered with
   flour* 10r
enlatado/a   *canned* 10r
enojado/a   *angry* 2
la ensalada   *salad* 3
enseguida   *immediately* 6
entender (ie)   *to understand* 4
entonces   *then* 8
el entorno   *surroundings*[S.L.5] 7r
la entrada   *appetizer* 3r; *ticket for
   admission* 3r, 8; *entrance* 5r
entrar   *to go in, to enter* 6
entre   *between, among* P
entregar   *to deliver* 5r
el/la entrenador/a   *coach* 7
el entrenamiento   *training* 10r
el entretenimiento   *entertainment* 3r
la entrevista   *interview* 9
el/la entrevistador/a   *interviewer* 9r
entrevistar   *to interview* 4r
el entusiasmo *enthusiasm*   10r
enviar   *to send* 9
el episodio   *episode* 4r
el equipaje   *luggage* 12
el equipo   *team* 7
eres   *you are (familiar)* P
es   *you are (formal), he/she is* P
la escala   *stopping point* 12r
el escaparate   *shop window* 6r
la escasez   *lack, scarcity* 7r
la escena   *scene* 8r
escoger (j)   *to choose* 1r
escolar   *adj. school* 4r

escribir   *to write* 3
el/la escritor/a   *writer* 13
el escritorio   *desk* P
escuchar   *to listen* Pr; *listen (to)* 1
la escuela   *school* 1r
el/la escultor/a   *sculptor* 13
ese/a   *that (adjective)* P
espacial   *adj. space* 9r
el espacio   *space* 7r
espacioso/a   *spacious* 5r
la espalda   *back* 11
español/a   *adj. Spanish* 1r, 2
el español   *n. Spanish* Pr, 1
la especia   *spice* 5r
especial   *special* 3r; **en especial**
   especially 8r
la especialidad   *specialty* 1r
la especie   *species* 3r
especificar (qu)   *to specify, to point
   out* 4r
el espectáculo   *show* 3r
el/la espectador/a   *spectator* 7r
el espejo   *mirror* 5; **el espejo**
   retrovisor *rearview mirror* 12
la esperanza   *hope* 10r
esperar   *to wait for* 9; *to hope,
   to expect* 10
las espinacas   *spinach* 10
el espíritu   *spirit, disposition* 7r
la esposa   *wife* 4
el esposo   *husband* 4
el esquí   *skiing, ski* 7
esquiar   *to ski* 7
la esquina   *corner* 11r, 12
está   *he/she is, you are (formal)* P
establecer(se) (zc)   *to establish, to
   settle* 11r
el estadio   *stadium* 3r
la estadística   *statistic* 14
el estado   *state* 1r; *condition* 7r
estándar   [S.L.6]*standard* 10r
estar   *to be* Pr, 1
estar a cargo   *to be in charge* 9r
estar de acuerdo   *to agree* 7
estar de moda   *to be fashionable* 6
estar en forma   *to keep fit* 4r
estar enamorado/a   *to be in love* 13
estás   *you are (familiar)* P
estatura   *height* 14r
este/a   *this* 1
el este   *east* 1r
el estéreo   *stereo* 5r
el estilo   *style* 5r
estirar   *to stretch* 11r
esto   *this* 4r
el estómago   *stomach* 3r, 11
estornudar   *to sneeze* 11
la estrategia   *strategy* 7r
estrecho/a   *narrow, tight* 6
el estrés   *stress* 12r

la estructura   *structure* 4r
el/la estudiante   *student* P
estudiantil   *adj student* 1r
estudiar   *to study* 1
el estudio   *study* 1r; *studying* 9r
estudioso/a   *studious* 1
la estufa   *stove* 5
la etapa   *stage* 4r
el evento   *event* 1r
la evidencia   *evidence* 12r
el examen   *test, examination* 1
examinar   *to examine* 11
excelente   *excellent* 1
excepcional   *exceptional* 5r
la excursión   *excursion* 3r
exhaustivamente   *exhaustingly* 12r
la experiencia   *experience* 1r, 9
el experimento   *experiment* 15r
el/la experto/a   *expert* 7r
la explicación   *explanation* 9r
la exportación   *export* 9r
expresar   *to express* 10r
extender(se) (ie)   *to extend,
   to expand* 2r
la extinción   *extinction* 5r
extranjero/a   *adj. foreign* 1r
extrovertido/a   *extroverted* Pr

F

la fábrica   *factory* 15r
fabuloso/a   *fabulous, great* 3
fácil   *easy* 1
fácilmente   *easily* 9r
facturar   *to check in (luggage)* 12
la falda   *skirt* 6
falso/a   *false* 1r
falta: hacer falta   *to need* 14r
la familia   *family* Pr
famoso/a   *famous* 1r
fanático/a   *fanatic* 4r
fantástico/a   *fantastic* 3r
el/la farmacéutico/a   *pharmacist* 11
fascinante   *fascinating* 4r
la fase   *phase* 1r
el fastidio   *annoyance* 4r
la fatiga   *fatigue* 10r
fatigado/a   *fatigued, tired* 10r
la fecha   *date* P
felicitar   *to congratulate* 7r
feliz   *happy* 2
feo/a   *ugly* 2
la feria   *fair* 1r
la ferretería   *hardware shop* 6r
la festividad   *festivity* 8r
festivo   *festive* 8r
fiable   *trustworthy* 14
la fibra   *fiber* 10r
la fiebre   *fever* 11

fielmente   *faithfully* 7r
la fiesta   *party* Pr, 3
la filosofía   *philosophy* 1r
el fin   *end* 7
fin de semana   *objective* 9r[S.L.7]
el fin de semana   *weekend* 1
el final   *end* 5r
finalista   *finalist* 7r
financiado/a   *financed* 11r
financiero   *financial* 14
la firma   *signature* 1r
la física   *physics* Pr
físicamente   *physically* 7r
el/la fisioterapista   *physiotherapist*
   11r
la flor   *flower* 5r, 7
la fobia   *phobia* 12r
los fondos   *money* 9r; *fund* 11r
la formación   *formation* 7r
la fórmula   *formula* 15r
la fortaleza   *fortress* 3r
la fortuna   *fortune* 1r
la foto(grafía)   *photo* 4
la fotocopiadora   *photocopier* 9r
fracturar(se)   *to fracture, break* 11
la frase   *phrase* 8r
la frecuencia   *frequency* 1r
el fregadero   *kitchen sink* 5
freír (i)   *to fry* 10
la frente   *forehead* 11
la fresa   *strawberry* 10
fresco/a   *cool* 7, *fresh* 10r
los frijoles   *beans* 3r
frío/a   *cold* 3
frito/a   *fried* 3
la fruta   *fruit* 3
la fuente   *fountain* 1r; *source* 8r
fuerte   *strong* 2
fumar   *to smoke* 11
el fútbol   *soccer* 7
el/la futbolista   *football player* 7r

G

la gabardina   *raincoat* 7r
las gafas de sol   *sunglasses* 6
la galleta   *cookie* 10
la gamba   *shrimp (in Spain)* 10r
el/la ganador/a   *winner* 7r
ganar   *to win* 7
el garaje   *garage* 5
la garganta   *throat* 11
la gasolina   *gasoline* 12r
gastar   *to spend* 6
la gelatina   *gelatin* 10
gemelo/a   *twin* 4
genealógico/a   *genealogical* 4r
generoso/a   *generous* Pr
el género   *type* 4r

genético/a   *genetic* 15r
la gente   *people* 8
la geografía   *geography* 1
el/la gerente (de ventas)   *(sales) manager* 9
gigante   *adj. giant* 5r
el gimnasio   *gymnasium* 1
el gobierno   *government* 13
la golondrina   *sparrow* 15r
gordo/a   *fat* 2
la gorra   *cap* 6
la grabadora   *tape recorder, cassette player* P
el grado   *degree* 7r; *grade* 8r
la graduación   *graduation* Pr
gradualmente   *gradually* 15r
graduarse   *to graduate* 14r
gráfico/a   *graphic* 1r
gramatical   *grammatical* 4r
gran   *great* 1r
grande   *big* 1
el grano   *grain* 10r
la grasa   *fat* 10r
la gravedad   *seriousness* 15r
la gripe   *flu* 11
grueso/a   *coarse* 7r
el grupo   *group* 1r
el guajolote   *turkey* 10r
el guante   *glove* 6
la guantera   *glove compartment* 12
guapo/a   *good-looking, handsome* 2
el guaraní   *monetary unit of Paraguay* 1r; *language spoken in Paraguay* 10r
guatemalteco/a   *Guatemalan* 2
la guayabera   *loose-fitting men's shirt* 6r
el gueto   *ghetto* 15r
el/la guía   *guide* 3r
la guitarra   *guitar* 3
el/la guitarrista   *guitar player* 13
gustar *to be pleasing to, to like* 6; le gusta(n) *you (formal) like* 2; me gusta(n) *I like* 2; te gusta(n) *you (familiar) like* 2; Me gustaría... *I would like . . .* 6
el gusto *liking, taste* 6r

H

haber   *to have (auxiliary verb)* 13
había   *there was, there were* 8
la habitación   *room* 5r
la habitación doble/sencilla   *double/single room* 12
el/la habitante   *inhabitant* 14
el hábito   *habit* 6r
hablar   *to speak* 1
Hace calor.   *It's hot.* 7

hacer (g)   *to do, make* 1r, 4
hacer cola   *to stand in line* 12
hacer el papel   *play the part* 6r
hacer escala   *to make a stopover* 12
hacer la cama   *to make the bed* 4
hacer la maleta   *to pack* 12r
hacer preguntas   *to ask questions* 4r
hacerse   *to become* 4r
hacia   *towards, near* 8r
la hamburguesa   *hamburger* 1r, 3
la hamburguesería   *hamburger place* 3r
la harina   *flour* 10
hay   *there is, there are* P
el helado   *ice cream* 3
el hemisferio   *hemisphere* 10r
la hermana   *sister* 4
el hermano   *brother* 4
hervir (ie, i)   *to boil* 10
el hielo   *ice* 7
la hierba/yerba   *herb* 3r
la hija   *daughter* 4
el hijo   *son* 4
hijo/a único/a   *only child* 4
hiperactivo/a   *hyperactive* 1r
hípico/a   *adj. horse* 7r
hispano/a   *Hispanic* 1r
el/la hispanohablante   *Spanish speaker* 13
la historia   *history* 1
el hogar   *home* 14
el hombre   *man* 4r
el hombre/la mujer de negocios   *businessman/woman* 9
el hombro   *shoulder* 11
hondureño/a   *Honduran* 5r
la honestidad   *honesty* 14
la hora   *hour, time* P
hora americana/inglesa   *precise time* Pr
la hora de llegada/salida   *arrival/departure time* 12
hora de salida   *dismissal time* 4r
el horario   *schedule* Pr
hornear   *to bake* 10r
el hospital   *hospital* 1r
hoy   *today* P
hoy en día   *nowadays* 4r, 8
el hueso   *bone* 11
el huevo   *egg* 3
huevo duro   *hard-boiled egg* 10r
humanidades   *humanities* 1
húmedo/a   *humid, damp* 10r

I

de ida y vuelta   *round trip* 12
idealista   *adj. idealistic* Pr
la identificación   *identification* Pr

el idioma   *language* 13
la iglesia   *church* 1r, 8
igual   *adj. the same* 1r; al igual que   *like, same as* 1r
la igualdad   *equality* 14
igualmente   *likewise* P
el imperio   *empire* 3r
el impermeable   *raincoat* 6
el implante   *implant* 15r
importante   *important* Pr; lo importante   *the important thing* 9
impresionante   *impressive* 1r
el impuesto   *tax* 12r
impulsivo/a   *impulsive* Pr
inapropiado/a   *inappropriate* 9r
el/la inca   *Inca* 3r
el incendio   *fire* 9
incentivar   *to encourage, to incite* 7r
inconcluso/a   *unfinished* 12r
incorrecto/a   *incorrect* 14r
indeciso/a   *undecided* 5r
independencia   *independence* 3r
independiente   *independent* Pr
indicado/a   *indicated, recommended* 8r
indicar   *to indicate* 9
inesperado   *unexpected* 8r
la infección   *infection* 11
infeccioso/a   *infectious* 11r
la influencia   *influence* 5r
influenciar   *to influence* 10r
informal   *informal* Pr
informática   *computer science* 1
el/la ingeniero/a   *engineer* 9
el inglés   *English* 1r
ingresar   *to be admitted* 1r
el ingreso   *income* 9r
el/la inmigrante   *immigrant* 13
el inodoro   *toilet* 5
inquieto/a   *restless* 7r
el instituto   *institute* 9r
el instrumento   *instrument* 3r
el/la integrante   *member* 11r
inteligente   *intelligent* Pr
la intención   *intention* 15r
el/la interesado/a   *interested (person), applicant* 9r
interesante   *interesting* Pr
interesar   *to interest* 6
el/la intérprete   *interpreter* 9
íntimo/a   *intimate, close* 1r
introducir (zc)   *to introduce* 7r
introvertido/a   *introvert* Pr
inventar   *to invent* 7r
investigar (gu)   *to investigate* 8r
la invitación   *invitation* 8
invitar   *to invite* 3r, 8
la inyección   *injection* 11
ir de compras   *to go shopping* 6
ir(se)   *to go away, to leave* 7

irónico/a   *ironic* 9r
ir   *to go* Pr, 3; **ir de compras**
   to go shopping 3r
la isla   *island* 6r
el itinerario   *itinerary* 12r
la izquierda   *left* 4r
a la izquierda/derecha   *to the*
   [S.L.8]*left/right* 12
el jabón   *soap* 5r

J

Januká *Hanukka* 3r
el jardín   *backyard, garden* 5
la jaula   *(bird)cage* 14r
el/la jefe/jefa   *boss* 9
el jesuita   *Jesuit* 10r
Jesús   *Jesus* 8r
el joropo   *typical Venezuelan*
   music 12r
joven   *young* 2
el/la joven   *young man/woman* 3
la joya   *jewel, jewelry* 5r
la joyería   *jewelry* 3r
el juego/partido   *game* 7
el/la juez   *judge* 9
el/la jugador/a   *player* 7
jugar (ue)   *to play (game, sport)* 4
jugar a los bolos   *to bowl* 7
el jugo   *juice* 3
el juguete   *toy* 6r
la jungla   *jungle* 5r
juntos/as   *together* 4

L

el labio   *lip* 11
el laboratorio   *laboratory* 1; **el**
   laboratorio de lenguas   *language*
   lab 1
lácteo/a   *dairy (product),*
   milky 10
al lado (de)   *next to* P
el lago   *lake* 7
la lámpara   *lamp* 5
la lana   *wool* 6
la langosta   *lobster* 10
lanzar (c)   *to throw* 7r
el lápiz   *pencil* P
[S.L.9]latinoamericano/a
   Latin-American 7r
el lavabo   *washbowl, bathroom*
   sink 5
la lavadora   *washer* 5
la lavandería   *laundry room* 5r
el lavaplatos   *dishwasher* 5
lavar(se)   *to wash (oneself)* 4

lavar(se) los dientes   *to brush one's*
   teeth 7
la leche   *milk* 3
la lechuga   *lettuce* 3
leer   *to read* 3
la legumbre   *legume, vegetable* 10r
lejos (de)   *far (from)* 5
el lempira   *monetary unit of*
   Honduras 5r
los lentes de contacto   *contact*
   lenses 2
el león   *lion* 3r
la letra   *letter* 9r
el letrero   *sign* 14r
levantar   *to raise* 7
levantarse   *to get up* 4
la ley   *law* 14r
liberado/a   *released* 15
la libra   *pound* 10r
libre   *free* 1r
la librería   *bookstore* 1
el libro   *book* P
ligero/a   *light* 15r
el limón   *lemon* 10
el limpiaparabrisas   *windshield*
   wiper 12
limpiar   *to clean* 5
limpio/a   *clean* 5
la lista de espera   *waiting list* 12
listo/a   *smart, ready* 2
la literatura   *literature* 1
la llamada   *call* 9
llamar   *to call* 3r
la llanta   *tire* 12
la llave   *key* 12
la llegada   *arrival* 8r
me llamo...   *my name is . . .* P
llegar   *to arrive* 1
llenar   *to fill (out)* 9
lleno/a   *full* 12
llevar   *to wear, to take* 6
llevarse bien   *to get along well* 13
llevarse mal   *to not get along* 2r, 13
llover (ue)   *to rain* 7
la lluvia   *rain* 7
la localización   *location* 5r
loco/a   *crazy* 6r
el/la locutor/a   *radio announcer* 9
el logro   *accomplishment* 8r
la loma   *hill* 5r
la longitud   *length* 7r
lo   *pron. you, him, it;* **lo** + *adj. the* 1r;
   lo que *what, that which* 1r
la lotería   *lottery* 5r
luego   *then* 1r; *after* 6r
el lugar   *place* Pr; **tener lugar** *to take*
   place 8r
lujoso/a   *luxurious* 6r
luna de miel   *honeymoon* 7r
de lunares   *polka-dotted* 6

M

la madera   *wood* 5r
la madrastra   *stepmother* 4
la madre   *mother* 4
el/la madrileño/a   *person from*
   Madrid 1r
la madrina   *godmother* 4
la madrugada   *early morning,*
   dawn 1r
magnífico/a   *great* 6
el maíz/elote   *corn* 10
la maleta   *suitcase* 12
el maletero   *trunk* 12
el maletín   *briefcase* 12
malo/a   *bad* 1
la mamá   *mom* 1r, 4
la mañana   *morning* P
mañana   *tomorrow* P
mandar   *to send* 5r, 9
el mandato   *order, command* 9r
manejar   *to drive* 12; *to manage,*
   to handle 15
la manera   *way* 4r
el mango   *mango* 10r
la mano   *hand* Pr, 11; **manos a la**
   obra *let's get to work* 1r
la manta   *blanket* 5
el mantel   *tablecloth* 10
mantener (g, ie)   *maintain* 8
la mantequilla   *butter* 10
el manual   *manual* 5r
la manzana   *apple* 10
la manzanilla   *camomile* 11r
el mapa   *map* 1
maquillar(se)   *to put on makeup* 7
máquina   *machine* 15r; **máquina de**
   escribir *typewriter* 9r; **la máquina**
   fotográfica *camera* 6r
maravilloso/a   *marvelous* 8
la marca   *brand name* 6r
el marcapasos   *pacemaker* 15r
la margarina   *margarine* 10
el mariachi   *Mexican band* 8r
la marinera   *typical Peruvian*
   music 12r
los mariscos   *shellfish;* 10
el mar   *sea* 1r; 3
más o menos   *more or less* P
más... que   *more . . . than, . . . -er*
   than (e.g., shorter than) 8
la masa   *dough* 10
las matemáticas   *mathematics* Pr
el material   *material* 8r
materno/a   *adj. mother,* 4r
el matrimonio   *marriage, wedding* 4r
máximo/a   *maximum* 7r
la mayonesa   *mayonnaise* 10
el/la mayor   *greater* 4r; **la mayor**
   parte *most* 1r

la mayoría   *the majority* 5r, 14
mayor   *older* 2
el/la mayor   *the oldest* 4
el médano   *slope* 7r
media   *half* P
la media   *average* 12r; adj. *middle* 4r
la media hermana   *half sister* 4
mediano/a   *average, medium (height)* 2
las medias   *stockings, socks* 6
la medicina   *medication* 11r
medicina   *medicine* 1
[S.L.10]el/la médico/a   *medical doctor* 9
el medio   *means* 2r
el medio ambiente   *environment* 15
el medio hermano   *half brother* 4
la megatienda   *superstore* 6r
la mejilla   *cheek* 11
mejor   *best* 7
mejorar   *to improve* 9
la melodía   *melody* 8
el/la menor   *the youngest* 4
menos   *minus, to (for telling time)* P
menos... que   *less than, fewer than* 8
el mensaje   *message* 4r
el menú   *menu* 3r
el mercado   *market* 6r; el mercado al aire libre   *open-air market* 6
el merengue   *typical music of the Dominican Republic* 11r
el mes   *month* P
la mesa   *table* P
la mesa de noche   *night stand* 5
el método   *method* 1r
el metro   *subway* 6r, 12; *meter* 6r
mexicano/a   *Mexican* 2
mi   *my* P
el micrófono   *microphone* 9r
el (horno) microondas   *microwave oven* 5
el microscopio   *microscope* 9r
mientras   *while* 8
el milagro   *miracle* 8r
el milenio   *millennium* 7r
la milla   *mile* 3r
la minería   *mining* 15r
minero/a   adj. *mining* 9r
el ministerio   *ministry* 14
mirar   *to look (at)* 1
el/la misionero/a   *missionary* 10r
lo mismo   *the same thing* 7r
el misterio   *mystery* 1r
la mitad   *half* 14
la mochila   *backpack* P
el/la modelo   *model* 3r
moderno/a   *modern* Pr
molestar   *to bother, be bothered by* 11
molida/picada   *ground beef* 10

monetario/a   *monetary* 5r
el monstruo   *monster* 9r
montar   *to ride* 1
montar en bicicleta   *to ride a bicycle* 1
moreno/a   *brunet, brunette* 2
morir (ue)   *to die* 13
el/la moro/a   *Moor* 1r
la mostaza   *mustard* 10
el mostrador   *counter* 12
mostrar (ue)   *to show* 6
el motivo   *motive* 8r
la moto(cicleta)   *motorcycle* 4r
mover (ue)   *to move* 8
la movilidad   *mobility* 8r
mucho/a   *much, a lot* 1r; *much, a lot* 2
mucho gusto   *pleased/nice to meet you* P
la mudanza   *move* 14r
la mueblería   *furniture store* 5r
la muestra   *sample* 3r
la multitud   *crowd* 14r
mundial   *worldwide* 7
la muñeca   *wrist* 11
el músculo   *muscle* 11
el museo   *museum* 1r
la música   *music* 1r, 3; música ambiental *background music* 4r
el/la músico/a   *musician* 9r

N

nacer (zc)   *to be born* 13
la nación   *nation* 3r
nadar   *to swim* 3
la naranja   *orange* 3
el narcotráfico   *drug traffic* 14r
la nariz   *nose* 11
la narración   *narration* 6r
el/la narrador/a   *narrator* 15r
la natación   *swimming* 7r
la natalidad   *birth* 14r
nativo/a   *native* 1r
la naturaleza   *nature* 7r
la náusea   *nausea* 11r
la nave espacial   *space ship* 15
navegable   *navigable* 10r
la navidad   *Christmas* 3r
necesitar   *to need* 1
negativo/a   *negative* 4r
el nervio   *nerve* 11
nervioso/a   *nervous* 2
nevar (ie)   *to snow* 7
ni siquiera   *not even* 15r
nicaragüense   *Nicaraguan* 2
la nieta   *granddaughter* 4
el nieto   *grandson* 4

la nieve   *snow* 7
la niñera   *nanny* 9r
ninguno/a   *not any, none* 7r
el/la niño/a   *child* 1r, 4
el nivel   *level* 14
no (ni)... ni   *neither . . . nor* 2
no sé   *I don't know* Pr
el nombre   *name* Pr
nocturno/a   adj. *night* 8r
nominado/a   *nominated* 8r
el norte   *north* 1r
norteamericano/a   *American* 1
nosotros/nosotras   *we* 1
la nota   *note, grade* 1
notable   *notable, noteworthy* 14
notablemente   *notably* 9r
la noticia   *news* 4
la novela   *novel* 1r, 13
el/la novelista   *novelist* 13
la novia   *fiancée, girlfriend* 4
el novio   *fiancé, boyfriend* 4
nublado/a   *cloudy* 7
nuestro/a(s)   *our* 1r
nuevo/a   *new* 1r, 2; nuevo sol *monetary unit of Peru* 1r
el número   *number* P
la nutrición   *nutrition* 10r
nutrido/a   *full, busy* 14r

O

el objetivo   *objective* 1r
la obra   *work* 1r, 13
obra de teatro   *play* 3r
obra maestra   *masterpiece* 13
el/la obrero/a   *worker* 9
obtener (g, ie)   *to obtain, to get* 3r
ocupado/a   *busy* 4
odiar   *to hate* 13
la oferta   *offer* 6r
la oficina   *office* 1
ofrecer (zc)   *to offer* 9
el oído   *(inner) ear* 11
oír (g)   *to hear* 4
ojalá   *I/we hope* 10
los ojos   *eyes* 2
ojos azules   *blue eyes* 2; ojos verdes *green eyes* 2
la ola   *wave* 7r
oliva: de oliva   *olive* 10r
olvidar   *to forget* 15
la operación   *operation* 11r
operar   *to operate* 11r
la opinión   *opinion* 1r
la oportunidad   *opportunity* 9
optativo/a   *optional* 15r
optimista   adj. *optimistic* Pr
la oración   *sentence* 4r

el orden   *order 4r*; el orden público
    law and order 9r; la orden *order,*
    command 9r
ordenado/a   *tidy 5*
el ordenador   *computer 1r*
ordenar   *to tidy up 5*
la oreja   *(outer) ear 11*
el/la organizador/a   *organizer 10r*
el oro   *gold 3r*
la orquesta   *orchestra 8*
la ortografía   *orthography 4r*
otavaleño/a   *from Otavalo,*
    Ecuador 10r
otro/a   *other, another 1r, 3*; otra vez
    again Pr, 7r; de vez en cuando *now*
    and then 10r
oxígeno   *oxygen 11r*

P

el/la paciente   *patient Pr, 9r*
[S.L.11]el padrastro   *stepfather 4*
el padre   *father 3r, 4*
los padres   *parents 4*
el padrino   *godfather 4*
pagar   *to pay 6*
la página   *page Pr*
el pago   *payment 6r*
el país   *country 1r; country, nation 3*
el pájaro   *bird 14r*
la palabra   *word Pr*
el palacio   *palace 1r*
la paloma   *dove 14r*
los palos   *golf clubs 7*
el pan   *bread 3*
la panadería   *bakery 6r*
el pánico   *panic 12r*
los pantalones   *pants 6*
los pantalones cortos   *shorts 6*
las pantimedias   *pantyhose 6*
el pañuelo   *handkerchief 6*
el papá   *dad 4*
la papa   *potato 3*
papas chorreadas   *Colombian typical*
    dish 4r; las papas fritas *French*
    fries 3
la papaya   *papaya 10r*
el papel   *paper 1r;* cambiar de papel
    switch roles Pr; hacer el papel *play*
    the part 6r
el paquete   *package 12*
el par   *pair 7r;* sin par *without*
    equal 1r
para   *for, to 1*
el parabrisas   *windshield 12*
el paracaídas   *parachute 15*
el parachoques   *bumper 12*
el paraguas   *umbrella 6*
paraguayo/a   *Paraguayan 10r*

parecer (zc)   *to seem 1r, 6*
el parentesco   *kinship 4r*
los parientes   *relatives 4*
el parque   *park 1r*
el párrafo   *paragraph 4r*
la participación   *participation 8r*
el/la participante   *participant 8r*
participar   *to participate 1r, 7*
particular: en particular   *especially 3r*
el partido   *game Pr*
la pasa   *raisin 10r*
el pasaje   *ticket 3r; passage 9r*
el/la pasajero/a   *passenger 12*
el pasaporte   *passport 12*
pasar   *to go through 4r; to spend*
    (time) 4; pour 5r; to happen 6r; to
    come in 9r; pasarlo bien *to have*
    fun 3r; pasar lista *to call roll*
    Pr; ¿Qué pasa?   *What's going on? 9r*
[S.L.12]pasar la aspiradora   *to*
    vacuum 5
el pasatiempo   *pastime 15r*
pasear   *to take a walk, to stroll 4*
el paseo   *walk 4r*
de pasillo/ventanilla   *aisle/window*
    seat 12
pasivo/a   *passive Pr*
el pastel   *pie, cake 8r*
la pastelería   *pastry shop 10*
la pastilla   *pill 11*
patinar   *to skate 7*
paulatinamente   *gradually 15r*
el pavo   *turkey 10*
el pecho   *chest 11*
pedir (i)   *to ask for 4*
peinar(se)   *to comb 4*
la pelea   *argument 4r*
pelear   *to fight 13*
la película   *film 3*
el peligro   *danger 5r*
peligroso/a   *dangerous 10r*
pelirrojo/a   *redhead 2*
el pelo   *hair 2*
pelo castaño   *brown hair 2*
pelo negro   *black hair 2*
la pelota   *ball 7*
la peluquería   *beauty salon,*
    barbershop 9[S.L.13]
el/la peluquero/a   *hairdresser 9*
[S.L.14]la península   *peninsula 7r*
pensar (ie)   *to think 1r, 4*
pensar + inf.   *to plan to + [verb] 4*
[S.L.15]peor   *worse, worst 8*
la pepa   *seed 10r*
el pepino   *cucumber 10*
pequeño/a   *small 1*
la pera   *pear 10*
perder (ie)   *to lose 7*
perderse (ie)   *to get lost 12*
la pérdida   *loss 15*

perdido/a   *lost 12r*
perezoso/a   *lazy 2*
perfeccionista   *perfectionist Pr*
el perfil   *profile 14*
el periódico   *newspaper 3*
el/la periodista   *journalist,*
    newspaperman/woman 7r, 9
permitir   *to permit, to allow 10*
pero   *but 1, 2*
el/la perro/a   *dog 4r, 5*
perseguir   *to chase 8r*
el personaje   *character 8r; person 9r*
la perspectiva   *perspective 9r*
peruano/a   *Peruvian 2*
el pescado   *fish 3*
la pesca   *fishing 15r*
pesimista   *pessimist Pr*
el peso   *weight 3r*
la pestaña   *eyelash 11*
el petróleo   *petroleum, oil 6r*
el/la pianista   *pianist 8r*
picado/a   *chopped, ground 10r*
la piedra   *stone 6r*
el pie   *foot 10r, 11;* a pie *on foot 10r*
la piel   *skin 11r*
la pierna   *leg 3r, 11*
la pieza   *piece, object 5r*
pilotear   *to pilot, to fly 12r*
el/la piloto   *pilot 9r*
la pimienta   *pepper 10*
el pimiento verde   *green pepper 10*
la piña   *pineapple 10*
la piñata   *pottery filled with*
    candies 8r
pintado/a   *painted 12r*
el/la pintor/a   *painter 13*
el pintor   *painter 5r*
la pintura   *painting 13*
pisar   *to step on 14r*
la piscina   *swimming pool 5*
el piso   *floor 5*
la pista   *clue 1r; slope, court,*
    track 7
el/la piyama   *pajama 6r*
la pizarra   *chalkboard P*
la pizzería   *pizza place 4r*
la placa   *plates 12*
el placer   *pleasure 8r*
planchar   *to iron 5*
planear   *to plan 12r*
el planeta   *planet 5r, 15*
el plano/a   *plan 5r; level 10r*
la planta baja   *first floor 5*
plástico/a   *plastic 9r*
la plata   *silver 10r*
el plátano/la banana   *banana 10*
el plato   *dish, plate 5, 10*
la playa   *beach 1*
la plaza (de toros)   *bullring 8*
el pliegue   *fold 10r*

el/la plomero/a *plumber* 9
el plomo *lead 15r*
la población *population* 13
poblado/a *inhabited 8r*
pobre *poor* 2
poder (ue) *to be able to, can* 4
el poema *poem 1r*
el/la poeta *poet 9r*
la polémica *polemic 7r*
el policía/la (mujer) policía
 policeman, policewoman 9
el poliéster *polyester* 6
la política *politics* 13
el/la político/a *politician 2r; political
 adj. 1r*
la pollera *typical Panamanian
 dress 12r*
el pollo *chicken* 3
el polo *pole 5r*
poner (g) *to put, to turn on* 4
poner la mesa *to set the table* 4
ponerse *to put on* 6
popularidad *popularity 7r*
popular *popular Pr*
por *by, 1r; por eso that's why 1r; por
 ejemplo for instance 1r; por lo
 menos at least 1r; por lo tanto
 therefore 10r*
por cierto *by the way* 9
por correo *by mail 9r, 9*
por lo menos *at least 1r*
[S.L.16]el porcentaje *percentage* 14
la porción *portion 10r*
portátil *portable* 15
portugués/a *Portuguese 1r*
las Posadas *Hispanic festivities 8r*
positivo/a *positive 5r*
el postre *dessert 3r*
la práctica *practice 1r; adj.
 practical 9r*
practicar *to practice* 1
el precio *price* 6
precioso/a *precious 6r; beautiful* 6
precisamente *precisely 7r*
la precisión *precision 4r*
predilecto/a *favorite 7r*
preferir (ie) *to prefer 1r, 4*
la pregunta *question Pr*
el premio *award, prize 6r, 13*
preocupar(se) *to worry 10r*
la preparación *preparation 1r*
preparar *to prepare* 5
el preparativo *preparation 5r, 8*
presente *present, here Pr*
prestar *to lend 6r*
primario/a *elementary 5r*
primero/a *first 1r*
el/la primo/a *cousin* 4
el príncipe *prince 5r*
privado/a *private Pr*

privilegiado/a *exceptional 7r*
probablemente *probably 3r*
probarse (ue) *to try on* 6
el problema *problem Pr*
proceder (de) *to come from* 14
la procesión *procession* 8
la productividad *productivity 15r*
el/la profesor/a *professor P*
el programa *program 1r*
programar *to program 12r*
la prohibición *prohibition 7r*
prohibir *to prohibit, to forbid* 10
prolongado/a *lengthy 10r*
el promedio *average* 14
la promesa *promise 7r*
el pronombre *pronoun 1r*
propio/a *own* 9
la protección *protection 15r*
la provincia *province 8r*
la (p)sicología *psychology* 1
el/la (p)sicólogo/a *psychologist* 9
el/la psiquiatra *psychiatrist 9r*
la publicidad *advertisement 9r*
público/a *public 1r*
el pueblo *town* 8
el puente *bridge 9r*
la puerta *door P*
la puerta (de salida) *gate* 12
puertorriqueño/a *Puerto Rican* 2
pues *(interj.) well 3r*
el puesto *position* 9
el pulmón *lung* 11
la pulsera *bracelet* 6
la puntuación *punctuation 6r*
puntual *punctual 7r*
el pupitre *student's desk P*

Q

que *that 1r, 2; lo que what 1r*
quedar *to fit, to be left over* 6
la quema *burning 8r*
querer (ie) *to want 1r, 4*
¿de quién? *whose?* 2
¿En qué puedo servirle(s)? *How may
 I help you?* 6
¿Quién es...? *Who is . . . ? P*
¡Qué lástima! *What a pity!* 1
¡Qué pena! *What a pity!* 8
¿Qué te/le(s) pasa? *What's wrong
 (with you)?* 11
¿Qué tiempo hace? *What's the
 weather like?* 7
la química *chemistry 1r*
químico/a *chemical 9r*
Quisiera... *I would like . . .* 6
quitar *to take away, to remove* 7
quitar(se) *to take off* 7
quizá(s)/tal vez *maybe* 10

R

el radiador *radiator 12r, 12*
el/la radio *radio* 5
el ramadán *Ramadan 3r*
rápido/a *fast* 3
la raqueta *racket* 7
el rato *time 3r*
el ratón *mouse* 15
la razón *reason 4r*
de rayas *striped* 6
realizar (c) *to carry out 4r, 14r;
 to take place 5r*
realmente *really 4r*
la rebaja *sale* 6
rebajado/a *marked down* 6
rebelde *rebellious Pr*
la recepción *reception 6r; front
 desk* 12
el/la recepcionista *receptionist 9r*
el receso *recess Pr*
la receta *recipe 10; prescription* 11
recetar *to prescribe* 11
el recibo *receipt 9r*
reciclar *recycle 14r*
recién *adv. recently 11r*
recoger (j) *to pick up* 5
recomendar *to recommend* 10
recordar (ue) *to remember* 8
el recuerdo *memory 8r*
el recurso *resource 6r, 15*
la red World Wide Web *7r, 7*
la referencia *reference 4r*
referir(se) (ie, i) *to refer 5r*
el refresco *soda* 3
el refrigerador *refrigerator* 5
regalar *to give (a present)* 6
el regalo *present* 6
regar (ie) *to water* 5
regatear *to bargain 6r*
la región *region 1r*
regresar *to come back* 5
la reja *iron grill 5r*
la relación *relationship 4r*
religioso/a *adj. religious Pr*
el relleno *filling 10r*
el reloj *clock P*
el remedio *remedy 11r*
la reparación *reparation, repair 7r*
repente: de repente *suddenly 8r*
el/la reportero/a *reporter 7r*
el reposo *rest 11r*
el/la representante *representative 5r*
representar *to represent* 7
la reproducción *reproduction 15r*
el repuesto *part 15r*
de res *beef/steak* 10
la reserva *reserve 3r, 15*
reservado/a *reserved 12r*

reservar   *to make a reservation* 8r, 12
el/la residente   *resident* 5r
resolver (ue)   *to solve* 6r
respecto: con respecto a   *in relation to* 4r
respetar   *to respect* 8
respirar   *to breathe* 11
responsable   *responsible* Pr
el resto   *rest* 4r
el resultado   *result, outcome* 4r
resumen: el resumen   *summary* 14r;
en resumen   *to summarize* 4r
la reunión   *meeting, gathering* 3
reunirse   *to get together* 8
revisar   *to inspect* 12
la revisión   *revision, inspection* 1r
la revista   *magazine* 1r, 3
el rey/la reina   *king/queen* 8
rico/a   *rich, wealthy* 2
el riel   *rail* 15r
el riesgo   *risk, danger* 9r
la riqueza   *wealth* 1r
el robot   *robot* 3r
la roca   *rock* 7r
la rodilla   *knee* 11
romper   *to break, tear* 13, 15
la ropa   *clothing* 5r; ropa interior   *underwear* 6r
rubio/a   *blond* 2
la rueda   *wheel* 12
el ruego   *plea* 14r
el ruido   *noise* 8
las ruinas   *ruins* 3r

S

la sábana   *sheet* 5
saber   *to know* 5
sacar (qu)   *to get, to take (out)* 1
sacar fotos   *to take photos* 12r
el saco   *blazer* 6
la sal   *salt* 4r, 10
la sala   *living room* 5
salir (g)   *to leave* 3r, 4
la salsa de tomate   *tomato sauce* 10
saltar   *to jump* 14
la salud   *health* 7r
saludable   *healthy* 10r
saludar(se)   *to greet* 13
el saludo   *greeting* Pr
la salvación   *salvation* 15r
salvadoreño/a   *Salvadoran* 5r
la sandalia   *sandal* 6
la sangre   *blood* 11
sano/a   *healthy* 10r, 10
sano/a y salvo/a   *safe and sound* 15
la sardana   *typical Catalonian dance* 1r
el secador   *hairdryer* 9r

la secadora   *dryer* 5
secar   *to dry* 5; secarse *to dry oneself* 4
la sección   *section* 3r
seco/a   *dry* 5
secundario/a   *secondary* 1r
la seda   *silk* 6
sedentario/a   *sedentary* 10r
seguido/a   *followed* 8r
seguidor/a   *follower* 10r
seguir (i)   *to follow, to go on* 4
seguir derecho   *to go straight ahead* 12
según   *according to* 1r, 13
segundo/a   *second* 1r
la seguridad   *safety, security* 5r, 8
el seguro   *insurance* 6r; *adj. sure* 5r; *n. safe* 12r
la selección   *selection* 7r
el sello   *stamp* 12
la selva   *jungle* 6r, 15
la semana   *week* P
Semana Santa   *Holy Week* 1r
semejante   *similar* 4r
la semejanza   *similarity* 4r
la semilla   *seed* 8r
el/la senador/a   *senator* 1r
la señal   *signal* 9
el señor   *lord* 8r
señor (Sr.)   *Mr.* P
señora (Sra.)   *Mrs.* P
señorita (Srta.)   *Miss* P
sentar(se) (ie)   *to sit down* 7
sentimental   *sentimental* Pr
el sentimiento   *feeling* 5r
sentir (ie, i)   *to feel* 5; *to be sorry* 11
sentirse (ie, i)   *to feel* 11
la separación   *separation* 14
ser   *to be* Pr, 2
el ser humano   *human being* 15
la serie   *series* 4r
serio/a   *serious* Pr, 11
la servilleta   *napkin* 10
servir (i)   *to serve* 3r, 4
severo/a   *severe, serious* 12r
el sexo   *sex* 8
si   *if* 1r, 3
sí   *yes* P
el siglo   *century* 1r
el significado   *meaning* 7r
siguiente   *adj. following* 1r
la silla   *chair* P
simbolizar   *to symbolize* 8r
el símbolo   *symbol* 8r
simpático/a   *nice, charming* 2
simplemente   *simply* 4r
simultáneamente   *simultaneously* 9r
sin   *without* 7
sin embargo   *nevertheless* 9
sincero/a   *sincere* Pr

el síntoma   *symptom* 11
la sirena   *siren* 9r
la situación   *situation, location* 4r
sobre   *on, above* P
el sobre   *envelope* 12
la sobrina   *niece* 4
el sobrino   *nephew* 4
la sociedad   *society* 13
la sociología   *sociology* 1
el sodio   *sodium* 10r
el sofá   *sofa* 5
el sol   *sun* 7
solicitar   *to apply (for)* 9
la solicitud   *application* 9
sólo   *adv. only* 1r
solo/a   *adj. one* 6r; *alone* 14
soltero/a   *single* 2
la solución   *solution* 6r
el sombrero   *hat* 6
el somnífero   *sleeping pill* 11r
son   *they, you (plural) are* P
la sopa   *soup* 3
sordo/a   *deaf* 15r
el sostén   *bra* 6
soy   *I am* P
su   *his, her, their, your (formal)* 1
suave   *soft* 8
subir   *to go up* 8r; *to increase* 10r; subir de peso *gain weight* 3r
sucio/a   *dirty* 5
la sucursal   *branch (business)* 14
la sudadera   *jogging suit, sweatshirt* 6
el sueldo   *salary* 9
el suéter   *sweater* 6
la sugerencia   *suggestion* 3r
sumar   *to add* 1r
la superación   *improvement* 9r; *overcoming* 2r
superar   *to surpass* 9r; *to overcome* 12r
el supermercado   *supermarket* 6r
la súplica   *plea* 14r
el sur   *south* 1r
el sureste   *southeast* 7r
el/la surfista   *surfer* 7r
suroeste   *southwest* 2r
el sustantivo   *noun* 10r
suyo (-a, -os, -as)   *(of) yours, his, hers, theirs* 5r

T

la tabla   *chart* 4r; *cutting board* 5r
el talento   *talent* 8r
la talla   *size* 6
el tamaño   *size* 4r
también   *also* 1
tampoco   *adv. neither, nor, either* 5r
tan... como   *as . . . as* 8

tan pronto   *as soon as* 11r
tanto/a como   *as much as* 8
tantos/as como   *as many as* 8
tarde   *late* 1r, 4
la tarea   *assignment, homework* Pr, 1
la tarjeta de crédito   *credit card* 6
la tarjeta de embarque   *boarding pass* 12
la tarjeta postal   *post card* 12
la tasa   *rate, interest* 14r
la taza   *cup* 10
el teatro   *theater* 3r, 8
el techo   *roof* 8r
la técnica   *technique* 12r
el/la técnico/a   *adj. technical* 9r; *technician* 9
la tecnología   *technology* 8r
el tejido   *weaving* 8r
la tela   *fabric* 6r
telefónico/a   *adj. telephone* 9r
el teléfono   *telephone* Pr, 3
la telenovela   *soap opera* 11r
la telepatía   *telepathy* 3r
el televisor   *television set* P
temer   *to fear* 11
el temperamento   *temperament* 9r
temprano   *early* 4
tender (ie)   *to hang (clothes); to make (a bed)* 5
el tenedor   *fork* 10
tener (g, ie)   *to have* Pr, 4; tener que + inf. *to have to + verb* 1r; tener lugar *to take place* 8r
tener deseos de +   inf. *to feel like, to want* 8
tener dolor de...   *to have a(n) . . . ache* 11
tener éxito   *to be successful* 13
tener mala cara   *to look terrible* 11
Tengo... años.   *I am . . . years old.* 2
tengo/tienes   *I/you have* 1
el/la tenista   *tennis player* 7
el tenis   *tennis* Pr, 7
la tensión (arterial)   *(blood) pressure* 11
el tequila   *Mexican liqueur* 8r
el termómetro   *thermometer* 11
la terraza   *terrace* 1r, 5
el territorio   *territory* 15r
la tía   *aunt* 4
tibio/a   *lukewarm* 10r
el tiempo   *time* Pr; tiempo libre *free time* 1r, 3
la tienda   *store* 6
tiene   *he/she has, you (formal) have* 2
la tierra   *land, soil* 15
tímido/a   *timid* Pr
el tío   *uncle* 4
típico/a   *typical* 1r, 3
el tipo   *type, style,* 3r; *kind* 10r

el título   *title* 4r
la tiza   *chalk* P
la toalla   *towel* 5
el tobillo   *ankle* 11
tocar   *to touch* 3; tocar un instrumento *to play an instrument* 3
todavía   *still, yet* 13
tolerante   *tolerant* 1r
tomar   *to take, to drink* 1
tomar apuntes   *to take notes* 1
tomar el sol   *to sunbathe* 3
tomar notas   *take notes* 1r
el tomate   *tomato* 3
tonto/a   *silly, foolish* 2
torcer(se) (ue)   *to twist* 11
el torneo   *tournament* 7r, 7
la toronja/el pomelo   *grapefruit* 10
la tortura   *torture* 10r
la tos   *cough* 11
toser   *to cough* 11
la tostada   *toast* 3
trabajador/a   *hardworking* 2
trabajar   *to work* 1
la tradición   *tradition* 8
tradicional   *traditional* Pr
traducir (zc)   *to translate* 7
traer (g)   *to bring* 4
el tráfico   *traffic* 12r
el traje   *suit* 6
el traje de baño   *bathing suit* 6
el traje pantalón   *pantsuit* 6
tranquilizante   *tranquilizer* 12r
tranquilo/a   *calm, tranquil* Pr, 2
el transbordador espacial   *space shuttle* 15
transparente   *transparent* 9r
el transporte   *transportation* 5r
a través de   *through* 13
el tren   *train* 11r, 12
el trigo   *wheat* 15r
triste   *sad* 2
el triunfo   *victory* 7r
el trofeo   *trophy* 7r
tropical   *tropical* 10r
tu   *your (familiar)* P
tú   *you (familiar)* P
el túnel   *tunnel* 3r
la túnica   *tunic* 8r
turístico/a   *adj. tourist* 7r
el turno   *turn, shift* 11r

U

la ubicación   *location* 5r
la úlcera   *ulcer* 11r
último/a   *last* 8
un/una   *a, an* P
un poco   *a little* 4

una vez   *once* 12
la unidad   *unity* 5r
unido/a   *united* 1r
el uniforme   *uniform* 3r
la unión   *union* 7r
la universidad   *university* 1
universitario/a   *adj. university* 1r
urbano/a   *urban* 12r
urgente   *urgent* 1r
urgentemente   *urgently* 9r
uruguayo/a   *Uruguayan* 7r
usar   *to use* 2
usted   *you (formal)* P; ustedes *you (plural)* 1
la uva   *grape* 10

V

las vacaciones   *vacation* 1r, 3
la vacante   *opening* 9
vacío/a   *empty* 12
la vainilla   *vanilla* 10
valer   *to be worth* 6
valiente   *brave* Pr
valioso/a   *valuable* 2r
el valle   *valley* 9r
el vallenato   *typical Colombian music* 4r
el valor   *value, price* 3r
el vaquero   *cowboy* 7r
los vaqueros/jeans   *jeans* 6
variable   *variable, changeable* 9r
la variante   *variant* 7r
varios/as   *various, several* 1r
el vaso   *glass* 3r, 10
el vecindario   *neighborhood* 5r
el/la vecino/a   *neighbor* 5r, 14
la vegetación   *vegetation* 15r
el vegetal/la verdura   *vegetable* 3
la vela   *candle* 4r
la velocidad   *speed* 12
la vena   *vein* 11
el/la vendedor/a   *salesman, saleswoman* 6r, 9
vender   *to sell* 6
venezolano/a   *Venezuelan* 2
venir (g, ie)   *to come* 4
la ventaja   *advantage* 14
la ventana   *window* P
la ventanilla   *window* 12
las ventas   *sales* 9
el verbo   *verb* 1r
¿Verdad?   *Right?* 1
la verdura   *vegetable* 10
verificar (qu)   *to verify* 4r
versátil   *versatile* 7r
ver   *to see* 1r, 3
el vestido   *dress* 6
vestir(se) (i)   *to dress, to get dressed* 4

el **vestuario** *dressing room 7r*
viajar *to travel* 12
la **vida** *life 1r,* 15
el **video** *video 1r*
la **videocasetera** *VCR* P
viejo/a *old* 2
el **viento** *wind* 7
el **vinagre** *vinegar* 10
el **viñedo** *vineyard 9r*
el **vino** *wine* 3; el **vino tinto** *red wine* 10
la **violencia** *violence* 8
el/la **violinista** *violinist 8r*
la **virgen** *virgin 8r*
virtual *virtual 3r*
la **visa** *visa 3r*
la **visita** *guest 5r*
visitar *to visit 1r,* 4

la **vista** *view 5r*
la **vitalidad** *vitality 1r*
la **vitamina** *vitamin 10r*
la **viuda** *widow* 14
el **viudo** *widower* 14
vivir *to live 1r,* 3
vivo/a *alive, living 4r*
el **vocabulario** *vocabulary* Pr
volador *flying 15r*
el **volante** *steering wheel* 12
volar (ue) *to fly 5r,* 12
el **voleibol** *volleyball* 7
la **voluntad** *will, will power 2r*
el/la **voluntario/a** *volunteer 14r*
volver (ue) *to return* 4
votar *to vote 12r*
la **voz** *voice 14r*
el **vuelo** *flight 3r,* 12

Y

y *and* P
ya *already 3r,* 13; **ya que** *since 8r;*
ya sea *whether 9r*
la **yema** *egg yolk 10r*
el **yogur** *yogurt* 10
yo *I* P

Z

la **zanahoria** *carrot* 10
la **zapatilla** *slipper* 6
el **zapato** *shoe* 6

ENGLISH TO SPANISH VOCABULARY [S.L.2]

A

a, an un/una
above arriba
absence la ausencia
to accept aceptar
access el acceso
accident el accidente
accompany acompañar
accomplishment el logro
according según
accountant el/la contador/a
accounting la contabilidad
to act actuar
action la acción
activity la actividad
actor/actress el actor/la actriz
ad (advertisement) el anuncio
to add sumar, añadir
additional adicional
address, direction la dirección
administrative administrativo/a
adolescent el/la adolescente
adult adulto/a
advance el avance
advantage la ventaja
advertisement la publicidad
advice el consejo
advisable aconsejable
affection, love el cariño
after, later, then después
again de vez en cuando [S.L.3]
against contra
agenda la agenda
agent el/la agente
to agree estar de acuerdo
to agree, access acceder
agreement la concordancia
agricultural agrícola
air conditioned climatizado/a
air conditioning el aire acondicionado
airline la aerolínea
aisle/window seat de pasillo/ventanilla
alarm la alarma
alarm clock el despertador
alcoholic alcohólico/a
alive, living vivo/a
alone solo/a

alphabet el alfabeto
already ya
also también
altar el altar
Amazonian amazónico/a
ambitious ambicioso/a
American americano/a, norteamericano/a
ancestor el antepasado
and y
Andean andino/a
angry enojado/a
anguish la angustia
anisette (licor) el anisado
ankle el tobillo
anniversary el aniversario
annoyance el fastidio
annual anual
to answer contestar
to answer, attend atender (ie)
anthropology la antropología
antibiotic el antibiótico
any, some algunos/as
apartment el apartamento
appearance el aspecto
appetite el apetito
appetizer, ticket for admission, entrance la entrada
to applaud aplaudir
apple la manzana
application la solicitud
to apply (for) solicitar
appropriate adecuado/a, apropiado/a
approval la aprobación
archaeological arqueológico/a
archaeology la arqueología
architect el/la arquitecto/a
architecture arquitectura
area el área
Argentinean argentino/a
to argue discutir
argument el argumento, la pelea
arm el brazo
armchair la butaca
arrival la llegada
arrival/departure time la hora de llegada/salida
to arrive llegar
arrogant arrogante
as, like *adv.* como

as . . . as tan... como
as many as tantos/as como
as much . . . as tanto/a como
as soon as tan pronto
ask for pedir (i)
asphyxia la asfixia
aspirin la aspirina
assassination, murder el asesinato
assignment, homework la tarea
astronaut el/la astronauta
at a
at least por lo menos
at random azar, el azar
at the present time actualmente, en la actualidad
athlete el/la atleta
athletic atlético/a
atmosphere la atmósfera
attendance la asistencia
attention, service la atención
attitude la actitud
attractive atractivo [S.L.4]
aunt la tía
authentic auténtico/a
author el/la autor/a
authoritarian autoritario/a
authority la autoridad
avenue la avenida
average el promedio
average, medium height mediano/a
average, middle *adj.* la media
avocado el aguacate
award, prize el premio

B

back la espalda
backpack la mochila
backyard, garden el jardín
bad malo/a
to bake hornear
bakery la panadería
balcony el balcón
ball la pelota
ballpoint pen el bolígrafo
banana el plátano/la banana
band la banda
bank el banco
banquet el banquete

baptism, christening   el bautizo
bar   el bar
barbecue   la barbacoa
to bargain   regatear
baseball   el béisbol
basically   básicamente
basket, hoop   el/la cesto/a
basketball   el baloncesto/basquetbol
bat   el bate
bathing suit   el traje de baño
bathroom   el baño
battery   la batería/el acumulador
to be   estar, ser; **be able to, can**
   poder (ue); **be admitted** ingresar;
   be bored aburrirse; **be born** nacer
   (zc); **be enough** bastar; **be**
   fashionable estar de moda; **be glad**
   (about) alegrarse (de); **be hot**
   (weather) hacer calor; **be in love**
   estar enamorado/a; **be pleasing to,**
   like gustar; **be successful** tener
   éxito; **be worth** valer; **be in charge**
   estar a cargo; **be fit** estar en forma
beach   la playa
beans   los frijoles
to beat   batir
beauty salon, barbershop   la
   peluquería
to become sick   enfermarse
bed   la cama
bedroom   el cuarto/dormitorio
beef/steak   de res
beer   la cerveza
before   antes
begin, start   comenzar (ie), empezar
   (ie, c)
beginning   el comienzo
behavior   el comportamiento
behind   detrás (de)
to believe   creer
below   abajo, continuación: a
   continuación
belt   el cinturón
benefit   el beneficio
best   mejor
between, among   entre
big   grande
bilingual   bilingüe
biology   la biología
biosphere   la biosfera
bird   el pájaro
birth   la natalidad
birthday   el cumpleaños
[S.L.5] blanket   la manta
blazer   el saco
blind   ciego/a
(city) block   la cuadra
blond   rubio/a
blood   la sangre
blouse   la blusa

[S.L.6] board of directors   la directiva
boarding pass   la tarjeta de
   embarque
boat   el bote
to boil   hervir (ie, i)
bone   el hueso
book   el libro
bookstore   la librería
boot   la bota
boring   aburrido/a
boss   el/la jefe/jefa
to bother, be bothered by   molestar
bottle   la botella
bowl   jugar a los bolos
bowling   los bolos
boxer shorts   el calzoncillo
boy   el chico
bra   el sostén
bracelet   la pulsera
brain   el cerebro
branch (business)   la sucursal
brand name   la marca
brave   valiente
Brazilian   brasileño/a
bread   el pan
to break   romper
to break down   descomponer
breakfast   el desayuno
to breathe   respirar
bridge   el puente
briefcase   el maletín
to bring   traer (g)
brother   el hermano
[S.L.7] brunet, brunette   moreno/a
to brush one's teeth   lavar(se) los
   dientes
to build   construir (y)
building   el edificio
bullfight   la corrida (de toros)
bullring   la plaza (de toros)
bumper   el parachoques
burning   la quema
bus   el autobús/bus
businessman/woman   el hombre/la
   mujer de negocios
busy   ocupado/a
but   pero
butter   la mantequilla
buy   comprar
by   por; **that's why** por eso; **for**
   instance por ejemplo; **at least**
   por lo menos; **therefore** por lo
   tanto

C

[S.L.8]cabin (on boat)   el camarote
cabin, cockpit   la cabina
cafeteria   la cafetería

cage   la jaula
calcium   el calcio
calculator   la calculadora
calculus   el cálculo
to call   la llamada, llamar
calm, tranquil   tranquilo/a
calorie   la caloría
camel   el camello
camomile   la manzanilla
camp   el campamento
campaign   la campaña
to cancel   cancelar
cancer   el cáncer
candle   la vela
candy/sweets   el dulce
canned   enlatado/a
Cantonese   cantonés/cantonesa
cap   la gorra
capital   la capital
captain   el capitán/la capitana
car   el auto(móvil)/coche/carro
cardboard   (de) cartón
career, race   la carrera
Caribbean   caribeño/a
carnival, Mardi Gras   el carnaval
carpet, rug   la alfombra
carrot   la zanahoria
to carry out, take place   realizar (c)
cart, wagon   la carreta
case   el caso
cash register, box   la caja
cash   en efectivo
cashier   el/la cajero/a
to catch   atrapar
Catholic   católico/a
cause   la causa
celebrate   celebrar
celebration   la celebración
cellular phone   el celular
cemetery   el cementerio
to center   centrar(se)
center   el centro; **shopping center**
   centro comercial
century   el siglo
ceremony   la ceremonia
chair   la silla
chalk   la tiza
chalkboard   la pizarra
champagne   el champaña
champion   el campeón/la campeona
championship   el campeonato
change, exchange   cambiar
channel, canal   el canal
character   el carácter
character, person   el personaje
charm   el encanto
chart, cutting board   la tabla
to chase   perseguir
to check in (luggage)   facturar
check   el cheque

checking account   la cuenta: cuenta corriente
cheek   la mejilla
chemical   químico/a
chemistry   la química
cherry   la cereza
chest   el pecho
chicken   el pollo
child   el/la niño/a
Chilean   chileno/a
chocolate   el chocolate
choose   escoger (j)
chop   la chuleta
chopped, ground   picado/a
Christmas   la navidad
church   la iglesia
circumstance   la circunstancia
city   la ciudad
[S.L.9] civilization   la civilización
to clarify   aclarar
to clean   limpiar; clean   limpio/a
clear   despejado/a
client   el/la cliente, el/la cliente/a
clinic, hospital   la clínica
clock   el reloj
closet, armoire   el armario
clothing   la ropa; underwear   ropa interior [S.L.10]
cloudy   nublado/a
clue   la pista
coach   el/la entrenador/a
coarse   grueso/a
coat   el abrigo
coconut   el coco
coffee, coffee house   el café; after-dinner drink plus café
cognate   el cognado
coherence   la coherencia
cold   el catarro, frío/a
collection   la colección
Colombian   colombiano/a
Colombian music and dance   la cumbia
Colombian typical dish   papas chorreadas
color, colorful   colorido
column   la columna
to comb   peinar(se)
to come   venir (g, ie)
to come back   regresar
to come from   proceder (de)
comfortable   cómodo/a
comic, funny   cómico/a
to comment, discuss   comentar
commerce   el comercio
commission   la comisión
communicate   comunicar(se) (qu)
community   la comunidad
company   la compañía/empresa
to compare   comparar

comparison   la comparación
compensation   la compensación
to compete   competir (i)
competition   la competencia
complex   complicado/a
composition   composición
computer   la computadora, el ordenador
computer science   informática
concert   el concierto
concierge   el/la conserje
condiment   el condimento
condition   la condición
condominium   el condominio
to congratulate   felicitar
congress, convention   el congreso
considerably   considerablemente
construction   la construcción
contact lenses   los lentes de contacto
contagion, spreading of a disease   el contagio
to contain   contener (g, ie)
contamination   la contaminación
contents,   contenido; controlled   el contenido
contest   el concurso
to continue   continuar
contract   el contrato, el contraste [S.L.11]
conversation   la conversación
to cook   cocinar
cooked   cocinado/a
cookie   la galleta
cool   fresco/a
to cool down   enfriar
to copy   copiar; copy   la copia
corn   el maíz/elote
corner   la esquina
correct   correcto/a
corresponding   correspondiente
cosmetic   el cosmético
cosmopolitan   cosmopolita
cost   costar (ue)
costume   el disfraz
costumed group   la comparsa
cotton   el algodón
cough   la tos, toser
counselor, adviser   el/la consejero/a
counter   el mostrador
country, nation   el país
courage   el coraje
course   el curso
court, golf course   la cancha
courtesy   la cortesía
cousin   el/la primo/a
to cover   cubrir
cowboy   el vaquero
crash   chocar (qu)
crazy   loco/a

cream   la crema
to create   crear
creative   creativo/a
credit card   la tarjeta de crédito
crime   el crimen
crisis   la crisis
crowd   la multitud
cruise   el crucero
Cuban   cubano/a
cucumber   el pepino
cultivation   el cultivo
cumin   el comino
cup   la taza
curiosity   la curiosidad
curious   curioso/a
curtain   la cortina
custom   la costumbre
customs   la aduana
to cut   cortar
cycling   el ciclismo
cyclist   el/la ciclista

D

dad   el papá
dairy (product), milky   lácteo/a
damage   el deterioro
to dance   bailar; dance   el baile
dance club   la discoteca
dancer   el/la bailarín/bailarina
danger   el peligro
dangerous   peligroso/a
data   los datos
date   la fecha
daughter   la hija
day   el día
dead   difunto/a, muerto/a
deaf   sordo/a
decorated   adornado/a
decuple, tenfold   el décuplo
deep-fried batter   el churro
defense   la defensa
deforestation   la deforestación
degree, grade   el grado
to delight, love   encantar
delighted   encantado/a
delinquency   la delincuencia
to deliver   entregar
demonstrative   el demostrativo
dense   denso/a
dentist   el/la dentista
department   el departamento
department store   el almacén
depressed   deprimido/a
to describe   describir
description   la descripción
desert   el desierto
to design   diseñar, el diseño
designer   el/la diseñador/a

desk   el escritorio
dessert   el postre
destination   el destino
devil   el diablo
diabetic   el/la diabético/a
dialog   el diálogo
diameter   el diámetro
dictionary   el diccionario
to die   morir (ue)
diet   la alimentación
difference   la diferencia
different   diferente
difficult   difícil
dining room   el comedor
dinner, supper   la cena, la
    comida
directory   el directorio
dirty   sucio/a
discount   el descuento
discrimination   la discriminación
dish, plate   el plato
dishwasher   el lavaplatos
dismissal time   hora de salida
disorganized   desorganizado/a
dissolved   disuelto/a
distance   la distancia
diverse, different   diverso
divorce   divorciarse, el divorcio
divorced   divorciado/a
to do, make   hacer (g); pack   hacer la
    maleta; ask questions   hacer
    preguntas; become   hacerse; play
    the part   hacer el papel
doctor   el/la doctor/a
doctor's office   el consultorio
dog   el perro, el/la perro/a
domestic   doméstico/a
Dominican   dominicano/a, el/la
    dominicano/a
door   la puerta
double   doble
double/single room   la habitación
    doble/sencilla
doubt   dudar
dough   la masa
dove   la paloma
downtown, center   el centro
drawing   el dibujo
dress   el vestido
to dress, get dressed   vestir(se) (i)
dresser   la cómoda
dressing room   el vestuario
to drink   beber; drink   la bebida
drive, manage, handle   manejar
driver   el/la chofer
drop   la caída
drug   la droga
drug traffic   el narcotráfico
to dry (oneself)   secar(se); dry   seco/a
dryer   la secadora

due to   debido a
during   durante
dynamic   dinámico/a

E

each, every, each   adj. cada
ear   el oído, la oreja
early   temprano
early morning, dawn   la
    madrugada [S.L.12]
earring   el arete
easily   fácilmente
east   el este
easy   fácil
to eat   comer
ecological   ecológico/a
economics, economy, inexpensive   la
    economía
Ecuadorian   ecuatoriano/a
edge   el borde
educated   educado/a
effect   el efecto
efficiency   la eficiencia
efficient   eficiente
egg   el huevo
egg yolk   la yema
elbow   el codo
electric   eléctrico/a
electrician   el/la electricista
electronic   electrónico/a
elegant   elegante
elementary   primario/a
elevator   el ascensor
to eliminate   eliminar
e-mail   el correo electrónico
emergency   la emergencia
emigrant   el/la emigrante
to emigrate   emigrar
empire   el imperio
employee   el/la empleado/a
empty   vacío/a
to encourage, incite   incentivar
end   el fin, el final
energetic   enérgico/a
energy   la energía
engineer   el/la ingeniero/a
English   el inglés
enlargement, expansion   la
    ampliación
entertainment   el entretenimiento, la
    diversión
enthusiasm   el entusiasmo
envelope   el sobre
environmental   ambiental, el medio
    ambiente
episode   el episodio
equality   la igualdad

eraser   el borrador
especially   particular: en particular
to establish, settle   establecer(se) (zc)
even   aun
event   el evento
every . . . hours   cada... horas
evidence   la evidencia
to examine   examinar
example   el ejemplo
excellent   excelente
exceptional   excepcional,
    privilegiado/a
excited   emocionado/a
excursion   la excursión
executive   el/la ejecutivo/a
exercise   el ejercicio
exhaustingly   exhaustivamente
expensive   caro/a
experience   la experiencia
experiment   el experimento
expert   el/la experto/a
explanation   la explicación
export   la exportación
to express   expresar
to extend, expand   extender(se) (ie)
extinction   la extinción
to extinguish, turn off, turn off the
    lights   apagar
extrovert   extrovertido/a
eyebrow   la ceja
eyelash   la pestaña
eyes   los ojos; blue eyes   ojos azules;
    brown eyes   café; green eyes   ojos
    verdes, ojos (de color)

F

fabric   la tela
fabulous, great   fabuloso/a
face   la cara
factory   la fábrica
fair   la feria
faithfully   fielmente
to fall   caer(se); fall asleep   dormirse
    (ue); fall in love   enamorarse
false   falso/a
family   la familia
famous   famoso/a
fan   el/la aficionado/a
fanatic   fanático/a
fantastic   fantástico/a
far (from)   lejos (de)
farewell   la despedida
fascinating   fascinante
fashion show   desfile de moda, desfile
    de modas
fast   rápido/a
fat   gordo/a, la grasa
father   el padre

fatigue   la fatiga
fatigued, tired   fatigado/a
favorite   predilecto/a
fear   temer
feed   alimentar
to feel   sentirse (ie, i); feel, be sorry sentir (ie, i)
to feel like, want   tener deseos de + inf.
feeling   el sentimiento
festive   festivo
festivity   la festividad
fever   la fiebre
fiancé, boyfriend   el novio
fiancée, girlfriend   la novia [S.L.13] fiber   la fibra
field   el campo
to fight   pelear
figure   la cifra
to fill (out)   llenar
filling   el relleno
film   la película
finalist   finalista
financed   financiado/a
financial   financiero
to find   encontrar (ue)
finger   el dedo
to finish   acabar
fire   el incendio
firefighter   el/la bombero/a
fireplace   la chimenea
first   primero/a
first floor   la planta baja
fish   el pescado
fishing   la pesca
to fit, be left over   quedar
to fix, repair   arreglar
flight   el vuelo
flight attendant   el/la auxiliar de vuelo
float   la carroza
floor   el piso
flour   la harina
flower   la flor
flu   la gripe
to fly   volar (ue)
flying   volador
fold   el pliegue
to fold, bend, turn   doblar
to follow, go on   seguir (i)
followed   seguido/a
follower   adepto/a, seguidor/a
following   *adj.* siguiente
food   el alimento
foot   el pie; on foot   a pie
football player   el/la futbolista
for   para
forehead   la frente
foreign   *adj.* extranjero/a
forest   el bosque; rain forest   bosque tropical

to forget   olvidar
fork   el tenedor
formation   la formación
former, old   antiguo/a
formula   la fórmula
fortress   la fortaleza
fortune   la fortuna
forward   adelante; later on   más adelante [S.L.14]
fountain, source   la fuente
fracture, break   fracturar(se)
free   libre; free time   tiempo libre
freeway   la autopista
to freeze   congelar(se)
French fries   las papas fritas
frequency   la frecuencia
fresh   fresco/a
fried   frito/a
friend   el/la amigo/a
front desk   la recepción
fruit   la fruta
to fry   freír (i)
full   lleno/a
full, busy   nutrido/a
funny, amusing   divertido/a
furnished   amueblado/a
furniture store   la mueblería

G

to gain weight   engordar
game   el juego/partido, el partido
garage   el garaje
garbage, trash   la basura
garlic   el ajo
gasoline   la gasolina
gate   la puerta (de salida)
gelatin   la gelatina
genealogical   genealógico/a
generous   generoso/a
genetic   genético/a
geography   la geografía
gesture   el ademán
to get along well   llevarse bien; get lost   perderse (ie); get married casarse; get off, come down   bajar; lose weight   bajar de peso; get together   reunirse; get up levantarse; get, take (out)   sacar
ghetto   el gueto
giant   gigante *adj.*
girl   la chica
to give (a present)   regalar; give advice   aconsejar; give, hand   dar
glass   el vaso
glass, drink   la copa
glove   el guante
glove compartment   la guantera

to go   ir; go shopping   ir de compras;
go away, leave   ir(se); go bed, lie down   acostar(se); go in, enter entrar; go shopping   ir de compras; go straight ahead   seguir (i) derecho; go through; spend (time); pour, happen, come in have fun [S.L.15]pasar, pasarlo bien; call roll   pasar lista; What's going on?   ¿Qué pasa?; go up, increase subir; gain weight   subir de peso
God   Dios
godchild   el/la ahijado/a
godfather   el padrino
godmother   la madrina
gold   el oro
golf clubs   los palos
good luck   buena suerte
good-looking, handsome   guapo/a [S.L.16]goods   los bienes; real estate bienes raíces
[S.L.17]government   el gobierno
gradually   gradualmente, paulatinamente
to graduate   graduarse
graduation   la graduación
grain   el grano
grammatical   gramatical
granddaughter   la nieta
grandfather   el abuelo
grandmother   la abuela
grandson   el nieto
grape   la uva
grapefruit   la toronja/el pomelo
graphic   gráfico/a
great   gran, magnífico/a
greater   el/la mayor
[S.L.18]green pepper   el pimiento verde [S.L.19]
to greet   saludar(se)
greeting   el saludo
ground beef   molida/picada
group   el grupo
growth   el crecimiento
Guatemalan   guatemalteco/a
guest   la visita
guide   el/la guía
guitar   la guitarra
guitar player   el/la guitarrista
gymnasium   el gimnasio

H

habit   el hábito
hair   el cabello, el pelo; black hair pelo negro; brown hair   pelo castaño
hairdresser   el/la peluquero/a

hairdryer   el secador
half   la mitad, media
half brother   el medio hermano
half sister   la media hermana
hamburger   la hamburguesa
hamburger place   la hamburguesería
hand   la mano; **let's get to work**
   manos a la obra
handicraft   la artesanía; **handicrafts**
   adj. artesanal
handkerchief   el pañuelo
to hang (clothes), make (a bed)
   tender (ie)
Hanukka   Januká
happy   feliz
happy, glad   alegre, contento/a
hard   duro/a
hard-boiled egg   huevo duro,
hardware shop   la ferretería
hardworking   trabajador/a
hat   el sombrero
to hate   odiar
to have (**auxiliary verb**)   haber, tener
   (g, ie); **have a good time, have a**
   good time/fun divertirse (ie, i);
   have a(n) . . . ache tener dolor
   de...; **have breakfast** desayunar;
   have dinner cenar; **have just + past**
   participle acabar de + inf.; **have**
   lunch almorzar (ue); **have**
   tener (g, ie); **+ inf. have + verb**
   tener que; [S.L.20]**take place**
   tener lugar
[S.L.21] **he**   él
he/she has, you (formal) have   tiene
he/she is, you are (formal)   está
head   la cabeza
health   la salud; **healthy** saludable,
   sano/a
to hear   oír (g)
heart   el corazón
heating   la calefacción
height   estatura
Hello?   ¿Aló?
to help   ayudar; **help** la ayuda
hemisphere   el hemisferio
herb   la hierba/yerba
here   aquí
highway   la carretera
hill   la loma
hip   la cadera
to hire   contratar
his, her, their, your (formal)   su
   [S.L.22]
Hispanic   hispano/a
Hispanic festivities   las Posadas
history   la historia
hole   el agujero
Holy Week   Semana Santa
home   el hogar

Honduran   hondureño/a
honesty   la honestidad
honeymoon   luna de miel
hood   el capó
hope   la esperanza
horse   *adj.* hípico/a
hospital   el hospital
hot   caliente
hour, time   la hora
house, home,   *adj.* casero/a
   [S.L.23]la casa
housewife, homemaker   el ama de
   casa
How is it going?   ¿Cómo te va?
How may I help you?   ¿En qué puedo
   servirle(s)?
How much is it?   ¿Cuánto cuesta?
human being   el ser humano
humanities   humanidades
humid, damp   húmedo/a
to hurt   doler (ue)
husband   el esposo
hyperactive   hiperactivo/a

I

I am . . . years old   Tengo... años
I am   soy
I don't know   no sé [S.L.24]
I   yo
I/we hope   ojalá
I/you have   tengo/tienes
ice   el hielo
ice cream   el helado
idealistic   *adj.* idealista
identification   la identificación
if   si
illiteracy   el analfabetismo; **illiterate**
   analfabeto/a
illness   la enfermedad
immediately   enseguida
immigrant   el/la inmigrante
implant   el implante
important   importante
impressive   impresionante
to improve   mejorar
improvement, overcoming   la
   superación
impulsive   impulsivo/a
in   en
in advance   anterioridad: con
   anterioridad
in advance, before   *adv.* antes
in cubes   el cubo: en cubitos
in fact, really   en realidad/realmente
in front of   delante de, enfrente (de)
in relation   respecto: con respecto a
in search of   busca: en busca de
in the affirmative   afirmativamente

inappropriate   inapropiado/a
Inca   el/la inca
income   el ingreso
incorrect   incorrecto/a
independence   independencia;
   independent independiente
to indicate   indicar
indicated, recommended   indicado/a
inexpensive, cheap   barato/a
infection   la infección
infectious   infeccioso/a
to influence   influenciar, la influencia
informal   informal
inhabitant   el/la habitante
inhabited   poblado/a
injection   la inyección
inside, in   dentro
to inspect   revisar
institute   el instituto
instrument   el instrumento
insurance,   **sure** (*adj.*), **safe** (*n.*) el
   seguro
intelligent   inteligente
intention   la intención
to interest   interesar; **interested**
   (person), applicant el/la
   interesado/a; **interesting**
   interesante
interpreter   el/la intérprete
[S.L.25]interview   entrevistar, la
   entrevista; **interviewer** el/la
   entrevistador/a
intimate, close   íntimo/a
to introduce   introducir (zc)
introvert   introvertido/a
to invent   inventar; **investigate**
   investigar (gu)
invitation   la invitación
to invite   invitar
to iron   planchar
iron grill   la reja
ironic   irónico/a
island   la isla
It's hot   Hace calor
itinerary   el itinerario

J

jacket   la chaqueta
jeans   los vaqueros/jeans
Jesuit   el jesuita
Jesus   Jesús
jewel, jewelry   la joya; **jewelry** la
   joyería
jogging suit, sweatshirt   la sudadera
to jot down   anotar
journalist, newspaperman/woman
   el/la periodista
joy   la alegría

judge   el/la juez
juice   el jugo
to jump   saltar
jungle   la selva, la jungla

K

kept, preserved   conservado/a
key   la llave
king/queen   el rey/la reina
kinship   el parentesco
to kiss   besar
kitchen   la cocina
kitchen sink   el fregadero
knee   la rodilla
knife   el cuchillo
to know   saber
to know, meet   conocer (zc)

L

laboratory   el laboratorio
lack, scarcity   la escasez
lake   el lago
lamp   la lámpara
to land   aterrizar (c)
land, soil   la tierra
language   el idioma
language lab   el laboratorio de
   lenguas
language spoken in Paraguay   el
   guaraní
to last   durar; last, final   último/a
late   tarde, atrasado/a
Latin-American   latinoamericano/a
laundry room   la lavandería
law   la ley
lawn   el césped
lawyer   el/la abogado/a
layer   la capa
lazy   perezoso/a
lead   el plomo
to learn   aprender
leather   de cuero
to leave (behind), leave   dejar, salir (g)
lecture   la conferencia
left   la izquierda
leg   la pierna
legume, vegetable   la legumbre
lemon   el limón
to lend   prestar
length   la longitud
lengthy   prolongado/a
less than, fewer than   menos que
letter   la letra [S.L.26]
letter carrier   el/la cartero/a
lettuce   la lechuga
level   el nivel

librarian   el/la bibliotecario/a
library   la biblioteca
life   la vida
light   ligero/a
lightly covered with flour
   enharinado/a
to like   caer bien; you (familiar) like
   te gusta(n); you (formal) like   le
   gusta(n); I like   me gusta(n); I
   would like . . .   Me gustaría...,
   Quisiera...
likewise   igualmente
liking, taste   el gusto
lion   el león
lip   el labio
to listen, listen (to)   escuchar
literature   la literatura
little   un poco
to live   vivir
living room   la sala
lobster   la langosta
location   la localización, la ubicación
to lock up   encerrar (ie); locked up
   encerrado/a
lodging   el alojamiento
long   largo/a
to look (at)   mirar
to look for   buscar
to look terrible   tener mala cara
loose-fitting men's shirt   la guayabera
lord   el señor
to lose   perder (ie)
to lose weight   adelgazar (c)
loss   la pérdida
lost   perdido/a
lot   bastante bien
lottery   la lotería
to love   amar
lover   el/la amante
luggage   el equipaje
lukewarm   tibio/a
lunch   el almuerzo
lung   el pulmón
luxurious   lujoso/a

M

machine   máquina; camera   la
   máquina fotográfica; typewriter
   máquina de escribir
of Madrid   madrileño/a
[S.L.27] magazine   la revista
mail   por correo
mailbox   el buzón
to maintain   mantener (g, ie)
the majority   la mayoría
to make a reservation   reservar
to make a stopover   hacer
   escala

to make the bed   hacer la cama
man   el hombre
manager   el/la gerente (de ventas)
mango   el mango
manual   el manual
map   el mapa
margarine   la margarina
marked down   rebajado/a
market   el mercado
marriage, wedding   el matrimonio
married   casado/a
marvelous   maravilloso/a
masterpiece   obra maestra
material   el material
mathematics   las matemáticas
maximum   máximo/a
maybe   quizá(s)/tal vez
mayonnaise   la mayonesa
meaning   el significado
means   el medio
meat   la carne
medical doctor   el/la médico/a
medication, medicine   la
   medicina
meeting, gathering   la reunión
melody   la melodía
member   el/la integrante
memory   el recuerdo
menu   el menú; menu, letter   la carta
message   el mensaje
method   el método
Mexican   mexicano/a
Mexican band   el mariachi
Mexican liqueur   el tequila
microphone   el micrófono
microscope   el microscopio
microwave oven   el (horno)
   microondas
mile   la milla
milk   la leche
millennium   el milenio
mining   adj. la minería, minero/a
ministry   el ministerio
minus (for telling time)   menos
miracle   el milagro
mirror   el espejo
Miss   señorita (Srta.)
missionary   el/la misionero/a
mobility   la movilidad
model   el/la modelo
modern   moderno/a
mom   la mamá
monetary   monetario/a; monetary
   unit of Bolivia   el boliviano;
   monetary unit of Costa Rica and El
   Salvador   el colón; monetary unit of
   Honduras   el lempira; monetary unit
   of Nicaragua   el córdoba; monetary
   unit of Panamá   el balboa;
   monetary unit of Paraguay;

monetary unit of Peru nuevo sol;
[S.L.28]**monetary unit of Venezuela**
el bolívar
money el dinero
money, funds los fondos
monster el monstruo
month el mes
Moor el/la moro/a
more . . . than, . . . -er than (e.g.,
shorter than) más... que
more or less más o menos
morning la mañana
most la mayor parte
mother la madre; **mother** *adj.*
materno/a
motive el motivo
motorcycle la moto(cicleta)
mouse el ratón
mouth la boca
to move mover (ue); **move** la
mudanza
movies el cine
Mr. señor (Sr.)
Mrs. señora (Sra.)
much, a lot mucho/a
muscle el músculo
museum el museo
music la música; **background music**
música ambiental
musician el/la músico/a
mustard la mostaza
my mi
my name is . . . me llamo...
mystery el misterio

N

name el nombre
nanny la niñera
napkin la servilleta
narration la narración; **narrator**
el/la narrador/a
narrow, tight estrecho/a
nation la nación
native nativo/a
nature la naturaleza
nausea la náusea
navigable navegable
near (close to) cerca (de)
neck el cuello
necklace el collar
to need hacer falta, necesitar
negative negativo/a
neighbor el/la vecino/a
neighborhood el barrio, el vecindario
neither . . . nor no (ni)... ni
neither, nor, either *adv.* tampoco
nephew el sobrino
nerve el nervio

nervous nervioso/a
nevertheless sin embargo
new nuevo/a;
[S.L.29] **news** la noticia
newspaper el periódico
next al lado (de)
Nicaraguan nicaragüense
nice agradable; **nice, charming**
simpático/a
niece la sobrina
night *adj.* nocturno/a
night stand la mesa de noche
nightgown el camisón
noise el ruido
nominated nominado/a
north el norte
nose la nariz
not any, none ninguno/a
not even ni siquiera
to not get along llevarse mal
notable, noteworthy notable; **notably**
notablemente
note, grade la nota
notebook el cuaderno
noun el sustantivo
novel la novela
novelist el/la novelista
now ahora
now and then otra vez [S.L.30]
nowadays hoy en día
number el número
nurse el/la enfermero/a
nutrition la nutrición

O

objective el objetivo, fin de
to obtain, get obtener (g, ie)
of, from de
of course desde luego, ¡Cómo no!,
¡Claro!
of the del (contraction of *de* + *el*)
offer la oferta, ofrecer (zc)
office la oficina
oil el aceite
old mayor, viejo/a; **oldest** el/la
mayor
olive la aceituna, oliva: de oliva
on top encima
on, above sobre
once una vez
one *adj.* solo/a [S.L.31]
onion la cebolla
only *adv.* sólo
only child hijo/a único/a
open-air market el mercado al aire
libre
opening la vacante
operate operar

operation la operación
opinion la opinión
opportunity la oportunidad
opposite, contrary contrario/a
optimistic *adj.* optimista
optional optativo/a
orange la naranja
orchestra la orquesta
order el orden; **law and order** el
orden público; **order, command** la
orden, el mandato
organizer el/la organizador/a
orthography la ortografía
of Otavalo, Ecuador otavaleño/a
other, another otro/a; **again**
otra vez
ought to, should deber
our nuestro/a(s)
outdoors al aire libre
outskirts las afueras
outstanding, distinguished destacado/a
over there allá
own propio/a
oxygen oxígeno

P

P.O. box el apartado postal (de
correos)
pacemaker el marcapasos
package el paquete
page la página
painted pintado/a
painter el pintor, el/la pintor/a
painting la pintura
pair el par; **without equal** sin par
pajama el/la piyama
palace el palacio
panic el pánico
pants los pantalones
pantsuit el traje pantalón
pantyhose las pantimedias
papaya la papaya
paper el papel; **switch roles**
cambiar de papel; **play the part**
hacer el papel
parachute el paracaídas
parade el desfile
paragraph el párrafo
Paraguayan paraguayo/a
parents los padres
park el parque
part el repuesto
participant el/la participante;
participate participar; **participation**
la participación
partner, classmate el/la compañero/a
party la fiesta
passenger el/la pasajero/a

passive   pasivo/a
passport   el pasaporte
pastime   el pasatiempo
pastry shop   la pastelería
patient   *n.* el/la paciente
to pay   pagar
payment   el pago
pea   la arveja
pear   la pera
peasant   el/la campesino/a
pencil   el lápiz
peninsula   la península
penning (of bulls)   el encierro (de los toros)
people   la gente
pepper   la pimienta, el ají
percentage   el porcentaje
perfectionist   perfeccionista
to permit, allow   permitir
[S.L.32]perspective   la perspectiva
Peruvian   peruano/a
pessimist   pesimista
petroleum, oil   el petróleo
pharmacist   el/la farmacéutico/a
phase   la fase
philosophy   la filosofía
phobia   la fobia
photo   la foto (grafía)
photocopier   la fotocopiadora
phrase   la frase
physically   físicamente
physics   la física
physiotherapist   el/la fisioterapista
pianist   el/la pianista
to pick up   recoger (j)
picture   el cuadro
pie, cake   el pastel
piece, object   la pieza
pigeonhole   el casillero
pill   la pastilla
pillow   la almohada
pilot   el/la piloto; to pilot, fly   pilotear
pin   el alfiler
pineapple   la piña
pizza place   la pizzería
place   el lugar; to take place   tener lugar
plaid   de cuadros
to plan   planear; plan + verb   pensar + inf.
plan, level   el plano/a
plane   el avión
planet   el planeta
plastic   plástico/a
plates   la placa
play (an instrument)   tocar (un instrumento)
play (game, sport)   jugar (ue)
player   el/la jugador/a

plea   el ruego, la súplica
pleased/nice meet you   mucho gusto
pleasure   el placer
plumber   el/la plomero/a
poem   el poema
poet   el/la poeta
pole   el polo
polemic   la polémica
policeman, policewoman   el policía/la (mujer) policía
political science   las ciencias políticas
politician, political (*adj.*)   el/la político/a
politics   la política
polka-dotted   de lunares
polluted, contaminated   contaminado/a
polyester   el poliéster
poor   pobre
popular   popular; popularity   popularidad
population   la población
pork   el cerdo
portable   portátil
portion   la porción
Portuguese   portugués/a
position   el puesto
positive   positivo/a
post card   la tarjeta postal
potato   la papa
pottery [S.L.33]filled with candies   la piñata
poultry, foul   las aves
pound   la libra
to practice   practicar; practice, practical *adj.*   la práctica
precious, beautiful   precioso/a
precise time   hora americana/inglesa
precisely   precisamente
precision   la precisión
to prefer   preferir (ie)
pregnant   embarazada
preparation   el preparativo, la preparación
to prepare   preparar
to prescribe   recetar
present time   la actualidad
present, current   actual; present, here   presente
present, gift   el regalo
preservation   la conservación
to press   apretar (ie)
pressure   la tensión (arterial)
pretty   bonito/a
price   el precio
prince   el príncipe
private   privado/a
probably   probablemente

problem   el problema
procession   la procesión
productivity   la productividad
professor   el/la profesor/a
profile   el perfil
to program   programar; program   el programa,
to prohibit, forbid   prohibir
prohibition   la prohibición
promise   la promesa
pronoun   el pronombre
protection   la protección
province   la provincia
psychiatrist   el/la psiquiatra
psychologist   el/la (p)sicólogo/a
psychology   la (p)sicología
public   público/a
Puerto Rican   puertorriqueño/a
punctual   puntual
punctuation   la puntuación
purse   la bolsa
to put to bed   acostar (ue);
   put on makeup   maquillar(se);
   put on   ponerse; put, turn on   poner (g)

Q

quack doctor   el/la curandero/a
quality   la calidad
quantity, amount   la cantidad
quarter   cuarto
question   la pregunta
quiet   callado/a

R

racket   la raqueta
radiator   el radiador
radio   el/la radio
radio announcer   el/la locutor/a
rail   el riel
rain   la lluvia, llover (ue)
raincoat   el impermeable, la gabardina
rain forest   el bosque tropical
to raise   levantar
raisin   la pasa
Ramadan   el ramadán
rate, interest   la tasa
raw fish dish   el ceviche
to read   leer
ready   dispuesto/a
really   realmente
rearview mirror   el espejo retrovisor
reason   la razón

rebellious   rebelde
receipt   el recibo
recently   *adv.* recién
reception   la recepción; **receptionist**
   el/la recepcionista
recess   el receso
recipe, prescription   la receta
to recommend   recomendar
recycle   reciclar
redhead   pelirrojo/a
to refer   referir(se) (ie, i)
reference   la referencia
refrigerator   el refrigerador
region   la región
relationship   la relación
relatives   los parientes
released   liberado/a
religious   *adj.* religioso/a
remedy   el remedio
to remember   recordar (ue)
to rent   alquilar, el alquiler
reparation, repair   la reparación
reporter   el/la reportero/a
to represent   representar;
   representative el/la
   representante
reproduction   la reproducción
reserve   la reserva
reserved   reservado/a
resident   el/la residente
resource   el recurso
to respect   respetar
responsible   responsable
to rest   descansar; **rest** el descanso, el
   reposo, el resto
restless   inquieto/a
result, outcome   el resultado
résumé   el currículum
to return   volver (ue)
revision, inspection   la revisión
rib   la costilla
rice   el arroz
rich, wealthy   rico/a
to ride   montar; **ride a bicycle**
   montar en bicicleta **right (legal)** el
   derecho, **(direction)** la derecha;
   Right? ¿Verdad?
ring   el anillo
risk, danger   el riesgo
river basin   la cuenca
road, way   el camino
robe   la bata
robot   el robot
rock   la roca
rocket   el cohete
roof   el techo
room   la habitación
round trip   de ida y vuelta
ruins   las ruinas
to run   correr

S

to take photos   sacar (qu) fotos
sad   triste
safe and sound   sano/a y salvo/a
safe box   la caja fuerte
safety, security   la seguridad
salad   la ensalada
salad dressing   el aderezo
salary   el sueldo
sale   la rebaja
sales   las ventas
salesman, saleswoman   el/la
   vendedor/a
salesperson   el/la dependiente/a
salt   la sal
Salvadoran   salvadoreño/a
salvation   la salvación
same   *adj.* igual; **same thing** lo
   mismo; **like, same as** al igual que
sample   la muestra
sand   la arena
sandal   la sandalia
sandy   arenoso/a
to save   ahorrar
sawdust   el aserrín
to say, tell   decir (g, i)
scarf   la bufanda
scene   la escena
schedule   el horario
school   *n.* la escuela, *adj.* escolar
sciences   ciencias
scientist   el/la científico/a
sculptor   el/la escultor/a
sea   el mar
seat   el asiento
seaweed   el alga
second   segundo/a
secondary   secundario/a
section   la sección
sedentary   sedentario/a
to see   ver
seed   la pepa, la semilla
to seem   parecer (zc)
selection   la selección
to sell   vender
senator   el/la senador/a
to send   enviar, mandar
sentence   la oración
sentimental   sentimental
separation   la separación
series   la serie
serious   serio/a
seriousness   la gravedad
to serve   servir (i)
to set the table   poner la mesa
set, group,   el conjunto; **joint** *adj.*
   conjunto
severe, serious   severo/a
sex   el sexo

sharp   en punto
to shave   afeitar(se)
she   ella
sheet   la sábana
shellfish   los mariscos
ship/boat   el barco
shirt   la camisa
shoe   el zapato
shop window   el escaparate
shopping center   el centro comercial
short (in length)   corto/a; **short (in
   stature)** bajo/a
short course of studies   el cursillo
shorts   los pantalones cortos
shoulder   el hombro
to show   mostrar (ue); **show** el
   espectáculo
shower   la ducha
shrimp   el camarón; **shrimp (in Spain)**
   la gamba
sick   *adj.* enfermo/a
sign   el letrero
signal   la señal
signature   la firma
silk   la seda
silly, foolish   tonto/a
silver   la plata
similar   semejante
similarity   la semejanza
simply   simplemente
simultaneously   simultáneamente
since   desde, ya que
sincere   sincero/a
to sing   cantar
singer   el/la cantante
single   soltero/a
siren   la sirena
sister   la hermana
to sit down   sentar(se) (ie)
situation, location   la situación
size   el tamaño, la talla
to skate   patinar
to ski   esquiar
skiing, ski   el esquí
skin   la piel
skirt   la falda
sky   el cielo
to sleep   dormir (ue)
sleeping pill   el somnífero
slipper   la zapatilla
slope   el médano, la bajada
slope, court, track   la pista
slowly   despacio
small meat pie   la empanada; **typical
   Bolivian meat pies** empanadas
   salteñas
[S.L.34]small   pequeño/a
smart, ready   listo/a
to smoke   fumar
to sneeze   estornudar

to snow   nevar (ie); **snow**   la nieve
soap   el jabón
soap opera   la telenovela
soccer   el fútbol
society   la sociedad
sociology   la sociología
sock   el calcetín
soda   el refresco
sodium   el sodio
sofa   el sofá
soft   suave
solid color   de color entero
solution   la solución
to solve   resolver (ue)
something   algo
son   el hijo
song   la canción
sorrounding   el entorno
soup   la sopa
sour   agrio/a
south   el sur
southeast   el sureste
southwest   suroeste
space   el espacio, *adj.* espacial
spaceship   la nave espacial
space shuttle   el transbordador
    espacial
spacious   espacioso/a
Spanish   el español, *adj.* español/a
Spanish American   *adj.* criollo/a
Spanish speaker   el/la
    hispanohablante
sparrow   la golondrina
to speak   hablar
special   especial; **especially**   en
    especial
specialty   la especialidad
species   la especie
specific   determinado/a
to specify, point out   especificar (qu)
spectator   el/la espectador/a
speed   la velocidad
to spend   gastar
spice   la especia
spinach   las espinacas
spirit, disposition   el espíritu
spoon   la cuchara
spoon(full)   la cucharada
sport   *adj.* deportivo/a
sportsman/woman   el/la deportista
square   cuadrado/a
stadium   el estadio
stage   la etapa
stamp   el sello
to stand in line   hacer cola
standard   estándar [S.L.35]
state, condition   el estado
statistic   la estadística
steak   el bistec
steering wheel   el volante

to step on   pisar
stepfather   el padrastro
stepmother   la madrastra
stereo   el estéreo
still, yet   aún, todavía
stockings, socks   las medias
stomach   el estómago
stone   la piedra
to stop   detener (g, ie)
stopping point   la escala
store   la tienda
story   el cuento
stove   la estufa
strategy   la estrategia
strawberry   la fresa
street   la calle
stress   el estrés
to stretch   estirar
striped   de rayas
strong   fuerte
structure   la estructura
student   el/la alumno/a, el/la
    estudiante, *adj.* estudiantil
student's desk   el pupitre
studious   estudioso/a
to study   estudiar; **study, studying**   el
    estudio
style   el estilo
subway, meter   el metro
suddenly   de repente
sugar   el/la azúcar
suggestion   la sugerencia
suit   el traje
suitcase   la maleta
summary   el resumen; **to summarize**
    en resumen
summit, top   la cima
sun   el sol
to sunbathe   tomar el sol
sunglasses   las gafas de sol
supermarket   el supermercado
superstore   la megatienda
support   el apoyo
surfer   el/la surfista
surgeon   el/la cirujano/a
to surpass, overcome   superar
sweater   el suéter
sweep   barrer
to swim   nadar; **swimming**   la
    natación
swimming pool   la piscina
symbol   el símbolo; **to symbolize**
    simbolizar
symptom   el síntoma

T

table   la mesa
tablecloth   el mantel

to take a bath, bathe   bañar(se);
    take a nap   dormir la siesta;
    take a walk, stroll   pasear;
    take advantage   aprovechar;
    take away, remove   quitar; **take
    care of**   cuidar(se); **take notes**
    tomar apuntes; **take notes**
    tomar notas; **take off**   despegar,
    quitar(se); **take, drink**   tomar
talent   el talento
to talk, converse   conversar; **talkative**
    conversador/a
tall   alto/a
tape recorder, cassette player   la
    grabadora
tax   el impuesto
team   el equipo
to tear   romper
teaspoon   la cucharadita, la
    cucharita
technical   *adj.* el/la técnico/a;
    technician   el/la técnico/a
technique   la técnica
technology   la tecnología
telepathy   la telepatía
telephone   el teléfono, el teléfono, *adj.*
    telefónico/a
television set   el televisor
to tell, count   contar (ue)
temperament   el temperamento
tennis   el tenis
tennis player   el/la tenista
terrace   la terraza
territory   el territorio
to terrorize   aterrorizar (c)
test, examination   el examen
that   (*adj.*) ese/a, que
thaw   el deshielo
the (contraction of *a + el*)   al;
    the   lo; **the important thing**   lo
    importante; [S.L.36] [S.L.37]
    [S.L.38]
[S.L.39]theater   el teatro
then   entonces; **then, after**
    luego
there   ahí, allí
there is, there are   hay; **there was,
    there were**   había
thermometer   el termómetro
they   ellos/ellas; **they, you (plural) are**
    son
thin   delgado/a
thing   la cosa
to think   pensar (ie)
this   este/a, esto
this way   así
threaten, menace   amenazar (c)
throat   la garganta
through   a través de
throw   lanzar (c)

ticket, passage   el billete, el boleto/pasaje; **ticket for admission** la entrada
tidy   ordenado/a
to tidy up   ordenar
tie   la corbata
tile   el azulejo
time   el rato, el tiempo; **free time** tiempo libre
timid   tímido/a
tire   la llanta
tired   cansado/a
title   el título
toast   la tostada
today   hoy
together   juntos/as
toilet   el inodoro
tolerant   tolerante
tomato   el tomate
tomato sauce   la salsa de tomate
tomorrow   mañana
tooth   el diente
torture   la tortura
to touch   tocar
tourist   *adj.* turístico/a
tournament   el torneo
toward, near   hacia
towel   la toalla
town   el pueblo
toy   el juguete
tradition   la tradición; **traditional** tradicional
traffic   el tráfico
train   el tren
training   el entrenamiento
tranquilizer   tranquilizante
to translate   traducir (zc)
transparent   transparente
transportation   el transporte
to travel   viajar; **travel agency** la agencia de viajes; **travel agent** el/la agente de viajes; **traveler's check** el cheque de viajero
tray   la bandeja
tree   el árbol
trophy   el trofeo
tropical   tropical
truck   el camión
true, certain   *adv.* cierto
trunk   el maletero
trust   la confianza
trustworthy   fiable
to try on   probarse (ue)
T-shirt   la camiseta
tub   la bañadera
tunic   la túnica
tunnel   el túnel
turkey   el guajolote, el pavo
turn, shift   el turno
twin   gemelo/a

to twist   torcer(se) (ue)
type   el género; **type, style, kind** el tipo
type of soup   el ajiaco
typical   típico/a, típico/a; **typical Catalonian dance** la sardana; **typical Chilean music** la cueca; **typical Colombian music** el vallenato; **typical music of the Dominican Republic** el merengue; **typical Panamanian dress** la pollera; **typical Peruvian music** la marinera; **typical Venezuelan music** el joropo

U

[S.L.40]U
ugly   feo/a
ulcer   la úlcera
umbrella   el paraguas
umpire, referee   el árbitro
uncle   el tío
undecided   indeciso/a
under   debajo (de)
to understand   entender (ie)
unemployed   desempleado/a
unexpected   inesperado
unfinished   inconcluso/a
uniform   el uniforme
union   la unión
united   unido/a
unity   la unidad
university   la universidad, *adj.* universitario/a
unknown   desconocido/a
unpleasant   antipático/a
urban   urbano/a
urgent   urgente; **urgently** urgentemente
Uruguayan   uruguayo/a
to use   usar
used to, accustomed   acostumbrado/a

V

vacation   las vacaciones
to vacuum   pasar la aspiradora; **vacuum cleaner** la aspiradora
valley   el valle
valuable   valioso/a
value, price   el valor
vanilla   la vainilla
variable, changeable   variable
variant   la variante
various, several   varios/as
VCR   la videocasetera

vegetable   el vegetal, la verdura
vegetation   la vegetación
vein   la vena
Venezuelan   venezolano/a
verb   el verbo
to verify   verificar (qu)
versatile   versátil
victory   el triunfo
video   el video
view   la vista
vinegar   el vinagre
vineyard   el viñedo
violence   la violencia
violinist   el/la violinista
virgin   la virgen
virtual   virtual
visa   la visa
to visit   visitar
vitality   la vitalidad
vitamin   la vitamina
vocabulary   el vocabulario
voice   la voz
volleyball   el voleibol
volunteer   el/la voluntario/a
to vote   votar

W

waist   la cintura
to wait for, hope, expect   esperar
waiter/waitress   el/la camarero/a
waiting list   la lista de espera
to wake up   despertar(se) (ie)
to walk   caminar; **walk** el paseo, la caminata
walker   el/la caminante
wallet   la billetera
to want   querer (ie)
warming   el calentamiento
to wash (oneself)   lavar(se)
washbowl, bathroom sink   el lavabo
washer   la lavadora
wastepaper basket   el cesto
to water   regar (ie); **water** el agua, *adj.* acuático/a
wave   la ola
way   la manera, por cierto
we   nosotros/nosotras
weak   débil
wealth   la riqueza
to wear, take   llevar
to wear a costume   disfrazarse
weaving   el tejido
[S.L.41]wedding   la boda
week   la semana
weekend   el fin de semana
weight   el peso
well   *(interj.)* pues
what, that which   lo que

What a pity! ¡Qué lástima!, ¡Qué pena!
What is he/she/it like? ¿Cómo es?
What's the weather like? ¿Qué tiempo hace?
What's wrong (with you)? ¿Qué te/le(s) pasa?
What's your name? (familiar) ¿Cómo te llamas?
What's your name? (formal) ¿Cómo se llama usted?
wheat el trigo
wheel la rueda
when *adv.* cuando
where (*interrog.*) dónde
Where (to)? ¿Adónde?
Where is . . . ? ¿Dónde está...?
whether ya sea
while mientras
Who is . . . ? ¿Quién es...?
whose? ¿de quién?
wide ancho/a

widow la viuda
widower el viudo
wife la esposa
will, will power la voluntad
to win ganar
wind el viento
window la ventana, la ventanilla
windshield el parabrisas
windshield wiper el limpiaparabrisas
wine el vino; **red wine** el vino tinto
winner el/la ganador/a
to wish, want desear
with con; **with me** conmigo; **with you (familiar)** contigo
without sin
wood la madera
wool la lana
word la palabra
to work trabajar; **work** la obra; **play** obra de teatro
worker el/la obrero/a
World Wide Web la red

worldwide mundial
to worry preocupar(se)
worse, worst peor
wrist la muñeca
to write escribir
writer el/la escritor/a

Y

year el año
yes sí
yogurt el yogur
you (familiar) tú; **you (formal)** usted; **you (plural)** ustedes; **you, him, it** lo; [S.L.42] [S.L.43] **you are (familiar)** eres, estás; **you are (formal), he/she is** es
young joven; **young man/woman** el/la joven; **youngest** el/la menor
your (familiar) tu
yours, his, hers, theirs suyo(-a, -os, -as)

CREDITS

INDEX OF LANGUAGE FUNCTIONS

INDEX

A

a
  with article, 105, 177, 443
  with **ir**, 105
  personal, 177, 441, 443
acabar de + infinitive, 478
accent marks
  diphthongs, 369
  double object pronouns, 333
  present participle, 255
  preterit, 215
  question forms, 40
  rules for, 73, 104, 138, 177, 299
activities/plans, 94–95, 127
actualmente, 325
addresses, 16
adjective clauses, indicative vs.
    subjunctive in, 443–44
adjectives
  agreement, 67
  comparative forms, 295–96, 297
  demonstrative, 181–82
  with **estar**, 70
  as nouns, 299
  ordinal numbers, 166, 187
  past participles as, 481
  possessive, 74, 446–47
  with **ser**, 70
  shortened forms, 187
  stressed possessive adjectives,
      446–47
  superlative forms, 299
adverbial conjunctions, subjunctive vs.
    indicative, 508–09
adverbs
  comparative forms, 295–96, 297
  formation with **-mente**, 138
  superlative forms, 299
affirmative and negative expressions,
    440–41
air travel, 432–34, 467
al + infinitive, 515
alphabet, 8
-ar verbs
  conditional, 475
  formal commands, 335–36
  future, 449
  imperfect indicative, 290
  imperfect subjunctive, 539

informal commands, 403
  present indicative, 32
  present participle, 172
  present subjunctive, 365
  preterit, 215
articles
  contraction with **a**, 105,
    177, 443
  contraction with **de**, 70
  gender and number, 35–36
artists, 470–72, 495, 499

B

body language, 5
body, parts of, 91, 394, 429

C

caer bien/mal, 222–23
-car verbs. *See* spelling-change verbs
cardinal numbers, 14–15, 108–09
cars, 436
celebrations, 282–84, 286–87, 317
classrooms, 11, 19–20, 21
clothing, 206–07, 241
cognates, 10
colors, 64
comic strips, 80
commands
  formal, 335–36
  informal, 403
comparisons of equality, 297
comparisons of inequality,
    295–96
conditional
  formation and use of, 475
  with *if*-clauses, 541
conjunctions, 380, 508–09
conmigo, contigo, 258
conocer
  imperfect indicative, 330
  present indicative, 184
  present subjunctive, 366
  preterit, 330
  uses of, 184
contractions
  al, 105, 177, 443
  del, 70

cooking, 97–99, 363
correspondence, 438
courtesy, 6

D

daily activities, 250–51
dance and music, 470
dar, 219
days and dates, 16–17
de, with article, 70
deber + infinitive, 102
decir
  commands, 403
  conditional, 475
  future, 449
  past participle, 478
  present indicative, 135
  present subjunctive, 366
  preterit, 260
democracy, 527
demonstrative adjectives, 181–82
demonstrative pronouns, 182
dependent clauses
  adjectival, 443–44
  adverbial, 508–09
  if-clauses, 541
  relative pronouns, 410
  subjunctive forms, 367–68,
      371–72, 401
descriptions, of people, 91
direct object pronouns
  commands, 336, 403
  and indirect object pronouns,
      333
  in present perfect indicative, 478
  use of, 176–77
dónde + **está**, 12

E

economic issues, 349, 553
entertainment, 121
environmental issues, 534–35,
    557
-er verbs
  conditional, 475
  formal commands, 335–36
  future, 449
  imperfect indicative, 290

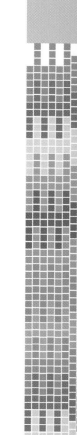

Mar Caribe

OCÉANO ATLÁNTICO

Barranquilla
Cartagena
Maracaibo
Caracas
Barquisimeto
Medellín
VENEZUELA
Río Orinoco
Georgetown
Paramaribo
Manizales
GUYANA
Cayenne
SURINAM
GUAYANA FRANCESA (Francia)
Bogotá
Cali
COLOMBIA
Salto Ángel
Quito
ECUADOR
Ecuador
Guayaquil
Cuenca
Río Amazonas
Belém
CORDILLERA DE LOS ANDES
Iquitos
Manaus
Fortaleza
Islas Galápagos (Ec.)
Cajamarca
Río Madeira
BRASIL
Recife
Trujillo
Río Branco
PERÚ
Lima
Machu Picchu
Salvador
Ayacucho
Cuzco
BOLIVIA
Brasília
Arequipa
Lago Titicaca
La Paz
Arica
Cochabamba
Santa Cruz
Belo Horizonte
Iquique
Sucre
Potosí
PARAGUAY
São Paulo
Río de Janeiro

OCÉANO PACÍFICO

I. Pinta
I. Fernandina
I. Marchena
I. San Salvador
Santa Cruz
I. Isabela
I. Santa Cruz
Puerto Ayora
Puerto Villamil
I. San Cristóbal
Puerto Baquerizo Moreno
ISLAS GALÁPAGOS (ECUADOR)

Antofagasta
Salta
Asunción
Salto Iguazú
Santos
Trópico de Capricornio
CHILE
San Miguel de Tucumán
ARGENTINA
Pôrto Alegre
Coquimbo
Córdoba
Río Paraná
Río Uruguay
Rivera

OCÉANO PACÍFICO
Cabo Norte
Volcán Katiki
Hanga Roa
Cabo Cumming
Mataveri
ISLA de PASCUA (CHILE)

Valparaíso
Mendoza
Rosario
URUGUAY
Santiago
Buenos Aires
Montevideo
La Plata
Río de la Plata
OCÉANO ATLÁNTICO
Concepción
Bahía Blanca

CORDILLERA DE LOS ANDES
Desierto de Atacama

OCÉANO PACÍFICO

Puerto Montt

Estrecho de Magallanes
Islas Malvinas (Br.)
Punta Arenas
TIERRA DEL FUEGO
Cabo de Hornos

América del Sur